BRITISH MORALISTS

BRITISH MORALISTS

MORALISTS

1650–1800

SELECTED AND EDITED
WITH COMPARATIVE NOTES AND
ANALYTICAL INDEX

BY

D. D. RAPHAEL

*Formerly Edward Caird Professor of
Political and Social Philosophy
in the University of Glasgow*

II

HUME–BENTHAM
AND INDEX

HACKETT PUBLISHING COMPANY, INC.
INDIANAPOLIS/CAMBRIDGE

Republication of this work was made possible
by the gracious support of Oxford University Press,
which first published it in 1969.

For further information, please contact
Hackett Publishing Company, Inc.
P.O. Box 44937
Indianapolis, Indiana 46244-0937

www.hackettpublishing.com

10 09 08 07 06   3 4 5 6 7 8 9

Library of Congress Cataloging-in-Publication Data

British moralists, 1650–1800/selected and edited with comparative notes and an-
    alytic index by D. D. Raphael.
        p.   cm.
    Reprint. Originally published: Oxford: Clarendon Press, 1969.
    Includes bibliographical references and index.
    Contents: 1. Hobbes–Gay.   2. Hume–Bentham and index.
    ISBN 0-87220-118-X (v. 1: alk. paper),—ISBN 0-87220-119-8 (v. 2: alk.
    paper).—ISBN 0-87220-121-X (set: alk. paper).—ISBN 0-87220-116-3 (v.
    1. pbk.: alk. paper).—ISBN 0-87220-117-1 (v. 2: pbk.: alk. paper).—ISBN
    0-87220-120-1 (set: pbk.: alk. paper).
    1. Ethics, Modern—17th century.   2. Ethics, Modern—18th century.   3.
    Ethics, British.   I. Raphael, D. D. (David Daiches), 1916–
    BJ801.B75   1991
    170'.941'09032—dc20   90-85423
                                                                        CIP

ISBN-13: 978-0-87220-119-4 (v. 2: cloth)
ISBN-13: 978-0-87220-117-0 (v. 2: pbk.)

CONTENTS OF VOLUME II

§§

DAVID HUME   479–634

DAVID HARTLEY   635–654

RICHARD PRICE   655–762

ADAM SMITH   763–844

WILLIAM PALEY   845–855

THOMAS REID   856–945

JEREMY BENTHAM   946–999

BIBLIOGRAPHICAL NOTE   p. 347

INDEX   p. 361

DAVID HUME

1711–1776

I. *A TREATISE OF HUMAN NATURE*

[First printed, 1739–40. Reprinted here from the first
edition, with misprints corrected and spelling modified]

II. *AN ENQUIRY CONCERNING THE PRINCIPLES OF MORALS*

[First printed, 1751. Reprinted here from the finally
revised version published in the posthumous 1777
edition of *Essays and Treatises on Several Subjects*, with
misprints corrected and spelling modified]

SUPPLEMENTARY EXTRACTS FROM

I. *AN ENQUIRY CONCERNING HUMAN UNDERSTANDING*

[First printed, 1748, under the title *Philosophical Essays
concerning Human Understanding*. Reprinted here from
the 1777 edition of *Essays and Treatises on Several
Subjects*, with spelling modified]

II. *TWO LETTERS TO FRANCIS HUTCHESON*

[Written in 1739 and 1740. Reprinted here, by kind
permission of the late Professor J. Y. T. Greig and of
the Delegates of the Clarendon Press, from *The Letters
of David Hume*, edited by J. Y. T. Greig, 1932, with
spelling modified and reduction of initial capital letters]

DAVID HUME

A Treatise of Human Nature

BOOK II—OF THE PASSIONS

PART III—*Of the will and direct passions*

SECT. III—OF THE INFLUENCING MOTIVES OF THE WILL

Nothing is more usual in philosophy, and even in common life, **479** than to talk of the combat of passion and reason, to give the preference to reason, and assert that men are only so far virtuous as they conform themselves to its dictates. Every rational creature, it is said, is obliged to regulate his actions by reason; and if any other motive or principle challenge the direction of his conduct, he ought to oppose it, till it be entirely subdued, or at least brought to a conformity with that superior principle. On this method of thinking the greatest part of moral philosophy, ancient and modern, seems to be founded; nor is there an ampler field, as well for metaphysical arguments, as popular declamations, than this supposed pre-eminence of reason above passion. The eternity, invariableness, and divine origin of the former have been displayed to the best advantage: the blindness, inconstancy, and deceitfulness of the latter have been as strongly insisted on. In order to show the fallacy of all this philosophy, I shall endeavour to prove *first*, that reason alone can never be a motive to any action of the will; and *secondly*, that it can never oppose passion in the direction of the will.

The understanding exerts itself after two different ways, as it **480** judges from demonstration or probability; as it regards the abstract relations of our ideas, or those relations of objects, of which experience only gives us information. I believe it scarce will be asserted, that the first species of reasoning alone is ever the cause of any action. As its proper province is the world of ideas, and as the will always places us in that of realities, demonstration and volition seem, upon that account, to be totally removed from each other. Mathematics, indeed, are useful in all mechanical operations, and arithmetic in almost every art and profession: but it is not of themselves they have any influence. Mechanics are the art of regulating the motions of bodies *to some designed end or purpose*; and the reason why we employ arithmetic in fixing the proportions of numbers, is only that we may discover the proportions of their influence and operation. A merchant is desirous of knowing the sum total of his accounts with any person: why? but that he may learn what sum will have the same *effects* in paying his debt, and going to market, as all the particular articles taken together. Abstract or demonstrative reasoning, therefore, never influences any of our actions, but only as it directs our judgement concerning causes and effects; which leads us to the second operation of the understanding.

481 It is obvious, that when we have the prospect of pain or pleasure from any object, we feel a consequent emotion of aversion or propensity, and are carried to avoid or embrace what will give us this uneasiness or satisfaction. It is also obvious, that this emotion rests not here, but making us cast our view on every side, comprehends whatever objects are connected with its original one by the relation of cause and effect. Here then reasoning takes place to discover this relation; and according as our reasoning varies, our actions receive a subsequent variation. But it is evident in this case, that the impulse arises not from reason, but is only directed by it. It is from the prospect of pain or pleasure that the aversion or propensity arises towards any object: and these emotions extend themselves to the causes and effects of that object, as they are pointed out to us by reason and experience. It can never in the least concern us to know, that such objects are causes, and such others effects, if both the causes and effects be indifferent to us. Where the objects themselves do not affect us, their connection can never give them any influence; and it is plain, that as reason is nothing but the discovery of this connection, it cannot be by its means that the objects are able to affect us.

482 Since reason alone can never produce any action, or give rise to volition, I infer, that the same faculty is as incapable of preventing volition, or of disputing the preference with any passion or emotion. This consequence is necessary. It is impossible reason could have the

latter effect of preventing volition, but by giving an impulse in a contrary direction to our passion; and that impulse, had it operated alone, would have been able to produce volition. Nothing can oppose or retard the impulse of passion, but a contrary impulse; and if this contrary impulse ever arises from reason, that latter faculty must have an original influence on the will, and must be able to cause, as well as hinder any act of volition. But if reason has no original influence, it is impossible it can withstand any principle, which has such an efficacy, or ever keep the mind in suspense a moment. Thus it appears, that the principle, which opposes our passion, cannot be the same with reason, and is only called so in an improper sense. We speak not strictly and philosophically when we talk of the combat of passion and of reason. Reason is, and ought only to be the slave of the passions, and can never pretend to any other office than to serve and obey them. As this opinion may appear somewhat extraordinary, it may not be improper to confirm it by some other considerations.

A passion is an original existence, or, if you will, modification of **483** existence, and contains not any representative quality, which renders it a copy of any other existence or modification. When I am angry, I am actually possessed with the passion, and in that emotion have no more a reference to any other object, than when I am thirsty, or sick, or more than five foot high. It is impossible, therefore, that this passion can be opposed by, or be contradictory to truth and reason; since this contradiction consists in the disagreement of ideas, considered as copies, with those objects, which they represent.

What may at first occur on this head, is, that as nothing can be contrary to truth or reason, except what has a reference to it, and as the judgements of our understanding only have this reference, it must follow, that passions can be contrary to reason only so far as they are *accompanied* with some judgement or opinion. According to this principle, which is so obvious and natural, it is only in two senses, that any affection can be called unreasonable. First, when a passion, such as hope or fear, grief or joy, despair or security, is founded on the supposition of the existence of objects, which really do not exist. Secondly, when in exerting any passion in action, we choose means insufficient for the designed end, and deceive ourselves in our judgement of causes and effects. Where a passion is neither founded on false suppositions, nor chooses means insufficient for the end, the understanding can neither justify nor condemn it. It is not contrary to reason to prefer the destruction of the whole world to the scratching of my finger. It is not contrary to reason for me to choose my total ruin, to prevent the least uneasiness of an Indian or person wholly unknown to me. It is as little contrary to reason to prefer even my own acknowledged lesser good to my greater, and have a more ardent affection for the former than the latter. A trivial good may, from certain circumstances, produce a desire superior to what arises from the greatest and most valuable enjoyment; nor is there any thing more extraordinary in this, than in mechanics to see one pound weight raise up a hundred by the advantage of its situation. In short, a passion must be accompanied with some false judgement, in order to its being unreasonable; and even then it is not the passion, properly speaking, which is unreasonable, but the judgement.

484   The consequences are evident. Since a passion can never, in any sense, be called unreasonable, but when founded on a false supposition, or when it chooses means insufficient for the designed end, it is impossible, that reason and passion can ever oppose each other, or dispute for the government of the will and actions. The moment we perceive the falsehood of any supposition, or the insufficiency of any means, our passions yield to our reason without any opposition. I may desire any fruit as of an excellent relish; but whenever you convince me of my mistake, my longing ceases. I may will the performance of certain actions as means of obtaining any desired good; but as my willing of these actions is only secondary, and founded on the supposition, that they are causes of the proposed effect; as soon as I discover the falsehood of that supposition, they must become indifferent to me.

485   It is natural for one, that does not examine objects with a strict philosophic eye, to imagine, that those actions of the mind are entirely the same, which produce not a different sensation, and are not immediately distinguishable to the feeling and perception. Reason, for instance, exerts itself without producing any sensible emotion; and except in the more sublime disquisitions of philosophy, or in the frivolous subtleties of the schools, scarce ever conveys any pleasure or uneasiness. Hence it proceeds, that every action of the mind, which operates with the same calmness and tranquillity, is confounded with reason by all those, who judge of things from the first view and appearance. Now it is certain, there are certain

calm desires and tendencies,[1] which, though they be real passions, produce little emotion in the mind, and are more known by their effects than by the immediate feeling or sensation. These desires are of two kinds; either certain instincts originally implanted in our natures, such as benevolence and resentment, the love of life, and kindness to children; or the general appetite to good, and aversion to evil, considered merely as such. When any of these passions are calm, and cause no disorder in the soul, they are very readily taken for the determinations of reason, and are supposed to proceed from the same faculty, with that, which judges of truth and falsehood. Their nature and principles have been supposed the same, because their sensations are not evidently different.

Beside these calm passions, which often determine the will, there are certain violent emotions of the same kind, which have likewise a great influence on that faculty. When I receive any injury from another, I often feel a violent passion of resentment, which makes me desire his evil and punishment, independent of all considerations of pleasure and advantage to myself. When I am immediately threatened with any grievous ill, my fears, apprehensions, and aversions rise to a great height, and produce a sensible emotion.

The common error of metaphysicians has lain in ascribing the **486** direction of the will entirely to one of these principles, and supposing the other to have no influence. Men often act knowingly against their interest: for which reason the view of the greatest possible good does not always influence them. Men often counteract a violent passion in prosecution of their interests and designs: it is not therefore the present uneasiness alone, which determines them.[2] In general we may observe, that both these principles operate on the will; and where they are contrary, that either of them prevails, according to the *general* character or *present* disposition of the person. What we call strength of mind, implies the prevalence of the calm passions above the violent; though we may easily observe, there is no man so constantly possessed of this virtue, as never on any occasion to yield to the solicitations of passion and desire. From these variations of temper proceeds the great difficulty of deciding concerning the actions and resolutions of men, where there is any contrariety of motives and passions.

[1 Cf. Hutcheson, §§ 331, 357, 369; Butler, § 382.]
[2 Contrast Locke, §§ 174-5.]

BOOK III—OF MORALS

PART I—*Of virtue and vice in general*

SECT. I—MORAL DISTINCTIONS NOT DERIVED FROM REASON

* * * *

487 It has been observed, that nothing is ever present to the mind but its perceptions; and that all the actions of seeing, hearing, judging, loving, hating, and thinking, fall under this denomination. The mind can never exert itself in any action, which we may not comprehend under the term of *perception*; and consequently that term is no less applicable to those judgements, by which we distinguish moral good and evil, than to every other operation of the mind. To approve of one character, to condemn another, are only so many different perceptions.

Now as perceptions resolve themselves into two kinds, viz. *impressions* and *ideas*, this distinction gives rise to a question, with which we shall open up our present inquiry concerning morals, *Whether it is by means of our* ideas *or impressions we distinguish betwixt vice and virtue, and pronounce an action blameable or praise-worthy?* This will immediately cut off all loose discourses and declamations, and reduce us to something precise and exact on the present subject.

488 Those who affirm that virtue is nothing but a conformity to reason; that there are eternal fitnesses and unfitnesses of things, which are the same to every rational being that considers them; that the immutable measures of right and wrong impose an obligation, not only on human creatures, but also on the Deity himself: all these systems concur in the opinion, that morality, like truth, is discerned merely by ideas, and by their juxtaposition and comparison. In order, therefore, to judge of these systems, we need only consider, whether it be possible, from reason alone, to distinguish betwixt moral good and evil, or whether there must concur some other principles to enable us to make that distinction.

489 If morality had naturally no influence on human passions and actions, it were in vain to take such pains to inculcate it; and nothing would be more fruitless than that multitude of rules and precepts, with which all moralists abound. Philosophy is commonly divided into *speculative* and *practical*; and as morality is always comprehended under the latter division, it is supposed to influence our passions and actions, and to go beyond the calm and indolent judgements of the understanding. And this is confirmed by common experience, which informs us, that men are often governed by their duties, and are deterred from some actions by the opinion of injustice, and impelled to others by that of obligation.

Since morals, therefore, have an influence on the actions and affections, it follows, that they cannot be derived from reason; and that because reason alone, as we have already proved, can never have any such influence. Morals excite passions, and produce or prevent actions. Reason of itself is utterly impotent in this particular. The rules of morality, therefore, are not conclusions of our reason.

No one, I believe, will deny the justness of this inference; nor is there any other means of evading it, than by denying that principle, on which it is founded. As long as it is allowed, that reason has no influence on our passions and actions, it is in vain to pretend, that morality is discovered only by a deduction of reason. An active principle can never be founded on an inactive; and if reason be inactive in itself, it must remain so in all its shapes and appearances, whether it exerts itself in natural or moral subjects, whether it considers the powers of external bodies, or the actions of rational beings.

It would be tedious to repeat all the arguments, by which I have 490 proved[a], that reason is perfectly inert, and can never either prevent or produce any action or affection. It will be easy to recollect what has been said upon that subject. I shall only recall on this occasion one of these arguments, which I shall endeavour to render still more conclusive, and more applicable to the present subject.

Reason is the discovery of truth or falsehood. Truth or falsehood consists in an agreement or disagreement either to the *real* relations of ideas, or to *real* existence and matter of fact. Whatever, therefore, is not susceptible of this agreement or disagreement, is incapable of being true or false, and can never be an object of our reason. Now it is evident our passions, volitions, and actions, are not susceptible of any such agreement or disagreement; being original facts and realities, complete in themselves, and implying no reference to other passions, volitions, and actions. It is impossible, therefore, they can

---

[a] Book II. Part III. Sect. 3 [i.e. §§ 479–86].

be pronounced either true or false, and be either contrary or conformable to reason.

This argument is of double advantage to our present purpose. For it proves *directly*, that actions do not derive their merit from a conformity to reason, nor their blame from a contrariety to it; and it proves the same truth more *indirectly*, by showing us, that as reason can never immediately prevent or produce any action by contradicting or approving of it, it cannot be the source of moral good and evil, which are found to have that influence. Actions may be laudable or blameable; but they cannot be reasonable or unreasonable: laudable or blameable, therefore, are not the same with reasonable or unreasonable. The merit and demerit of actions frequently contradict, and sometimes control our natural propensities. But reason has no such influence. Moral distinctions, therefore, are not the offspring of reason. Reason is wholly inactive, and can never be the source of so active a principle as conscience, or a sense of morals.

491 But perhaps it may be said, that though no will or action can be immediately contradictory to reason, yet we may find such a contradiction in some of the attendants of the action, that is, in its causes or effects. The action may cause a judgement, or may be *obliquely* caused by one, when the judgement concurs with a passion; and by an abusive way of speaking, which philosophy will scarce allow of, the same contrariety may, upon that account, be ascribed to the action. How far this truth or falsehood may be the source of morals, it will now be proper to consider.

It has been observed, that reason, in a strict and philosophical sense, can have an influence on our conduct only after two ways: either when it excites a passion by informing us of the existence of something which is a proper object of it; or when it discovers the connection of causes and effects, so as to afford us means of exerting any passion. These are the only kinds of judgement, which can accompany our actions, or can be said to produce them in any manner; and it must be allowed, that these judgements may often be false and erroneous. A person may be affected with passion, by supposing a pain or pleasure to lie in an object, which has no tendency to produce either of these sensations, or which produces the contrary to what is imagined. A person may also take false measures for the attaining his end, and may retard, by his foolish conduct, instead of forwarding the execution of any project. These false judgements may be thought to affect the passions and actions, which are connected with them, and may be said to render them unreasonable, in a figurative and improper way of speaking. But though this be acknowledged, it is easy to observe, that these errors are so far from being the source of all immorality, that they are commonly very innocent, and draw no manner of guilt upon the person who is so unfortunate as to fall into them. They extend not beyond a mistake of *fact*, which moralists have not generally supposed criminal, as being perfectly involuntary. I am more to be lamented than blamed, if I am mistaken with regard to the influence of objects in producing pain or pleasure, or if I know not the proper means of satisfying my desires. No one can ever regard such errors as a defect in my moral character. A fruit, for instance, that is really disagreeable, appears to me at a distance, and through mistake I fancy it to be pleasant and delicious. Here is one error. I choose certain means of reaching this fruit, which are not proper for my end. Here is a second error; nor is there any third one, which can ever possibly enter into our reasonings concerning actions. I ask, therefore, if a man, in this situation, and guilty of these two errors, is to be regarded as vicious and criminal, however unavoidable they might have been? Or if it be possible to imagine, that such errors are the sources of all immorality?

And here it may be proper to observe, that if moral distinctions **492** be derived from the truth or falsehood of those judgements, they must take place wherever we form the judgements; nor will there be any difference, whether the question be concerning an apple or a kingdom, or whether the error be avoidable or unavoidable. For as the very essence of morality is supposed to consist in an agreement or disagreement to reason, the other circumstances are entirely arbitrary, and can never either bestow on any action the character of virtuous or vicious, or deprive it of that character. To which we may add, that this agreement or disagreement, not admitting of degrees, all virtues and vices would of course be equal.

Should it be pretended, that though a mistake of *fact* be not **493** criminal, yet a mistake of *right* often is; and that this may be the source of immorality: I would answer, that it is impossible such a mistake can ever be the original source of immorality, since it supposes a real right and wrong; that is, a real distinction in morals, independent of these judgements. A mistake, therefore, of right may become a species of immorality; but it is only a secondary one, and is founded on some other, antecedent to it.

494   As to those judgements which are the *effects* of our actions, and which, when false, give occasion to pronounce the actions contrary to truth and reason; we may observe, that our actions never cause any judgement, either true or false, in ourselves, and that it is only on others they have such an influence. It is certain, that an action, on many occasions, may give rise to false conclusions in others; and that a person, who through a window sees any lewd behaviour of mine with my neighbour's wife, may be so simple as to imagine she is certainly my own. In this respect my action resembles somewhat a lie or falsehood;[1] only with this difference, which is material, that I perform not the action with any intention of giving rise to a false judgement in another,[2] but merely to satisfy my lust and passion. It causes, however, a mistake and false judgement by accident; and the falsehood of its effects may be ascribed, by some odd figurative way of speaking, to the action itself. But still I can see no pretext of reason for asserting, that the tendency to cause such an error is the first spring or original source of all immorality[a].

495   [a] One might think it were entirely superfluous to prove this, if a late author,[3] who has had the good fortune to obtain some reputation, had not seriously affirmed, that such a falsehood is the foundation of all guilt and moral deformity. That we may discover the fallacy of his hypothesis, we need only consider, that a false conclusion is drawn from an action, only by means of an obscurity of natural principles, which makes a cause be secretly interrupted in its operation, by contrary causes, and renders the connection betwixt two objects uncertain and variable. Now, as a like uncertainty and variety of causes take place, even in natural objects, and produce a like error in our judgement, if that tendency to produce error were the very essence of vice and immorality, it should follow, that even inanimate objects might be vicious and immoral.

It is in vain to urge, that inanimate objects act without liberty and choice. For as liberty and choice are not necessary to make an action produce in us an erroneous conclusion, they can be, in no respect, essential to morality; and I do not readily perceive, upon this system, how they can ever come to be regarded by it. If the tendency to cause error be the origin of immorality, that tendency and immorality would in every case be inseparable.

Add to this, that if I had used the precaution of shutting the windows, while I indulged myself in those liberties with my neighbour's wife, I should have been guilty of no immorality; and that because my action, being perfectly concealed, would have had no tendency to produce any false conclusion.

For the same reason, a thief, who steals in by a ladder at a window, and takes all imaginable care to cause no disturbance, is in no respect criminal. For either he will

---

[1 Cf. Wollaston, § 278.]   [2 Cf. Hutcheson, § 368.]
[3 Wollaston.]

Thus upon the whole, it is impossible, that the distinction betwixt moral good and evil, can be made by reason; since that distinction has an influence upon our actions, of which reason alone is incapable. Reason and judgement may, indeed, be the mediate cause of an action, by prompting, or by directing a passion: but it is not pretended, that a judgement of this kind, either in its truth or falsehood, is attended with virtue or vice. And as to the judgements, which are caused by our judgements, they can still less bestow those moral qualities on the actions, which are their causes.

But to be more particular, and to show, that those eternal immutable fitnesses and unfitnesses of things cannot be defended by sound philosophy, we may weigh the following considerations. **497**

If the thought and understanding were alone capable of fixing the boundaries of right and wrong, the character of virtuous and vicious either must lie in some relations of objects, or must be a matter of

---

not be perceived, or if he be, it is impossible he can produce any error, nor will any one, from these circumstances, take him to be other than what he really is.

It is well known, that those who are squint-sighted, do very readily cause mistakes in others, and that we imagine they salute or are talking to one person, while they address themselves to another. Are they therefore, upon that account, immoral?

Besides, we may easily observe, that in all those arguments there is an evident reasoning in a circle. A person who takes possession of *another*'s goods, and uses them as his *own*, in a manner declares them to be his own;[1] and this falsehood is the source of the immorality of injustice. But is property, or right, or obligation, intelligible, without an antecedent morality? **496**

A man that is ungrateful to his benefactor, in a manner affirms, that he never received any favours from him. But in what manner? Is it because it is his duty to be grateful? But this supposes, that there is some antecedent rule of duty and morals. Is it because human nature is generally grateful, and makes us conclude, that a man who does any harm never received any favour from the person he harmed? But human nature is not so generally grateful, as to justify such a conclusion. Or if it were, is an exception to a general rule in every case criminal, for no other reason than because it is an exception?

But what may suffice entirely to destroy this whimsical system is, that it leaves us under the same difficulty to give a reason why truth is virtuous and falsehood vicious, as to account for the merit or turpitude of any other action. I shall allow, if you please, that all immorality is derived from this supposed falsehood in action, provided you can give me any plausible reason, why such a falsehood is immoral. If you consider rightly of the matter, you will find yourself in the same difficulty as at the beginning.

This last argument is very conclusive; because, if there be not an evident merit or turpitude annexed to this species of truth or falsehood, it can never have any influence upon our actions. For, who ever thought of forbearing any action, because others might possibly draw false conclusions from it? Or, who ever performed any, that he might give rise to true conclusions?

[1 Cf. Wollaston, §§ 278, 287.]

fact, which is discovered by our reasoning. This consequence is evident. As the operations of human understanding divide themselves into two kinds, the comparing of ideas, and the inferring of matter of fact; were virtue discovered by the understanding; it must be an object of one of these operations, nor is there any third operation of the understanding, which can discover it. There has been an opinion very industriously propagated by certain philosophers, that morality is susceptible of demonstration;[1] and though no one has ever been able to advance a single step in those demonstrations; yet it is taken for granted, that this science may be brought to an equal certainty with geometry or algebra. Upon this supposition, vice and virtue must consist in some relations; since it is allowed on all hands, that no matter of fact is capable of being demonstrated. Let us, therefore, begin with examining this hypothesis, and endeavour, if possible, to fix those moral qualities, which have been so long the objects of our fruitless researches. Point out distinctly the relations, which constitute morality or obligation, that we may know wherein they consist, and after what manner we must judge of them.

498   If you assert, that vice and virtue consist in relations susceptible of certainty and demonstration, you must confine yourself to those *four* relations, which alone admit of that degree of evidence; and in that case you run into absurdities, from which you will never be able to extricate yourself. For as you make the very essence of morality to lie in the relations, and as there is no one of these relations but what is applicable, not only to an irrational, but also to an inanimate object; it follows, that even such objects must be susceptible of merit or demerit. *Resemblance, contrariety, degrees in quality,* and *proportions in quantity and number*; all these relations belong as properly to matter, as to our actions, passions, and volitions. It is unquestionable, therefore, that morality lies not in any of these relations, nor the sense of it in their discovery[b].

b As a proof, how confused our way of thinking on this subject commonly is, we may observe, that those who assert, that morality is demonstrable, do not say, that morality lies in the relations, and that the relations are distinguishable by reason. They only say, that reason can discover such an action, in such relations, to be virtuous, and such another vicious. It seems they thought it sufficient, if they could bring the word, Relation, into the proposition, without troubling themselves whether it was to the purpose or not. But here, I think, is plain argument. Demonstrative reason discovers only relations. But that reason, according to this hypothesis, discovers also vice and

[1 Cf. Locke, §§ 154, 189; Clarke, §§ 224, 239; Balguy, §§ 456–60.]

Should it be asserted, that the sense of morality consists in the discovery of some relation, distinct from these, and that our enumeration was not complete, when we comprehended all demonstrable relations under the four general heads: to this I know not what to reply, till some one be so good as to point out to me this new relation. It is impossible to refute a system, which has never yet been explained. In such a manner of fighting in the dark, a man loses his blows in the air, and often places them where the enemy is not present.

I must, therefore, on this occasion, rest contented with requiring **499** the two following conditions of any one that would undertake to clear up this system. *First*, as moral good and evil belong only to the actions of the mind, and are derived from our situation with regard to external objects, the relations, from which these moral distinctions arise, must lie only betwixt internal actions, and external objects, and must not be applicable either to internal actions, compared among themselves, or to external objects, when placed in opposition to other external objects. For as morality is supposed to attend certain relations, if these relations could belong to internal actions considered singly, it would follow, that we might be guilty of crimes in ourselves, and independent of our situation, with respect to the universe: and in like manner, if these moral relations could be applied to external objects, it would follow, that even inanimate beings would be susceptible of moral beauty and deformity. Now it seems difficult to imagine, that any relation can be discovered betwixt our passions, volitions and actions, compared to external objects, which relation might not belong either to these passions and volitions, or to these external objects, compared among *themselves*.

But it will be still more difficult to fulfil the *second* condition, **500** requisite to justify this system. According to the principles of those who maintain an abstract rational difference betwixt moral good and evil, and a natural fitness and unfitness of things, it is not only supposed, that these relations, being eternal and immutable, are the same, when considered by every rational creature, but their *effects*

---

virtue. These moral qualities, therefore, must be relations. When we blame any action, in any situation, the whole complicated object, of action and situation, must form certain relations, wherein the essence of vice consists. This hypothesis is not otherwise intelligible. For what does reason discover, when it pronounces any action vicious? Does it discover a relation or a matter of fact? These questions are decisive, and must not be eluded.

are also supposed to be necessarily the same; and it is concluded they have no less, or rather a greater, influence in directing the will of the Deity, than in governing the rational and virtuous of our own species. These two particulars are evidently distinct. It is one thing to know virtue, and another to conform the will to it. In order, therefore, to prove, that the measures of right and wrong are eternal laws, *obligatory* on every rational mind, it is not sufficient to show the relations upon which they are founded: we must also point out the connection betwixt the relation and the will; and must prove that this connection is so necessary, that in every well-disposed mind, it must take place and have its influence; though the difference betwixt these minds be in other respects immense and infinite. Now besides what I have already proved, that even in human nature no relation can ever alone produce any action; besides this, I say, it has been shown, in treating of the understanding, that there is no connection of cause and effect, such as this is supposed to be, which is discoverable otherwise than by experience, and of which we can pretend to have any security by the simple consideration of the objects. All beings in the universe, considered in themselves, appear entirely loose and independent of each other. It is only by experience we learn their influence and connection; and this influence we ought never to extend beyond experience.

Thus it will be impossible to fulfil the *first* condition required to the system of eternal rational measures of right and wrong; because it is impossible to show those relations, upon which such a distinction may be founded: and it is as impossible to fulfil the *second* condition; because we cannot prove *a priori*, that these relations, if they really existed and were perceived, would be universally forcible and obligatory.

501   But to make these general reflections more clear and convincing, we may illustrate them by some particular instances, wherein this character of moral good or evil is the most universally acknowledged. Of all crimes that human creatures are capable of committing, the most horrid and unnatural is ingratitude, especially when it is committed against parents, and appears in the more flagrant instances of wounds and death. This is acknowledged by all mankind, philosophers as well as the people; the question only arises among philosophers, whether the guilt or moral deformity of this action be discovered by demonstrative reasoning, or be felt by an internal sense, and by means of some sentiment, which the reflecting on such an action naturally occasions. This question will soon be decided against the former opinion, if we can show the same relations in other objects, without the notion of any guilt or iniquity attending them. Reason or science is nothing but the comparing of ideas, and the discovery of their relations; and if the same relations have different characters, it must evidently follow, that those characters are not discovered merely by reason. To put the affair, therefore, to this trial, let us choose any inanimate object, such as an oak or elm; and let us suppose, that by the dropping of its seed, it produces a sapling below it, which springing up by degrees, at last overtops and destroys the parent tree: I ask, if in this instance there be wanting any relation, which is discoverable in parricide or ingratitude? Is not the one tree the cause of the other's existence; and the latter the cause of the destruction of the former, in the same manner as when a child murders his parent? It is not sufficient to reply, that a choice or will is wanting. For in the case of parricide, a will does not give rise to any *different* relations, but is only the cause from which the action is derived; and consequently produces the *same* relations, that in the oak or elm arise from some other principles. It is a will or choice, that determines a man to kill his parent; and they are the laws of matter and motion, that determine a sapling to destroy the oak, from which it sprung. Here then the same relations have different causes; but still the relations are the same: and as their discovery is not in both cases attended with a notion of immorality, it follows, that that notion does not arise from such a discovery.

But to choose an instance, still more resembling; I would fain ask **502** any one, why incest in the human species is criminal, and why the very same action, and the same relations in animals have not the smallest moral turpitude and deformity? If it be answered, that this action is innocent in animals, because they have not reason sufficient to discover its turpitude; but that man, being endowed with that faculty, which *ought* to restrain him to his duty, the same action instantly becomes criminal to him; should this be said, I would reply, that this is evidently arguing in a circle. For before reason can perceive this turpitude, the turpitude must exist; and consequently is independent of the decisions of our reason, and is their object more properly than their effect. According to this system, then, every animal, that has sense, and appetite, and will;

that is, every animal, must be susceptible of all the same virtues and vices, for which we ascribe praise and blame to human creatures. All the difference is, that our superior reason may serve to discover the vice or virtue, and by that means may augment the blame or praise: but still this discovery supposes a separate being in these moral distinctions, and a being, which depends only on the will and appetite, and which, both in thought and reality, may be distinguished from the reason. Animals are susceptible of the same relations, with respect to each other, as the human species, and therefore would also be susceptible of the same morality, if the essence of morality consisted in these relations. Their want of a sufficient degree of reason may hinder them from perceiving the duties and obligations of morality, but can never hinder these duties from existing; since they must antecedently exist, in order to their being perceived. Reason must find them, and can never produce them. This argument deserves to be weighed, as being, in my opinion, entirely decisive.

503   Nor does this reasoning only prove, that morality consists not in any relations, that are the objects of science; but if examined, will prove with equal certainty, that it consists not in any *matter of fact*, which can be discovered by the understanding. This is the *second* part of our argument; and if it can be made evident, we may conclude, that morality is not an object of reason. But can there be any difficulty in proving, that vice and virtue are not matters of fact, whose existence we can infer by reason? Take any action allowed to be vicious: wilful murder, for instance. Examine it in all lights, and see if you can find that matter of fact, or real existence, which you call *vice*. In whichever way you take it, you find only certain passions, motives, volitions and thoughts. There is no other matter of fact in the case. The vice entirely escapes you, as long as you consider the object. You never can find it, till you turn your reflection into your own breast, and find a sentiment of disapprobation, which arises in you, towards this action. Here is a matter of fact; but it is the object of feeling, not of reason. It lies in yourself, not in the object. So that when you pronounce any action or character to be vicious, you mean nothing, but that from the constitution of your nature you have a feeling or sentiment of blame from the contemplation of it. Vice and virtue, therefore, may be compared to sounds, colours, heat and cold, which, according to modern philosophy, are

not qualities in objects, but perceptions in the mind: and this discovery in morals, like that other in physics, is to be regarded as a considerable advancement of the speculative sciences; though, like that too, it has little or no influence on practice. Nothing can be more real, or concern us more, than our own sentiments of pleasure and uneasiness; and if these be favourable to virtue, and unfavourable to vice, no more can be requisite to the regulation of our conduct and behaviour.

I cannot forbear adding to these reasonings an observation, which **504** may, perhaps, be found of some importance. In every system of morality, which I have hitherto met with, I have always remarked, that the author proceeds for some time in the ordinary way of reasoning, and establishes the being of a God, or makes observations concerning human affairs; when of a sudden I am surprised to find, that instead of the usual copulations of propositions, *is*, and *is not*, I meet with no proposition that is not connected with an *ought*, or an *ought not*. This change is imperceptible; but is, however, of the last consequence. For as this *ought*, or *ought not*, expresses some new relation or affirmation, it is necessary that it should be observed and explained; and at the same time that a reason should be given, for what seems altogether inconceivable, how this new relation can be a deduction from others, which are entirely different from it. But as authors do not commonly use this precaution, I shall presume to recommend it to the readers; and am persuaded, that this small attention would subvert all the vulgar systems of morality, and let us see, that the distinction of vice and virtue is not founded merely on the relations of objects, nor is perceived by reason.

SECT. II—MORAL DISTINCTIONS DERIVED FROM A MORAL SENSE

Thus the course of the argument leads us to conclude, that since **505** vice and virtue are not discoverable merely by reason, or the comparison of ideas, it must be by means of some impression or sentiment they occasion, that we are able to mark the difference betwixt them. Our decisions concerning moral rectitude and depravity are evidently perceptions; and as all perceptions are either impressions or ideas, the exclusion of the one is a convincing argument for the other. Morality, therefore, is more properly felt than judged of; though this feeling or sentiment is commonly so soft and gentle, that we are apt to confound it with an idea, according to our common custom of taking all things for the same, which have any near resemblance to each other.

506 The next question is, Of what nature are these impressions, and after what manner do they operate upon us? Here we cannot remain long in suspense, but must pronounce the impression arising from virtue, to be agreeable, and that proceeding from vice to be uneasy. Every moment's experience must convince us of this. There is no spectacle so fair and beautiful as a noble and generous action; nor any which gives us more abhorrence than one that is cruel and treacherous. No enjoyment equals the satisfaction we receive from the company of those we love and esteem; as the greatest of all punishments is to be obliged to pass our lives with those we hate or contemn. A very play or romance may afford us instances of this pleasure, which virtue conveys to us; and pain, which arises from vice.

Now since the distinguishing impressions, by which moral good or evil is known, are nothing but *particular* pains or pleasures; it follows, that in all inquiries concerning these moral distinctions, it will be sufficient to show the principles, which make us feel a satisfaction or uneasiness from the survey of any character, in order to satisfy us why the character is laudable or blameable. An action, or sentiment, or character is virtuous or vicious; why? because its view causes a pleasure or uneasiness of a particular kind. In giving a reason, therefore, for the pleasure or uneasiness, we sufficiently explain the vice or virtue. To have the sense of virtue, is nothing but to *feel* a satisfaction of a particular kind from the contemplation of a character. The very *feeling* constitutes our praise or admiration. We go no farther; nor do we inquire into the cause of the satisfaction. We do not infer a character to be virtuous, because it pleases: but in feeling that it pleases after such a particular manner, we in effect feel that it is virtuous. The case is the same as in our judgements concerning all kinds of beauty, and tastes, and sensations. Our approbation is implied in the immediate pleasure they convey to us.

507 I have objected to the system, which establishes eternal rational measures of right and wrong, that it is impossible to show, in the actions of reasonable creatures, any relations, which are not found in external objects; and therefore, if morality always attended these relations, it were possible for inanimate matter to become virtuous or

vicious. Now it may, in like manner, be objected to the present system, that if virtue and vice be determined by pleasure and pain, these qualities must, in every case, arise from the sensations; and consequently any object, whether animate or inanimate, rational or irrational, might become morally good or evil, provided it can excite a satisfaction or uneasiness. But though this objection seems to be the very same, it has by no means the same force, in the one case as in the other. For, *first*, it is evident, that under the term *pleasure*, we comprehend sensations, which are very different from each other, and which have only such a distant resemblance, as is requisite to make them be expressed by the same abstract term. A good composition of music and a bottle of good wine equally produce pleasure; and what is more, their goodness is determined merely by the pleasure. But shall we say upon that account, that the wine is harmonious, or the music of a good flavour? In like manner an inanimate object, and the character or sentiments of any person may, both of them, give satisfaction; but as the satisfaction is different, this keeps our sentiments concerning them from being confounded, and makes us ascribe virtue to the one, and not to the other. Nor is every sentiment of pleasure or pain, which arises from characters and actions, of that *peculiar* kind, which makes us praise or condemn. The good qualities of an enemy are hurtful to us; but may still command our esteem and respect. It is only when a character is considered in general, without reference to our particular interest, that it causes such a feeling or sentiment, as denominates it morally good or evil. It is true, those sentiments, from interest and morals, are apt to be confounded, and naturally run into one another. It seldom happens, that we do not think an enemy vicious, and can distinguish betwixt his opposition to our interest and real villainy or baseness. But this hinders not, but that the sentiments are, in themselves, distinct; and a man of temper and judgement may preserve himself from these illusions. In like manner, though it is certain a musical voice is nothing but one that naturally gives a *particular* kind of pleasure; yet it is difficult for a man to be sensible, that the voice of an enemy is agreeable, or to allow it to be musical. But a person of a fine ear, who has the command of himself, can separate these feelings, and give praise to what deserves it.

Secondly, we may call to remembrance the preceding system of **508** the passions, in order to remark a still more considerable difference among our pains and pleasures. Pride and humility, love and hatred, are excited, when there is any thing presented to us, that both bears a relation to the object of the passion, and produces a separate sensation related to the sensation of the passion. Now virtue and vice are attended with these circumstances. They must necessarily be placed either in ourselves or others, and excite either pleasure or uneasiness; and therefore must give rise to one of these four passions; which clearly distinguishes them from the pleasure and pain arising from inanimate objects, that often bear no relation to us: and this is, perhaps, the most considerable effect that virtue and vice have upon the human mind.

509   It may now be asked *in general*, concerning this pain or pleasure, that distinguishes moral good and evil, *From what principles is it derived, and whence does it arise in the human mind?* To this I reply, *first*, that it is absurd to imagine, that in every particular instance, these sentiments are produced by an *original* quality and *primary* constitution. For as the number of our duties is, in a manner, infinite, it is impossible that our original instincts should extend to each of them, and from our very first infancy impress on the human mind all that multitude of precepts, which are contained in the completest system of ethics. Such a method of proceeding is not conformable to the usual maxims, by which nature is conducted, where a few principles produce all that variety we observe in the universe, and every thing is carried on in the easiest and most simple manner. It is necessary, therefore, to abridge these primary impulses, and find some more general principles, upon which all our notions of morals are founded.

510   But in the *second* place, should it be asked, Whether we ought to search for these principles in *nature*, or whether we must look for them in some other origin? I would reply, that our answer to this question depends upon the definition of the word, Nature, than which there is none more ambiguous and equivocal. If *nature* be opposed to miracles, not only the distinction betwixt vice and virtue is natural, but also every event, which has ever happened in the world, *excepting those miracles, on which our religion is founded*. In saying, then, that the sentiments of vice and virtue are natural in this sense, we make no very extraordinary discovery.

But *nature* may also be opposed to rare and unusual; and in this sense of the word, which is the common one, there may often arise disputes concerning what is natural or unnatural; and one may in general affirm, that we are not possessed of any very precise standard, by which these disputes can be decided. Frequent and rare depend upon the number of examples we have observed; and as this number may gradually increase or diminish, it will be impossible to fix any exact boundaries betwixt them. We may only affirm on this head, that if ever there was any thing, which could be called natural in this sense, the sentiments of morality certainly may; since there never was any nation of the world, nor any single person in any nation, who was utterly deprived of them, and who never, in any instance, showed the least approbation or dislike of manners. These sentiments are so rooted in our constitution and temper, that without entirely confounding the human mind by disease or madness, it is impossible to extirpate and destroy them.

But *nature* may also be opposed to artifice, as well as to what is rare and unusual; and in this sense it may be disputed, whether the notions of virtue be natural or not. We readily forget, that the designs, and projects, and views of men are principles as necessary in their operation as heat and cold, moist and dry: but taking them to be free and entirely our own, it is usual for us to set them in opposition to the other principles of nature. Should it, therefore, be demanded, whether the sense of virtue be natural or artificial, I am of opinion, that it is impossible for me at present to give any precise answer to this question. Perhaps it will appear afterwards, that our sense of some virtues is artificial, and that of others natural. The discussion of this question will be more proper, when we enter upon an exact detail of each particular vice and virtue[a].

Mean while it may not be amiss to observe from these definitions **511** of *natural* and *unnatural*, that nothing can be more unphilosophical than those systems, which assert, that virtue is the same with what is natural, and vice with what is unnatural. For in the first sense of the word, Nature, as opposed to miracles, both vice and virtue are equally natural; and in the second sense, as opposed to what is unusual, perhaps virtue will be found to be the most unnatural. At least it must be owned, that heroic virtue, being as unusual, is as little natural as the most brutal barbarity. As to the third sense of the word, it is certain, that both vice and virtue are equally artificial, and out of nature. For however it may be disputed, whether the notion of a

---

[a] In the following discourse, *natural* is also opposed sometimes to *civil*, sometimes to *moral*. The opposition will always discover the sense, in which it is taken.

merit or demerit in certain actions be natural or artificial, it is evident, that the actions themselves are artificial, and are performed with a certain design and intention; otherwise they could never be ranked under any of these denominations. It is impossible, therefore, that the character of natural and unnatural can ever, in any sense, mark the boundaries of vice and virtue.

Thus we are still brought back to our first position, that virtue is distinguished by the pleasure, and vice by the pain, that any action, sentiment or character gives us by the mere view and contemplation. This decision is very commodious; because it reduces us to this simple question, *Why any action or sentiment upon the general view or survey, gives a certain satisfaction or uneasiness*, in order to show the origin of its moral rectitude or depravity, without looking for any incomprehensible relations and qualities, which never did exist in nature, nor even in our imagination, by any clear and distinct conception. I flatter myself I have executed a great part of my present design by a state of the question, which appears to me so free from ambiguity and obscurity.

PART II—*Of justice and injustice*

SECT. I—JUSTICE, WHETHER A NATURAL OR ARTIFICIAL VIRTUE?

512   I have already hinted, that our sense of every kind of virtue is not natural; but that there are some virtues, that produce pleasure and approbation by means of an artifice or contrivance, which arises from the circumstances and necessity of mankind. Of this kind I assert *justice* to be; and shall endeavour to defend this opinion by a short, and, I hope, convincing argument, before I examine the nature of the artifice, from which the sense of that virtue is derived.

It is evident, that when we praise any actions, we regard only the motives that produced them, and consider the actions as signs or indications of certain principles in the mind and temper. The external performance has no merit. We must look within to find the moral quality. This we cannot do directly; and therefore fix our attention on actions, as on external signs. But these actions are still considered as signs; and the ultimate object of our praise and approbation is the motive, that produced them.

After the same manner, when we require any action, or blame a person for not performing it, we always suppose, that one in that situation should be influenced by the proper motive of that action, and we esteem it vicious in him to be regardless of it. If we find, upon inquiry, that the virtuous motive was still powerful over his breast, though checked in its operation by some circumstances unknown to us, we retract our blame, and have the same esteem for him, as if he had actually performed the action, which we require of him.

It appears, therefore, that all virtuous actions derive their merit **513** only from virtuous motives, and are considered merely as signs of those motives. From this principle I conclude, that the first virtuous motive, which bestows a merit on any action, can never be a regard to the virtue of that action, but must be some other natural motive or principle. To suppose, that the mere regard to the virtue of the action, may be the first motive, which produced the action, and rendered it virtuous, is to reason in a circle. Before we can have such a regard, the action must be really virtuous; and this virtue must be derived from some virtuous motive: and consequently the virtuous motive must be different from the regard to the virtue of the action. A virtuous motive is requisite to render an action virtuous. An action must be virtuous, before we can have a regard to its virtue. Some virtuous motive, therefore, must be antecedent to that regard.

Nor is this merely a metaphysical subtlety; but enters into all our reasonings in common life, though perhaps we may not be able to place it in such distinct philosophical terms. We blame a father for neglecting his child. Why? because it shows a want of natural affection, which is the duty of every parent. Were not natural affection a duty, the care of children could not be a duty; and it were impossible we could have the duty in our eye in the attention we give to our offspring. In this case, therefore, all men suppose a motive to the action distinct from a sense of duty.

Here is a man, that does many benevolent actions; relieves the distressed, comforts the afflicted, and extends his bounty even to the greatest strangers. No character can be more amiable and virtuous. We regard these actions as proofs of the greatest humanity. This humanity bestows a merit on the actions. A regard to this merit is, therefore, a secondary consideration, and derived from the antecedent principle of humanity, which is meritorious and laudable.

In short, it may be established as an undoubted maxim, *that no action can be virtuous, or morally good, unless there be in human nature some motive to produce it, distinct from the sense of its morality.*

514   But may not the sense of morality or duty produce an action, without any other motive? I answer, It may: but this is no objection to the present doctrine. When any virtuous motive or principle is common in human nature, a person, who feels his heart devoid of that motive, may hate himself upon that account, and may perform the action without the motive, from a certain sense of duty, in order to acquire by practice, that virtuous principle, or at least, to disguise to himself, as much as possible, his want of it. A man that really feels no gratitude in his temper, is still pleased to perform grateful actions, and thinks he has, by that means, fulfilled his duty. Actions are at first only considered as signs of motives: but it is usual, in this case, as in all others, to fix our attention on the signs, and neglect, in some measure, the thing signified. But though, on some occasions, a person may perform an action merely out of regard to its moral obligation, yet still this supposes in human nature some distinct principles, which are capable of producing the action, and whose moral beauty renders the action meritorious.

Now to apply all this to the present case; I suppose a person to have lent me a sum of money, on condition that it be restored in a few days; and also suppose, that after the expiration of the term agreed on, he demands the sum: I ask, *What reason or motive have I to restore the money?* It will, perhaps, be said, that my regard to justice, and abhorrence of villainy and knavery, are sufficient reasons for me, if I have the least grain of honesty, or sense of duty and obligation. And this answer, no doubt, is just and satisfactory to man in his civilized state, and when trained up according to a certain discipline and education. But in his rude and more *natural* condition, if you are pleased to call such a condition natural, this answer would be rejected as perfectly unintelligible and sophistical. For one in that situation would immediately ask you, *Wherein consists this honesty and justice, which you find in restoring a loan, and abstaining from the property of others?* It does not surely lie in the external action. It must, therefore, be placed in the motive, from which the external action is derived. This motive can never be a regard to the honesty of the action. For it is a plain fallacy to say, that a virtuous motive is requisite to render an action honest, and at the same time that a regard to the honesty is the motive of the action. We can never have a regard to the virtue of an action, unless the action be antecedently virtuous. No action can be virtuous, but so far as it proceeds from a virtuous motive. A virtuous motive, therefore, must precede the regard to the virtue; and it is impossible, that the virtuous motive and the regard to the virtue can be the same.

It is requisite, then, to find some motive to acts of justice and 515 honesty, distinct from our regard to the honesty; and in this lies the great difficulty. For should we say, that a concern for our private interest or reputation is the legitimate motive to all honest actions; it would follow, that wherever that concern ceases, honesty can no longer have place. But it is certain, that self-love, when it acts at its liberty, instead of engaging us to honest actions, is the source of all injustice and violence; nor can a man ever correct those vices, without correcting and restraining the *natural* movements of that appetite.

But should it be affirmed, that the reason or motive of such actions 516 is the *regard to public interest,* to which nothing is more contrary than examples of injustice and dishonesty; should this be said, I would propose the three following considerations, as worthy of our attention. *First,* public interest is not naturally attached to the observation of the rules of justice; but is only connected with it, after an artificial convention for the establishment of these rules, as shall be shown more at large hereafter. *Secondly,* if we suppose, that the loan was secret, and that it is necessary for the interest of the person, that the money be restored in the same manner (as when the lender would conceal his riches), in that case the example ceases, and the public is no longer interested in the actions of the borrower; though I suppose there is no moralist, who will affirm, that the duty and obligation ceases. *Thirdly,* experience sufficiently proves, that men, in the ordinary conduct of life, look not so far as the public interest, when they pay their creditors, perform their promises, and abstain from theft, and robbery, and injustice of every kind. That is a motive too remote and too sublime to affect the generality of mankind, and operate with any force in actions so contrary to private interest as are frequently those of justice and common honesty.

In general, it may be affirmed, that there is no such passion in human 517 minds, as the love of mankind, merely as such, independent of personal qualities, of services, or of relation to ourself. It is true, there is no human, and indeed no sensible, creature, whose happiness or misery does not, in some measure, affect us, when brought near

to us, and represented in lively colours: but this proceeds merely
from sympathy, and is no proof of such an universal affection to
mankind, since this concern extends itself beyond our own species.
An affection betwixt the sexes is a passion evidently implanted in
human nature; and this passion not only appears in its peculiar
symptoms, but also in inflaming every other principle of affection,
and raising a stronger love from beauty, wit, kindness, than what
would otherwise flow from them. Were there an universal love
among all human creatures, it would appear after the same manner.
Any degree of a good quality would cause a stronger affection than
the same degree of a bad quality would cause hatred; contrary to
what we find by experience. Men's tempers are different, and some
have a propensity to the tender, and others to the rougher, affections:
but in the main, we may affirm, that man in general, or human
nature, is nothing but the object both of love and hatred, and requires some other cause, which by a double relation of impressions
and ideas, may excite these passions. In vain would we endeavour to
elude this hypothesis. There are no phenomena that point out any
such kind affection to men, independent of their merit, and every
other circumstance. We love company in general; but it is as we
love any other amusement. An Englishman in Italy is a friend: a
European in China; and perhaps a man would be beloved as such,
were we to meet him in the moon. But this proceeds only from the
relation to ourselves; which in these cases gathers force by being
confined to a few persons.

518   If public benevolence, therefore, or a regard to the interests of
mankind, cannot be the original motive to justice, much less can
private benevolence, or a *regard to the interests of the party concerned*, be
this motive. For what if he be my enemy, and has given me just cause
to hate him? What if he be a vicious man, and deserves the hatred of
all mankind? What if he be a miser, and can make no use of what I
would deprive him of? What if he be a profligate debauchee, and
would rather receive harm than benefit from large possessions?
What if I be in necessity, and have urgent motives to acquire something to my family? In all these cases, the original motive to justice
would fail; and consequently the justice itself, and along with it all
property, right, and obligation.

A rich man lies under a moral obligation to communicate to those
in necessity a share of his superfluities. Were private benevolence

the original motive to justice, a man would not be obliged to leave others in the possession of more than he is obliged to give them. At least the difference would be very inconsiderable. Men generally fix their affections more on what they are possessed of, than on what they never enjoyed: for this reason, it would be greater cruelty to dispossess a man of any thing, than not to give it him. But who will assert, that this is the only foundation of justice?

Besides, we must consider, that the chief reason, why men attach themselves so much to their possessions is, that they consider them as their property, and as secured to them inviolably by the laws of society. But this is a secondary consideration, and dependent on the preceding notions of justice and property.

A man's property is supposed to be fenced against every mortal, in every possible case. But private benevolence is, and ought to be, weaker in some persons, than in others: and in many, or indeed in most persons, must absolutely fail. Private benevolence, therefore, is not the original motive of justice.

From all this it follows, that we have no real or universal motive 519 for observing the laws of equity, but the very equity and merit of that observance; and as no action can be equitable or meritorious, where it cannot arise from some separate motive, there is here an evident sophistry and reasoning in a circle. Unless, therefore, we will allow, that nature has established a sophistry, and rendered it necessary and unavoidable, we must allow, that the sense of justice and injustice is not derived from nature, but arises artificially, though necessarily, from education and human conventions.

I shall add, as a corollary to this reasoning, that since no action can 520 be laudable or blameable, without some motives or impelling passions, distinct from the sense of morals, these distinct passions must have a great influence on that sense. It is according to their general force in human nature, that we blame or praise. In judging of the beauty of animal bodies, we always carry in our eye the economy of a certain species; and where the limbs and features observe that proportion, which is common to the species, we pronounce them handsome and beautiful. In like manner we always consider the *natural* and *usual* force of the passions, when we determine concerning vice and virtue; and if the passions depart very much from the common measures on either side, they are always disapproved as vicious. A man naturally loves his children better than his nephews, his nephews better than his cousins, his cousins better than strangers, where every thing else is equal. Hence arise our common measures of duty, in preferring the one to the other. Our sense of duty always follows the common and natural course of our passions.

521   To avoid giving offence, I must here observe, that when I deny justice to be a natural virtue, I make use of the word, *natural*, only as opposed to *artificial*. In another sense of the word; as no principle of the human mind is more natural than a sense of virtue; so no virtue is more natural than justice. Mankind is an inventive species; and where an invention is obvious and absolutely necessary, it may as properly be said to be natural as any thing that proceeds immediately from original principles, without the intervention of thought or reflection. Though the rules of justice be *artificial*, they are not *arbitrary*. Nor is the expression improper to call them *Laws of Nature*; if by natural we understand what is common to any species, or even if we confine it to mean what is inseparable from the species.

SECT. II—OF THE ORIGIN OF JUSTICE AND PROPERTY

522   We now proceed to examine two questions, viz. *concerning the manner, in which the rules of justice are established by the artifice of men*; and *concerning the reasons, which determine us to attribute to the observance or neglect of these rules a moral beauty and deformity*. These questions will appear afterwards to be distinct. We shall begin with the former.

Of all the animals, with which this globe is peopled, there is none towards whom nature seems, at first sight, to have exercised more cruelty than towards man, in the numberless wants and necessities, with which she has loaded him, and in the slender means, which she affords to the relieving these necessities. In other creatures these two particulars generally compensate each other. If we consider the lion as a voracious and carnivorous animal, we shall easily discover him to be very necessitous; but if we turn our eye to his make and temper, his agility, his courage, his arms, and his force, we shall find, that his advantages hold proportion with his wants. The sheep and ox are deprived of all these advantages; but their appetites are moderate, and their food is of easy purchase. In man alone, this unnatural conjunction of infirmity, and of necessity, may be observed in its greatest perfection. Not only the food, which is required for his sustenance, flies his search and approach, or at least requires his labour to be produced, but he must be possessed of clothes and lodging, to defend him against the injuries of the weather; though to consider him only in himself, he is provided neither with arms, nor force, nor other natural abilities, which are in any degree answerable to so many necessities.

It is by society alone he is able to supply his defects, and raise **523** himself up to an equality with his fellow-creatures, and even acquire a superiority above them. By society all his infirmities are compensated; and though in that situation his wants multiply every moment upon him, yet his abilities are still more augmented, and leave him in every respect more satisfied and happy, than it is possible for him, in his savage and solitary condition, ever to become. When every individual person labours apart, and only for himself, his force is too small to execute any considerable work; his labour being employed in supplying all his different necessities, he never attains a perfection in any particular art; and as his force and success are not at all times equal, the least failure in either of these particulars must be attended with inevitable ruin and misery. Society provides a remedy for these *three* inconveniences. By the conjunction of forces, our power is augmented: by the partition of employments, our ability increases: and by mutual succour we are less exposed to fortune and accidents. It is by this additional *force*, *ability*, and *security*, that society becomes advantageous.

But in order to form society, it is requisite not only that it be ad- **524** vantageous, but also that men be sensible of these advantages; and it is impossible, in their wild uncultivated state, that by study and reflection alone, they should ever be able to attain this knowledge. Most fortunately, therefore, there is conjoined to those necessities, whose remedies are remote and obscure, another necessity, which having a present and more obvious remedy, may justly be regarded as the first and original principle of human society. This necessity is no other than that natural appetite betwixt the sexes, which unites them together, and preserves their union, till a new tie takes place in their concern for their common offspring. This new concern becomes also a principle of union betwixt the parents and offspring, and forms a more numerous society; where the parents govern by the advantage of their superior strength and wisdom, and at the same time are restrained in the exercise of their authority by that natural affection, which they bear their children. In a little time, custom and habit operating on the tender minds of the children, makes them sensible of the advantages, which they may reap from society, as well as fashions them by degrees for it, by rubbing off those rough corners and untoward affections, which prevent their coalition.

525   For it must be confessed, that however the circumstances of human nature may render an union necessary, and however those passions of lust and natural affection may seem to render it unavoidable; yet there are other particulars in our *natural temper*, and in our *outward circumstances*, which are very incommodious, and are even contrary to the requisite conjunction. Among the former, we may justly esteem our *selfishness* to be the most considerable. I am sensible, that, generally speaking, the representations of this quality have been carried much too far; and that the descriptions, which certain philosophers delight so much to form of mankind in this particular, are as wide of nature as any accounts of monsters, which we meet with in fables and romances. So far from thinking, that men have no affection for any thing beyond themselves, I am of opinion, that though it be rare to meet with one, who loves any single person better than himself; yet it is as rare to meet with one, in whom all the kind affections, taken together, do not overbalance all the selfish. Consult common experience: do you not see, that though the whole expense of the family be generally under the direction of the master of it, yet there are few that do not bestow the largest part of their fortunes on the pleasures of their wives, and the education of their children, reserving the smallest portion for their own proper use and entertainment? This is what we may observe concerning such as have those endearing ties; and may presume, that the case would be the same with others, were they placed in a like situation.

But though this generosity must be acknowledged to the honour of human nature, we may at the same time remark, that so noble an affection, instead of fitting men for large societies, is almost as contrary to them, as the most narrow selfishness. For while each person loves himself better than any other single person, and in his love to others bears the greatest affection to his relations and acquaintance, this must necessarily produce an opposition of passions, and a consequent opposition of actions; which cannot but be dangerous to the new-established union.

It is however worth while to remark, that this contrariety of **526** passions would be attended with but small danger, did it not concur with a peculiarity in our *outward circumstances*, which affords it an opportunity of exerting itself. There are three different species of goods, which we are possessed of; the internal satisfaction of our minds, the external advantages of our body, and the enjoyment of such possessions as we have acquired by our industry and good fortune. We are perfectly secure in the enjoyment of the first. The second may be ravished from us, but can be of no advantage to him who deprives us of them. The last only are both exposed to the violence of others, and may be transferred without suffering any loss or alteration; while at the same time, there is not a sufficient quantity of them to supply every one's desires and necessities. As the improvement, therefore, of these goods is the chief advantage of society, so the *instability* of their possession, along with their *scarcity*, is the chief impediment.

In vain should we expect to find, in *uncultivated nature*, a remedy to this inconvenience; or hope for any inartificial principle of the human mind, which might control those partial affections, and make us overcome the temptations arising from our circumstances.

★   ★   ★   ★

The remedy, then, is not derived from nature, but from *artifice*; **527** or more properly speaking, nature provides a remedy in the judgement and understanding, for what is irregular and incommodious in the affections. For when men, from their early education in society, have become sensible of the infinite advantages that result from it, and have besides acquired a new affection to company and conversation; and when they have observed, that the principal disturbance in society arises from those goods, which we call external, and from their looseness and easy transition from one person to another; they must seek for a remedy, by putting these goods, as far as possible, on the same footing with the fixed and constant advantages of the mind and body. This can be done after no other manner, than by a convention entered into by all the members of the society to bestow stability on the possession of those external goods, and leave every one in the peaceable enjoyment of what he may acquire by his fortune and industry. By this means, every one knows what he may safely possess; and the passions are restrained in their partial and contradictory motions. Nor is such a restraint contrary to these passions; for if so, it could never be entered into, nor maintained; but it is only contrary to their heedless and impetuous movement. Instead of departing from our own interest, or from that of our nearest friends, by abstaining from the possessions of others, we cannot better consult both these interests, than by such a convention; because it is by that means we maintain society, which is so necessary to their well-being and subsistence, as well as to our own.

528   This convention is not of the nature of a *promise*: for even promises themselves, as we shall see afterwards, arise from human conventions. It is only a general sense of common interest; which sense all the members of the society express to one another, and which induces them to regulate their conduct by certain rules. I observe, that it will be for my interest to leave another in the possession of his goods, *provided* he will act in the same manner with regard to me. He is sensible of a like interest in the regulation of his conduct. When this common sense of interest is mutually expressed, and is known to both, it produces a suitable resolution and behaviour. And this may properly enough be called a convention or agreement betwixt us, though without the interposition of a promise; since the actions of each of us have a reference to those of the other, and are performed upon the supposition, that something is to be performed on the other part. Two men, who pull the oars of a boat, do it by an agreement or convention, though they have never given promises to each other. Nor is the rule concerning the stability of possession the less derived from human conventions, that it arises gradually, and acquires force by a slow progression, and by our repeated experience of the inconviences of transgressing it. On the contrary, this experience assures us still more, that the sense of interest has become common to all our fellows, and gives us a confidence of the future regularity of their conduct: and it is only on the expectation of this, that our moderation and abstinence are founded. In like manner are languages gradually established by human conventions without any promise. In like manner do gold and silver become the common measures of exchange, and are esteemed sufficient payment for what is of a hundred times their value.

529   After this convention, concerning abstinence from the possessions of others, is entered into, and every one has acquired a stability in his possessions, there immediately arise the ideas of justice and injustice; as also those of *property*, *right*, and *obligation*. The latter are altogether unintelligible without first understanding the former. Our property is nothing but those goods, whose constant possession is established by the laws of society; that is, by the laws of justice. Those, therefore, who make use of the words *property*, or *right*, or *obligation*, before they have explained the origin of justice, or even make use of them in that explication, are guilty of a very gross fallacy, and can never reason upon any solid foundation. A man's property is some object related to him. This relation is not natural, but moral, and founded on justice. It is very preposterous, therefore, to imagine, that we can have any idea of property, without fully comprehending the nature of justice, and showing its origin in the artifice and contrivance of men. The origin of justice explains that of property. The same artifice gives rise to both. As our first and most natural sentiment of morals is founded on the nature of our passions, and gives the preference to ourselves and friends, above strangers; it is impossible there can be naturally any such thing as a fixed right or property, while the opposite passions of men impel them in contrary directions, and are not restrained by any convention or agreement.

No one can doubt, that the convention for the distinction of **530** property, and for the stability of possession, is of all circumstances the most necessary to the establishment of human society, and that after the agreement for the fixing and observing of this rule, there remains little or nothing to be done towards settling a perfect harmony and concord. All the other passions, beside this of interest, are either easily restrained, or are not of such pernicious consequence, when indulged. *Vanity* is rather to be esteemed a social passion, and a bond of union among men. *Pity* and *love* are to be considered in the same light. And as to *envy* and *revenge*, though pernicious, they operate only by intervals, and are directed against particular persons, whom we consider as our superiors or enemies. This avidity alone, of acquiring goods and possessions for ourselves and our nearest friends, is insatiable, perpetual, universal, and directly destructive of society. There scarce is any one, who is not actuated by it; and there is no one, who has not reason to fear from it, when it acts without any restraint, and gives way to its first and most natural movements. So that upon the whole, we are to esteem the difficulties in the establishment of society, to be greater or less, according to those we encounter in regulating and restraining this passion.

*　　　*　　　*　　　*

531　Now as it is by establishing the rule for the stability of possession, that this passion restrains itself; if that rule be very abstruse, and of difficult invention; society must be esteemed, in a manner, accidental, and the effect of many ages. But if it be found, that nothing can be more simple and obvious than that rule; that every parent, in order to preserve peace among his children, must establish it; and that these first rudiments of justice must every day be improved, as the society enlarges: if all this appear evident, as it certainly must, we may conclude, that it is utterly impossible for man to remain any considerable time in that savage condition, which precedes society; but that his very first state and situation may justly be esteemed social. This, however, hinders not, but that philosophers may, if they please, extend their reasoning to the supposed *state of nature*; provided they allow it to be a mere philosophical fiction, which never had, and never could have any reality. Human nature being composed of two principal parts, which are requisite in all its actions, the affections and understanding; it is certain, that the blind motions of the former, without the direction of the latter, incapacitate men for society: and it may be allowed us to consider separately the effects, that result from the separate operations of these two component parts of the mind. The same liberty may be permitted to moral, which is allowed to natural philosophers; and it is very usual with the latter to consider any motion as compounded and consisting of two parts separate from each other, though at the same time they acknowledge it to be in itself uncompounded and inseparable.

This *state of nature*, therefore, is to be regarded as a mere fiction, not unlike that of the *golden age*, which poets have invented; only with this difference, that the former is described as full of war, violence and injustice; whereas the latter is painted out to us, as the most charming and most peaceable condition, that can possibly be imagined. The seasons, in that first age of nature, were so temperate, if we may believe the poets, that there was no necessity for men to provide themselves with clothes and houses as a security against the violence of heat and cold. The rivers flowed with wine and milk: the oaks yielded honey; and nature spontaneously produced her greatest delicacies. Nor were these the chief advantages of that happy age. The storms and tempests were not alone removed from nature; but those more furious tempests were unknown to human breasts, which now cause such uproar, and engender such confusion. Avarice, ambition, cruelty, selfishness, were never heard of: cordial affection, compassion, sympathy, were the only movements, with which the human mind was yet acquainted. Even the distinction of *mine* and *thine* was banished from that happy race of mortals, and carried with them the very notions of property and obligation, justice and injustice.

This, no doubt, is to be regarded as an idle fiction; but yet deserves our attention, because nothing can more evidently show the origin of those virtues, which are the subjects of our present inquiry. I have already observed, that justice takes its rise from human conventions; and that these are intended as a remedy to some inconveniences, which proceed from the concurrence of certain *qualities* of the human mind with the *situation* of external objects. The qualities of the mind are *selfishness* and *limited generosity*: and the situation of external objects is their *easy change*, joined to their *scarcity* in comparison of the wants and desires of men. But however philosophers may have been bewildered in those speculations, poets have been guided more infallibly, by a certain taste or common instinct, which in most kinds of reasoning goes farther than any of that art and philosophy, with which we have been yet acquainted. They easily perceived, if every man had a tender regard for another, or if nature supplied abundantly all our wants and desires, that the jealousy of interest, which justice supposes, could no longer have place; nor would there be any occasion for those distinctions and limits of property and possession, which at present are in use among mankind. Increase to a sufficient degree the benevolence of men, or the bounty of nature, and you render justice useless, by supplying its place with much nobler virtues, and more valuable blessings. The selfishness of men is animated by the few possessions we have, in proportion to our wants; and it is to restrain this selfishness, that men have been obliged to separate themselves from the community, and to distinguish betwixt their own goods and those of others.

Nor need we have recourse to the fictions of poets to learn this; but beside the reason of the thing, may discover the same truth by common experience and observation. It is easy to remark, that a

532

cordial affection renders all things common among friends; and that married people in particular mutually lose their property, and are unacquainted with the *mine* and *thine*, which are so necessary, and yet cause such disturbance in human society. The same effect arises from any alteration in the circumstances of mankind; as when there is such a plenty of any thing as satisfies all the desires of men: in which case the distinction of property is entirely lost, and every thing remains in common. This we may observe with regard to air and water, though the most valuable of all external objects; and may easily conclude, that if men were supplied with every thing in the same abundance, or if *every one* had the same affection and tender regard for *every one* as for himself; justice and injustice would be equally unknown among mankind.

Here then is a proposition, which, I think, may be regarded as certain, *that it is only from the selfishness and confined generosity of man, along with the scanty provision nature has made for his wants, that justice derives its origin.*

★   ★   ★   ★

533 We come now to the *second* question we proposed, viz. *Why we annex the idea of virtue to justice, and of vice to injustice.* This question will not detain us long after the principles, which we have already established. All we can say of it at present will be dispatched in a few words: and for farther satisfaction, the reader must wait till we come to the *third* part of this book. The *natural* obligation to justice, viz. interest,[1] has been fully explained; but as to the *moral* obligation, or the sentiment of right and wrong, it will first be requisite to examine the natural virtues, before we can give a full and satisfactory account of it.

534 After men have found by experience, that their selfishness and confined generosity, acting at their liberty, totally incapacitate them for society; and at the same time have observed, that society is necessary to the satisfaction of those very passions, they are naturally induced to lay themselves under the restraint of such rules, as may render their commerce more safe and commodious. To the imposition then, and observance of these rules, both in general, and in every particular instance, they are at first induced only by a regard to

[1 Cf. Balguy, § 460.]

interest; and this motive, on the first formation of society, is sufficiently strong and forcible. But when society has become numerous, and has increased to a tribe or nation, this interest is more remote; nor do men so readily perceive, that disorder and confusion follow upon every breach of these rules, as in a more narrow and contracted society. But though in our own actions we may frequently lose sight of that interest, which we have in maintaining order, and may follow a lesser and more present interest, we never fail to observe the prejudice we receive, either mediately or immediately, from the injustice of others; as not being in that case either blinded by passion, or biased by any contrary temptation. Nay when the injustice is so distant from us, as no way to affect our interest, it still displeases us; because we consider it as prejudicial to human society, and pernicious to every one that approaches the person guilty of it. We partake of their uneasiness by *sympathy*; and as every thing, which gives uneasiness in human actions, upon the general survey, is called Vice, and whatever produces satisfaction, in the same manner, is denominated Virtue; this is the reason why the sense of moral good and evil follows upon justice and injustice. And though this sense, in the present case, be derived only from contemplating the actions of others, yet we fail not to extend it even to our own actions. The *general rule* reaches beyond those instances, from which it arose; while at the same time we naturally *sympathize* with others in the sentiments they entertain of us. *Thus self-interest is the original motive to the* establishment *of justice: but a* sympathy *with public interest is the source of the* moral approbation, *which attends that virtue.*

*   *   *   *

SECT. V—OF THE OBLIGATION OF PROMISES

That the rule of morality, which enjoins the performance of **535** promises, is not *natural*, will sufficiently appear from these two propositions, which I proceed to prove, viz. *that a promise would not be intelligible, before human conventions had established it*; and *that even if it were intelligible, it would not be attended with any moral obligation.*

I say, *first*, that a promise is not intelligible naturally, nor antecedent to human conventions; and that a man, unacquainted with society, could never enter into any engagements with another, even though they could perceive each other's thoughts by intuition. If promises be natural and intelligible, there must be some act of the mind attending these words, *I promise*; and on this act of the mind must the obligation depend. Let us, therefore, run over all the faculties of the soul, and see which of them is exerted in our promises.

536 The act of the mind, expressed by a promise, is not a *resolution* to perform any thing: for that alone never imposes any obligation. Nor is it a *desire* of such a performance: for we may bind ourselves without such a desire, or even with an aversion, declared and avowed. Neither is it the *willing* of that action,[1] which we promise to perform: for a promise always regards some future time, and the will has an influence only on present actions. It follows, therefore, that since the act of the mind, which enters into a promise, and produces its obligation, is neither the resolving, desiring, nor willing any particular performance, it must necessarily be the *willing* of that *obligation*, which arises from the promise. Nor is this only a conclusion of philosophy; but is entirely conformable to our common ways of thinking and of expressing ourselves, when we say that we are bound by our own consent, and that the obligation arises from our mere will and pleasure. The only question, then, is, whether there be not a manifest absurdity in supposing this act of the mind, and such an absurdity as no man could fall into, whose ideas are not confounded with prejudice and the fallacious use of language.

537 All morality depends upon our sentiments; and when any action, or quality of the mind, pleases us *after a certain manner*, we say it is virtuous; and when the neglect, or non-performance of it, displeases us *after a like manner*, we say that we lie under an obligation to perform it. A change of the obligation supposes a change of the sentiment; and a creation of a new obligation supposes some new sentiment to arise. But it is certain we can naturally no more change our own sentiments, than the motions of the heavens; nor by a single act of our will, that is, by a promise, render any action agreeable or disagreeable, moral or immoral; which, without that act, would have produced contrary impressions, or have been endowed with different qualities. It would be absurd, therefore, to will any new obligation, that is, any new sentiment of pain or pleasure; nor is it possible, that men could naturally fall into so gross an absurdity.

[1 Contrast Hobbes, § 102.]

A promise, therefore, is *naturally* something altogether unintelligible, nor is there any act of the mind belonging to it[a].

But, *secondly*, if there was any act of the mind belonging to it, it **538** could not *naturally* produce any obligation. This appears evidently from the foregoing reasoning. A promise creates a new obligation. A new obligation supposes new sentiments to arise. The will never creates new sentiments. There could not naturally, therefore, arise any obligation from a promise, even supposing the mind could fall into the absurdity of willing that obligation.

The same truth may be proved still more evidently by that reasoning, which proved justice in general to be an artificial virtue. No action can be required of us as our duty, unless there be implanted in human nature some actuating passion or motive, capable of producing the action. This motive cannot be the sense of duty. A sense of duty supposes an antecedent obligation: and where an action is not required by any natural passion, it cannot be required by any natural obligation; since it may be omitted without proving any defect or imperfection in the mind and temper, and consequently without any vice. Now it is evident we have no motive leading us to the performance of promises, distinct from a sense of duty. If we thought, that promises had no moral obligation, we never should feel any inclination to observe them. This is not the case with the natural virtues. Though there was no obligation to relieve the miserable,

---

[a] Were morality discoverable by reason, and not by sentiment, it would be still more evident, that promises could make no alteration upon it. Morality is supposed to consist in relation. Every new imposition of morality, therefore, must arise from some new relation of objects; and consequently the will could not produce *immediately* any change in morals, but could have that effect only by producing a change upon the objects. But as the moral obligation of a promise is the pure effect of the will, without the least change in any part of the universe; it follows, that promises have no *natural* obligation.

Should it be said, that this act of the will being in effect a new object, produces new relations and new duties; I would answer, that this is a pure sophism, which may be detected by a very moderate share of accuracy and exactness. To will a new obligation, is to will a new relation of objects; and therefore, if this new relation of objects were formed by the volition itself, we should in effect will the volition; which is plainly absurd and impossible. The will has here no object to which it could tend; but must return upon itself *in infinitum*. The new obligation depends upon new relations. The new relations depend upon a new volition. The new volition has for object a new obligation, and consequently new relations, and consequently a new volition; which volition again has in view a new obligation, relation and volition, without any termination. It is impossible, therefore, we could ever will a new obligation; and consequently it is impossible the will could ever accompany a promise, or produce a new obligation of morality.

our humanity would lead us to it; and when we omit that duty, the immorality of the omission arises from its being a proof, that we want the natural sentiments of humanity. A father knows it to be his duty to take care of his children: but he has also a natural inclination to it. And if no human creature had that inclination, no one could lie under any such obligation. But as there is naturally no inclination to observe promises, distinct from a sense of their obligation; it follows, that fidelity is no natural virtue, and that promises have no force, antecedent to human conventions.

539   If any one dissent from this, he must give a regular proof of these two propositions, viz. *that there is a peculiar act of the mind, annexed to promises*; and *that consequent to this act of the mind, there arises an inclination to perform, distinct from a sense of duty.* I presume, that it is impossible to prove either of these two points; and therefore I venture to conclude, that promises are human inventions, founded on the necessities and interests of society.

540   In order to discover these necessities and interests, we must consider the same qualities of human nature, which we have already found to give rise to the preceding laws of society. Men being naturally selfish, or endowed only with a confined generosity, they are not easily induced to perform any action for the interest of strangers, except with a view to some reciprocal advantage, which they had no hope of obtaining but by such a performance. Now as it frequently happens, that these mutual performances cannot be finished at the same instant, it is necessary, that one party be contented to remain in uncertainty, and depend upon the gratitude of the other for a return of kindness. But so much corruption is there among men, that, generally speaking, this becomes but a slender security; and as the benefactor is here supposed to bestow his favours with a view to self-interest, this both takes off from the obligation, and sets an example of selfishness, which is the true mother of ingratitude. Were we, therefore, to follow the natural course of our passions and inclinations, we should perform but few actions for the advantage of others, from disinterested views; because we are naturally very limited in our kindness and affection: and we should perform as few of that kind, out of a regard to interest; because we cannot depend upon their gratitude. Here then is the mutual commerce of good offices in a manner lost among mankind, and every one reduced to his own skill and industry for his well-being and

subsistence. The invention of the law of nature, concerning the *stability* of possession, has already rendered men tolerable to each other; that of the *transference* of property and possession by consent has begun to render them mutually advantageous: but still these laws of nature, however strictly observed, are not sufficient to render them so serviceable to each other, as by nature they are fitted to become. Though possession be *stable*, men may often reap but small advantage from it, while they are possessed of a greater quantity of any species of goods than they have occasion for, and at the same time suffer by the want of others. The *transference* of property, which is the proper remedy for this inconvenience, cannot remedy it entirely; because it can only take place with regard to such objects as are *present* and *individual*, but not to such as are *absent* or *general*. One cannot transfer the property of a particular house, twenty leagues distant; because the consent cannot be attended with delivery, which is a requisite circumstance. Neither can one transfer the property of ten bushels of corn, or five hogsheads of wine, by the mere expression and consent; because these are only general terms, and have no direct relation to any particular heap of corn, or barrels of wine. Besides, the commerce of mankind is not confined to the barter of commodities, but may extend to services and actions, which we may exchange to our mutual interest and advantage. Your corn is ripe to-day; mine will be so to-morrow. It is profitable for us both, that I should labour with you to-day, and that you should aid me to-morrow. I have no kindness for you, and know you have as little for me. I will not, therefore, take any pains upon your account; and should I labour with you upon my own account, in expectation of a return, I know I should be disappointed, and that I should in vain depend upon your gratitude. Here then I leave you to labour alone: you treat me in the same manner. The seasons change; and both of us lose our harvests for want of mutual confidence and security.

All this is the effect of the natural and inherent principles and 541 passions of human nature; and as these passions and principles are inalterable, it may be thought, that our conduct, which depends on them, must be so too, and that it would be in vain, either for moralists or politicians, to tamper with us, or attempt to change the usual course of our actions, with a view to public interest. And indeed, did the success of their designs depend upon their success in correcting the selfishness and ingratitude of men, they would never make any progress, unless aided by omnipotence, which is alone able to new-mould the human mind, and change its character in such fundamental articles. All they can pretend to, is, to give a new direction to those natural passions, and teach us that we can better satisfy our appetites in an oblique and artificial manner, than by their headlong and impetuous motion. Hence I learn to do a service to another, without bearing him any real kindness; because I foresee, that he will return my service, in expectation of another of the same kind, and in order to maintain the same correspondence of good offices with me or with others. And accordingly, after I have served him, and he is in possession of the advantage arising from my action, he is induced to perform his part, as foreseeing the consequences of his refusal.

But though this self-interested commerce of men begins to take place, and to predominate in society, it does not entirely abolish the more generous and noble intercourse of friendship and good offices. I may still do services to such persons as I love, and am more particularly acquainted with, without any prospect of advantage; and they may make me a return in the same manner, without any view but that of recompensing my past services. In order, therefore, to distinguish those two different sorts of commerce, the interested and the disinterested, there is a *certain form of words* invented for the former, by which we bind ourselves to the performance of any action. This form of words constitutes what we call a *promise*, which is the sanction of the interested commerce of mankind. When a man says *he promises any thing*, he in effect expresses a *resolution* of performing it; and along with that, by making use of this *form of words*, subjects himself to the penalty of never being trusted again in case of failure. A resolution is the natural act of the mind, which promises express: but were there no more than a resolution in the case, promises would only declare our former motives, and would not create any new motive or obligation. They are the conventions of men, which create a new motive, when experience has taught us, that human affairs would be conducted much more for mutual advantage, were there certain *symbols* or *signs* instituted, by which we might give each other security of our conduct in any particular incident. After these signs are instituted, whoever uses them is immediately bound by his interest to execute his engagements, and must never expect to be trusted any more, if he refuse to perform what he promised.

Nor is that knowledge, which is requisite to make mankind **542** sensible of this interest in the *institution* and *observance* of promises, to be esteemed superior to the capacity of human nature, however savage and uncultivated. There needs but a very little practice of the world, to make us perceive all these consequences and advantages. The shortest experience of society discovers them to every mortal; and when each individual perceives the same sense of interest in all his fellows, he immediately performs his part of any contract, as being assured, that they will not be wanting in theirs. All of them, by concert, enter into a scheme of actions, calculated for common benefit, and agree to be true to their word; nor is there any thing requisite to form this concert or convention, but that every one have a sense of interest in the faithful fulfilling of engagements, and express that sense to other members of the society. This immediately causes that interest to operate upon them; and interest is the *first* obligation to the performance of promises.

Afterwards a sentiment of morals concurs with interest, and be- **543** comes a new obligation upon mankind. This sentiment of morality, in the performance of promises, arises from the same principles as that in the abstinence from the property of others. *Public interest, education,* and *the artifices of politicians,* have the same effect in both cases. The difficulties, that occur to us, in supposing a moral obligation to attend promises, we either surmount or elude. For instance; the expression of a resolution is not commonly supposed to be obligatory; and we cannot readily conceive how the making use of a certain form of words should be able to cause any material difference. Here, therefore, we *feign* a new act of the mind, which we call the *willing* an obligation; and on this we suppose the morality to depend. But we have proved already, that there is no such act of the mind, and consequently that promises impose no natural obligation.

To confirm this, we may subjoin some other reflections concerning that will, which is supposed to enter into a promise, and to cause its obligation. It is evident, that the will alone is never supposed to cause the obligation, but must be expressed by words or signs, in order to impose a tie upon any man. The expression being once brought in as subservient to the will, soon becomes the principal part of the promise; nor will a man be less bound by his word, though he secretly give a different direction to his intention, and withhold himself both from a resolution, and from willing an obligation. But though the expression makes on most occasions the whole of the promise, yet it does not always so; and one, who should make use of any expression, of which he knows not the meaning, and which he uses without any intention of binding himself, would not certainly be bound by it. Nay, though he knows its meaning, yet if he uses it in jest only, and with such signs as show evidently he has no serious intention of binding himself, he would not lie under any obligation of performance; but it is necessary, that the words be a perfect expression of the will, without any contrary signs. Nay, even this we must not carry so far as to imagine, that one, whom, by our quickness of understanding, we conjecture, from certain signs, to have an intention of deceiving us, is not bound by his expression or verbal promise, if we accept of it; but must limit this conclusion to those cases, where the signs are of a different kind from those of deceit. All these contradictions are easily accounted for, if the obligation of promises be merely a human invention for the convenience of society; but will never be explained, if it be something *real* and *natural*, arising from any action of the mind or body.

544 I shall farther observe, that since every new promise imposes a new obligation of morality on the person who promises, and since this new obligation arises from his will; it is one of the most mysterious and incomprehensible operations that can possibly be imagined, and may even be compared to *transubstantiation*, or *holy orders*[a], where a certain form of words, along with a certain intention, changes entirely the nature of an external object, and even of a human creature. But though these mysteries be so far alike, it is very remarkable, that they differ widely in other particulars, and that this difference may be regarded as a strong proof of the difference of their origins. As the obligation of promises is an invention for the interest of society, it is warped into as many different forms as that interest requires, and even runs into direct contradictions, rather than lose sight of its object. But as those other monstrous doctrines are mere priestly inventions, and have no public interest in view, they are less disturbed in their progress by new obstacles; and it must be owned, that, after the first absurdity, they follow more directly the current of reason and good sense. Theologians clearly perceived, that the

---

[a] I mean so far, as holy orders are supposed to produce the *indelible character*. In other respects they are only a legal qualification.

external form of words, being mere sound, require an intention to make them have any efficacy; and that this intention being once considered as a requisite circumstance, its absence must equally prevent the effect, whether avowed or concealed, whether sincere or deceitful. Accordingly they have commonly determined, that the intention of the priest makes the sacrament, and that when he secretly withdraws his intention, he is highly criminal in himself; but still destroys the baptism, or communion, or holy orders. The terrible consequences of this doctrine were not able to hinder its taking place; as the inconveniences of a similar doctrine, with regard to promises, have prevented that doctrine from establishing itself. Men are always more concerned about the present life than the future; and are apt to think the smallest evil, which regards the former, more important than the greatest, which regards the latter.

We may draw the same conclusion, concerning the origin of 545 promises, from the *force*, which is supposed to invalidate all contracts, and to free us from their obligation. Such a principle is a proof, that promises have no natural obligation, and are mere artificial contrivances for the convenience and advantage of society. If we consider aright of the matter, force is not essentially different from any other motive of hope or fear, which may induce us to engage our word, and lay ourselves under any obligation. A man, dangerously wounded, who promises a competent sum to a surgeon to cure him, would certainly be bound to performance; though the case be not so much different from that of one, who promises a sum to a robber, as to produce so great a difference in our sentiments of morality, if these sentiments were not built entirely on public interest and convenience.

PART III—*Of the other virtues and vices*

SECT. I—OF THE ORIGIN OF THE NATURAL VIRTUES AND VICES

We come now to the examination of such virtues and vices as are 546 entirely natural, and have no dependence on the artifice and contrivance of men. The examination of these will conclude this system of morals.

*　　　*　　　*　　　*

We may begin with considering anew the nature and force of *sympathy*. The minds of all men are similar in their feelings and operations; nor can any one be actuated by any affection, of which all others are not, in some degree, susceptible. As in strings equally wound up, the motion of one communicates itself to the rest; so all the affections readily pass from one person to another, and beget correspondent movements in every human creature. When I see the *effects* of passion in the voice and gesture of any person, my mind immediately passes from these effects to their causes, and forms such a lively idea of the passion, as is presently converted into the passion itself. In like manner, when I perceive the *causes* of any emotion, my mind is conveyed to the effects, and is actuated with a like emotion. Were I present at any of the more terrible operations of surgery, it is certain, that even before it begun, the preparation of the instruments, the laying of the bandages in order, the heating of the irons, with all the signs of anxiety and concern in the patient and assistants, would have a great effect upon my mind, and excite the strongest sentiments of pity and terror. No passion of another discovers itself immediately to the mind. We are only sensible of its causes or effects. From *these* we infer the passion: and consequently *these* give rise to our sympathy.

547   Our sense of beauty depends very much on this principle; and where any object has a tendency to produce pleasure in its possessor, it is always regarded as beautiful; as every object, that has a tendency to produce pain, is disagreeable and deformed. Thus the conveniency of a house, the fertility of a field, the strength of a horse, the capacity, security, and swift-sailing of a vessel, form the principal beauty of these several objects. Here the object, which is denominated beautiful, pleases only by its tendency to produce a certain effect. That effect is the pleasure or advantage of some other person. Now the pleasure of a stranger, for whom we have no friendship, pleases us only by sympathy. To this principle, therefore, is owing the beauty, which we find in every thing that is useful. How considerable a part this is of beauty will easily appear upon reflection. Wherever an object has a tendency to produce pleasure in the possessor, or in other words, is the proper *cause* of pleasure, it is sure to please the spectator, by a delicate sympathy with the possessor. Most of the works of art are esteemed beautiful, in proportion to their fitness for the use of man, and even many of the productions of nature derive

their beauty from that source. Handsome and beautiful, on most occasions, is not an absolute but a relative quality, and pleases us by nothing but its tendency to produce an end that is agreeable[a].

The same principle produces, in many instances, our sentiments **548** of morals, as well as those of beauty. No virtue is more esteemed than justice, and no vice more detested than injustice; nor are there any qualities, which go farther to the fixing the character, either as amiable or odious. Now justice is a moral virtue, merely because it has that tendency to the good of mankind; and, indeed, is nothing but an artificial invention to that purpose. The same may be said of allegiance, of the laws of nations, of modesty, and of good-manners. All these are mere human contrivances for the interest of society. And since there is a very strong sentiment of morals, which in all nations, and all ages, has attended them, we must allow, that the reflecting on the tendency of characters and mental qualities, is sufficient to give us the sentiments of approbation and blame. Now as the means to an end can only be agreeable, where the end is agreeable; and as the good of society, where our own interest is not concerned, or that of our friends, pleases only by sympathy: it follows, that sympathy is the source of the esteem, which we pay to all the artificial virtues.

Thus it appears, *that* sympathy is a very powerful principle in **549** human nature, *that* it has a great influence on our taste of beauty, and *that* it produces our sentiment of morals in all the artificial virtues. From thence we may presume, that it also gives rise to many of the other virtues; and that qualities acquire our approbation, because of their tendency to the good of mankind. This presumption must become a certainty, when we find that most of those qualities, which we *naturally* approve of, have actually that tendency, and render a man a proper member of society: while the qualities, which we *naturally* disapprove of, have a contrary tendency, and render any intercourse with the person dangerous or disagreeable. For having found, that such tendencies have force enough to produce the strongest sentiment of morals, we can never reasonably, in these cases, look for any other cause of approbation or blame; it being an

---

[a] Decentior equus cujus astricta sunt ilia; sed idem velocior. Pulcher aspectu sit athleta, cujus lacertos exercitatio expressit; idem certamini paratior. Nunquam vero *species* ab *utilitate* dividitur. Sed hoc quidem discernere, modici judicii est. *Quinct.* lib. 8.

inviolable maxim in philosophy, that where any particular cause is sufficient for an effect, we ought to rest satisfied with it, and ought not to multiply causes without necessity. We have happily attained experiments in the artificial virtues, where the tendency of qualities to the good of society, is the *sole* cause of our approbation, without any suspicion of the concurrence of another principle. From thence we learn the force of that principle. And where that principle may take place, and the quality approved of is really beneficial to society, a true philosopher will never require any other principle to account for the strongest approbation and esteem.

550 That many of the natural virtues have this tendency to the good of society, no one can doubt of. Meekness, beneficence, charity, generosity, clemency, moderation, equity, bear the greatest figure among the moral qualities, and are commonly denominated the *social* virtues, to mark their tendency to the good of society. This goes so far, that some philosophers have represented all moral distinctions as the effect of artifice and education, when skilful politicians endeavoured to restrain the turbulent passions of men, and make them operate to the public good, by the notions of honour and shame.[1] This system, however, is not consistent with experience. For, *first*, there are other virtues and vices beside those which have this tendency to the public advantage and loss. *Secondly*, had not men a natural sentiment of approbation and blame, it could never be excited by politicians;[2] nor would the words *laudable* and *praiseworthy*, *blameable* and *odious*, be any more intelligible, than if they were a language perfectly unknown to us, as we have already observed. But though this system be erroneous, it may teach us, that moral distinctions arise, in a great measure, from the tendency of qualities and characters to the interests of society, and that it is our concern for that interest, which makes us approve or disapprove of them. Now we have no such extensive concern for society but from sympathy; and consequently it is that principle, which takes us so far out of ourselves, as to give us the same pleasure or uneasiness in the characters of others, as if they had a tendency to our own advantage or loss.

551 The only difference betwixt the natural virtues and justice lies in this, that the good, which results from the former, arises from every

[1 Cf. Mandeville, §§ 264, 267, 269.]
[2 Cf. Hutcheson, § 311.]

single act, and is the object of some natural passion: whereas a single act of justice, considered in itself, may often be contrary to the public good; and it is only the concurrence of mankind, in a general scheme or system of action, which is advantageous. When I relieve persons in distress, my natural humanity is my motive; and so far as my succour extends, so far have I promoted the happiness of my fellow-creatures. But if we examine all the questions, that come before any tribunal of justice, we shall find, that, considering each case apart, it would as often be an instance of humanity to decide contrary to the laws of justice as conformable to them. Judges take from a poor man to give to a rich; they bestow on the dissolute the labour of the industrious; and put into the hands of the vicious the means of harming both themselves and others. The whole scheme, however, of law and justice is advantageous to the society; and it was with a view to this advantage, that men, by their voluntary conventions, established it. After it is once established by these conventions, it is *naturally* attended with a strong sentiment of morals; which can proceed from nothing but our sympathy with the interests of society. We need no other explication of that esteem, which attends such of the natural virtues, as have a tendency to the public good.

I must farther add, that there are several circumstances, which 552 render this hypothesis much more probable with regard to the natural than the artificial virtues. It is certain, that the imagination is more affected by what is particular, than by what is general; and that the sentiments are always moved with difficulty, where their objects are, in any degree, loose and undetermined: now every particular act of justice is not beneficial to society, but the whole scheme or system: and it may not, perhaps, be any individual person, for whom we are concerned, who receives benefit from justice, but the whole society alike. On the contrary, every particular act of generosity, or relief of the industrious and indigent, is beneficial; and is beneficial to a particular person, who is not undeserving of it. It is more natural, therefore, to think, that the tendencies of the latter virtue will affect our sentiments, and command our approbation, than those of the former; and therefore, since we find, that the approbation of the former arises from their tendencies, we may ascribe, with better reason, the same cause to the approbation of the latter. In any number of similar effects, if a cause can be discovered for one, we ought to extend that cause to all the other effects, which can be accounted for by it: but much more, if these other effects be attended with peculiar circumstances, which facilitate the operation of that cause.

553 Before I proceed farther, I must observe two remarkable circumstances in this affair, which may seem objections to the present system. The first may be thus explained. When any quality, or character, has a tendency to the good of mankind, we are pleased with it, and approve of it; because it presents the lively idea of pleasure; which idea affects us by sympathy, and is itself a kind of pleasure. But as this sympathy is very variable, it may be thought, that our sentiments of morals must admit of all the same variations. We sympathize more with persons contiguous to us, than with persons remote from us: with our acquaintance, than with strangers: with our countrymen, than with foreigners. But notwithstanding this variation of our sympathy, we give the same approbation to the same moral qualities in China as in England. They appear equally virtuous, and recommend themselves equally to the esteem of a judicious spectator. The sympathy varies without a variation in our esteem. Our esteem, therefore, proceeds not from sympathy.

554 To this I answer: The approbation of moral qualities most certainly is not derived from reason, or any comparison of ideas; but proceeds entirely from a moral taste, and from certain sentiments of pleasure or disgust, which arise upon the contemplation and view of particular qualities or characters. Now it is evident, that those sentiments, whence-ever they are derived, must vary according to the distance or contiguity of the objects; nor can I feel the same lively pleasure from the virtues of a person, who lived in Greece two thousand years ago, that I feel from the virtues of a familiar friend and acquaintance. Yet I do not say, that I esteem the one more than the other: and therefore, if the variation of the sentiment, without a variation of the esteem, be an objection, it must have equal force against every other system, as against that of sympathy. But to consider the matter aright, it has no force at all; and it is the easiest matter in the world to account for it. Our situation, with regard both to persons and things, is in continual fluctuation; and a man, that lies at a distance from us, may, in a little time, become a familiar acquaintance. Besides, every particular man has a peculiar position with regard to others; and it is impossible we could ever converse together on any reasonable terms, were each of us to consider characters and persons, only as they appear from his peculiar point of view. In order, therefore, to prevent those continual *contradictions*, and arrive at a more *stable* judgement of things, we fix on some *steady* and *general* points of view; and always, in our thoughts, place ourselves in them, whatever may be our present situation. In like manner, external beauty is determined merely by pleasure; and it is evident, a beautiful countenance cannot give so much pleasure, when seen at the distance of twenty paces, as when it is brought nearer us. We say not, however, that it appears to us less beautiful: because we know what effect it will have in such a position, and by that reflection we correct its momentary appearance.

In general, all sentiments of blame or praise are variable, according to our situation of nearness or remoteness, with regard to the person blamed or praised, and according to the present disposition of our mind. But these variations we regard not in our general decisions, but still apply the terms expressive of our liking or dislike, in the same manner, as if we remained in one point of view. Experience soon teaches us this method of correcting our sentiments, or at least, of correcting our language, where the sentiments are more stubborn and inalterable. Our servant, if diligent and faithful, may excite stronger sentiments of love and kindness than Marcus Brutus, as represented in history; but we say not upon that account, that the former character is more laudable than the latter. We know, that were we to approach equally near to that renowned patriot, he would command a much higher degree of affection and admiration. Such corrections are common with regard to all the senses; and indeed it were impossible we could ever make use of language, or communicate our sentiments to one another, did we not correct the momentary appearances of things, and overlook our present situation.

★　　★　　★　　★

I now proceed to the *second* remarkable circumstance, which I **555** proposed to take notice of. Where a person is possessed of a character, that in its natural tendency is beneficial to society, we esteem him virtuous, and are delighted with the view of his character, even though particular accidents prevent its operation, and incapacitate him from being serviceable to his friends and country. Virtue in rags is still virtue; and the love, which it procures, attends a man into a dungeon or desert, where the virtue can no longer be exerted in action, and is lost to all the world. Now this may be esteemed an objection to the present system. Sympathy interests us in the good of mankind; and if sympathy were the source of our esteem for virtue, that sentiment of approbation could only take place, where the virtue actually attained its end, and was beneficial to mankind. Where it fails of its end, it is only an imperfect means; and therefore can never acquire any merit from that end. The goodness of an end can bestow a merit on such means alone as are complete, and actually produce the end.

556   To this we may reply, that where any object, in all its parts, is fitted to attain any agreeable end, it naturally gives us pleasure, and is esteemed beautiful, even though some external circumstances be wanting to render it altogether effectual. It is sufficient if every thing be complete in the object itself. A house, that is contrived with great judgement for all the commodities of life, pleases us upon that account; though perhaps we are sensible, that no-one will ever dwell in it. A fertile soil, and a happy climate, delight us by a reflection on the happiness which they would afford the inhabitants, though at present the country be desert and uninhabited. A man, whose limbs and shape promise strength and activity, is esteemed handsome, though condemned to perpetual imprisonment. The imagination has a set of passions belonging to it, upon which our sentiments of beauty much depend. These passions are moved by degrees of liveliness and strength, which are inferior to *belief*, and independent of the real existence of their objects. Where a character is, in every respect, fitted to be beneficial to society, the imagination passes easily from the cause to the effect, without considering that there are still some circumstances wanting to render the cause a complete one. *General rules* create a species of probability, which sometimes influences the judgement, and always the imagination.

It is true, when the cause is complete, and a good disposition is attended with good fortune, which renders it really beneficial to society, it gives a stronger pleasure to the spectator, and is attended with a more lively sympathy. We are more affected by it; and yet we do not say that it is more virtuous, or that we esteem it more. We know, that an alteration of fortune may render the benevolent disposition entirely impotent; and therefore we separate, as much as possible, the fortune from the disposition. The case is the same, as when we correct the different sentiments of virtue, which proceed from its different distances from ourselves. The passions do not always follow our corrections; but these corrections serve sufficiently to regulate our abstract notions, and are alone regarded, when we pronounce in general concerning the degrees of vice and virtue.

It is observed by critics, that all words or sentences, which are difficult to the pronunciation, are disagreeable to the ear. There is no difference, whether a man hear them pronounced, or read them silently to himself. When I run over a book with my eye, I imagine I hear it all; and also, by the force of imagination, enter into the uneasiness, which the delivery of it would give the speaker. The uneasiness is not real; but as such a composition of words has a natural tendency to produce it, this is sufficient to affect the mind with a painful sentiment, and render the discourse harsh and disagreeable. It is a similar case, where any real quality is, by accidental circumstances, rendered impotent, and is deprived of its natural influence on society.

Upon these principles we may easily remove any contradiction, 557 which may appear to be betwixt the *extensive sympathy*, on which our sentiments of virtue depend, and that *limited generosity*, which I have frequently observed to be natural to men, and which justice and property suppose, according to the precedent reasoning. My sympathy with another may give me the sentiment of pain and disapprobation, when any object is presented, that has a tendency to give him uneasiness; though I may not be willing to sacrifice any thing of my own interest, or cross any of my passions, for his satisfaction. A house may displease me by being ill-contrived for the convenience of the owner; and yet I may refuse to give a shilling towards the rebuilding of it. Sentiments must touch the heart, to make them control our passions: but they need not extend beyond the imagination, to make them influence our taste. When a building seems clumsy and tottering to the eye, it is ugly and disagreeable; though we be fully assured of the solidity of the workmanship. It is a kind of fear, which causes this sentiment of disapprobation; but the passion is not the same with that which we feel, when obliged to stand under a wall, that we really think tottering and insecure. The *seeming tendencies* of objects affect the mind: and the emotions they excite are of a like species with those, which proceed from the *real consequences* of objects, but their feeling is different. Nay, these emotions are so different in their feeling, that they may often be contrary, without destroying each other; as when the fortifications of a city belonging to an enemy are esteemed beautiful upon account of their strength, though we could wish that they were entirely destroyed. The imagination adheres to the *general* views of things, and distinguishes the feelings they produce, from those which arise from our particular and momentary situation.

*   *   *   *

558   There have been many systems of morality advanced by philosophers in all ages; but if they are strictly examined, they may be reduced to two, which alone merit our attention. Moral good and evil are certainly distinguished by our *sentiments*, not by *reason*: but these sentiments may arise either from the mere species or appearance of characters and passions, or from reflections on their tendency to the happiness of mankind, and of particular persons. My opinion is, that both these causes are intermixed in our judgements of morals; after the same manner as they are in our decisions concerning most kinds of external beauty: though I am also of opinion, that reflections on the tendencies of actions have by far the greatest influence, and determine all the great lines of our duty. There are, however, instances, in cases of less moment, wherein this immediate taste or sentiment produces our approbation. Wit, and a certain easy and disengaged behaviour, are qualities *immediately agreeable* to others, and command their love and esteem. Some of these qualities produce satisfaction in others by particular *original* principles of human nature, which cannot be accounted for: others may be resolved into principles, which are more general. This will best appear upon a particular inquiry.

559   As some qualities acquire their merit from their being *immediately agreeable* to others, without any tendency to public interest; so some are denominated virtuous from their being *immediately agreeable* to the person himself, who possesses them. Each of the passions and operations of the mind has a particular feeling, which must be either agreeable or disagreeable. The first is virtuous, the second vicious. This particular feeling constitutes the very nature of the passion; and therefore needs not be accounted for.

But however directly the distinction of vice and virtue may seem to flow from the immediate pleasure or uneasiness, which particular qualities cause to ourselves or others; it is easy to observe, that it has also a considerable dependence on the principle of *sympathy* so often insisted on. We approve of a person, who is possessed of qualities *immediately agreeable* to those, with whom he has any commerce; though perhaps we ourselves never reaped any pleasure from them. We also approve of one, who is possessed of qualities, that are *immediately agreeable* to himself; though they be of no service to any mortal. To account for this we must have recourse to the foregoing principles.

Thus, to take a general review of the present hypothesis: every **560** quality of the mind is denominated virtuous, which gives pleasure by the mere survey; as every quality, which produces pain, is called vicious. This pleasure and this pain may arise from four different sources. For we reap a pleasure from the view of a character, which is naturally fitted to be useful to others, or to the person himself, or which is agreeable to others, or to the person himself. One may, perhaps, be surprised, that amidst all these interests and pleasures, we should forget our own, which touch us so nearly on every other occasion. But we shall easily satisfy ourselves on this head, when we consider, that every particular person's pleasure and interest being different, it is impossible men could ever agree in their sentiments and judgements, unless they chose some common point of view, from which they might survey their object, and which might cause it to appear the same to all of them. Now in judging of characters, the only interest or pleasure, which appears the same to every spectator, is that of the person himself, whose character is examined; or that of persons, who have a connection with him. And though such interests and pleasures touch us more faintly than our own, yet being more constant and universal, they counterbalance the latter even in practice, and are alone admitted in speculation as the standard of virtue and morality. They alone produce that particular feeling or sentiment, on which moral distinctions depend.

As to the good or ill desert of virtue or vice, it is an evident consequence of the sentiments of pleasure or uneasiness. These sentiments produce love or hatred; and love or hatred, by the original constitution of human passion, is attended with benevolence or anger; that is, with a desire of making happy the person we love, and miserable the person we hate. We have treated of this more fully on another occasion.

SECT. VI—CONCLUSION OF THIS BOOK

561   Thus upon the whole I am hopeful, that nothing is wanting to an accurate proof of this system of ethics. We are certain, that sympathy is a very powerful principle in human nature. We are also certain, that it has a great influence on our sense of beauty, when we regard external objects, as well as when we judge of morals. We find, that it has force sufficient to give us the strongest sentiments of approbation, when it operates alone, without the concurrence of any other principle; as in the cases of justice, allegiance, chastity, and good-manners. We may observe, that all the circumstances requisite for its operation are found in most of the virtues; which have, for the most part, a tendency to the good of society, or to that of the person possessed of them. If we compare all these circumstances, we shall not doubt, that sympathy is the chief source of moral distinctions; especially when we reflect, that no objection can be raised against this hypothesis in one case, which will not extend to all cases. Justice is certainly approved of for no other reason, than because it has a tendency to the public good: and the public good is indifferent to us, except so far as sympathy interests us in it. We may presume the like with regard to all the other virtues, which have a like tendency to the public good. They must derive all their merit from our sympathy with those, who reap any advantage from them: as the virtues, which have a tendency to the good of the person possessed of them, derive their merit from our sympathy with him.

Most people will readily allow, that the useful qualities of the mind are virtuous, because of their utility. This way of thinking is so natural, and occurs on so many occasions, that few will make any scruple of admitting it. Now this being once admitted, the force of sympathy must necessarily be acknowledged. Virtue is considered as means to an end. Means to an end are only valued so far as the end is valued. But the happiness of strangers affects us by sympathy alone. To that principle, therefore, we are to ascribe the sentiment of approbation, which arises from the survey of all those virtues, that are useful to society, or to the person possessed of them. These form the most considerable part of morality.

★ ★ ★ ★

An Enquiry concerning the Principles of Morals

SECT. I—OF THE GENERAL PRINCIPLES OF MORALS

*   *   *   *

There has been a controversy started of late, much better worth **562** examination, concerning the general foundation of MORALS; whether they be derived from REASON, or from SENTIMENT; whether we attain the knowledge of them by a chain of argument and induction, or by an immediate feeling and finer internal sense; whether, like all sound judgement of truth and falsehood, they should be the same to every rational intelligent being; or whether, like the perception of beauty and deformity, they be founded entirely on the particular fabric and constitution of the human species.

*   *   *   *

But though this question, concerning the general principles of **563** morals, be curious and important, it is needless for us, at present, to employ farther care in our researches concerning it. For if we can be so happy, in the course of this inquiry, as to discover the true origin of morals, it will then easily appear how far either sentiment or reason enters into all determinations of this nature*. In order to attain this purpose, we shall endeavour to follow a very simple method: we shall analyse that complication of mental qualities, which form what, in common life, we call PERSONAL MERIT: we shall consider every attribute of the mind, which renders a man an object either of esteem and affection, or of hatred and contempt; every habit or sentiment or faculty, which, if ascribed to any person, implies either praise or blame, and may enter into any panegyric or satire of his character and manners. The quick sensibility, which, on this head, is so universal among mankind, gives a philosopher suffi-cient assurance, that he can never be considerably mistaken in fram-ing the catalogue, or incur any danger of misplacing the objects of his contemplation: he needs only enter into his own breast for a

* See Appendix I [i.e. §§ 594–607].

moment, and consider whether or not he should desire to have this or that quality ascribed to him, and whether such or such an imputation would proceed from a friend or an enemy. The very nature of language guides us almost infallibly in forming a judgement of this nature; and as every tongue possesses one set of words which are taken in a good sense, and another in the opposite, the least acquaintance with the idiom suffices, without any reasoning, to direct us in collecting and arranging the estimable or blameable qualities of men. The only object of reasoning is to discover the circumstances on both sides, which are common to these qualities; to observe that particular in which the estimable qualities agree on the one hand, and the blameable on the other; and thence to reach the foundation of ethics, and find those universal principles, from which all censure or approbation is ultimately derived. As this is a question of fact, not of abstract science, we can only expect success, by following the experimental method, and deducing general maxims from a comparison of particular instances. The other scientifical method, where a general abstract principle is first established, and is afterwards branched out into a variety of inferences and conclusions, may be more perfect in itself, but suits less the imperfection of human nature, and is a common source of illusion and mistake in this as well as in other subjects. Men are now cured of their passion for hypotheses and systems in natural philosophy, and will hearken to no arguments but those which are derived from experience. It is full time they should attempt a like reformation in all moral disquisitions; and reject every system of ethics, however subtle or ingenious, which is not founded on fact and observation.

We shall begin our inquiry on this head by the consideration of the social virtues, benevolence and justice. The explication of them will probably give us an opening by which the others may be accounted for.

SECT. II—OF BENEVOLENCE

★   ★   ★   ★

PART II

564   We may observe, that, in displaying the praises of any humane, beneficent man, there is one circumstance which never fails to be amply insisted on, namely, the happiness and satisfaction, derived to society from his intercourse and good offices. To his parents, we are apt to say, he endears himself by his pious attachment and duteous care, still more than by the connections of nature. His children never feel his authority, but when employed for their advantage. With him, the ties of love are consolidated by beneficence and friendship. The ties of friendship approach, in a fond observance of each obliging office, to those of love and inclination. His domestics and dependants have in him a sure resource; and no longer dread the power of fortune, but so far as she exercises it over him. From him the hungry receive food, the naked clothing, the ignorant and slothful skill and industry. Like the sun, an inferior minister of providence, he cheers, invigorates, and sustains the surrounding world.

If confined to private life, the sphere of his activity is narrower; but his influence is all benign and gentle. If exalted into a higher station, mankind and posterity reap the fruit of his labours.

As these topics of praise never fail to be employed, and with success, where we would inspire esteem for any one; may it not thence be concluded, that the UTILITY, resulting from the social virtues, forms, at least, a *part* of their merit, and is one source of that approbation and regard so universally paid to them?

*   *   *   *

In all determinations of morality, this circumstance of public 565 utility is ever principally in view; and wherever disputes arise, either in philosophy or common life, concerning the bounds of duty, the question cannot, by any means, be decided with greater certainty, than by ascertaining, on any side, the true interests of mankind. If any false opinion, embraced from appearances, has been found to prevail; as soon as farther experience and sounder reasoning have given us juster notions of human affairs; we retract our first sentiment, and adjust anew the boundaries of moral good and evil.

*   *   *   *

Upon the whole, then, it seems undeniable, *that* nothing can bestow more merit on any human creature than the sentiment of benevolence in an eminent degree; and *that* a *part*, at least, of its merit arises from its tendency to promote the interests of our species, and bestow happiness on human society. We carry our view into the salutary consequences of such a character and disposition; and whatever has so benign an influence, and forwards so desirable an end, is beheld with complacency and pleasure. The social virtues are never regarded without their beneficial tendencies, nor viewed as barren and unfruitful. The happiness of mankind, the order of society, the harmony of families, the mutual support of friends, are always considered as the result of their gentle dominion over the breasts of men.

How considerable a *part* of their merit we ought to ascribe to their utility, will better appear from future disquisitions*; as well as the reason, why this circumstance has such a command over our esteem and approbation†.

SECT. III—OF JUSTICE

PART I

566 That JUSTICE is useful to society, and consequently that *part* of its merit, at least, must arise from that consideration, it would be a superfluous undertaking to prove. That public utility is the *sole* origin of justice, and that reflections on the beneficial consequences of this virtue are the *sole* foundation of its merit; this proposition, being more curious and important, will better deserve our examination and inquiry.

567 Let us suppose, that nature has bestowed on the human race such profuse *abundance* of all *external* conveniencies, that, without any uncertainty in the event, without any care or industry on our part, every individual finds himself fully provided with whatever his most voracious appetites can want, or luxurious imagination wish or desire. His natural beauty, we shall suppose, surpasses all acquired ornaments: the perpetual clemency of the seasons renders useless all clothes or covering: the raw herbage affords him the most delicious fare; the clear fountain, the richest beverage. No laborious occupation required: no tillage: no navigation. Music, poetry, and contemplation form his sole business: conversation, mirth, and friendship his sole amusement.

It seems evident, that, in such a happy state, every other social virtue would flourish, and receive tenfold increase; but the cautious,

*Sect. 3d and 4th.   †Sect. 5th.

jealous virtue of justice would never once have been dreamed of. For what purpose make a partition of goods, where every one has already more than enough? Why give rise to property, where there cannot possibly be any injury? Why call this object *mine*, when, upon the seizing of it by another, I need but stretch out my hand to possess myself of what is equally valuable? Justice, in that case, being totally USELESS, would be an idle ceremonial, and could never possibly have place in the catalogue of virtues.

We see, even in the present necessitous condition of mankind, that, wherever any benefit is bestowed by nature in an unlimited abundance, we leave it always in common among the whole human race, and make no subdivisions of right and property. Water and air, though the most necessary of all objects, are not challenged as the property of individuals; nor can any man commit injustice by the most lavish use and enjoyment of these blessings. In fertile extensive countries, with few inhabitants, land is regarded on the same footing. And no topic is so much insisted on by those, who defend the liberty of the seas, as the unexhausted use of them in navigation. Were the advantages, procured by navigation, as inexhaustible, these reasoners had never had any adversaries to refute; nor had any claims ever been advanced of a separate, exclusive dominion over the ocean.

It may happen, in some countries, at some periods, that there be established a property in water, none in land*; if the latter be in greater abundance than can be used by the inhabitants, and the former be found, with difficulty, and in very small quantities.

Again; suppose, that, though the necessities of the human race **568** continue the same as at present, yet the mind is so enlarged, and so replete with friendship and generosity, that every man has the utmost tenderness for every man, and feels no more concern for his own interest than for that of his fellows: it seems evident, that the USE of justice would, in this case, be suspended by such an extensive benevolence, nor would the divisions and barriers of property and obligation have ever been thought of. Why should I bind another, by a deed or promise, to do me any good office, when I know that he is already prompted, by the strongest inclination, to seek my happiness, and would, of himself, perform the desired service; except the hurt, he thereby receives, be greater than the benefit accruing to me? in which case, he knows, that, from my innate

*Genesis, chap. xiii, and xxi.

humanity and friendship, I should be the first to oppose myself to his imprudent generosity. Why raise landmarks between my neighbour's field and mine, when my heart has made no division between our interests; but shares all his joys and sorrows with the same force and vivacity as if originally my own? Every man, upon this supposition, being a second self to another, would trust all his interests to the discretion of every man; without jealousy, without partition, without distinction. And the whole human race would form only one family; where all would lie in common, and be used freely, without regard to property; but cautiously too, with as entire regard to the necessities of each individual, as if our own interests were most intimately concerned.

In the present disposition of the human heart, it would, perhaps, be difficult to find complete instances of such enlarged affections; but still we may observe, that the case of families approaches towards it; and the stronger the mutual benevolence is among the individuals, the nearer it approaches; till all distinction of property be, in a great measure, lost and confounded among them. Between married persons, the cement of friendship is by the laws supposed so strong as to abolish all division of possessions; and has often, in reality, the force ascribed to it. And it is observable, that, during the ardour of new enthusiasms, when every principle is inflamed into extravagance, the community of goods has frequently been attempted; and nothing but experience of its inconveniencies, from the returning or disguised selfishness of men, could make the imprudent fanatics adopt anew the ideas of justice and of separate property. So true is it, that this virtue derives its existence entirely from its necessary *use* to the intercourse and social state of mankind.

569   To make this truth more evident, let us reverse the foregoing suppositions; and carrying every thing to the opposite extreme, consider what would be the effect of these new situations. Suppose a society to fall into such want of all common necessaries, that the utmost frugality and industry cannot preserve the greater number from perishing, and the whole from extreme misery: it will readily, I believe, be admitted, that the strict laws of justice are suspended, in such a pressing emergence, and give place to the stronger motives of necessity and self-preservation. Is it any crime, after a shipwreck, to seize whatever means or instrument of safety one can lay hold of, without regard to former limitations of property? Or if a city besieged were perishing with hunger; can we imagine, that men will see any means of preservation before them, and lose their lives, from a scrupulous regard to what, in other situations, would be the rules of equity and justice? The USE and TENDENCY of that virtue is to procure happiness and security, by preserving order in society: but where the society is ready to perish from extreme necessity, no greater evil can be dreaded from violence and injustice; and every man may now provide for himself by all the means, which prudence can dictate, or humanity permit. The public, even in less urgent necessities, opens granaries, without the consent of proprietors; as justly supposing, that the authority of magistracy may, consistent with equity, extend so far: but were any number of men to assemble, without the tie of laws or civil jurisdiction; would an equal partition of bread in a famine, though effected by power and even violence, be regarded as criminal or injurious?

Suppose likewise, that it should be a virtuous man's fate to fall **570** into the society of ruffians, remote from the protection of laws and government; what conduct must he embrace in that melancholy situation? He sees such a desperate rapaciousness prevail; such a disregard to equity, such contempt of order, such stupid blindness to future consequences, as must immediately have the most tragical conclusion, and must terminate in destruction to the greater number, and in a total dissolution of society to the rest. He, mean while, can have no other expedient than to arm himself, to whomever the sword he seizes, or the buckler, may belong: to make provision of all means of defence and security: and his particular regard to justice being no longer of USE to his own safety or that of others, he must consult the dictates of self-preservation alone, without concern for those who no longer merit his care and attention.

When any man, even in political society, renders himself, by his crimes, obnoxious to the public, he is punished by the laws in his goods and person; that is, the ordinary rules of justice are, with regard to him, suspended for a moment, and it becomes equitable to inflict on him, for the *benefit* of society, what, otherwise, he could not suffer without wrong or injury.

The rage and violence of public war; what is it but a suspension of justice among the warring parties, who perceive, that this virtue is now no longer of any *use* or advantage to them? The laws of war, which then succeed to those of equity and justice, are rules calculated for the *advantage* and *utility* of that particular state, in which men are now placed. And were a civilized nation engaged with barbarians, who observed no rules even of war; the former must also suspend their observance of them, where they no longer serve to any purpose; and must render every action or rencounter as bloody and pernicious as possible to the first aggressors.

571   Thus, the rules of equity or justice depend entirely on the particular state and condition, in which men are placed, and owe their origin and existence to that UTILITY, which results to the public from their strict and regular observance. Reverse, in any considerable circumstance, the condition of men: produce extreme abundance or extreme necessity: implant in the human breast perfect moderation and humanity, or perfect rapaciousness and malice: by rendering justice totally *useless*, you thereby totally destroy its essence, and suspend its obligation upon mankind.

The common situation of society is a medium amidst all these extremes. We are naturally partial to ourselves, and to our friends; but are capable of learning the advantage resulting from a more equitable conduct. Few enjoyments are given us from the open and liberal hand of nature; but by art, labour, and industry, we can extract them in great abundance. Hence the ideas of property become necessary in all civil society: hence justice derives its usefulness to the public: and hence alone arises its merit and moral obligation.

*   *   *   *

572   The more we vary our views of human life, and the newer and more unusual the lights are, in which we survey it, the more shall we be convinced, that the origin here assigned for the virtue of justice is real and satisfactory.

Were there a species of creatures, intermingled with men, which, though rational, were possessed of such inferior strength, both of body and mind, that they were incapable of all resistance, and could never, upon the highest provocation, make us feel the effects of their resentment; the necessary consequence, I think, is, that we should be bound, by the laws of humanity, to give gentle usage to these creatures, but should not, properly speaking, lie under any restraint of justice with regard to them, nor could they possess any right or property, exclusive of such arbitrary lords. Our intercourse with them could not be called society, which supposes a degree of equality;

but absolute command on the one side, and servile obedience on the other. Whatever we covet, they must instantly resign: our permission is the only tenure, by which they hold their possessions: our compassion and kindness the only check, by which they curb our lawless will: and as no inconvenience ever results from the exercise of a power, so firmly established in nature, the restraints of justice and property, being totally *useless*, would never have place in so unequal a confederacy.

This is plainly the situation of men, with regard to animals; and how far these may be said to possess reason, I leave it to others to determine. The great superiority of civilized Europeans above barbarous Indians, tempted us to imagine ourselves on the same footing with regard to them, and made us throw off all restraints of justice, and even of humanity, in our treatment of them. In many nations, the female sex are reduced to like slavery, and are rendered incapable of all property, in opposition to their lordly masters. But though the males, when united, have, in all countries, bodily force sufficient to maintain this severe tyranny; yet such are the insinuation, address, and charms of their fair companions, that women are commonly able to break the confederacy, and share with the other sex in all the rights and privileges of society.

Were the human species so framed by nature as that each individual possessed within himself every faculty, requisite both for his own preservation and for the propagation of his kind: were all society and intercourse cut off between man and man, by the primary intention of the supreme Creator: it seems evident, that so solitary a being would be as much incapable of justice, as of social discourse and conversation. Where mutual regards and forbearance serve to no manner of purpose, they would never direct the conduct of any reasonable man. The headlong course of the passions would be checked by no reflection on future consequences. And as each man is here supposed to love himself alone, and to depend only on himself and his own activity for safety and happiness, he would, on every occasion, to the utmost of his power, challenge the preference above every other being, to none of which he is bound by any ties, either of nature or of interest. **573**

But suppose the conjunction of the sexes to be established in nature, a family immediately arises; and particular rules being found requisite for its subsistence, these are immediately embraced; though without comprehending the rest of mankind within their prescriptions. Suppose, that several families unite together into one society, which is totally disjoined from all others, the rules, which preserve peace and order, enlarge themselves to the utmost extent of that society; but becoming then entirely useless, lose their force when carried one step farther. But again suppose, that several distinct societies maintain a kind of intercourse for mutual convenience and advantage, the boundaries of justice still grow larger, in proportion to the largeness of men's views, and the force of their mutual connections. History, experience, reason sufficiently instruct us in this natural progress of human sentiments, and in the gradual enlargement of our regards to justice, in proportion as we become acquainted with the extensive utility of that virtue.

*   *   *   *

SECT. V—WHY UTILITY PLEASES

PART I

574   It seems so natural a thought to ascribe to their utility the praise, which we bestow on the social virtues, that one would expect to meet with this principle every where in moral writers, as the chief foundation of their reasoning and inquiry. In common life, we may observe, that the circumstance of utility is always appealed to; nor is it supposed, that a greater eulogy can be given to any man, than to display his usefulness to the public, and enumerate the services, which he has performed to mankind and society. What praise, even of an inanimate form, if the regularity and elegance of its parts destroy not its fitness for any useful purpose! And how satisfactory an apology for any disproportion or seeming deformity, if we can show the necessity of that particular construction for the use intended! A ship appears more beautiful to an artist, or one moderately skilled in navigation, where its prow is wide and swelling beyond its poop, than if it were framed with a precise geometrical regularity, in contradiction to all the laws of mechanics. A building, whose doors and windows were exact squares, would hurt the eye by that very proportion; as ill adapted to the figure of a human creature, for whose service the fabric was intended. What wonder then, that a man, whose habits and conduct are hurtful to society, and dangerous or pernicious to every one who has an intercourse with him, should, on that account, be an object of disapprobation, and communicate to every spectator the strongest sentiment of disgust and hatred*.

But perhaps the difficulty of accounting for these effects of useful- **575** ness, or its contrary, has kept philosophers from admitting them into their systems of ethics, and has induced them rather to employ any other principle, in explaining the origin of moral good and evil. But it is no just reason for rejecting any principle, confirmed by experience, that we cannot give a satisfactory account of its origin, nor are able to resolve it into other more general principles. And if we would employ a little thought on the present subject, we need be at no loss to account for the influence of utility, and to deduce it from principles, the most known and avowed in human nature.

★   ★   ★   ★

Usefulness is agreeable, and engages our approbation. This is a matter of fact, confirmed by daily observation. But, *useful*? For what? For some body's interest, surely. Whose interest then? Not our own only: for our approbation frequently extends farther. It must, therefore, be the interest of those, who are served by the character or action approved of; and these we may conclude, however remote, are not totally indifferent to us. By opening up this principle, we shall discover one great source of moral distinctions.

* We ought not to imagine, because an inanimate object may be useful as well as a man, that therefore it ought also, according to this system, to merit the appellation of *virtuous*. The sentiments, excited by utility, are, in the two cases, very different; and the one is mixed with affection, esteem, approbation, etc., and not the other.[1] In like manner, an inanimate object may have good colour and proportions as well as a human figure. But can we ever be in love with the former? There are a numerous set of passions and sentiments, of which thinking rational beings are, by the original constitution of nature, the only proper objects: and though the very same qualities be transferred to an insensible, inanimate being, they will not excite the same sentiments. The beneficial qualities of herbs and minerals are, indeed, sometimes called their *virtues*; but this is an effect of the caprice of language, which ought not to be regarded in reasoning. For though there be a species of approbation attending even inanimate objects, when beneficial, yet this sentiment is so weak, and so different from that which is directed to beneficent magistrates or statesmen; that they ought not to be ranked under the same class or appellation.

A very small variation of the object, even where the same qualities are preserved, will destroy a sentiment. Thus, the same beauty, transferred to a different sex, excites no amorous passion, where nature is not extremely perverted.

[1 Cf. Hutcheson, § 307.]

PART II

576 Self-love is a principle in human nature of such extensive energy, and the interest of each individual is, in general, so closely connected with that of the community, that those philosophers were excusable, who fancied, that all our concern for the public might be resolved into a concern for our own happiness and preservation. They saw every moment, instances of approbation or blame, satisfaction or displeasure towards characters and actions; they denominated the objects of these sentiments, *virtues*, or *vices*; they observed, that the former had a tendency to increase the happiness, and the latter the misery of mankind; they asked, whether it were possible that we could have any general concern for society, or any disinterested resentment of the welfare or injury of others; they found it simpler to consider all these sentiments as modifications of self-love; and they discovered a pretence, at least, for this unity of principle, in that close union of interest, which is so observable between the public and each individual.

But notwithstanding this frequent confusion of interests, it is easy to attain what natural philosophers, after Lord Bacon, have affected to call the *experimentum crucis*, or that experiment, which points out the right way in any doubt or ambiguity. We have found instances, in which private interest was separate from public; in which it was even contrary: and yet we observed the moral sentiment to continue, notwithstanding this disjunction of interests. And wherever these distinct interests sensibly concurred, we always found a sensible increase of the sentiment, and a more warm affection to virtue, and detestation of vice, or what we properly call, *gratitude* and *revenge*. Compelled by these instances, we must renounce the theory, which accounts for every moral sentiment by the principle of self-love. We must adopt a more public affection, and allow, that the interests of society are not, even on their own account, entirely indifferent to us. Usefulness is only a tendency to a certain end; and it is a contradiction in terms, that any thing pleases as means to an end, where the end itself no wise affects us. If usefulness, therefore, be a source of moral sentiment, and if this usefulness be not always considered with a reference to self; it follows, that every thing, which contributes to the happiness of society, recommends itself directly to our approbation and good-will. Here is a principle, which accounts, in great part, for the origin of morality: and what need we seek for abstruse and remote systems, when there occurs one so obvious and natural★?

★   ★   ★   ★

If any man from a cold insensibility, or narrow selfishness of **577** temper, is unaffected with the images of human happiness or misery, he must be equally indifferent to the images of vice and virtue: as, on the other hand, it is always found, that a warm concern for the interests of our species is attended with a delicate feeling of all moral distinctions; a strong resentment of injury done to men; a lively approbation of their welfare. In this particular, though great superiority is observable of one man above another; yet none are so entirely indifferent to the interest of their fellow-creatures, as to perceive no distinctions of moral good and evil, in consequence of the different tendencies of actions and principles. How, indeed, can we suppose it possible in any one, who wears a human heart, that if there be subjected to his censure, one character or system of conduct, which is beneficial, and another, which is pernicious, to his species or community, he will not so much as give a cool preference to the former, or ascribe to it the smallest merit or regard? Let us suppose such a person ever so selfish; let private interest have engrossed ever so much his attention; yet in instances, where that is not concerned, he must unavoidably feel *some* propensity to the good of mankind, and make it an object of choice, if every thing else be equal. Would any man, who is walking along, tread as willingly on another's gouty toes, whom he has no quarrel with, as on the hard flint and pavement? There is here surely a difference in the case. We surely take into consideration the happiness and misery of others, in weighing the several motives of action, and incline to the former, where no private regards draw us to seek our own promotion or advantage by the injury of our fellow-creatures. And if the principles

★ It is needless to push our researches so far as to ask, why we have humanity or a fellow-feeling with others. It is sufficient, that this is experienced to be a principle in human nature. We must stop somewhere in our examination of causes; and there are, in every science, some general principles, beyond which we cannot hope to find any principle more general. No man is absolutely indifferent to the happiness and misery of others. The first has a natural tendency to give pleasure; the second, pain. This every one may find in himself. It is not probable, that these principles can be resolved into principles more simple and universal, whatever attempts may have been made to that purpose. But if it were possible, it belongs not to the present subject; and we may here safely consider these principles as original: happy, if we can render all the consequences sufficiently plain and perspicuous!

of humanity are capable, in many instances, of influencing our actions, they must, at all times, have *some* authority over our sentiments, and give us a general approbation of what is useful to society, and blame of what is dangerous or pernicious. The degrees of these sentiments may be the subject of controversy; but the reality of their existence, one should think, must be admitted, in every theory or system.

578   A creature, absolutely malicious and spiteful, were there any such in nature, must be worse than indifferent to the images of vice and virtue. All his sentiments must be inverted, and directly opposite to those, which prevail in the human species. Whatever contributes to the good of mankind, as it crosses the constant bent of his wishes and desires, must produce uneasiness and disapprobation; and on the contrary, whatever is the source of disorder and misery in society, must, for the same reason, be regarded with pleasure and complacency. Timon, who, probably from his affected spleen, more than any inveterate malice, was denominated the man-hater, embraced Alcibiades, with great fondness. *Go on my boy!* cried he, *acquire the confidence of the people: you will one day, I foresee, be the cause of great calamities to them**. Could we admit the two principles of the Manicheans, it is an infallible consequence, that their sentiments of human actions, as well as of every thing else, must be totally opposite, and that every instance of justice and humanity, from its necessary tendency, must please the one deity and displease the other. All mankind so far resemble the good principle, that, where interest or revenge or envy perverts not our disposition, we are always inclined, from our natural philanthropy, to give the preference to the happiness of society, and consequently to virtue, above its opposite. Absolute, unprovoked, disinterested malice has never, perhaps, place in any human breast;[1] or if it had, must there pervert all the sentiments of morals, as well as the feelings of humanity. If the cruelty of Nero be allowed entirely voluntary, and not rather the effect of constant fear and resentment; it is evident, that Tigellinus, preferably to Seneca or Burrhus, must have possessed his steady and uniform approbation.

579   A statesman or patriot, who serves our own country, in our own time, has always a more passionate regard paid to him, than one

* Plutarch in vita Alc.

[1 Hutcheson, §§ 326, 329, 336, 338.]

whose beneficial influence operated on distant ages or remote nations; where the good, resulting from his generous humanity, being less connected with us, seems more obscure, and affects us with a less lively sympathy. We may own the merit to be equally great, though our sentiments are not raised to an equal height, in both cases. The judgement here corrects the inequalities of our internal emotions and perceptions; in like manner, as it preserves us from error, in the several variations of images, presented to our external senses. The same object, at a double distance, really throws on the eye a picture of but half the bulk; yet we imagine that it appears of the same size in both situations; because we know, that, on our approach to it, its image would expand on the eye, and that the difference consists not in the object itself, but in our position with regard to it. And, indeed, without such a correction of appearances, both in internal and external sentiment, men could never think or talk steadily on any subject; while their fluctuating situations produce a continual variation on objects, and throw them into such different and contrary lights and positions*.

The more we converse with mankind, and the greater social **580** intercourse we maintain, the more shall we be familiarized to these general preferences and distinctions, without which our conversation and discourse could scarcely be rendered intelligible to each other. Every man's interest is peculiar to himself, and the aversions and desires, which result from it, cannot be supposed to affect others in a like degree. General language, therefore, being formed for general use, must be moulded on some more general views, and must affix the epithets of praise or blame, in conformity to sentiments, which arise from the general interests of the community. And if these

---

* For a like reason, the tendencies of actions and characters, not their real accidental consequences, are alone regarded in our moral determinations or general judgements; though in our real feeling or sentiment, we cannot help paying greater regard to one whose station, joined to virtue, renders him really useful to society, than to one, who exerts the social virtues only in good intentions and benevolent affections. Separating the character from the fortune, by an easy and necessary effort of thought, we pronounce these persons alike, and give them the same general praise. The judgement corrects or endeavours to correct the appearance: but is not able entirely to prevail over sentiment.

Why is this peach-tree said to be better than that other; but because it produces more or better fruit? And would not the same praise be given it, though snails or vermin had destroyed the peaches, before they came to full maturity? In morals too, is not *the tree known by the fruit?* And cannot we easily distinguish between nature and accident, in the one case as well as in the other?

sentiments, in most men, be not so strong as those, which have a reference to private good; yet still they must make some distinction, even in persons the most depraved and selfish; and must attach the notion of good to a beneficent conduct, and of evil to the contrary. Sympathy, we shall allow, is much fainter than our concern for ourselves, and sympathy with persons remote from us, much fainter than that with persons near and contiguous; but for this very reason, it is necessary for us, in our calm judgements and discourse concerning the characters of men, to neglect all these differences, and render our sentiments more public and social. Besides that we ourselves often change our situation in this particular, we every day meet with persons, who are in a situation different from us, and who could never converse with us, were we to remain constantly in that position and point of view, which is peculiar to ourselves. The intercourse of sentiments, therefore, in society and conversation, makes us form some general unalterable standard, by which we may approve or disapprove of characters and manners. And though the heart takes not part entirely with those general notions, nor regulates all its love and hatred, by the universal, abstract differences of vice and virtue, without regard to self, or the persons with whom we are more intimately connected; yet have these moral differences a considerable influence, and being sufficient, at least, for discourse, serve all our purposes in company, in the pulpit, on the theatre, and in the schools*.

581   Thus, in whatever light we take this subject, the merit, ascribed to the social virtues, appears still uniform, and arises chiefly from that regard, which the natural sentiment of benevolence engages us to pay to the interests of mankind and society. If we consider the principles of the human make, such as they appear to daily experience and observation, we must, *a priori*, conclude it impossible for such a creature as man to be totally indifferent to the well or ill-being of his fellow-creatures, and not readily, of himself, to pronounce, where nothing gives him any particular bias, that what promotes their

---

* It is wisely ordained by nature, that private connections should commonly prevail over universal views and considerations; otherwise our affections and actions would be dissipated and lost, for want of a proper limited object. Thus a small benefit done to ourselves, or our near friends, excites more lively sentiments of love and approbation than a great benefit done to a distant commonwealth: but still we know here, as in all the senses, to correct these inequalities by reflection, and retain a general standard of vice and virtue, founded chiefly on general usefulness.

happiness is good, what tends to their misery is evil, without any farther regard or consideration. Here then are the faint rudiments, at least, or outlines, of a *general* distinction between actions; and in proportion as the humanity of the person is supposed to increase his connection with those who are injured or benefited, and his lively conception of their misery or happiness; his consequent censure or approbation acquires proportionable vigour. There is no necessity, that a generous action, barely mentioned in an old history or remote gazette, should communicate any strong feelings of applause and admiration. Virtue, placed at such a distance, is like a fixed star, which, though to the eye of reason, it may appear as luminous as the sun in his meridian, is so infinitely removed, as to affect the senses, neither with light nor heat. Bring this virtue nearer, by our acquaintance or connection with the persons, or even by an eloquent recital of the case; our hearts are immediately caught, our sympathy enlivened, and our cool approbation converted into the warmest sentiments of friendship and regard. These seem necessary and infallible consequences of the general principles of human nature, as discovered in common life and practice.

Again; reverse these views and reasonings: consider the matter **582** *a posteriori*; and weighing the consequences, inquire if the merit of social virtue be not, in a great measure, derived from the feelings of humanity, with which it affects the spectators. It appears to be matter of fact, that the circumstance of *utility*, in all subjects, is a source of praise and approbation: that it is constantly appealed to in all moral decisions concerning the merit and demerit of actions: that it is the *sole* source of that high regard paid to justice, fidelity, honour, allegiance, and chastity: that it is inseparable from all the other social virtues, humanity, generosity, charity, affability, lenity, mercy, and moderation: and, in a word, that it is a foundation of the chief part of morals, which has a reference to mankind and our fellow-creatures.

★   ★   ★   ★

SECT. VII—OF QUALITIES IMMEDIATELY AGREEABLE TO OURSELVES

Whoever has passed an evening with serious melancholy people, **583** and has observed how suddenly the conversation was animated, and what sprightliness diffused itself over the countenance, discourse, and behaviour of every one, on the accession of a good-humoured, lively companion; such a one will easily allow, that CHEERFULNESS carries great merit with it, and naturally conciliates the good-will of mankind. No quality, indeed, more readily communicates itself to all around; because no one has a greater propensity to display itself, in jovial talk and pleasant entertainment. The flame spreads through the whole circle; and the most sullen and morose are often caught by it. That the melancholy hate the merry, even though Horace says it, I have some difficulty to allow; because I have always observed, that, where the jollity is moderate and decent, serious people are so much the more delighted, as it dissipates the gloom, with which they are commonly oppressed; and gives them an unusual enjoyment.

From this influence of cheerfulness, both to communicate itself, and to engage approbation, we may perceive, that there is another set of mental qualities, which, without any utility or any tendency to farther good, either of the community or of the possessor, diffuse a satisfaction on the beholders, and procure friendship and regard. Their immediate sensation, to the person possessed of them, is agreeable: others enter into the same humour, and catch the sentiment, by a contagion or natural sympathy: and as we cannot forbear loving whatever pleases, a kindly emotion arises towards the person, who communicates so much satisfaction. He is a more animating spectacle: his presence diffuses over us more serene complacency and enjoyment: our imagination, entering into his feelings and disposition, is affected in a more agreeable manner, than if a melancholy, dejected, sullen, anxious temper were presented to us. Hence the affection and approbation, which attend the former: the aversion and disgust, with which we regard the latter★.

★ ★ ★ ★

584 The merit of BENEVOLENCE, arising from its utility, and its tendency to promote the good of mankind, has been already explained, and is, no doubt, the source of a *considerable* part of that esteem, which is so universally paid to it. But it will also be allowed, that the very

---

★ There is no man, who, on particular occasions, is not affected with all the disagreeable passions, fear, anger, dejection, grief, melancholy, anxiety, etc. But these, so far as they are natural, and universal, make no difference between one man and another, and can never be the object of blame. It is only when the disposition gives a *propensity* to any of these disagreeable passions, that they disfigure the character, and by giving uneasiness, convey the sentiment of disapprobation to the spectator.

softness and tenderness of the sentiment, its engaging endearments, its fond expressions, its delicate attentions, and all that flow of mutual confidence and regard, which enters into a warm attachment of love and friendship: it will be allowed, I say, that these feelings, being delightful in themselves, are necessarily communicated to the spectators, and melt them into the same fondness and delicacy. The tear naturally starts in our eye on the apprehension of a warm sentiment of this nature: our breast heaves, our heart is agitated, and every humane tender principle of our frame is set in motion, and gives us the purest and most satisfactory enjoyment.

When poets form descriptions of Elysian fields, where the blessed inhabitants stand in no need of each other's assistance, they yet represent them as maintaining a constant intercourse of love and friendship, and soothe our fancy with the pleasing image of these soft and gentle passions. The idea of tender tranquillity in a pastoral Arcadia is agreeable from a like principle, as has been observed above*.

Who would live amidst perpetual wrangling, and scolding, and mutual reproaches? The roughness and harshness of these emotions disturb and displease us: we suffer by contagion and sympathy; nor can we remain indifferent spectators, even though certain, that no pernicious consequences would ever follow from such angry passions.

As a certain proof, that the whole merit of benevolence is not derived from its usefulness, we may observe, that, in a kind way of blame, we say, a person is *too good*; when he exceeds his part in society, and carries his attention for others beyond the proper bounds. In like manner, we say a man is *too high-spirited, too intrepid, too indifferent about fortune*: reproaches, which really, at bottom, imply more esteem than many panegyrics. Being accustomed to rate the merit and demerit of characters chiefly by their useful or pernicious tendencies, we cannot forbear applying the epithet of blame, when we discover a sentiment, which rises to a degree, that is hurtful: but it may happen, at the same time, that its noble elevation, or its engaging tenderness so seizes the heart, as rather to increase our friendship and concern for the person†.

*   *   *   *

* Sect. v. Part 2.

† Cheerfulness could scarce admit of blame from its excess, were it not that dissolute mirth, without a proper cause or subject, is a sure symptom and characteristic of folly, and on that account disgustful.

585   These are some instances of the several species of merit, that are valued for the immediate pleasure, which they communicate to the person possessed of them. No views of utility or of future beneficial consequences enter into this sentiment of approbation; yet is it of a kind similar to that other sentiment, which arises from views of a public or private utility. The same social sympathy, we may observe, or fellow-feeling with human happiness or misery, gives rise to both; and this analogy, in all the parts of the present theory, may justly be regarded as a confirmation of it.

SECT. IX—CONCLUSION

PART I

586   It may justly appear surprising, that any man, in so late an age, should find it requisite to prove, by elaborate reasoning, that PERSONAL MERIT consists altogether in the possession of mental qualities, *useful* or *agreeable* to the *person himself* or to *others*. It might be expected, that this principle would have occurred even to the first rude, unpractised inquirers concerning morals, and been received from its own evidence, without any argument or disputation. Whatever is valuable in any kind, so naturally classes itself under the division of *useful* or *agreeable*, the *utile* or the *dulce*, that it is not easy to imagine, why we should ever seek farther, or consider the question as a matter of nice research or inquiry. And as every thing useful or agreeable must possess these qualities with regard either to the *person himself* or to *others*, the complete delineation or description of merit seems to be performed as naturally as a shadow is cast by the sun, or an image is reflected upon water. If the ground, on which the shadow is cast, be not broken and uneven; nor the surface, from which the image is reflected, disturbed and confused; a just figure is immediately presented, without any art or attention. And it seems a reasonable presumption, that systems and hypotheses have perverted our natural understanding; when a theory, so simple and obvious, could so long have escaped the most elaborate examination.

       ★   ★   ★   ★

587   And as every quality, which is useful or agreeable to ourselves or others, is, in common life, allowed to be a part of personal merit;

so no other will ever be received, where men judge of things by their natural, unprejudiced reason, without the delusive glosses of superstition and false religion. Celibacy, fasting, penance, mortification, self-denial, humility, silence, solitude, and the whole train of monkish virtues; for what reason are they every where rejected by men of sense, but because they serve to no manner of purpose; neither advance a man's fortune in the world, nor render him a more valuable member of society; neither qualify him for the entertainment of company, nor increase his power of self-enjoyment? We observe, on the contrary, that they cross all these desirable ends; stupefy the understanding and harden the heart, obscure the fancy and sour the temper. We justly, therefore, transfer them to the opposite column, and place them in the catalogue of vices; nor has any superstition force sufficient among men of the world, to pervert entirely these natural sentiments. A gloomy, hair-brained enthusiast, after his death, may have a place in the calendar; but will scarcely ever be admitted, when alive, into intimacy and society, except by those who are as delirious and dismal as himself.

It seems a happiness in the present theory, that it enters not into **588** that vulgar dispute concerning the *degrees* of benevolence or self-love, which prevail in human nature; a dispute which is never likely to have any issue, both because men, who have taken part, are not easily convinced, and because the phenomena, which can be produced on either side, are so dispersed, so uncertain, and subject to so many interpretations, that it is scarcely possible accurately to compare them, or draw from them any determinate inference or conclusion. It is sufficient for our present purpose, if it be allowed, what surely, without the greatest absurdity, cannot be disputed, that there is some benevolence, however small, infused into our bosom; some spark of friendship for human kind; some particle of the dove, kneaded into our frame, along with the elements of the wolf and serpent. Let these generous sentiments be supposed ever so weak; let them be insufficient to move even a hand or finger of our body; they must still direct the determinations of our mind, and where every thing else is equal, produce a cool preference of what is useful and serviceable to mankind, above what is pernicious and dangerous. A *moral distinction*, therefore, immediately arises; a general sentiment of blame and approbation; a tendency, however faint, to the objects of the one, and a proportionable aversion to those of the other. Nor will those reasoners, who so earnestly maintain the predominant selfishness of human kind, be any wise scandalized at hearing of the weak sentiments of virtue, implanted in our nature. On the contrary, they are found as ready to maintain the one tenet as the other; and their spirit of satire (for such it appears, rather than of corruption) naturally gives rise to both opinions; which have, indeed, a great and almost an indissoluble connection together.

589   Avarice, ambition, vanity, and all passions vulgarly, though improperly, comprised under the denomination of *self-love*, are here excluded from our theory concerning the origin of morals, not because they are too weak, but because they have not a proper direction, for that purpose. The notion of morals, implies some sentiment common to all mankind, which recommends the same object to general approbation, and makes every man, or most men, agree in the same opinion or decision concerning it. It also implies some sentiment, so universal and comprehensive as to extend to all mankind, and render the actions and conduct, even of the persons the most remote, an object of applause or censure, according as they agree or disagree with that rule of right which is established. These two requisite circumstances belong alone to the sentiment of humanity here insisted on. The other passions produce, in every breast, many strong sentiments of desire and aversion, affection and hatred; but these neither are felt so much in common, nor are so comprehensive, as to be the foundation of any general system and established theory of blame or approbation.

590   When a man denominates another his *enemy*, his *rival*, his *antagonist*, his *adversary*, he is understood to speak the language of self-love, and to express sentiments, peculiar to himself, and arising from his particular circumstances and situation. But when he bestows on any man the epithets of *vicious* or *odious* or *depraved*, he then speaks another language, and expresses sentiments, in which, he expects, all his audience are to concur with him. He must here, therefore, depart from his private and particular situation, and must choose a point of view, common to him with others: he must move some universal principle of the human frame, and touch a string, to which all mankind have an accord and symphony. If he mean, therefore, to express, that this man possesses qualities, whose tendency is pernicious to society, he has chosen this common point of view, and

has touched the principle of humanity, in which every man, in some degree, concurs. While the human heart is compounded of the same elements as at present, it will never be wholly indifferent to public good, nor entirely unaffected with the tendency of characters and manners. And though this affection of humanity may not generally be esteemed so strong as vanity or ambition, yet, being common to all men, it can alone be the foundation of morals, or of any general system of blame or praise. One man's ambition is not another's ambition; nor will the same event or object satisfy both: but the humanity of one man is the humanity of every one; and the same object touches this passion in all human creatures.

But the sentiments, which arise from humanity, are not only the **591** same in all human creatures, and produce the same approbation or censure; but they also comprehend all human creatures; nor is there any one whose conduct or character is not, by their means, an object, to every one, of censure or approbation. On the contrary, those other passions, commonly denominated selfish, both produce different sentiments in each individual, according to his particular situation; and also contemplate the greater part of mankind with the utmost indifference and unconcern. Whoever has a high regard and esteem for me flatters my vanity; whoever expresses contempt mortifies and displeases me: but as my name is known but to a small part of mankind, there are few, who come within the sphere of this passion, or excite, on its account, either my affection or disgust. But if you represent a tyrannical, insolent, or barbarous behaviour, in any country or in any age of the world; I soon carry my eye to the pernicious tendency of such a conduct, and feel the sentiment of repugnance and displeasure towards it. No character can be so remote as to be, in this light, wholly indifferent to me. What is beneficial to society or to the person himself must still be preferred. And every quality or action, of every human being, must, by this means, be ranked under some class or denomination, expressive of general censure or applause.

What more, therefore, can we ask to distinguish the sentiments, **592** dependent on humanity, from those connected with any other passion, or to satisfy us, why the former are the origin of morals, not the latter? Whatever conduct gains my approbation, by touching my humanity, procures also the applause of all mankind, by affecting the same principle in them: but what serves my avarice or ambition pleases these passions in me alone, and affects not the avarice and ambition of the rest of mankind. There is no circumstance of conduct in any man, provided it have a beneficial tendency, that is not agreeable to my humanity, however remote the person: but every man, so far removed as neither to cross nor serve my avarice and ambition, is regarded as wholly indifferent by those passions. The distinction, therefore, between these species of sentiment being so great and evident, language must soon be moulded upon it, and must invent a peculiar set of terms, in order to express those universal sentiments of censure or approbation, which arise from humanity, or from views of general usefulness and its contrary. VIRTUE and VICE become then known: morals are recognized: certain general ideas are framed of human conduct and behaviour: such measures are expected from men, in such situations: this action is determined to be conformable to our abstract rule; that other, contrary. And by such universal principles are the particular sentiments of self-love frequently controlled and limited.

★   ★   ★   ★

593   Another spring of our constitution, that brings a great addition of force to moral sentiment, is, the love of fame; which rules, with such uncontrolled authority, in all generous minds, and is often the grand object of all their designs and undertakings. By our continual and earnest pursuit of a character, a name, a reputation in the world, we bring our own deportment and conduct frequently in review, and consider how they appear in the eyes of those who approach and regard us. This constant habit of surveying ourselves, as it were, in reflection, keeps alive all the sentiments of right and wrong, and begets, in noble natures, a certain reverence for themselves as well as others; which is the surest guardian of every virtue. The animal conveniencies and pleasures sink gradually in their value; while every inward beauty and moral grace is studiously acquired, and the mind is accomplished in every perfection, which can adorn or embellish a rational creature.

Here is the most perfect morality with which we are acquainted: here is displayed the force of many sympathies. Our moral sentiment is itself a feeling chiefly of that nature: and our regard to a character with others seems to arise only from a care of preserving a character with ourselves; and in order to attain this end, we find it necessary to prop our tottering judgement on the correspondent approbation of mankind.

★   ★   ★   ★

APPENDIX I—CONCERNING MORAL SENTIMENT

If the foregoing hypothesis be received, it will now be easy for us **594** to determine the question first started★, concerning the general principles of morals; and though we postponed the decision of that question, lest it should then involve us in intricate speculations, which are unfit for moral discourses, we may resume it at present, and examine how far either *reason* or *sentiment* enters into all decisions of praise or censure.

One principal foundation of moral praise being supposed to lie in the usefulness of any quality or action; it is evident, that *reason* must enter for a considerable share in all decisions of this kind; since nothing but that faculty can instruct us in the tendency of qualities and actions, and point out their beneficial consequences to society and to their possessor. In many cases, this is an affair liable to great controversy: doubts may arise; opposite interests may occur; and a preference must be given to one side, from very nice views, and a small overbalance of utility. This is particularly remarkable in questions with regard to justice; as is, indeed, natural to suppose, from that species of utility, which attends this virtue. Were every single instance of justice, like that of benevolence, useful to society; this would be a more simple state of the case, and seldom liable to great controversy. But as single instances of justice are often pernicious in their first and immediate tendency, and as the advantage to society results only from the observance of the general rule, and from the concurrence and combination of several persons in the same equitable conduct; the case here becomes more intricate and involved. The various circumstances of society; the various consequences of any practice; the various interests, which may be proposed: these, on many occasions, are doubtful, and subject to great discussion and inquiry. The object of municipal laws is to fix all the questions with regard to justice: the debates of civilians; the reflections of politicians; the precedents of history and public records, are all directed to the same purpose. And a very accurate *reason* or

★ Sect. I [i.e. § 562; cf. §§ 479–511].

judgement is often requisite, to give the true determination, amidst such intricate doubts arising from obscure or opposite utilities.

595   But though reason, when fully assisted and improved, be sufficient to instruct us in the pernicious or useful tendency of qualities and actions; it is not alone sufficient to produce any moral blame or approbation. Utility is only a tendency to a certain end; and were the end totally indifferent to us, we should feel the same indifference towards the means. It is requisite a *sentiment* should here display itself, in order to give a preference to the useful above the pernicious tendencies. This sentiment can be no other than a feeling for the happiness of mankind, and a resentment of their misery; since these are the different ends which virtue and vice have a tendency to promote. Here, therefore, *reason* instructs us in the several tendencies of actions, and *humanity* makes a distinction in favour of those which are useful and beneficial.

This partition between the faculties of understanding and sentiment, in all moral decisions, seems clear from the preceding hypothesis. But I shall suppose that hypothesis false: it will then be requisite to look out for some other theory, that may be satisfactory; and I dare venture to affirm, that none such will ever be found, so long as we suppose reason to be the sole source of morals. To prove this, it will be proper to weigh the five following considerations.

596   I. It is easy for a false hypothesis to maintain some appearance of truth, while it keeps wholly in generals, makes use of undefined terms, and employs comparisons, instead of instances. This is particularly remarkable in that philosophy, which ascribes the discernment of all moral distinctions to reason alone, without the concurrence of sentiment. It is impossible that, in any particular instance, this hypothesis can so much as be rendered intelligible; whatever specious figure it may make in general declamations and discourses. Examine the crime of *ingratitude*, for instance; which has place, wherever we observe good-will, expressed and known, together with good-offices performed, on the one side, and a return of ill-will or indifference, with ill-offices or neglect on the other: anatomize all these circumstances, and examine, by your reason alone, in what consists the demerit or blame: you never will come to any issue or conclusion.

597   Reason judges either of *matter of fact* or of *relations*. Inquire then, *first*, where is that matter of fact, which we here call *crime*; point it

out; determine the time of its existence; describe its essence or nature; explain the sense or faculty, to which it discovers itself. It resides in the mind of the person, who is ungrateful. He must, therefore, feel it, and be conscious of it. But nothing is there, except the passion of ill-will or absolute indifference. You cannot say, that these, of themselves, always, and in all circumstances, are crimes. No: they are only crimes, when directed towards persons, who have before expressed and displayed good-will towards us. Consequently, we may infer, that the crime of ingratitude is not any particular individual *fact*; but arises from a complication of circumstances, which, being presented to the spectator, excites the *sentiment* of blame, by the particular structure and fabric of his mind.

This representation, you say, is false. Crime, indeed, consists not **598** in a particular *fact*, of whose reality we are assured by *reason*: but it consists in certain *moral relations*, discovered by reason, in the same manner as we discover, by reason, the truths of geometry or algebra. But what are the relations, I ask, of which you here talk? In the case stated above, I see first good-will and good-offices in one person; then ill-will and ill-offices in the other. Between these, there is the relation of *contrariety*.[1] Does the crime consist in that relation? But suppose a person bore me ill-will or did me ill-offices; and I, in return, were indifferent towards him, or did him good-offices: here is the same relation of *contrariety*; and yet my conduct is often highly laudable. Twist and turn this matter as much as you will, you can never rest the morality on relation; but must have recourse to the decisions of sentiment.

When it is affirmed, that two and three are equal to the half of **599** ten; this relation of equality, I understand perfectly. I conceive, that if ten be divided into two parts, of which one has as many units as the other; and if any of these parts be compared to two added to three, it will contain as many units as that compound number. But when you draw thence a comparison to moral relations, I own that I am altogether at a loss to understand you. A moral action, a crime, such as ingratitude, is a complicated object. Does the morality consist in the relation of its parts to each other? How? After what manner? Specify the relation: be more particular and explicit in your propositions; and you will easily see their falsehood.

No, say you, the morality consists in the relation of actions to the

[1 See Balguy, §§ 456–8.]

rule of right; and they are denominated good or ill, according as they agree or disagree with it. What then is this rule of right? In what does it consist? How is it determined? By reason, you say, which examines the moral relations of actions. So that moral relations are determined by the comparison of actions to a rule. And that rule is determined by considering the moral relations of objects. Is not this fine reasoning?

600 All this is metaphysics, you cry: that is enough: there needs nothing more to give a strong presumption of falsehood. Yes, reply I: here are metaphysics surely: but they are all on your side, who advance an abstruse hypothesis, which can never be made intelligible, nor quadrate with any particular instance or illustration. The hypothesis which we embrace is plain. It maintains, that morality is determined by sentiment. It defines virtue to be *whatever mental action or quality gives to a spectator the pleasing sentiment of approbation*; and vice the contrary. We then proceed to examine a plain matter of fact, to wit, what actions have this influence: we consider all the circumstances, in which these actions agree: and thence endeavour to extract some general observations with regard to these sentiments. If you call this metaphysics, and find any thing abstruse here, you need only conclude, that your turn of mind is not suited to the moral sciences.

601 II. When a man, at any time, deliberates concerning his own conduct (as, whether he had better, in a particular emergence, assist a brother or a benefactor), he must consider these separate relations, with all the circumstances and situations of the persons, in order to determine the superior duty and obligation: and in order to determine the proportion of lines in any triangle, it is necessary to examine the nature of that figure, and the relations which its several parts bear to each other. But notwithstanding this appearing similarity in the two cases, there is, at bottom, an extreme difference between them. A speculative reasoner concerning triangles or circles considers the several known and given relations of the parts of these figures; and thence infers some unknown relation, which is dependent on the former. But in moral deliberations, we must be acquainted, beforehand, with all the objects, and all their relations to each other; and from a comparison of the whole, fix our choice or approbation. No new fact to be ascertained: no new relation to be discovered. All the circumstances of the case are supposed to be laid before us, ere we can fix any sentence of blame or approbation. If any material circumstance be yet unknown or doubtful, we must first employ our inquiry or intellectual faculties to assure us of it; and must suspend for a time all moral decision or sentiment. While we are ignorant, whether a man were aggressor or not, how can we determine whether the person who killed him, be criminal or innocent? But after every circumstance, every relation is known, the understanding has no farther room to operate, nor any object on which it could employ itself. The approbation or blame, which then ensues, cannot be the work of the judgement, but of the heart; and is not a speculative proposition or affirmation, but an active feeling or sentiment. In the disquisitions of the understanding, from known circumstances and relations, we infer some new and unknown. In moral decisions, all the circumstances and relations must be previously known; and the mind, from the contemplation of the whole, feels some new impression of affection or disgust, esteem or contempt, approbation or blame.

Hence the great difference between a mistake of *fact* and one of **602** *right*; and hence the reason why the one is commonly criminal and not the other. When Oedipus killed Laius, he was ignorant of the relation, and from circumstances, innocent and involuntary, formed erroneous opinions concerning the action which he committed. But when Nero killed Agrippina, all the relations between himself and the person, and all the circumstances of the fact, were previously known to him: but the motive of revenge, or fear, or interest, prevailed in his savage heart over the sentiments of duty and humanity. And when we express that detestation against him, to which he, himself, in a little time, became insensible; it is not, that we see any relations, of which he was ignorant; but that, from the rectitude of our disposition, we feel sentiments, against which he was hardened, from flattery and a long perseverance in the most enormous crimes. In these sentiments, then, not in a discovery of relations of any kind, do all moral determinations consist. Before we can pretend to form any decision of this kind, every thing must be known and ascertained on the side of the object or action. Nothing remains but to feel, on our part, some sentiment of blame or approbation; whence we pronounce the action criminal or virtuous.

III. This doctrine will become still more evident, if we compare **603** moral beauty with natural, to which, in many particulars, it bears so near a resemblance. It is on the proportion, relation, and position of parts, that all natural beauty depends; but it would be absurd thence to infer, that the perception of beauty, like that of truth in geometrical problems, consists wholly in the perception of relations, and was performed entirely by the understanding or intellectual faculties. In all the sciences, our mind, from the known relations, investigates the unknown: but in all decisions of taste or external beauty, all the relations are beforehand obvious to the eye; and we thence proceed to feel a sentiment of complacency or disgust, according to the nature of the object, and disposition of our organs.

Euclid has fully explained all the qualities of the circle; but has not, in any proposition, said a word of its beauty. The reason is evident. The beauty is not a quality of the circle. It lies not in any part of the line, whose parts are equally distant from a common centre. It is only the effect, which that figure produces upon the mind, whose peculiar fabric or structure renders it susceptible of such sentiments. In vain would you look for it in the circle, or seek it, either by your senses or by mathematical reasonings, in all the properties of that figure.

Attend to Palladio and Perrault, while they explain all the parts and proportions of a pillar: they talk of the cornice and frieze and base and entablature and shaft and architrave; and give the description and position of each of these members. But should you ask the description and position of its beauty, they would readily reply, that the beauty is not in any of the parts or members of a pillar, but results from the whole, when that complicated figure is presented to an intelligent mind, susceptible to those finer sensations. Till such a spectator appear, there is nothing but a figure of such particular dimensions and proportions: from his sentiments alone arise its elegance and beauty.

604   Again; attend to Cicero, while he paints the crimes of a Verres or a Catiline; you must acknowledge that the moral turpitude results, in the same manner, from the contemplation of the whole, when presented to a being, whose organs have such a particular structure and formation. The orator may paint rage, insolence, barbarity on the one side: meekness, suffering, sorrow, innocence on the other: but if you feel no indignation or compassion arise in you from this complication of circumstances, you would in vain ask him, in what consists the crime or villainy, which he so vehemently exclaims against: at what time, or on what subject it first began to exist: and what has for a few months afterwards become of it, when every disposition and thought of all the actors is totally altered or annihilated. No satisfactory answer can be given to any of these questions, upon the abstract hypothesis of morals; and we must at last acknowledge, that the crime or immorality is no particular fact or relation, which can be the object of the understanding: but arises entirely from the sentiment of disapprobation, which, by the structure of human nature, we unavoidably feel on the apprehension of barbarity or treachery.

IV. Inanimate objects may bear to each other all the same relations, **605** which we observe in moral agents; though the former can never be the object of love or hatred, nor are consequently susceptible of merit or iniquity. A young tree, which overtops and destroys its parent, stands in all the same relations with Nero, when he murdered Agrippina; and if morality consisted merely in relations, would, no doubt, be equally criminal.

V. It appears evident, that the ultimate ends of human actions can **606** never, in any case, be accounted for by *reason*, but recommend themselves entirely to the sentiments and affections of mankind, without any dependence on the intellectual faculties. Ask a man, *why he uses exercise*; he will answer, *because he desires to keep his health*. If you then inquire, *why he desires health*, he will readily reply, *because sickness is painful*. If you push your inquiries farther, and desire a reason, *why he hates pain*, it is impossible he can ever give any. This is an ultimate end, and is never referred to any other object.[1]

Perhaps, to your second question, *why he desires health*, he may also reply, that *it is necessary for the exercise of his calling*. If you ask, *why he is anxious on that head*, he will answer, *because he desires to get money*. If you demand *Why? It is the instrument of pleasure*, says he. And beyond this it is an absurdity to ask for a reason. It is impossible there can be a progress *in infinitum*; and that one thing can always be a reason, why another is desired. Something must be desirable on its own account, and because of its immediate accord or agreement with human sentiment and affection.

Now as virtue is an end, and is desirable on its own account, without fee or reward, merely for the immediate satisfaction which it conveys; it is requisite that there should be some sentiment, which it

[1 Cf. Hutcheson, §§ 362–3; Gay, § 470.]

touches; some internal taste or feeling, or whatever you please to call it, which distinguishes moral good and evil, and which embraces the one and rejects the other.

607 Thus the distinct boundaries and offices of *reason* and of *taste* are easily ascertained. The former conveys the knowledge of truth and falsehood: the latter gives the sentiment of beauty and deformity, vice and virtue. The one discovers objects, as they really stand in nature, without addition or diminution: the other has a productive faculty, and gilding or staining all natural objects with the colours, borrowed from internal sentiment, raises, in a manner, a new creation. Reason, being cool and disengaged, is no motive to action, and directs only the impulse received from appetite or inclination, by showing us the means of attaining happiness or avoiding misery: taste, as it gives pleasure or pain, and thereby constitutes happiness or misery, becomes a motive to action, and is the first spring or impulse to desire and volition. From circumstances and relations, known or supposed, the former leads us to the discovery of the concealed and unknown: after all circumstances and relations are laid before us, the latter makes us feel from the whole a new sentiment of blame or approbation. The standard of the one, being founded on the nature of things, is eternal and inflexible, even by the will of the Supreme Being: the standard of the other, arising from the internal frame and constitution of animals, is ultimately derived from that Supreme Will, which bestowed on each being its peculiar nature, and arranged the several classes and orders of existence.

APPENDIX IV—OF SOME VERBAL DISPUTES

608 Nothing is more usual than for philosophers to encroach upon the province of grammarians; and to engage in disputes of words, while they imagine, that they are handling controversies of the deepest importance and concern. It was in order to avoid altercations, so frivolous and endless, that I endeavoured to state with the utmost caution the object of our present inquiry; and proposed simply to collect on the one hand, a list of those mental qualities which are the object of love or esteem, and form a part of personal merit, and on the other hand, a catalogue of those qualities, which are the object of censure or reproach, and which detract from the character of the person, possessed of them; subjoining some reflections concerning the origin of these sentiments of praise or blame. On all occasions, where there might arise the least hesitation, I avoided the terms *virtue* and *vice*; because some of those qualities, which I classed among the objects of praise, receive, in the English language, the appellation of *talents*, rather than of virtues; as some of the blameable or censurable qualities are often called *defects*, rather than vices. It may now, perhaps, be expected, that, before we conclude this moral inquiry, we should exactly separate the one from the other; should mark the precise boundaries of virtues and talents, vices and defects; and should explain the reason and origin of that distinction. But in order to excuse myself from this undertaking, which would, at last, prove only a grammatical inquiry, I shall subjoin the four following reflections, which shall contain all that I intend to say on the present subject.

First, I do not find, that in the English, or any other modern **609** tongue, the boundaries are exactly fixed between virtues and talents, vices and defects, or that a precise definition can be given of the one as contradistinguished from the other. Were we to say, for instance, that the esteemable qualities alone, which are voluntary, are entitled to the appellation of virtues; we should soon recollect the qualities of courage, equanimity, patience, self-command; with many others, which almost every language classes under this appellation, though they depend little or not at all on our choice. Should we affirm, that the qualities alone, which prompt us to act our part in society, are entitled to that honourable distinction; it must immediately occur, that these are indeed the most valuable qualities, and are commonly denominated the *social* virtues; but that this very epithet supposes, that there are also virtues of another species. Should we lay hold of the distinction between *intellectual* and *moral* endowments, and affirm the last alone to be the real and genuine virtues, because they alone lead to action; we should find, that many of those qualities, usually called intellectual virtues, such as prudence, penetration, discernment, discretion, had also a considerable influence on conduct. The distinction between the *heart* and the *head* may also be adopted: the qualities of the first may be defined such as in their immediate exertion are accompanied with a feeling or sentiment; and these alone may be called the genuine virtues: but industry, frugality, temperance, secrecy, perseverance, and many other laudable powers or habits, generally styled virtues, are exerted without any immediate sentiment in the person possessed of them; and are only known to him by their effects. It is fortunate, amidst all this seeming perplexity, that the question, being merely verbal, cannot possibly be of any importance. A moral, philosophical discourse needs not enter into all these caprices of language, which are so variable in different dialects, and in different ages of the same dialect. But on the whole, it seems to me, that, though it is always allowed, that there are virtues of many different kinds, yet, when a man is called *virtuous*, or is denominated a man of virtue, we chiefly regard his social qualities, which are, indeed, the most valuable. It is, at the same time, certain, that any remarkable defect in courage, temperance, economy, industry, understanding, dignity of mind, would bereave even a very good-natured, honest man of this honourable appellation. Who did ever say, except by way of irony, that such a one was a man of great virtue, but an egregious blockhead?

610   But, *secondly*, it is no wonder, that languages should not be very precise in marking the boundaries between virtues and talents, vices and defects; since there is so little distinction made in our internal estimation of them. It seems indeed certain, that the *sentiment* of conscious worth, the self-satisfaction proceeding from a review of a man's own conduct and character; it seems certain, I say, that this sentiment, which, though the most common of all others, has no proper name in our language*, arises from the endowments of courage and capacity, industry and ingenuity, as well as from any other mental excellencies. Who, on the other hand, is not deeply mortified with reflecting on his own folly and dissoluteness, and feels not a secret sting or compunction, whenever his memory presents any past occurrence, where he behaved with stupidity or ill-manners? No time can efface the cruel ideas of a man's own foolish conduct, or of affronts, which cowardice or impudence[1] has brought upon him. They still haunt his solitary hours, damp his

---

* The term, pride, is commonly taken in a bad sense; but this sentiment seems indifferent, and may be either good or bad, according as it is well or ill founded, and according to the other circumstances which accompany it. The French express this sentiment by the term, *amour propre*, but as they also express self-love as well as vanity, by the same term, there arises thence a great confusion in Rochefoucauld, and many of their moral writers.

[1 *Sic* in all the editions approved by Hume. Amendment by some editors to 'imprudence' is, I think, mistaken.]

most aspiring thoughts, and show him, even to himself, in the most contemptible and most odious colours imaginable.

What is there too we are more anxious to conceal from others than such blunders, infirmities, and meannesses, or more dread to have exposed by raillery and satire? And is not the chief object of vanity, our bravery or learning, our wit or breeding, our eloquence or address, our taste or abilities? These we display with care, if not with ostentation; and we commonly show more ambition of excelling in them, than even in the social virtues themselves, which are, in reality, of such superior excellence. Good-nature and honesty, especially the latter, are so indispensably required, that, though the greatest censure attends any violation of these duties, no eminent praise follows such common instances of them, as seem essential to the support of human society. And hence the reason, in my opinion, why, though men often extol so liberally the qualities of their heart, they are shy in commending the endowments of their head: because the latter virtues, being supposed more rare and extraordinary, are observed to be the more usual objects of pride and self-conceit; and when boasted of, beget a strong suspicion of these sentiments.

It is hard to tell, whether you hurt a man's character most by **611** calling him a knave or a coward, and whether a beastly glutton or drunkard be not as odious and contemptible, as a selfish, ungenerous miser. Give me my choice, and I would rather, for my own happiness and self-enjoyment, have a friendly, humane heart, than possess all the other virtues of Demosthenes and Philip united: but I would rather pass with the world for one endowed with extensive genius and intrepid courage, and should thence expect stronger instances of general applause and admiration. The figure which a man makes in life, the reception which he meets with in company, the esteem paid him by his acquaintance; all these advantages depend as much upon his good sense and judgement, as upon any other part of his character. Had a man the best intentions in the world, and were the farthest removed from all injustice and violence, he would never be able to make himself be much regarded, without a moderate share, at least, of parts and understanding.

What is it then we can here dispute about? If sense and courage, **612** temperance and industry, wisdom and knowledge confessedly form a considerable part of *personal merit*: if a man, possessed of these qualities, is both better satisfied with himself, and better entitled to the good-will, esteem, and services of others, than one entirely destitute of them; if, in short, the *sentiments* are similar, which arise from these endowments and from the social virtues; is there any reason for being so extremely scrupulous about a *word*, or disputing whether they be entitled to the denomination of virtues? It may, indeed, be pretended, that the sentiment of approbation, which those accomplishments produce, besides its being *inferior*, is also somewhat *different* from that, which attends the virtues of justice and humanity. But this seems not a sufficient reason for ranking them entirely under different classes and appellations. The character of Caesar and that of Cato, as drawn by Sallust, are both of them virtuous, in the strictest and most limited sense of the word; but in a different way: nor are the sentiments entirely the same, which arise from them. The one produces love; the other, esteem: the one is amiable; the other awful: we should wish to meet the one character in a friend; the other we should be ambitious of in ourselves. In like manner the approbation, which attends temperance or industry or frugality, may be somewhat different from that which is paid to the social virtues, without making them entirely of a different species. And, indeed, we may observe, that these endowments, more than the other virtues, produce not, all of them, the same kind of approbation. Good sense and genius beget esteem and regard: wit and humour excite love and affection.

*   *   *   *

An Enquiry concerning Human Understanding

SECT. VIII—OF LIBERTY AND NECESSITY

PART I

It might reasonably be expected, in questions, which have been **613** canvassed and disputed with great eagerness, since the first origin of science and philosophy, that the meaning of all the terms, at least, should have been agreed upon among the disputants; and our inquiries, in the course of two thousand years, been able to pass from words to the true and real subject of the controversy. For how easy it may seem to give exact definitions of the terms employed in reasoning, and make these definitions, not the mere sound of words, the object of future scrutiny and examination? But if we consider the matter more narrowly, we shall be apt to draw a quite opposite conclusion. From this circumstance alone, that a controversy has been long kept on foot, and remains still undecided, we may presume, that there is some ambiguity in the expression, and that the disputants affix different ideas to the terms employed in the controversy. . . .

This has been the case in the long disputed question concerning liberty and necessity; and to so remarkable a degree, that, if I be not much mistaken, we shall find, that all mankind, both learned and ignorant, have always been of the same opinion with regard to this subject, and that a few intelligible definitions would immediately have put an end to the whole controversy. . . .

I hope, therefore, to make it appear, that all men have ever agreed in the doctrine both of necessity and of liberty, according to any reasonable sense, which can be put on these terms; and that the whole controversy has hitherto turned merely upon words. We shall begin with examining the doctrine of necessity.

It is universally allowed, that matter, in all its operations, is **614** actuated by a necessary force, and that every natural effect is so precisely determined by the energy of its cause, that no other effect, in such particular circumstances, could possibly have resulted from it. The degree and direction of every motion is, by the laws of nature, prescribed with such exactness, that a living creature may as soon arise from the shock of two bodies, as motion in any other degree or direction than what is actually produced by it. Would we, therefore, form a just and precise idea of *necessity*, we must consider whence that idea arises, when we apply it to the operation of bodies.

It seems evident, that, if all the scenes of nature were continually shifted in such a manner, that no two events bore any resemblance to each other, but every object was entirely new, without any similitude to whatever had been seen before, we should never, in that case, have attained the least idea of necessity, or of a connection among these objects. We might say, upon such a supposition, that one object or event has followed another; not that one was produced by the other. The relation of cause and effect must be utterly unknown to mankind. Inference and reasoning concerning the operations of nature would, from that moment, be at an end; and the memory and senses remain the only canals, by which the knowledge of any real existence could possibly have access to the mind. Our idea, therefore, of necessity and causation arises entirely from the uniformity, observable in the operations of nature; where similar objects are constantly conjoined together, and the mind is determined by custom to infer the one from the appearance of the other. These two circumstances form the whole of that necessity, which we ascribe to matter. Beyond the constant *conjunction* of similar objects, and the consequent *inference* from one to the other, we have no notion of any necessity, or connection.

If it appear, therefore, that all mankind have ever allowed, without any doubt or hesitation, that these two circumstances take place in the voluntary actions of men, and in the operations of mind; it must follow, that all mankind have ever agreed in the doctrine of necessity, and that they have hitherto disputed, merely for not understanding each other.

615 As to the first circumstance, the constant and regular conjunction of similar events; we may possibly satisfy ourselves by the following considerations. It is universally acknowledged, that there is a great uniformity among the actions of men, in all nations and ages, and that human nature remains still the same, in its principles and operations. The same motives always produce the same actions: the same events follow from the same causes. Ambition, avarice, self-love, vanity, friendship, generosity, public spirit; these passions, mixed in various degrees, and distributed through society, have been, from the beginning of the world, and still are, the source of all the actions and enterprises, which have ever been observed among mankind. Would you know the sentiments, inclinations, and course of life of the Greeks and Romans? Study well the temper and actions of the French and English: you cannot be much mistaken in transferring to the former *most* of the observations, which you have made with regard to the latter. Mankind are so much the same, in all times and places, that history informs us of nothing new or strange in this particular. Its chief use is only to discover the constant and universal principles of human nature, by showing men in all varieties of circumstances and situations, and furnishing us with materials, from which we may form our observations, and become acquainted with the regular springs of human action and behaviour. These records of wars, intrigues, factions, and revolutions, are so many collections of experiments, by which the politician or moral philosopher fixes the principles of his science; in the same manner as the physician or natural philosopher becomes acquainted with the nature of plants, minerals, and other external objects, by the experiments, which he forms concerning them. Nor are the earth, water, and other elements, examined by Aristotle, and Hippocrates, more like to those, which at present lie under our observation, than the men, described by Polybius and Tacitus, are to those, who now govern the world.

Should a traveller, returning from a far country, bring us an account of men, wholly different from any, with whom we were ever acquainted; men, who were entirely divested of avarice, ambition, or revenge; who knew no pleasure but friendship, generosity, and public spirit; we should immediately, from these circumstances, detect the falsehood, and prove him a liar, with the same certainty as if he had stuffed his narration with stories of centaurs and dragons, miracles and prodigies. And if we would explode any forgery in history, we cannot make use of a more convincing argument, than to prove, that the actions, ascribed to any person, are directly contrary to the course of nature, and that no human motives, in such circumstances, could ever induce him to such a conduct. The veracity of Quintus Curtius is as much to be suspected, when he describes the supernatural courage of Alexander, by which he was hurried on singly to attack multitudes, as when he describes his supernatural force and activity, by which he was able to resist them. So readily and universally do we acknowledge a uniformity in human motives and actions as well as in the operations of body.

★　　★　　★　　★

616　We must not, however, expect, that this uniformity of human actions should be carried to such a length, as that all men, in the same circumstances, will always act precisely in the same manner, without making any allowance for the diversity of characters, prejudices, and opinions. Such a uniformity in every particular, is found in no part of nature. On the contrary, from observing the variety of conduct in different men, we are enabled to form a greater variety of maxims, which still suppose a degree of uniformity and regularity.

Are the manners of men different in different ages and countries? We learn thence the great force of custom and education, which mould the human mind from its infancy, and form it into a fixed and established character. Is the behaviour and conduct of the one sex very unlike that of the other? It is thence we become acquainted with the different characters, which nature has impressed upon the sexes, and which she preserves with constancy and regularity. Are the actions of the same person much diversified in the different periods of his life, from infancy to old age? This affords room for many general observations concerning the gradual change of our sentiments and inclinations, and the different maxims, which prevail in the different ages of human creatures. Even the characters, which are peculiar to each individual, have a uniformity in their influence; otherwise our acquaintance with the persons and our observation of their conduct, could never teach us their dispositions, or serve to direct our behaviour with regard to them.

617　I grant it possible to find some actions, which seem to have no regular connection with any known motives, and are exceptions to all the measures of conduct, which have ever been established for the government of men. But if we would willingly know, what judgement should be formed of such irregular and extraordinary actions; we may consider the sentiments, commonly entertained with regard to those irregular events, which appear in the course of nature, and the operations of external objects. All causes are not conjoined to their usual effects, with like uniformity. An artificer, who handles only dead matter, may be disappointed of his aim, as well as the politician, who directs the conduct of sensible and intelligent agents.

The vulgar, who take things according to their first appearance, attribute the uncertainty of events to such an uncertainty in the causes as makes the latter often fail of their usual influence; though they meet with no impediment in their operation. But philosophers, observing, that, almost in every part of nature, there is contained a vast variety of springs and principles, which are hid, by reason of their minuteness or remoteness, find, that it is at least possible the contrariety of events may not proceed from any contingency in the cause, but from the secret operation of contrary causes. This possibility is converted into certainty by farther observation; when they remark, that, upon an exact scrutiny, a contrariety of effects always betrays a contrariety of causes, and proceeds from their mutual opposition. A peasant can give no better reason for the stopping of any clock or watch than to say that it does not commonly go right: but an artist easily perceives, that the same force in the spring or pendulum has always the same influence on the wheels; but fails of its usual effect, perhaps by reason of a grain of dust, which puts a stop to the whole movement. From the observation of several parallel instances, philosophers form a maxim, that the connection between all causes and effects is equally necessary, and that its seeming uncertainty in some instances proceeds from the secret opposition of contrary causes.

Thus for instance, in the human body, when the usual symptoms of health or sickness disappoint our expectation; when medicines operate not with their wonted powers; when irregular events follow from any particular cause; the philosopher and physician are not surprised at the matter, nor are ever tempted to deny, in general, the necessity and uniformity of those principles, by which the animal economy is conducted. They know, that a human body is a mighty complicated machine: that many secret powers lurk in it, which are altogether beyond our comprehension: that to us it must often appear very uncertain in its operations: and that therefore the irregular events, which outwardly discover themselves, can be no proof, that the laws of nature are not observed with the greatest regularity in its internal operations and government.

618   The philosopher, if he be consistent, must apply the same reasoning to the actions and volitions of intelligent agents. The most irregular and unexpected resolutions of men may frequently be accounted for by those, who know every particular circumstance of their character and situation. A person of an obliging disposition gives a peevish answer: but he has the toothache, or has not dined. A stupid fellow discovers an uncommon alacrity in his carriage: but he has met with a sudden piece of good fortune. Or even when an action, as sometimes happens, cannot be particularly accounted for, either by the person himself or by others; we know, in general, that the characters of men are, to a certain degree, inconstant and irregular. This is, in a manner, the constant character of human nature; though it be applicable, in a more particular manner, to some persons, who have no fixed rule for their conduct, but proceed in a continued course of caprice and inconstancy. The internal principles and motives may operate in a uniform manner, notwithstanding these seeming irregularities; in the same manner as the winds, rain, clouds, and other variations of the weather are supposed to be governed by steady principles; though not easily discoverable by human sagacity and inquiry.

619   Thus it appears, not only that the conjunction between motives and voluntary actions is as regular and uniform, as that between the cause and effect in any part of nature; but also that this regular conjunction has been universally acknowledged among mankind, and has never been the subject of dispute, either in philosophy or common life. Now, as it is from past experience, that we draw all inferences concerning the future, and as we conclude, that objects will always be conjoined together, which we find to have always been conjoined; it may seem superfluous to prove, that this experienced uniformity in human actions is a source, whence we draw *inferences* concerning them. But in order to throw the argument into a greater variety of lights, we shall also insist, though briefly, on this latter topic.

★   ★   ★   ★

620   And indeed, when we consider how aptly *natural* and *moral* evidence link together, and form only one chain of argument, we shall make no scruple to allow, that they are of the same nature, and derived from the same principles. A prisoner, who has neither money nor interest, discovers the impossibility of his escape, as well when he considers the obstinacy of the gaoler, as the walls and bars, with which he is surrounded; and, in all attempts for his freedom, chooses rather to work upon the stone and iron of the one, than upon the inflexible nature of the other. The same prisoner, when conducted to the scaffold, foresees his death as certainly from the constancy and fidelity of his guards, as from the operation of the axe or wheel. His mind runs along a certain train of ideas: the refusal of the soldiers to consent to his escape; the action of the executioner; the separation of the head and body; bleeding, convulsive motions, and death. Here is a connected chain of natural causes and voluntary actions; but the mind feels no difference between them, in passing from one link to another: nor is less certain of the future event than if it were connected with the objects present to the memory or senses, by a train of causes, cemented together by what we are pleased to call a *physical* necessity. The same experienced union has the same effect on the mind, whether the united objects be motives, volition, and actions; or figure and motion. We may change the name of things; but their nature and their operation on the understanding never change.

$$\star \qquad \star \qquad \star \qquad \star$$

I have frequently considered, what could possibly be the reason, **621** why all mankind, though they have ever, without hesitation, acknowledged the doctrine of necessity, in their whole practice and reasoning, have yet discovered such a reluctance to acknowledge it in words, and have rather shown a propensity, in all ages, to profess the contrary opinion. The matter, I think, may be accounted for, after the following manner. If we examine the operations of body, and the production of effects from their causes, we shall find, that all our faculties can never carry us farther in our knowledge of this relation, than barely to observe, that particular objects are *constantly conjoined* together, and that the mind is carried, by a *customary transition*, from the appearance of one to the belief of the other. But though this conclusion concerning human ignorance be the result of the strictest scrutiny of this subject, men still entertain a strong propensity to believe, that they penetrate farther into the powers of nature, and perceive something like a necessary connection between the cause and the effect. When again they turn their reflections towards the operations of their own minds, and *feel* no such connection of the motive and the action; they are thence apt to suppose, that there is a difference between the effects, which result from material force, and those which arise from thought and intelligence. But being once convinced, that we know nothing farther of causation of any kind, than merely the *constant conjunction* of objects, and the consequent *inference* of the mind from one to another, and finding, that these two circumstances are universally allowed to have place in voluntary actions; we may be more easily led to own the same necessity common to all causes. And though this reasoning may contradict the systems of many philosophers, in ascribing necessity to the determinations of the will, we shall find, upon reflection, that they dissent from it in words only, not in their real sentiment. Necessity, according to the sense, in which it is here taken, has never yet been rejected, nor can ever, I think, be rejected by any philosopher. It may only, perhaps, be pretended, that the mind can perceive, in the operations of matter, some farther connection between the cause and effect; and a connection that has not place in the voluntary actions of intelligent beings. Now whether it be so or not, can only appear upon examination; and it is incumbent on these philosophers to make good their assertion, by defining or describing that necessity, and pointing it out to us in the operations of material causes.

622   It would seem, indeed, that men begin at the wrong end of this question concerning liberty and necessity, when they enter upon it by examining the faculties of the soul, the influence of the understanding, and the operations of the will. Let them first discuss a more simple question, namely, the operations of body and of brute unintelligent matter; and try whether they can there form any idea of causation and necessity, except that of a constant conjunction of objects, and subsequent inference of the mind from one to another. If these circumstances form, in reality, the whole of that necessity, which we conceive in matter, and if these circumstances be also universally acknowledged to take place in the operations of the mind, the dispute is at an end; at least, must be owned to be thenceforth merely verbal. But as long as we will rashly suppose, that we have some farther idea of necessity and causation in the operations of external objects; at the same time, that we can find nothing farther, in the voluntary actions of the mind; there is no possibility of bringing the question to any determinate issue, while we proceed upon so erroneous a supposition. The only method of undeceiving us, is, to mount up higher; to examine the narrow extent of science when applied to material causes; and to convince ourselves, that all we know of them, is, the constant conjunction and inference above mentioned. We may, perhaps, find, that it is with difficulty we are induced to fix such narrow limits to human understanding: but we can afterwards find no difficulty when we come to apply this doctrine to the actions of the will. For as it is evident, that these have a regular conjunction with motives and circumstances and characters, and as we always draw inferences from one to the other, we must be obliged to acknowledge in words, that necessity, which we have already avowed, in every deliberation of our lives, and in every step of our conduct and behaviour*.

* The prevalence of the doctrine of liberty may be accounted for, from another **623** cause, viz. a false sensation or seeming experience which we have, or may have, of liberty or indifference, in many of our actions. The necessity of any action, whether of matter or of mind, is not, properly speaking, a quality in the agent, but in any thinking or intelligent being, who may consider the action; and it consists chiefly in the determination of his thoughts to infer the existence of that action from some preceding objects; as liberty, when opposed to necessity, is nothing but the want of that determination, and a certain looseness or indifference, which we feel, in passing, or not passing, from the idea of one object to that of any succeeding one. Now we may observe, that, though, in *reflecting* on human actions, we seldom feel such a looseness or indifference, but are commonly able to infer them with considerable certainty from their motives, and from the disposition of the agent; yet it frequently happens, that, in *performing* the actions themselves, we are sensible of something like it: and as all resembling objects are readily taken for each other, this has been employed as a demonstrative and even intuitive proof of human liberty. We feel, that our actions are subject to our will, on most occasions; and imagine we feel, that the will itself is subject to nothing, because, when by a denial of it we are provoked to try, we feel, that it moves easily every way, and produces an image of itself, (or a *Velleity*, as it is called in the schools) even on that side, on which it did not settle. This image, or faint motion, we persuade ourselves, could, at that time, have been completed into the thing itself; because, should that be denied, we find, upon a second trial, that, at present, it can. We consider not, that the fantastical desire of showing liberty, is here the motive of our actions. And it seems certain, that, however we may imagine we feel a liberty within ourselves, a spectator can commonly infer our actions from our motives and character; and even where he cannot, he concludes in general, that he might, were he perfectly acquainted with every circumstance of our situation and temper, and the most secret springs of our complexion and disposition. Now this is the very essence of necessity, according to the foregoing doctrine.

624   But to proceed in this reconciling project with regard to the question of liberty and necessity; the most contentious question of metaphysics, the most contentious science; it will not require many words to prove, that all mankind have ever agreed in the doctrine of liberty as well as in that of necessity, and that the whole dispute, in this respect also, has been hitherto merely verbal. For what is meant by liberty, when applied to voluntary actions? We cannot surely mean, that actions have so little connection with motives, inclinations, and circumstances, that one does not follow with a certain degree of uniformity from the other, and that one affords no inference by which we can conclude the existence of the other. For these are plain and acknowledged matters of fact. By liberty, then, we can only mean *a power of acting or not acting, according to the determinations of the will*;[1] that is, if we choose to remain at rest, we may; if we choose to move, we also may. Now this hypothetical liberty is universally allowed to belong to every one, who is not a prisoner and in chains.[2] Here then is no subject of dispute.

625   Whatever definition we may give of liberty, we should be careful to observe two requisite circumstances; *first*, that it be consistent with plain matter of fact; *secondly*, that it be consistent with itself. If we observe these circumstances, and render our definition intelligible, I am persuaded that all mankind will be found of one opinion with regard to it.

It is universally allowed, that nothing exists without a cause of its existence, and that chance, when strictly examined, is a mere negative word, and means not any real power, which has any where, a being in nature. But it is pretended, that some causes are necessary, some not necessary. Here then is the advantage of definitions. Let any one *define* a cause, without comprehending, as a part of the definition, a *necessary connection* with its effect; and let him show distinctly the origin of the idea, expressed by the definition; and I shall readily give up the whole controversy. But if the foregoing explication of the matter be received, this must be absolutely impracticable. Had not objects a regular conjunction with each other, we should never have entertained any notion of cause and effect; and this regular conjunction produces that inference of the under-

[1 Cf. Hobbes, §§ 90, 98; Locke, §§ 164, 169.]   [2 Cf. Hobbes, §§ 82, 96.]

standing, which is the only connection, that we can have any comprehension of. Whoever attempts a definition of cause, exclusive of these circumstances, will be obliged, either to employ unintelligible terms, or such as are synonymous[1] to the term, which he endeavours to define*. And if the definition above mentioned be admitted; liberty, when opposed to necessity, not to constraint, is the same thing with chance; which is universally allowed to have no existence.

PART II

There is no method of reasoning more common, and yet none more blameable, than, in philosophical disputes, to endeavour the refutation of any hypothesis, by a pretence of its dangerous consequences to religion and morality. When any opinion leads to absurdities, it is certainly false; but it is not certain that an opinion is false, because it is of dangerous consequence. Such topics, therefore, ought entirely to be forborne; as serving nothing to the discovery of truth, but only to make the person of an antagonist odious. This I observe in general, without pretending to draw any advantage from it. I frankly submit to an examination of this kind, and shall venture to affirm, that the doctrines, both of necessity and of liberty, as above explained, are not only consistent with morality, but are absolutely essential to its support.

Necessity may be defined two ways, conformably to the two definitions of *cause*, of which it makes an essential part. It consists either in the constant conjunction of like objects, or in the inference of the understanding from one object to another. Now necessity, in both these senses, (which, indeed, are, at bottom, the same) has universally, though tacitly, in the schools, in the pulpit, and in common life, been allowed to belong to the will of man; and no one has ever pretended to deny, that we can draw inferences concerning human actions, and that those inferences are founded on the experienced union of like actions, with like motives, inclinations, and circumstances. The only particular, in which any one can differ, is,

626

627

[1 Cf. Hutcheson, § 373.]

* Thus, if a cause be defined, *that which produces any thing*; it is easy to observe, that *producing* is synonymous to *causing*. In like manner, if a cause be defined, *that by which any thing exists*; this is liable to the same objection. For what is meant by these words, *by which*? Had it been said, that a cause is *that* after which *any thing constantly exists*; we should have understood the terms. For this is, indeed, all we know of the matter. And this constancy forms the very essence of necessity, nor have we any other idea of it.

that either, perhaps, he will refuse to give the name of necessity to this property of human actions: but as long as the meaning is understood, I hope the word can do no harm: or that he will maintain it possible to discover something farther in the operations of matter. But this, it must be acknowledged, can be of no consequence to morality or religion, whatever it may be to natural philosophy or metaphysics. We may here be mistaken in asserting, that there is no idea of any other necessity or connection in the actions of body: but surely we ascribe nothing to the actions of the mind, but what every one does, and must readily allow of. We change no circumstance in the received orthodox system with regard to the will, but only in that with regard to material objects and causes. Nothing therefore can be more innocent, at least, than this doctrine.

628   All laws being founded on rewards and punishments, it is supposed as a fundamental principle, that these motives have a regular and uniform influence on the mind, and both produce the good and prevent the evil actions. We may give to this influence what name we please; but, as it is usually conjoined with the action, it must be esteemed a *cause*, and be looked upon as an instance of that necessity, which we would here establish.

The only proper object of hatred or vengeance, is a person or creature, endowed with thought and consciousness; and when any criminal or injurious actions excite that passion, it is only by their relation to the person, or connection with him. Actions are, by their very nature, temporary and perishing; and where they proceed not from some *cause* in the character and disposition of the person who performed them, they can neither redound to his honour, if good; nor infamy, if evil. The actions themselves may be blameable; they may be contrary to all the rules of morality and religion: but the person is not answerable for them; and as they proceeded from nothing in him, that is durable and constant, and leave nothing of that nature behind them, it is impossible he can, upon their account, become the object of punishment or vengeance. According to the principle, therefore, which denies necessity, and consequently causes, a man is as pure and untainted, after having committed the most horrid crime, as at the first moment of his birth, nor is his character any wise concerned in his actions; since they are not derived from it, and the wickedness of the one can never be used as a proof of the depravity of the other.

Men are not blamed for such actions, as they perform ignorantly and casually, whatever may be the consequences. Why? but because the principles of these actions are only momentary, and terminate in them alone. Men are less blamed for such actions as they perform hastily and unpremeditately, than for such as proceed from deliberation. For what reason? but because a hasty temper, though a constant cause or principle in the mind, operates only by intervals, and infects not the whole character. Again, repentance wipes off every crime, if attended with a reformation of life and manners. How is this to be accounted for? but by asserting, that actions render a person criminal, merely as they are proofs of criminal principles in the mind; and when, by an alteration of these principles, they cease to be just proofs, they likewise cease to be criminal. But, except upon the doctrine of necessity, they never were just proofs, and consequently never were criminal.

It will be equally easy to prove, and from the same arguments, **629** that *liberty*, according to that definition above mentioned, in which all men agree, is also essential to morality, and that no human actions, where it is wanting, are susceptible of any moral qualities, or can be the objects either of approbation or dislike. For as actions are objects of our moral sentiment, so far only as they are indications of the internal character, passions, and affections; it is impossible that they can give rise either to praise or blame, where they proceed not from these principles, but are derived altogether from external violence.

★   ★   ★   ★

Two Letters to Francis Hutcheson

[Letter of 17 September 1739. No. 13 in J. Y. T. Greig's edition of *The Letters of David Hume*.]

Sir

630   I am much obliged to you for your reflections on my papers.[1] I have perused them with care, and find they will be of use to me. You have mistaken my meaning in some passages; which upon examination I have found to proceed from some ambiguity or defect in my expression.

What affected me most in your remarks is your observing, that there wants a certain warmth in the cause of virtue, which, you think, all good men would relish, and could not displease amidst abstract inquiries. I must own, this has not happened by chance, but is the effect of a reasoning either good or bad. There are different ways of examining the mind as well as the body. One may consider it either as an anatomist or as a painter; either to discover its most secret springs and principles or to describe the grace and beauty of its actions. I imagine it is impossible to conjoin these two views. Where you pull off the skin, and display all the minute parts, there appears something trivial, even in the noblest attitudes and most vigorous actions: nor can you ever render the object graceful or engaging but by clothing the parts again with skin and flesh, and presenting only their bare outside. An anatomist, however, can give very good advice to a painter or statuary: and in like manner, I am persuaded, that a metaphysician may be very helpful to a moralist; though I cannot easily conceive these two characters united in the same work. Any warm sentiment of morals, I am afraid, would have the air of declamation amidst abstract reasonings, and would be esteemed contrary to good taste. And though I am much more ambitious of being esteemed a friend to virtue, than a writer of taste; yet I must always carry the latter in my eye, otherwise I must despair of ever being serviceable to virtue. I hope these reasons will satisfy you; though at the same time, I intend to make a new trial,

[1 The manuscript, before publication, of Book III of the *Treatise*.]

if it be possible to make the moralist and metaphysician agree a little better.

I cannot agree to your sense of *natural*. It is founded on final **631** causes; which is a consideration, that appears to me pretty uncertain and unphilosophical. For pray, what is the end of man? Is he created for happiness or for virtue? For this life or for the next? For himself or for his Maker? Your definition of *natural* depends upon solving these questions, which are endless, and quite wide of my purpose. I have never called justice unnatural, but only artificial.[1] *Atque ipsa utilitas justi prope mater et aequi.* Says one of the best moralists of antiquity.[2] Grotius and Pufendorf, to be consistent, must assert the same.

Whether natural abilities be virtues is a dispute of words.[3] I think **632** I follow the common use of language. . . . Were benevolence the only virtue no characters could be mixed, but would depend entirely on their degrees of benevolence. Upon the whole, I desire to take my catalogue of virtues from Cicero's *Offices*, not from the *Whole Duty of Man*. I had, indeed, the former book in my eye in all my reasonings.

I have many other reflections to communicate to you; but it would be troublesome. I shall therefore conclude with telling you, that I intend to follow your advice in altering most of those passages you have remarked as defective in point of prudence; though I must own, I think you a little too delicate. Except a man be in orders, or be immediately concerned in the instruction of youth, I do not think his character depends upon his philosophical speculations, as the world is now modelled; and a little liberty seems requisite to bring into the public notice a book that is calculated for so few readers. I hope you will allow me the freedom of consulting you when I am in any difficulty; and believe me to be

Dear Sir

Your most obliged humble servant

DAVID HUME.

P.S.

I cannot forbear recommending another thing to your considera- **633** tion. Actions are not virtuous nor vicious; but only so far as they are proofs of certain qualities or durable principles in the mind.[4] This is

[1 Cf. §§ 510–12, 521.]   [2 Horace, *Satires*, I. iii.]   [3 Cf. §§ 608–12.]
[4 Cf. § 512.]

a point I should have established more expressly than I have done. Now I desire you to consider, if there be any quality, that is virtuous, without having a tendency either to the public good or to the good of the person, who possesses it. If there be none without these tendencies, we may conclude, that their merit is derived from sympathy. I desire you would only consider the tendencies of qualities, not their actual operation, which depends on chance.[1] Brutus riveted the chains of Rome faster by his opposition; but the natural tendency of his noble dispositions, his public spirit and magnanimity, was to establish her liberty.

You are a great admirer of Cicero, as well as I am. Please to review the 4th Book, *de finibus bonorum et malorum*; where you find him prove against the Stoics, that if there be no other goods but virtue, it is impossible there can be any virtue; because the mind would then want all motives to begin its actions upon: and it is on the goodness or badness of the motives that the virtue of the action depends. This proves, that to every virtuous action there must be a motive or impelling passion distinct from the virtue, and that virtue can never be the sole motive to any action.[2] You do not assent to this; though I think there is no proposition more certain or important. I must own my proofs were not distinct enough, and must be altered. You see with what reluctance I part with you; though I believe it is time I should ask your pardon for so much trouble.

[Letter of 16 March 1740. No. 16 in Greig's edition.]

Dear Sir

           ★   ★   ★   ★

634   I must consult you in a point of prudence. I have concluded a reasoning with these two sentences. *When you pronounce any action or character to be vicious, you mean nothing but that from the particular constitution of your nature you have a feeling or sentiment of blame from the contemplation of it. Vice and virtue, therefore, may be compared to sounds, colours, heat and cold, which, according to modern philosophy, are not qualities in objects but perceptions in the mind: and this discovery in morals, like that other in physics, is to be regarded as a mighty advancement of the speculative sciences; though like that too, it has little or no influence on practice.*[3] Is not this laid a little too strong? I desire your opinion of

[1 Cf. § 579 *n*.]   [2 Cf. § 513.]   [3 Cf. § 503.]

it, though I cannot entirely promise to conform myself to it. I wish from my heart, I could avoid concluding, that since morality, according to your opinion as well as mine, is determined merely by sentiment, it regards only human nature and human life. This has been often urged against you,[1] and the consequences are very momentous. If you make any alterations on your performances, I can assure you, there are many who desire you would more fully consider this point; if you think that the truth lies on the popular side. Otherwise common prudence, your character, and situation forbid you touch upon it. If morality were determined by reason, that is the same to all rational beings: but nothing but experience can assure us, that the sentiments are the same. What experience have we with regard to superior beings? How can we ascribe to them any sentiments at all? They have implanted those sentiments in us for the conduct of life like our bodily sensations, which they possess not themselves. I expect no answer to these difficulties in the compass of a letter. It is enough if you have patience to read so long a letter as this. I am Dear Sir

Your most obedient humble servant
DAVID HUME.

[1] The criticism considered by Hutcheson, §§ 364, 366, and by Balguy, § 438, is not quite the same as Hume's conclusion but is related to it.]

DAVID HARTLEY

1705–1757

OBSERVATIONS ON MAN,
his Frame, his Duty, and his Expectations

[First printed, 1749. Reprinted here from the first edition, with reduction of initial capital letters and slight modification of spelling]

DAVID HARTLEY

Observations on Man

THE PREFACE

The work here offered to the public consists of papers written at **635** different times, but taking their rise from the following occasion.

About eighteen years ago I was informed, that the Rev. Mr. Gay, then living, asserted the possibility of deducing all our intellectual pleasures and pains from association. This put me upon considering the power of association. Mr. Gay published his sentiments on this matter,[1] about the same time, in a Dissertation on the fundamental Principle of Virtue, prefixed to Mr. Archdeacon Law's translation of Archbishop King's Origin of Evil.

From inquiring into the power of association I was led to examine both its consequences, in respect of morality and religion, and its physical cause. By degrees many disquisitions foreign to the doctrine of association, or at least not immediately connected with it, intermixed themselves. I have here put together all my separate papers on these subjects, digesting them in such order as they seemed naturally to suggest; and adding such things as were necessary to make the whole appear more complete and systematical.

*   *   *   *

PART I

INTRODUCTION

Man consists of two parts, body and mind. **636**

The first is subjected to our senses and inquiries, in the same manner as the other parts of the external material world.

The last is that substance, agent, principle, etc. to which we refer the sensations, ideas, pleasures, pains, and voluntary motions.

[1 Cf. Gay, §§ 475–8.]

Sensations are those internal feelings of the mind, which arise from the impressions made by external objects upon the several parts of our bodies.

All our other internal feelings may be called *ideas*. Some of these appear to spring up in the mind of themselves, some are suggested by words, others arise in other ways. Many writers comprehend *sensations* under *ideas*; but I everywhere use these words in the senses here ascribed to them.

The ideas which resemble sensations, are called *ideas of sensation*: all the rest may therefore be called *intellectual ideas*.

It will appear in the course of these observations, that the *ideas of sensation* are the elements of which all the rest are compounded. Hence *ideas of sensation* may be termed *simple*, *intellectual* ones *complex*.

637 The *pleasures* and *pains* are comprehended under the sensations and ideas, as these are explained above. For all our pleasures and pains are internal feelings, and, conversely, all our internal feelings seem to be attended with some degree either of *pleasure* or *pain*. However, I shall, for the most part, give the names of *pleasure* and *pain* only to such degrees as are considerable; referring all low, evanescent ones to the head of *mere sensations* and *ideas*.

The pleasures and pains may be ranged under seven general classes; viz.

1. sensation;
2. imagination;
3. ambition;
4. self-interest;
5. sympathy;
6. theopathy; and,
7. the moral sense; according as they arise from,

1. the impressions made on the external senses;
2. natural or artificial beauty or deformity;
3. the opinions of others concerning us;
4. our possession or want of the means of happiness, and security from, or subjection to, the hazards of misery;
5. the pleasures and pains of our fellow-creatures;
6. the affections excited in us by the contemplation of the Deity; or,
7. moral beauty and deformity.

★   ★   ★   ★

My chief design in the following chapter, is, briefly, to explain, **638**
establish, and apply the doctrines of *vibrations* and *association*. The
first of these doctrines is taken from the hints concerning the performance of sensation and motion, which Sir Isaac Newton has given
at the end of his *Principia*, and in the *Questions* annexed to his *Optics*;
the last, from what Mr. Locke, and other ingenious persons since
his time, have delivered concerning the influence of *association* over
our opinions and affections, and its use in explaining those things
in an accurate and precise way, which are commonly referred to the
power of habit and custom, in a general and indeterminate one.

The doctrine of *vibrations* may appear at first sight to have no
connection with that of *association*; however, if these doctrines be
found in fact to contain the laws of the bodily and mental powers
respectively, they must be related to each other, since the body and
mind are. One may expect, that *vibrations* should infer *association* as
their effect, and *association* point to *vibrations* as its cause. I will
endeavour, in the present chapter, to trace out this mutual relation.

⋆　　⋆　　⋆　　⋆

SECT. II—OF IDEAS, THEIR GENERATION AND ASSOCIATIONS;
AND OF THE AGREEMENT OF THE DOCTRINE OF VIBRATIONS
WITH THE PHENOMENA OF IDEAS

PROP. 8—*Sensations, by being often repeated, leave certain vestiges,* **639**
types, or images, of themselves, which may be called, simple ideas of
sensation.

⋆　　⋆　　⋆　　⋆

PROP. 9—*Sensory vibrations, by being often repeated, beget, in the
medullary substance of the brain, a disposition to diminutive vibrations,
which may also be called vibratiuncles and miniatures, corresponding to
themselves respectively.*

⋆　　⋆　　⋆　　⋆

PROP. 10—*Any sensations A, B, C, etc. by being associated with one
another a sufficient number of times, get such a power over the corresponding*

ideas a, b, c, etc. that any one of the sensations A, when impressed alone, shall be able to excite in the mind b, c, etc. the ideas of the rest.

Sensations may be said to be associated together, when their impressions are either made precisely at the same instant of time, or in the contiguous successive instants. We may therefore distinguish association into two sorts, the synchronous, and the successive.

The influence of association over our ideas, opinions, and affections, is so great and obvious, as scarce to have escaped the notice of any writer who has treated of these, though the word *association*, in the particular sense here affixed to it, was first brought into use by Mr. Locke. But all that has been delivered by the ancients and moderns, concerning the power of habit, custom, example, education, authority, party-prejudice, the manner of learning the manual and liberal arts, etc. goes upon this doctrine as its foundation, and may be considered as the detail of it, in various circumstances. I here begin with the simplest case, and shall proceed to more and more complex ones continually, till I have exhausted what has occurred to me upon this subject.

*   *   *   *

640 PROP. 11—*Any vibrations, A, B, C, etc. by being associated together a sufficient number of times, get such a power over a, b, c, etc. the corresponding miniature vibrations, that any of the vibrations A, when impressed alone, shall be able to excite b, c, etc. the miniatures of the rest.*

*   *   *   *

PROP. 12—*Simple ideas will run into complex ones, by means of association.*

*   *   *   *

PROP. 13—*When simple ideas run into a complex one, according to the foregoing proposition, we are to suppose, that the simple miniature vibrations corresponding to those simple ideas run, in like manner, into a complex miniature vibration, corresponding to the resulting complex idea.*

*   *   *   *

CHAP. IV—OF THE SIX CLASSES OF INTELLECTUAL PLEASURES
AND PAINS

641   I have now dispatched the history and analysis of the sensations, motions, and ideas; and endeavoured to suit them, as well as I could,

to the principles laid down in the first chapter. My next business, is to inquire particularly into the rise and gradual increase of the pleasures and pains of imagination, ambition, self-interest, sympathy, theopathy, and the moral sense; and to see how far these can be deduced, in the particular forms and degrees that are found to prevail, in fact, from the sensible pleasures and pains, by means of the general law of association. As to that of vibrations, it seems of little importance in this part of the work, whether it be adopted or not. If any other law can be made the foundation of association, or consistent with it, it may also be made consistent with the analysis of the intellectual pleasures and pains, which I shall here give. I do not think there is any other law that can; on the contrary, there seems to be so peculiar an aptness in the doctrine of vibrations, for explaining many of the phenomena of the passions, as almost excludes all others.

Now it will be a sufficient proof, that all the intellectual pleasures and pains are deducible ultimately from the sensible ones, if we can show of each intellectual pleasure and pain in particular, that it takes its rise from other pleasures and pains, either sensible or intellectual. For thus none of the intellectual pleasures and pains can be original. But the sensible pleasures and pains are evidently originals. They are therefore the only ones, i.e. they are the common source from whence all the intellectual pleasures and pains are ultimately derived.

When I say, that the intellectual pleasures A and B are deducible from one another, I do not mean, that A receives back again from B that lustre which it had conferred upon it; for this would be to argue in a circle; but that whereas both A and B borrow from a variety of sources, as well as from each other, they may, and indeed must, transfer by association part of the lustre borrowed from foreign sources upon each other.

If we admit the power of association, and can also show, that associations, sufficient in kind and degree, concur, in fact, in the several instances of our intellectual pleasures and pains, this will, of itself, exclude all other causes for these pleasures and pains, such as instinct for instance. If we cannot trace out associations sufficient in kind and degree, still it will not be necessary to have recourse to other causes, because great allowances are to be made for the novelty, complexness, and intricacy of the subject. However, on the other hand, analogy may perhaps lead us to conclude, that as instinct prevails much, and reason a little, in brutes, so instinct ought to prevail a little in us. Let the facts speak for themselves.

SECT. IV—OF THE PLEASURES AND PAINS OF SYMPATHY

642 PROP. 97—*To examine how far the pleasures and pains of sympathy are agreeable to the foregoing theory.*

The sympathetic affections may be distinguished into four classes; viz.

First, those by which we rejoice at the happiness of others.

Secondly, those by which we grieve for their misery.

Thirdly, those by which we rejoice at their misery.

And, fourthly, those by which we grieve for their happiness.

Of the first kind are sociality, good-will, generosity, and gratitude. Of the second, compassion and mercy. Of the third, moroseness, anger, revenge, jealousy, cruelty, and malice. And of the fourth, emulation and envy.

It is easy to be conceived, that association should produce affections of all these four kinds, since in the intercourses of life the pleasures and pains of one are, in various ways, intermixed with, and dependent upon, those of others, so as to have clusters of their miniatures excited, in all the possible ways in which the happiness or misery of one can be combined with the happiness or misery of another; i.e. in the four above-mentioned. I will now enter upon the detail of the rise and progress of each of them.

643 *Of the affections by which we rejoice at the happiness of others*

The first of these is sociality, or the pleasure which we take in the mere company and conversation of others, particularly of our friends and acquaintance, and which is attended with mutual affability, complaisance, and candour. Now most of the pleasures which children receive are conferred upon them by others, their parents, attendants, or play-fellows. And the number of the pleasures which they receive in this way, is far greater than that of the pains brought upon them by others. Indeed the hurts, and bodily injuries, which they meet with, are chiefly from themselves; and the denials of gratifications are either very few in number, or, if they be more frequent, give little uneasiness. It appears therefore, that, according to the doctrine of association, children ought to be pleased, in general, with the sight and company of all their acquaintance. And the same things, with some alterations, hold in respect of adults, through the whole course, and general tenor, of human life.

★   ★   ★   ★

Good-will, or benevolence, when understood in a limited sense, **644** may be termed that pleasing affection which engages us to promote the welfare of others to the best of our power. If it carry us so far as to forego great pleasures, or endure great pains, it is called generosity. But good-will and benevolence, in a general sense, are put for all the sympathetic affections of the first and second class, viz. those by which we either rejoice in, and promote, the happiness of others, or grieve for, and endeavour to remove, their misery; as ill-will and malevolence, understood in a general sense also, are put for the contrary affections, viz. those of the third and fourth class.

Benevolence, in the limited sense, is nearly connected with sociality, and has the same sources. It has also a high degree of honour and esteem annexed to it, procures us many advantages, and returns of kindness, both from the person obliged and others; and is most closely connected with the hope of reward in a future state, and with the pleasures of religion, and of self-approbation, or the moral sense. And the same things hold with respect to generosity in a much higher degree. It is easy therefore to see, how such associations may be formed in us, as to engage us to forego great pleasure, or endure great pain, for the sake of others; how these associations may be attended with so great a degree of pleasure as to overrule the positive pain endured, or the negative one from the foregoing of a pleasure; and yet how there may be no direct, explicit expectation of reward, either from God or man, by natural consequence, or express appointment, not even of the concomitant pleasure which engages the agent to undertake the benevolent or generous action. And this I take to be a proof from the doctrine of association, that there is, and must be, such a thing as pure disinterested benevolence; also a just account of the origin and nature of it.

Gratitude includes benevolence, and therefore has the same sources with some additional ones; these last are the explicit or implicit recollection of the benefits and pleasures received, the hope

of future ones, the approbation of the moral character of the benefactor, and the pleasures from the honour and esteem attending
gratitude, much enhanced by the peculiar baseness and shamefulness
of ingratitude.

645   *Of the affections by which we grieve for the misery of others*

Compassion is the uneasiness which a man feels at the misery of
another. Now this in children seems to be grounded upon such
associations as these that follow: the very appearance and idea of any
kind of misery which they have experienced, or of any signs of
distress which they understand, raise up in their nervous systems a
state of misery from mere memory, on account of the strength of
their imaginations; and because the connection between the adjuncts
of pain, and the actual infliction of it, has not yet been sufficiently
broken by experience, as in adults.—When several children are
educated together, the pains, the denials of pleasures, and the sorrows, which affect one, generally extend to all in some degree, often
in an equal one.—When their parents, attendants, etc. are sick or
afflicted, it is usual to raise in their minds the nascent ideas of pains
and miseries, by such words and signs as are suited to their capacities;
they also find themselves laid under many restraints on this account.
And when these and such-like circumstances have raised the desires
and endeavours to remove the causes of these their own internal
uneasy feelings, or, which is the same thing, of these miseries of
others (in all which they are much influenced, as in other like cases,
by the great disposition to imitate, before spoken of); and a variety
of internal feelings and desires of this kind are so blended and associated together, as that no part can be distinguished separately from
the rest; the child may properly be said to have compassion.

The same sources of compassion remain, though with some
alterations, during our whole progress through life; and an attentive
person may plainly discern the constituent parts of his compassion,
while they are yet the mere internal, and, as one may say, selfish
feelings above-mentioned; and before they have put on the nature
of compassion by coalescence with the rest.

Agreeably to this method of reasoning, it may be observed, that
persons whose nerves are easily irritable, and those who have experienced great trials and afflictions, are, in general, more disposed

to compassion than others; and that we are most apt to pity in those diseases and calamities, which we either have felt already, or apprehend ourselves in danger of feeling hereafter.[1]

★   ★   ★   ★

SECT. VI—OF THE PLEASURES AND PAINS OF THE MORAL SENSE

PROP. 99—*To examine how far the pleasures and pains of the moral* **646** *sense are agreeable to the foregoing theory.*

There are certain tempers of mind, with the actions flowing from them, as of piety, humility, resignation, gratitude, etc. towards God; of benevolence, charity, generosity, compassion, humility, gratitude, etc. towards men; of temperance, patience, contentment, etc. in respect of a person's own private enjoyments or sufferings; which when he believes himself to be possessed of, and reflects upon, a pleasing consciousness and self-approbation rise up in his mind, exclusively of any direct explicit consideration of advantage likely to accrue to himself, from his possession of these good qualities. In like manner the view of them in others raises up a disinterested love and esteem for those others. And the opposite qualities of impiety, profaneness, uncharitableness, resentment, cruelty, envy, ingratitude, intemperance, lewdness, selfishness, etc. are attended with the condemnation both of ourselves and others. This is, in general, the state of the case; but there are many particular differences, according to the particular education, temper, profession, sex, etc. of each person.

Or, which is the same thing, the secondary ideas belonging to virtue and vice, duty and sin, innocence and guilt, merit and demerit, right and wrong, moral good and moral evil, just and unjust, fit and unfit, obligation and prohibition, etc. in one man, bear a great resemblance to those belonging to the same words in another, or to the corresponding words, if they have different languages; and yet do not exactly coincide, but differ more or less, according to the difference in education, temper, etc.

Now both this general resemblance, and these particular differences, in our ideas, and consequent approbation or disapprobation, seem to admit of an analysis and explanation from the following particulars.

[1 Cf. Hobbes, §§ 10, 32.]

647 First, children are, for the most part, instructed in the difference and opposition between virtue and vice, duty and sin, etc.; and have some general descriptions of the virtues and vices inculcated upon them. They are told, that the first are good, pleasant, beautiful, noble, fit, worthy of praise and reward, etc.; the last odious, painful, shameful, worthy of punishment, etc.; so that the pleasing and displeasing associations, previously annexed to these words in their minds, are, by means of that confidence which they place in their superiors, transferred upon the virtues and vices respectively. And the mutual intercourses of life have the same effect in a less degree, with respect to adults, and those children who receive little or no instruction from their parents or superiors. Virtue is in general approved, and set off by all the encomiums, and honourable appellations, that any other thing admits of, and vice loaded with censures and reproaches of all kinds, in all good conversation and books. And this happens oftener than the contrary, even in bad ones; so that as far as men are influenced in their judgements by those of others, the balance is, upon the whole, on the side of virtue.

648 Secondly, there are many immediate good consequences, which attend upon virtue, as many ill ones do upon vice, and that during our whole progress through life. . . . Now these pleasures and pains, by often recurring in various combinations, and by being variously transferred upon each other, from the great affinity between the several virtues, and their rewards, with each other; also between the several vices, and their punishments, with each other; will at last beget in us a general, mixed, pleasing idea and consciousness, when we reflect upon our own virtuous affections or actions; a sense of guilt, and an anxiety, when we reflect on the contrary; and also raise in us the love and esteem of virtue, and the hatred of vice in others.

649 Thirdly, the many benefits which we receive immediately from, or which have some evident, though distant, connection with the piety, benevolence, and temperance of others; also the contrary mischiefs from their vices; lead us first to the love and hatred of the persons themselves by association, as explained under the head of sympathy, and then by farther associations to the love and hatred of the virtues and vices, considered abstractedly, and without any regard to our own interest; and that whether we view them in ourselves or others. As our love and esteem for virtue in others is much increased by the pleasing consciousness, which our own practice of it affords to ourselves, so the pleasure of this consciousness is much increased by our love of virtue in others.

Fourthly, the great suitableness of all the virtues to each other, and **650** to the beauty, order, and perfection of the world, animate and inanimate, impresses a very lovely character upon virtue; and the contrary self-contradiction, deformity, and mischievous tendency of vice, render it odious, and matter of abhorrence to all persons that reflect upon these things; and beget a language of this kind, which is borrowed, in great measure, from the pleasures and pains of imagination, and applied with a peculiar force and fitness to this subject from its great importance.

Fifthly, the hopes and fears which arise from the consideration of **651** a future state, are themselves pleasures and pains of a high nature. When therefore a sufficient foundation has been laid by a practical belief of religion, natural and revealed, by the frequent view of, and meditation upon, death, by the loss of departed friends, by bodily pains, by worldly disappointments and afflictions, for forming strong associations of the pleasures of these hopes with duty, and the pains of these fears with sin, the reiterated impressions of those associations will at last make duty itself a pleasure, and convert sin into a pain, giving a lustre and deformity respectively to all their appellations; and that without any express recollection of the hopes and fears of another world, just as in other cases of association.

Sixthly, all meditations upon God, who is the inexhaustible **652** fountain, and infinite abyss, of all perfection, both natural and moral; also all the kinds of prayer, i.e. all the ways of expressing our love, hope, trust, resignation, gratitude, reverence, fear, desire, etc. towards him; transfer, by association, all the perfection, greatness, and gloriousness of his natural attributes upon his moral ones, i.e. upon moral rectitude. We shall by this means learn to be merciful, holy, and perfect, because God is so; and to love mercy, holiness, and perfection, wherever we see them.

And thus we may perceive, that all the pleasures and pains of **653** sensation, imagination, ambition, self-interest, sympathy, and theopathy, as far as they are consistent with one another, with the frame of our natures, and with the course of the world, beget in us a moral sense, and lead us to the love and approbation of virtue, and to the fear, hatred, and abhorrence of vice. This moral sense therefore carries its own authority with it,[1] inasmuch as it is the sum total of all the rest, and the ultimate result from them; and employs the force and authority of the whole nature of man against any particular part of it, that rebels against the determinations and commands of the conscience or moral judgement.

It appears also, that the moral sense carries us perpetually to the pure love of God, as our highest and ultimate perfection, our end, centre, and only resting-place, to which yet we can never attain.

When the moral sense is advanced to considerable perfection, a person may be made to love and hate, merely because he ought; i.e. the pleasures of moral beauty and rectitude, and the pains of moral deformity and unfitness, may be transferred, and made to coalesce almost instantaneously.

★   ★   ★   ★

654   The moral sense or judgement here spoken of, is sometimes considered as an instinct, sometimes as determinations of the mind, grounded on the eternal reasons and relations of things. Those who maintain either of these opinions may, perhaps, explain them so as to be consistent with the foregoing analysis of the moral sense from association. But if by instinct be meant a disposition communicated to the brain, and in consequence of this, to the mind, or to the mind alone, so as to be quite independent of association; and by a moral instinct, such a disposition producing in us moral judgements concerning affections and actions; it will be necessary, in order to support the opinion of a moral instinct, to produce instances, where moral judgements arise in us independently of prior associations determining thereto.

In like manner, if by founding the morality of actions, and our judgement concerning this morality, on the eternal reasons and relations of things, be meant, that the reasons drawn from the relations of things, by which the morality or immorality of certain actions is commonly proved, and which, with the relations, are called eternal, from their appearing the same, or nearly the same, to the mind at all times, would determine the mind to form the corresponding moral judgement independently of prior associations, this ought also to be proved by the allegation of proper instances. To me it appears, that the instances are, as far as we can judge of them, of an

[1 Cf. Butler, §§ 379–81, 399–402, 406.]

opposite nature, and favour the deduction of all our moral judgements, approbations, and disapprobations, from association alone. However, some associations are formed so early, repeated so often, riveted so strong, and have so close a connection with the common nature of man, and the events of life which happen to all, as, in a popular way of speaking, to claim the appellation of original and natural dispositions; and to appear like instincts, when compared with dispositions evidently factitious; also like axioms, and intuitive propositions, eternally true according to the usual phrase, when compared with moral reasonings of a compound kind. But I have endeavoured to show in these papers, that all reasoning, as well as affection, is the mere result of association.

RICHARD PRICE

1723–1791

A REVIEW OF THE PRINCIPAL QUESTIONS IN MORALS

[First printed, 1758, with the title *A Review of the Principal Questions and Difficulties in Morals*. Reprinted here from the third edition, 1787, with misprints corrected, spelling modified, initial capital letters reduced, and some footnotes omitted]

RICHARD PRICE

———

A Review of the Principal Questions in Morals

CHAP. I—OF THE ORIGIN OF OUR IDEAS OF RIGHT AND WRONG

In considering the actions of moral agents, we shall find in our- **655** selves three different perceptions concerning them, which are necessary to be carefully distinguished.

The *first,* is our perception of right and wrong.

The *second,* is our perception of beauty and deformity.

The *third* we express, when we say, that actions are of *good* or *ill* desert.

Each of these perceptions I propose separately to examine, but particularly the *first,* with which I shall begin.

It is proper the reader should carefully attend to the state of the question here to be considered; which, as clearly as I can, I shall lay before him.

SECT. I—THE QUESTION STATED CONCERNING THE FOUNDATION OF MORALS

Some actions we all feel ourselves irresistibly determined to ap- **656** prove, and others to disapprove. Some actions we cannot but think *right,* and others *wrong,* and of all actions we are led to form some opinion, as either *fit* to be performed or *unfit;* or neither fit nor unfit to be performed; that is, *indifferent.* What the power within us is, which thus determines, is the question to be considered.

A late very distinguished writer, Dr. Hutcheson, deduces our **657** moral ideas from a *moral sense;* meaning by this *sense,* a power within us, different from reason, which renders certain actions pleasing and others displeasing to us. As we are so made, that certain impressions on our bodily organs shall excite certain ideas in our minds, and that certain outward forms, when presented to us, shall be the necessary occasions of pleasure or pain. In like manner, according to Dr. Hutcheson, we are so made, that certain affections and actions of moral agents shall be the necessary occasions of agreeable or disagreeable sensations in us, and procure our love or dislike of them. He has indeed well shown, that we have a faculty determining us *immediately* to approve or disapprove actions, abstracted from all views of private advantage; and that the highest pleasures of life depend upon this faculty. Had he proceeded no farther, and intended nothing more by the *moral sense*, than our *moral faculty* in general, little room would have been left for any objections: but then he would have meant by it nothing *new*, and he could not have been considered as the *discoverer* of it★. From the term *sense*, which he applies to it, from his rejection of all the arguments that have been used to prove it to be an intellectual power, and from the whole of his language on this subject; it is evident, he considered it as the effect of a *positive constitution* of our minds, or as an *implanted* and *arbitrary* principle[1] by which a *relish* is given us for certain moral objects and forms and aversion to others, similar to the relishes and aversions created by any of our other senses. In other words; our ideas of morality, if this account is right, have the same origin with our ideas of the sensible qualities of bodies, the harmony of sounds†, or the beauties of painting or sculpture; that is, the mere good pleasure of our Maker adapting the mind and its organs in a particular manner to certain objects. Virtue (as those who embrace this scheme say) is an affair of taste. Moral right and wrong, signify nothing *in the objects themselves* to which they are applied, any more than agreeable and harsh; sweet and bitter; pleasant and painful; but only *certain effects in us*. Our perception of *right*, or moral good, in actions, is that agreeable *emotion*, or feeling, which certain actions produce in

---

★ In the Preface to his *Treatise on the Passions*, he tells us; (after taking notice of some gentlemen, who, by what he had writ, had been convinced of a *moral sense*;) that they had made him a *compliment which he did not think belonged to him, as if the world were indebted to him for the discovery of it.*

† If any person wants to be convinced, that this is a just representation of Dr. Hutcheson's sentiments, he need only read his *Illustrations on the Moral Sense*, and particularly the 4th section at the conclusion [i.e. Hutcheson, § 371]. See also a *Note* at the end of the first of Mr. Hume's *Philosophical Essays*.

[1 Cf. Balguy, §§ 438, 444.]

us; and of *wrong*, or moral evil, the contrary. They are particular modifications of our minds, or impressions which they are made to receive from the contemplation of certain actions, which the contrary actions *might* have occasioned, had the Author of nature so pleased; and which to suppose to belong to these actions themselves, is as absurd as to ascribe the pleasure or uneasiness, which the observation of a particular form gives us, to the form itself. It is therefore, by this account, improper to say of an action, that it *is right*, in much the same sense that it is improper to say of an object of taste, that it is *sweet*; or of *pain*, that it is *in* fire.

The present inquiry therefore is; whether this be a true account of virtue or not; whether it *has* or has *not* a foundation in the *nature* of its object; whether *right* and *wrong* are real characters of *actions*, or only qualities of our *minds*; whether, in short, they denote what actions *are*, or only *sensations* derived from the particular frame and structure of our natures.

*   *   *   *

As to the schemes which found morality on self-love, on positive **658** laws and compacts, or the divine will; they must either mean, that moral good and evil are only other words for *advantageous* and *disadvantageous*, *willed* and *forbidden*.[1] Or they relate to a very different question; that is, not to the question, what is the nature and true *account* of virtue; but, what is the *subject-matter* of it.

As far as the former may be the intention of the schemes I have mentioned, they afford little room for controversy. Right and wrong when applied to actions which are commanded or forbidden by the will of God, or that produce good or harm, do not signify merely, that such actions are commanded or forbidden, or that they are useful or hurtful, but a *sentiment* concerning them and our consequent approbation or disapprobation of the performance of them. Were not this true, it would be palpably absurd in any case to ask, whether it is *right* to obey a command, or *wrong* to disobey it; and the propositions, *obeying a command is right*, or *producing happiness is right*, would be most trifling, as expressing no more than that obeying a command, is obeying a command, or producing happiness, is producing happiness.[2] Besides; on the supposition, that right and wrong denote only the relations of actions to will and law, or to

[1 Cf. Cudworth, § 120.]   [2 Cf. Hutcheson, §§ 350–1; Butler, § 411.]

happiness and misery, there could be no dispute about the faculty that perceives right and wrong, since it must be owned by all, that these relations are objects of the investigations of *reason*.

Happiness requires something in its own nature, or in ours, to give it influence, and to determine our desire of it and approbation of pursuing it. In like manner; all laws, will, and compacts suppose *antecedent right* to give them effect; and, instead of being the *constituents* of right, they owe their whole force and obligation to it.

659 Having premised these observations; the question now returns— What is the power within us that perceives the distinctions of *right* and *wrong*?

My answer is. The UNDERSTANDING.

In order to prove this, it is necessary to enter into a particular inquiry into the origin of our ideas in general, and the distinct provinces of the *understanding* and of *sense*.

SECT. II—OF THE ORIGIN OF OUR IDEAS IN GENERAL

660 SENSATION and REFLECTION have been commonly reckoned the sources of all our ideas: and Mr. Locke has taken no small pains to prove this. How much soever, on the whole, I admire his excellent *Essay*, I cannot think him sufficiently clear or explicit on this subject. It is hard to determine exactly what he meant by *sensation* and *reflection*. If by the former we understand, the effects arising from the impressions made on our minds by external objects; and by the latter, the notice the mind takes of its own operations; it will be impossible to derive some of the most important of our ideas from them. This is the explanation Mr. Locke gives of them in the beginning of his *Essay*. But it seems probable that what he chiefly meant, was, that all our ideas are either derived *immediately* from these two sources, or ultimately *grounded* upon ideas so derived; or, in other words, that they furnish us with all the subjects, materials, and occasions of knowledge, comparison, and internal perception. This, however, by no means renders them in any proper sense, the sources of all our ideas: nor indeed does it appear, notwithstanding all he has said of the operations of the mind about its ideas, that he thought we had any faculty different from sensation and reflection which could give rise to any *simple ideas*; or that was capable of more than compounding, dividing, abstracting, or enlarging ideas previously in the mind. But be this as it may, what I am going to observe, will, I believe, be found true.

The power, I assert, that *understands*; or the faculty within us that **661** discerns *truth*, and that compares all the objects of thought, and *judges* of them, is a spring of new ideas★.

As, perhaps, this has not been enough attended to, and as the question to be discussed, is; whether our *moral ideas* are derived from the *understanding* or from a *sense*; it will be necessary to state distinctly the different natures and provinces of sense and reason.

To this purpose we may observe, first, that the power which **662** judges of the perceptions of the senses, and contradicts their decisions; which discovers the nature of the sensible qualities of objects, inquires into their causes, and distinguishes between what is real and what is not real in them, must be a power within us which is superior to sense.

Again, it is plain that one sense cannot judge of the objects of another; the eye, for instance, of harmony, or the ear of colours. The faculty therefore which views and compares the objects of *all* the senses, cannot be sense.[1] When, for instance, we consider sound and colour together, we observe in them *essence, number, identity, diversity*, etc. and determine their reality to consist, not in being properties of *external substances*, but in being modifications of *our souls*. The power which takes cognizance of all this, and gives rise to these notions, must be a power capable of subjecting all things alike to its inspection, and of acquainting itself with necessary truth and existence.

★ The reader is desired to remember, that by *ideas*, I mean here almost constantly *simple ideas*, or original and uncompounded perceptions of the mind. That our ideas of right and wrong are of this sort, will be particularly observed hereafter. It may also be right to take notice, that I all along speak of the understanding, in the most confined and proper sense of it. What gives occasion for observing this, is the division which has been made by some writers, of all the powers of the soul into understanding and will; the former comprehending under it, all the powers of external and internal sensation, as well as those of judging and reasoning; and the latter, all the affections of the mind, as well as the power of acting and determining.

There may be further some occasion for observing, that the two acts of the understanding, being intuition and deduction, I have in view the former. It is plain, on the contrary, that those writers, who argue against referring our moral ideas to reason, have generally the latter only in view.

———

[1 Cf. Cudworth, § 131.]

663   Sense consists in the obtruding of certain impressions upon us, independently of our wills; but it cannot perceive what they are, or whence they are derived. It lies prostrate under its object,[1] and is only a capacity in the soul of having its own state altered by the influence of particular causes. It must therefore remain a stranger to the objects and causes affecting it.

Were not *sense* and *knowledge* entirely different, we should rest satisfied with sensible impressions, such as light, colours, and sounds, and inquire no farther about them, at least when the impressions are strong and vigorous: whereas, on the contrary, we necessarily desire some farther acquaintance with them, and can never be satisfied till we have subjected them to the survey of reason.—Sense presents *particular* forms to the mind; but cannot rise to any *general* ideas. It is the intellect that examines and compares the presented forms, that rises above individuals to universal and abstract ideas; and thus looks downward upon objects, takes in at one view an infinity of particulars, and is capable of discovering general truths.[1]—Sense sees only the *outside* of things, reason acquaints itself with their *natures*.—Sensation is only a mode of feeling in the mind; but knowledge implies an active and vital energy of the mind.[1] Feeling pain, for example, is the effect of sense; but the understanding is employed when pain itself is made an object of the mind's reflection, or held up before it, in order to discover its nature and causes. Mere sense can perceive nothing in the most exquisite work of art; suppose a plant, or the body of an animal; but what is painted in the eye, or what might be described on paper. It is the intellect that must perceive in it order and proportion; variety and regularity; design, connection, art, and power; aptitudes, dependencies, correspondencies, and adjustment of parts so as to subserve an end, and compose one perfect whole*; things which can never be represented on a sensible organ, and the ideas of which cannot be passively communicated, or stamped on the mind by the operation of external objects.—Sense cannot perceive any of the modes of thinking beings; these can be discovered only by the mind's survey of itself.

* See Dr. Cudworth's Treatise *of eternal and immutable Morality*, Book IV. Chap. 2. where he observes, that the mind perceives, by occasion of outward objects, as much more than is represented to it by sense, as a learned man perceives in the best written book, more than an illiterate person or brute. . . .

[1 Cf. Cudworth, § 132.]

In a word, it appears that *sense* and *understanding* are faculties of **664** the soul totally different: the one being conversant only about *particulars*; the other about *universals*: the one not *discerning*, but *suffering*; the other not *suffering*, but *discerning*; and signifying the soul's *power* of surveying and examining all things, in order to judge of them; which *power*, perhaps, can hardly be better defined, than by calling it, in Plato's language, the power in the soul to which belongs καταληψις του οντος, or the apprehension of TRUTH*.

But, in order farther to show how little a way mere sense (and let **665** me add *imagination*, a faculty nearly allied to *sense*) can go, and how far we are dependent on our higher reasonable powers for many of our fundamental ideas; I would instance in the following particulars.

The idea of *solidity* has been generally reckoned among the ideas we owe to sense; and yet perhaps it would be difficult to prove, that we ever had actual experience of that *impenetrability* which we include in it, and consider as essential to all bodies.

*   *   *   *

Again, what is meant by the *vis inertiae*, or *inactivity* of matter, is rather a perception of reason, than an idea conveyed to the mind by sense.

*   *   *   *

The idea of *substance*, likewise, is an idea to which our minds are necessarily carried, beyond what mere sensation suggests to us; which can show us nothing but accidents, sensible qualities, and the outsides of things. It is the understanding that discovers the general distinction between substance and accident; nor can any perception be more unavoidable, than that motion implies *something* that moves; *extension* something *extended*; and, in general, *modes* something *modified*.

The idea of *duration* is an idea accompanying all our ideas, and **666** included in every notion we can frame of reality and existence. What the observation of the train of thoughts following one another in our minds, or the constant flux of external objects, suggests, is *succession*; an idea which, in common with all others, presupposes that of *duration*; but is as different from it as the idea of motion, or figure. It would, I think, have been much properer to have said, that the

* Most of these observations concerning the difference between sense and knowledge, may be found in Plato's *Theaetetus*; and in the Treatise quoted in the last note.

reflection on the succession of ideas in our minds is that by which we estimate the *quantity* of duration intervening between two events; than, that we owe to it the idea of duration.

Observations to the same purpose might be made concerning *space*. This, as well as duration, is included in every reflection we can make on our own existence, or that of other things; it being self-evidently the same with *denying* the existence of a thing, to say, that it exists *no where*. We, and all things, exist in *time* and *place*; and therefore, as self-conscious and intelligent beings, we must have ideas of them.

What may be farther worth observing concerning space and duration, is, that we perceive intuitively their *necessary existence*. The very notion of annihilation being the removal of a thing from space and duration; to suppose these themselves annihilated, would be to suppose their separation from themselves. In the same intuitive manner we perceive they can have no *bounds*, and thus acquire the idea of *infinity*.

★   ★   ★   ★

There are other objects which the same faculty, with equal evidence, perceives to be *contingent*; or whose actual existence it sees to be not *necessary*, but only *possible*.

Thus, the understanding, by employing its attention about different objects, and observing what is or is not *true* of them, acquires the different ideas of necessity, infinity, contingency, possibility, and impossibility

667   The next ideas I shall instance in are those of *power* and *causation*. Some of the ideas already mentioned imply them; but they require our particular notice and attention.

★   ★   ★   ★

What we observe by our external senses, is properly no more than that one thing *follows* another★, or the *constant conjunction* of certain events; as of the melting of wax, with placing it in the flame of a candle; and, in general, of such and such alterations in the qualities

---

★ Several observations to this purpose are made by Malebranche, who (it is well known) has maintained, that nothing in nature is ever the proper *cause* or *efficient* of another, but only the *occasion*; the Deity, according to him, being the sole agent in all effects and events. But Mr. Hume has more particularly insisted on the observation here made, with a very different view. See his *Phil. Essays*. [Cf. Hume,§§ 614, 621–2.]

of bodies, with such and such circumstances of their situation. That one thing is the *cause* of another, or *produces* it, we never see: nor is it indeed true, in numberless instances where men commonly think they observe it: and were it in no one instance true; I mean, were there no object that contributed, by its own proper force, to the production of any new event; were the *apparent* causes of things universally only their *occasions* or *concomitants*; (which is nearly the real case, according to some philosophical principles;) yet still we should have the same ideas of cause, and effect, and power. Our certainty that every new event requires some cause, depends no more on experience than our certainty of any other the most obvious subject of intuition. In the idea of every *change* is included that of its being an *effect*.

★   ★   ★   ★

It should be observed, that I have not said that we have no idea of power, except from the understanding. Activity and self-determination are as essential to spirit, as the contrary are to matter; and therefore inward consciousness gives us the idea of that particular sort of power which they imply. But the universal source of the idea of power, as we conceive it necessary to the production of all that happens, and of our notions of influence, connection, aptitude, and dependence in general, must be the understanding.

★   ★   ★   ★

With respect to all the ideas now mentioned, particularly the last, **668** it is worth observing, that were it as difficult to find out their true origin, as it is to deduce them from the common sources explained by writers on these subjects, it would surely be very unreasonable to conclude, that we have no such ideas. And yet this is the very conclusion some have drawn★. If then we indeed have such ideas; and if, besides, they have a foundation in truth, and are ideas of somewhat really existing correspondent to them, what difficulty can there be in granting they may be apprehended by that faculty whose object is truth? But if we have no such ideas, or if they denote nothing real besides the qualities of our own minds; I need not say into what an abyss of scepticism we are plunged.

Let me add, in the last place, that our *abstract ideas* seem most **669**

* See Mr. Hume's *Philosophical Essays*, p. 104, etc. [But contrast Hume, § 625.]

properly to belong to the understanding. They are, undoubtedly, essential to all its operations; every act of judgement implying some abstract or universal idea. Were they formed by the mind in the manner generally represented, it seems unavoidable to conceive that it *has* them at the very time that it is supposed to be employed in *forming* them. Thus; from any *particular* idea of a triangle, it is said we can frame the *general* one; but does not the very reflection said to be necessary to this, on a greater or lesser triangle, imply, that the general idea is already in the mind? How else should it know how to go to work, or what to reflect on?—That the universality consists in the *idea*; and not merely in the *name* as used to signify a number of particulars *resembling* that which is the immediate object of reflection, is plain; because, was the idea to which the name answers and which it recalls into the mind, only a particular one, we could not know to what other ideas to apply it, or what particular objects had the resemblance necessary to bring them within the meaning of the name.

★　　★　　★　　★

670　　When I consider these things, I cannot help wondering, that, in inquiring into the origin of our ideas, the understanding, which, though not first in time, is the most important source of our ideas, should have been overlooked. It has, indeed, been always considered, as the source of *knowledge*: but it should have been more attended to, that as the source of knowledge, it is likewise the source of new ideas, and that it cannot be one of these without being the other. The various kinds of *agreement* and *disagreement* between our ideas, which Mr. Locke says, it is its office to discover and trace, are so many new simple ideas, obtained by its discernment. Thus; when it considers the two angles made by a right line, standing in any direction on another, and perceives the *agreement* between them and two right angles; what is this *agreement* besides their *equality*? And is not the idea of this *equality* a new simple idea, acquired by the understanding, wholly different from that of the two angles compared, and denoting self-evident truth?—In much the same manner in other cases, knowledge and intuition suppose somewhat perceived in their objects, denoting simple ideas to which themselves gave rise.—This is true of our ideas of *proportion*; of our ideas of *identity* and *diversity, existence, connection, cause* and *effect, power, possibility* and *impossibility*; and let me add, though prematurely, of our ideas of moral *right* and *wrong*. The first concerns *quantity*; the last *actions*; the rest *all things*. They comprehend the most considerable part of what we can desire to *know* of things, and are the objects of almost all reasonings and disquisitions.

In short. As bodily sight discovers to us *visible* objects; so does the understanding, (the eye of the mind, and infinitely more penetrating) discover to us *intelligible* objects; and thus, in a like sense with bodily vision, becomes the inlet of new ideas.—

★   ★   ★   ★

It is an observation very necessary to be made, before we leave 671 what we are now upon, that the source of ideas on which I have insisted, is different from the power of *reasoning*, and ought, by no means, to be confounded with it. This consists in investigating certain relations between objects, ideas of which must have been previously in the mind: that is; it supposes us already to have the ideas we want to trace; and therefore cannot give rise to new ideas. No mind can be engaged in investigating it knows not what; or in endeavouring to find out any thing concerning an object, of which it has no conception. When, from the view of objects to which they belong self-evidently, we have gained ideas of proportion, identity, connection, etc. we employ deduction, or reasoning, to trace these amongst other objects, and in other instances, where they cannot be perceived immediately.

SECT. III—OF THE ORIGIN OF OUR IDEAS OF MORAL RIGHT AND WRONG

Let us now return to our first inquiry, and apply the foregoing 672 observations to our ideas of *right* and *wrong* in particular.

It is a very necessary previous observation, that our ideas of *right* and *wrong* are simple ideas, and must therefore be ascribed to some power of *immediate* perception in the human mind. He that doubts this, need only try to give definitions of them, which shall amount to more than synonymous expressions.[1] Most of the confusion in which the question concerning the foundation of morals has been

[1 Cf. Hutcheson, § 358.]

involved has proceeded from inattention to this remark. There are, undoubtedly, some actions that are *ultimately* approved, and for justifying which no reason can be assigned; as there are some ends, which are *ultimately* desired, and for choosing which no reason can be given.[1] Were not this true; there would be an infinite progression of reasons and ends, and therefore nothing could be at all approved or desired.

673   Supposing then, that we have a power *immediately* perceiving right and wrong: the point I am now to endeavour to prove, is, that this power is the *understanding*, agreeably to the assertion at the end of the *first* section. I cannot but flatter myself, that the main obstacle to the acknowledgement of this, has been already removed, by the observations made in the preceding section, to show that the understanding is a power of immediate perception, which gives rise to new original ideas; nor do I think it possible that there should have been many disputes on this subject had this been properly considered.

But, in order more explicitly and distinctly to evince what I have asserted (in the only way the nature of the question seems capable of) let me,

674   *First,* observe, that it implies no absurdity, but evidently *may* be true. It is undeniable, that many of our ideas are derived from our INTUITION of truth, or the discernment of the natures of things by the understanding. This therefore *may* be the source of our moral ideas. It is at least *possible,* that *right* and *wrong* may denote what we *understand* and *know* concerning certain objects, in like manner with proportion and disproportion, connection and repugnancy, contingency and necessity, and the other ideas before-mentioned.—I will add, that nothing has been offered which has any tendency to prove the contrary. All that can appear, from the objections and reasonings of the author of the *Inquiry into the original of our ideas of beauty and virtue,* is only, what has been already observed, and what does not in the least affect the point in debate: namely, that the words *right* and *wrong, fit* and *unfit,* express simple and undefinable ideas. But that the power perceiving them is properly a *sense* and not *reason*; that these ideas denote nothing *true* of actions, nothing in the *nature* of actions; this, he has left entirely without proof. He appears, indeed, to have taken for granted, that if virtue and vice are *immediately*

[1 Cf. Hutcheson, §§ 362–3; Gay, § 470; Hume, § 606.]

perceived, they must be perceptions of an *implanted* sense. But no conclusion could have been more hasty. For will any one take upon him to say, that all powers of immediate perception must be arbitrary and implanted; or that there can be no simple ideas denoting any thing besides the qualities and passions of the mind?—In short. Whatever some writers have said to the contrary, it is certainly a point not yet decided, that virtue is wholly factitious, and to be *felt*, not *understood*.

As there are some propositions, which, when attended to, necessarily determine all minds to *believe* them: and as (which will be shown hereafter) there are some ends, whose natures are such, that, when perceived, all beings immediately and necessarily *desire* them: so is it very credible, that, in like manner, there are some actions whose natures are such, that, when observed, all rational beings immediately and necessarily *approve* them.

I do not at all care what follows from Mr. Hume's assertion, that **675** all our ideas are either *impressions, or *copies of impressions*; or from Mr. Locke's assertion that they are all *deducible from* SENSATION *and* REFLECTION.—The first of these assertions is, I think, destitute of all proof; supposes, when applied in this as well as many other cases, the point in question; and, when pursued to its consequences, ends in the destruction of all truth and the subversion of our intellectual faculties.—The other wants much explication to render it consistent with any tolerable account of the original of our moral ideas: nor does there seem to be any thing necessary to convince a person, that all our ideas are not deducible from sensation and reflection, except taken in a very large and comprehensive sense, besides considering how Mr. Locke derives from them our *moral ideas*. He places them among our ideas of relations, and represents *rectitude* as signifying the conformity of actions to some rules or laws; which rules or laws, he says, are either *the will of God*, the *decrees of the magistrate, or the fashion of the country*:[1] from whence it follows, that it is an absurdity to apply *rectitude* to rules and laws themselves;[2] to suppose the *divine* will to be directed by it; or to consider it as *itself* a rule and law. But, it is undoubted, that this great man would have detested these consequences; and, indeed, it is sufficiently evident, that he was strangely

* See Mr. Hume's *Treatise of Human Nature*, and *Philosophical Essays*.

[1 Cf. Locke, §§ 183–8.]   [2 Cf. § 658.]

embarrassed in his notions on this, as well as some other subjects. But,

676   *Secondly*, I know of no better way of determining this point, than by referring those who doubt about it to common sense, and putting them upon considering the nature of their own perceptions.—Could we suppose a person, who, when he perceived an external object, was at a loss to determine whether he perceived it by means of his organs of sight or touch; what better method could be taken to satisfy him? There is no possibility of doubting in any such cases. And it seems not more difficult to determine in the present case.

Were the question; what that perception is, which we have of number, diversity, causation or proportion; and whether our ideas of them signify truth and reality perceived by the understanding, or impressions made by the objects to which we ascribe them, on our minds; were, I say, this the question; would it not be sufficient to appeal to every man's consciousness?—These perceptions seem to me to have no greater pretence to be denominated perceptions of the understanding, than *right* and *wrong*.

677   It is true, some impressions of pleasure or pain, satisfaction or disgust, generally attend our perceptions of virtue and vice. But these are merely their effects and concomitants, and not the perceptions themselves, which ought no more to be confounded with them, than a particular truth (like that for which Pythagoras offered a hecatomb) ought to be confounded with the pleasure that may attend the discovery of it. Some emotion or other accompanies, perhaps, all our perceptions; but more remarkably our perceptions of right and wrong. And this, as will be again observed in the next chapter, is what has led to the mistake of making them to signify nothing but impressions, which error some have extended to all objects of knowledge; and thus have been led into an extravagant and monstrous scepticism.

678   But to return; let any one compare the ideas arising from our *powers of sensation*, with those arising from our *intuition of the natures of things*, and inquire which of them his ideas of right and wrong most resemble. On the issue of such a comparison may we safely rest this question. It is scarcely conceivable that any one can impartially attend to the nature of his own perceptions, and determine that, when he thinks gratitude or beneficence to be *right*, he perceives nothing *true* of them, and *understands* nothing, but only receives an impression from a *sense*. Was it possible for a person to question, whether his idea of *equality* was gained from sense or intelligence; he might soon be convinced, by considering, whether he is not sure, that certain lines or figures are *really* equal, and that their equality must be perceived by all minds, as soon as the objects themselves are perceived.—In the same manner may we satisfy ourselves concerning the origin of the idea of *right*: for have we not a like consciousness, that we discern the one, as well as the other, *in* certain objects? Upon what possible grounds can we pronounce the one to be *sense*, and the other *reason*? Would not a being purely intelligent, having happiness within his reach, *approve* of securing it for himself? Would not he *think* this right; and would it not *be* right? When we contemplate the happiness of a species, or of a world, and pronounce concerning the actions of reasonable beings which promote it, that they are *right*; is this judging erroneously? Or is it no determination of judgement at all, but a species of mental taste?—Are not such actions *really right*? Or is every apprehension of rectitude in them false and delusive, just as the like apprehension is concerning the effects of external and internal sensation, when taken to belong to the causes producing them?

It seems beyond contradiction certain, that every being must **679** *desire* happiness for himself; and can those natures of things, from which the *desire* of happiness and *aversion* to misery necessarily arise, leave, at the same time, a rational nature totally indifferent as to any *approbation* of actions procuring the one, or preventing the other? Is there nothing that any *understanding* can perceive to be amiss in a creature's bringing upon himself, or others, calamities and ruin? Is there nothing truly wrong in the absolute and eternal misery of an innocent being?—'It *appears* wrong to us.'—And what reason can you have for doubting, whether it appears what *it is*?—Should a being, after being flattered with hopes of bliss, and having his expectations raised by encouragements and promises, find himself, without reason, plunged into irretrievable torments; would he not *justly* complain? Would he want a *sense* to cause the idea of *wrong* to arise in his mind?—Can goodness, gratitude, and veracity, appear to any mind under the same characters, with cruelty, ingratitude, and treachery?—Darkness may as soon appear to be light.

It would, I doubt, be to little purpose to plead further here, the **680** natural and universal apprehensions of mankind, that our ideas of right and wrong belong to the understanding, and denote real characters of actions; because it will be easy to reply, that they have a like opinion of the *sensible qualities* of bodies; and that nothing is more common than for men to mistake their own sensations for the properties of the objects producing them, or to apply to the object itself, what they find always accompanying it, whenever observed. Let it therefore be observed,

681   *Thirdly*, that if right and wrong denote effects of sensation, it must imply the greatest absurdity to suppose them applicable to actions: that is; the ideas of *right* and *wrong* and of *action*, must in this case be incompatible; as much so, as the idea of pleasure and a regular form, or of pain and the collisions of bodies.—All sensations, as such, are modes of consciousness, or feelings of a sentient being, which must be of a nature totally different from the particular causes which produce them. A *coloured body*, if we speak accurately, is the same absurdity with a *square sound*. We need no experiments to prove that heat, cold, colours, tastes, etc. are not real qualities of bodies; because the ideas of matter and of these qualities, are incompatible.— But is there indeed any such incompatibility between *actions* and *right*? Or any such absurdity in affirming the one of the other?—Are the ideas of them as different as the idea of a sensation, and its cause?

*   *   *   *

682   How strange would it be to maintain, that there is no possibility of *mistaking* with respect to right and wrong*; that the apprehensions of all beings, on this subject, are alike just, since all sensation must be alike *true* sensation?—Is there a greater absurdity, than to suppose, that the *moral rectitude* of an action is nothing absolute and unvarying; but capable, like all the modifications of pleasure and pain, of being intended and remitted, of increasing and lessening, of rising and sinking with the force and liveliness of our feelings? Would it be less ridiculous to suppose this of the relations between given quantities, of the equality of numbers, or the figure of bodies?

683   In the last place; let it be considered, that all actions, undoubtedly, have a *nature*. That is, *some character* certainly belongs to them, and somewhat there is to be *truly* affirmed of them. This may be, that some of them are right, others wrong. But if this is not allowed; if

---

* It will be observed presently, that the ancient sceptics asserted universally there could be no such thing as *error*; and for the very reason here assigned.

no actions are, *in themselves*, either right or wrong, or any thing of a moral and obligatory nature, which can be an object to the understanding; it follows, that, in themselves, they *are* all indifferent. This is what is essentially true of them, and this is what all understandings, that perceive right, must perceive them to be. But are we not conscious, that we perceive the contrary? And have we not as much reason to believe the contrary, as to believe or trust at all our own discernment?

★   ★   ★   ★

In short; it seems sufficient to overthrow any scheme, that such consequences, as the following, should rise from it:—That no one being can judge one end to be better than another, or believe a real moral difference between actions; without giving his assent to an impossibility; without mistaking the *affections of his own mind* for *truth*, and *sensation* for *knowledge*.—That there being nothing intrinsically proper or improper, just or unjust; there is nothing *obligatory*★; but all beings enjoy, from the reasons of things and the nature of actions, liberty to act as they will.

The following important corollary arises from these arguments: **684**
That morality is *eternal and immutable*.

Right and wrong, it appears, denote what actions *are*. Now whatever any thing *is*, that it is, not by will, or decree, or power, but by *nature and necessity*.[1] Whatever a triangle or circle is, that it is unchangeably and eternally. It depends upon no will or power, whether the three angles of a triangle and two right ones shall be *equal*; whether the periphery of a circle and its diameter shall be *incommensurable*; or whether matter shall be *divisible, moveable, passive*, and *inert*. Every object of the understanding has an indivisible and invariable essence; from whence arise its properties, and numberless truths concerning it. Omnipotence does not consist in a power to alter the nature of things, and to destroy necessary truth

---

★ Moral right and wrong, and moral obligation or duty, must remain, or vanish together. They necessarily accompany one another, and make but as it were one idea. As far as the former are fictitious and imaginary, the latter must be so too. This connection or coincidence between moral rectitude and obligation, will be at large considered hereafter [cf. §§ 708 ff.].

[1 Cf. Cudworth, § 120.]

(for this is contradictory, and would infer the destruction of all wisdom, and knowledge) but in an absolute command over all *particular, external* existences, to create or destroy them, or produce any possible changes among them.—The natures of things then being immutable; whatever we suppose the natures of actions to be, they must be immutably. If they are indifferent, this indifference is itself immutable, and there neither is nor can be any one thing that, *in reality*, we *ought* to do rather than another. The same is to be said of right and wrong, of moral good and evil, as far as they express *real characters* of actions. They must immutably and necessarily belong to those actions of which they are *truly* affirmed.

*   *   *   *

CHAP. II—OF OUR IDEAS OF THE BEAUTY AND DEFORMITY
OF ACTIONS

685   Having considered our ideas of *right* and *wrong*; I come now to consider our ideas of *beauty*, and its contrary.

This is the *second* kind of sentiment, or perception, with respect to actions, which I noticed at the beginning of the preceding chapter. Little need be said to show, that it is different from the former. We are plainly conscious of more than the bare discernment of right and wrong, or the cool judgement of reason concerning the natures of actions. We often say of some actions, not only that they are *right*, but that they are *amiable*; and of others, not only that they are *wrong*, but *odious* and *shocking*. Every one must see, that these epithets denote the *delight*; or on the contrary, the *horror* and *detestation felt* by ourselves; and, consequently, signify not any real qualities or characters of actions, but the *effects in us*, or the particular pleasure and pain, attending the consideration of them.

'What then is the true account of these perceptions? Must they not arise entirely from an arbitrary structure of our minds, by which certain objects, when observed, are rendered the occasions of certain sensations and affections? And therefore, in this instance, are we not under a necessity of recurring to a *sense*? Can there be any connection, except such as arises from implanted principles, between any perceptions and particular modifications of pleasure and pain in the perceiving mind?'

I answer; that there *may* be such a connection; and that I think, there *is* such a connection in many instances; and particularly in this instance.

Why or how the impressions made by *external objects* on our 686 bodily organs, produce the sensations constantly attending them, it is not possible for us to discover. The same is true of the sensations and affections of mind produced by the objects of many of the *internal senses*. In such instances, we can conceive of no connection between the effects in us and their apparent causes; and the only account we can give is, that 'such is our frame; so God has seen fit to adapt our faculties and particular objects to one another.' But this is far from being true *universally*. There are objects which have a *natural aptitude* to please or displease our minds. And thus in the *spiritual* world, the case is the same, as in the *corporeal*; where, though there are events which we cannot explain, and numberless causes and effects of which, for want of being acquainted with the inward structure and constitution of bodies, we know no more than their existence: there are also causes the manner of whose operation we understand; and events, between which we discern a necessary connection.

One account, therefore, of the sentiments we are examining, is; 'that such are the *natures* of certain actions, that, when perceived, there must result certain emotions and affections.'

That there are objects which have a natural aptitude to please or 687 offend, and between which and the contemplating mind there is a necessary congruity or incongruity, seems to me unquestionable.— For, what shall we say of supreme and complete excellence? Is what we mean by this only a particular kind of sensation; or, if something real and objective, can it be contemplated without emotion? Must there be the aid of a sense to make the character of the *Deity* appear *amiable*; or, would pure and abstract reason be indifferent to it? Is there any thing more necessary to cause it to be loved and admired besides *knowing* it? The more it is known, and the better it is understood, must it not the more delight?

Again, a reasonable being, void of all superadded determinations or senses, who knows what order and happiness are, would, I think, unavoidably, receive *pleasure* from the survey of an universe where perfect order prevailed; and the contrary prospect of universal confusion and misery would *offend* him.

But his own happiness and misery are, undeniably, objects, which no being can contemplate with indifference. Of which in the next chapter.

What is thus true, in these and other instances, is particularly evident in the present case. It is not indeed plainer, that, in any instances, there are correspondencies and connections of things among themselves; or that one motion has a tendency to produce another; than it is, that virtue is naturally adapted to *please* every observing mind; and vice the contrary.—I cannot perceive an action to be right, without *approving* it; or *approve* it, without being conscious of some degree of *satisfaction* and complacency. I cannot perceive an action to be wrong, without *disapproving* it; or *disapprove* it, without being *displeased* with it. Right actions then, as such, must be *grateful*, and wrong ones *ungrateful* to us. The one must appear *amiable*, and the other *unamiable* and *base*.

*   *   *   *

688 To return therefore from this digression. The observations now made will not account for all our feelings and affections with respect to virtue and vice. Our intellectual faculties are in their infancy. The lowest degrees of reason are sufficient to discover *moral distinctions* in general; because these are self-evident, and included in the ideas of certain actions and characters. They must, therefore, appear to all who are capable of making actions the objects of their reflection. But the extent to which they appear, and the accuracy and force with which they are discerned; and, consequently, their influence, must, so far as they are the objects of pure intelligence, be in proportion to the strength and improvement of the rational faculties of beings and their acquaintance with truth and the natures of things.

From hence, it must appear, that in men it is necessary that the *rational principle*, or the *intellectual discernment* of *right* and *wrong*, should be aided by *instinctive determinations*.—The dictates of mere reason, being slow, and deliberate, would be otherwise much too weak. The condition in which we are placed, renders many urgent passions necessary for us; and these cannot but often interfere with our sentiments of rectitude. Reason alone, (imperfect as it is in us) is by no means sufficient to defend us against the danger to which, in such circumstances, we are exposed. Our Maker has, therefore, wisely provided remedies for its imperfections; and established a due balance in our frame by annexing to our intellectual perceptions sensations and instincts, which give them greater weight and force.

In short. The truth seems to be that, 'in contemplating the actions of moral agents, we have both a *perception of the understanding*, and a *feeling of the heart*;[1] and that the latter, or the effects in us accompanying our moral perceptions, depend on two causes. Partly, on the positive constitution of our natures: but principally on the essential congruity or incongruity between moral ideas and our intellectual faculties.'

*   *   *   *

It was, probably, in consequence of not duly considering the **689** difference I have now insisted on between the *honestum* and *pulchrum* (the δίκαιον and καλόν); or of not carefully distinguishing between the discernment of the mind, and the sensations attending it in our moral perceptions; that the author of the *Inquiry into the Original of our Ideas of Beauty and Virtue*, was led to derive all our ideas of virtue from an implanted sense. Moral good and evil, he every where describes, by the effects accompanying the perception of them. The *rectitude* of an action is, with him, the same with its *gratefulness* to the observer; and wrong, the contrary. But what can be more evident, than that *right* and *pleasure*, *wrong* and *pain*, are as different as a cause and its effect; what is *understood*, and what is *felt*; absolute truth, and its *agreeableness* to the mind?—Let it be granted, as undoubtedly it must, that some degree of pleasure is inseparable from the observation of virtuous actions★: it is just as unreasonable to infer from hence, that the discernment of virtue is nothing distinct from the reception of this pleasure; as it would be to infer, as some have done, that solidity, extension, and figure are only *particular modes of sensation*; because attended, whenever they are perceived, with some sensations of sight or touch, and impossible to be conceived by the imagination without them.

An able writer on these subjects, tells us that, after some †doubts, **690** he at last satisfied himself, that all beauty, whether natural or moral, is a species of absolute truth; as resulting from, or consisting in, the

---

★ The virtue of an action, Mr. Hume says, is its *pleasing* us after *a particular manner*. *Treatise of Human Nature*, Vol. iii. page 103 [i.e. Hume, § 537].

† See Mr. Balguy's *Tracts on the Foundation of Moral Goodness*, p. 61 [i.e. Balguy, § 443 *n*.].

[1 Cf. Butler, § 429.]

necessary relations and congruities of ideas. It is not easy to say what this means. *Natural beauty* will be considered presently. And as to *moral beauty*, one would think, that the meaning must be, that it denotes a real quality of certain actions. But the word *beauty* seems always to refer to the reception of pleasure; and the *beauty*, therefore, of an action or character, must signify its being such as *pleases us*, or has an aptness to *please* when perceived: nor can it be just to conceive more in the action itself, or to affirm more of it, than *this aptness*, or that objective goodness or rectitude on which it depends. Beauty and loveliness are synonymous; but an object *self-lovely* can only mean an object, by its nature, fitted to engage love.

*   *   *   *

I have already noticed the opinion that *natural beauty* is a real quality of objects.—It seems impossible for any one to conceive the objects themselves to be endowed with more than a particular order of parts, and with *powers*, or an *affinity* to our perceptive faculties, thence arising; and, if we call this *beauty*, then it is an absolute, inherent quality of certain objects; and equally existent whether any mind discerns it or not. But, surely, order and regularity are, more properly, the *causes* of beauty than *beauty itself*.

*   *   *   *

CHAP. III—OF THE ORIGIN OF OUR DESIRES AND AFFECTIONS

*   *   *   *

691 As all moral approbation and disapprobation, and our ideas of beauty and deformity, have been ascribed to an INTERNAL SENSE; meaning by this, not 'any inward power of perception,' but 'an *implanted power*, different from *reason*;' so, all our desires and affections have, in like manner, been ascribed to INSTINCT, *meaning by instinct, not merely 'the immediate desire of an object,'* but 'the *reason* of this desire; or an *implanted propension*.'—The former opinion I have already at large examined. I am now to examine the latter.

'Is then all desire to be considered as *wholly instinctive*? Is it, in particular, owing to nothing but an original bias given our natures, which they might have either wanted or have received in a contrary direction; that we are at all concerned for our own good, or for the good of others?'

As far as this inquiry relates to *private* good, we may without hesi- **692** tation answer in the negative. The desire of happiness for *ourselves*, certainly arises not from INSTINCT. The full and adequate account of it, is, *the nature of happiness*. It is impossible, but that creatures capable of pleasant and painful sensations, should *love and choose* the one, and *dislike and avoid* the other. No being, who knows what happiness and misery are, can be supposed indifferent to them, without a plain contradiction. Pain is not a *possible* object of *desire*; nor happiness, of *aversion*. No power whatsoever can cause a creature, in the agonies of torture and misery, to be pleased with his state, to like it for itself, or to wish to remain so. Nor can any power cause a creature rejoicing in bliss to *dislike* his state, or be *afraid* of its continuance. Then only can this happen, when pain can be *agreeable*, and pleasure *disagreeable*; that is, when pain can be pleasure; and pleasure, pain.

From hence I infer, that it is by no means, in general, an absurd **693** method of explaining our affections, to derive them from the natures of things and of beings. For thus without doubt we are to account for one of the most important and active of all our affections. To the preference and desire of *private happiness* by all beings, nothing more is requisite than to *know* what it *is*.—'And may not this be true, likewise, of *public* happiness? May not benevolence be *essential* to *intelligent* beings, as well as self-love to *sensible beings*?'

But to enter a little more minutely into the discussion of this point. Let us, again, put the case of a being *purely* reasonable. It is evident, that (though by supposition void of *implanted* biases) he would not want all principles of action, and all inclinations. It has been shown he would perceive VIRTUE, and possess affection to it, in proportion to the degree of his knowledge. The nature of *happiness* also would engage him to choose and desire it for *himself*. And is it credible that, at the same time, he would be necessarily indifferent about it for *others*? Can it be supposed to have that in it, which would determine him to seek it for *himself*; and yet to have nothing in it, which could engage him to approve of it for *others*? Would the nature of things, upon this supposition, be consistent? Would he not be capable of seeing, that the happiness of others is to them as important as his is to him; and that it is in itself equally valuable and desirable, whoever possesses it?

★   ★   ★   ★

694 But it must not be forgotten, that, in men, the sentiments **and** tendencies of our intelligent nature are, in a great degree, mingled with the effects of arbitrary constitution. It is necessary this observation, before insisted on, should be here called to mind. Rational and dispassionate benevolence would, in us, be a principle much too weak, and utterly insufficient for the purposes of our present state. And the same is true of our other rational principles and desires.

And this, perhaps, will afford us a good reason for distinguishing between *affections* and *passions*. The former, which we apply indiscriminately to all reasonable beings, may most properly signify the desires founded in the reasonable nature itself, and essential to it; such as self-love, benevolence, and the love of truth.—These, when strengthened by instinctive determinations, take the latter denomination; or are, properly, *passions*.—Those tendencies within us that are merely instinctive, such as hunger, thirst, etc. we commonly call *appetites* or *passions* indifferently, but seldom or never *affections*.

★　　　★　　　★　　　★

CHAP. IV—OF OUR IDEAS OF GOOD AND ILL DESERT

695 It is needless to say any thing to show that the ideas of good and ill desert necessarily arise in us upon considering certain actions and characters; or, that we conceive virtue as always *worthy*, and vice as the contrary. These ideas are plainly a species of the ideas of right and wrong. There is, however, the following difference between them, which may be worth mentioning. The epithets, *right* and *wrong*, are, with strict propriety, applied only to *actions*; but *good* and *ill desert* belong rather to the *agent*. It is the *agent* alone, that is capable of happiness or misery; and, therefore, it is he alone that properly can be said to *deserve* these.

I apprehend no great difficulty in explaining these ideas. They suppose virtue practised, or neglected; and regard the treatment due to beings in consequence of this. They signify the propriety which there is in making virtuous agents happy, and in discountenancing the vicious. When we say, a man *deserves* well, we mean, that his character is such, that we *approve* of showing him *favour*; or that it is *right* he should be happier than if he had been of a contrary character. We cannot but love a virtuous agent, and desire his happiness above that of others. Reason determines at once, that he *ought* to be the better for his virtue.—A vicious being, on the contrary, as such, we cannot but hate and condemn. Our concern for his happiness is necessarily diminished; nor can any truth appear more self-evidently to our minds, than that it is improper he should prosper in his wickedness, or that happiness should be conferred on him to the same degree that it is on others of worthy characters; or that it would have been conferred on himself, had he been virtuous.

Different characters require different treatment. Virtue affords a **696** *reason* for communicating happiness to the agent. Vice is a *reason* for withdrawing favour, and for punishing.—This seems to be very intelligible. But in order farther to explain this point, it is necessary to observe particularly, that the *whole* foundation of the sentiments now mentioned is by no means this; 'the tendency of virtue to the happiness of the world, and of vice to its misery; or the public utility of the one, and perniciousness of the other.'—We have an *immediate* approbation of making the virtuous happy, and discouraging the vicious, abstracted from all consequences. Were there but two beings in the universe, one of whom was virtuous, the other vicious; or, were we to conceive two such beings, in other respects alike, governed apart from the rest of the world, and removed for ever from the notice of all other creatures; we should still approve of a different treatment of them. That the good being should be less happy, or a greater sufferer, than his evil fellow-being, would appear to us wrong.

*   *   *   *

The moral worth or MERIT of an agent, then, is, 'his virtue considered as implying the fitness, that good should be communicated to him preferably to others; and as disposing all observers to esteem, and love him, and study his happiness.'—Virtue naturally, and of itself, recommends to favour and happiness, qualifies for them, and renders the being possessed of it the proper object of encouragement and reward. It is, in a like sense, we say that a person, who has been a benefactor to another, *deserves* well of him; that benefits received ought to be acknowledged and recompensed; and, that the person who bestows them is, preferably to others, the proper object of our regard and benevolence.

I deny not, but that one circumstance of great importance, upon **697** which is grounded the fitness of countenancing virtue and dis-countenancing vice among reasonable beings, is, the manifest tendency of this to prevent misery, and to preserve order and happiness in the world. What I assert is, that it is not *all* that renders such a procedure right; but that, setting aside the consideration of public interest, it would still remain right to make a distinction between the lots of the virtuous and vicious. Vice is of ESSENTIAL DEMERIT; and virtue is *in itself rewardable*. For, once more, let us imagine an order of reasonable beings made to pass through a particular stage of exis-tence, at the end of which they are annihilated: among whom, during the period they existed, no distinction was made on account of their different characters: virtue was not favoured, nor vice pun-ished: happiness and misery were distributed promiscuously; the guilty often prosperous, and flourishing; the good, as often afflicted and distressed, and sometimes brought to untimely ends by the oppression of their more happy, though wicked fellow-beings: the *most* wicked, generally, the *least* sufferers; and the *most* upright, the *least* happy. Notwithstanding all this, the quantity of happiness enjoyed may be conceived to exceed the ill. But will any one say, that, were there no connection between such beings and the rest of the universe, there would be nothing in the disposition of its affairs that would be wrong?—It will be said, for nothing else can be said, 'that such a state of reasonable beings cannot be approved because there would have been *more* happiness among them, had their differ-ent lots been ordered agreeably to the rules of distributive justice.' But is it so unavoidable to see this, that every one's disapprobation must be always immediately determined by it? Is there no other kind of wrong in so governing a system of beings, than in producing a *smaller* quantity of happiness rather than a *greater*? Or can the view of such beings give as much satisfaction to an unbiased mind, as if there had been among them, upon the whole, the same quantity of happiness, but distributed with a regard to their moral characters?

698　　In the case of a single, solitary evil being, it may perhaps be very true, that the only thing that could justify putting him into a state of absolute misery, would be its conduciveness to his reformation. But the reason why we approve of using methods to accomplish his reformation, is not merely this; 'that it is expedient to his happiness.' For were this true, it would, in a moral view, be indifferent whether he was made happy in consequence of being *punished* and thus reformed, or in consequence of such an extraordinary communication of advantages as should counteract and overbalance any sufferings necessarily occasioned by his vices. Can we equally approve these opposite methods of treating such a being? Supposing the same quantity of happiness enjoyed, is it indifferent whether a being enjoys it in a course of wickedness, or of virtue?—It would be extravagant to assert, that there is no *possible* method whereby a being can, in any degree, escape the hurtful effects of his vices, or lose the beneficial effects of his virtue. We see enough in the present world to convince us of the contrary.

★   ★   ★   ★

CHAP. V—OF THE RELATION OF MORALITY TO THE DIVINE NATURE; THE RECTITUDE OF OUR FACULTIES; AND THE GROUNDS OF BELIEF

Morality has been represented as necessary and immutable. There **699** is an objection to this, which to some has appeared of considerable weight, and which it will be proper to examine.

It may seem 'that this is setting up something distinct from God, which is independent of him, and equally eternal and necessary.'[1]

It is easy to see that this difficulty affects morality, no more than it does all truth. If for this reason, we must give up the unalterable natures of right and wrong, and make them dependent on the divine will; we must, for the same reason, give up all necessary truth, and assert the possibility of contradictions.

What I have hitherto aimed at has been, to prove that morality is a branch of *necessary truth*, and that it has the same foundation with it. If this is acknowledged, the main point I contend for is granted, and I shall be very willing that truth and morality should stand and fall together. This subject however cannot be pursued far enough, and morality traced to its source, without entering into the consideration of the difficulty now proposed; which naturally occurs in all inquiries of this sort.

In the first place, therefore, let it be observed, that something **700** there certainly is which we must allow not to be dependent on the will of God. For instance; this will itself; his own existence; his

[1 Cf. Cudworth, § 127.]

eternity and immensity; the difference between power and impotence, wisdom and folly, truth and falsehood, existence and non-existence.

To suppose these dependent on his will, is so extravagant, that no one can assert it. It would imply, that he is a changeable and precarious being, and render it impossible for us to form any consistent ideas of his existence and attributes. But these must be the creatures of will, if all truth be so.—There is another view of this notion, which shows that it overthrows the divine attributes and existence. For,

701   *Secondly*, mind supposes truth; and intelligence, something intelligible. Wisdom supposes certain *objects* about which it is conversant; and knowledge, *knowables*.—An eternal, necessary *mind* supposes eternal, necessary *truth*; and infinite knowledge, infinite knowables. If then there were no infinity of knowables; no eternal, necessary, independent truths; there could be no infinite, independent, necessary *mind* or *intelligence*; because there would be nothing to be certainly and eternally known. Just as, if there were nothing *possible*, there could be no *power*; or, if there were no necessary *infinity* of possibles, there could be no necessary, *infinite* power; because power supposes objects, and eternal, necessary, infinite power, an infinity of eternal and necessary *possibles*.

In like manner it may be said, that if there were no *moral distinctions*, there could be no *moral attributes in the Deity*. If there were nothing eternally and unalterably right and wrong, there could be nothing meant by his eternal, unalterable rectitude or holiness.—It is evident, therefore, that annihilating truth, possibility, or moral differences, is indeed annihilating all mind, all power, all goodness; and that so far as we make the former precarious, dependent, or limited; so far we make the latter so too.

702   Hence we see clearly, that to conceive of truth as depending on God's will, is to conceive of his intelligence and knowledge as depending on his will. And is it possible, that any one can think this as reasonable, as, on the contrary, to conceive of his *will* (which, from the nature of it, *requires something* to guide and determine it) as dependent on and regulated by his *understanding*?[1]—What can be more preposterous, than to make the Deity nothing but will; and to exalt this on the ruins of all his attributes?

[1 Cf. Cudworth, § 128.]

But it may still be urged, that these observations remove not the difficulty; but rather strengthen it. We are still left to conceive of 'certain objects, distinct from Deity, which are necessary and independent; and on which too his existence and attributes are founded; and without which, we cannot so much as form any idea of them.' I answer; we ought to distinguish between the *will* of God and his *nature*. It by no means follows, because they are independent of his *will*, that they are also independent of his *nature*. To conceive thus of them would indeed involve us in the greatest inconsistencies. Wherever, or in whatever objects, *necessity* and *infinity* occur to our thoughts, the divine, eternal nature is to be acknowledged.

★   ★   ★   ★

I shall conclude this chapter with a few observations on the **703** general grounds of belief and assent. These may be all comprehended under the three following heads.

The first is immediate consciousness or FEELING. It is absurd to ask a reason for our believing what we *feel*, or are inwardly conscious of. A thinking being must necessarily have a capacity of discovering some things in this way. It is from hence particularly we acquire the knowledge of our own existence, and of the several operations, passions, and sensations of our minds. And it is also under this head I would comprehend the information we derive from our powers of recollection or memory.

The *second* ground of belief is INTUITION; by which I mean the **704** mind's survey of its own ideas, and the relations between them, and the notice it takes of what is or is not true and false, consistent and inconsistent, possible and impossible in the natures of things. It is to this, as has been explained at large in the first chapter, we owe our belief of all self-evident truths; our ideas of the general, abstract affections and relations of things; our moral ideas, and whatsoever else we discover, without making use of any process of reasoning.—It is on this power of intuition, essential, in some degree or other, to all rational minds, that the whole possibility of all reasoning is founded. To it the last appeal is ever made. Many of its perceptions are capable, by attention, of being rendered more clear; and many of the truths discovered by it, may be illustrated by an advantageous representation of them, or by being viewed in particular lights; but seldom will admit of proper proof.—Some truths there must be, which can appear only by their own light, and which are incapable of proof; otherwise nothing could be proved, or known; in the same manner as, if there were no letters, there could be no words, or if there were no simple and undefinable ideas, there could be no complex ideas.—I might mention many instances of truths discernible no other way than *intuitively*, which learned men have strangely confounded and obscured, by supposing them subjects of *reasoning and deduction*. One of the most important instances, the subject of this treatise affords us; and another we have, in our notions of the necessity of a *cause* of whatever begins to exist, and our general ideas of *power and connection**: and, sometimes, reason has been ridiculously employed to prove even our own existence.

705   The *third* ground of belief is ARGUMENTATION *or* DEDUCTION. This we have recourse to when intuition fails us; and it is, as just now hinted, highly necessary, that we carefully distinguish between these two, mark their differences and limits, and observe what information we owe to the one or the other of them.—Our ideas are such, that, by comparing them amongst themselves, we can find out numberless truths concerning them, and, consequently, concerning actually existent objects, as far as correspondent to them, which would be otherwise undiscoverable. Thus, a particular relation between two ideas, which cannot be discerned by any immediate comparison, may appear, to the greatest satisfaction, by the help of a proper, intermediate idea, whose relation to each is either self-evident, or made out by some precedent reasoning.

*   *   *   *

706   It may be worth observing, that all we believe on any of these grounds is not equally evident to us. This is obvious with respect to the last, which supplies us with all the degrees of evidence, from that producing full certainty, to the lowest probability. *Intuition*, likewise, is found in very various degrees. It is sometimes clear and perfect, and sometimes faint and obscure. Several propositions in geometry would appear very likely to it, though we had no demonstrations of them.—Neither do *consciousness*, *memory*, and *reflection on ourselves* convince us equally of all we discover by them.

*   *   *   *

* See the second section of the first chapter, § 667.

CHAP. VI—OF FITNESS, AND MORAL OBLIGATION, AND THE
VARIOUS FORMS OF EXPRESSION, WHICH HAVE BEEN USED
BY DIFFERENT WRITERS IN EXPLAINING MORALITY

After the account that has been given of the nature and origin of **707**
our ideas of morality; it will be easy to perceive the meaning of
several terms and phrases, which are commonly used in speaking on
this subject.

Fitness and *unfitness* most frequently denote the congruity or incongruity, aptitude or inaptitude of any means to accomplish an end.
But when applied to actions, they generally signify the same with
right and *wrong*; nor is it often hard to determine in which of these
senses these words are to be understood. It is worth observing, that
fitness, in the former sense, is equally undefinable with *fitness* in the
latter; or, that it is as impossible to express, in any other than synonymous words,[1] what we mean, when we say of certain objects,
'that they have a *fitness* to one another; or are *fit* to answer certain
purposes,' as it is when we say, 'reverencing the Deity is *fit*, or
beneficence is *fit* to be practised.' In the first of these instances, none
can avoid owning the absurdity of making an arbitrary sense the
source of the idea of *fitness*, and of concluding that it signifies
nothing real in objects, and that no one thing can be properly the
means of another. In both cases the term *fit*, signifies a simple perception of the understanding.

Morally good and *evil*, *reasonable* and *unreasonable*, are epithets also
commonly applied to actions, evidently meaning the same with
right and *wrong*, *fit* and *unfit*.

Approving an action is the same with discerning it to be *right*; as
assenting to a proposition is the same with discerning it to be *true*.

But *obligation* is the term most necessary to be here considered; **708**
and to the explication of it, the best part of this chapter shall be
devoted.

Obligation to action, and *rightness* of action, are plainly coincident
and identical; so far so, that we cannot form a notion of the one,
without taking in the other. This may appear to any one upon considering, whether he can point out any difference between what is
right, *meet* or *fit* to be done, and what *ought* to be done. It is not
indeed plainer, that figure implies something figured, solidity

[¹ Cf. § 672; Hutcheson, §§ 358, 373; Hume, § 625 *n.*]

resistance, or an effect a cause, than it is that *rightness* implies *ought-ness* (if I may be allowed this word) or *obligatoriness*. And as easily can we conceive of figure without extension, or motion without a change of place, as that it can be *fit* for us to do an action, and yet that it may not be what we *should* do, what it is our *duty* to do, or what we are under an *obligation* to do.—*Right, fit ought, should, duty, obligation*, convey, then, ideas necessarily including one another. From hence it follows,

709 *First*, that virtue, *as such*, has a real obligatory power antecedently to all positive laws, and independently of all will; for obligation, we see, is involved in the very nature of it.[1] To affirm, that the performance of that, which, to omit, would be wrong, is not obligatory, unless conducive to private good or enjoined by a superior power, is a manifest contradiction. It is to say, that it is not true, that a thing is what it is; or that we are *obliged* to do what we *ought* to do; unless it be the object of a command, or, in some manner, privately useful. —If there are any actions fit to be done by an agent, besides such as tend to his own happiness, those actions, by the terms, are *obligatory*, independently of their influence on his happiness.—Whatever it is *wrong* to do, that it is our *duty* not to do, whether enjoined or not by any positive law*.—I cannot conceive of any thing much more evident than this.—It appears, therefore, that those who maintain that all obligation is to be deduced from positive laws, the divine will, or self-love, assert what (if they mean any thing contrary to what is here said) implies, that the words *right* and *just* stand for no real and distinct characters of actions; but signify merely what is *willed* and *commanded*,[2] or conducive to private advantage, whatever that be; so that any thing may be both right and wrong, morally good and evil, at the same time and in any circumstances, as it may be commanded or forbidden by different laws and wills; and any the most pernicious effects will become just, and fit to be produced by any being, if but the smallest degree of clear advantage or pleasure may result to him from them.

710 Those who say, nothing can oblige but the will of God, generally

* It is obvious, that this is very different from saying (what it would be plainly absurd to say) that every action, the performance of which, in certain circumstances is wrong, will continue wrong, let the circumstances be ever so much altered, or by whatever authority it is commanded.

[1 Cf. Butler, § 381.]   [2 Cf. § 658; Cudworth, § 120.]

resolve the power of this to oblige to the annexed rewards and punishments. And thus, in reality, they subvert entirely the independent natures of moral good and evil; and are forced to maintain, that nothing can *oblige*, but the prospect of pleasure to be obtained, or pain to be avoided. If this be true, it follows that *vice* is, properly, no more than *imprudence*; that nothing is right or wrong, just or unjust, any farther than it affects self-interest; and that a being, independently and completely happy, cannot have any moral perceptions. The justness of these inferences cannot be denied by one, who will attend to the coincidence here insisted on between obligation and virtue.

But to pursue this point farther; let me ask, would a person who either believes there is no God, or that he does not concern himself with human affairs, feel no *moral obligations*, and therefore not be at all *accountable*? Would one, who should happen not to be convinced, that virtue tends to his happiness here or hereafter, be released from every *bond* of duty and morality? Or, would he, if he believed no future state, and that, in any instance, virtue was against his *present* interest, be truly *obliged*, in these instances, to be wicked?[1]—These consequences must follow, if obligation depends entirely on the knowledge of the will of a superior, or on the connection between actions and private interest.—But, indeed, the very expression, *virtue tends to our happiness*, and the supposition that, in certain cases, it may be inconsistent with it, imply that it may exist independently of any connection with private interest; and would have no sense, if it signified only the relation of actions to private interest. For then, to suppose virtue to be inconsistent with our happiness, would be the same with supposing, that what is *advantageous* to us, may be *disadvantageous* to us.[2]

It is strange to find those who plead for self-interest, as the only 711 ground of moral obligation, asserting that, when virtue clashes with present enjoyments, all motives to it cease, supposing no future state. For, upon their principles, the truth is not, that all motives to practise virtue, would, in these circumstances, cease, but that virtue itself would cease; nay, would be changed into vice; and what would otherwise have been fit and just, become unlawful and wrong: for, being under an obligation in these circumstances not to do what appeared to us fit, it could not in reality *be* fit; we could not do it

[1 Cf. Butler, § 380.]   [2 Cf. § 658.]

without violating our duty, and therefore certainly, not without doing wrong. Thus, all who find not their *present* account in virtue, would, upon these principles (setting aside another world) be under an obligation to be wicked. Or, to speak more properly, the subject-matter of virtue and vice (that is, the relation of particular actions to private good) would be altered; what was before *wickedness* would become *virtue*, and what was before *virtue* would become *wickedness*. —It should be carefully minded that, as far as another world creates *obligation*, it creates *virtue*; for it is an absurdity too gross to be maintained, that we may act contrary to our obligations, and yet act virtuously.

712 Another observation worthy our notice in this place, is, that rewards and punishments suppose, in the very idea of them, moral obligation, and are founded upon it. They do not *make* it, but *enforce* it. They are the *sanctions* of virtue, and not its *efficients*. A reward supposes something done to *deserve* it, or a conformity to *obligation subsisting previously to it*; and punishment is always inflicted on account of some breach of *obligation*. Were we under no obligations, antecedently to the proposal of rewards and punishments, it would be a contradiction to suppose us subjects capable of them.—A person without any light besides that of nature, and supposed ignorant of a future state of rewards and punishments and the will of the Deity, might discover these by reasoning from his natural notions of morality and duty. But were the latter dependent on the former, and not *vice versa*; this could not be said, nor should we have any principles left, from which to learn the will of the Deity, and the conditions of his favour to us.

713 *Secondly*, from the account given of *obligation*, it follows that *rectitude* is a *law* as well as a *rule* to us; that it not only *directs*, but *binds* all, as far as it is perceived.—With respect to its being a *rule*, we may observe, that a rule of action signifying some measure or standard to which we are to conform our actions, or some information we possess concerning what we ought to do, there can, in this sense, be no *other* rule of action; all besides, to which this name can be properly given, implying it, or signifying only helps to the discovery of it. To perceive or to be informed how it is *right* to act, is the very notion of a *direction* to act. And it must be added, that it is such a direction as implies *authority*,[1] and which we cannot disregard

[1 Cf. Butler, §§ 379–81, 399–402.]

or neglect without remorse and pain. Reason is the guide, the *natural* and *authoritative* guide of a rational being.[1] Where he has no discernment of right and wrong, there, and there only, is he (morally speaking) *free*. But where he has this discernment, where *moral good* appears to him, and he cannot avoid pronouncing concerning an action, that it is fit to be done, and evil to omit it; here he is tied in the most strict and absolute manner, in bonds that no power in nature can dissolve, and from which he can at no time, or in any single instance, break loose, without offering the most unnatural violence to himself; without making an inroad into his own soul, and immediately pronouncing his own sentence.

That is properly a *law* to us, which we always and unavoidably feel and own ourselves *obliged* to obey; and which, as we obey or disobey it, is attended with the immediate sanctions of inward triumph and self-applause, or of inward shame and self-reproach, together with the secret apprehensions of the favour or displeasure of a superior righteous power, and the anticipations of *future* rewards, and punishments.[2]—That has proper *authority* over us, to which, if we refuse submission, we transgress our duty, incur guilt, and expose ourselves to just vengeance. All this is certainly true of our moral judgement, and contained in the idea of it.

*　　　*　　　*　　　*

Thirdly, from the account given of obligation, it appears how **714** absurd it is to inquire, what *obliges* us to practise virtue? as if obligation was no part of the idea of virtue, but something adventitious and foreign to it; that is, as if what was *due*, might not be our *duty*, or what was *wrong*, *unlawful*; or as if it might not be true, that what it is *fit* to do, we *ought* to do, and that what we *ought* to do, we are *obliged* to do.—To ask, why are we *obliged* to practise virtue, to abstain from what is wicked, or perform what is just, is the very same as to ask, why we are *obliged* to do what we are *obliged* to do?—It is not possible to avoid wondering at those, who have so unaccountably embarrassed themselves, on a subject that one would think was attended with no difficulty; and who, because they cannot find any thing in *virtue and duty themselves*, which can induce us to pay a regard to them in our practice, fly to self-love, and maintain that from hence alone are derived all inducement and obligation.

[1 Cf. Butler, §§ 406, 427 *n*., 429 *n*.]   [2 Cf. Butler, § 399.]

715   *Fourthly*, from what has been observed, it may appear, in what sense obligation is ascribed to God. It is no more than ascribing to him the perception of rectitude, or saying, that there are certain ends, and certain measures in the administration of the world, which he approves, and which are *better* to be pursued than others.—Great care, however, should be taken, what language we here use. *Obligation* is a word to which many persons have affixed several ideas, which should by no means be retained when we speak of God. Our language and our conceptions, whenever he is the subject of them, are *always* extremely defective and inadequate, and *often* very erroneous.—There are many who think it absurd and shocking to attribute any thing of *obligation* or *law* to a being who is necessarily sufficient and independent, and to whom nothing can be prior or superior. How, I conceive, we are to frame our apprehensions on this subject, has already, in some measure, appeared. It should, methinks, be enough to satisfy such persons, that the obligations ascribed to the Deity arise entirely from and exist in his own nature; and that the eternal, unchangeable LAW, by which it has been said, he is directed in all his actions, is no other than HIMSELF; *his own infinite, eternal, all perfect understanding.*

716   *Fifthly*, what has been said also shows us, on what the obligations of religion and the divine will are founded. They are plainly branches of universal rectitude. Our obligation to obey God's will means nothing, but that obedience is *due* to it, or that it is *right and fit* to comply with it. What an absurdity is it then, to make obligation *subsequent* to the divine will, and the *creature* of it? For why, upon this supposition, does not *all* will oblige equally? If there be any thing which gives the preference to one will above another; that, by the terms, is *moral rectitude.* What would any laws or will of any being signify, what influence could they have on the determinations of a moral agent, was there no good reason for complying with them, no obligation to regard them, no *antecedent right* of command?—To affirm that we are *obliged* in any case, but not in virtue of *reason and right*, is to say, that in that case we are not obliged at all.

*   *   *   *

717   Farther, what has been said will show us, what judgement to form concerning several accounts and definitions, which have been given of obligation. It is easy here to perceive the perplexity arising from attempting to define words expressing simple perceptions of the mind.—An ingenious and able writer* defines obligation to be *a state of the mind into which it is brought by perceiving a reason for action.* Let this definition be substituted wherever the words *duty, should, obliged,* occur; and it will soon be seen how defective it is.[1] The meaning of it is plainly, that obligation denotes that attraction or excitement which the mind feels upon perceiving right and wrong. But this is the *effect* of obligation perceived, rather than *obligation itself.* Besides, it is proper to say, that the duty or obligation to act is a reason for acting; and then this definition will stand thus: *obligation is a state of the mind into which it is brought by perceiving obligation to act.*— This author divides obligation into *external* and *internal*; by the former, meaning the excitement we feel to pursue pleasure as *sensible agents*; and, by the latter, the excitement we feel to pursue virtue as *reasonable and moral agents.*[2] But, as merely sensible beings, we are incapable of obligation; otherwise it might be properly applied to brutes, which, I think, it never is. What, in these instances, produces confusion, is not distinguishing between perception and the effect of it; between *obligation* and a *motive*. All motives are not obligations; though the contrary is true, that wherever there is obligation, there is also a motive to action.—Some perhaps, by *obligation,* may only mean such a motive to act, as shall have the greatest influence, and be most likely to determine us, and as far as this is all that is intended, it may be allowed, that the obligation to practise virtue depends greatly, as mankind are now situated, on its connection with private interest, and the views of future rewards and punishments.

Obligation has, by several writers, been styled, the *necessity of* **718** *doing a thing in order to be happy.*†[3] I have already taken sufficient

---

* Mr. Balguy. See his *tracts on the foundation of moral goodness and the law of truth.* [Cf. Balguy, § 450.]

† 'The whole force of obligation (says Bishop Cumberland in his *treatise* of the laws of nature, chap. v. sect. ii.) is this, that the legislator hath annexed to the observance of his laws, good, to the transgression, evil; and those natural: in prospect whereof men are moved to perform actions, rather agreeing than disagreeing with the laws.'— Ibid. sect. 27. 'I think that moral obligation may be thus universally and properly defined. Obligation is that act of a legislator, by which he declares that actions conformable to his law are necessary to those for whom the law is made. An action is then

---

[1 Cf. §§ 658, 710; Hutcheson, § 350; Butler, § 411.]
[2 Cf. Balguy, §§ 450, 455, 460.]   [3 Cf. Gay, § 463.]

notice of the opinion from which this definition is derived; and therefore shall here only ask, what, if this be the only sense of obligation, is meant when we say, a man is *obliged* to study his own happiness? Is it not obvious that *obliged*, in this proposition, signifies, not the necessity of doing a thing in order to be happy, which would make it ridiculous;[1] but only, that it is *right* to study our own happiness, and *wrong* to neglect it?

★   ★   ★   ★

719   The sense of obligation given by Dr. Hutcheson★, agrees in some measure, with the account here given of it. Then, he says, a *person is obliged to an action, when every spectator, or he himself, upon reflection, must approve his action and disapprove omitting it.* This account, however, is not perfectly accurate; for though obligation to act, and reflex approbation and disapprobation do, *in one*† sense, always accompany and imply one another; yet they seem as different as an *act* and an *object* of the mind, or as perception and the truth perceived. It is not exactly the same to say, it is our *duty* to do a thing; and to say, we *approve* of doing it. The one is the quality of the action, the other the *discernment* of that quality. Yet, such is the connection between these, that it is not very necessary to distinguish them; and, in common language, the term *obligation* often stands for the sense and judgement of the mind concerning what is fit or unfit to be done. It would, nevertheless, I imagine, prevent some confusion, and keep our ideas more distinct and clear, to remember, that a man's consciousness that an action ought to be done, or the *judgement concerning*

understood to be necessary to a rational agent, when it is certainly one of the causes necessarily required to that happiness, which he naturally and consequently necessarily desires.' . . .

★ *Illustrations on the Moral Sense.* Sect. 1. [And cf. Hutcheson, § 346.]

† The reason of adding this restriction is this. A man may, through involuntary error, approve of doing what he *ought* not to do, or think that to be his duty, which is really contrary to it; and yet it is too, in this case, really his duty to act agreeably to his judgement.—There are then two views of obligation, which, if not attended to, will be apt to produce confusion.—*In one sense,* a man's being *obliged* to act in a particular manner depends on his knowing it; and in *another sense,* it does not. Was not the *former* true, we might be contracting guilt, when acting with the fullest approbation of our consciences: and was not the *latter* true, it would not be sense ever to speak of *showing* another what his *obligations* are, or how it is *incumbent upon him* to act.—This entirely coincides with the distinction of virtue into *absolute* and *relative,* hereafter to be explained, Chap. VIII.

[1 Cf. §§ 658, 675, 710, 717.]

obligation and inducing or inferring it, cannot, properly speaking, be *obligation itself*; and that, however variously and loosely this word may be used, its primary and original signification coincides with *rectitude*.

*   *   *   *

There is an objection to what has been now said of obligation, **720** which deserves to be considered*.—It may be asked, 'Are there not many actions, of which it cannot be said, that we are *bound* to perform them, which yet are *right* to be performed; and the actual performance of which appears to us even more amiable, than if they had been strictly our duty; such as requital of good for evil, and acts of generosity and kindness?'

I answer, that allowing this, the most that can follow from it is, not that rectitude does not imply obligation, but that it does not imply it absolutely and universally, or so far as that there can be no sense in which actions are denominated *right*, which does not carry in it *obligation*. The nature of rectitude may vary, according to the objects or actions to which it is ascribed. All right actions are not so in precisely the same sense; and it might, with little prejudice to what is above asserted, be granted, that some things are right in such a sense as yet not to be our indispensable duty. But then let it be remembered: that it holds universally and incontestably, that whatever is right in such a sense, as that the omission of it would be wrong, is always and indispensably obligatory. And, in the next place, that though the idea of *rightness* may be more general than that of *fitness*, *duty*, or *obligation*; so that there may be instances to which we apply the one, but not the other; yet this cannot be said of *wrong*. The idea of this, and of obligation, are certainly of the same extent; I mean, that though there may be cases in which it cannot be said, that what we approve as right, *ought* to have been done; yet there are no cases in which it cannot be said, that what is wrong to be done, or omitted, *ought not* to be done or omitted.

But, not to dwell on this: it will be found on careful inquiry that the objection now mentioned does not require any such restrictions of what has been advanced as, at first sight, may appear to be necessary; and the following observations will, perhaps, show this.

---

* See *Essays on the Principles of Morality and natural Religion* [by Lord Kames], Part I. Essay ii. Chap. 3.

721   In the *first* place, beneficence, *in general*, is undoubtedly a duty; and it is only with respect to the *particular* acts and instances of it that we are at liberty. A certain person, suppose, performs an act of kindness to another: we say, he *might* not have done it, or he was not *obliged* to do it; that is, he was not obliged to do this *particular* kind act. But to be kind in some instances or other; to do all the good he can to his fellow-creatures, every one is obliged; and we necessarily look upon that person as blame-worthy and guilty who aims not at this; but contents himself with barely abstaining from injury and mischief. A certain part of our fortunes and labour we *owe* to those about us, and *should* employ in doing good; but the particular objects and methods of beneficence are not absolutely fixed. Here we are left to our own choice, and may not be in any sense bound; that is, there may be nothing in any particular objects or methods of beneficence, which render it fit and right *they* should be chosen rather than others. If a man endeavours to do all the good which is suitable to his station and abilities, we never condemn him for not doing it in a particular way, or for rejecting particular objects that are offered to him; except these objects are such, that it is right he should *prefer* them. As far as this happens, so far, even here, *duty* takes place. Thus, *ceteris paribus*, it is right, friends, relations, and benefactors should be preferred to strangers; and, whoever does otherwise, acts contrary to his *duty*.

722   Again; the precise limits of some general duties cannot be determined by us. No one can tell *exactly* to what degree he ought to be beneficent, and how far he is obliged to exert himself for the benefit of other men. No person, for instance, can determine accurately, how far, in many cases, his own good ought to give way to that of another, what number of distressed persons he ought to relieve, or what portion *precisely* of his fortune he ought to lay out in charity, or of his time and labour in direct endeavours to serve the public.

In order to form a judgement in these cases, there are so many particulars to be considered in our own circumstances and abilities, and in the state of mankind and the world, that we cannot but be in some uncertainty. There are indeed degrees of *defect* and *excess*, which we easily and certainly see to be wrong: but there is a great variety of intermediate degrees, concerning which we cannot absolutely pronounce, that one of them rather than another ought to be chosen.—The same is true of the *general* duty of worshipping God.

Many of the *particular* circumstances attending it, and the precise degree of frequency with which it should be performed, are not distinctly marked out to us. In this, as well as the preceding instance, our consciences, within certain limits, are *free*★, and for a very good reason; namely, because we have no distinct apprehensions of *rectitude* to guide us. To the same degree and extent that we see this, we are *bound*, in these as much as in any other cases. Whenever any degree of beneficence, or any particular circumstances and frequency of divine worship, or any behaviour in any possible instances, appear, *all things considered*, BEST; they become *obligatory*. It is impossible to put a case, in which we shall not be *obliged* to conform ourselves to the *right* of it, whatever that is. Even what, at any time, or in any circumstances, is, upon the whole, only more *proper* to be done, *ought* then to be done; and to suppose the contrary, would be to take away the whole sense and meaning of such an assertion.

In short, the following general reasoning will hold universally.— **723** Let a person be supposed to have under his consideration, any action proposed to be performed by him. The performance of it must be either right, or wrong, or indifferent. Now it is self-evident, that, if it is not the last, it must be one of the other two, and that obligation will ensue: for what can be plainer than that it is a contradiction to say, we may act as we will, when it is not *indifferent* how we act?— If it is *wrong*, obligation to forbear is implied.—If *right*, this may be true only of such *kind* of actions, as relieving the miserable, or worshipping the Deity in general; and then, it is only these *general duties* that are obligatory, which may be consistent with complete liberty and perfect indifference, in regard to the *particular action* in view.— Or, it may be true of this *particular* action, and then it is no longer indifferent; yet still, there may be liberty as to the time and manner of doing it. But if even the time and manner are not indifferent, then is he also as to these *obliged*.

'But what shall we say, to the *greater amiableness* of the actions **724** under consideration? How can there be greater virtue, or any virtue at all, in doing particular actions which beforehand were indifferent, and which without any blame we might have omitted?'—The

---

★ The latitude here taken notice of is one thing that allows so much room and scope for unfairness and disingenuity; and which renders it generally certain, that a backward unwilling heart that is not strongly attached to virtue, and possessed with an inward relish for it, will err on the deficient side.

answer is very easy. What denominates an agent virtuous, and entitles him to praise, is his acting from a regard to goodness and right. Now, the performance of particular instances of duty, or producing particular effects which have nothing in them that requires our preference, may, as much as any actions whatsoever, proceed from this regard. Relieving a miserable object is virtue, though there may be no reason that obliges a person to select this object in particular out of many others. Worshipping God may arise from a general sense of duty, though it is known that the particular times and manner in which it is done, have nothing morally better in them.—And as to the *greater* merit we apprehend in many actions of this kind (as, in many instances of generosity, kindness, charity, and forgiveness of injuries) it is plainly to be accounted for, in the following manner.—As every action of an agent is *in him* so far virtuous, as he was determined to it by a regard to virtue; so the more of this regard it discovers, the more we must admire it. And it is plain, it is more discovered, and a stronger virtuous principle proved, by fixing (in cases where the limits of duty are not exactly defined) upon the greater rather than the less. A person acts more apparently from good motives, and shows a greater degree of benevolence, and is therefore deservedly more applauded, who chooses to devote *more* of his fortune, his time and his labour, to promote the happiness of his fellow-creatures, or to serve his neighbours or his country, when he knows not but that if he had devoted *less*, he would have done all that was in reason incumbent upon *him*, and deserved just commendation. And even when there is *overdoing*, and a person is led to visible extremes and an undue neglect of his private concerns, we always approve, except we suspect the influence of some indirect motives. Some of these observations will be again more particularly insisted on, when I come to consider the difference which they imply and require us to keep in view, between the virtue of the *action*, and the virtue of the *agent*.

725   I shall only say farther on this subject, that it appears to be so far from being true, that the performance of *mere* duty produces no love or friendship to the agent, (as has been asserted) that, on the contrary, he who, however tempted and opposed, discharges his whole duty, and endeavours faithfully and uniformly to *be* and *do* in all respects just what he *ought* to *be* and *do*, is the object of our highest love and

friendship: to aim at acting *beyond* obligation, being the same with aiming at acting *contrary* to obligation; and doing *more* than is fit to be done, the same with *doing wrong*.

Having now given, what appears to me, the true account of the nature and foundation of moral good and evil and of moral obligation, I will add, as a supplement to this chapter, an examination of some of the forms of expression, which several eminent writers have used on this subject.

The meaning and design of these expressions will appear, after considering, that all actions being necessarily right, indifferent, or wrong; what determines which of these an action should be accounted is the *truth of the case*; or the relations and circumstances of the agent and the objects. In certain relations there is a certain conduct right. There are certain manners of behaviour which we unavoidably approve, as soon as these relations are known. Change the relations, and a different manner of behaviour becomes right. Nothing is clearer than that what is due or undue, proper or improper to be done, must vary according to the different natures and circumstances of beings. If a particular treatment of *one* nature is right; it is impossible that the same treatment of a *different* nature, or of *all* natures, should be right.

From hence arose the expressions, *acting suitably to the natures of things*; *treating things as they are*; *conformity to truth*; *agreement and disagreement, congruity and incongruity between actions and relations*. These expressions are of no use, and have little meaning, if considered as intended to *define* virtue; for they evidently *presuppose* it. Treating an object as being what *it is*, is treating it as *it is right such* an object should be treated. Conforming ourselves to truth means the same with conforming ourselves to the true state and relations we are in; which is the same with doing what such a state and such relations *require*, or what is *right* in them. In given circumstances, there is something peculiar and determinate *best* to be done; which, when these circumstances cease, ceases with them, and other obligations arise. This naturally leads us to speak of *suiting* actions to circumstances, natures, and characters; and of the *agreement* and *repugnancy* between them. Nor, when thus considered, is there any thing in such ways of speaking, not proper and intelligible. But, at the same time, it is very obvious, that they are only different phrases for *right*

726

and *wrong*; and it is to be wished that those who have made use of them had attended more to this, and avoided the ambiguity and confusion arising from seeming to deny an *immediate perception* of morality without any deductions of reasoning; and from attempting to give definitions of words which admit not of them. Were any one to define *pleasure*, to be the *agreement* between a faculty and its object; what instruction would such a definition convey? Would it be amiss to ask, what this *agreement* is; and whether any thing be meant by it, different from the *pleasure itself*, which the object is fitted to produce by its influence on the faculty?

727   It is well known that Mr. Wollaston, in a work which has obtained great and just reputation, places the whole notion of moral good and evil in *signifying* and *denying* truth.[1] Supposing his meaning to be, that all virtue and vice may be reduced to these *particular instances* of them; nothing can be more plain, than that it leaves the nature and origin of our ideas of them as much as ever undetermined: for it acquaints us not, whence our ideas of right in observing truth and wrong in violating it, arise;[2] but supposes these to be perceptions of self-evident truths, as indeed they are, but not more so, than our ideas of the other principles of morality.—The evil of ingratitude and cruelty is not the same with that of denying truth, or affirming a lie: nor can the *formal ratio and notion* of it (as Mr. Wollaston speaks[3]) be justly said to consist in this; because there may be no intention to deny any thing true, or to produce an assent to any thing false.[4] Ingratitude and cruelty would be wrong, though there were no rational creatures in the world besides the agent, and though he could have no design to declare a falsehood; which is a quite distinct species of evil.—A person, who neglects the worship due to God, may have no thought of denying his existence, or of conveying any such opinion to others. It is true, he acts as if he did not exist, that is, in a manner which nothing else can justify, or which, upon any other supposition, is inexcusable; and therefore, *figuratively speaking*, may be said to *contradict* truth, and to declare himself to be self-originated and self-sufficient⋆. It is probable, this eminent writer meant in

⋆ How plain is it here, that the very thing that gives ground for the application of this language in this instance, is our perceiving, antecedently to this application, that such a manner of acting, in such circumstances, is *wrong*? The same is true in all other

[1 Cf. Wollaston, § 280.]   [2 Cf. Hume, § 496.]
[3 Cf. Wollaston, § 293.]   [4 Cf. Hutcheson, § 368; Hume, § 494.]

reality but little more than this; and the language he has introduced, I would not, by any means, be thought absolutely to condemn. All I aim at, is to guard against making a wrong application of it.

*   *   *   *

It should be further considered, that neither do these forms of **728** expression direct us to proper *criteria*, by which we may be enabled to judge in all cases what is morally good or evil. For if, after weighing the state and circumstances of a case, we do not perceive how it is proper to act; it would be trifling to direct us, for this end, to consider what is *agreeable* to them. When, in given circumstances, we cannot determine what is *right*, we must be also equally unable to determine what is *suitable* to those circumstances. It is indeed very proper and just to direct us, in order to judge of an action, to endeavour to discover the whole *truth* with respect to its probable or possible consequences, the circumstances and qualifications of the object, and the relations of the agent; for this, as was before said, is what determines its moral nature; and no more can be intended by representing *truth* and *relations* as *criteria* of virtue.

'The language we are considering then expressing neither *definitions* nor *proper criteria* of virtue, of what use is it? and what is designed by it?'—I answer, that it is evidently designed to show, that morality *is founded* in truth and reason; or that it is equally necessary and immutable, and perceived by the same power, with the natural proportions and essential differences of things.

*   *   *   *

CHAP. VII—OF THE SUBJECT-MATTER OF VIRTUE, OR ITS
PRINCIPAL HEADS AND DIVISIONS

There remain yet three questions to be considered in relation to **729** virtue.

First, to what particular course of action we give this name, or what are the chief *heads* of virtue.

Secondly, what is the *principle* or *motive*, from which a virtuous agent, as such, acts.

Thirdly, what is meant by the different *degrees* of virtue, in different

instances: nor, independently of this perception, could we ever know when to say, that an action affirms or denies truth. How then does such language explain and define right and wrong?

actions and characters, and how we estimate them.—Each of these questions shall be examined in the order in which they are here proposed.

730   There would be less occasion for the first of these inquiries, if several writers had not maintained, that the *whole* of virtue consists in BENEVOLENCE. Nothing better can be offered on this point, than what is said under the fifth observation in the *Dissertation on the Nature of Virtue*, annexed to Bishop Butler's *Analogy*.[1]

*　　　*　　　*　　　*

A disapprobation in the human mind of ingratitude, injustice, and deceit, none deny. The point under examination is, the *ground* of this disapprobation; whether it arises solely from views of inconvenience to others and confusion in society occasioned by them; or whether there be not also *immediate wrong* apprehended in them, independently of their effects. The instances and considerations here produced seem sufficiently to determine this. It appears, that they are disapproved when productive of no harm, and even when in some degree beneficial.

'Shall it be still urged that, in cases of this kind, our disapprobation is owing to the idea of a plan or system of common utility established by custom in the mind with which these vices are apprehended to be inconsistent; or to a habit acquired of considering them as of general pernicious tendency, by which we are insensibly influenced, whenever, in any particular circumstances or instances, we contemplate them?'—But why must we have recourse to the influence of habits and associations in this case? This has been the refuge of those, who would resolve all our moral perceptions into views of private advantage, and may serve to evade almost any evidence which can be derived from the experience we have of the workings of our minds and the motives of our actions. In the cases which have been mentioned, we may remove entirely the idea of a public, and suppose no persons existing whose state they can at all influence; or, we may suppose all memory of the action to be for ever lost as soon as done, and the agent to foresee this; and yet, the same ideas of the ingratitude, injustice, or violation of truth will remain.

*　　　*　　　*　　　*

[1 i.e. Butler, §§ 434–5.]

It is further to be observed on this argument, that in these cases it **731**
does not appear that mankind in general much attended to distant
consequences. Children, particularly, cannot be supposed to consider
consequences, or to have any fixed ideas of a public or a community;
and yet, we observe in them the same aversion to falsehood and relish
for truth, as in the rest of mankind. There is indeed no less evidence,
that, in the cases specified, we approve and disapprove *immediately*,
than there is that we do so, when we consider benevolence or cruelty.
It has been urged against those who derive all our desires and actions
from self-love, that they find out views and reasonings for men,
which never entered the minds of most of them; and which, in all
probability, none attended to in the common course of their thoughts
and pursuits.—The same may be urged against those, who derive all
our sentiments of moral good and evil from our approbation of
benevolence and disapprobation of the want of it; and both, in my
opinion, have undertaken tasks almost equally impracticable.

★   ★   ★   ★

Perhaps, he who should maintain, that we have no affection **732**
properly resting in *ourselves*, but that all our desires and aversions
arise from a prospect of advantage or detriment to *others*, would not
assert what would be much less defensible than what those assert who
maintain the reverse of this, and deny all *disinterested benevolence*.—In
like manner, to assert that our approbation of *beneficence* is to be resolved into our approbation of *veracity*, or that the whole of morality
consists in *signifying and denying truth*, would not be much more unreasonable than the contrary assertion, that our approbation of
veracity and of all that is denominated virtue, is resolvable into the
approbation of *beneficence*. But why must there be in the human mind
approbation only of one sort of actions? Why must all moral good
be reduced to one particular species of it, and kind affections, with
the actions flowing from them, be represented, as alone capable of
appearing to our moral faculty *virtuous*?

★   ★   ★   ★

How unreasonable is that love of uniformity and simplicity which
inclines men thus to seek them where it is so difficult to find them?
It is this that, on other subjects, has often led men astray. What
mistakes and extravagances in natural philosophy have been produced, by the desire of discovering *one* principle which shall account

for all effects? I deny not but that in the human mind, as well as in the material world, the most wonderful simplicity takes place; but we ought to learn to wait, till we can, by careful observation and inquiry, find out wherein it consists; and not suffer ourselves rashly to determine any thing concerning it, or to receive any general causes and principles which cannot be proved by experience.

*   *   *   *

733   Having premised these observations, I shall now proceed to enumerate some of the most important *branches of virtue*, or *heads of rectitude and duty*.

What requires the first place is our DUTY TO GOD, or the whole of that regard, subjection and homage we owe him. These seem unquestionably objects of moral approbation, independently of all considerations of utility. They are considered as indispensably obligatory, and yet the principle upon which they are practised cannot be an intention, in any manner, to be useful or profitable to the object of them.

*   *   *   *

What has been now said, is, in some degree, applicable to superiors and benefactors among created beings; and the grounds of duty to them, are, in their general nature, the same with those of our duty to the Deity. A fellow-man may be raised so much above us in station and character, and so little within the reach of any of the effects of what we can do, that the reason of the respect and submission we pay him, and of our general behaviour to him, cannot be any view to his benefit, but *principally*, or *solely*, the sense of what is in itself right, decent, or becoming.

*   *   *   *

734   The *second* branch of virtue, which we may take notice of, is that which has *ourselves* for its object. There is, undoubtedly, a certain manner of conduct terminating in ourselves, which is properly matter of *duty* to us. It is too absurd to be maintained by any one, that no relation which an action may have to our own happiness or misery, can (supposing other beings unconcerned) have any influence in determining, whether it is or is not to be done, or make it appear to rational and calm reflection otherwise than *morally indifferent*.—It is contradictory to suppose, that the same necessity which makes an end to us, and determines us to the choice and desire* of it, should be unaccompanied with an approbation of using the means of attaining it. It is, in reality, no more morally indifferent, how we employ our faculties, and what we do relating to our own interest, than it is how we behave to our fellow-creatures. If it is my duty to promote the good of *another*, and to abstain from hurting him; the same, most certainly, must be my duty with regard to *myself*. It would be contrary to all reason to deny this; or to assert that I *ought* to consult the good of another, but not my own; or that the advantage an action will produce to another makes it right to be done, but that an equal advantage to myself leaves me at liberty to do or omit it.—So far is this from being true, that it will be strange, if any one can avoid acknowledging that it is right and fit that a being should, when all circumstances on both sides are equal, *prefer* himself to another; reserve, for example, to *himself*, a certain means of enjoyment he possesses rather than part with it to a *stranger*, to whom it will not be *more* beneficial.

It is evident, that this affords us another instance of right behaviour, **735** the principle of which is not kind affection, and which no views of public utility, or sympathy with others can possibly explain. What can prove more incontestably that actions evidencing kind affections are not the only ones we approve, than our approving in many cases of the prevalency of self-love against them, and our being conscious that in these cases it *should* thus prevail?

*   *   *   *

It should not, however, be overlooked, that acting with a view to private advantage does not so generally and certainly prove a virtuous intention, as acting with a view to public good; and that, in rejecting an evil, or embracing a good to ourselves, when it is sensible and at hand, and no opposition arises from any interfering desires and propensions, the virtuous effort and design, and consequently the degree of virtue in the agent, can be but small. But of this more will be said hereafter.

*   *   *   *

Thirdly, another part of rectitude is BENEFICENCE, or the study **736** of the good of others. Public happiness is an object that must

* See last Section of Chapter I, § 679.

necessarily determine all minds to prefer and desire it. It is of essential and unchangeable value and importance; and there is not any thing which appears to our thoughts with greater light and evidence, or of which we have more undeniably an intuitive perception, than that it is *right* to promote and pursue it.—So important a part of virtue is this, and so universally acknowledged, that it is become a considerable subject of debate, whether it be not the *whole* of virtue.

As, under the preceding head, it has been observed, that it would be strange that the good of another should make an action fit to be performed, but our own good not; the contrary observation may be here made; namely, that it cannot be consistently supposed that our own good should make an action fit to be performed, but that of others not.

✱   ✱   ✱   ✱

737   *Fourthly*, the next head of virtue proper to be mentioned is GRATITUDE. The consideration that we have received benefits, lays us under *peculiar* obligations to the persons who have conferred them; and renders that behaviour, which to others may be innocent, to them criminal. That this is not to be looked upon as the effect merely of the utility of gratitude, appears, I think, sufficiently from the citation at the beginning of this chapter.[1]

With respect to this part of virtue, it is proper to observe, that it is but one out of a great variety of instances, wherein particular facts and circumstances constitute a fitness of a different behaviour to different persons, independently of its consequences. The different moral qualifications of different persons; their different degrees of nearness to us in various respects; and numberless circumstances in their situations, and characters, have the like effect, and give just reason, in innumerable instances, for a preference of some of them to others. Some of these circumstances may be of so little moment in themselves, that almost any appearance or possibility of greater good may suspend their influence; although when there is no such appearance, they have a full effect in determining what is *right*. A fact of the same kind with this, I shall have occasion to mention under the head of *justice*.

What will be most beneficial, or productive of the greatest public good, I acknowledge to be the most general and leading considera-

---

[1 i.e. the reference, in § 730, to Butler, §§ 434–5.]

tion in all our inquiries concerning *right*; and so important is it, when the public interest depending is very considerable, that it may set aside every obligation which would otherwise arise from the common rules of justice, from promises, private interest, friendship, gratitude, and all particular attachments and connections.

Fifthly, VERACITY is a most important part of virtue. Of this a good **738** deal has been already said. As it has some dependence upon *different sentiments* and *affections* with respect to *truth* and *falsehood*, it will not be improper to be a little particular in giving an account of the foundation of these.

∗   ∗   ∗   ∗

Under this head, I would comprehend impartiality and honesty of mind in our inquiries after truth, as well as a sacred regard to it in all we say; fair and ingenuous dealing; such an openness and simplicity of temper as exclude guile and prevarication, and all the contemptible arts of craft, equivocation and hypocrisy; fidelity to our engagements; sincerity and uprightness in our transactions with ourselves as well as others; and the careful avoiding of all secret attempts to deceive ourselves, and to evade or disguise the truth in examining our own characters.

Some of these particulars, though they belong to the division of **739** rectitude I have now in view, and which has truth for its object; yet are not properly included in the signification of *veracity*.—But it requires our notice, that fidelity to promises is *properly* a branch or instance of *veracity*.—∗The nature and obligation of *promises* have been said to be attended with great difficulties; which makes it necessary to desire this observation may be particularly considered.

By a *promise* some declaration is made, or assurance given to another, which brings us under an obligation to act or not to act, from which we should have been otherwise free. Such an obligation never flows merely from declaring a *resolution* or *intention*;[1] and therefore a promise must mean more than this; and the whole difference is, that the one relates to the *present*, the other to *future* time.—When I say I *intend* to do an action, I affirm only a present

---

∗ See Treatise of Human Nature. Vol. III. Book III. part II. Sect. V [i.e. Hume, §§ 535–45].

[1 Cf. Hume, § 536.]

fact.—But to *promise*, is to declare that such a thing *shall* be done, or that such and such events *shall* happen. In this case, it is not enough to acquit me from the charge of falsehood, that I *intend* to do what I promise, but it must be actually done, agreeably to the assurances given. After declaring a *resolution* to do an action, a man is under no obligation actually to do it, because he did not say he would; his word and veracity are not engaged; and the non-performance cannot infer the guilt of violating truth. On the contrary, when a person declares he *will* do any action, he becomes obliged to do it, and cannot afterwards omit it, without incurring the imputation of declaring falsehood, as really as if he had declared what he knew to be a false past or present fact; and in much the same manner as he would have done, if he had pretended to know, and had accordingly asserted, that a certain event would happen at a certain time which yet did not then happen. There is, however, a considerable difference between this last case, and the falsehood implied in breaking promises and engagements; for the object of these is something, the existence of which depends on ourselves, and which we have in our power to bring to pass; and therefore here the falsehood must be known and wilful, and entirely imputable to our own neglect and guilt. But in the case of events predicted which are not subject to our dominion, the blame, as far as there may be any, must arise from pretending to knowledge which we really want, and asserting absolutely what we are not sure of.

740   To *promise* then, being to assert a fact dependent on ourselves, with an intention to produce faith in it and reliance upon it, as certainly to happen; the obligation to keep a promise is the same with the obligation to regard truth; and the intention of it cannot be, in the sense some have asserted, to will or create a new obligation;[1] unless it can be pretended that the obligation to veracity is *created* by the mere breath of men every time they speak, or make any professions. If indeed we mean by creating a new obligation, that the producing a particular effect or performance of an external action becomes fit, in consequence of some new situation of a person (or some preceding acts of his own) which was not fit before; it may be very well acknowledged; nor is there any thing in the least mysterious in it. Thus, performance becomes our duty after a promise, in the same sense that repentance becomes our duty in consequence

[1 Cf. Hume, § 536.]

of doing wrong, reparation of an injury, in consequence of committing it, or a particular manner of conduct, in consequence of placing ourselves in particular circumstances and relations of life.

As a confirmation of this account, if any confirmation was necessary, it might be observed, that false declarations in general, and violations of engagements admit of the same extenuations or aggravations according to the different degrees of solemnity with which they are made, and the different importance of the subjects of them.

The last part of virtue, I shall mention, is JUSTICE: meaning by this **741** word, that part of virtue which regards *property* and *commerce*.

The origin of the idea of *property* is the same with that of right and wrong in general. It denotes such a relation of a particular object to a particular person, as infers or implies, that it is fit he should have the disposal of it rather than others, and wrong to deprive him of it. This is what every one means by calling a thing his *right*, or saying that it is *his own*.

Upon this there are two questions that may be asked. *First*, how an object obtains this relation to a person?—*Secondly*, into what we are to resolve, and how we are to account for, the right and wrong we perceive in these instances?

The writers of Ethics are very well agreed in their answers to the **742** first of these questions. An object, it is obvious, will acquire the relation to a person which has been mentioned, in consequence of first possession; in consequence of its being the fruit of his labour; by donation, succession, and many other ways not necessary to be here enumerated.

It is far from being so generally agreed, what account ought to be given of this: but I cannot find any particular difficulties attending it. Numberless are the facts and circumstances, which vary and modify the general law of right, and alter the relations of particular effects to it. Taking possession of an object, and disposing of it as I please, abstracted from all particular circumstances attending such conduct, is innocent; but suppose the object was before possessed by another, the fruit of whose labour it was, and who consents not to be deprived of it, and then this conduct becomes wrong; not merely upon the account of its consequences, but *immediately* wrong.— Taking to ourselves any of the means of enjoyment, when quite loose from our fellow-creatures, or not related to them in any of the ways which determine property, cannot be the same with doing this, when the contrary is true; nor is it possible to frame the same moral judgement concerning an action in these different circumstances.—That *first possession, prescription, donation, succession,* etc. should be circumstances which alter the *nature of a case,* determine right and wrong, and induce obligation, where otherwise we should have been free, is not less conceivable than that benefits received, private or public interest, the will of certain beings, or any of the other considerations before insisted on, should have this effect. There is no other account to be given of this, than that 'such is truth, such the nature of things.' And this account, wherever it distinctly appears, is ultimate and satisfactory, and leaves nothing further for the mind to desire.

★   ★   ★   ★

743   It may tend to remove some further difficulties which may occur to one who considers this subject, to remark, that amongst near relations and intimate friends, and also with respect to useful objects of which there is no scarcity, the ideas of property are always relaxed in proportion to the intimacy of the relation or friendship, and the degree of plenty.[1] The reason in the first case may be chiefly the consent of the proprietors, which, where known or reasonably presumed, always removes the unlawfulness of taking and employing what belongs to them. Between married persons there has been a formal surrender of their respective possessions to one another: and between intimate friends, though no professions may have passed directly expressing such a surrender, there is always understood to prevail such an union as implies it.[1] In the latter case, there is also a tacit and presumed surrender; for it cannot be conceived that any one should be unwilling to resign, or that he should at all attach himself to any thing, the loss of which he can immediately and with perfect ease repair.—Besides; inquiries concerning rights are only proper, as far as an object is of some value real or imaginary, mediate or immediate. To ask to whom belongs the property of what is of no value, is trifling and absurd: it is the same as to ask who ought to have the use of what is of no use. Now any *particular portion* of natural supplies which are so common as to bear no price, as water or air,[2] is to be deemed really worthless, and so far no object of

<hr>

[1 Cf. Hume, §§ 532, 567–8.]   [2 Cf. Hume, §§ 532, 567.]

property. It is not certainly in the least wonderful, that objects procurable without any trouble; which can be the produce of no one's labour; which when taken from persons are always replaced immediately by others of the same value; and a sufficient quantity of which none can want: it is not, I say, in the least wonderful that objects of this kind should be incapable of acquiring the relation of property to particular persons, and that no injustice should be possible to be committed by any seizure of them. No objections then can, with any reason, be derived from hence against the account that has been given of property.

The particular rules of *justice* are various, and there are many **744** instances in which it is difficult to determine what it requires. Of these it is not requisite that I should take any notice: but it is very proper to observe, that, though I cannot allow public good to be the *sole* original of justice, yet, undoubtedly, it has great influence upon it, and is *one* important ground of many of its maxims. It gives a very considerable additional force to the *rights* of men, and, in some cases, entirely creates them.

★　　　★　　　★　　　★

I omit taking any particular notice here of *justice*, as it signifies the due treatment of beings according to their different moral characters, or the equitable distribution of rewards and punishments; because it has been particularly considered elsewhere★.

These then are the main and leading branches of virtue. It may not **745** be possible properly to comprehend all the particular instances of it under any number of heads. It is by attending to the different relations, circumstances, and qualifications of beings, and the natures and tendencies of objects, and by examining into the whole truth of every case, that we judge what *is* or *is not to be* done. And as there is an endless variety of cases, and the situations of agents and objects are ever changing; the universal law of rectitude, though in the abstract idea of it always invariably the same, must be continually varying in its *particular* demands and obligations.

This leads me to observe, that however different from one another the heads which have been enumerated are, yet, from the very

★ See Chap. IV [especially §§ 696–8].

notion of them, as *heads of virtue*, it is plain, that they all run up to one general idea, and should be considered as only different modifications and views of one original, all-governing law. It is the same authority that enjoins, the same truth and right that oblige, the same eternal reason that commands in them all. Virtue thus considered, is necessarily *one* thing. No part of it can be separated from another.

*   *   *   *

746   But though the heads of virtue before-mentioned agree thus far in requiring the same course of action, yet they often also interfere. Though upon the whole, or when considered as making one *general system or plan of conduct*, there is a strict coincidence between them, yet in examining *single acts* and *particular cases*, we find that they lead us contrary ways.—This perhaps has not been enough attended to, and therefore I shall particularly insist upon it.

What creates the difficulty in morals of determining what is right or wrong, in many particular cases, is chiefly the interference now mentioned in such cases between the different general principles of virtue.—Thus, the pursuit of the happiness of others is a duty, and so is the pursuit of private happiness; and though, on the whole, these are inseparably connected, in many particular instances, one of them cannot be pursued without giving up the other. When the public happiness is very great, and the private very inconsiderable, no difficulties appear. We pronounce as confidently, that the one ought to give way to the other, as we do, that either alone ought to be pursued. But when the former is diminished, and the latter increased to a certain degree, doubt arises; and we may thus be rendered entirely incapable of determining what we ought to choose. We have the most satisfactory perception, that we ought to study our own good, and, within certain limits, prefer it to that of another; but who can say how far, mark precisely these limits, and inform us in all cases of opposition between them, where right and wrong and indifference take place?—In like manner; the nearer attachments of nature or friendship, the obligations to veracity, fidelity, gratitude, or justice, may interfere with private and public good, and it is not possible for us to judge always and accurately, what degrees or circumstances of any one of these compared with the others, will or will not cancel its obligation, and justify the violation of it.—It is thus likewise, that the different foundations of property give rise to contrary claims, and that sometimes it becomes very hard to say which of different titles to an object is the best.—If we examine the various intricate and disputed cases in morality, we shall, I believe, find that it is always some interference of this kind that produces the obscurity. Truth and right in all circumstances, require one determinate way of acting; but so variously may different obligations combine with or oppose each other in particular cases, and so imperfect are our discerning faculties, that it cannot but happen, that we should be frequently in the dark,[1] and that different persons should judge differently, according to the different views they have of the several moral principles. Nor is this less unavoidable, or more to be wondered at, than that in matters of mere speculation, we should be at a loss to know what is true, when the arguments for and against a proposition appear nearly equal.

The principles themselves, it should be remembered, are self- 747 evident; and to conclude the contrary, or to assert that there are no moral distinctions, because of the obscurity attending several cases wherein a competition arises between the several principles of morality, is very unreasonable.

★　　　★　　　★　　　★

These observations may be of some use in helping us to determine, how far and in what sense, morality is capable of demonstration.[2] There are undoubtedly a variety of moral principles and maxims, which, to gain assent, need only to be understood: and I see not why such propositions as these, 'gratitude is due to benefactors; reverence is due to our Creator; it is right to study our own happiness; an innocent being ought not to be absolutely miserable; it is wrong to take from another the fruit of his labour,' and others of the like kind, may not be laid down and used as axioms, the truth of which appears as irresistibly as the truth of those which are the foundation of geometry. But the case is very different when we come to consider *particular* effects. What is meant by demonstrating morality, can only be reducing these under the general self-evident principles of morality, or making out with certainty their relation to them. It would be happy for us were this always possible. We should then be eased of many painful doubts, know universally and infallibly what

----

[1 Contrast Butler, § 405.]   [2 Cf. Locke, §§ 154, 189.]

we should do and avoid, and have nothing to attend to besides conforming our practice to our knowledge. How impracticable this is
every one must see.—Were benevolence the only virtuous principle,
we could by no means apply it always without any danger of mistake
to action; because we cannot be more sure, a particular external
action is an instance of beneficence, than we are of the tendencies and
consequences of that action. The same holds true upon the supposition that self-love is the only principle of virtue. Until we can in
every particular know what is good or bad for ourselves and others,
and discover the powers and qualities of objects, and what will
result from any application of them to one another, we cannot
always demonstrate what either of these principles requires, but
must continue liable to frequent and unavoidable errors in our moral
judgement.—In like manner, what our duty to God, the regard due
to the properties and rights of others, and gratitude require, we must
be at a loss about, as far as in any circumstances we cannot be sure
what the will of God is, where property is lodged, or who our benefactors are and what are our obligations to them.—Thus, if we consider the several moral principles singly (or as liable to no limitations
from one another) we find that we must frequently be very uncertain
how it is best to act.

748   But if we further recollect, that in order to discover what is right
in a case, we ought to extend our views to all the different *heads* of
virtue, to examine how far each is concerned, and compare their
respective influence and demands; and that at the same time (as just
now explained) they often interfere; a second source of insuperable
difficulties will appear. It is not alone sufficient to satisfy us that an
action is to be done, that we know it will be the means of good to
others: we are also to consider how it affects ourselves, what it is in
regard to justice, and all the other circumstances the case may involve must be taken in, and weighed, if we would form a true judgement concerning it. In reality, before we can be capable of deducing
demonstrably, accurately and particularly, the whole rule of *right* in
every instance, we must possess universal and unerring knowledge.
It must be above the power of any finite understanding to do this.
He only who knows all truth, is acquainted with the whole law of
truth in all its importance, perfection and extent.

749   Once more; we may, by considerations of this kind, be helped in
forming a judgement of the different sentiments and practices in

several points of morality, which have obtained in different countries and ages. The foregoing general principles all men at all times have agreed in. It cannot be shown that there have ever been any human beings who have had no ideas of property and justice, of the rectitude of veracity, gratitude, benevolence, prudence, and religious worship. All the difference has been about particular usages and practices, of which it is impossible but different persons must have different ideas, according to the various opinions they entertain of their relation to the universally acknowledged moral principles, or of their ends, connections, and tendencies.—Those who plead for passive obedience and non-resistance, think that to be required by divine command, or public good; which others, with more reason, think to be reproachful to human nature, and destructive of the very end of magistracy and government.—Those nations amongst whom the customs of exposing children and aged persons have prevailed, approved of these customs upon the opinion of their being conducive to the general advantage, and friendly to the sufferers themselves.

*   *   *   *

CHAP. VIII—OF THE NATURE AND ESSENTIALS OF VIRTUE IN PRACTICE, AS DISTINGUISHED FROM ABSOLUTE VIRTUE; AND, THE PRINCIPLE OF ACTION IN A VIRTUOUS AGENT

Before I enter on the discussion of the principal point to be con- **750** sidered in this chapter, it is necessary a distinction on which what will be said is founded, and to which I have before had occasion to refer, should be distinctly explained: I mean, the distinction of virtue into ABSTRACT or ABSOLUTE virtue, and PRACTICAL or RELATIVE virtue.

*   *   *   *

ABSTRACT virtue is, most properly, a quality of the external action or event. It denotes what an action is, considered independently of the *sense* of the agent; or what, *in itself* and *absolutely*, it is right such an agent, in *such* circumstances, should do; and what, if he judged truly, he would judge he ought to do.—PRACTICAL *virtue*, on the contrary, has a necessary relation to, and dependence upon, the opinion of the agent concerning his actions. It signifies what he ought to do, *upon supposition* of his having such and such sentiments.

—In a sense, not entirely different from this, good actions have
been by some divided into such as are *materially* good, and such as are
formally so.—Moral agents are liable to mistake the circumstances they
are in, and, consequently, to form erroneous judgements concerning
their own obligations. This supposes, that these obligations have a
real existence, independent of their judgements. But, when they are
in any manner mistaken, it is not to be imagined, that then nothing
remains obligatory; for there is a sense in which it may be said, that
what any being, in the sincerity of his heart, *thinks* he ought to do,
he *indeed* ought to do, and would be justly blameable if he omitted
to do, though contradictory to what, in the former sense, is his duty.
—It would be trifling to object to this, that it implies, that an
action may, at the same time, be both right and wrong; for it implies
this only, as the rightness and wrongness of actions are considered
in different views. A magistrate who should adjudge an estate to the
person whose right it *appears* to be, upon a great overbalance of
evidence, would certainly do right in *one* sense; though, should the
opposite claimant, after all, prove to be the true proprietor, he would
as certainly do wrong in *another* sense.

*   *   *   *

751   I have applied the epithets *real* and *absolute* to the first kind of
virtue, for an obvious reason; but care should be taken not to
imagine, that the latter is not also, in a different sense and view, *real*
virtue. It is truly and absolutely right, that a being should do what
the reason of his mind, though perhaps unhappily misinformed,
requires of him; or what, according to his best judgement, he is
persuaded to be the will of God. If he neglects this, he becomes
necessarily and justly the object of his own dislike, and forfeits all
pretensions to integrity.

These different kinds of rectitude have such an affinity that we are
very prone to confound them in our thoughts and discourses; and a
particular attention is necessary, in order to know when we speak
of the one or the other. It is hardly possible, in writing on morality,
to avoid blending them in our language, and frequently including
both, even in the same sentence. But enough has been said to enable
an attentive person to see when and how this is done, and to prepare
the way for that explanation of the nature and essentials of PRACTICAL
virtue, to which I shall now proceed.

What first of all offers itself here, is, that *practical* virtue supposes **752** LIBERTY.—Whether all will acknowledge this or not, it cannot be omitted.

The *liberty* I here mean is the same with the power of *acting* and *determining*: and it is self-evident, that where such a power is wanting, there can be no moral capacities. As far as it is true of a being that he *acts*, so far he must *himself* be the cause of the action, and therefore not necessarily determined to act. Let any one try to put a sense on the expressions; *I will; I act;* which is consistent with supposing, that the volition or action does not proceed from myself. Virtue supposes determination, and determination supposes a determiner; and a determiner that determines not himself, is a palpable contradiction. Determination requires an efficient cause. If this cause is the being himself, I plead for no more. If not, then it is no longer *his* determination; that is, *he* is no longer the determiner, but the motive, or whatever else any one will say to be the cause of the determination. To ask, what effects *our* determinations, is the very same with asking who did an action, after being informed that such a one did it. In short; who must not *feel* the absurdity of saying, *my* volitions are produced by a *foreign* cause, that is, are not *mine;* I determine *voluntarily,* and yet *necessarily?*—We have, in truth, the same constant and necessary consciousness of liberty, that we have that we think, choose, will, or even exist; and whatever to the contrary any persons may say, it is impossible for them in earnest to think they have no active, self-moving powers, and are not the causes of *their own* volitions, or not to ascribe to *themselves,* what they must be conscious *they* think and do.

But, not to enter much further into a question which has been **753** strangely darkened by fallacious reasonings, and where there is so much danger of falling into a confusion of ideas, I would only observe, that it is hard to say what virtue and vice, commendation and blame, mean, if they do not suppose *agency,* free choice, and an absolute dominion over our resolutions.—It has always been the *general,* and it is evidently the *natural* sense of mankind, that they cannot be accountable for what they have no power to avoid. Nothing can be more glaringly absurd, than applauding or reproaching ourselves for what we were no more the causes of, than our own beings, and what it was no more possible for us to prevent, than the returns of the seasons, or the revolutions of the planets. The whole language of men, all their practical sentiments and schemes, and the whole frame and order of human affairs, are founded upon the notion of liberty, and are utterly inconsistent with the supposition, that nothing is made to depend on ourselves, or that our purposes and determinations are not subjected to our own command, but the result of physical laws, not possible to be resisted.

If, upon examination, any of the advocates of the doctrine of necessity should find, that what they mean by necessity is not inconsistent with the ideas of *agency* and *self-determination*, there will be little room for farther disputes; and that liberty, which I insist upon as essential to morality, will be acknowledged; nor will it be at all necessary to take into consideration, or to pay much regard to any difficulties relating* to the nature of that influence we commonly ascribe to motives.

754 *Secondly, intelligence* is another requisite of practical morality. Some degree of this is necessary to the perception of moral good and evil; and without this perception, there can be no moral agency. It must not be imagined, that liberty comprehends or infers intelligence; for all the inferior orders of beings possess true liberty. Self-motion and activity, of some kind, are essential to every conscious, living being. There seems no difference between wanting all spontaneity, and being quite inanimate.—But though liberty does not suppose intelligence, yet intelligence plainly supposes liberty. For what has been now affirmed of all sensitive natures, is much more unexceptionably true of intelligent natures. A thinking, designing, reasoning being, without liberty, without any inward, spontaneous,

---

* With respect to this, however, one may observe, that there seems to be very little mysterious in a man's choosing to follow his judgement and desires, or in his actually doing what he is *inclined* to do; which is what we mean when we say, motives determine him: though, at the same time it be very plain, that motives can have no concern in *effecting* his determination, or that there is no *physical connection* between his judgement and views, and the actions consequent upon them. What would be more absurd than to say, that our inclinations act upon us, or compel us; that our desires and fears *put* us into motion, or *produce* our volitions; that is, are *agents*? And yet, what is more conceivable, than that they may be the *occasions* of our putting *ourselves* into motion?—That there is an essential and total difference between the ideas of an *efficient cause* and an *account* or *occasion*, it would be trifling to go about to prove. What sense would there be in saying, that the *situation* of a body, which may properly be the occasion of its being struck by another body, is the *efficient* of its motion or its *impeller*?—A particular discussion of this question may be found in the CORRESPONDENCE between Dr. Priestley and Dr. Price, on the subjects of MATERIALISM and NECESSITY. 8vo. printed for Mr. Johnson in St. Paul's Churchyard.

active, self-directing principle, is what no one can frame any idea of. So unreasonable are all objections to the making of free creatures; and so absurd to ask, why men were made so. But,

Thirdly, the main point now to be insisted on is, 'that an agent **755** cannot be justly denominated *virtuous*, except he acts from a consciousness of rectitude, and with a regard to it as his *rule* and *end*.' Though this observation appears to me undoubtedly true, and of the greatest importance on this subject; yet I know there are many, whose assent to it will not be easily gained; and, therefore, it will be proper that I should endeavour particularly to explain and prove it.

Liberty and *reason* constitute the *capacity* of virtue. It is the *intention* that gives it *actual being* in a character.—The reader must not here forget the distinction before explained. To mere theoretical virtue, or (if I may so speak) the abstract reasons and fitnesses of things, praise-worthiness is not applicable. It is the actual conformity of the wills of moral agents to what they see or believe to be the fitnesses of things, that is the object of our praise and esteem. One of these may, perhaps, very properly be called the *virtue of the action*, in contradistinction from the other, which may be called the *virtue of the agent*. To the former, no particular intention is requisite; for what is *objectively* right, may be done from any motive good or bad; and, therefore, from hence alone, no merit is communicated to the agent; nay, it is consistent with the greatest guilt. On the contrary, to the other the particular intention is what is most essential. When this is good, there is so far virtue, whatever is true of the *matter* of the action; for an agent, who does what is *objectively wrong*, may often be entitled to commendation.

It may possibly be of some advantage towards elucidating this **756** matter, to conceive that only as, in strict propriety, *done* by a moral agent, which he *intends* to do. What arises beyond or contrary to his intention, however it may eventually happen, or be derived, by the connection of natural causes, from his determination, should not be imputed to him. Our own determinations alone are, most properly, our actions. These alone we have absolute power over, and are responsible for. It is at least worth considering, in what different senses, we are said to do what we did, and what we did not *design* to do. The causality or efficiency implied in these cases, is certainly far from being the same.—There seems indeed scarcely any thing more evident, than that there are two views or senses, in which we commonly speak of actions. Sometimes we mean by them, the determinations or volitions themselves of a being, of which the intention is an essential part: and sometimes we mean the real event, or external effect produced. With respect to a being possessed of infinite knowledge and power, these are always coincident. What such a being designs and determines to do, is always the same with the actual event produced. But we have no reason to think this true of any inferior beings.

757   In further explaining and proving what I have now in view, it will be proper to show, 'that the perception of right and wrong does *excite* to action, and is alone a sufficient *principle* of action;' after which we shall be better prepared for judging, 'how far, without it, there can be *practical virtue*.'

Experience, and the reason of the thing, will, if we attentively consult them, soon satisfy us about the first of these points. All men continually feel, that the perception of right and wrong excites to action; and it is so much their natural and unavoidable sense that this is true, that there are few or none, who, upon having it at first proposed to them, would not wonder at its being questioned.

*   *   *   *

But further, it seems extremely evident, that excitement belongs to the very ideas of moral right and wrong, and is essentially inseparable from the apprehension of them. The account in a former chapter of *obligation*, is enough to show this.—When we are conscious that an action is *fit* to be done, or that it *ought* to be done, it is not conceivable that we can remain *uninfluenced*, or want a *motive* to action. It would be to little purpose to argue much with a person, who would deny this; or who would maintain, that the *becomingness* or *reasonableness* of an action is no reason *for* doing it; and the *immorality* or *unreasonableness* of an action, no reason *against* doing it. An affection or inclination to rectitude cannot be separated from the view of it. The knowledge of what is right, without any approbation of it, or concern to practise it, is not conceivable or possible. And this knowledge will certainly be attended with *correspondent, actual practice*, whenever there is nothing to oppose it. Why a *reasonable* being acts *reasonably*; why he has a disposition to follow reason, and is not without aversion to wrong; why he chooses to do what he knows he *should* do, and cannot be wholly indifferent, whether he abstains from that which he knows is evil and criminal, and *not to be done*, are questions which need not, and which deserve not to be answered.

Instincts, therefore, as before observed in other instances, are not necessary to the choice of ends. The intellectual nature is its own law. It has, within itself, a spring and guide of action which it cannot suppress or reject.

*   *   *   *

It being therefore apparent that the determination of our minds **758** concerning the nature of actions as morally good or bad, suggests a motive to do or avoid them; it being also plain that this determination or judgement, though often not the prevailing, yet is always the first, the proper, and most natural and intimate spring and guide of the actions of reasonable beings: let us now inquire, whether it be not further the *only* spring of action in a reasonable being, as far as he can be deemed morally good and worthy; whether it be not the *only* principle from which all actions flow which engage our esteem of the agents; or, in other words, whether virtue be not itself the end of a virtuous agent as such.

If we consider that alone as most properly *done* by an agent, which he *designs* to do, and that what was no way an object of his design is not strictly imputable to him, or at least cannot give him any claim to merit or praise, it will follow that he cannot be properly said to practise virtue who does not *design* to practise it, to whom it is no object of regard, or who has it not at all in his view. It seems indeed as evident as we can wish any thing to be, that an action which is under no influence or direction from a *moral judgement*, cannot be in the practical sense *moral*; that when virtue is not pursued or intended, there is no virtue in the agent. Morally good intention, without any idea of moral good, is a contradiction. To act virtuously is to obey or follow reason: but can this be done without knowing and designing it?

I know, indeed, that according to the account some have given of **759** virtue, it presupposes an intention in the agent different from that to itself,[1] because, according to this account, it denotes only the emotion arising in us upon observing actions flowing from certain

[1 Presumably a reference to Hume's view that it presupposes a *motive* different from the sense of duty. See Hume, §§ 513–14, 633.]

motives and affections, and, in the original constitution of our
natures, is applicable alike to actions flowing from *any* motives. Were
this account true, it would be a gross fallacy to suppose that a sense of
virtue and duty, or any regard to moral good, can ever influence to
action. But this consequence cannot be regarded by one who
believes not the opinion which implies it; nor is it with me a small
objection to this opinion, that such a consequence arises from it.

If a person can justly be styled *virtuous* and *praise-worthy*, when he
never reflects upon virtue, and the reason of his acting is not taken
from any consideration of it, intelligence certainly is not necessary
to moral agency, and brutes are full as capable of virtue and moral
merit as we are.—Besides, might not a person with equal reason be
reckoned *public spirited*, who without any view to public good,
should accidentally make a discovery that enriches his country? May
not that course of behaviour be as well styled *ambitious*, to which the
love of honour and power did not excite; or that *selfish*, which did
not aim at private interest; or that *friendly*, which was attended with
no friendly intention?

*   *   *   *

760   But it may be asked, 'is not *benevolence* a virtuous principle? And
do we not approve all actions proceeding from it?'—I answer, benevolence, it has been shown, is of two kinds, *rational* and *instinctive*.
Rational benevolence entirely coincides with rectitude, and the actions
proceeding from it, with the actions proceeding from a regard to
rectitude. And the same is to be said of all those affections and
desires, which would arise in a nature as intelligent. It is not possible
that endeavours to obtain an end which, as reasonable, we cannot but
love and choose, should not be by reason approved; or that what is
necessarily desirable to all beings, should not be also *necessarily right to
be pursued*.

But *instinctive benevolence* is no principle of virtue, nor are any
actions flowing merely from it virtuous. As far as this influences, so
far something else than reason and goodness influences, and so much
I think is to be subtracted from the moral worth of any action or
character. This observation agrees perfectly with the common sentiments and determinations of mankind. Wherever the influence of
mere natural temper or inclination appears, and a particular conduct
is known to proceed from hence, we may, it is true, love the person,

as we commonly do the inferior creatures when they discover mild-ness and tractableness of disposition; but no regard to him as a *virtuous* agent will arise within us.

★　　　★　　　★　　　★

Actions proceeding from universal, calm, and dispassionate bene-　**761** volence, are by all esteemed more virtuous and amiable than actions producing equal or greater moments of good, directed to those to whom nature has more particularly linked us, and arising from kind determinations in our minds which are more confined and urgent. The reason is, that in the former case the operations of instinct have less effect, and are less sensible, and the attention to what is morally good and right is more explicit and prevalent. Were we prompted to the acts of universal benevolence in the same manner that parents are to the care of their children, we should not conceive of them as more virtuous. These facts cannot be explained consistently with the notion, that virtue consists in acting from kind affections which cannot be derived from intelligence, and are incapable, in their immediate exercise, of being attended with any influence from it. For why then should not the virtue be greatest where the kind impulse is strongest? Why should it, on the contrary, in such a case, be least of all, and entirely vanish, when all use of reason is precluded, and nothing but the force of instinct appears? Why, in particular, should resisting our strongest instincts, and following steadily in contradiction to them★, the determinations of cool unbiased reason, be considered as the very highest virtue? Probably, those who plead for this opinion would give it up, and acknowledge what is now asserted, could they be convinced that benevolence is essential to intelligence, and not merely an implanted principle or instinct.

All these observations may very justly be applied to self-love. *Reasonable and calm* self-love, as well as the *love of mankind*, is entirely a virtuous principle. They are both parts of the idea of virtue. Where this is greatest, there will be the most ardent and active bene-volence, and likewise the greatest degree of true prudence, the highest concern about bettering ourselves to the utmost, and the most effectual and constant pursuit of private happiness and perfection,

---

★ More to this purpose has been said by Mr. Balguy, in his *Tract on the Foundation of Moral Goodness* [especially §§ 441–2].

in opposition to whatever hindrances and temptations to neglect them may be thrown in our way.

★ ★ ★ ★

762   But to return to the main purpose of this chapter.—What has been said of virtuous actions may easily be applied to vicious actions. These can be no farther *in the agent* vicious, than he knew or might have known them to be so. The wrong can be no farther chargeable upon *him*, than he *saw* it, and acted in opposition to his *sense* of it. Or, to speak agreeably to a foregoing observation, and perhaps more properly, the *viciousness* in an action is no farther the agent's, than the *vicious* action is his; and no more of the vicious action is his, than was included in his intention.

★ ★ ★ ★

Let it not be imagined that what has been now asserted, has a tendency to render men negligent in their inquiries. Though a crazy or drunken man may not be *immediately* blameable in doing many actions in themselves very evil, yet for a man to put himself into a state in which he knows he shall be liable to do such actions, is extremely wicked. The difference is not great, between doing what we foresee may cause us to do an evil blindly and unknowingly, and doing the evil deliberately.

★ ★ ★ ★

ADAM SMITH

1723–1790

THE THEORY OF MORAL SENTIMENTS

[First printed, 1759. Reprinted here from the enlarged sixth edition, 1790, with misprints corrected and spelling slightly modified]

ADAM SMITH

———

The Theory of Moral Sentiments

PART I—OF THE PROPRIETY OF ACTION

SECT. I—*Of the sense of propriety*

CHAP. I—OF SYMPATHY

How selfish soever man may be supposed, there are evidently **763** some principles in his nature, which interest him in the fortune of others, and render their happiness necessary to him, though he derives nothing from it except the pleasure of seeing it. Of this kind is pity or compassion, the emotion which we feel for the misery of others, when we either see it, or are made to conceive it in a very lively manner. That we often derive sorrow from the sorrow of others, is a matter of fact too obvious to require any instances to prove it; for this sentiment, like all the other original passions of human nature, is by no means confined to the virtuous and humane, though they perhaps may feel it with the most exquisite sensibility. The greatest ruffian, the most hardened violator of the laws of society, is not altogether without it.

As we have no immediate experience of what other men feel, we **764** can form no idea of the manner in which they are affected, but by conceiving what we ourselves should feel in the like situation. Though our brother is upon the rack, as long as we ourselves are at our ease, our senses will never inform us of what he suffers. They never did, and never can, carry us beyond our own person, and it is by the imagination only that we can form any conception of what are his sensations. Neither can that faculty help us to this any other way, than by representing to us what would be our own, if we were in his case. It is the impressions of our own senses only, not those of his, which our imaginations copy. By the imagination we place ourselves in his situation, we conceive ourselves enduring all the same torments, we enter as it were into his body, and become in some measure the same person with him, and thence form some idea of his sensations, and even feel something which, though weaker in degree, is not altogether unlike them. His agonies, when they are thus brought home to ourselves, when we have thus adopted and made them our own, begin at last to affect us, and we then tremble and shudder at the thought of what he feels. For as to be in pain or distress of any kind excites the most excessive sorrow, so to conceive or to imagine that we are in it, excites some degree of the same emotion, in proportion to the vivacity or dullness of the conception.

That this is the source of our fellow-feeling for the misery of others, that it is by changing places in fancy with the sufferer, that we come either to conceive or to be affected by what he feels, may be demonstrated by many obvious observations, if it should not be thought sufficiently evident of itself. When we see a stroke aimed and just ready to fall upon the leg or arm of another person, we naturally shrink and draw back our own leg or our own arm; and when it does fall, we feel it in some measure, and are hurt by it as well as the sufferer. The mob, when they are gazing at a dancer on the slack rope, naturally writhe and twist and balance their own bodies, as they see him do, and as they feel that they themselves must do if in his situation. Persons of delicate fibres and a weak constitution of body complain, that in looking on the sores and ulcers which are exposed by beggars in the streets, they are apt to feel an itching or uneasy sensation in the correspondent part of their own bodies. The horror which they conceive at the misery of those wretches affects that particular part in themselves more than any other; because that horror arises from conceiving what they themselves would suffer, if they really were the wretches whom they are looking upon, and if that particular part in themselves was actually affected in the same miserable manner. The very force of this conception is sufficient, in their feeble frames, to produce that itching or uneasy sensation complained of. Men of the most robust make, observe that in looking upon sore eyes they often feel a very sensible soreness in their own, which proceeds from the same reason; that organ being in the strongest man more delicate, than any other part of the body is in the weakest.

765   Neither is it those circumstances only, which create pain or sorrow, that call forth our fellow-feeling. Whatever is the passion which arises from any object in the person principally concerned, an analogous emotion springs up, at the thought of his situation, in the breast of every attentive spectator. Our joy for the deliverance of those heroes of tragedy or romance who interest us, is as sincere as our grief for their distress, and our fellow-feeling with their misery is not more real than that with their happiness. We enter into their gratitude towards those faithful friends who did not desert them in their difficulties; and we heartily go along with their resentment against those perfidious traitors who injured, abandoned, or deceived them. In every passion of which the mind of man is susceptible, the emotions of the by-stander always correspond to what, by bringing the case home to himself, he imagines should be the sentiments of the sufferer.

Pity and compassion are words appropriated to signify our fellow-feeling with the sorrow of others. Sympathy, though its meaning was, perhaps, originally the same, may now, however, without much impropriety, be made use of to denote our fellow-feeling with any passion whatever.

Upon some occasions sympathy may seem to arise merely from **766** the view of a certain emotion in another person. The passions, upon some occasions, may seem to be transfused from one man to another, instantaneously, and antecedent to any knowledge of what excited them in the person principally concerned. Grief and joy, for example, strongly expressed in the look and gestures of any one, at once affect the spectator with some degree of a like painful or agreeable emotion. A smiling face is, to every body that sees it, a cheerful object; as a sorrowful countenance, on the other hand, is a melancholy one.

This, however, does not hold universally, or with regard to every passion. There are some passions of which the expressions excite no sort of sympathy, but before we are acquainted with what gave occasion to them, serve rather to disgust and provoke us against them. The furious behaviour of an angry man is more likely to exasperate us against himself than against his enemies. As we are unacquainted with his provocation, we cannot bring his case home to ourselves, nor conceive any thing like the passions which it excites. But we plainly see what is the situation of those with whom he is angry, and to what violence they may be exposed from so enraged an adversary. We readily, therefore, sympathize with their fear or resentment, and are immediately disposed to take part against the man from whom they appear to be in so much danger.

767   If the very appearances of grief and joy inspire us with some degree of the like emotions, it is because they suggest to us the general idea of some good or bad fortune that has befallen the person in whom we observe them: and in these passions this is sufficient to have some little influence upon us. The effects of grief and joy terminate in the person who feels those emotions, of which the expressions do not, like those of resentment, suggest to us the idea of any other person for whom we are concerned, and whose interests are opposite to his. The general idea of good or bad fortune, there-fore, creates some concern for the person who has met with it, but the general idea of provocation excites no sympathy with the anger of the man who has received it. Nature, it seems, teaches us to be more averse to enter into this passion, and, till informed of its cause, to be disposed rather to take part against it.

Even our sympathy with the grief or joy of another, before we are informed of the cause of either, is always extremely imperfect. General lamentations, which express nothing but the anguish of the sufferer, create rather a curiosity to inquire into his situation, along with some disposition to sympathize with him, than any actual sympathy that is very sensible. The first question which we ask is, What has befallen you? Till this be answered, though we are uneasy both from the vague idea of his misfortune, and still more from torturing ourselves with conjectures about what it may be, yet our fellow-feeling is not very considerable.

768   Sympathy, therefore, does not arise so much from the view of the passion, as from that of the situation which excites it. We sometimes feel for another, a passion of which he himself seems to be altogether incapable; because, when we put ourselves in his case, that passion arises in our breast from the imagination, though it does not in his from the reality. We blush for the impudence and rudeness of another, though he himself appears to have no sense of the im-propriety of his own behaviour; because we cannot help feeling with what confusion we ourselves should be covered, had we behaved in so absurd a manner.

Of all the calamities to which the condition of mortality exposes mankind, the loss of reason appears, to those who have the least spark of humanity, by far the most dreadful, and they behold that last stage of human wretchedness, with deeper commiseration than any other. But the poor wretch, who is in it, laughs and sings perhaps, and is altogether insensible of his own misery. The anguish which humanity feels, therefore, at the sight of such an object, cannot be the reflection of any sentiment of the sufferer. The compassion of the spectator must arise altogether from the consideration of what he himself would feel if he was reduced to the same unhappy situation, and, what perhaps is impossible, was at the same time able to regard it with his present reason and judgement.

What are the pangs of a mother, when she hears the moanings of her infant that during the agony of disease cannot express what it feels? In her idea of what it suffers, she joins, to its real helplessness, her own consciousness of that helplessness, and her own terrors for the unknown consequences of its disorder; and out of all these, forms, for her own sorrow, the most complete image of misery and distress. The infant, however, feels only the uneasiness of the present instant, which can never be great. With regard to the future, it is perfectly secure, and in its thoughtlessness and want of foresight, possesses an antidote against fear and anxiety, the great tormentors of the human breast, from which, reason and philosophy will, in vain, attempt to defend it, when it grows up to a man.

We sympathize even with the dead, and overlooking what is of **769** real importance in their situation, that awful futurity which awaits them, we are chiefly affected by those circumstances which strike our senses, but can have no influence upon their happiness. It is miserable, we think, to be deprived of the light of the sun; to be shut out from life and conversation; to be laid in the cold grave, a prey to corruption and the reptiles of the earth; to be no more thought of in this world, but to be obliterated, in a little time, from the affections, and almost from the memory, of their dearest friends and relations. Surely, we imagine, we can never feel too much for those who have suffered so dreadful a calamity. The tribute of our fellow-feeling seems doubly due to them now, when they are in danger of being forgot by every body; and, by the vain honours which we pay to their memory, we endeavour, for our own misery, artificially to keep alive our melancholy remembrance of their misfortune. That our sympathy can afford them no consolation seems to be an addition to their calamity; and to think that all we can do is unavailing, and that, what alleviates all other distress, the regret, the love, and the lamentations of their friends, can yield no comfort to them, serves only to exasperate our sense of their misery. The happiness of the dead, however, most assuredly, is affected by none of these circumstances; nor is it the thought of these things which can ever disturb the profound security of their repose. The idea of that dreary and endless melancholy, which the fancy naturally ascribes to their condition, arises altogether from our joining to the change which has been produced upon them, our own consciousness of that change, from our putting ourselves in their situation, and from our lodging, if I may be allowed to say so, our own living souls in their inanimated bodies, and thence conceiving what would be our emotions in this case. It is from this very illusion of the imagination, that the foresight of our own dissolution is so terrible to us, and that the idea of those circumstances, which undoubtedly can give us no pain when we are dead, makes us miserable while we are alive. And from thence arises one of the most important principles in human nature, the dread of death, the great poison to the happiness, but the great restraint upon the injustice of mankind, which, while it afflicts and mortifies the individual, guards and protects the society.

CHAP. III—OF THE MANNER IN WHICH WE JUDGE OF THE PROPRIETY OR IMPROPRIETY OF THE AFFECTIONS OF OTHER MEN, BY THEIR CONCORD OR DISSONANCE WITH OUR OWN

770   When the original passions of the person principally concerned are in perfect concord with the sympathetic emotions of the spectator, they necessarily appear to this last just and proper, and suitable to their objects; and, on the contrary, when, upon bringing the case home to himself, he finds that they do not coincide with what he feels, they necessarily appear to him unjust and improper, and unsuitable to the causes which excite them. To approve of the passions of another, therefore, as suitable to their objects, is the same thing as to observe that we entirely sympathize with them; and not to approve of them as such, is the same thing as to observe that we do not entirely sympathize with them. The man who resents the injuries that have been done to me, and observes that I resent them precisely as he does, necessarily approves of my resentment. The man whose sympathy keeps time to my grief, cannot but admit the reasonableness of my sorrow. He who admires the same poem, or the same

picture, and admires them exactly as I do, must surely allow the justness of my admiration. He who laughs at the same joke, and laughs along with me, cannot well deny the propriety of my laughter. On the contrary, the person who, upon these different occasions, either feels no such emotion as that which I feel, or feels none that bears any proportion to mine, cannot avoid disapproving my sentiments on account of their dissonance with his own. If my animosity goes beyond what the indignation of my friend can correspond to; if my grief exceeds what his most tender compassion can go along with; if my admiration is either too high or too low to tally with his own; if I laugh loud and heartily when he only smiles, or, on the contrary, only smile when he laughs loud and heartily; in all these cases, as soon as he comes from considering the object, to observe how I am affected by it, according as there is more or less disproportion between his sentiments and mine, I must incur a greater or less degree of his disapprobation: and upon all occasions his own sentiments are the standards and measures by which he judges of mine.

To approve of another man's opinions is to adopt those opinions, **771** and to adopt them is to approve of them. If the same arguments which convince you convince me likewise, I necessarily approve of your conviction; and if they do not, I necessarily disapprove of it: neither can I possibly conceive that I should do the one without the other. To approve or disapprove, therefore, of the opinions of others is acknowledged, by every body, to mean no more than to observe their agreement or disagreement with our own. But this is equally the case with regard to our approbation or disapprobation of the sentiments or passions of others.

There are, indeed, some cases in which we seem to approve **772** without any sympathy or correspondence of sentiments, and in which, consequently, the sentiment of approbation would seem to be different from the perception of this coincidence. A little attention, however, will convince us that even in these cases our approbation is ultimately founded upon a sympathy or correspondence of this kind. I shall give an instance in things of a very frivolous nature, because in them the judgements of mankind are less apt to be perverted by wrong systems. We may often approve of a jest, and think the laughter of the company quite just and proper, though we ourselves do not laugh, because, perhaps, we are in a grave humour, or happen to have our attention engaged with other objects. We have learned, however, from experience, what sort of pleasantry is upon most occasions capable of making us laugh, and we observe that this is one of that kind. We approve, therefore, of the laughter of the company, and feel that it is natural and suitable to its object; because, though in our present mood we cannot easily enter into it, we are sensible that upon most occasions we should very heartily join in it.

The same thing often happens with regard to all the other passions. A stranger passes by us in the street with all the marks of the deepest affliction; and we are immediately told that he has just received the news of the death of his father. It is impossible that, in this case, we should not approve of his grief. Yet it may often happen, without any defect of humanity on our part, that, so far from entering into the violence of his sorrow, we should scarce conceive the first movements of concern upon his account. Both he and his father, perhaps, are entirely unknown to us, or we happen to be employed about other things, and do not take time to picture out in our imagination the different circumstances of distress which must occur to him. We have learned, however, from experience, that such a misfortune naturally excites such a degree of sorrow, and we know that if we took time to consider his situation, fully and in all its parts, we should, without doubt, most sincerely sympathize with him. It is upon the consciousness of this conditional sympathy, that our approbation of his sorrow is founded, even in those cases in which that sympathy does not actually take place; and the general rules derived from our preceding experience of what our sentiments would commonly correspond with, correct upon this, as upon many other occasions, the impropriety of our present emotions.

773 The sentiment of affection of the heart from which any action proceeds, and upon which its whole virtue or vice must ultimately depend, may be considered under two different aspects, or in two different relations; first, in relation to the cause which excites it, or the motive which gives occasion to it; and secondly, in relation to the end which it proposes, or the effect which it tends to produce.

In the suitableness or unsuitableness, in the proportion or disproportion which the affection seems to bear to the cause or object which excites it, consists the propriety or impropriety, the decency or ungracefulness of the consequent action.

In the beneficial or hurtful nature of the effects which the affection aims at, or tends to produce, consists the merit or demerit of the action, the qualities by which it is entitled to reward, or is deserving of punishment.

Philosophers have, of late years, considered chiefly the tendency **774** of affections, and have given little attention to the relation which they stand in to the cause which excites them. In common life, however, when we judge of any person's conduct, and of the sentiments which directed it, we constantly consider them under both these aspects. When we blame in another man the excesses of love, of grief, of resentment, we not only consider the ruinous effects which they tend to produce, but the little occasion which was given for them. The merit of his favourite, we say, is not so great, his misfortune is not so dreadful, his provocation is not so extraordinary, as to justify so violent a passion. We should have indulged, we say; perhaps, have approved of the violence of his emotion, had the cause been in any respect proportioned to it.

When we judge in this manner of any affection, as proportioned **775** or disproportioned to the cause which excites it, it is scarce possible that we should make use of any other rule or canon but the correspondent affection in ourselves. If, upon bringing the case home to our own breast, we find that the sentiments which it gives occasion to, coincide and tally with our own, we necessarily approve of them, as proportioned and suitable to their objects; if otherwise, we necessarily disapprove of them, as extravagant and out of proportion.

Every faculty in one man is the measure by which he judges of the like faculty in another. I judge of your sight by my sight, of your ear by my ear, of your reason by my reason, of your resentment by my resentment, of your love by my love. I neither have, nor can have, any other way of judging about them.

CHAP. IV—THE SAME SUBJECT CONTINUED

We may judge of the propriety or impropriety of the sentiments **776** of another person by their correspondence or disagreement with our own, upon two different occasions; either, first, when the objects which excite them are considered without any peculiar relation, either to ourselves or to the person whose sentiments we judge of;

or, secondly, when they are considered as peculiarly affecting one or other of us.

1. With regard to those objects which are considered without any peculiar relation either to ourselves or to the person whose sentiments we judge of; wherever his sentiments entirely correspond with our own, we ascribe to him the qualities of taste and good judgement. The beauty of a plain, the greatness of a mountain, the ornaments of a building, the expression of a picture, the composition of a discourse, the conduct of a third person, the proportions of different quantities and numbers, the various appearances which the great machine of the universe is perpetually exhibiting, with the secret wheels and springs which produce them; all the general subjects of science and taste, are what we and our companions regard as having no peculiar relation to either of us. We both look at them from the same point of view, and we have no occasion for sympathy, or for that imaginary change of situations from which it arises, in order to produce, with regard to these, the most perfect harmony of sentiments and affections. If, notwithstanding, we are often differently affected, it arises either from the different degrees of attention, which our different habits of life allow us to give easily to the several parts of those complex objects, or from the different degrees of natural acuteness in the faculty of the mind to which they are addressed.

*   *   *   *

777   2. With regard to those objects, which affect in a particular manner either ourselves or the person whose sentiments we judge of, it is at once more difficult to preserve this harmony and correspondence, and at the same time, vastly more important. My companion does not naturally look upon the misfortune that has befallen me, or the injury that has been done me, from the same point of view in which I consider them. They affect me much more nearly. We do not view them from the same station, as we do a picture, or a poem, or a system of philosophy, and are, therefore, apt to be very differently affected by them. But I can much more easily overlook the want of this correspondence of sentiments with regard to such indifferent objects as concern neither me nor my companion, than with regard to what interests me so much as the misfortune that has befallen me, or the injury that has been done me. Though you despise that picture, or that poem, or even that system of philosophy, which I admire, there is little danger of our quarrelling upon that account. Neither of us can reasonably be much interested about them. They ought all of them to be matters of great indifference to us both; so that, though our opinions may be opposite, our affections may still be very nearly the same. But it is quite otherwise with regard to those objects by which either you or I are particularly affected. Though your judgements in matters of speculation, though your sentiments in matters of taste, are quite opposite to mine, I can easily overlook this opposition; and if I have any degree of temper, I may still find some entertainment in your conversation, even upon those very subjects. But if you have either no fellow-feeling for the misfortunes I have met with, or none that bears any proportion to the grief which distracts me; or if you have either no indignation at the injuries I have suffered, or none that bears any proportion to the resentment which transports me, we can no longer converse upon these subjects. We become intolerable to one another. I can neither support your company, nor you mine. You are confounded at my violence and passion, and I am enraged at your cold insensibility and want of feeling.

In all such cases, that there may be some correspondence of sentiments between the spectator and the person principally concerned, **778** the spectator must, first of all, endeavour, as much as he can, to put himself in the situation of the other, and to bring home to himself every little circumstance of distress which can possibly occur to the sufferer. He must adopt the whole case of his companion with all its minutest incidents; and strive to render as perfect as possible, that imaginary change of situation upon which his sympathy is founded.

After all this, however, the emotions of the spectator will still be very apt to fall short of the violence of what is felt by the sufferer. Mankind, though naturally sympathetic, never conceive, for what has befallen another, that degree of passion which naturally animates the person principally concerned. That imaginary change of situation, upon which their sympathy is founded, is but momentary. The thought of their own safety, the thought that they themselves are not really the sufferers, continually intrudes itself upon them; and though it does not hinder them from conceiving a passion somewhat analogous to what is felt by the sufferer, hinders them from conceiving any thing that approaches to the same degree of violence.

The person principally concerned is sensible of this, and at the same time passionately desires a more complete sympathy. He longs for that relief which nothing can afford him but the entire concord of the affections of the spectators with his own. To see the emotions of their hearts, in every respect, beat time to his own, in the violent and disagreeable passions, constitutes his sole consolation. But he can only hope to obtain this by lowering his passion to that pitch, in which the spectators are capable of going along with him. He must flatten, if I may be allowed to say so, the sharpness of its natural tone, in order to reduce it to harmony and concord with the emotions of those who are about him. What they feel, will, indeed, always be, in some respects, different from what he feels, and compassion can never be exactly the same with original sorrow; because the secret consciousness that the change of situations, from which the sympathetic sentiment arises, is but imaginary, not only lowers it in degree, but, in some measure, varies it in kind, and gives it a quite different modification. These two sentiments, however, may, it is evident, have such a correspondence with one another, as is sufficient for the harmony of society. Though they will never be unisons, they may be concords, and this is all that is wanted or required.

779   In order to produce this concord, as nature teaches the spectators to assume the circumstances of the person principally concerned, so she teaches this last in some measure to assume those of the spectators. As they are continually placing themselves in his situation, and thence conceiving emotions similar to what he feels; so he is as constantly placing himself in theirs, and thence conceiving some degree of that coolness about his own fortune, with which he is sensible that they will view it. As they are constantly considering what they themselves would feel, if they actually were the sufferers, so he is as constantly led to imagine in what manner he would be affected if he was only one of the spectators of his own situation. As their sympathy makes them look at it, in some measure, with his eyes, so his sympathy makes him look at it, in some measure, with theirs, especially when in their presence and acting under their observation: and as the reflected passion, which he thus conceives, is much weaker than the original one, it necessarily abates the violence of what he felt before he came into their presence, before he began to recollect in what manner they would be affected by it, and to view his situation in this candid and impartial light.

The mind, therefore, is rarely so disturbed, but that the company **780**
of a friend will restore it to some degree of tranquillity and sedate-
ness. The breast is, in some measure, calmed and composed the
moment we come into his presence. We are immediately put in
mind of the light in which he will view our situation, and we begin
to view it ourselves in the same light; for the effect of sympathy is
instantaneous. We expect less sympathy from a common acquaintance than from a friend: we cannot open to the former all those
little circumstances which we can unfold to the latter: we assume,
therefore, more tranquillity before him, and endeavour to fix our
thoughts upon those general outlines of our situation which he is
willing to consider. We expect still less sympathy from an assembly
of strangers, and we assume, therefore, still more tranquillity before
them, and always endeavour to bring down our passion to that
pitch, which the particular company we are in may be expected to
go along with. Nor is this only an assumed appearance: for if we are
at all masters of ourselves, the presence of a mere acquaintance will
really compose us, still more than that of a friend; and that of an
assembly of strangers still more than that of an acquaintance.

Society and conversation, therefore, are the most powerful
remedies for restoring the mind to its tranquillity, if, at any time, it
has unfortunately lost it; as well as the best preservatives of that
equal and happy temper, which is so necessary to self-satisfaction
and enjoyment. Men of retirement and speculation, who are apt to
sit brooding at home over either grief or resentment, though they
may often have more humanity, more generosity, and a nicer sense
of honour, yet seldom possess that equality of temper which is so
common among men of the world.

CHAP. V—OF THE AMIABLE AND RESPECTABLE VIRTUES

Upon these two different efforts, upon that of the spectator to **781**
enter into the sentiments of the person principally concerned, and
upon that of the person principally concerned, to bring down his
emotions to what the spectator can go along with, are founded two
different sets of virtues. The soft, the gentle, the amiable[1] virtues,
the virtues of candid condescension and indulgent humanity, are

[1 Cf. Hume, § 612.]

founded upon the one: the great, the awful[1] and respectable, the virtues of self-denial, of self-government, of that command of the passions which subjects all the movements of our nature to what our own dignity and honour, and the propriety of our own conduct require, take their origin from the other.

*   *   *   *

782   And hence it is, that to feel much for others and little for ourselves, that to restrain our selfish, and to indulge our benevolent affections, constitutes the perfection of human nature; and can alone produce among mankind that harmony of sentiments and passions in which consists their whole grace and propriety. As to love our neighbour as we love ourselves is the great law of Christianity, so it is the great precept of nature to love ourselves only as we love our neighbour, or what comes to the same thing, as our neighbour is capable of loving us.

As taste and good judgement, when they are considered as qualities which deserve praise and admiration, are supposed to imply a delicacy of sentiment and an acuteness of understanding not commonly to be met with; so the virtues of sensibility and self-command are not apprehended to consist in the ordinary, but in the uncommon degrees of those qualities. The amiable virtue of humanity requires, surely, a sensibility, much beyond what is possessed by the rude vulgar of mankind. The great and exalted virtue of magnanimity undoubtedly demands much more than that degree of self-command, which the weakest of mortals is capable of exerting. As in the common degree of the intellectual qualities, there are no abilities; so in the common degree of the moral, there is no virtue. Virtue is excellence, something uncommonly great and beautiful, which rises far above what is vulgar and ordinary. The amiable virtues consist in that degree of sensibility which surprises by its exquisite and unexpected delicacy and tenderness. The awful and respectable, in that degree of self-command which astonishes by its amazing superiority over the most ungovernable passions of human nature.

783   There is, in this respect, a considerable difference between virtue and mere propriety; between those qualities and actions which deserve to be admired and celebrated, and those which simply deserve to be approved of. Upon many occasions, to act with the most perfect propriety, requires no more than that common and

[1 Cf. Hume, § 612.]

ordinary degree of sensibility or self-command which the most worthless of mankind are possessed of, and sometimes even that degree is not necessary. Thus, to give a very low instance, to eat when we are hungry, is certainly, upon ordinary occasions, perfectly right and proper, and cannot miss being approved of as such by every body. Nothing, however, could be more absurd than to say it was virtuous.

On the contrary, there may frequently be a considerable degree of virtue in those actions which fall short of the most perfect propriety; because they may still approach nearer to perfection than could well be expected upon occasions in which it was so extremely difficult to attain it: and this is very often the case upon those occasions which require the greatest exertions of self-command. There are some situations which bear so hard upon human nature, that the greatest degree of self-government, which can belong to so imperfect a creature as man, is not able to stifle, altogether, the voice of human weakness, or reduce the violence of the passions to that pitch of moderation, in which the impartial spectator can entirely enter into them. Though in those cases, therefore, the behaviour of the sufferer fall short of the most perfect propriety, it may still deserve some applause, and even in a certain sense, may be denominated virtuous. It may still manifest an effort of generosity and magnanimity of which the greater part of men are incapable; and though it fails of absolute perfection, it may be a much nearer approximation towards perfection, than what, upon such trying occasions, is commonly either to be found or to be expected.

In cases of this kind, when we are determining the degree of **784** blame or applause which seems due to any action, we very frequently make use of two different standards. The first is the idea of complete propriety and perfection, which, in those difficult situations, no human conduct ever did, or ever can come up to; and in comparison with which the actions of all men must for ever appear blameable and imperfect. The second is the idea of that degree of proximity or distance from this complete perfection, which the actions of the greater part of men commonly arrive at. Whatever goes beyond this degree, how far soever it may be removed from absolute perfection, seems to deserve applause; and whatever falls short of it, to deserve blame.

*   *   *   *

PART II—OF MERIT AND DEMERIT; OR, OF THE OBJECTS OF REWARD AND PUNISHMENT

SECT. I—*Of the sense of merit and demerit*

INTRODUCTION

785　There is another set of qualities ascribed to the actions and conduct of mankind, distinct from their propriety or impropriety, their decency or ungracefulness, and which are the objects of a distinct species of approbation and disapprobation. These are Merit and Demerit, the qualities of deserving reward, and of deserving punishment.

It has already been observed,[1] that the sentiment or affection of the heart, from which any action proceeds, and upon which its whole virtue or vice depends, may be considered under two different aspects, or in two different relations: first, in relation to the cause or object which excites it; and, secondly, in relation to the end which it proposes, or to the effect which it tends to produce: that upon the suitableness or unsuitableness, upon the proportion or disproportion, which the affection seems to bear to the cause or object which excites it, depends the propriety or impropriety, the decency or ungracefulness of the consequent action; and that upon the beneficial or hurtful effects which the affection proposes or tends to produce, depends the merit or demerit, the good or ill desert of the action to which it gives occasion. Wherein consists our sense of the propriety or impropriety of actions, has been explained in the former part of this discourse. We come now to consider, wherein consists that of their good or ill desert.

CHAP. I—THAT WHATEVER APPEARS TO BE THE PROPER OBJECT OF GRATITUDE, APPEARS TO DESERVE REWARD; AND THAT, IN THE SAME MANNER, WHATEVER APPEARS TO BE THE PROPER OBJECT OF RESENTMENT, APPEARS TO DESERVE PUNISHMENT

786　To us, therefore, that action must appear to deserve reward, which appears to be the proper and approved object of that sentiment, which most immediately and directly prompts us to reward, or to do good to another. And in the same manner, that action must appear to deserve punishment, which appears to be the proper and

[1 § 773.]

approved object of that sentiment which most immediately and directly prompts us to punish, or to inflict evil upon another.

The sentiment which most immediately and directly prompts us to reward, is gratitude; that which most immediately and directly prompts us to punish, is resentment.

To us, therefore, that action must appear to deserve reward, which appears to be the proper and approved object of gratitude; as, on the other hand, that action must appear to deserve punishment, which appears to be the proper and approved object of resentment.

To reward, is to recompense, to remunerate, to return good for good received. To punish, too, is to recompense, to remunerate, though in a different manner; it is to return evil for evil that has been done.

There are some other passions, besides gratitude and resentment, **787** which interest us in the happiness or misery of others; but there are none which so directly excite us to be the instruments of either. The love and esteem which grow upon acquaintance and habitual approbation, necessarily lead us to be pleased with the good fortune of the man who is the object of such agreeable emotions, and consequently, to be willing to lend a hand to promote it. Our love, however, is fully satisfied, though his good fortune should be brought about without our assistance. All that this passion desires is to see him happy, without regarding who was the author of his prosperity. But gratitude is not to be satisfied in this manner. If the person to whom we owe many obligations, is made happy without our assistance, though it pleases our love, it does not content our gratitude. Till we have recompensed him, till we ourselves have been instrumental in promoting his happiness, we feel ourselves still loaded with that debt which his past services have laid upon us.

The hatred and dislike, in the same manner, which grow upon **788** habitual disapprobation, would often lead us to take a malicious pleasure in the misfortune of the man whose conduct and character excite so painful a passion. But though dislike and hatred harden us against all sympathy, and sometimes dispose us even to rejoice at the distress of another, yet, if there is no resentment in the case, if neither we nor our friends have received any great personal provocation, these passions would not naturally lead us to wish to be instrumental in bringing it about. Though we could fear no punishment in consequence of our having had some hand in it, we would rather that it should happen by other means. To one under the dominion of violent hatred it would be agreeable, perhaps, to hear, that the person whom he abhorred and detested was killed by some accident. But if he had the least spark of justice, which, though this passion is not very favourable to virtue, he might still have, it would hurt him excessively to have been himself, even without design, the occasion of this misfortune. Much more would the very thought of voluntarily contributing to it shock him beyond all measure. He would reject with horror even the imagination of so execrable a design; and if he could imagine himself capable of such an enormity, he would begin to regard himself in the same odious light in which he had considered the person who was the object of his dislike. But it is quite otherwise with resentment: if the person who had done us some great injury, who had murdered our father or our brother, for example, should soon afterwards die of a fever, or even be brought to the scaffold upon account of some other crime, though it might soothe our hatred, it would not fully gratify our resentment. Resentment would prompt us to desire, not only that he should be punished, but that he should be punished by our means, and upon account of that particular injury which he had done to us. Resentment cannot be fully gratified, unless the offender is not only made to grieve in his turn, but to grieve for that particular wrong which we have suffered from him. He must be made to repent and be sorry for this very action, that others, through fear of the like punishment, may be terrified from being guilty of the like offence. The natural gratification of this passion tends, of its own accord, to produce all the political ends of punishment; the correction of the criminal, and the example to the public.

Gratitude and resentment, therefore, are the sentiments which most immediately and directly prompt to reward and to punish. To us, therefore, he must appear to deserve reward, who appears to be the proper and approved object of gratitude; and he to deserve punishment, who appears to be that of resentment.

CHAP. II—OF THE PROPER OBJECTS OF GRATITUDE AND RESENTMENT

789 To be the proper and approved object either of gratitude or resentment, can mean nothing but to be the object of that gratitude, and of that resentment, which naturally seems proper, and is approved of.

But these, as well as all the other passions of human nature, seem proper and are approved of, when the heart of every impartial spectator entirely sympathizes with them, when every indifferent by-stander entirely enters into, and goes along with them.

He, therefore, appears to deserve reward, who, to some person or persons, is the natural object of a gratitude which every human heart is disposed to beat time to, and thereby applaud: and he, on the other hand, appears to deserve punishment, who in the same manner is to some person or persons the natural object of a resentment which the breast of every reasonable man is ready to adopt and sympathize with. To us, surely, that action must appear to deserve reward, which every body who knows of it would wish to reward, and therefore delights to see rewarded: and that action must as surely appear to deserve punishment, which every body who hears of it is angry with, and upon that account rejoices to see punished.

1. As we sympathize with the joy of our companions when in 790 prosperity, so we join with them in the complacency and satisfaction with which they naturally regard whatever is the cause of their good fortune. We enter into the love and affection which they conceive for it, and begin to love it too. We should be sorry for their sakes if it was destroyed, or even if it was placed at too great a distance from them, and out of the reach of their care and protection, though they should lose nothing by its absence except the pleasure of seeing it. If it is man who has thus been the fortunate instrument of the happiness of his brethren, this is still more peculiarly the case. When we see one man assisted, protected, relieved by another, our sympathy with the joy of the person who receives the benefit serves only to animate our fellow-feeling with his gratitude towards him who bestows it. When we look upon the person who is the cause of his pleasure with the eyes with which we imagine he must look upon him, his benefactor seems to stand before us in the most engaging and amiable light. We readily therefore sympathize with the grateful affection which he conceives for a person to whom he has been so much obliged; and consequently applaud the returns which he is disposed to make for the good offices conferred upon him. As we entirely enter into the affection from which these returns proceed, they necessarily seem every way proper and suitable to their object.

791   2. In the same manner, as we sympathize with the sorrow of our fellow-creature whenever we see his distress, so we likewise enter into his abhorrence and aversion for whatever has given occasion to it. Our heart, as it adopts and beats time to his grief, so is it likewise animated with that spirit by which he endeavours to drive away or destroy the cause of it. The indolent and passive fellow-feeling, by which we accompany him in his sufferings, readily gives way to that more vigorous and active sentiment by which we go along with him in the effort he makes, either to repel them, or to gratify his aversion to what has given occasion to them. This is still more peculiarly the case, when it is man who has caused them. When we see one man oppressed or injured by another, the sympathy which we feel with the distress of the sufferer seems to serve only to animate our fellow-feeling with his resentment against the offender. We are rejoiced to see him attack his adversary in his turn, and are eager and ready to assist him whenever he exerts himself for defence, or even for vengeance within a certain degree. If the injured should perish in the quarrel, we not only sympathize with the real resentment of his friends and relations, but with the imaginary resentment which in fancy we lend to the dead, who is no longer capable of feeling that or any other human sentiment. But as we put ourselves in his situation, as we enter, as it were, into his body, and in our imaginations, in some measure, animate anew the deformed and mangled carcass of the slain, when we bring home in this manner his case to our own bosoms, we feel upon this, as upon many other occasions, an emotion which the person principally concerned is incapable of feeling, and which yet we feel by an illusive sympathy with him. The sympathetic tears which we shed for that immense and irretrievable loss, which in our fancy he appears to have sustained, seem to be but a small part of the duty which we owe him. The injury which he has suffered demands, we think, a principal part of our attention. We feel that resentment which we imagine he ought to feel, and which he would feel, if in his cold and lifeless body there remained any consciousness of what passes upon earth. His blood, we think, calls aloud for vengeance. The very ashes of the dead seem to be disturbed at the thought that his injuries are to pass unrevenged. The horrors which are supposed to haunt the bed of the murderer, the ghosts which, superstition imagines, rise from their graves to demand vengeance upon those who brought them to an untimely end, all take their origin from this natural sympathy with the imaginary resentment of the slain. And with regard, at least, to this most dreadful of all crimes, Nature, antecedent to all reflections upon the utility of punishment, has in this manner stamped upon the human heart, in the strongest and most indelible characters, an immediate and instinctive approbation of the sacred and necessary law of retaliation.

CHAP. III—THAT WHERE THERE IS NO APPROBATION OF THE CONDUCT OF THE PERSON WHO CONFERS THE BENEFIT, THERE IS LITTLE SYMPATHY WITH THE GRATITUDE OF HIM WHO RECEIVES IT: AND THAT, ON THE CONTRARY, WHERE THERE IS NO DISAPPROBATION OF THE MOTIVES OF THE PERSON WHO DOES THE MISCHIEF, THERE IS NO SORT OF SYMPATHY WITH THE RESENTMENT OF HIM WHO SUFFERS IT

It is to be observed, however, that, how beneficial soever on the **792** one hand, or how hurtful soever on the other, the actions or intentions of the person who acts may have been to the person who is, if I may say so, acted upon, yet if in the one case there appears to have been no propriety in the motives of the agent, if we cannot enter into the affections which influenced his conduct, we have little sympathy with the gratitude of the person who receives the benefit: or if, in the other case, there appears to have been no impropriety in the motives of the agent, if, on the contrary, the affections which influenced his conduct are such as we must necessarily enter into, we can have no sort of sympathy with the resentment of the person who suffers. Little gratitude seems due in the one case, and all sort of resentment seems unjust in the other. The one action seems to merit little reward, the other to deserve no punishment.

1. First, I say, that wherever we cannot sympathize with the **793** affections of the agent, wherever there seems to be no propriety in the motives which influenced his conduct, we are less disposed to enter into the gratitude of the person who received the benefit of his actions. A very small return seems due to that foolish and profuse generosity which confers the greatest benefits from the most trivial motives, and gives an estate to a man merely because his name and surname happen to be the same with those of the giver. Such services do not seem to demand any proportionable recompense. Our contempt for the folly of the agent hinders us from thoroughly

entering into the gratitude of the person to whom the good office has been done. His benefactor seems unworthy of it. As when we place ourselves in the situation of the person obliged, we feel that we could conceive no great reverence for such a benefactor, we easily absolve him from a great deal of that submissive veneration and esteem which we should think due to a more respectable character; and provided he always treats his weak friend with kindness and humanity, we are willing to excuse him from many attentions and regards which we should demand to a worthier patron.

★   ★   ★   ★

794   2. Secondly, I say, that wherever the conduct of the agent appears to have been entirely directed by motives and affections which we thoroughly enter into and approve of, we can have no sort of sympathy with the resentment of the sufferer, how great soever the mischief which may have been done to him. When two people quarrel, if we take part with, and entirely adopt the resentment of one of them, it is impossible that we should enter into that of the other. Our sympathy with the person whose motives we go along with, and whom therefore we look upon as in the right, cannot but harden us against all fellow-feeling with the other, whom we necessarily regard as in the wrong. Whatever this last, therefore, may have suffered, while it is no more than what we ourselves should have wished him to suffer, while it is no more than what our own sympathetic indignation would have prompted us to inflict upon him, it cannot either displease or provoke us. When an inhuman murderer is brought to the scaffold, though we have some compassion for his misery, we can have no sort of fellow-feeling with his resentment, if he should be so absurd as to express any against either his prosecutor or his judge. The natural tendency of their just indignation against so vile a criminal is indeed the most fatal and ruinous to him. But it is impossible that we should be displeased with the tendency of a sentiment, which, when we bring the case home to ourselves, we feel that we cannot avoid adopting.

CHAP. IV—RECAPITULATION OF THE FOREGOING CHAPTERS

795   1. We do not, therefore, thoroughly and heartily sympathize with the gratitude of one man towards another, merely because this other has been the cause of his good fortune, unless he has been the cause of it from motives which we entirely go along with. Our heart must adopt the principles of the agent, and go along with all the affections which influenced his conduct, before it can entirely sympathize with, and beat time to, the gratitude of the person who has been benefited by his actions. If in the conduct of the benefactor there appears to have been no propriety, how beneficial soever its effects, it does not seem to demand, or necessarily to require, any proportionable recompense.

But when to the beneficent tendency of the action is joined the propriety of the affection from which it proceeds, when we entirely sympathize and go along with the motives of the agent, the love which we conceive for him upon his own account, enhances and enlivens our fellow-feeling with the gratitude of those who owe their prosperity to his good conduct. His actions seem then to demand, and, if I may say so, to call aloud for a proportionable recompense. We then entirely enter into that gratitude which prompts to bestow it. The benefactor seems then to be the proper object of reward, when we thus entirely sympathize with, and approve of, that sentiment which prompts to reward him. When we approve of, and go along with, the affection from which the action proceeds, we must necessarily approve of the action, and regard the person towards whom it is directed, as its proper and suitable object.

2. In the same manner, we cannot at all sympathize with the 796 resentment of one man against another, merely because this other has been the cause of his misfortune, unless he has been the cause of it from motives which we cannot enter into. Before we can adopt the resentment of the sufferer, we must disapprove of the motives of the agent, and feel that our heart renounces all sympathy with the affections which influenced his conduct. If there appears to have been no impropriety in these, how fatal soever the tendency of the action which proceeds from them to those against whom it is directed, it does not seem to deserve any punishment, or to be the proper object of any resentment.

But when to the hurtfulness of the action is joined the impropriety of the affection from whence it proceeds, when our heart rejects with abhorrence all fellow-feeling with the motives of the agent, we then heartily and entirely sympathize with the resentment of the sufferer. Such actions seem then to deserve, and, if I may say so, to call aloud for, a proportionable punishment; and we entirely enter into, and thereby approve of, that resentment which prompts to inflict it. The offender necessarily seems then to be the proper object of punishment, when we thus entirely sympathize with, and thereby approve of, that sentiment which prompts to punish. In this case too, when we approve, and go along with, the affection from which the action proceeds, we must necessarily approve of the action, and regard the person against whom it is directed, as its proper and suitable object.

CHAP. V—THE ANALYSIS OF THE SENSE OF MERIT AND DEMERIT

797 1. As our sense, therefore, of the propriety of conduct arises from what I shall call a direct sympathy with the affections and motives of the person who acts, so our sense of its merit arises from what I shall call an indirect sympathy with the gratitude of the person who is, if I may say so, acted upon.

As we cannot indeed enter thoroughly into the gratitude of the person who receives the benefit, unless we beforehand approve of the motives of the benefactor, so, upon this account, the sense of merit seems to be a compounded sentiment, and to be made up of two distinct emotions; a direct sympathy with the sentiments of the agent, and an indirect sympathy with the gratitude of those who receive the benefit of his actions.

*   *   *   *

798 2. In the same manner as our sense of the impropriety of conduct arises from a want of sympathy, or from a direct antipathy to the affections and motives of the agent, so our sense of its demerit arises from what I shall here too call an indirect sympathy with the resentment of the sufferer.

As we cannot indeed enter into the resentment of the sufferer, unless our heart beforehand disapproves the motives of the agent, and renounces all fellow-feeling with them; so upon this account the sense of demerit, as well as that of merit, seems to be a compounded sentiment, and to be made up of two distinct emotions; a direct antipathy to the sentiments of the agent, and an indirect sympathy with the resentment of the sufferer.

*   *   *   *

[The following paragraph concludes a long footnote appended to Chapter V as a whole.]

Before I conclude this note, I must take notice of a difference **799** between the approbation of propriety and that of merit or beneficence. Before we approve of the sentiments of any person as proper and suitable to their objects, we must not only be affected in the same manner as he is, but we must perceive this harmony and correspondence of sentiments between him and ourselves. Thus, though upon hearing of a misfortune that had befallen my friend, I should conceive precisely that degree of concern which he gives way to; yet till I am informed of the manner in which he behaves, till I perceive the harmony between his emotions and mine, I cannot be said to approve of the sentiments which influence his behaviour. The approbation of propriety therefore requires, not only that we should entirely sympathize with the person who acts, but that we should perceive this perfect concord between his sentiments and our own. On the contrary, when I hear of a benefit that has been bestowed upon another person, let him who has received it be affected in what manner he pleases, if, by bringing his case home to myself, I feel gratitude arise in my own breast, I necessarily approve of the conduct of his benefactor, and regard it as meritorious, and the proper object of reward. Whether the person who has received the benefit conceives gratitude or not, cannot, it is evident, in any degree alter our sentiments with regard to the merit of him who has bestowed it. No actual correspondence of sentiments, therefore, is here required. It is sufficient that if he was grateful, they would correspond; and our sense of merit is often founded upon one of those illusive sympathies, by which, when we bring home to ourselves the case of another, we are often affected in a manner in which the person principally concerned is incapable of being affected. There is a similar difference between our disapprobation of demerit, and that of impropriety.

PART III—OF THE FOUNDATION OF OUR JUDGEMENTS CONCERNING OUR OWN SENTIMENTS AND CONDUCT, AND OF THE SENSE OF DUTY

CHAP. I—OF THE PRINCIPLE OF SELF-APPROBATION AND OF SELF-DISAPPROBATION

In the two foregoing parts of this discourse, I have chiefly con- **800** sidered the origin and foundation of our judgements concerning the sentiments and conduct of others. I come now to consider more particularly the origin of those concerning our own.

The principle by which we naturally either approve or disapprove of our own conduct, seems to be altogether the same with that by which we exercise the like judgements concerning the conduct of other people. We either approve or disapprove of the conduct of another man according as we feel that, when we bring his case home to ourselves, we either can or cannot entirely sympathize with the sentiments and motives which directed it. And, in the same manner, we either approve or disapprove of our own conduct, according as we feel that, when we place ourselves in the situation of another man, and view it, as it were, with his eyes and from his station, we either can or cannot entirely enter into and sympathize with the sentiments and motives which influenced it. We can never survey our own sentiments and motives, we can never form any judgement concerning them; unless we remove ourselves, as it were, from our own natural station, and endeavour to view them as at a certain distance from us. But we can do this in no other way than by endeavouring to view them with the eyes of other people, or as other people are likely to view them. Whatever judgement we can form concerning them, accordingly, must always bear some secret reference, either to what are, or to what, upon a certain condition, would be, or to what, we imagine, ought to be the judgement of others. We endeavour to examine our own conduct as we imagine any other fair and impartial spectator would examine it. If, upon placing ourselves in his situation, we thoroughly enter into all the passions and motives which influenced it, we approve of it, by sympathy with the approbation of this supposed equitable judge. If otherwise, we enter into his disapprobation, and condemn it.

801   Were it possible that a human creature could grow up to manhood in some solitary place, without any communication with his own species, he could no more think of his own character, of the propriety or demerit of his own sentiments and conduct, of the beauty or deformity of his own mind, than of the beauty or deformity of his own face. All these are objects which he cannot easily see, which naturally he does not look at, and with regard to which he is provided with no mirror which can present them to his view. Bring him into society, and he is immediately provided with the mirror[1]

[1 Cf. Hume, § 593.]

which he wanted before. It is placed in the countenance and behaviour of those he lives with, which always mark when they enter
into, and when they disapprove of his sentiments; and it is here that
he first views the propriety and impropriety of his own passions,
the beauty and deformity of his own mind. To a man who from
his birth was a stranger to society, the objects of his passions, the
external bodies which either pleased or hurt him, would occupy his
whole attention. The passions themselves, the desires or aversions,
the joys or sorrows, which those objects excited, though of all
things the most immediately present to him, could scarce ever be
the objects of his thoughts. The idea of them could never interest
him so much as to call upon his attentive consideration. The consideration of his joy could in him excite no new joy, nor that of his
sorrow any new sorrow, though the consideration of the causes of
those passions might often excite both. Bring him into society, and
all his own passions will immediately become the cause of new
passions. He will observe that mankind approve of some of them,
and are disgusted by others. He will be elevated in the one case,
and cast down in the other: his desires and aversions, his joys and
sorrows, will now often become the causes of new desires and
new aversions, new joys and new sorrows: they will now, therefore, interest him deeply, and often call upon his most attentive
consideration.

Our first ideas of personal beauty and deformity, are drawn from **802**
the shape and appearance of others, not from our own. We soon
become sensible, however, that others exercise the same criticism
upon us. We are pleased when they approve of our figure, and are
disobliged when they seem to be disgusted. We become anxious to
know how far our appearance deserves either their blame or approbation. We examine our persons limb by limb, and by placing ourselves before a looking-glass, or by some such expedient, endeavour,
as much as possible, to view ourselves at the distance and with
the eyes of other people. If, after this examination, we are satisfied
with our own appearance, we can more easily support the most
disadvantageous judgements of others. If, on the contrary, we are
sensible that we are the natural objects of distaste, every appearance of
their disapprobation mortifies us beyond all measure. A man who is
tolerably handsome, will allow you to laugh at any little irregularity
in his person; but all such jokes are commonly unsupportable to one

who is really deformed. It is evident, however, that we are anxious about our own beauty and deformity, only upon account of its effect upon others. If we had no connection with society, we should be altogether indifferent about either.

803 In the same manner our first moral criticisms are exercised upon the characters and conduct of other people; and we are all very forward to observe how each of these affects us. But we soon learn, that other people are equally frank with regard to our own. We become anxious to know how far we deserve their censure or applause, and whether to them we must necessarily appear those agreeable or disagreeable creatures which they represent us. We begin, upon this account, to examine our own passions and conduct, and to consider how these must appear to them, by considering how they would appear to us if in their situation. We suppose ourselves the spectators of our own behaviour, and endeavour to imagine what effect it would, in this light, produce upon us. This is the only looking-glass by which we can, in some measure, with the eyes of other people, scrutinize the propriety of our own conduct. If in this view it pleases us, we are tolerably satisfied. We can be more indifferent about the applause, and, in some measure, despise the censure of the world; secure that, however misunderstood or misrepresented, we are the natural and proper objects of approbation. On the contrary, if we are doubtful about it, we are often, upon that very account, more anxious to gain their approbation, and, provided we have not already, as they say, shaken hands with infamy, we are altogether distracted at the thoughts of their censure, which then strikes us with double severity.

804 When I endeavour to examine my own conduct, when I endeavour to pass sentence upon it, and either to approve or condemn it, it is evident that, in all such cases, I divide myself, as it were, into two persons; and that I, the examiner and judge, represent a different character from that other I, the person whose conduct is examined into and judged of. The first is the spectator, whose sentiments with regard to my own conduct I endeavour to enter into, by placing myself in his situation, and by considering how it would appear to me, when seen from that particular point of view. The second is the agent, the person whom I properly call myself, and of whose conduct, under the character of a spectator, I was endeavouring to form some opinion. The first is the judge; the second the person judged of.

But that the judge should, in every respect, be the same with the person judged of, is as impossible, as that the cause should, in every respect, be the same with the effect.

To be amiable and to be meritorious; that is, to deserve love and to deserve reward, are the great characters of virtue; and to be odious and punishable, of vice. But all these characters have an immediate reference to the sentiments of others. Virtue is not said to be amiable, or to be meritorious, because it is the object of its own love, or of its own gratitude; but because it excites those sentiments in other men. The consciousness that it is the object of such favourable regards, is the source of that inward tranquillity and self-satisfaction with which it is naturally attended, as the suspicion of the contrary gives occasion to the torments of vice. What so great happiness as to be beloved, and to know that we deserve to be beloved? What so great misery as to be hated, and to know that we deserve to be hated?

CHAP. II—OF THE LOVE OF PRAISE, AND OF THAT OF PRAISEWORTHINESS; AND OF THE DREAD OF BLAME, AND OF THAT OF BLAME-WORTHINESS

Man naturally desires, not only to be loved, but to be lovely; or 805 to be that thing which is the natural and proper object of love. He naturally dreads, not only to be hated, but to be hateful; or to be that thing which is the natural and proper object of hatred. He desires, not only praise, but praise-worthiness; or to be that thing which, though it should be praised by nobody, is, however, the natural and proper object of praise. He dreads, not only blame, but blame-worthiness; or to be that thing which, though it should be blamed by nobody, is, however, the natural and proper object of blame.

The love of praise-worthiness is by no means derived altogether 806 from the love of praise. Those two principles, though they resemble one another, though they are connected, and often blended with one another, are yet, in many respects, distinct and independent of one another.

The love and admiration which we naturally conceive for those whose character and conduct we approve of, necessarily dispose us to desire to become ourselves the objects of the like agreeable sentiments, and to be as amiable and as admirable as those whom we love and admire the most. Emulation, the anxious desire that we ourselves should excel, is originally founded in our admiration of the excellence of others. Neither can we be satisfied with being merely admired for what other people are admired. We must at least believe ourselves to be admirable for what they are admirable. But, in order to attain this satisfaction, we must become the impartial spectators of our own character and conduct. We must endeavour to view them with the eyes of other people, or as other people are likely to view them. When seen in this light, if they appear to us as we wish, we are happy and contented. But it greatly confirms this happiness and contentment when we find that other people, viewing them with those very eyes with which we, in imagination only, were endeavouring to view them, see them precisely in the same light in which we ourselves had seen them. Their approbation necessarily confirms our own self-approbation. Their praise necessarily strengthens our own sense of our own praise-worthiness. In this case, so far is the love of praise-worthiness from being derived altogether from that of praise; that the love of praise seems, at least in a great measure, to be derived from that of praise-worthiness.

*   *   *   *

807   Praise and blame express what actually are; praise-worthiness and blame-worthiness, what naturally ought to be the sentiments of other people with regard to our character and conduct. The love of praise is the desire of obtaining the favourable sentiments of our brethren. The love of praise-worthiness is the desire of rendering ourselves the proper objects of those sentiments. So far those two principles resemble and are akin to one another. The like affinity and resemblance take place between the dread of blame and that of blame-worthiness.

*   *   *   *

808   Very few men can be satisfied with their own private consciousness that they have attained those qualities, or performed those actions, which they admire and think praise-worthy in other people; unless it is, at the same time, generally acknowledged that they possess the one, or have performed the other; or, in other words, unless they have actually obtained that praise which they think due both to the one and to the other. In this respect, however, men differ

considerably from one another. Some seem indifferent about the praise, when, in their own minds, they are perfectly satisfied that they have attained the praise-worthiness. Others appear much less anxious about the praise-worthiness than about the praise.

No man can be completely, or even tolerably satisfied, with **809** having avoided every thing blame-worthy in his conduct; unless he has likewise avoided the blame or the reproach. A wise man may frequently neglect praise, even when he has best deserved it; but, in all matters of serious consequence, he will most carefully endeavour so to regulate his conduct as to avoid, not only blame-worthiness, but, as much as possible, every probable imputation of blame. He will never, indeed, avoid blame by doing any thing which he judges blame-worthy; by omitting any part of his duty, or by neglecting any opportunity of doing any thing which he judges to be really and greatly praise-worthy. But, with these modifications, he will most anxiously and carefully avoid it. To show much anxiety about praise, even for praise-worthy actions, is seldom a mark of great wisdom, but generally of some degree of weakness. But, in being anxious to avoid the shadow of blame or reproach, there may be no weakness, but frequently the most praise-worthy prudence.

'Many people,' says Cicero, 'despise glory, who are yet most severely mortified by unjust reproach; and that most inconsistently.' This inconsistency, however, seems to be founded in the unalterable principles of human nature.

The all-wise Author of Nature has, in this manner, taught man to **810** respect the sentiments and judgements of his brethren; to be more or less pleased when they approve of his conduct, and to be more or less hurt when they disapprove of it. He has made man, if I may say so, the immediate judge of mankind; and has, in this respect, as in many others, created him after his own image, and appointed him his vicegerent upon earth, to superintend the behaviour of his brethren. They are taught by nature, to acknowledge that power and jurisdiction which has thus been conferred upon him, to be more or less humbled and mortified when they have incurred his censure, and to be more or less elated when they have obtained his applause.

But though man has, in this manner, been rendered the immediate **811** judge of mankind, he has been rendered so only in the first instance; and an appeal lies from his sentence to a much higher tribunal, to the tribunal of their own consciences, to that of the supposed impartial and well-informed spectator, to that of the man within the breast, the great judge and arbiter of their conduct. The jurisdictions of those two tribunals are founded upon principles which, though in some respects resembling and akin, are, however, in reality different and distinct. The jurisdiction of the man without, is founded altogether in the desire of actual praise, and in the aversion to actual blame. The jurisdiction of the man within, is founded altogether in the desire of praise-worthiness, and in the aversion to blame-worthiness; in the desire of possessing those qualities, and performing those actions, which we love and admire in other people; and in the dread of possessing those qualities, and performing those actions, which we hate and despise in other people. If the man without should applaud us, either for actions which we have not performed, or for motives which had no influence upon us; the man within can immediately humble that pride and elevation of mind which such groundless acclamations might otherwise occasion, by telling us, that as we know that we do not deserve them, we render ourselves despicable by accepting them. If, on the contrary, the man without should reproach us, either for actions which we never performed, or for motives which had no influence upon those which we may have performed; the man within may immediately correct this false judgement, and assure us, that we are by no means the proper objects of that censure which has so unjustly been bestowed upon us. But in this and in some other cases, the man within seems sometimes, as it were, astonished and confounded by the vehemence and clamour of the man without. The violence and loudness, with which blame is sometimes poured out upon us, seems to stupefy and benumb our natural sense of praise-worthiness and blame-worthiness; and the judgements of the man within, though not, perhaps, absolutely altered or perverted, are, however, so much shaken in the steadiness and firmness of their decision, that their natural effect, in securing the tranquillity of the mind, is frequently in a great measure destroyed. We scarce dare to absolve ourselves, when all our brethren appear loudly to condemn us. The supposed impartial spectator of our conduct seems to give his opinion in our favour with fear and hesitation; when that of all the real spectators, when that of all those with whose eyes and from whose station he endeavours to consider it, is unanimously and violently against us. In such cases, this demigod within the breast appears, like the demigods of the poets, though partly of immortal, yet partly too of mortal extraction. When his judgements are steadily and firmly directed by the sense of praise-worthiness and blame-worthiness, he seems to act suitably to his divine extraction: but when he suffers himself to be astonished and confounded by the judgements of ignorant and weak man, he dis-covers his connection with mortality, and appears to act suitably, rather to the human, than to the divine, part of his origin.

*   *   *   *

CHAP. IV—OF THE NATURE OF SELF-DECEIT, AND OF THE ORIGIN AND USE OF GENERAL RULES

In order to pervert the rectitude of our own judgements concern- **812** ing the propriety of our own conduct, it is not always necessary that the real and impartial spectator should be at a great distance. When he is at hand, when he is present, the violence and injustice of our own selfish passions are sometimes sufficient to induce the man within the breast to make a report very different from what the real circumstances of the case are capable of authorizing.

There are two different occasions upon which we examine our own conduct, and endeavour to view it in the light in which the impartial spectator would view it: first, when we are about to act; and secondly, after we have acted. Our views are apt to be very partial in both cases; but they are apt to be most partial when it is of most importance that they should be otherwise.

When we are about to act, the eagerness of passion will seldom **813** allow us to consider what we are doing, with the candour of an indifferent person. The violent emotions which at that time agitate us, discolour our views of things, even when we are endeavouring to place ourselves in the situation of another, and to regard the objects that interest us in the light in which they will naturally appear to him. The fury of our own passions constantly calls us back to our own place, where every thing appears magnified and mis-represented by self-love. Of the manner in which those objects would appear to another, of the view which he would take of them, we can obtain, if I may say so, but instantaneous glimpses, which vanish in a moment, and which, even while they last, are not alto-gether just. We cannot even for that moment divest ourselves entirely of the heat and keenness with which our peculiar situation inspires us, nor consider what we are about to do with the complete impartiality of an equitable judge. The passions, upon this account, as father Malebranche says,[1] all justify themselves, and seem reasonable and proportioned to their objects, as long as we continue to feel them.

814 When the action is over, indeed, and the passions which prompted it have subsided, we can enter more coolly into the sentiments of the indifferent spectator. What before interested us is now become almost as indifferent to us as it always was to him, and we can now examine our own conduct with his candour and impartiality. The man of to-day is no longer agitated by the same passions which distracted the man of yesterday: and when the paroxysm of emotion, in the same manner as when the paroxysm of distress, is fairly over, we can identify ourselves, as it were, with the ideal man within the breast, and, in our own character, view, as in the one case, our own situation, so in the other, our own conduct, with the severe eyes of the most impartial spectator. But our judgements now are often of little importance in comparison of what they were before; and can frequently produce nothing but vain regret and unavailing repentance; without always securing us from the like errors in time to come.

★   ★   ★   ★

815 So partial are the views of mankind with regard to the propriety of their own conduct, both at the time of action and after it; and so difficult is it for them to view it in the light in which any indifferent spectator would consider it. But if it was by a peculiar faculty, such as the moral sense is supposed to be, that they judged of their own conduct, if they were endued with a particular power of perception, which distinguished the beauty or deformity of passions and affections; as their own passions would be more immediately exposed to the view of this faculty, it would judge with more accuracy concerning them, than concerning those of other men, of which it had only a more distant prospect.

816 This self-deceit, this fatal weakness of mankind, is the source of half the disorders of human life. If we saw ourselves in the light in which others see us, or in which they would see us if they knew all, a reformation would generally be unavoidable. We could not otherwise endure the sight.

[1 Cf. Hutcheson, § 322.]

Nature, however, has not left this weakness, which is of so much importance, altogether without a remedy; nor has she abandoned us entirely to the delusions of self-love. Our continual observations upon the conduct of others, insensibly lead us to form to ourselves certain general rules concerning what is fit and proper either to be done or to be avoided. Some of their actions shock all our natural sentiments. We hear every body about us express the like detestation against them. This still further confirms, and even exasperates our natural sense of their deformity. It satisfies us that we view them in the proper light, when we see other people view them in the same light. We resolve never to be guilty of the like, nor ever, upon any account, to render ourselves in this manner the objects of universal disapprobation. We thus naturally lay down to ourselves a general rule, that all such actions are to be avoided, as tending to render us odious, contemptible, or punishable, the objects of all those sentiments for which we have the greatest dread and aversion. Other actions, on the contrary, call forth our approbation, and we hear every body around us express the same favourable opinion concerning them. Every body is eager to honour and reward them. They excite all those sentiments for which we have by nature the strongest desire; the love, the gratitude, the admiration of mankind. We become ambitious of performing the like; and thus naturally lay down to ourselves a rule of another kind, that every opportunity of acting in this manner is carefully to be sought after.

It is thus that the general rules of morality are formed. They are **817** ultimately founded upon experience of what, in particular instances, our moral faculties, our natural sense of merit and propriety, approve, or disapprove of. We do not originally approve or condemn particular actions; because, upon examination, they appear to be agreeable or inconsistent with a certain general rule. The general rule, on the contrary, is formed, by finding from experience, that all actions of a certain kind, or circumstanced in a certain manner, are approved or disapproved of. To the man who first saw an inhuman murder, committed from avarice, envy, or unjust resentment, and upon one too that loved and trusted the murderer, who beheld the last agonies of the dying person, who heard him, with his expiring breath, complain more of the perfidy and ingratitude of his false friend, than of the violence which had been done to him, there could be no occasion, in order to conceive how horrible such an action was, that he should reflect, that one of the most sacred rules of conduct was what prohibited the taking away the life of an innocent person, that this was a plain violation of that rule, and consequently a very blameable action. His detestation of this crime, it is evident, would arise instantaneously and antecedent to his having formed to himself any such general rule. The general rule, on the contrary, which he might afterwards form, would be founded upon the detestation which he felt necessarily arise in his own breast, at the thought of this, and every other particular action of the same kind.

★ ★ ★ ★

818 When these general rules, indeed, have been formed, when they are universally acknowledged and established, by the concurring sentiments of mankind, we frequently appeal to them as to the standards of judgement, in debating concerning the degree of praise or blame that is due to certain actions of a complicated and dubious nature. They are upon these occasions commonly cited as the ultimate foundations of what is just and unjust in human conduct; and this circumstance seems to have misled several very eminent authors, to draw up their systems in such a manner, as if they had supposed that the original judgements of mankind with regard to right and wrong, were formed like the decisions of a court of judicatory, by considering first the general rule, and then, secondly, whether the particular action under consideration fell properly within its comprehension.

819 Those general rules of conduct, when they have been fixed in our mind by habitual reflection, are of great use in correcting the misrepresentations of self-love concerning what is fit and proper to be done in our particular situation. The man of furious resentment, if he was to listen to the dictates of that passion, would perhaps regard the death of his enemy, as but a small compensation for the wrong, he imagines, he has received; which, however, may be no more than a very slight provocation. But his observations upon the conduct of others, have taught him how horrible all such sanguinary revenges appear. Unless his education has been very singular, he has laid it down to himself as an inviolable rule, to abstain from them upon all occasions. This rule preserves its authority with him, and renders him incapable of being guilty of such a violence. Yet the fury of his own temper may be such, that had this been the first time in which

he considered such an action, he would undoubtedly have determined it to be quite just and proper, and what every impartial spectator would approve of. But that reverence for the rule which past
experience has impressed upon him, checks the impetuosity of his
passion, and helps him to correct the too partial views which self-
love might otherwise suggest, of what was proper to be done in his
situation. If he should allow himself to be so far transported by
passion as to violate this rule, yet, even in this case, he cannot throw
off altogether the awe and respect with which he has been accustomed to regard it.

★　　　★　　　★　　　★

CHAP. V—OF THE INFLUENCE AND AUTHORITY OF THE GENERAL
RULES OF MORALITY, AND THAT THEY ARE JUSTLY REGARDED
AS THE LAWS OF THE DEITY

The regard to those general rules of conduct, is what is properly **820**
called a sense of duty, a principle of the greatest consequence in
human life, and the only principle by which the bulk of mankind
are capable of directing their actions. Many men behave very
decently, and through the whole of their lives avoid any considerable
degree of blame, who yet, perhaps, never felt the sentiment upon
the propriety of which we found our approbation of their conduct,
but acted merely from a regard to what they saw were the established
rules of behaviour.

★　　　★　　　★　　　★

This reverence is still further enhanced by an opinion which is **821**
first impressed by nature, and afterwards confirmed by reasoning
and philosophy, that those important rules of morality are the commands and laws of the Deity, who will finally reward the obedient,
and punish the transgressors of their duty.

This opinion or apprehension, I say, seems first to be impressed by
nature. Men are naturally led to ascribe to those mysterious beings,
whatever they are, which happen, in any country, to be the
objects of religious fear, all their own sentiments and passions. . . .
And thus religion, even in its rudest form, gave a sanction to the
rules of morality, long before the age of artificial reasoning and
philosophy. That the terrors of religion should thus enforce the

natural sense of duty, was of too much importance to the happiness of mankind, for nature to leave it dependent upon the slowness and uncertainty of philosophical researches.

822 These researches, however, when they came to take place, confirmed those original anticipations of nature. Upon whatever we suppose that our moral faculties are founded, whether upon a certain modification of reason, upon an original instinct, called a moral sense, or upon some other principle of our nature, it cannot be doubted, that they were given us for the direction of our conduct in this life. They carry along with them the most evident badges of this authority,[1] which denote that they were set up within us to be the supreme arbiters of all our actions, to superintend all our senses, passions, and appetites, and to judge how far each of them was either to be indulged or restrained. Our moral faculties are by no means, as some have pretended, upon a level in this respect with the other faculties and appetites of our nature, endowed with no more right to restrain these last, than these last are to restrain them. No other faculty or principle of action judges of any other. Love does not judge of resentment, nor resentment of love. Those two passions may be opposite to one another, but cannot, with any propriety, be said to approve or disapprove of one another. But it is the peculiar office of those faculties now under our consideration to judge, to bestow censure or applause upon all the other principles of our nature. They may be considered as a sort of senses of which those principles are the objects. Every sense is supreme over its own objects. There is no appeal from the eye with regard to the beauty of colours, nor from the ear with regard to the harmony of sounds, nor from the taste with regard to the agreeableness of flavours. Each of those senses judges in the last resort of its own objects. Whatever gratifies the taste is sweet, whatever pleases the eye is beautiful, whatever soothes the ear is harmonious. The very essence of each of those qualities consists in its being fitted to please the sense to which it is addressed. It belongs to our moral faculties, in the same manner to determine when the ear ought to be soothed, when the eye ought to be indulged, when the taste ought to be gratified, when and how far every other principle of our nature ought either to be indulged or restrained. What is agreeable to our moral faculties, is fit, and right, and proper to be done; the contrary, wrong,

[1 Cf. Butler, §§ 379–81, 399–402, 406; Hartley, § 653; Price, § 713.]

unfit, and improper. The sentiments which they approve of, are graceful and becoming: the contrary, ungraceful and unbecoming. The very words, right, wrong, fit, improper, graceful, unbecoming, mean only what pleases or displeases those faculties.

Since these, therefore, were plainly intended to be the governing **823** principles of human nature,[1] the rules which they prescribe are to be regarded as the commands and laws of the Deity, promulgated by those vicegerents which he has thus set up within us. All general rules are commonly denominated laws: thus the general rules which bodies observe in the communication of motion, are called the laws of motion. But those general rules which our moral faculties observe in approving or condemning whatever sentiment or action is subjected to their examination, may much more justly be denominated such. They have a much greater resemblance to what are properly called laws, those general rules which the sovereign lays down to direct the conduct of his subjects. Like them they are rules to direct the free actions of men: they are prescribed most surely by a lawful superior, and are attended too with the sanction of rewards and punishments. Those vicegerents of God within us, never fail to punish the violation of them, by the torments of inward shame, and self-condemnation; and on the contrary, always reward obedience with tranquillity of mind, with contentment, and self-satisfaction.

*   *   *   *

PART IV—OF THE EFFECT OF UTILITY UPON THE SENTIMENT OF APPROBATION

CHAP. I—OF THE BEAUTY WHICH THE APPEARANCE OF UTILITY BESTOWS UPON ALL THE PRODUCTIONS OF ART, AND OF THE EXTENSIVE INFLUENCE OF THIS SPECIES OF BEAUTY

That utility is one of the principal sources of beauty has been **824** observed by every body, who has considered with any attention what constitutes the nature of beauty. The conveniency of a house gives pleasure to the spectator as well as its regularity, and he is as much hurt when he observes the contrary defect, as when he sees the correspondent windows of different forms, or the door not placed exactly in the middle of the building. That the fitness of any

[1 Cf. Butler, § 395.]

system or machine to produce the end for which it was intended, bestows a certain propriety and beauty upon the whole, and renders the very thought and contemplation of it agreeable, is so very obvious that nobody has overlooked it.

The cause too, why utility pleases, has of late been assigned by an ingenious and agreeable philosopher,[1] who joins the greatest depth of thought to the greatest elegance of expression, and possesses the singular and happy talent of treating the abstrusest subjects not only with the most perfect perspicuity, but with the most lively eloquence. The utility of any object, according to him, pleases the master by perpetually suggesting to him the pleasure or conveniency which it is fitted to promote. Every time he looks at it, he is put in mind of this pleasure; and the object in this manner becomes a source of perpetual satisfaction and enjoyment. The spectator enters by sympathy into the sentiments of the master, and necessarily views the object under the same agreeable aspect. When we visit the palaces of the great, we cannot help conceiving the satisfaction we should enjoy if we ourselves were the masters, and were possessed of so much artful and ingeniously contrived accommodation. A similar account is given why the appearance of inconveniency should render any object disagreeable both to the owner and to the spectator.

825 But that this fitness, this happy contrivance of any production of art, should often be more valued, than the very end for which it was intended; and that the exact adjustment of the means for attaining any conveniency or pleasure, should frequently be more regarded, than that very conveniency or pleasure, in the attainment of which their whole merit would seem to consist, has not, so far as I know, been yet taken notice of by any body. That this however is very frequently the case, may be observed in a thousand instances, both in the most frivolous and in the most important concerns of human life.

When a person comes into his chamber, and finds the chairs all standing in the middle of the room, he is angry with his servant, and rather than see them continue in that disorder, perhaps takes the trouble himself to set them all in their places with their backs to the wall. The whole propriety of this new situation arises from its superior conveniency in leaving the floor free and disengaged. To attain this conveniency he voluntarily puts himself to more trouble

[1 Hume; cf. §§ 547, 574–5.]

than all he could have suffered from the want of it; since nothing was more easy, than to have set himself down upon one of them, which is probably what he does when his labour is over. What he wanted therefore, it seems, was not so much this conveniency, as that arrangement of things which promotes it. Yet it is this conveniency which ultimately recommends that arrangement, and bestows upon it the whole of its propriety and beauty.

*   *   *   *

Nor is it only with regard to such frivolous objects that our **826** conduct is influenced by this principle; it is often the secret motive of the most serious and important pursuits of both private and public life.

The poor man's son, whom heaven in its anger has visited with ambition, when he begins to look around him, admires the condition of the rich. He finds the cottage of his father too small for his accommodation, and fancies he should be lodged more at his ease in a palace. He is displeased with being obliged to walk a-foot, or to endure the fatigue of riding on horseback. He sees his superiors carried about in machines, and imagines that in one of these he could travel with less inconveniency. He feels himself naturally indolent, and willing to serve himself with his own hands as little as possible; and judges, that a numerous retinue of servants would save him from a great deal of trouble. He thinks if he had attained all these, he would sit still contentedly, and be quiet, enjoying himself in the thought of the happiness and tranquillity of his situation. He is enchanted with the distant idea of this felicity. It appears in his fancy like the life of some superior rank of beings, and, in order to arrive at it, he devotes himself for ever to the pursuit of wealth and greatness. To obtain the conveniencies which these afford, he submits in the first year, nay in the first month of his application, to more fatigue of body and more uneasiness of mind than he could have suffered through the whole of his life from the want of them. He studies to distinguish himself in some laborious profession. With the most unrelenting industry he labours night and day to acquire talents superior to all his competitors. He endeavours next to bring those talents into public view, and with equal assiduity solicits every opportunity of employment. For this purpose he makes his court to all mankind; he serves those whom he hates, and is obsequious to

those whom he despises. Through the whole of his life he pursues
the idea of a certain artificial and elegant repose which he may never
arrive at, for which he sacrifices a real tranquillity that is at all times
in his power, and which, if in the extremity of old age he should at
last attain to it, he will find to be in no respect preferable to that
humble security and contentment which he had abandoned for it.
It is then, in the last dregs of life, his body wasted with toil and
diseases, his mind galled and ruffled by the memory of a thousand
injuries and disappointments which he imagines he has met with
from the injustice of his enemies, or from the perfidy and ingratitude
of his friends, that he begins at last to find that wealth and greatness
are mere trinkets of frivolous utility, no more adapted for procuring
ease of body or tranquillity of mind than the tweezer-cases of the
lover of toys; and like them too, more troublesome to the person
who carries them about with him than all the advantages they can
827 afford him are commodious. . . . If we examine, however, why the
spectator distinguishes with such admiration the condition of the
rich and the great, we shall find that it is not so much upon account
of the superior ease or pleasure which they are supposed to enjoy,
as of the numberless artificial and elegant contrivances for promoting
this ease or pleasure. He does not even imagine that they are really
happier than other people: but he imagines that they possess more
means of happiness. And it is the ingenious and artful adjustment of
those means to the end for which they were intended, that is the
principal source of his admiration. But in the languor of disease
and the weariness of old age, the pleasures of the vain and empty
distinctions of greatness disappear. To one, in this situation, they are
no longer capable of recommending those toilsome pursuits in which
they had formerly engaged him. In his heart he curses ambition, and
vainly regrets the ease and indolence of youth, pleasures which are
fled for ever, and which he has foolishly sacrificed for what, when he
has got it, can afford him no real satisfaction. In this miserable aspect
does greatness appear to every man when reduced either by spleen
or disease to observe with attention his own situation, and to consider what it is that is really wanting to his happiness. Power and
riches appear then to be, what they are, enormous and operose
machines contrived to produce a few trifling conveniencies to the
body, consisting of springs the most nice and delicate, which must
be kept in order with the most anxious attention, and which in spite

of all our care are ready every moment to burst into pieces, and to crush in their ruins their unfortunate possessor. They are immense fabrics, which it requires the labour of a life to raise, which threaten every moment to overwhelm the person that dwells in them, and which while they stand, though they may save him from some smaller inconveniencies, can protect him from none of the severer inclemencies of the season. They keep off the summer shower, not the winter storm, but leave him always as much, and sometimes more exposed than before, to anxiety, to fear, and to sorrow; to disease, to danger, and to death.

But though this splenetic philosophy, which in time of sickness or **828** low spirits is familiar to every man, thus entirely depreciates those great objects of human desire, when in better health and in better humour, we never fail to regard them under a more agreeable aspect. Our imagination, which in pain and sorrow seems to be confined and cooped up within our own persons, in times of ease and prosperity expands itself to every thing around us. We are then charmed with the beauty of that accommodation which reigns in the palaces and economy of the great; and admire how every thing is adapted to promote their ease, to prevent their wants, to gratify their wishes, and to amuse and entertain their most frivolous desires. If we consider the real satisfaction which all these things are capable of affording, by itself and separated from the beauty of that arrangement which is fitted to promote it, it will always appear in the highest degree contemptible and trifling. But we rarely view it in this abstract and philosophical light. We naturally confound it in our imagination with the order, the regular and harmonious movement of the system, the machine or economy by means of which it is produced. The pleasures of wealth and greatness, when considered in this complex view, strike the imagination as something grand and beautiful and noble, of which the attainment is well worth all the toil and anxiety which we are so apt to bestow upon it.

And it is well that nature imposes upon us in this manner. It is **829** this deception which rouses and keeps in continual motion the industry of mankind. It is this which first prompted them to cultivate the ground, to build houses, to found cities and commonwealths, and to invent and improve all the sciences and arts, which ennoble and embellish human life; which have entirely changed the whole face of the globe, have turned the rude forests of nature into agreeable and fertile plains, and made the trackless and barren ocean a new fund of subsistence, and the great high road of communication to the different nations of the earth. The earth by these labours of mankind has been obliged to redouble her natural fertility, and to maintain a greater multitude of inhabitants. It is to no purpose, that the proud and unfeeling landlord views his extensive fields, and without a thought for the wants of his brethren, in imagination consumes himself the whole harvest that grows upon them. The homely and vulgar proverb, that the eye is larger than the belly, never was more fully verified than with regard to him. The capacity of his stomach bears no proportion to the immensity of his desires, and will receive no more than that of the meanest peasant. The rest he is obliged to distribute among those, who prepare, in the nicest manner, that little which he himself makes use of, among those who fit up the palace in which this little is to be consumed, among those who provide and keep in order all the different baubles and trinkets, which are employed in the economy of greatness; all of whom thus derive from his luxury and caprice, that share of the necessaries of life, which they would in vain have expected from his humanity or his justice. The produce of the soil maintains at all times nearly that number of inhabitants which it is capable of maintaining. The rich only select from the heap what is most precious and agreeable. They consume little more than the poor, and in spite of their natural selfishness and rapacity, though they mean only their own conveniency, though the sole end which they propose from the labours of all the thousands whom they employ, be the gratification of their own vain and insatiable desires, they divide with the poor the produce of all their improvements. They are led by an invisible hand to make nearly the same distribution of the necessaries of life, which would have been made, had the earth been divided into equal portions among all its inhabitants, and thus without intending it, without knowing it, advance the interest of the society, and afford means to the multiplication of the species. When Providence divided the earth among a few lordly masters, it neither forgot nor abandoned those who seemed to have been left out in the partition. These last too enjoy their share of all that it produces. In what constitutes the real happiness of human life, they are in no respect inferior to those who would seem so much above them. In ease of body and peace of mind, all the different ranks of life are nearly upon a level, and the beggar,

who suns himself by the side of the highway, possesses that security
which kings are fighting for.

★   ★   ★   ★

CHAP. II—OF THE BEAUTY WHICH THE APPEARANCE OF UTILITY
BESTOWS UPON THE CHARACTERS AND ACTIONS OF MEN; AND
HOW FAR THE PERCEPTION OF THIS BEAUTY MAY BE REGARDED
AS ONE OF THE ORIGINAL PRINCIPLES OF APPROBATION

The characters of men, as well as the contrivances of art, or the **830**
institutions of civil government, may be fitted either to promote or
to disturb the happiness both of the individual and of the society.
The prudent, the equitable, the active, resolute, and sober character
promises prosperity and satisfaction, both to the person himself
and to every one connected with him. The rash, the insolent, the
slothful, effeminate, and voluptuous, on the contrary, forebodes
ruin to the individual, and misfortune to all who have any thing to
do with him. The first turn of mind has at least all the beauty which
can belong to the most perfect machine that was ever invented for
promoting the most agreeable purpose: and the second, all the deformity of the most awkward and clumsy contrivance. What institution of government could tend so much to promote the happiness
of mankind as the general prevalence of wisdom and virtue? All
government is but an imperfect remedy for the deficiency of these.
Whatever beauty, therefore, can belong to civil government upon
account of its utility, must in a far superior degree belong to these.
On the contrary, what civil policy can be so ruinous and destructive
as the vices of men? The fatal effects of bad government arise from
nothing, but that it does not sufficiently guard against the mischiefs
which human wickedness gives occasion to.

This beauty and deformity which characters appear to derive from **831**
their usefulness or inconveniency, are apt to strike, in a peculiar
manner, those who consider, in an abstract and philosophical light,
the actions and conduct of mankind. When a philosopher goes to
examine why humanity is approved of, or cruelty condemned, he
does not always form to himself, in a very clear and distinct manner,
the conception of any one particular action either of cruelty or of
humanity, but is commonly contented with the vague and indeterminate idea which the general names of those qualities suggest to

him. But it is in particular instances only that the propriety or impropriety, the merit or demerit of actions is very obvious and discernible. It is only when particular examples are given that we perceive distinctly either the concord or disagreement between our own affections and those of the agent, or feel a social gratitude arise towards him in the one case, or a sympathetic resentment in the other. When we consider virtue and vice in an abstract and general manner, the qualities by which they excite these several sentiments seem in a great measure to disappear, and the sentiments themselves become less obvious and discernible. On the contrary, the happy effects of the one and the fatal consequences of the other seem then to rise up to the view, and as it were to stand out and distinguish themselves from all the other qualities of either.

832   The same ingenious and agreeable author who first explained why utility pleases, has been so struck with this view of things, as to resolve our whole approbation of virtue into a perception of this species of beauty which results from the appearance of utility. No qualities of the mind, he observes, are approved of as virtuous, but such as are useful or agreeable either to the person himself or to others;[1] and no qualities are disapproved of as vicious, but such as have a contrary tendency. And Nature, indeed, seems to have so happily adjusted our sentiments of approbation and disapprobation, to the conveniency both of the individual and of the society, that after the strictest examination it will be found, I believe, that this is universally the case. But still I affirm, that it is not the view of this utility or hurtfulness which is either the first or principal source of our approbation and disapprobation. These sentiments are no doubt enhanced and enlivened by the perception of the beauty or deformity which results from this utility or hurtfulness. But still, I say, they are originally and essentially different from this perception.

833   For first of all, it seems impossible that the approbation of virtue should be a sentiment of the same kind with that by which we approve of a convenient and well-contrived building; or that we should have no other reason for praising a man than that for which we commend a chest of drawers.[2]

And secondly, it will be found, upon examination, that the useful-ness of any disposition of mind is seldom the first ground of our

[1 Cf. Hume, §§ 560, 586.]   [2 But see Hume, § 574 n.]

approbation; and that the sentiment of approbation always involves in it a sense of propriety quite distinct from the perception of utility. We may observe this with regard to all the qualities which are approved of as virtuous, both those which, according to this system, are originally valued as useful to ourselves, as well as those which are esteemed on account of their usefulness to others.

★　　★　　★　　★

PART VII—OF SYSTEMS OF MORAL PHILOSOPHY

SECT. III—*Of the different systems which have been formed concerning the principle of approbation*

INTRODUCTION

After the inquiry concerning the nature of virtue, the next **834** question of importance in Moral Philosophy, is concerning the principle of approbation, concerning the power or faculty of the mind which renders certain characters agreeable or disagreeable to us, makes us prefer one tenor of conduct to another, denominate the one right and the other wrong, and consider the one as the object of approbation, honour, and reward; the other as that of blame, censure, and punishment.

Three different accounts have been given of this principle of approbation. According to some, we approve and disapprove both of our own actions and of those of others, from self-love only, or from some view of their tendency to our own happiness or disadvantage: according to others, reason, the same faculty by which we distinguish between truth and falsehood, enables us to distinguish between what is fit and unfit both in actions and affections: according to others, this distinction is altogether the effect of immediate sentiment and feeling, and arises from the satisfaction or disgust with which the view of certain actions or affections inspires us. Self-love, reason, and sentiment, therefore, are the three different sources which have been assigned for the principle of approbation.

Before I proceed to give an account of those different systems, **835** I must observe, that the determination of this second question, though of the greatest importance in speculation, is of none in practice.[1] The question concerning the nature of virtue necessarily has some influence upon our notions of right and wrong in many particular cases. That concerning the principle of approbation can possibly have no such effect. To examine from what contrivance or mechanism within, those different notions or sentiments arise, is a mere matter of philosophical curiosity.

CHAP. III—OF THOSE SYSTEMS WHICH MAKE SENTIMENT THE PRINCIPLE OF APPROBATION

836   Those systems which make sentiment the principle of approbation may be divided into two different classes.

I. According to some, the principle of approbation is founded upon a sentiment of a peculiar nature, upon a particular power of perception exerted by the mind at the view of certain actions or affections; some of which affecting this faculty in an agreeable and others in a disagreeable manner, the former are stamped with the characters of right, laudable, and virtuous; the latter with those of wrong, blameable, and vicious. This sentiment being of a peculiar nature distinct from every other, and the effect of a particular power of perception, they give it a particular name, and call it a moral sense.

II. According to others, in order to account for the principle of approbation, there is no occasion for supposing any new power of perception which had never been heard of before: Nature, they imagine, acts here, as in all other cases, with the strictest economy, and produces a multitude of effects from one and the same cause; and sympathy, a power which has always been taken notice of, and with which the mind is manifestly endowed, is, they think, sufficient to account for all the effects ascribed to this peculiar faculty.

837   I. Dr. Hutcheson* had been at great pains to prove that the principle of approbation was not founded on self-love. He had demonstrated too that it could not arise from any operation of reason. Nothing remained, he thought, but to suppose it a faculty of a peculiar kind, with which Nature had endowed the human mind, in order to produce this one particular and important effect. When self-love and reason were both excluded, it did not occur to

* Inquiry concerning Virtue.

[1 Cf. Hume, §§ 503, 634.]

him that there was any other known faculty of the mind which could in any respect answer this purpose.

This new power of perception he called a moral sense, and supposed it to be somewhat analogous to the external senses. As the bodies around us, by affecting these in a certain manner, appear to possess the different qualities of sound, taste, odour, colour; so the various affections of the human mind, by touching this particular faculty in a certain manner, appear to possess the different qualities of amiable and odious, of virtuous and vicious, of right and wrong.

★　　　★　　　★　　　★

But notwithstanding all the pains which this ingenious philo- **838** sopher has taken to prove that the principle of approbation is founded in a peculiar power of perception, somewhat analogous to the external senses, there are some consequences, which he acknowledges to follow from this doctrine, that will, perhaps, be regarded by many as a sufficient confutation of it. The qualities, he allows★, which belong to the objects of any sense, cannot, without the greatest absurdity, be ascribed to the sense itself. Who ever thought of calling the sense of seeing black or white, the sense of hearing loud or low, or the sense of tasting sweet or bitter? And, according to him, it is equally absurd to call our moral faculties virtuous or vicious, morally good or evil. These qualities belong to the objects of those faculties, not to the faculties themselves. If any man, therefore, was so absurdly constituted as to approve of cruelty and injustice as the highest virtues, and to disapprove of equity and humanity as the most pitiful vices, such a constitution of mind might indeed be regarded as inconvenient both to the individual and to the society, and likewise as strange, surprising, and unnatural in itself; but it could not, without the greatest absurdity, be denominated vicious or morally evil.

Yet surely if we saw any man shouting with admiration and applause at a barbarous and unmerited execution, which some insolent tyrant had ordered, we should not think we were guilty of any great absurdity in denominating this behaviour vicious and morally evil in the highest degree, though it expressed nothing but depraved moral faculties, or an absurd approbation of this horrid action, as of

★ Illustrations upon the Moral Sense, sect. i. p. 237, et seq.; third edition [i.e. Hutcheson, § 364].

what was noble, magnanimous, and great. Our heart, I imagine, at the sight of such a spectator, would forget for a while its sympathy with the sufferer, and feel nothing but horror and detestation, at the thought of so execrable a wretch. We should abominate him even more than the tyrant who might be goaded on by the strong passions of jealousy, fear, and resentment, and upon that account be more excusable. But the sentiments of the spectator would appear altogether without cause or motive, and therefore most perfectly and completely detestable. There is no perversion of sentiment or affection which our heart would be more averse to enter into, or which it would reject with greater hatred and indignation than one of this kind; and so far from regarding such a constitution of mind as being merely something strange or inconvenient, and not in any respect vicious or morally evil, we should rather consider it as the very last and most dreadful stage of moral depravity.

★   ★   ★   ★

839 It may be said, perhaps, that though the principle of approbation is not founded upon any power of perception that is in any respect analogous to the external senses, it may still be founded upon a peculiar sentiment[1] which answers this one particular purpose and no other. Approbation and disapprobation, it may be pretended, are certain feelings or emotions which arise in the mind upon the view of different characters and actions; and as resentment might be called a sense of injuries, or gratitude a sense of benefits, so these may very properly receive the name of a sense of right and wrong, or of a moral sense.

But this account of things, though it may not be liable to the same objections with the foregoing, is exposed to others which are equally unanswerable.

840 First of all, whatever variations any particular emotion may undergo, it still preserves the general features which distinguish it to be an emotion of such a kind, and these general features are always more striking and remarkable than any variation which it may undergo in particular cases. Thus anger is an emotion of a particular kind: and accordingly its general features are always more distinguishable than all the variations it undergoes in particular cases. Anger against a

[1 Cf. Hume, §§ 506–7.]

man is, no doubt, somewhat different from anger against a woman, and that again from anger against a child. In each of those three cases, the general passion of anger receives a different modification from the particular character of its object, as may easily be observed by the attentive. But still the general features of the passion predominate in all these cases. To distinguish these, requires no nice observation: a very delicate attention, on the contrary, is necessary to discover their variations: every body takes notice of the former; scarce any body observes the latter. If approbation and disapprobation, therefore, were, like gratitude and resentment, emotions of a particular kind, distinct from every other, we should expect that in all the variations which either of them might undergo, it would still retain the general features which mark it to be an emotion of such a particular kind, clear, plain, and easily distinguishable. But in fact it happens quite otherwise. If we attend to what we really feel when upon different occasions we either approve or disapprove, we shall find that our emotion in one case is often totally different from that in another, and that no common features can possibly be discovered between them. Thus the approbation with which we view a tender, delicate, and humane sentiment, is quite different from that with which we are struck by one that appears great, daring, and magnanimous.[1] Our approbation of both may, upon different occasions, be perfect and entire; but we are softened by the one, and we are elevated by the other, and there is no sort of resemblance between the emotions which they excite in us. But, according to that system which I have been endeavouring to establish, this must necessarily be the case. As the emotions of the person whom we approve of, are, in those two cases, quite opposite to one another, and as our approbation arises from sympathy with those opposite emotions, what we feel upon the one occasion, can have no sort of resemblance to what we feel upon the other. But this could not happen if approbation consisted in a peculiar emotion which had nothing in common with the sentiments we approved of, but which arose at the view of those sentiments, like any other passion at the view of its proper object. The same thing holds true with regard to disapprobation. Our horror for cruelty has no sort of resemblance to our contempt for mean-spiritedness. It is quite a different species of discord which we feel at the view of those two different vices, between our own

[1 Cf. §§ 781–2; and cf. Hume himself, § 612.]

minds and those of the person whose sentiments and behaviour we consider.

841 Secondly, I have already observed, that not only the different passions or affections of the human mind which are approved or disapproved of, appear morally good or evil, but that proper and improper approbation appear, to our natural sentiments, to be stamped with the same characters. I would ask, therefore, how it is, that, according to this system, we approve or disapprove of proper or improper approbation? To this question there is, I imagine, but one reasonable answer, which can possibly be given. It must be said, that when the approbation with which our neighbour regards the conduct of a third person coincides with our own, we approve of his approbation, and consider it as, in some measure, morally good; and that, on the contrary, when it does not coincide with our own sentiments, we disapprove of it, and consider it as, in some measure, morally evil. It must be allowed, therefore, that, at least in this one case, the coincidence or opposition of sentiments, between the observer and the person observed, constitutes moral approbation or disapprobation. And if it does so in this one case, I would ask, why not in every other? to what purpose imagine a new power of perception in order to account for those sentiments?

842 Against every account of the principle of approbation, which makes it depend upon a peculiar sentiment, distinct from every other, I would object; that it is strange that this sentiment, which Providence undoubtedly intended to be the governing principle of human nature, should hitherto have been so little taken notice of, as not to have got a name in any language. The word moral sense is of very late formation, and cannot yet be considered as making part of the English tongue. The word approbation has but within these few years been appropriated to denote peculiarly any thing of this kind. In propriety of language we approve of whatever is entirely to our satisfaction, of the form of a building, of the contrivance of a machine, of the flavour of a dish of meat. The word conscience does not immediately denote any moral faculty by which we approve or disapprove. Conscience supposes, indeed, the existence of some such faculty, and properly signifies our consciousness of having acted agreeably or contrary to its directions. When love, hatred, joy, sorrow, gratitude, resentment, with so many other passions which are all supposed to be the subjects of this principle, have made

themselves considerable enough to get titles to know them by, is it not surprising that the sovereign of them all should hitherto have been so little heeded, that, a few philosophers excepted, nobody has yet thought it worth while to bestow a name upon it?

When we approve of any character or action, the sentiments 843 which we feel, are, according to the foregoing system, derived from four sources, which are in some respects different from one another. First, we sympathize with the motives of the agent; secondly, we enter into the gratitude of those who receive the benefit of his actions; thirdly, we observe that his conduct has been agreeable to the general rules by which those two sympathies generally act; and, last of all, when we consider such actions as making a part of a system of behaviour which tends to promote the happiness either of the individual or of the society, they appear to derive a beauty from this utility, not unlike that which we ascribe to any well-contrived machine. After deducting, in any one particular case, all that must be acknowledged to proceed from some one or other of these four principles, I should be glad to know what remains, and I shall freely allow this overplus to be ascribed to a moral sense, or to any other peculiar faculty, provided any body will ascertain precisely what this overplus is. It might be expected, perhaps, that if there was any such peculiar principle, such as this moral sense is supposed to be, we should feel it, in some particular cases, separated and detached from every other, as we often feel joy, sorrow, hope, and fear, pure and unmixed with any other emotion. This however, I imagine, cannot even be pretended. I have never heard any instance alleged in which this principle could be said to exert itself alone and unmixed with sympathy or antipathy, with gratitude or resentment, with the perception of the agreement or disagreement of any action to an established rule, or last of all with that general taste for beauty and order which is excited by inanimated as well as by animated objects.

II. There is another system which attempts to account for the 844 origin of our moral sentiments from sympathy, distinct from that which I have been endeavouring to establish. It is that which places virtue in utility, and accounts for the pleasure with which the spectator surveys the utility of any quality from sympathy with the happiness of those who are affected by it. This sympathy is different both from that by which we enter into the motives of the agent, and from that by which we go along with the gratitude of the persons who are benefited by his actions. It is the same principle with that by which we approve of a well-contrived machine. But no machine can be the object of either of those two last-mentioned sympathies. I have already, in the fourth part of this discourse, given some account of this system.[1]

[1 See §§ 824, 832–3.]

WILLIAM PALEY

1743–1805

THE PRINCIPLES OF MORAL AND POLITICAL PHILOSOPHY

[First printed, 1785. Reprinted here from the sixteenth edition, 1806, with misprints corrected and spelling slightly modified]

WILLIAM PALEY

===

The Principles of Moral and Political Philosophy

BOOK I—PRELIMINARY CONSIDERATIONS

CHAP. VII—VIRTUE

Virtue is '*the doing good to mankind, in obedience to the will of God,* **845**
and for the sake of everlasting happiness.'

According to which definition, 'the good of mankind' is the subject; the 'will of God,' the rule;[1] and 'everlasting happiness,' the motive of human virtue.

*   *   *   *

BOOK II—MORAL OBLIGATION

CHAP. I—THE QUESTION, *WHY AM I OBLIGED TO KEEP MY WORD?* CONSIDERED

Why am I *obliged* to keep my word?   **846**

Because it is right, says one.—Because it is agreeable to the fitness of things, says another.—Because it is conformable to reason and nature, says a third.—Because it is conformable to truth, says a fourth.—Because it promotes the public good, says a fifth.—Because it is required by the will of God, concludes a sixth.

Upon which different accounts, two things are observable:—
FIRST, that they all ultimately coincide.

The fitness of things, means their fitness to produce happiness: the nature of things, means that actual constitution of the world, by which some things, as such and such actions, for example, produce

[1 Cf. Gay, § 464.]

happiness, and others misery: reason is the principle, by which we discover or judge of this constitution: truth, is this judgement expressed or drawn out into propositions. So that it necessarily comes to pass, that what promotes the public happiness, or happiness on the whole, is agreeable to the fitness of things, to nature, to reason, and to truth: and such (as will appear by-and-by) is the divine character, that what promotes the general happiness, is required by the will of God;[1] and what has all the above properties, must needs be *right*; for, right means no more than conformity to the rule we go by, whatever that rule be.

And this is the reason that moralists, from whatever different principles they set out, commonly meet in their conclusions; that is, they enjoin the same conduct, prescribe the same rules of duty, and, with a few exceptions, deliver upon dubious cases the same determinations.

847 SECONDLY, it is to be observed, that these answers all leave the matter *short*; for, the inquirer may turn round upon his teacher with a second question, in which he will expect to be satisfied, namely, *why* am I obliged to do what is right; to act agreeably to the fitness of things; to conform to reason, nature, or truth; to promote the public good, or to obey the will of God?

The proper method of conducting the inquiry is, FIRST, to examine what we mean, when we say a man is *obliged* to do any thing, and THEN to show *why* he is obliged to do the thing which we have proposed as an example, namely, 'to keep his word.'

CHAP. II—WHAT WE MEAN WHEN WE SAY A MAN IS *OBLIGED* TO DO A THING

848 A man is said to be *obliged*, '*when he is urged by a violent motive resulting from the command of another*.'

I. 'The motive must be violent.' If a person, who has done me some little service, or has a small place in his disposal, ask me upon some occasion for my vote, I may possibly give it him, from a motive of gratitude or expectation: but I should hardly say that I was *obliged* to give it him; because the inducement does not rise high enough. Whereas if a father or a master, any great benefactor, or one

[1 Cf. Gay, § 465.]

on whom my fortune depends, require my vote, I give it him of course: and my answer to all who ask me why I voted so and so, is, that my father or my master *obliged* me; that I had received so many favours from, or had so great a dependence upon, such a one, that I was *obliged* to vote as he directed me.

SECONDLY, 'It must result from the command of another.' Offer a man a gratuity for doing any thing, for seizing, for example, an offender, he is not *obliged* by your offer to do it; nor would he say he is; though he may be *induced, persuaded, prevailed upon, tempted.* If a magistrate or the man's immediate superior command it, he considers himself as *obliged* to comply, though possibly he would lose less by a refusal in this case, than in the former.

I will not undertake to say that the words *obligation* and *obliged* are **849** used uniformly in this sense, or always with this distinction: nor is it possible to tie down popular phrases to any constant signification: but wherever the motive is violent enough, and coupled with the idea of command, authority, law, or the will of a superior, there, I take it, we always reckon ourselves to be *obliged*.

And from this account of obligation it follows, that we can be obliged to nothing, but what we ourselves are to gain or lose something by: for nothing else can be a 'violent motive' to us. As we should not be obliged to obey the laws, or the magistrate, unless rewards or punishments, pleasure or pain, somehow or other, depended upon our obedience; so neither should we, without the same reason, be obliged to do what is right, to practise virtue, or to obey the commands of God.

CHAP. III—THE QUESTION, *WHY AM I OBLIGED TO KEEP MY WORD?* RESUMED

Let it be remembered, that to be *obliged*, 'is to be urged by a **850** violent motive, resulting from the command of another.'

And then let it be asked, Why am I *obliged* to keep my word? and the answer will be, Because I am 'urged to do so by a violent motive' (namely, the expectation of being after this life rewarded, if I do, or punished for it, if I do not,) 'resulting from the command of another,' (namely, of God).

This solution goes to the bottom of the subject, as no further question can reasonably be asked.

Therefore, private happiness is our motive, and the will of God our rule.

851   When I first turned my thoughts to moral speculations, an air of mystery seemed to hang over the whole subject; which arose, I believe, from hence,—that I supposed, with many authors whom I had read, that to be *obliged* to do a thing, was very different from being *induced* only to do it; and that the obligation to practise virtue, to do what is right, just, etc. was quite another thing, and of another kind, than the obligation which a soldier is under to obey his officer, a servant his master; or any of the civil and ordinary obligations of human life. Whereas, from what has been said it appears, that moral obligation is like all other obligations; and that *obligation* is nothing more than an *inducement* of sufficient strength, and resulting, in some way, from the command of another.

852   There is always understood to be a difference between an act of *prudence* and an act of *duty*. Thus, if I distrusted a man who owed me a sum of money, I should reckon it an act of prudence to get another person bound with him; but I should hardly call it an act of duty. On the other hand, it would be thought a very unusual and loose kind of language, to say, that, as I had made such a promise, it was *prudent* to perform it; or that, as my friend, when he went abroad, placed a box of jewels in my hands, it would be *prudent* in me to preserve it for him till he returned.

Now, in what, you will ask, does the difference consist? inasmuch as, according to our account of the matter, both in the one case and the other, in acts of duty as well as acts of prudence, we consider solely what we ourselves shall gain or lose by the act.

The difference, and the only difference, is this; that, in the one case we consider what we shall gain or lose in the present world; in the other case, we consider also what we shall gain or lose in the world to come.

★   ★   ★   ★

CHAP. IV—THE WILL OF GOD

853   As the will of God is our rule, to inquire what is our duty, or what we are obliged to do, in any instance, is, in effect, to inquire, what is the will of God in that instance? which consequently becomes the whole business of morality.

Now there are two methods of coming at the will of God on any point:

I. By his express declarations, when they are to be had, and which must be sought for in Scripture.

II. By what we can discover of his designs and disposition from his works; or, as we usually call it, the light of nature.

*   *   *   *

The method of coming at the will of God, concerning any action, by the light of nature, is to inquire into 'the tendency of the action to promote or diminish the general happiness.' This rule proceeds upon the presumption, that God Almighty wills and wishes the happiness of his creatures; and, consequently, that those actions, which promote that will and wish, must be agreeable to him; and the contrary.

*   *   *   *

CHAP. VI—UTILITY

So then actions are to be estimated by their tendency*. Whatever **854** is expedient, is right. It is the utility of any moral rule alone which constitutes the obligation of it.

But to all this there seems a plain objection, viz. that many actions are useful, which no man in his senses will allow to be right. There are occasions, in which the hand of the assassin would be very useful. The present possessor of some great estate employs his influence and fortune, to annoy, corrupt, or oppress all about him. His estate would devolve, by his death, to a successor of an opposite character. It is useful, therefore, to dispatch such a one as soon as possible out of the way; as the neighbourhood will exchange thereby a pernicious tyrant for a wise and generous benefactor. It might be useful to rob a miser, and give the money to the poor; as the money, no doubt, would produce more happiness, by being laid out in food and clothing for half a dozen distressed families, than by continuing locked up

---

* Actions in the abstract are right or wrong, according to their *tendency*; the agent is virtuous or vicious, according to his *design*. Thus, if the question be, Whether relieving common beggars be right or wrong? we inquire into the *tendency* of such a conduct to the public advantage or inconvenience. If the question be, Whether a man remarkable for this sort of bounty is to be esteemed virtuous for that reason? we inquire into his *design*, whether his liberality sprang from charity or from ostentation? It is evident that our concern is with actions in the abstract.

in a miser's chest. It may be useful to get possession of a place, a piece of preferment, or of a seat in parliament, by bribery or false swearing: as by means of them we may serve the public more effectually than in our private station. What then shall we say? Must we admit these actions to be right, which would be to justify assassination, plunder, and perjury; or must we give up our principle, that the criterion of right is utility?

It is not necessary to do either.

The true answer is this; that these actions, after all, are not useful, and for that reason, and that alone, are not right.

855   To see this point perfectly, it must be observed that the bad consequences of actions are twofold, *particular* and *general*.

The particular bad consequence of an action is, the mischief which that single action directly and immediately occasions.

The general bad consequence is, the violation of some necessary or useful *general* rule.

Thus, the particular bad consequence of the assassination above described, is the fright and pain which the deceased underwent; the loss he suffered of life, which is as valuable to a bad man, as to a good one, or more so; the prejudice and affliction, of which his death was the occasion, to his family, friends, and dependants.

The general bad consequence is the violation of this necessary general rule, that no man be put to death for his crimes, but by public authority.

Although, therefore, such an action have no particular bad consequences, or greater particular good consequences, yet it is not useful, by reason of the general consequence, which is of more importance, and which is evil. And the same of the other two instances, and of a million more, which might be mentioned.

But as this solution supposes, that the moral government of the world must proceed by general rules, it remains that we show the necessity of this.

THOMAS REID

1710–1796

ESSAYS ON THE ACTIVE POWERS OF MAN

[First printed, 1788. Reprinted here from the first edition, with reduction of initial capital letters and slight modification of spelling]

THOMAS REID

―――

Essays on the Active Powers of Man

ESSAY III—OF THE PRINCIPLES OF ACTION

PART III—*Of the rational principles of action*

CHAP. I—THERE ARE RATIONAL PRINCIPLES OF ACTION IN MAN

Mechanical principles of action produce their effect without any **856** will or intention on our part. We may, by a voluntary effort, hinder the effect; but if it be not hindered by will and effort, it is produced without them.

Animal principles of action require intention and will in their operation, but not judgement. They are, by ancient moralists, very properly called *caecae cupidines*, blind desires.

Having treated of these two classes, I proceed to the third, the *rational* principles of action in man; which have that name, because they can have no existence in beings not endowed with reason, and, in all their exertions, require, not only intention and will, but judgement or reason.

That talent which we call *reason*, by which men that are adult and **857** of a sound mind, are distinguished from brutes, idiots, and infants, has, in all ages, among the learned and unlearned, been conceived to have two offices, to regulate our belief, and to regulate our actions and conduct.

Whatever we believe, we think agreeable to reason, and, on that account, yield our assent to it. Whatever we disbelieve, we think contrary to reason, and, on that account, dissent from it. Reason therefore is allowed to be the principle by which our belief and opinions ought to be regulated.

But reason has been no less universally conceived to be a principle, by which our actions ought to be regulated.

To act reasonably, is a phrase no less common in all languages, than to judge reasonably. We immediately approve of a man's conduct, when it appears that he had good reason for what he did. And every action we disapprove, we think unreasonable, or contrary to reason.

A way of speaking so universal among men, common to the learned and the unlearned in all nations, and in all languages, must have a meaning. To suppose it to be words without meaning,[1] is to treat, with undue contempt, the common sense of mankind.

858   Supposing this phrase to have a meaning, we may consider in what way reason may serve to regulate human conduct, so that some actions of men are to be denominated reasonable, and others unreasonable.

I take it for granted, that there can be no exercise of reason without judgement, nor, on the other hand, any judgement of things, abstract and general, without some degree of reason.

If, therefore, there be any principles of action in the human constitution, which, in their nature, necessarily imply such judgement, they are the principles which we may call rational, to distinguish them from animal principles, which imply desire and will, but not judgement.

859   Every deliberate human action must be done either as the means, or as an end; as the means to some end, to which it is subservient, or as an end, for its own sake, and without regard to any thing beyond it.

That it is a part of the office of reason to determine, what are the proper means to any end which we desire, no man ever denied. But some philosophers, particularly Mr Hume,[2] think that it is no part of the office of reason to determine the ends we ought to pursue, or the preference due to one end above another. This, he thinks, is not the office of reason, but of taste or feeling.

If this be so, reason cannot, with any propriety, be called a principle of action. Its office can only be to minister to the principles of action, by discovering the means of their gratification. Accordingly Mr Hume maintains,[3] that reason is no principle of action; but that it is, and ought to be, the servant of the passions.

860   I shall endeavour to show, that, among the various ends of human

[1 See Hume, §§ 490–1.]   [2 See Hume, §§ 480–1, 594–5, 606–7.]
[3 See Hume, § 482.]

actions, there are some, of which, without reason, we could not even form a conception; and that, as soon as they are conceived, a regard to them is, by our constitution, not only a principle of action, but a leading and governing principle, to which all our animal principles are subordinate, and to which they ought to be subject.

These I shall call *rational* principles; because they can exist only in beings endowed with reason, and because, to act from these principles, is what has always been meant by acting according to reason.

The ends of human actions I have in view, are two, to wit, what is good for us upon the whole, and what appears to be our duty. They are very strictly connected, lead to the same course of conduct,[1] and co-operate with each other; and, on that account, have commonly been comprehended under one name, that of *reason*. But as they may be disjoined, and are really distinct principles of action, I shall consider them separately.

CHAP. II—OF REGARD TO OUR GOOD ON THE WHOLE

It will not be denied that man, when he comes to years of under- **861** standing, is led by his rational nature, to form the conception of what is good for him upon the whole.

★　　　★　　　★　　　★

In the first part of life we have many enjoyments of various kinds; but very similar to those of brute-animals.

They consist in the exercise of our senses and powers of motion, the gratification of our appetites, and the exertions of our kind affections. These are chequered with many evils of pain, and fear, and disappointment, and sympathy with the sufferings of others.

But the goods and evils of this period of life are of short duration, and soon forgot. The mind being regardless of the past, and unconcerned about the future, we have then no other measure of good but the present desire; no other measure of evil but the present aversion.

★　　　★　　　★　　　★

As we grow up to understanding, we extend our view both **862** forward and backward. We reflect upon what is past, and, by the lamp of experience, discern what will probably happen in time to

[1 Cf. Butler, §§ 408–9.]

come. We find that many things which we eagerly desired, were too dearly purchased, and that things grievous for the present, like nauseous medicines, may be salutary in the issue.

We learn to observe the connections of things, and the consequences of our actions; and, taking an extended view of our existence, past, present, and future, we correct our first notions of good and ill, and form the conception of what is good or ill upon the whole; which must be estimated, not from the present feeling, or from the present animal desire or aversion, but from a due consideration of its consequences, certain or probable, during the whole of our existence.

That which, taken with all its discoverable connections and consequences, brings more good than ill, I call *good upon the whole*.

That brute-animals have any conception of this good, I see no reason to believe. And it is evident, that man cannot have the conception of it, till reason is so far advanced, that he can seriously reflect upon the past, and take a prospect of the future part of his existence.

It appears therefore, that the very conception of what is good or ill for us upon the whole, is the offspring of reason, and can be only in beings endowed with reason. And if this conception give rise to any principle of action in man, which he had not before, that principle may very properly be called a rational principle of action.

★   ★   ★   ★

863   I observe, in the *next* place, that as soon as we have the conception of what is good or ill for us upon the whole, we are led, by our constitution, to seek the good and avoid the ill; and this becomes not only a principle of action, but a leading or governing principle,[1] to which all our animal principles ought to be subordinate.

★   ★   ★   ★

It appears that it is not without just cause, that this principle of action has in all ages been called *reason*, in opposition to our animal principles, which in common language are called by the general name of the *passions*.

The first not only operates in a calm and cool manner,[2] like reason, but implies real judgement in all its operations. The second, to wit,

[1 Cf. Butler, §§ 400, 409.]
[2 Cf. Butler, §§ 382, 393, 400; Hutcheson, § 357; Price, § 761.]

the passions, are blind desires of some particular object,[1] without any judgement or consideration, whether it be good for us upon the whole, or ill.

It appears also, that the fundamental maxim of prudence, and of **864** all good morals, that the passions ought, in all cases, to be under the dominion of reason, is not only self-evident, when rightly understood, but is expressed according to the common use and propriety of language.

The contrary maxim maintained by Mr Hume,[2] can only be defended by a gross and palpable abuse of words. For, in order to defend it, he must include under the *passions*,[3] that very principle which has always, in all languages, been called *reason*, and never was, in any language, called a *passion*. And from the meaning of the word *reason* he must exclude the most important part of it, by which we are able to discern and to pursue what appears to be good upon the whole. And thus, including the most important part of reason under passion, and making the least important part of reason to be the whole, he defends his favourite paradox, that reason is, and ought to be, the servant of the passions.

To judge of what is true or false in speculative points, is the office **865** of speculative reason; and to judge of what is good or ill for us upon the whole, is the office of practical reason. Of true and false there are no degrees; but of good and ill there are many degrees, and many kinds; and men are very apt to form erroneous opinions concerning them; misled by their passions, by the authority of the multitude, and by other causes.

Wise men, in all ages, have reckoned it a chief point of wisdom, to make a right estimate of the goods and evils of life. They have laboured to discover the errors of the multitude on this important point, and to warn others against them.

$$\ast \qquad \ast \qquad \ast \qquad \ast$$

From this we may see, that this rational principle of a regard to **866** our good upon the whole, gives us the conception of a *right* and a *wrong* in human conduct, at least of a *wise* and a *foolish*. It produces a kind of self-approbation,[4] when the passions and appetites are kept

---

[1 Cf. Butler, §§ 401, 414.]   [2 See Hume, §§ 479–84.]
[3 See Hume, § 485.]   [4 Cf. Butler, § 433.]

in their due subjection to it; and a kind of remorse and compunction, when it yields to them.

In these respects, this principle is so similar to the moral principle, or conscience, and so interwoven with it, that both are commonly comprehended under the name of *reason*. This similarity led many of the ancient philosophers, and some among the moderns, to resolve conscience, or a sense of duty, entirely into a regard to what is good for us upon the whole.

That they are distinct principles of action, though both lead to the same conduct in life, I shall have occasion to show, when I come to treat of *conscience*.

CHAP. V—OF THE NOTION OF DUTY, RECTITUDE, MORAL OBLIGATION

867   A being endowed with the animal principles of action only, may be capable of being trained to certain purposes by discipline, as we see many brute-animals are, but would be altogether incapable of being governed by law.

The subject of law must have the conception of a general rule of conduct, which, without some degree of reason, he cannot have. He must likewise have a sufficient inducement to obey the law, even when his strongest animal desires draw him the contrary way.

This inducement may be a sense of interest, or a sense of duty, or both concurring.

These are the only principles I am able to conceive, which can reasonably induce a man to regulate all his actions according to a certain general rule or law. They may therefore be justly called the *rational* principles of action, since they can have no place but in a being endowed with reason, and since it is by them only, that man is capable either of political or of moral government.

★   ★   ★   ★

868   A man is prudent when he consults his real interest, but he cannot be virtuous, if he has no regard to duty.

I proceed now to consider this regard to duty as a rational principle of action in man, and as that principle alone by which he is capable either of virtue or vice.

I shall first offer some observations with regard to the general notion of duty, and its contrary, or of right and wrong in human conduct, and then consider how we come to judge and determine certain things in human conduct to be right, and others to be wrong.

With regard to the notion or conception of duty, I take it to be **869** too simple to admit of a logical definition.[1]

We can define it only by synonymous words or phrases, or by its properties and necessary concomitants,[2] as when we say that it is what we ought to do, what is fair and honest, what is approvable, what every man professes to be the rule of his conduct, what all men praise, and what is in itself laudable, though no man should praise it.

I observe, in the *next* place, that the notion of duty cannot be **870** resolved into that of interest, or what is most for our happiness.[3]

Every man may be satisfied of this who attends to his own conceptions, and the language of all mankind shows it. When I say, this is my interest, I mean one thing; when I say, it is my duty, I mean another thing. And though the same course of action, when rightly understood, may be both my duty and my interest, the conceptions are very different. Both are reasonable motives to action, but quite distinct in their nature.

I presume it will be granted, that in every man of real worth, there **871** is a principle of honour, a regard to what is honourable or dishonourable, very distinct from a regard to his interest. It is folly in a man to disregard his interest, but to do what is dishonourable is baseness. The first may move our pity, or, in some cases, our contempt, but the last provokes our indignation.

As these two principles are different in their nature, and not resolvable into one, so the principle of honour is evidently superior in dignity to that of interest.

No man would allow him to be a man of honour, who should plead his interest to justify what he acknowledged to be dishonourable; but to sacrifice interest to honour never costs a blush.

★   ★   ★   ★

This principle of honour, which is acknowledged by all men who pretend to character, is only another name for what we call a regard to duty, to rectitude, to propriety of conduct. It is a moral obligation

[1 Cf. Price, § 672.]   [2 Cf. Hutcheson, § 358; Price, § 672.]
[3 Cf. Price, § 710.]

which obliges a man to do certain things because they are right, and not to do other things because they are wrong.

*　　*　　*　　*

Men of rank call it *honour*, and too often confine it to certain virtues that are thought most essential to their rank. The vulgar call it *honesty*, *probity*, *virtue*, *conscience*. Philosophers have given it the names of *the moral sense, the moral faculty, rectitude*.

872　The universality of this principle in men that are grown up to years of understanding and reflection, is evident. The words that express it, the names of the virtues which it commands, and of the vices which it forbids, the *ought* and *ought not* which express its dictates, make an essential part of every language.[1] The natural affections of respect to worthy characters, of resentment of injuries, of gratitude for favours, of indignation against the worthless, are parts of the human constitution which suppose a right and a wrong in conduct. Many transactions that are found necessary in the rudest societies go upon the same supposition. In all testimony, in all promises, and in all contracts, there is necessarily implied a moral obligation on one party, and a trust in the other, grounded upon this obligation.

The variety of opinions among men in points of morality, is not greater, but, as I apprehend, much less than in speculative points; and this variety is as easily accounted for, from the common causes of error, in the one case as in the other; so that it is not more evident, that there is a real distinction between true and false, in matters of speculation, than that there is a real distinction between right and wrong in human conduct.

*　　*　　*　　*

873　If we examine the abstract notion of duty, or moral obligation, it appears to be neither any real quality of the action considered by itself, nor of the agent considered without respect to the action, but a certain relation between the one and the other.

When we say a man ought to do such a thing, the *ought*, which expresses the moral obligation, has a respect, on the one hand, to the person who ought, and, on the other, to the action which he ought to do. Those two correlates are essential to every moral obligation;

[1 Cf. Butler, § 429.]

take away either, and it has no existence. So that, if we seek the place of moral obligation among the categories, it belongs to the category of *relation*.

    ★   ★   ★   ★

Perhaps it may not be improper to point out briefly the circum- **874** stances, both in the action and in the agent, which are necessary to constitute moral obligation. The universal agreement of men in these, shows that they have one and the same notion of it.

With regard to the action, it must be a voluntary action, or presta- tion of the person obliged, and not of another. There can be no moral obligation upon a man to be six feet high. Nor can I be under a moral obligation that another person should do such a thing. His actions must be imputed to himself, and mine only to me, either for praise or blame.

    ★   ★   ★   ★

The person obliged must have understanding and will, and some **875** degree of active power. He must not only have the natural faculty of understanding, but the means of knowing his obligation. An invincible ignorance of this destroys all moral obligation.

The opinion of the agent in doing the action gives it its moral denomination. If he does a materially good action, without any belief of its being good, but from some other principle, it is no good action in him. And if he does it with the belief of its being ill, it is ill in him.[1]

Thus, if a man should give to his neighbour a potion which he really believes will poison him, but which, in the event, proves salutary, and does much good; in moral estimation, he is a poisoner, and not a benefactor.

These qualifications of the action and of the agent, in moral obligation, are self-evident; and the agreement of all men in them shows, that all men have the same notion and a distinct notion of moral obligation.

CHAP. VI—OF THE SENSE OF DUTY

We are next to consider, how we learn to judge and determine, **876** that this is right, and that is wrong.

The abstract notion of moral good and ill would be of no use to

[1 Cf. Price, §§ 750–1, 755.]

direct our life, if we had not the power of applying it to particular actions, and determining what is morally good, and what is morally ill.

Some philosophers, with whom I agree, ascribe this to an original power or faculty in man, which they call the *moral sense*, the *moral faculty*, *conscience*. Others think, that our moral sentiments may be accounted for without supposing any original sense or faculty appropriated to that purpose, and go into very different systems to account for them.

I am not, at present, to take any notice of those systems, because the opinion first mentioned seems to me to be the truth, to wit, that, by an original power of the mind, when we come to years of understanding and reflection, we not only have the notions of right and wrong in conduct, but perceive certain things to be right, and others to be wrong.

877　The name of the *moral sense*, though more frequently given to conscience since Lord Shaftesbury and Dr Hutcheson wrote, is not new.[1] The *sensus recti et honesti* is a phrase not unfrequent among the ancients, neither is the *sense of duty* among us.

It has got this name of *sense*, no doubt, from some analogy which it is conceived to bear to the external senses.[2] And if we have just notions of the office of the external senses, the analogy is very evident, and I see no reason to take offence, as some have done, at the name of the *moral sense*.

878　The offence taken at this name seems to be owing to this, that philosophers have degraded the senses too much, and deprived them of the most important part of their office.

We are taught, that, by the senses, we have only certain ideas which we could not have otherwise. They are represented as powers by which we have sensations and ideas, not as powers by which we judge.

This notion of the senses I take to be very lame, and to contradict what nature and accurate reflection teach concerning them.

A man who has totally lost the sense of seeing, may retain very distinct notions of the various colours; but he cannot judge of colours, because he has lost the sense by which alone he could judge. By my eyes I not only have the ideas of a square and a circle, but I perceive this surface to be a square, that to be a circle.

[1 Contrast Smith, § 842.]　　　　[2 Cf. Smith, §§ 837-8.]

By my ear, I not only have the idea of sounds, loud and soft, acute and grave, but I immediately perceive and judge this sound to be loud, that to be soft, this to be acute, that to be grave. Two or more synchronous sounds I perceive to be concordant, others to be discordant.

These are judgements of the senses. They have always been called and accounted such, by those whose minds are not tinctured by philosophical theories. They are the immediate testimony of nature by our senses; and we are so constituted by nature, that we must receive their testimony, for no other reason but because it is given by our senses.

In vain do sceptics endeavour to overturn this evidence by metaphysical reasoning. Though we should not be able to answer their arguments, we believe our senses still, and rest our most important concerns upon their testimony.

If this be a just notion of our external senses, as I conceive it is, **879** our moral faculty may, I think, without impropriety, be called the *moral sense*.

In its dignity it is, without doubt, far superior to every other power of the mind; but there is this analogy between it and the external senses, that, as by them we have not only the original conceptions of the various qualities of bodies, but the original judgements that this body has such a quality, that such another; so by our moral faculty, we have both the original conceptions of right and wrong in conduct, of merit and demerit, and the original judgements that this conduct is right, that is wrong; that this character has worth, that, demerit.

The testimony of our moral faculty, like that of the external senses, is the testimony of nature, and we have the same reason to rely upon it.

The truths immediately testified by the external senses are the first principles from which we reason, with regard to the material world, and from which all our knowledge of it is deduced.

The truths immediately testified by our moral faculty, are the first principles of all moral reasoning, from which all our knowledge of our duty must be deduced.

* * * *

All reasoning must be grounded on first principles. This holds in moral reasoning, as in all other kinds. There must therefore be in morals, as in all other sciences, first or self-evident principles, on which all moral reasoning is grounded, and on which it ultimately rests. From such self-evident principles, conclusions may be drawn synthetically with regard to the moral conduct of life; and particular duties or virtues may be traced back to such principles, analytically. But, without such principles, we can no more establish any conclusion in morals, than we can build a castle in the air, without any foundation.

★   ★   ★   ★

ESSAY IV—OF THE LIBERTY OF MORAL AGENTS

CHAP. IV—OF THE INFLUENCE OF MOTIVES

880   The modern advocates for the doctrine of necessity lay the stress of their cause upon the influence of motives.

'Every deliberate action, they say, must have a motive. When there is no motive on the other side, this motive must determine the agent: when there are contrary motives, the strongest must prevail: we reason from men's motives to their actions, as we do from other causes to their effects:[1] if man be a free agent, and be not governed by motives, all his actions must be mere caprice, rewards and punishments can have no effect,[2] and such a being must be absolutely ungovernable.'

In order therefore to understand distinctly, in what sense we ascribe moral liberty to man, it is necessary to understand what influence we allow to motives. To prevent misunderstanding, which has been very common upon this point, I offer the following observations:

881   1. I grant that all rational beings are influenced, and ought to be influenced by motives. But the influence of motives is of a very different nature from that of efficient causes.[3] They are neither causes nor agents. They suppose an efficient cause, and can do nothing without it. We cannot, without absurdity, suppose a motive, either to act, or to be acted upon; it is equally incapable of action and of passion; because it is not a thing that exists, but a thing that is conceived; it is what the schoolmen called an *ens rationis*. Motives, therefore, may *influence* to action, but they do not act. They may be compared to advice, or exhortation, which leaves a man still

[1 Cf. Hume, § 619.]   [2 Cf. Hume, § 628.]   [3 Cf. Price, § 753 n.]

at liberty. For in vain is advice given when there is not a power either to do, or to forbear what it recommends. In like manner, motives suppose liberty in the agent, otherwise they have no influence at all.

It is a law of nature, with respect to matter, that every motion, and change of motion, is proportional to the force impressed, and in the direction of that force. The scheme of necessity supposes a similar law to obtain in all the actions of intelligent beings; which, with little alteration, may be expressed thus: every action, or change of action, in an intelligent being, is proportional to the force of motives impressed, and in the direction of that force.

The law of nature respecting matter, is grounded upon this principle: that matter is an inert, inactive substance, which does not act, but is acted upon; and the law of necessity must be grounded upon the supposition, that an intelligent being is an inert, inactive substance, which does not act, but is acted upon.

⋆   ⋆   ⋆   ⋆

5. When it is said, that of contrary motives the strongest always **882** prevails, this can neither be affirmed nor denied with understanding, until we know distinctly what is meant by the strongest motive.

I do not find, that those who have advanced this as a self-evident axiom, have ever attempted to explain what they mean by the strongest motive, or have given any rule by which we may judge which of two motives is the strongest.

How shall we know whether the strongest motive always prevails, if we know not which is strongest? There must be some test by which their strength is to be tried, some balance in which they may be weighed, otherwise, to say that the strongest motive always prevails, is to speak without any meaning. We must therefore search for this test or balance, since they who have laid so much stress upon this axiom, have left us wholly in the dark as to its meaning. I grant, that when the contrary motives are of the same kind, and differ only in quantity, it may be easy to say which is the strongest. Thus a bribe of a thousand pounds is a stronger motive than a bribe of a hundred pounds. But when the motives are of different kinds, as, money and fame, duty and worldly interest, health and strength, riches and honour, by what rule shall we judge which is the strongest motive?

Either we measure the strength of motives, merely by their **883** prevalence, or by some other standard distinct from their prevalence.

If we measure their strength merely by their prevalence, and by the strongest motive mean only the motive that prevails, it will be true indeed that the strongest motive prevails; but the proposition will be identical, and mean no more than that the strongest motive is the strongest motive. From this surely no conclusion can be drawn.

884 If it should be said, that by the strength of a motive is not meant its prevalence, but the cause of its prevalence; that we measure the cause by the effect, and from the superiority of the effect conclude the superiority of the cause, as we conclude that to be the heaviest weight which bears down the scale: I answer, that, according to this explication of the axiom, it takes for granted that motives are the causes, and the sole causes of actions. Nothing is left to the agent, but to be acted upon by the motives, as the balance is by the weights. The axiom supposes, that the agent does not act, but is acted upon; and, from this supposition, it is concluded that he does not act. This is to reason in a circle, or rather it is not reasoning but begging the question.

Contrary motives may very properly be compared to advocates pleading the opposite sides of a cause at the bar. It would be very weak reasoning to say, that such an advocate is the most powerful pleader, because sentence was given on his side. The sentence is in the power of the judge, not of the advocate. It is equally weak reasoning, in proof of necessity, to say, such a motive prevailed, therefore it is the strongest; since the defenders of liberty maintain that the determination was made by the man, and not by the motive.

885 We are therefore brought to this issue, that unless some measure of the strength of motives can be found distinct from their prevalence, it cannot be determined, whether the strongest motive always prevails or not. If such a measure can be found and applied, we may be able to judge of the truth of this maxim, but not otherwise.

Every thing that can be called a motive, is addressed either to the animal or to the rational part of our nature. Motives of the former kind are common to us with the brutes; those of the latter are peculiar to rational beings. We shall beg leave, for distinction's sake, to call the former, *animal* motives, and the latter, *rational*.

886 Hunger is a motive in a dog to eat; so is it in a man. According to the strength of the appetite, it gives a stronger or a weaker impulse to eat. And the same thing may be said of every other appetite and passion. Such animal motives give an impulse to the agent, to which he yields with ease; and, if the impulse be strong, it cannot be resisted without an effort which requires a greater or a less degree of self-command. Such motives are not addressed to the rational powers. Their influence is immediately upon the will. We feel their influence, and judge of their strength, by the conscious effort which is necessary to resist them.

When a man is acted upon by contrary motives of this kind, he finds it easy to yield to the strongest. They are like two forces pushing him in contrary directions. To yield to the strongest, he needs only to be passive. By exerting his own force, he may resist; but this requires an effort of which he is conscious. The strength of motives of this kind is perceived, not by our judgement, but by our feeling; and that is the strongest of contrary motives, to which he can yield with ease, or which it requires an effort of self-command to resist; and this we may call the *animal test* of the strength of motives.

If it be asked, whether, in motives of this kind, the strongest always prevails? I would answer, that in brute-animals I believe it does. They do not appear to have any self-command; an appetite or passion in them is overcome only by a stronger contrary one. On this account, they are not accountable for their actions, nor can they be the subjects of law.

But in men who are able to exercise their rational powers, and have any degree of self-command, the strongest animal motive does not always prevail. The flesh does not always prevail against the spirit, though too often it does. And if men were necessarily determined by the strongest animal motive, they could no more be accountable, or capable of being governed by law, than brutes are.

Let us next consider rational motives, to which the name of *motive* **887** is more commonly and more properly given. Their influence is upon the judgement, by convincing us that such an action ought to be done, that it is our duty, or conducive to our real good, or to some end which we have determined to pursue.

They do not give a blind impulse to the will as animal motives do. They convince, but they do not impel, unless, as may often happen, they excite some passion of hope, or fear, or desire. Such passions may be excited by conviction, and may operate in its aid as other animal motives do. But there may be conviction without passion; and the conviction of what we ought to do, in order to some end which we have judged fit to be pursued, is what I call a *rational motive*.

Brutes, I think, cannot be influenced by such motives. They have not the conception of *ought* and *ought not*. Children acquire these conceptions as their rational powers advance; and they are found in all of ripe age, who have the human faculties.

If there be any competition between rational motives, it is evident, that the strongest, in the eye of reason, is that which it is most our duty and our real happiness to follow. Our duty and our real happiness are ends which are inseparable; and they are the ends which every man, endowed with reason, is conscious he ought to pursue in preference to all others. This we may call the *rational test* of the strength of motives. A motive which is the strongest, according to the animal test, may be, and very often is the weakest according to the rational.

888   The grand and the important competition of contrary motives is between the animal, on the one hand, and the rational on the other. This is the conflict between the flesh and the spirit, upon the event of which the character of men depends.

If it be asked, which of these is the strongest motive? The answer is, that the first is commonly strongest, when they are tried by the animal test. If it were not so, human life would be no state of trial. It would not be a warfare, nor would virtue require any effort or self-command. No man would have any temptation to do wrong. But, when we try the contrary motives by the rational test, it is evident, that the rational motive is always the strongest.

And now, I think, it appears, that the strongest motive, according to either of the tests I have mentioned, does not always prevail.

In every wise and virtuous action, the motive that prevails is the strongest according to the rational test, but commonly the weakest according to the animal. In every foolish, and in every vicious action, the motive that prevails is commonly the strongest according to the animal test, but always the weakest according to the rational.

889   6. It is true, that we reason from men's motives to their actions, and, in many cases, with great probability, but never with absolute certainty. And to infer from this, that men are necessarily determined by motives, is very weak reasoning.

For let us suppose, for a moment, that men have moral liberty, I would ask, what use may they be expected to make of this liberty? It may surely be expected, that, of the various actions within the sphere of their power, they will choose what pleases them most for the present, or what appears to be most for their real, though distant good. When there is a competition between these motives, the foolish will prefer present gratification; the wise the greater and more distant good.

Now, is not this the very way in which we see men act? Is it not from the presumption that they act in this way, that we reason from their motives to their actions? Surely it is. Is it not weak reasoning, therefore, to argue, that men have not liberty, because they act in that very way in which they would act if they had liberty? It would surely be more like reasoning to draw the contrary conclusion from the same premises.

7. Nor is it better reasoning to conclude, that, if men are not **890** necessarily determined by motives, all their actions must be capricious.

To resist the strongest animal motives when duty requires, is so far from being capricious, that it is, in the highest degree, wise and virtuous. And we hope this is often done by good men.

To act against rational motives, must always be foolish, vicious, or capricious. And, it cannot be denied, that there are too many such actions done. But is it reasonable to conclude, that because liberty may be abused by the foolish and the vicious, therefore it can never be put to its proper use, which is to act wisely and virtuously?

8. It is equally unreasonable to conclude, that if men are not neces- **891** sarily determined by motives, rewards and punishments would have no effect. With wise men they will have their due effect; but not always with the foolish and the vicious.

Let us consider what effect rewards and punishments do really, and in fact, produce, and what may be inferred from that effect, upon each of the opposite systems of liberty and of necessity.

I take it for granted that, in fact, the best and wisest laws, both human and divine, are often transgressed, notwithstanding the rewards and punishments that are annexed to them. If any should deny this fact, I know not how to reason with him.

From this fact, it may be inferred with certainty, upon the supposition of necessity, that, in every instance of transgression, the motive of reward or punishment was not of sufficient strength to produce obedience to the law. This implies a fault in the lawgiver; but there can be no fault in the transgressor, who acts mechanically by the force of motives. We might as well impute a fault to the balance, when it does not raise a weight of two pounds by the force of one pound.

Upon the supposition of necessity, there can be neither reward nor punishment, in the proper sense, as those words imply good and ill desert. Reward and punishment are only tools employed to produce a mechanical effect. When the effect is not produced, the tool must be unfit or wrong applied.

Upon the supposition of liberty, rewards and punishments will have a proper effect upon the wise and the good; but not so upon the foolish and the vicious, when opposed by their animal passions or bad habits; and this is just what we see to be the fact. Upon this supposition the transgression of the law implies no defect in the law, no fault in the lawgiver; the fault is solely in the transgressor. And it is upon this supposition only, that there can be either reward or punishment, in the proper sense of the words, because it is only on this supposition, that there can be good or ill desert.

ESSAY V—of morals

CHAP. IV—WHETHER AN ACTION DESERVING MORAL APPRO-BATION, MUST BE DONE WITH THE BELIEF OF ITS BEING MORALLY GOOD

892 There is no part of philosophy more subtle and intricate than that which is called *The Theory of Morals*. Nor is there any more plain and level to the apprehension of man than the practical part of morals.

In the former, the Epicurean, the Peripatetic and the Stoic, had each his different system of old; and almost every modern author of reputation has a system of his own. At the same time, there is no branch of human knowledge, in which there is so general an agreement among ancients and moderns, learned and unlearned, as in the practical rules of morals.

From this discord in the theory, and harmony in the practical part, we may judge, that the rules of morality stand upon another and a firmer foundation than the theory. And of this it is easy to perceive the reason.

For, in order to know what is right and what is wrong in human conduct, we need only listen to the dictates of our conscience when the mind is calm and unruffled, or attend to the judgement we form of others in like circumstances. But, to judge of the various theories of morals, we must be able to analyse and dissect, as it were, the active powers of the human mind, and especially to analyse accurately that conscience or moral power by which we discern right from wrong.

The conscience may be compared to the eye in this, as in many other respects. The learned and the unlearned see objects with equal distinctness. The former have no title to dictate to the latter, as far as the eye is judge, nor is there any disagreement about such matters. But, to dissect the eye, and to explain the theory of vision, is a difficult point, wherein the most skilful have differed.

From this remarkable disparity between our decisions in the theory **893** of morals and in the rules of morality, we may, I think, draw this conclusion, that wherever we find any disagreement between the practical rules of morality, which have been received in all ages, and the principles of any of the theories advanced upon this subject, the practical rules ought to be the standard by which the theory is to be corrected, and that it is both unsafe and unphilosophical to warp the practical rules, in order to make them tally with a favourite theory.

The question to be considered in this chapter belongs to the practical part of morals, and therefore is capable of a more easy and more certain determination. And, if it be determined in the affirmative, I conceive that it may serve as a touchstone to try some celebrated theories which are inconsistent with that determination, and which have led the theorists to oppose it by very subtle metaphysical arguments.

Every question about what is or is not the proper object of moral **894** approbation, belongs to practical morals, and such is the question now under consideration: whether actions deserving moral approbation must be done with the belief of their being morally good? Or, whether an action, done without any regard to duty or to the dictates of conscience, can be entitled to moral approbation?[1]

★　　　★　　　★　　　★

... It appears evident, therefore, that those actions only can truly be called virtuous, or deserving of moral approbation, which the agent believed to be right, and to which he was influenced, more or less, by that belief.

[1 Cf. Price, § 755, 758.]

If it should be objected, that this principle makes it to be of no consequence to a man's morals, what his opinions may be, providing he acts agreeably to them, the answer is easy.

Morality requires, not only that a man should act according to his judgement, but that he should use the best means in his power that his judgement be acccording to truth. If he fail in either of these points, he is worthy of blame;[1] but, if he fail in neither, I see not wherein he can be blamed.

★ ★ ★ ★

895 The last objection I shall mention is a metaphysical one urged by Mr Hume.

It is a favourite point in his system of morals, that justice is not a natural but an artificial virtue.[2] To prove this, he has exerted the whole strength of his reason and eloquence. And as the principle we are considering stood in his way, he takes pains to refute it.

'Suppose, says he,[3] a person to have lent me a sum of money, on condition that it be restored in a few days. After the expiration of the term he demands the sum. I ask, what reason or motive have I to restore the money? It will perhaps be said, that my regard to justice and abhorrence of villainy and knavery are sufficient reasons for me.' And this, he acknowledges, would be a satisfactory answer to a man in his civilized state, and when trained up according to a certain discipline and education. 'But in his rude and more natural condition, says he, if you are pleased to call such a condition natural, this answer would be rejected as perfectly unintelligible and sophistical.

'For wherein consists this honesty and justice? Not surely in the external action. It must, therefore, consist in the motive from which the external action is derived. This motive can never be a regard to the honesty of the action. For it is a plain fallacy to say, that a virtuous motive is requisite to render an action honest, and, at the same time, that a regard to the honesty is the motive to the action. We can never have a regard to the virtue of an action, unless the action be antecedently virtuous.'

And, in another place,[4] 'To suppose that the mere regard to the virtue of the action is that which rendered it virtuous, is to reason in

[1 Cf. Price, § 762.]   [2 See Hume, §§ 512–21, 548, 631.]
[3 See Hume, § 514.]   [4 See Hume, § 513.]

a circle. An action must be virtuous, before we can have a regard to its virtue. Some virtuous motive, therefore, must be antecedent to that regard. Nor is this merely a metaphysical subtlety,' etc. *Treatise of Hum. Nature, book* 3. *part* 2. *sect.* 1.

I am not to consider at this time, how this reasoning is applied to support the author's opinion, that justice is not a natural but an artificial virtue. I consider it only as far as it opposes the principle I have been endeavouring to establish, that, to render an action truly virtuous, the agent must have some regard to its rectitude. And I conceive the whole force of the reasoning amounts to this:

When we judge an action to be good or bad, it must have been so in its own nature antecedent to that judgement, otherwise the judgement is erroneous. If, therefore, the action be good in its nature, the judgement of the agent cannot make it bad, nor can his judgement make it good if, in its nature, it be bad. For this would be to ascribe to our judgement a strange magical power to transform the nature of things, and to say, that my judging a thing to be what it is not, makes it really to be what I erroneously judge it to be. This, I think, is the objection in its full strength. And, in answer to it,

First, if we could not loose this metaphysical knot, I think we **896** might fairly and honestly cut it, because it fixes an absurdity upon the clearest and most indisputable principles of morals and of common sense. For I appeal to any man whether there be any principle of morality, or any principle of common sense, more clear and indisputable than that which we just now quoted from the Apostle Paul, that although a thing be not unclean in itself, yet to him that esteemeth it to be unclean, to him it is unclean. But the metaphysical argument makes this absurd. For, says the metaphysician, if the thing was not unclean in itself, you judged wrong in esteeming it to be unclean; and what can be more absurd, than that your esteeming a thing to be what it is not, should make it what you erroneously esteem it to be?

Let us try the edge of this argument in another instance. Nothing is more evident, than that an action does not merit the name of benevolent, unless it be done from a belief that it tends to promote the good of our neighbour. But this is absurd, says the metaphysician. For, if it be not a benevolent action in itself, your belief of its tendency cannot change its nature. It is absurd, that your erroneous belief should make the action to be what you believe it to be. Nothing is more evident, than that a man who tells the truth, believing it to be a lie, is guilty of falsehood; but the metaphysician would make this to be absurd.

In a word, if there be any strength in this argument, it would follow, that a man might be, in the highest degree, virtuous, without the least regard to virtue; that he might be very benevolent, without ever intending to do a good office; very malicious, without ever intending any hurt; very revengeful, without ever intending to retaliate an injury; very grateful, without ever intending to return a benefit; and a man of strict veracity, with an intention to lie. We might, therefore, reject this reasoning, as repugnant to self-evident truths, though we were not able to point out the fallacy of it.

897 2. But let us try, in the *second* place, whether the fallacy of this argument may not be discovered.

We ascribe moral goodness to actions considered abstractly, without any relation to the agent. We likewise ascribe moral goodness to an agent on account of an action he has done; we call it a good action, though, in this case, the goodness is properly in the man, and is only by a figure ascribed to the action. Now, it is to be considered, whether *moral goodness*, when applied to an action considered abstractly, has the same meaning as when we apply it to a man on account of that action; or whether we do not unawares change the meaning of the word, according as we apply it to the one or to the other.[1]

The action, considered abstractly, has neither understanding nor will; it is not accountable, nor can it be under any moral obligation. But all these things are essential to that moral goodness which belongs to a man; for, if a man had not understanding and will, he could have no moral goodness. Hence it follows necessarily, that the moral goodness which we ascribe to an action considered abstractly, and that which we ascribe to a person for doing that action, are not the same. The meaning of the word is changed when it is applied to these different subjects.

898 This will be more evident, when we consider what is meant by the moral goodness which we ascribe to a man for doing an action, and what by the goodness which belongs to the action considered abstractly. A good action in a man is that in which he applied his intellectual powers properly, in order to judge what he ought to do,

[1 Cf. Price, §§ 719 n., 750.]

and acted according to his best judgement. This is all that can be required of a moral agent; and in this his moral goodness, in any good action, consists. But is this the goodness which we ascribe to an action considered abstractly? No, surely. For the action, considered abstractly, is neither endowed with judgement nor with active power; and, therefore, can have none of that goodness which we ascribe to the man for doing it.

But what do we mean by goodness in an action considered abstractly? To me it appears to lie in this, and in this only, that it is an action which ought to be done by those who have the power and opportunity, and the capacity of perceiving their obligation to do it. I would gladly know of any man, what other moral goodness can be in an action considered abstractly. And this goodness is inherent in its nature, and inseparable from it. No opinion or judgement of an agent can in the least alter its nature.

Suppose the action to be that of relieving an innocent person out **899** of great distress. This surely has all the moral goodness that an action considered abstractly can have. Yet it is evident, that an agent, in relieving a person in distress, may have no moral goodness, may have great merit, or may have great demerit.

Suppose, *first*, that mice cut the cords which bound the distressed person, and so bring him relief. Is there moral goodness in this act of the mice?

Suppose, *secondly*, that a man maliciously relieves the distressed person, in order to plunge him into greater distress. In this action, there is surely no moral goodness, but much malice and inhumanity.

If, in the *last* place, we suppose a person, from real sympathy and humanity, to bring relief to the distressed person, with considerable expense or danger to himself; here is an action of real worth, which every heart approves and every tongue praises. But wherein lies the worth? Not in the action considered by itself, which was common to all the three, but in the man who, on this occasion, acted the part which became a good man. He did what his heart approved, and therefore he is approved by God and man.

Upon the whole, if we distinguish between that goodness which **900** may be ascribed to an action considered by itself, and that goodness which we ascribe to a man when he puts it in execution, we shall find a key to this metaphysical lock. We admit, that the goodness of an action, considered abstractly, can have no dependence upon the opinion or belief of an agent, any more than the truth of a proposition depends upon our believing it to be true. But, when a man exerts his active power well or ill, there is a moral goodness or turpitude which we figuratively impute to the action, but which is truly and properly imputable to the man only; and this goodness or turpitude depends very much upon the intention of the agent, and the opinion he had of his action.

This distinction has been understood in all ages by those who gave any attention to morals, though it has been variously expressed. The Greek moralists gave the name of καθῆκον to an action good in itself; such an action might be done by the most worthless. But an action done with a right intention, which implies real worth in the agent, they called κατόρθωμα. The distinction is explained by Cicero in his Offices. He calls the first *officium medium*, and the second *officium perfectum*, or *rectum*. In the scholastic ages, an action good in itself was said to be *materially* good, and an action done with a right intention was called *formally* good. This last way of expressing the distinction is still familiar among theologians; but Mr Hume seems not to have attended to it, or to have thought it to be words without any meaning.

901   Mr Hume, in the section already quoted,[1] tells us with great assurance, 'In short, it may be established as an undoubted maxim, that no action can be virtuous or morally good, unless there be in human nature some motive to produce it, distinct from the sense of its morality.' And upon this maxim he founds many of his reasonings on the subject of morals.

Whether it be consistent with Mr Hume's own system, that an action may be produced merely from the sense of its morality, without any motive of agreeableness or utility, I shall not now inquire. But, if it be true, and I think it evident to every man of common understanding, that a judge or an arbiter acts the most virtuous part when his sentence is produced by no other motive but a regard to justice and a good conscience; nay, when all other motives distinct from this are on the other side: if this I say be true, then that undoubted maxim of Mr Hume must be false, and all the conclusions built upon it must fall to the ground.

★   ★   ★   ★

[1 See Hume, § 513.]

CHAP. VI—OF THE NATURE AND OBLIGATION OF
A CONTRACT

★ ★ ★ ★

The operations of the human mind may be divided into two **902** classes, the solitary and the social. As promises and contracts belong to the last class, it may be proper to explain this division.

I call those operations *solitary*, which may be performed by a man in solitude, without intercourse with any other intelligent being.

I call those operations *social*, which necessarily imply social intercourse with some other intelligent being who bears a part in them.

A man may see, and hear, and remember, and judge, and reason; he may deliberate and form purposes, and exectue them, without the intervention of any other intelligent being. They are solitary acts. But when he asks a question for information, when he testifies a fact, when he gives a command to his servant, when he makes a promise, or enters into a contract, these are social acts of mind, and can have no existence without the intervention of some other intelligent being, who acts a part in them. Between the operations of the mind, which, for want of a more proper name, I have called *solitary*, and those I have called *social*, there is this very remarkable distinction, that, in the solitary, the expression of them by words, or any other sensible sign, is accidental. They may exist, and be complete, without being expressed, without being known to any other person. But, in the social operations, the expression is essential. They cannot exist without being expressed by words or signs, and known to the other party.

If nature had not made man capable of such social operations of mind, and furnished him with a language to express them, he might think, and reason, and deliberate, and will; he might have desires and aversions, joy and sorrow; in a word, he might exert all those operations of mind, which the writers in logic and pneumatology have so copiously described; but, at the same time, he would still be a solitary being, even when in a crowd; it would be impossible for him to put a question, or give a command, to ask a favour, or testify a fact, to make a promise or a bargain.

I take it to be the common opinion of philosophers, that the social **903** operations of the human mind are not specifically different from the

solitary, and that they are only various modifications or composi-
tions of our solitary operations, and may be resolved into them.

It is, for this reason probably, that, in enumerating the operations
of the mind, the solitary only are mentioned, and no notice at all
taken of the social, though they are familiar to every man, and have
names in all languages.

I apprehend, however, it will be found extremely difficult, if not
impossible, to resolve our social operations into any modification or
composition of the solitary: and that an attempt to do this, would
prove as ineffectual as the attempts that have been made to resolve
all our social affections into the selfish. The social operations appear
to be as simple in their nature as the solitary. They are found in
every individual of the species, even before the use of reason.

904   The power which man has of holding social intercourse with his
kind, by asking and refusing, threatening and supplicating, commanding and obeying, testifying and promising, must either be a
distinct faculty given by our Maker, and a part of our constitution,
like the powers of seeing, and hearing, or it must be a human invention. If men have invented this art of social intercourse, it must
follow, that every individual of the species must have invented it for
himself. It cannot be taught; for though, when once carried to a
certain pitch, it may be improved by teaching; yet it is impossible
it can begin in that way, because all teaching supposes a social intercourse and language already established between the teacher and the
learner. This intercourse must, from the very first, be carried on by
sensible signs; for the thoughts of other men can be discovered in no
other way. I think it is likewise evident, that this intercourse, in its
beginning at least, must be carried on by natural signs, whose meaning is understood by both parties, previous to all compact or agreement. For there can be no compact without signs, nor without
social intercourse.

                ★   ★   ★   ★

905   An observation or two, with regard to the nature of a contract,
will be sufficient for the present purpose.

It is obvious that the prestation promised must be understood by
both parties. One party engages to do such a thing, another accepts
of this engagement. An engagement to do, one does not know what,
can neither be made nor accepted. It is no less obvious, that a contract is a voluntary transaction.

But it ought to be observed, that the will, which is essential to a contract, is only a will to engage, or to become bound. We must beware of confounding this will, with a will to perform what we have engaged.[1] The last can signify nothing else than an intention and fixed purpose to do what we have engaged to do. The will to become bound, and to confer a right upon the other party, is indeed the very essence of a contract; but the purpose of fulfilling our engagement, is no part of the contract at all.

A purpose is a solitary act of mind, which lays no obligation on 906 the person, nor confers any right on another. A fraudulent person may contract with a fixed purpose of not performing his engagement. But this purpose makes no change with regard to his obligation.[2] He is as much bound as the honest man, who contracts with a fixed purpose of performing.

As the contract is binding without any regard to the purpose, so there may be a purpose without any contract. A purpose is no contract, even when it is declared to the person for whose benefit it is intended. I may say to a man, I intend to do such a thing for your benefit, but I come under no engagement. Every man understands the meaning of this speech, and sees no contradiction in it: whereas, if a purpose declared were the same thing with a contract, such a speech would be a contradiction, and would be the same as if one should say, I promise to do such a thing, but I do not promise.

All this is so plain to every man of common sense, that it would have been unnecessary to be mentioned, had not so acute a man as Mr Hume grounded some of the contradictions he finds in a contract, upon confounding a will to engage in a contract with a will or purpose to perform the engagement.[3]

$$\ast \qquad \ast \qquad \ast \qquad \ast$$

CHAP. VII—THAT MORAL APPROBATION IMPLIES
A REAL JUDGEMENT

The approbation of good actions, and disapprobation of bad, are 907 so familiar to every man come to years of understanding, that it seems strange there should be any dispute about their nature.

Whether we reflect upon our own conduct, or attend to the conduct of others with whom we live, or of whom we hear or read,

[1 Cf. Hume, § 536.]   [2 Cf. Hume, § 543.]
[3 But contrast Hume, § 536.]

we cannot help approving of some things, disapproving of others, and regarding many with perfect indifference.

These operations of our minds we are conscious of every day, and almost every hour we live. Men of ripe understanding are capable of reflecting upon them, and of attending to what passes in their own thoughts on such occasions; yet, for half a century, it has been a serious dispute among philosophers, what this approbation and disapprobation is, whether there be a real judgement included in it, which, like all other judgements, must be true or false; or, whether it include no more but some agreeable or uneasy feeling, in the person who approves or disapproves.

Mr Hume observes[1] very justly, that this is a controversy *started of late*. Before the modern system of ideas and impressions was introduced, nothing would have appeared more absurd, than to say, that when I condemn a man for what he has done, I pass no judgement at all about the man, but only express some uneasy feeling in myself. Nor did the new system produce this discovery at once, but gradually, by several steps, according as its consequences were more accurately traced, and its spirit more thoroughly imbibed by successive philosophers.

908

Descartes and Mr Locke went no farther than to maintain that the secondary qualities of body, heat and cold, sound, colour, taste and smell, which we perceive and judge to be in the external object, are mere feelings or sensations in our minds, there being nothing in bodies themselves to which these names can be applied; and that the office of the external senses is not to judge of external things, but only to give us ideas or sensations, from which we are by reasoning to deduce the existence of a material world without us, as well as we can.

Arthur Collier and Bishop Berkeley discovered, from the same principles, that the primary, as well as the secondary, qualities of bodies, such as extension, figure, solidity, motion, are only sensations in our minds; and therefore, that there is no material world without us at all.

The same philosophy, when it came to be applied to matters of taste, discovered that beauty and deformity are not any thing in the objects, to which men, from the beginning of the world, ascribed them, but certain feelings in the mind of the spectator.

[1 See Hume, § 562.]

The next step was an easy consequence from all the preceding, that moral approbation and disapprobation are not judgements, which must be true or false, but barely, agreeable and uneasy feelings or sensations.

Mr Hume made the last step in this progress, and crowned the system by what he calls his *hypothesis*, to wit, that belief is more properly an act of the sensitive, than of the cogitative part of our nature.

Beyond this I think no man can go in this track; sensation or feeling is all, and what is left to the cogitative part of our nature, I am not able to comprehend.

I have had occasion to consider each of these paradoxes, excepting **909** that which relates to morals, in *Essays on the Intellectual Powers of Man*; and, though they be strictly connected with each other, and with the system which has produced them, I have attempted to show, that they are inconsistent with just notions of our intellectual powers, no less than they are with the common sense and common language of mankind. And this, I think, will likewise appear with regard to the conclusion relating to morals, to wit, that moral approbation is only an agreeable feeling, and not a real judgement.

To prevent ambiguity as much as possible, let us attend to the meaning of *feeling* and of *judgement*. These operations of the mind, perhaps, cannot be logically defined; but they are well understood, and easily distinguished, by their properties and adjuncts.

Feeling, or sensation, seems to be the lowest degree of animation **910** we can conceive. We give the name of *animal* to every being that feels pain or pleasure; and this seems to be the boundary between the inanimate and animal creation.

We know no being of so low a rank in the creation of God, as to possess this animal power only without any other.

We commonly distinguish *feeling* from *thinking*, because it hardly deserves the name; and though it be, in a more general sense, a species of thought, is least removed from the passive and inert state of things inanimate.

A feeling must be agreeable, or uneasy, or indifferent. It may be weak or strong. It is expressed in language either by a single word, or by such a contexture of words as may be the subject or predicate of a proposition, but such as cannot by themselves make a proposition. For it implies neither affirmation nor negation; and therefore

cannot have the qualities of true or false, which distinguish propositions from all other forms of speech, and judgements from all other
acts of the mind.

That I have such a feeling, is indeed an affirmative proposition, and
expresses testimony grounded upon an intuitive judgement. But the
feeling is only one term of this proposition; and it can only make a
proposition when joined with another term, by a verb affirming
or denying.

911   As feeling distinguishes the animal nature from the inanimate; so
judging seems to distinguish the rational nature from the merely
animal.

Though judgement in general is expressed by one word in language, as the most complex operations of the mind may be; yet a
particular judgement can only be expressed by a sentence, and by
that kind of sentence which logicians call a *proposition*, in which there
must necessarily be a verb in the indicative mood, either expressed
or understood.

Every judgement must necessarily be true or false, and the same
may be said of the proposition which expresses it. It is a determination
of the understanding, with regard to what is true, or false, or dubious.

In judgement, we can distinguish the object about which we
judge, from the act of the mind in judging of that object. In mere
feeling there is no such distinction. The object of judgement must be
expressed by a proposition; and belief, disbelief or doubt, always
accompanies the judgement we form. If we judge the proposition
to be true, we must believe it; if we judge it to be false, we must
disbelieve it; and if we be uncertain whether it be true or false,
we must doubt.

The *toothache*, the *headache*, are words which express uneasy feelings; but to say that they express a judgement would be ridiculous.

That the sun is greater than the earth, is a proposition, and therefore
the object of judgement; and when affirmed or denied, believed or
disbelieved, or doubted, it expresses judgement; but to say that it
expresses only a feeling in the mind of him that believes it, would be
ridiculous.

912   These two operations of mind, when we consider them separately,
are very different, and easily distinguished. When we feel without
judging, or judge without feeling, it is impossible, without very
gross inattention, to mistake the one for the other.

But in many operations of the mind, both are inseparably conjoined under one name; and when we are not aware that the operation is complex, we may take one ingredient to be the whole, and overlook the other.

In former ages, that moral power, by which human actions ought **913** to be regulated, was called *reason*, and considered both by philosophers, and by the vulgar, as the power of judging what we ought, and what we ought not to do.

This is very fully expressed by Mr Hume, in his Treatise of Human Nature, Book II, Part III. § 3.[1] 'Nothing is more usual in philosophy, and even in common life, than to talk of the combat of passion and reason, to give the preference to reason, and assert that men are only so far virtuous as they conform themselves to its dictates. Every rational creature, it is said, is obliged to regulate his actions by reason; and if any other motive or principle challenge the direction of his conduct, he ought to oppose it, till it be entirely subdued, or, at least, brought to a conformity to that superior principle. On this method of thinking, the greatest part of moral philosophy, ancient and modern, seems to be founded.'

That those philosophers attended chiefly to the judging power of our moral faculty, appears from the names they gave to its operations, and from the whole of their language concerning it.

The modern philosophy has led men to attend chiefly to their sensations and feelings, and thereby to resolve into mere feeling, complex acts of the mind, of which feeling is only one ingredient.

I had occasion, in the preceding Essays, to observe, that several **914** operations of the mind, to which we give one name, and consider as one act, are compounded of more simple acts inseparably united in our constitution, and that in these, sensation or feeling often makes one ingredient.

Thus the appetites of hunger and thirst are compounded of an uneasy sensation, and the desire of food or drink. In our benevolent affections, there is both an agreeable feeling, and a desire of happiness to the object of our affection; and malevolent affections have ingredients of a contrary nature.

In these instances, sensation or feeling is inseparably conjoined with desire. In other instances, we find sensation inseparably conjoined with judgement or belief, and that in two different ways. In

[1 See Hume, § 479.]

some instances, the judgement or belief seems to be the consequence of the sensation, and to be regulated by it. In other instances, the sensation is the consequence of the judgement.

915　When we perceive an external object by our senses, we have a sensation conjoined with a firm belief of the existence and sensible qualities of the external object. Nor has all the subtlety of metaphysics been able to disjoin what nature has conjoined in our constitution. Descartes and Locke endeavoured, by reasoning, to deduce the existence of external objects from our sensations, but in vain. Subsequent philosophers, finding no reason for this connection, endeavoured to throw off the belief of external objects as being unreasonable; but this attempt is no less vain. Nature has doomed us to believe the testimony of our senses, whether we can give a good reason for doing so or not.

In this instance, the belief or judgement is the consequence of the sensation, as the sensation is the consequence of the impression made on the organ of sense.

916　But in most of the operations of mind in which judgement or belief is combined with feeling, the feeling is the consequence of the judgement, and is regulated by it.

Thus, an account of the good conduct of a friend at a distance gives me a very agreeable feeling, and a contrary account would give me a very uneasy feeling; but these feelings depend entirely upon my belief of the report.

In hope, there is an agreeable feeling, depending upon the belief or expectation of good to come: fear is made up of contrary ingredients; in both, the feeling is regulated by the degree of belief.

In the respect we bear to the worthy, and in our contempt of the worthless, there is both judgement and feeling, and the last depends entirely upon the first.

The same may be said of gratitude for good offices and resentment of injuries.

917　Let me now consider how I am affected when I see a man exerting himself nobly in a good cause. I am conscious that the effect of his conduct on my mind is complex, though it may be called by one name. I look up to his virtue, I approve, I admire it. In doing so, I have pleasure indeed, or an agreeable feeling; this is granted. But I find myself interested in his success and in his fame. This is affection; it is love and esteem, which is more than mere feeling.

The man is the object of this esteem; but in mere feeling there is no object.

I am likewise conscious, that this agreeable feeling in me, and this esteem of him, depend entirely upon the judgement I form of his conduct. I judge that this conduct merits esteem; and, while I thus judge, I cannot but esteem him, and contemplate his conduct with pleasure. Persuade me that he was bribed, or that he acted from some mercenary or bad motive, immediately my esteem and my agreeable feeling vanish.

In the approbation of a good action, therefore, there is feeling indeed, but there is also esteem of the agent; and both the feeling and the esteem depend upon the judgement we form of his conduct.

When I exercise my moral faculty about my own actions or those **918** of other men, I am conscious that I judge as well as feel. I accuse and excuse, I acquit and condemn, I assent and dissent, I believe and disbelieve, and doubt. These are acts of judgement, and not feelings.

Every determination of the understanding, with regard to what is true or false, is judgement. That I ought not to steal, or to kill, or to bear false witness, are propositions, of the truth of which I am as well convinced as of any proposition in Euclid. I am conscious that I judge them to be true propositions; and my consciousness makes all other arguments unnecessary, with regard to the operations of my own mind.

That other men judge, as well as feel, in such cases, I am convinced, because they understand me when I express my moral judgement, and express theirs by the same terms and phrases.

Suppose that, in a case well known to both, my friend says, *Such* **919** *a man did well and worthily, his conduct is highly approvable.* This speech, according to all rules of interpretation, expresses my friend's judgement of the man's conduct. This judgement may be true or false, and I may agree in opinion with him, or I may dissent from him without offence, as we may differ in other matters of judgement.

Suppose, again, that, in relation to the same case, my friend says, *The man's conduct gave me a very agreeable feeling.*

This speech, if approbation be nothing but an agreeable feeling, must have the very same meaning with the first, and express neither more nor less. But this cannot be, for two reasons.

First, because there is no rule in grammar or rhetoric, nor any **920** usage in language, by which these two speeches can be construed, so as to have the same meaning. The *first* expresses plainly an opinion or judgement of the conduct of the man, but says nothing of the speaker. The *second* only testifies a fact concerning the speaker, to wit, that he had such a feeling.

921   *Another* reason why these two speeches cannot mean the same thing is, that the first may be contradicted without any ground of offence, such contradiction being only a difference of opinion, which, to a reasonable man, gives no offence. But the second speech cannot be contradicted without an affront; for, as every man must know his own feelings, to deny that a man had a feeling which he affirms he had, is to charge him with falsehood.

922   If moral approbation be a real judgement, which produces an agreeable feeling in the mind of him who judges, both speeches are perfectly intelligible, in the most obvious and literal sense. Their meaning is different, but they are related, so that the one may be inferred from the other, as we infer the effect from the cause, or the cause from the effect. I know, that what a man judges to be a very worthy action, he contemplates with pleasure; and what he contemplates with pleasure must, in his judgement, have worth. But the judgement and the feeling are different acts of his mind, though connected as cause and effect. He can express either the one or the other with perfect propriety; but the speech which expresses his feeling is altogether improper and inept to express his judgement, for this evident reason, that judgement and feeling, though in some cases connected, are things in their nature different.

923   If we suppose, on the other hand, that moral approbation is nothing more than an agreeable feeling, occasioned by the contemplation of an action, the second speech above mentioned has a distinct meaning, and expresses all that is meant by moral approbation. But the first speech either means the very same thing, (which cannot be, for the reasons already mentioned) or it has no meaning.

Now, we may appeal to the reader, whether, in conversation upon human characters, such speeches as the first are not as frequent, as familiar, and as well understood, as any thing in language; and whether they have not been common in all ages that we can trace, and in all languages?

924   This doctrine, therefore, that moral approbation is merely a feeling without judgement, necessarily carries along with it this consequence, that a form of speech, upon one of the most common topics

of discourse, which either has no meaning, or a meaning irreconcilable to all rules of grammar or rhetoric, is found to be common and familiar in all languages and in all ages of the world, while every man knows how to express the meaning, if it have any, in plain and proper language.

Such a consequence I think sufficient to sink any philosophical opinion on which it hangs.

A particular language may have some oddity, or even absurdity, introduced by some man of eminence, from caprice or wrong judgement, and followed, by servile imitators, for a time, till it be detected, and, of consequence, discountenanced and dropped; but that the same absurdity should pervade all languages, through all ages, and that, after being detected and exposed, it should still keep its countenance and its place in language as much as before, this can never be while men have understanding.

It may be observed by the way, that the same argument may be **925** applied, with equal force, against those other paradoxical opinions of modern philosophy, which we before mentioned as connected with this, such as, that beauty and deformity are not at all in the objects to which language universally ascribes them, but are merely feelings in the mind of the spectator; that the secondary qualities are not in external objects, but are merely feelings or sensations in him that perceives them; and, in general, that our external and internal senses are faculties by which we have sensations or feelings only, but by which we do not judge.

That every form of speech, which language affords to express our judgements, should, in all ages, and in all languages, be used to express what is no judgement; and that feelings, which are easily expressed in proper language, should as universally be expressed by language altogether improper and absurd, I cannot believe; and therefore must conclude, that if language be the expression of thought, men judge of the primary and secondary qualities of body by their external senses, of beauty and deformity by their taste, and of virtue and vice by their moral faculty.

A truth so evident as this is, can hardly be obscured and brought **926** into doubt, but by the abuse of words. And much abuse of words there has been upon this subject. To avoid this, as much as possible, I have used the word *judgement*, on one side, and *sensation* or *feeling*, upon the other; because these words have been least liable to abuse or ambiguity. But it may be proper to make some observations upon other words that have been used in this controversy.

Mr Hume, in his Treatise of Human Nature, has employed two sections upon it, the titles of which are, *Moral Distinctions not derived from Reason,* and *Moral Distinctions derived from a Moral Sense.*[1]

When he is not, by custom, led unawares to speak of reason like other men, he limits that word to signify only the power of judging in matters merely speculative. Hence he concludes, 'that reason of itself is inactive and perfectly inert.'[2] That 'actions may be laudable or blameable, but cannot be reasonable or unreasonable.'[3] That 'it is not contrary to reason, to prefer the destruction of the whole world to the scratching of my finger.'[4] That 'it is not contrary to reason, for me to choose my total ruin to prevent the least uneasiness of an Indian, or of a person wholly unknown to me.'[4] That 'reason is, and ought only to be, the slave of the passions, and can never pretend to any other office, than to serve and obey them.'[5]

If we take the word *reason* to mean what common use, both of philosophers, and of the vulgar, hath made it to mean, these maxims are not only false, but licentious. It is only his abuse of the words *reason* and *passion,* that can justify them from this censure.

The meaning of a common word is not to be ascertained by philosophical theory, but by common usage; and if a man will take the liberty of limiting or extending the meaning of common words at his pleasure, he may, like Mandeville, insinuate the most licentious paradoxes with the appearance of plausibility. I have before made some observations upon the meaning of this word, Essay II. chap. 2. and Essay III. part. 3. chap. 1.[6] to which the reader is referred.

927 When Mr Hume derives moral distinctions from a moral sense, I agree with him in words, but we differ about the meaning of the word *sense.* Every power to which the name of a sense has been given, is a power of judging of the objects of that sense, and has been accounted such in all ages; the moral sense therefore is the power of judging in morals. But Mr Hume will have the moral sense to be only a power of feeling, without judging: this I take to be an abuse of a word.

Authors who place moral approbation in feeling only, very often

[1 See Hume, §§ 487-511.] [2 See Hume, §§ 489-90.]
[3 § 490.]   [4 § 483.]   [5 § 482.]
[6 §§ 857-60. Cf. also §§ 863-4.]

use the word *sentiment*,[1] to express feeling without judgement. This I take likewise to be an abuse of a word. Our moral determinations may, with propriety, be called *moral sentiments*. For the word *sentiment*, in the English language, never, as I conceive, signifies mere feeling, but judgement accompanied with feeling. It was wont to signify opinion or judgement of any kind, but, of late, is appropriated to signify an opinion or judgement, that strikes, and produces some agreeable or uneasy emotion. So we speak of sentiments of respect, of esteem, of gratitude. But I never heard the pain of the gout, or any other mere feeling, called a sentiment.

Even the word *judgement* has been used by Mr Hume to express **928** what he maintains to be only a feeling. Treatise of Human Nature, part 3. page 3.[2] 'The term *perception* is no less applicable to those *judgements* by which we distinguish moral good and evil, than to every other operation of the mind.' Perhaps he used this word inadvertently; for I think there cannot be a greater abuse of words, than to put judgement for what he held to be mere feeling.

All the words most commonly used, both by philosophers and by the vulgar, to express the operations of our moral faculty, such as, *decision*, *determination*, *sentence*, *approbation*, *disapprobation*, *applause*, *censure*, *praise*, *blame*, necessarily imply judgement in their meaning. When, therefore, they are used by Mr Hume, and others who hold his opinion, to signify feelings only, this is an abuse of words. If these philosophers wish to speak plainly and properly, they must, in discoursing of morals, discard these words altogether, because their established signification in the language, is contrary to what they would express by them.

They must likewise discard from morals the words *ought* and *ought* **929** *not*, which very properly express judgement, but cannot be applied to mere feelings. Upon these words Mr Hume has made a particular observation in the conclusion of his first section above mentioned. I shall give it in his own words, and make some remarks upon it.

'I cannot forbear adding to these reasonings, an observation which may, perhaps, be found of some importance. In every system of morality which I have hitherto met with, I have always remarked, that the author proceeds for some time in the ordinary way of reasoning, and establishes the being of a God, or makes observations

[1 Reid is thinking of Hume and Smith.]
[2 See Hume, § 487. Reid's reference to 'part 3' is a mistake for Book (or Volume) III.]

concerning human affairs; when, of a sudden, I am surprised to find, that, instead of the usual copulations of propositions, *is*, and *is not*, I meet with no proposition that is not connected with an *ought*, or an *ought not*. This change is imperceptible, but is, however, of the last consequence. For as this *ought* or *ought not* expresses some new relation or affirmation, it is necessary that it should be observed and explained; and, at the same time, that a reason should be given for what seems altogether inconceivable; how this new relation can be a deduction from others which are entirely different from it. But as authors do not commonly use this precaution, I shall presume to recommend it to the readers; and am persuaded, that this small attention would subvert all the vulgar systems of morality, and let us see, that the distinction of vice and virtue, is not founded merely on the relations of objects, nor is perceived by reason.'[1]

We may here observe, that it is acknowledged, that the words *ought* and *ought not* express some relation or affirmation; but a relation or affirmation which Mr Hume thought inexplicable, or, at least, inconsistent with his system of morals. He must, therefore, have thought, that they ought not to be used in treating of that subject.

930   He likewise makes two demands, and, taking it for granted that they cannot be satisfied, is persuaded, that an attention to this is sufficient to subvert all the vulgar systems of morals.

The *first* demand is, that *ought* and *ought not* be explained.

To a man that understands English, there are surely no words that require explanation less. Are not all men taught, from their early years, that they ought not to lie, nor steal, nor swear falsely? But Mr Hume thinks, that men never understood what these precepts mean, or rather that they are unintelligible. If this be so, I think indeed it will follow, that all the vulgar systems of morals are subverted.

Dr Johnson, in his Dictionary, explains the word *ought* to signify, being obliged by duty; and I know no better explication that can be given of it. The reader will see what I thought necessary to say concerning the moral relation expressed by this word, in Essay III. part 3. chap. 5.[2]

The *second* demand is, that a reason should be given why this relation should be a deduction from others which are entirely different from it.

[1 See Hume, § 504.]   [2 §§ 867–75.]

This is to demand a reason for what does not exist. The first principles of morals are not deductions. They are self-evident; and their truth, like that of other axioms, is perceived without reasoning or deduction. And moral truths that are not self-evident, are deduced, not from relations quite different from them, but from the first principles of morals.

In a matter so interesting to mankind, and so frequently the **931** subject of conversation among the learned and the unlearned as morals is, it may surely be expected, that men will express both their judgements and their feelings with propriety, and consistently with the rules of language. An opinion, therefore, which makes the language of all ages and nations, upon this subject, to be improper, contrary to all rules of language, and fit to be discarded, needs no other refutation.

As mankind have, in all ages, understood *reason* to mean the power by which not only our speculative opinions, but our actions ought to be regulated, we may say, with perfect propriety, that all vice is contrary to reason; that, by reason, we are to judge of what we ought to do, as well as of what we ought to believe.

But though all vice be contrary to reason, I conceive that it would not be a proper definition of vice to say, that it is a conduct contrary to reason, because this definition would apply equally to folly, which all men distinguish from vice.

There are other phrases which have been used on the same side **932** of the question, which I see no reason for adopting, such as, *acting contrary to the relations of things, contrary to the reason of things, to the fitness of things, to the truth of things, to absolute fitness.* These phrases have not the authority of common use, which, in matters of language, is great. They seem to have been invented by some authors, with a view to explain the nature of vice; but I do not think they answer that end. If intended as definitions of vice, they are improper; because, in the most favourable sense they can bear, they extend to every kind of foolish and absurd conduct, as well as to that which is vicious.

I shall conclude this chapter with some observations upon the five **933** arguments which Mr Hume has offered upon this point in his Enquiry.[1]

The *first* is, that it is impossible that the hypothesis he opposes,

[1 See Hume, §§ 596–606.]

can, in any particular instance, be so much as rendered intelligible, whatever specious figure it may make in general discourse. 'Examine, says he,[1] the crime of *ingratitude*, anatomize all its circumstances, and examine, by your reason alone, in what consists the demerit or blame, you will never come to any issue or conclusion.'

I think it unnecessary to follow him through all the accounts of ingratitude which he conceives may be given by those whom he opposes, because I agree with him in that which he himself adopts,[2] to wit, 'that this crime arises from a complication of circumstances, which, being presented to the spectator, excites the sentiment of blame by the particular structure and fabric of his mind.'

This he thought a true and intelligible account of the criminality of ingratitude. So do I. And therefore I think the hypothesis he opposes is intelligible, when applied to a particular instance.

Mr Hume, no doubt, thought, that the account he gives of ingratitude is inconsistent with the hypothesis he opposes, and could not be adopted by those who hold that hypothesis. He could be led to think so, only by taking for granted one of these two things. Either, *first*, that the *sentiment of blame* is a feeling only, without judgement; or *secondly*, that whatever is excited by the particular fabric and structure of the mind must be feeling only, and not judgement. But I cannot grant either the one or the other.

934   For, as to the *first*, it seems evident to me, that both *sentiment* and *blame* imply judgement; and, therefore, that the *sentiment of blame* is a judgement accompanied with feeling, and not mere feeling without judgement.

The *second* can as little be granted; for no operation of mind, whether judgement or feeling, can be excited but by that particular structure and fabric of the mind which makes us capable of that operation.

By that part of our fabric which we call *the faculty of seeing*, we judge of visible objects; by *taste*, another part of our fabric, we judge of beauty and deformity; by that part of our fabric, which enables us to form abstract conceptions, to compare them, and perceive their relations, we judge of abstract truths; and by that part of our fabric which we call the *moral faculty*, we judge of virtue and vice. If we suppose a being without any moral faculty in his fabric, I grant that he could not have the sentiments of blame and moral approbation.

[1 See Hume, § 596.]   [2 § 597.]

There are, therefore, judgements, as well as feelings, that are **935** excited by the particular structure and fabric of the mind. But there is this remarkable difference between them, that every judgement is, in its own nature, true or false; and though it depends upon the fabric of a mind, whether it have such a judgement or not, it depends not upon that fabric whether the judgement be true or not. A true judgement will be true, whatever be the fabric of the mind; but a particular structure and fabric is necessary, in order to our perceiving that truth. Nothing like this can be said of mere feelings, because the attributes of true or false do not belong to them.

Thus I think it appears, that the hypothesis which Mr Hume opposes is not unintelligible, when applied to the particular instance of ingratitude; because the account of ingratitude which he himself thinks true and intelligible, is perfectly agreeable to it.

The *second* argument amounts to this: that in moral deliberation, **936** we must be acquainted before-hand with all the objects and all their relations. After these things are known, the understanding has no farther room to operate. Nothing remains but to feel, on our part, some sentiment of blame or approbation.[1]

Let us apply this reasoning to the office of a judge. In a cause that comes before him, he must be made acquainted with all the objects, and all their relations. After this, his understanding has no farther room to operate. Nothing remains, on his part, but to feel the right or the wrong; and mankind have, very absurdly, called him a *judge*; he ought to be called a *feeler*.

To answer this argument more directly: the man who deliberates, after all the objects and relations mentioned by Mr Hume are known to him, has a point to determine; and that is, whether the action under his deliberation ought to be done or ought not. In most cases, this point will appear self-evident to a man who has been accustomed to exercise his moral judgement; in some cases it may require reasoning.

In like manner, the judge, after all the circumstances of the cause are known, has to judge, whether the plaintiff has a just plea or not.

The *third* argument is taken from the analogy between moral **937** beauty and natural, between moral sentiment and taste. As beauty is not a quality of the object, but a certain feeling of the spectator, so virtue and vice are not qualities in the persons to whom language ascribes them, but feelings of the spectator.[2]

[1 See Hume, § 601.]   [2 See Hume, § 603.]

But is it certain that beauty is not any quality of the object? This is indeed a paradox of modern philosophy, built upon a philosophical theory; but a paradox so contrary to the common language and common sense of mankind, that it ought rather to overturn the theory on which it stands, than receive any support from it. And if beauty be really a quality of the object, and not merely a feeling of the spectator, the whole force of this argument goes over to the other side of the question.

'Euclid, he says,[1] has fully explained all the qualities of the circle, but has not, in any proposition, said a word of its beauty. The reason is evident. The beauty is not a quality of the circle.'

By the *qualities of the circle*, he must mean its properties; and there are here two mistakes.

First, Euclid has not fully explained all the properties of the circle. Many have been discovered and demonstrated which he never dreamt of.

Secondly, the reason why Euclid has not said a word of the beauty of the circle, is not, *that beauty is not a quality of the circle*; the reason is, that Euclid never digresses from his subject. His purpose was to demonstrate the mathematical properties of the circle. Beauty is a quality of the circle, not demonstrable by mathematical reasoning, but immediately perceived by a good taste. To speak of it would have been a digression from his subject; and that is a fault he is never guilty of.

938 The *fourth* argument is, that inanimate objects may bear to each other all the same relations which we observe in moral agents.[2]

If this were true, it would be very much to the purpose; but it seems to be thrown out rashly, without any attention to its evidence. Had Mr Hume reflected but a very little upon this dogmatical assertion, a thousand instances would have occurred to him in direct contradiction to it.

May not one animal be more tame, or more docile, or more cunning, or more fierce, or more ravenous, than another? Are these relations to be found in inanimate objects? May not one man be a better painter, or sculptor, or ship-builder, or tailor, or shoemaker, than another? Are these relations to be found in inanimate objects, or even in brute-animals? May not one moral agent be more just, more pious, more attentive to any moral duty, or more eminent in

[1 See Hume, § 603.]   [2 See Hume, § 605.]

any moral virtue, than another? Are not these relations peculiar to moral agents? But to come to the relations most essential to morality.

When I say that *I ought to do such an action*, that *it is my duty*, do not these words express a relation between me and a certain action in my power; a relation which cannot be between inanimate objects, or between any other objects but a moral agent and his moral actions; a relation which is well understood by all men come to years of understanding, and expressed in all languages?

Again, when in deliberating about two actions in my power, which cannot both be done, I say *this* ought to be preferred to the other; that justice, for instance, ought to be preferred to generosity; I express a moral relation between two actions of a moral agent, which is well understood, and which cannot exist between objects of any other kind.

There are, therefore, moral relations which can have no existence but between moral agents and their voluntary actions. To determine these relations is the object of morals; and to determine relations the province of judgement, and not of mere feeling.

The *last* argument is a chain of several propositions, which deserve **939** distinct consideration. They may, I think, be summed up in these four: 1. There must be ultimate ends of action, beyond which it is absurd to ask a reason of acting. 2. The ultimate ends of human actions can never be accounted for by reason; 3. but recommend themselves entirely to the sentiments and affections of mankind, without any dependence on the intellectual faculties. 4. As virtue is an end, and is desirable on its own account, without fee or reward, merely for the immediate satisfaction it conveys; it is requisite, that there should be some sentiment which it touches, some internal taste or feeling, or whatever you please to call it, which distinguishes moral good and evil, and which embraces the one and rejects the other.[1]

To the *first* of these propositions I entirely agree. The ultimate ends of action are what I have called *the principles of action*, which I have endeavoured, in the third Essay, to enumerate, and to class under three heads of mechanical, animal and rational.[2]

The *second* proposition needs some explication. I take its meaning **940** to be, that there cannot another end, for the sake of which an ultimate end is pursued: for the reason of an action means nothing but the end for which the action is done; and the reason of an end of

[1 See Hume, § 606.]   [2 Cf. § 856.]

action can mean nothing but another end, for the sake of which that end is pursued, and to which it is the means.

That this is the author's meaning is evident from his reasoning in confirmation of it. 'Ask a man, *why he uses exercise?* he will answer, *because he desires to keep his health.* If you then inquire, *why he desires health?* he will readily reply, *because sickness is painful.* If you push your inquiries further, and desire a reason why he hates pain, it is impossible he can ever give any. This is an ultimate end, and is never referred to any other object.'[1] To account by reason for an end, therefore, is to show another end, for the sake of which that end is desired and pursued. And that, in this sense, an ultimate end can never be accounted for by reason, is certain, because that cannot be an ultimate end which is pursued only for the sake of another end.

I agree therefore with Mr Hume in this second proposition, which indeed is implied in the first.

941   The *third* proposition is, that ultimate ends recommend themselves entirely to the sentiments and affections of mankind, without any dependence on the intellectual faculties.

By *sentiments* he must here mean feelings without judgement, and by *affections*, such affections as imply no judgement. For surely any operation that implies judgement, cannot be independent of the intellectual faculties.

This being understood, I cannot assent to this proposition.

The author seems to think it implied in the preceding, or a necessary consequence from it, that because an ultimate end cannot be accounted for by reason; that is, cannot be pursued merely for the sake of another end; therefore it can have no dependence on the intellectual faculties. I deny this consequence, and can see no force in it.

I think it not only does not follow from the preceding proposition, but that it is contrary to truth.

A man may act from gratitude as an ultimate end; but gratitude implies a judgement and belief of favours received, and therefore is dependent on the intellectual faculties. A man may act from respect to a worthy character as an ultimate end; but this respect necessarily implies a judgement of worth in the person, and therefore is dependent on the intellectual faculties.

942   I have endeavoured in the third Essay before mentioned, to show

[1 See Hume, § 606.]

that, beside the animal principles of our nature, which require will and intention, but not judgement, there are also in human nature rational principles of action, or ultimate ends, which have, in all ages, been called rational, and have a just title to that name, not only from the authority of language, but because they can have no existence but in beings endowed with reason, and because, in all their exertions, they require not only intention and will, but judgement or reason.[1]

Therefore, until it can be proved that an ultimate end cannot be dependent on the intellectual faculties, this third proposition, and all that hangs upon it, must fall to the ground.

The *last* proposition assumes, with very good reason, that virtue **943** is an ultimate end, and desirable on its own account. From which, if the third proposition were true, the conclusion would undoubtedly follow, that virtue has no dependence on the intellectual faculties. But as that proposition is not granted, nor proved, this conclusion is left without any support from the whole of the argument.

I should not have thought it worth while to insist so long upon **944** this controversy, if I did not conceive that the consequences which the contrary opinions draw after them are important.

If what we call *moral judgement* be no real judgement, but merely a feeling, it follows, that the principles of morals which we have been taught to consider as an immutable law to all intelligent beings, have no other foundation but an arbitrary structure and fabric in the constitution of the human mind: so that, by a change in our structure, what is immoral might become moral, virtue might be turned into vice, and vice into virtue. And beings of a different structure, according to the variety of their feelings, may have different, nay opposite, measures of moral good and evil.

It follows that, from our notions of morals, we can conclude nothing concerning a moral character in the Deity, which is the foundation of all religion, and the strongest support of virtue.

Nay, this opinion seems to conclude strongly against a moral character in the Deity, since nothing arbitrary or mutable can be conceived to enter into the description of a nature eternal, immutable, and necessarily existent. Mr Hume seems perfectly consistent with himself, in allowing of no evidence for the moral attributes of the Supreme Being, whatever there may be for his natural attributes.[2]

[1 Cf. §§ 856–60.]   [2 Cf. Hume, § 634.]

945   On the other hand, if moral judgement be a true and real judgement, the principles of morals stand upon the immutable foundation of truth, and can undergo no change by any difference of fabric, or structure of those who judge of them. There may be, and there are, beings, who have not the faculty of conceiving moral truths, or perceiving the excellence of moral worth, as there are beings incapable of perceiving mathematical truths; but no defect, no error of understanding, can make what is true to be false.

If it be true that piety, justice, benevolence, wisdom, temperance, fortitude, are in their own nature the most excellent and most amiable qualities of a human creature; that vice has an inherent turpitude, which merits disapprobation and dislike; these truths cannot be hid from him whose understanding is infinite, whose judgement is always according to truth, and who must esteem every thing according to its real value.

The Judge of all the earth, we are sure, will do right. He has given to men the faculty of perceiving the right and the wrong in conduct, as far as is necessary to our present state, and of perceiving the dignity of the one, and the demerit of the other; and surely there can be no real knowledge or real excellence in man, which is not in his Maker.

We may therefore justly conclude, that what we know in part, and see in part, of right and wrong, he sees perfectly; that the moral excellence which we see and admire in some of our fellow-creatures, is a faint but true copy of that moral excellence, which is essential to his nature; and that to tread the path of virtue, is the true dignity of our nature, an imitation of God, and the way to obtain his favour.

JEREMY BENTHAM

1748–1832

AN INTRODUCTION TO THE PRINCIPLES OF MORALS AND LEGISLATION

[First printed, 1780; first published, 1789. Reprinted here from the second, enlarged, edition, 1823, with misprints corrected, spelling slightly modified, and some footnotes omitted]

JEREMY BENTHAM

An Introduction to the Principles of Morals and Legislation

CHAP. I—OF THE PRINCIPLE OF UTILITY

I. Nature has placed mankind under the governance of two sovereign masters, *pain* and *pleasure*. It is for them alone to point out what we ought to do, as well as to determine what we shall do. On the one hand the standard of right and wrong, on the other the chain of causes and effects, are fastened to their throne. They govern us in all we do, in all we say, in all we think: every effort we can make to throw off our subjection, will serve but to demonstrate and confirm it. In words a man may pretend to abjure their empire: but in reality he will remain subject to it all the while. The *principle of utility** recognizes this subjection, and assumes it for the foundation of that system, the object of which is to rear the fabric of felicity by the hands of reason and of law. Systems which attempt to question it, deal in sounds instead of sense, in caprice instead of reason, in darkness instead of light.

* Note by the Author, July 1822.

To this denomination has of late been added, or substituted, the *greatest happiness* or *greatest felicity* principle: this for shortness, instead of saying at length *that principle* which states the greatest happiness of all those whose interest is in question, as being the right and proper, and only right and proper and universally desirable, end of human action: of human action in every situation, and in particular in that of a functionary or set of functionaries exercising the powers of Government. The word *utility* does not so clearly point to the ideas of *pleasure* and *pain* as the words *happiness* and *felicity* do: nor does it lead us to the consideration of the *number*, of the interests affected; to the *number*, as being the circumstance, which contributes, in the largest proportion, to the formation of the standard here in question; the *standard of right and wrong*, by which alone the propriety of human conduct, in every situation, can with propriety be tried. This want of a sufficiently manifest connection between the ideas of *happiness* and *pleasure* on the one hand, and the idea of *utility* on the other, I have every now and then found operating, and with but too much efficiency, as a bar to the acceptance, that might otherwise have been given, to this principle.

But enough of metaphor and declamation: it is not by such means that moral science is to be improved.

947 II. The principle of utility is the foundation of the present work: it will be proper therefore at the outset to give an explicit and determinate account of what is meant by it. By the principle* of utility is meant that principle which approves or disapproves of every action whatsoever, according to the tendency which it appears to have to augment or diminish the happiness of the party whose interest is in question: or, what is the same thing in other words, to promote or to oppose that happiness. I say of every action whatsoever; and therefore not only of every action of a private individual, but of every measure of government.

948 III. By utility is meant that property in any object, whereby it tends to produce benefit, advantage, pleasure, good, or happiness, (all this in the present case comes to the same thing) or (what comes again to the same thing) to prevent the happening of mischief, pain, evil, or unhappiness to the party whose interest is considered: if that party be the community in general, then the happiness of the community: if a particular individual, then the happiness of that individual.

949 IV. The interest of the community is one of the most general expressions that can occur in the phraseology of morals: no wonder that the meaning of it is often lost. When it has a meaning, it is this. The community is a fictitious *body*, composed of the individual persons who are considered as constituting as it were its *members*. The interest of the community then is, what?—the sum of the interests of the several members who compose it.

V. It is in vain to talk of the interest of the community, without understanding what is the interest of the individual.† A thing is said to promote the interest, or to be *for* the interest, of an individual, when it tends to add to the sum total of his pleasures: or, what comes to the same thing, to diminish the sum total of his pains.

950 VI. An action then may be said to be conformable to the principle of utility, or, for shortness sake, to utility, (meaning with respect to

---

* [Principle] ... The principle here in question may be taken for an act of the mind; a sentiment; a sentiment of approbation; a sentiment which, when applied to an action, approves of its utility, as that quality of it by which the measure of approbation or disapprobation bestowed upon it ought to be governed.

† [Interest, etc.] Interest is one of those words, which not having any superior *genus*, cannot in the ordinary way be defined.

the community at large) when the tendency it has to augment the happiness of the community is greater than any it has to diminish it.

VII. A measure of government (which is but a particular kind of action, performed by a particular person or persons) may be said to be conformable to or dictated by the principle of utility, when in like manner the tendency which it has to augment the happiness of the community is greater than any which it has to diminish it.

VIII. When an action, or in particular a measure of government, is supposed by a man to be conformable to the principle of utility, it may be convenient, for the purposes of discourse, to imagine a kind of law or dictate, called a law or dictate of utility: and to speak of the action in question, as being conformable to such law or dictate.

IX. A man may be said to be a partizan of the principle of utility, when the approbation or disapprobation he annexes to any action, or to any measure, is determined by, and proportioned to the tendency which he conceives it to have to augment or to diminish the happiness of the community: or in other words, to its conformity or unconformity to the laws or dictates of utility.

X. Of an action that is conformable to the principle of utility, one 951 may always say either that it is one that ought to be done, or at least that it is not one that ought not to be done. One may say also, that it is right it should be done; at least that it is not wrong it should be done: that it is a right action; at least that it is not a wrong action. When thus interpreted, the words *ought*, and *right* and *wrong*, and others of that stamp, have a meaning: when otherwise, they have none.

XI. Has the rectitude of this principle been ever formally con- 952 tested? It should seem that it had, by those who have not known what they have been meaning. Is it susceptible of any direct proof? It should seem not: for that which is used to prove every thing else, cannot itself be proved: a chain of proofs must have their commencement somewhere. To give such proof is as impossible as it is needless.

XII. Not that there is or ever has been that human creature breathing, however stupid or perverse, who has not on many, perhaps on most occasions of his life, deferred to it. By the natural constitution of the human frame, on most occasions of their lives men in general embrace this principle, without thinking of it: if not for the ordering of their own actions, yet for the trying of their own actions, as well as of those of other men. There have been, at the same time, not many, perhaps, even of the most intelligent, who have been disposed to embrace it purely and without reserve. There are even few who have not taken some occasion or other to quarrel with it, either on account of their not understanding always how to apply it, or on account of some prejudice or other which they were afraid to examine into, or could not bear to part with. For such is the stuff that man is made of: in principle and in practice, in a right track and in a wrong one, the rarest of all human qualities is consistency.

953 XIII. When a man attempts to combat the principle of utility, it is with reasons drawn, without his being aware of it, from that very principle itself.* His arguments, if they prove any thing, prove not that the principle is *wrong*, but that, according to the applications he supposes to be made of it, it is *misapplied*. Is it possible for a man to move the earth? Yes; but he must first find out another earth to stand upon.

954 XIV. To disprove the propriety of it by arguments is impossible; but, from the causes that have been mentioned, or from some confused or partial view of it, a man may happen to be disposed not to relish it. Where this is the case, if he thinks the settling of his opinions on such a subject worth the trouble, let him take the following steps, and at length, perhaps, he may come to reconcile himself to it.

1. Let him settle with himself, whether he would wish to discard this principle altogether; if so, let him consider what it is that all his reasonings (in matters of politics especially) can amount to?

2. If he would, let him settle with himself, whether he would judge and act without any principle, or whether there is any other he would judge and act by?

3. If there be, let him examine and satisfy himself whether the principle he thinks he has found is really any separate intelligible principle; or whether it be not a mere principle in words, a kind of phrase, which at bottom expresses neither more nor less than the mere averment of his own unfounded sentiments; that is, what in another person he might be apt to call caprice?

* 'The principle of utility, (I have heard it said) is a dangerous principle: it is dangerous on certain occasions to consult it.' This is as much as to say, what? that it is not consonant to utility, to consult utility: in short, that it is *not* consulting it, to consult it.

*   *   *   *

4. If he is inclined to think that his own approbation or disapprobation, annexed to the idea of an act, without any regard to its consequences, is a sufficient foundation for him to judge and act upon, let him ask himself whether his sentiment is to be a standard of right and wrong, with respect to every other man, or whether every man's sentiment has the same privilege of being a standard to itself?

5. In the first case, let him ask himself whether his principle is not despotical, and hostile to all the rest of human race?

6. In the second case, whether it is not anarchial, and whether at this rate there are not as many different standards of right and wrong as there are men? and whether even to the same man, the same thing, which is right to-day, may not (without the least change in its nature) be wrong to-morrow? and whether the same thing is not right and wrong in the same place at the same time? and in either case, whether all argument is not at an end? and whether, when two men have said, 'I like this,' and 'I don't like it,' they can (upon such a principle) have any thing more to say?

7. If he should have said to himself, No: for that the sentiment which he proposes as a standard must be grounded on reflection, let him say on what particulars the reflection is to turn? if on particulars having relation to the utility of the act, then let him say whether this is not deserting his own principle, and borrowing assistance from that very one in opposition to which he sets it up: or if not on those particulars, on what other particulars?

8. If he should be for compounding the matter, and adopting his own principle in part, and the principle of utility in part, let him say how far he will adopt it?

9. When he has settled with himself where he will stop, then let him ask himself how he justifies to himself the adopting it so far? and why he will not adopt it any farther?

10. Admitting any other principle than the principle of utility to be a right principle, a principle that it is right for a man to pursue; admitting (what is not true) that the word *right* can have a meaning without reference to utility, let him say whether there is any such thing as a *motive* that a man can have to pursue the dictates of it: if there is, let him say what that motive is, and how it is to be distinguished from those which enforce the dictates of utility: if not, then lastly let him say what it is this other principle can be good for?

CHAP. II—OF PRINCIPLES ADVERSE TO THAT OF UTILITY

955   I. If the principle of utility be a right principle to be governed by, and that in all cases, it follows from what has been just observed, that whatever principle differs from it in any case must necessarily be a wrong one. To prove any other principle, therefore, to be a wrong one, there needs no more than just to show it to be what it is, a principle of which the dictates are in some point or other different from those of the principle of utility: to state it is to confute it.

II. A principle may be different from that of utility in two ways: 1. By being constantly opposed to it: this is the case with a principle which may be termed the principle of *asceticism*. 2. By being sometimes opposed to it, and sometimes not, as it may happen: this is the case with another, which may be termed the principle of *sympathy* and *antipathy*.

956   III. By the principle of asceticism I mean that principle, which, like the principle of utility, approves or disapproves of any action, according to the tendency which it appears to have to augment or diminish the happiness of the party whose interest is in question; but in an inverse manner: approving of actions in as far as they tend to diminish his happiness; disapproving of them in as far as they tend to augment it.

      ★   ★   ★   ★

IX. The principle of asceticism seems originally to have been the reverie of certain hasty speculators, who having perceived, or fancied, that certain pleasures, when reaped in certain circumstances, have, at the long run, been attended with pains more than equivalent to them, took occasion to quarrel with every thing that offered itself under the name of pleasure. Having then got thus far, and having forgot the point which they set out from, they pushed on, and went so much further as to think it meritorious to fall in love with pain. Even this, we see, is at bottom but the principle of utility misapplied.

X. The principle of utility is capable of being consistently pursued; and it is but tautology to say, that the more consistently it is pursued, the better it must ever be for human-kind. The principle of asceticism never was, nor ever can be, consistently pursued by any living creature. Let but one tenth part of the inhabitants of this earth pursue it consistently, and in a day's time they will have turned it into a hell.

XI. Among principles adverse to that of utility, that which at this 957 day seems to have most influence in matters of government, is what may be called the principle of sympathy and antipathy. By the principle of sympathy and antipathy, I mean that principle which approves or disapproves of certain actions, not on account of their tending to augment the happiness, nor yet on account of their tending to diminish the happiness of the party whose interest is in question, but merely because a man finds himself disposed to approve or disapprove of them: holding up that approbation or disapprobation as a sufficient reason for itself, and disclaiming the necessity of looking out for any extrinsic ground. Thus far in the general department of morals: and in the particular department of politics, measuring out the quantum (as well as determining the ground) of punishment, by the degree of the disapprobation.

XII. It is manifest, that this is rather a principle in name than in reality: it is not a positive principle of itself, so much as a term employed to signify the negation of all principle. What one expects to find in a principle is something that points out some external consideration, as a means of warranting and guiding the internal sentiments of approbation and disapprobation: this expectation is but ill fulfilled by a proposition, which does neither more nor less than hold up each of those sentiments as a ground and standard for itself.

⋆　　⋆　　⋆　　⋆

XIV. The various systems that have been formed concerning the 958 standard of right and wrong, may all be reduced to the principle of sympathy and antipathy. One account may serve for all of them. They consist all of them in so many contrivances for avoiding the obligation of appealing to any external standard, and for prevailing upon the reader to accept of the author's sentiment or opinion as a reason for itself. The phrases different, but the principle the same.⋆

⋆ It is curious enough to observe the variety of inventions men have hit upon, and 959 the variety of phrases they have brought forward, in order to conceal from the world, and, if possible, from themselves, this very general and therefore very pardonable self-sufficiency.

1. One man says, he has a thing made on purpose to tell him what is right and what is wrong; and that it is called a *moral sense*: and then he goes to work at his ease, and says, such a thing is right, and such a thing is wrong—why? 'because my moral sense tells me it is.'

2. Another man comes and alters the phrase: leaving out *moral*, and putting in *common*, in the room of it. He then tells you, that his common sense teaches him what

is right and wrong, as surely as the other's moral sense did: meaning by common sense, a sense of some kind or other, which, he says, is possessed by all mankind: the sense of those, whose sense is not the same as the author's, being struck out of the account as not worth taking. This contrivance does better than the other; for a moral sense, being a new thing,[1] a man may feel about him a good while without being able to find it out: but common sense is as old as the creation; and there is no man but would be ashamed to be thought not to have as much of it as his neighbours. It has another great advantage: by appearing to share power, it lessens envy: for when a man gets up upon this ground, in order to anathematize those who differ from him, it is not by a *sic volo sic jubeo*, but by a *velitis jubeatis*.

3. Another man comes, and says, that as to a moral sense indeed, he cannot find that he has any such thing: that however he has an *understanding*, which will do quite as well. This understanding, he says, is the standard of right and wrong: it tells him so and so. All good and wise men understand as he does: if other men's understandings differ in any point from his, so much the worse for them: it is a sure sign they are either defective or corrupt.

4. Another man says, that there is an eternal and immutable Rule of Right: that that rule of right dictates so and so: and then he begins giving you his sentiments upon any thing that comes uppermost: and these sentiments (you are to take for granted) are so many branches of the eternal rule of right.

5. Another man, or perhaps the same man (it's no matter) says, that there are certain practices conformable, and others repugnant, to the Fitness of Things; and then he tells you, at his leisure, what practices are conformable and what repugnant: just as he happens to like a practice or dislike it.

6. A great multitude of people are continually talking of the Law of Nature; and then they go on giving you their sentiments about what is right and what is wrong: and these sentiments, you are to understand, are so many chapters and sections of the Law of Nature.

7. Instead of the phrase, Law of Nature, you have sometimes, Law of Reason, Right Reason, Natural Justice, Natural Equity, Good Order. Any of them will do equally well. This latter is most used in politics. The three last are much more tolerable than the others, because they do not very explicitly claim to be any thing more than phrases: they insist but feebly upon the being looked upon as so many positive standards of themselves, and seem content to be taken, upon occasion, for phrases expressive of the conformity of the thing in question to the proper standard, whatever that may be. On most occasions, however, it will be better to say *utility*: *utility* is clearer, as referring more explicitly to pain and pleasure.

8. We have one philosopher,[2] who says, there is no harm in any thing in the world but in telling a lie: and that if, for example, you were to murder your own father, this would only be a particular way of saying, he was not your father. Of course, when this philosopher sees any thing that he does not like, he says, it is a particular way of telling a lie. It is saying, that the act ought to be done, or may be done, when, *in truth*, it ought not to be done.

9. The fairest and openest of them all is that sort of man who speaks out, and says, I am of the number of the Elect: now God himself takes care to inform the Elect what is right: and that with so good effect, that let them strive ever so, they cannot help not only knowing it but practising it. If therefore a man wants to know what is right and what is wrong, he has nothing to do but to come to me.

960   It is upon the principle of antipathy that such and such acts are often reprobated on

---

[1 Cf. Smith, § 842; contrast Reid, § 877.]   [2 Wollaston.]

the score of their being *unnatural*: the practice of exposing children, established among the Greeks and Romans, was an unnatural practice. Unnatural, when it means any thing, means unfrequent: and there it means something; although nothing to the present purpose. But here it means no such thing: for the frequency of such acts is perhaps the great complaint. It therefore means nothing; nothing, I mean, which there is in the act itself. All it can serve to express is, the disposition of the person who is talking of it: the disposition he is in to be angry at the thoughts of it. Does it merit his anger? Very likely it may: but whether it does or no is a question, which, to be answered rightly, can only be answered upon the principle of utility.

Unnatural, is as good a word as moral sense, or common sense; and would be as good a foundation for a system. Such an act is unnatural; that is, repugnant to nature: for I do not like to practise it; and, consequently, do not practise it. It is therefore repugnant to what ought to be the nature of every body else.

The mischief common to all these ways of thinking and arguing (which, in truth, **961** as we have seen, are but one and the same method, couched in different forms of words) is their serving as a cloak, and pretence, and aliment, to despotism: if not a despotism in practice, a despotism however in disposition: which is but too apt, when pretence and power offer, to show itself in practice. The consequence is, that with intentions very commonly of the purest kind, a man becomes a torment either to himself or his fellow-creatures. If he be of the melancholy cast, he sits in silent grief, bewailing their blindness and depravity: if of the irascible, he declaims with fury and virulence against all who differ from him; blowing up the coals of fanaticism, and branding with the charge of corruption and insincerity, every man who does not think, or profess to think, as he does.

If such a man happens to possess the advantages of style, his book may do a considerable deal of mischief before the nothingness of it is understood.

These principles, if such they can be called, it is more frequent to see applied to morals **962** than to politics: but their influence extends itself to both. In politics, as well as morals, a man will be at least equally glad of a pretence for deciding any question in the manner that best pleases him, without the trouble of inquiry. If a man is an infallible judge of what is right and wrong in the actions of private individuals, why not in the measures to be observed by public men in the direction of those actions? accordingly (not to mention other chimeras) I have more than once known the pretended law of nature set up in legislative debates, in opposition to arguments derived from the principle of utility.

'But is it never, then, from any other considerations than those of utility, that we **963** derive our notions of right and wrong?' I do not know: I do not care. Whether a moral sentiment can be originally conceived from any other source than a view of utility, is one question: whether upon examination and reflection it can, in point of fact, be actually persisted in and justified on any other ground, by a person reflecting within himself, is another: whether in point of right it can properly be justified on any other ground, by a person addressing himself to the community, is a third. The two first are questions of speculation: it matters not, comparatively speaking, how they are decided. The last is a question of practice: the decision of it is of as much importance as that of any can be.

'I feel in myself,' (say you) 'a disposition to approve of such or such an action in a moral view: but this is not owing to any notions I have of its being a useful one to the community. I do not pretend to know whether it be an useful one or not: it may be, for aught I know, a mischievous one.' 'But is it then,' (say I) 'a mischievous one? examine; and if you can make yourself sensible that it is so, then, if duty means any thing, that is, moral duty, it is your *duty* at least to abstain from it: and more than that, if it is what lies in your power, and can be done without too great a sacrifice, to

XV. It is manifest, that the dictates of this principle will frequently coincide with those of utility, though perhaps without intending any such thing. Probably more frequently than not: and hence it is that the business of penal justice is carried on upon that tolerable sort of footing upon which we see it carried on in common at this day. For what more natural or more general ground of hatred to a practice can there be, than the mischievousness of such practice? What all men are exposed to suffer by, all men will be disposed to hate. It is far yet, however, from being a constant ground: for when a man suffers, it is not always that he knows what it is he suffers by. A man may suffer grievously, for instance, by a new tax, without being able to trace up the cause of his sufferings to the injustice of some neighbour, who has eluded the payment of an old one.

★   ★   ★   ★

965   XVIII. It may be wondered, perhaps, that in all this while no mention has been made of the *theological* principle; meaning that principle which professes to recur for the standard of right and wrong to the will of God. But the case is, this is not in fact a distinct principle. It is never any thing more or less than one or other of the three before-mentioned principles presenting itself under another shape. The *will* of God here meant cannot be his revealed will, as contained in the sacred writings: for that is a system which nobody ever thinks

endeavour to prevent it. It is not your cherishing the notion of it in your bosom, and giving it the name of virtue, that will excuse you.'

'I feel in myself,' (say you again) 'a disposition to detest such or such an action in a moral view; but this is not owing to any notions I have of its being a mischievous one to the community. I do not pretend to know whether it be a mischievous one or not: it may be not a mischievous one: it may be, for aught I know, an useful one.'—'May it indeed,' (say I) 'an useful one? but let me tell you then, that unless duty, and right and wrong, be just what you please to make them, if it really be not a mischievous one, and any body has a mind to do it, it is no duty of yours, but, on the contrary, it would be very wrong in you, to take upon you to prevent him: detest it within yourself as much as you please; that may be a very good reason (unless it be also a useful one) for your not doing it yourself: but if you go about, by word or deed, to do any thing to hinder him, or make him suffer for it, it is you, and not he, that have done wrong: it is not your setting yourself to blame his conduct, or branding it with the name of vice, that will make him culpable, or you blameless. Therefore, if you can make yourself content that he shall be of one mind, and you of another, about that matter, and so continue, it is well: but if nothing will serve you, but that you and he must needs be of the same mind, I'll tell you what you have to do: it is for you to get the better of your antipathy, not for him to truckle to it.'

of recurring to at this time of day, for the details of political administration: and even before it can be applied to the details of private conduct, it is universally allowed, by the most eminent divines of all persuasions, to stand in need of pretty ample interpretations; else to what use are the works of those divines? And for the guidance of these interpretations, it is also allowed, that some other standard must be assumed. The will then which is meant on this occasion, is that which may be called the *presumptive* will: that is to say, that which is presumed to be his will on account of the conformity of its dictates to those of some other principle. What then may be this other principle? it must be one or other of the three mentioned above: for there cannot, as we have seen, be any more. It is plain, therefore, that, setting revelation out of the question, no light can ever be thrown upon the standard of right and wrong, by any thing that can be said upon the question, what is God's will. We may be perfectly sure, indeed, that whatever is right is conformable to the will of God: but so far is that from answering the purpose of showing us what is right, that it is necessary to know first whether a thing is right, in order to know from thence whether it be conformable to the will of God.★

XIX. There are two things which are very apt to be confounded, **966** but which it imports us carefully to distinguish:—the motive or cause, which, by operating on the mind of an individual, is productive of any act: and the ground or reason which warrants a legislator, or other by-stander, in regarding that act with an eye of approbation When the act happens, in the particular instance in question, to be

★ The principle of theology refers every thing to God's pleasure. But what is God's pleasure? God does not, he confessedly does not now, either speak or write to us. How then are we to know what is his pleasure? By observing what is our own pleasure, and pronouncing it to be his. Accordingly, what is called the pleasure of God, is and must necessarily be (revelation apart) neither more nor less than the good pleasure of the person, whoever he be, who is pronouncing what he believes, or pretends, to be God's pleasure. How know you it to be God's pleasure that such or such an act should be abstained from? whence come you even to suppose as much? 'Because the engaging in it would, I imagine, be prejudicial upon the whole to the happiness of mankind;' says the partizan of the principle of utility: 'Because the commission of it is attended with a gross and sensual, or at least with a trifling and transient satisfaction;' says the partizan of the principle of asceticism: 'Because I detest the thoughts of it; and I cannot, neither ought I to be called upon to tell why;' says he who proceeds upon the principle of antipathy. In the words of one or other of these must that person necessarily answer (revelation apart) who professes to take for his standard the will of God.

productive of effects which we approve of, much more if we happen to observe that the same motive may frequently be productive, in other instances, of the like effects, we are apt to transfer our approbation to the motive itself, and to assume, as the just ground for the approbation we bestow on the act, the circumstance of its originating from that motive. It is in this way that the sentiment of antipathy has often been considered as a just ground of action. Antipathy, for instance, in such or such a case, is the cause of an action which is attended with good effects: but this does not make it a right ground of action in that case, any more than in any other. Still farther. Not only the effects are good, but the agent sees beforehand that they will be so. This may make the action indeed a perfectly right action: but it does not make antipathy a right ground of action. For the same sentiment of antipathy, if implicitly deferred to, may be, and very frequently is, productive of the very worst effects. Antipathy, therefore, can never be a right ground of action. No more, therefore, can resentment, which, as will be seen more particularly hereafter, is but a modification of antipathy. The only right ground of action, that can possibly subsist, is, after all, the consideration of utility, which, if it is a right principle of action, and of approbation, in any one case, is so in every other. Other principles in abundance, that is, other motives, may be the reasons why such and such an act *has* been done: that is, the reasons or causes of its being done: but it is this alone that can be the reason why it might or ought to have been done. Antipathy or resentment requires always to be regulated, to prevent its doing mischief: to be regulated by what? always by the principle of utility. The principle of utility neither requires nor admits of any other regulator than itself.

CHAP. III—OF THE FOUR SANCTIONS OR SOURCES OF PAIN AND PLEASURE

967 I. It has been shown that the happiness of the individuals, of whom a community is composed, that is their pleasures and their security, is the end and the sole end which the legislator ought to have in view: the sole standard, in conformity to which each individual ought, as far as depends upon the legislator, to be *made* to fashion his behaviour. But whether it be this or any thing else that is to be *done*, there is nothing by which a man can ultimately be *made* to do it, but either pain or pleasure. Having taken a general view of these two grand objects (viz. pleasure, and what comes to the same thing, immunity from pain) in the character of *final* causes; it will be necessary to take a view of pleasure and pain itself, in the character of *efficient* causes or means.

II. There are four distinguishable sources from which pleasure and **968** pain are in use to flow: considered separately, they may be termed the *physical*, the *political*, the *moral*, and the *religious*:[1] and inasmuch as the pleasures and pains belonging to each of them are capable of giving a binding force to any law or rule of conduct, they may all of them be termed *sanctions*.*

III. If it be in the present life, and from the ordinary course of nature, not purposely modified by the interposition of the will of any human being, nor by any extraordinary interposition of any superior invisible being, that the pleasure or the pain takes place or is expected, it may be said to issue from or to belong to the *physical sanction*.

IV. If at the hands of a *particular* person or set of persons in the community, who under names correspondent to that of *judge*, are chosen for the particular purpose of dispensing it, according to the will of the sovereign or supreme ruling power in the state, it may be said to issue from the *political sanction*.

V. If at the hands of such *chance* persons in the community, as the party in question may happen in the course of his life to have concerns with, according to each man's spontaneous disposition, and not according to any settled or concerted rule, it may be said to issue from the *moral* or *popular sanction*.†

---

* Sanctio, in Latin, was used to signify the *act of binding*, and, by a common grammatical transition, *any thing which serves to bind a man*: to wit, to the observance of such or such a mode of conduct. . . .

A Sanction then is a source of obligatory powers or *motives*: that is, of *pains* and *pleasures*; which, according as they are connected with such or such modes of conduct, operate, and are indeed the only things which can operate, as *motives*. See Chap. x. [Motives.]

† Better termed *popular*, as more directly indicative of its constituent cause; as likewise of its relation to the more common phrase *public opinion*, in French *opinion publique*, the name there given to that tutelary power, of which of late so much is said, and by which so much is done. The latter appellation is however unhappy and inexpressive; since if *opinion* is material, it is only in virtue of the influence it exercises over action, through the medium of the affections and the will.

[1 Cf. Locke, § 184; Gay, § 464.]

VI. If from the immediate hand of a superior invisible being, either in the present life, or in a future, it may be said to issue from the *religious sanction*.

969 VII. Pleasures or pains which may be expected to issue from the *physical, political,* or *moral* sanctions, must all of them be expected to be experienced, if ever, in the *present* life: those which may be expected to issue from the *religious* sanction, may be expected to be experienced either in the *present* life or in a *future*.

VIII. Those which can be experienced in the present life, can of course be no others than such as human nature in the course of the present life is susceptible of: and from each of these sources may flow all the pleasures or pains of which, in the course of the present life, human nature is susceptible. With regard to these then (with which alone we have in this place any concern) those of them which belong to any one of those sanctions, differ not ultimately in kind from those which belong to any one of the other three: the only difference there is among them lies in the circumstances that accompany their production. A suffering which befalls a man in the natural and spontaneous course of things, shall be styled, for instance, a *calamity*; in which case, if it be supposed to befall him through any imprudence of his, it may be styled a punishment issuing from the physical sanction. Now this same suffering, if inflicted by the law, will be what is commonly called a *punishment*; if incurred for want of any friendly assistance, which the misconduct, or supposed misconduct, of the sufferer has occasioned to be withholden, a punishment issuing from the *moral* sanction; if through the immediate interposition of a particular providence, a punishment issuing from the religious sanction.

*   *   *   *

CHAP. IV—VALUE OF A LOT OF PLEASURE OR PAIN, HOW TO BE MEASURED

970 I. Pleasures then, and the avoidance of pains, are the *ends* which the legislator has in view: it behoves him therefore to understand their *value*. Pleasures and pains are the *instruments* he has to work with: it behoves him therefore to understand their force, which is again, in other words, their value.

II. To a person considered *by himself*, the value of a pleasure or **971** pain considered *by itself*, will be greater or less, according to the four following circumstances:*

1. Its *intensity*.
2. Its *duration*.
3. Its *certainty* or *uncertainty*.
4. Its *propinquity* or *remoteness*.

III. These are the circumstances which are to be considered in esti- **972** mating a pleasure or a pain considered each of them by itself. But when the value of any pleasure or pain is considered for the purpose of estimating the tendency of any *act* by which it is produced, there are two other circumstances to be taken into the account; these are,

5. Its *fecundity*, or the chance it has of being followed by sensations of the *same* kind: that is, pleasures, if it be a pleasure: pains, if it be a pain.

6. Its *purity*, or the chance it has of *not* being followed by sensations of the *opposite* kind: that is, pains, if it be a pleasure: pleasures, if it be a pain.

These two last, however, are in strictness scarcely to be deemed properties of the pleasure or the pain itself; they are not, therefore, in strictness to be taken into the account of the value of that pleasure or that pain. They are in strictness to be deemed properties only of the act, or other event, by which such pleasure or pain has been produced; and accordingly are only to be taken into the account of the tendency of such act or such event.

IV. To a *number* of persons, with reference to each of whom the **973** value of a pleasure or a pain is considered, it will be greater or less, according to seven circumstances: to wit, the six preceding ones; viz.

1. Its *intensity*.
2. Its *duration*.
3. Its *certainty* or *uncertainty*.
4. Its *propinquity* or *remoteness*.
5. Its *fecundity*.
6. Its *purity*.
And one other; to wit:

* These circumstances have since been denominated *elements* or *dimensions* of *value* in a pleasure or a pain.

★   ★   ★   ★

7. Its *extent*; that is, the number of persons to whom it *extends*; or (in other words) who are affected by it.

974 V. To take an exact account then of the general tendency of any act, by which the interests of a community are affected, proceed as follows. Begin with any one person of those whose interests seem most immediately to be affected by it: and take an account,

1. Of the value of each distinguishable *pleasure* which appears to be produced by it in the *first* instance.

2. Of the value of each *pain* which appears to be produced by it in the *first* instance.

3. Of the value of each pleasure which appears to be produced by it *after* the first. This constitutes the *fecundity* of the first *pleasure* and the *impurity* of the first *pain*.

4. Of the value of each *pain* which appears to be produced by it after the first. This constitutes the *fecundity* of the first *pain*, and the *impurity* of the first pleasure.

5. Sum up all the values of all the *pleasures* on the one side, and those of all the pains on the other. The balance, if it be on the side of pleasure, will give the *good* tendency of the act upon the whole, with respect to the interests of that *individual* person; if on the side of pain, the *bad* tendency of it upon the whole.

6. Take an account of the *number* of persons whose interests appear to be concerned; and repeat the above process with respect to each. *Sum up* the numbers expressive of the degrees of *good* tendency, which the act has, with respect to each individual, in regard to whom the tendency of it is *good* upon the whole: do this again with respect to each individual, in regard to whom the tendency of it is *bad* upon the whole. Take the *balance*; which, if on the side of *pleasure*, will give the general *good tendency* of the act, with respect to the total number or community of individuals concerned; if on the side of pain, the general *evil tendency*, with respect to the same community.

975 VI. It is not to be expected that this process should be strictly pursued previously to every moral judgement, or to every legislative or judicial operation. It may, however, be always kept in view: and as near as the process actually pursued on these occasions approaches to it, so near will such process approach to the character of an exact one.

VII. The same process is alike applicable to pleasure and pain, in whatever shape they appear: and by whatever denomination they are distinguished: to pleasure, whether it be called *good* (which is properly the cause or instrument of pleasure[1]) or *profit* (which is distant pleasure, or the cause or instrument of distant pleasure,) or *convenience*, or *advantage, benefit, emolument, happiness*, and so forth: to pain, whether it be called *evil*, (which corresponds to *good*) or *mischief*, or *inconvenience*, or *disadvantage*, or *loss*, or *unhappiness*, and so forth.

VIII. Nor is this a novel and unwarranted, any more than it is a **976** useless theory. In all this there is nothing but what the practice of mankind, wheresoever they have a clear view of their own interest, is perfectly conformable to. An article of property, an estate in land, for instance, is valuable, on what account? On account of the pleasures of all kinds which it enables a man to produce, and, what comes to the same thing, the pains of all kinds which it enables him to avert. But the value of such an article of property is universally understood to rise or fall according to the length or shortness of the time which a man has in it: the certainty or uncertainty of its coming into possession: and the nearness or remoteness of the time at which, if at all, it is to come into possession. As to the *intensity* of the pleasures which a man may derive from it, this is never thought of, because it depends upon the use which each particular person may come to make of it; which cannot be estimated till the particular pleasures he may come to derive from it, or the particular pains he may come to exclude by means of it, are brought to view. For the same reason, neither does he think of the *fecundity* or *purity* of those pleasures.

Thus much for pleasure and pain, happiness and unhappiness, in *general*. We come now to consider the several particular kinds of pain and pleasure.

CHAP. VII—OF HUMAN ACTIONS IN GENERAL

I. The business of government is to promote the happiness of **977** the society, by punishing and rewarding. That part of its business which consists in punishing, is more particularly the subject of penal law. In proportion as an act tends to disturb that happiness, in

[1 Cf. Locke, §§ 160, 177, 183; Gay, § 467.]

proportion as the tendency of it is pernicious, will be the demand it creates for punishment. What happiness consists of we have already seen: enjoyment of pleasures, security from pains.

978   II. The general tendency of an act is more or less pernicious, according to the sum total of its consequences: that is, according to the difference between the sum of such as are good, and the sum of such as are evil.

III. It is to be observed, that here, as well as henceforward, wherever consequences are spoken of, such only are meant as are *material*. Of the consequences of any act, the multitude and variety must needs be infinite: but such of them only as are material are worth regarding. Now among the consequences of an act, be they what they may, such only, by one who views them in the capacity of a legislator, can be said to be material,* as either consist of pain or pleasure, or have an influence in the production of pain or pleasure.

★   ★   ★   ★

CHAP. VIII—OF INTENTIONALITY

979   I. So much with regard to the two first of the articles upon which the evil tendency of an action may depend: viz. the act itself, and the general assemblage of the circumstances with which it may have been accompanied. We come now to consider the ways in which the particular circumstances of *intention* may be concerned in it.

II. First, then, the intention or will may regard either of two objects: 1. The act itself: or, 2. Its consequences. Of these objects, that which the intention regards may be styled *intentional*. If it regards the act, then the act may be said to be intentional:† if the

---

* Or *of importance*.

† On this occasion the words *voluntary* and *involuntary* are commonly employed. These, however, I purposely abstain from, on account of the extreme ambiguity of their signification. By a voluntary act is meant sometimes, any act, in the performance of which the will has had any concern at all; in this sense it is synonymous to *intentional*: sometimes such acts only, in the production of which the will has been determined by motives not of a painful nature; in this sense it is synonymous to un-constrained, or *uncoerced*: sometimes such acts only, in the production of which the will has been determined by motives, which, whether of the pleasurable or painful kind, occurred to a man himself, without being suggested by any body else; in this sense it is synonymous to *spontaneous*. The sense of the word involuntary does not correspond completely to that of the word voluntary. Involuntary is used in opposition to intentional; and to unconstrained: but not to spontaneous. . . .

consequences, so also then may the consequences. If it regards both the act and consequences, the whole *action* may be said to be intentional. Whichever of those articles is not the object of the intention, may of course be said to be *unintentional*.

III. The act may very easily be intentional without the consequences; and often is so. Thus, you may intend to touch a man, without intending to hurt him: and yet, as the consequences turn out, you may chance to hurt him. **980**

IV. The consequences of an act may also be intentional, without the act's being intentional throughout; that is, without its being intentional in every stage of it: but this is not so frequent a case as the former. You intend to hurt a man, suppose, by running against him, and pushing him down: and you run towards him accordingly: but a second man coming in on a sudden between you and the first man, before you can stop yourself, you run against the second man, and by him push down the first.

V. But the consequences of an act cannot be intentional, without the act's being itself intentional in at least the first stage. If the act be not intentional in the first stage, it is no act of yours: there is accordingly no intention on your part to produce the consequences: that is to say, the individual consequences. All there can have been on your part is a distant intention to produce other consequences, of the same nature, by some act of yours, at a future time: or else, without any intention, a bare *wish* to see such event take place. The second man, suppose, runs of his own accord against the first, and pushes him down. You had intentions of doing a thing of the same nature: viz. To run against him, and push him down yourself; but you had done nothing in pursuance of those intentions: the individual consequences therefore of the act, which the second man performed in pushing down the first, cannot be said to have been on your part intentional. **981**

* * * *

XIII. It is frequent to hear men speak of a good intention, of a bad intention; of the goodness and badness of a man's intention: a circumstance on which great stress is generally laid. It is indeed of no small importance, when properly understood: but the import of it is to the last degree ambiguous and obscure. Strictly speaking, nothing can be said to be good or bad, but either in itself; which is **982** the case only with pain or pleasure: or on account of its effects; which is the case only with things that are the causes or preventives of pain and pleasure. But in a figurative and less proper way of speech, a thing may also be styled good or bad, in consideration of its cause. Now the effects of an intention to do such or such an act, are the same objects which we have been speaking of under the appellation of its *consequences*: and the causes of intention are called *motives*. A man's intention then on any occasion may be styled good or bad, with reference either to the consequences of the act, or with reference to his motives. If it be deemed good or bad in any sense, it must be either because it is deemed to be productive of good or of bad consequences, or because it is deemed to originate from a good or from a bad motive. But the goodness or badness of the consequences depend upon the circumstances. Now the circumstances are no objects of the intention. A man intends the act: and by his intention produces the act: but as to the circumstances, he does not intend *them*: he does not, inasmuch as they are circumstances of it, produce them. If by accident there be a few which he has been instrumental in producing, it has been by former intentions, directed to former acts, productive of those circumstances as the consequences: at the time in question he takes them as he finds them. Acts, with their consequences, are objects of the will as well as of the understanding: circumstances, as such, are objects of the understanding only. All he can do with these, as such, is to know or not to know them: in other words, to be conscious of them, or not conscious. To the title of Consciousness belongs what is to be said of the goodness or badness of a man's intention, as resulting from the consequences of the act: and to the head of Motives, what is to be said of his intention, as resulting from the motive.

CHAP. IX—OF CONSCIOUSNESS

★   ★   ★   ★

983 XIII. In ordinary discourse, when a man does an act of which the consequences prove mischievous, it is a common thing to speak of him as having acted with a good intention or with a bad intention, of his intention's being a good one or a bad one. The epithets good and bad are all this while applied, we see, to the intention: but the application of them is most commonly governed by a supposition formed with regard to the nature of the motive. The act, though eventually it prove mischievous, is said to be done with a good intention, when it is supposed to issue from a motive which is looked upon as a good motive: with a bad intention, when it is supposed to be the result of a motive which is looked upon as a bad motive. But the nature of the consequences intended, and the nature of the motive which gave birth to the intention, are objects which, though intimately connected, are perfectly distinguishable. The intention might therefore with perfect propriety be styled a good one, whatever were the motive. It might be styled a good one, when not only the consequences of the act *prove* mischievous, but the motive which gave birth to it *was* what is called a bad one. To warrant the speaking of the intention as being a good one, it is sufficient if the consequences of the act, had they proved what to the agent they seemed likely to be, *would* have been of a beneficial nature. And in the same manner the intention may be bad, when not only the consequences of the act prove beneficial, but the motive which gave birth to it was a good one.

XIV. Now, when a man has a mind to speak of your *intention* as **984** being good or bad, with reference to the consequences, if he speaks of it at all he must use the word intention, for there is no other. But if a man means to speak of the *motive* from which your intention originated, as being a good or a bad one, he is certainly not obliged to use the word intention: it is at least as well to use the word motive. By the supposition he means the motive; and very likely he may *not* mean the intention. For what is true of the one is very often not true of the other. The motive may be good when the intention is bad: the intention may be good when the motive is bad: whether they are both good or both bad, or the one good and the other bad, makes, as we shall see hereafter, a very essential difference with regard to the consequences. It is therefore much better, when motive is meant, never to say intention.

XV. An example will make this clear. Out of malice a man prosecutes you for a crime of which he believes you to be guilty, but of which in fact you are not guilty. Here the *consequences* of his conduct are mischievous: for they are mischievous to you at any rate, in virtue of the shame and anxiety which you are made to suffer while the prosecution is depending: to which is to be added, in case of your being convicted, the evil of the punishment. To you therefore they are mischievous; nor is there any one to whom they are beneficial. The man's *motive* was also what is called a bad one: for malice will be allowed by every body to be a bad motive. However, the *consequences* of his conduct, had they proved such as he believed them likely to be, would have been good: for in them would have been included the punishment of a criminal, which is a benefit to all who are exposed to suffer by a crime of the like nature. The *intention* therefore, in this case, though not in a common way of speaking the motive, might be styled a *good* one. But of motives more particularly in the next chapter.

★   ★   ★   ★

CHAP. X—OF MOTIVES

§ 1—*Different senses of the word* motive*

985 I. It is an acknowledged truth, that every kind of act whatever, and consequently every kind of offence, is apt to assume a different character, and be attended with different effects, according to the nature of the *motive* which gives birth to it. This makes it requisite to take a view of the several motives by which human conduct is liable to be influenced.

II. By a motive, in the most extensive sense in which the word is ever used with reference to a thinking being, is meant any thing that can contribute to give birth to, or even to prevent, any kind of action. Now the action of a thinking being is the act either of the body, or only of the mind: and an act of the mind is an act either of the intellectual faculty, or of the will. Acts of the intellectual faculty will sometimes rest in the understanding merely, without exerting any influence in the production of any acts of the will. Motives, which are not of a nature to influence any other acts than those, may be styled purely *speculative* motives, or motives resting in speculation. But as to these acts, neither do they exercise any influence over external acts, or over their consequences, nor consequently over any pain or any pleasure that may be in the number of

* Note by the author, July 1822.

★   ★   ★   ★

The word *inducement* has of late presented itself, as being in its signification more comprehensive than the word *motive*, and on some occasions more apposite.

such consequences. Now it is only on account of their tendency to produce either pain or pleasure, that any acts can be material. With acts, therefore, that rest purely in the understanding, we have not here any concern: nor therefore with any object, if any such there be, which, in the character of a motive, can have no influence on any other acts than those.

III. The motives with which alone we have any concern, are such **986** as are of a nature to act upon the will. By a motive then, in this sense of the word, is to be understood any thing whatsoever, which, by influencing the will of a sensitive being, is supposed to serve as a means of determining him to act, or voluntarily to forbear to act,* upon any occasion. Motives of this sort, in contradistinction to the former, may be styled *practical* motives, or motives applying to practice.

IV. Owing to the poverty and unsettled state of language, the **987** word *motive* is employed indiscriminately to denote two kinds of objects, which, for the better understanding of the subject, it is necessary should be distinguished. On some occasions it is employed to denote any of those really existing incidents from whence the act n question is supposed to take its rise. The sense it bears on these occasions may be styled its literal or *unfigurative* sense. On other occasions it is employed to denote a certain fictitious entity, a passion, an affection of the mind, an ideal being which upon the happening of any such incident is considered as operating upon the mind, and prompting it to take that course, towards which it is impelled by the influence of such incident. Motives of this class are Avarice, Indolence, Benevolence, and so forth; as we shall see more particularly farther on. This latter may be styled the *figurative* sense of the term *motive*.

V. As to the real incidents to which the name of motive is also **988** given, these too are of two very different kinds. They may be either, 1. The *internal* perception of any individual lot of pleasure or pain,

---

* When the effect or tendency of a motive is to determine a man to forbear to act, it may seem improper to make use of the term *motive*: since motive, properly speaking, means that which disposes an object to *move*. We must however use that improper term, or a term which, though proper enough, is scarce in use, the word *determinative*. By way of justification, or at least apology, for the popular usage in this behalf, it may be observed, that even forbearance to act, or the negation of motion (that is, of bodily motion) supposes an act done, when such forbearance is voluntary. It supposes, to wit, an act of the will, which is as much a positive act, as much a motion, as any other act of the thinking substance.

the expectation of which is looked upon as calculated to determine you to act in such or such a manner; as the pleasure of acquiring such a sum of money, the pain of exerting yourself on such an occasion, and so forth: Or, 2. Any *external* event, the happening whereof is regarded as having a tendency to bring about the perception of such pleasure or such pain: for instance, the coming up of a lottery ticket, by which the possession of the money devolves to you; or the breaking out of a fire in the house you are in, which makes it necessary for you to quit it. The former kind of motives may be termed interior, or internal: the latter exterior, or external.

989   VI. Two other senses of the term *motive* need also to be distinguished. Motive refers necessarily to action. It is a pleasure, pain, or other event, that prompts to action. Motive then, in one sense of the word, must be previous to such event. But, for a man to be governed by any motive, he must in every case look beyond that event which is called his action; he must look to the consequences of it: and it is only in this way that the idea of pleasure, of pain, or of any other event, can give birth to it. He must look, therefore, in every case, to some event posterior to the act in contemplation: an event which as yet exists not, but stands only in prospect. Now, as it is in all cases difficult, and in most cases unnecessary, to distinguish between objects so intimately connected, as the posterior possible object which is thus looked forward to, and the present existing object or event which takes place upon a man's looking forward to the other, they are both of them spoken of under the same appellation, *motive*. To distinguish them, the one first mentioned may be termed a motive in *prospect*, the other a motive in *esse*: and under each of these denominations will come as well exterior as internal motives. A fire breaks out in your neighbour's house: you are under apprehension of its extending to your own: you are apprehensive, that if you stay in it, you will be burnt: you accordingly run out of it. This then is the act: the others are all motives to it. The event of the fire's breaking out in your neighbour's house is an external motive, and that in *esse*: the idea or belief of the probability of the fire's extending to your own house, that of your being burnt if you continue, and the pain you feel at the thought of such a catastrophe, are all so many internal events, but still in *esse*: the event of the fire's actually extending to your own house, and that of your being actually burnt by it, external motives in prospect: the

pain you would feel at seeing your house a burning, and the pain you would feel while you yourself were burning, internal motives in prospect: which events, according as the matter turns out, may come to be in *esse*: but then of course they will cease to act as motives.

VII. Of all these motives, that which stands nearest to the act, to the production of which they all contribute, is that internal motive in *esse* which consists in the expectation of the internal motive in prospect: the pain or uneasiness you feel at the thoughts of being burnt.* All other motives are more or less remote: the motives in prospect, in proportion as the period at which they are expected to happen is more distant from the period at which the act takes place, and consequently later in point of time: the motives in *esse*, in proportion as they also are more distant from that period, and consequently earlier in point of time.†   **990**

VIII. It has already been observed, that with motives of which the influence terminates altogether in the understanding, we have nothing here to do. If then, amongst objects that are spoken of as motives with reference to the understanding, there be any which concern us here, it is only in as far as such objects may, through the medium of the understanding, exercise an influence over the will. It is in this way, and in this way only, that any objects, in virtue of any tendency they may have to influence the sentiment of belief, may in a practical sense act in the character of motives. Any objects, by tending to induce a belief concerning the existence, actual, or probable, of a practical motive; that is, concerning the probability of a motive in prospect, or the existence of a motive in *esse*; may exercise an influence on the will, and rank with those other   **991**

* Whether it be the expectation of being burnt, or the pain that accompanies that expectation, that is the immediate internal motive spoken of, may be difficult to determine. It may even be questioned, perhaps, whether they are distinct entities. Both questions, however, seem to be mere questions of words, and the solution of them altogether immaterial. Even the other kinds of motives, though for some purposes they demand a separate consideration, are, however, so intimately allied, that it will often be scarce practicable, and not always material, to avoid confounding them, as they have always hitherto been confounded.

† Under the term *esse* must be included as well *past* existence, with reference to a given period, as *present*. They are equally real, in comparison with what is as yet but future. Language is materially deficient, in not enabling us to distinguish with precision between *existence* as opposed to *unreality*, and *present* existence as opposed to past. The word existence in English, and *esse*, adopted by lawyers from the Latin, have the inconvenience of appearing to confine the existence in question to some single period considered as being present.

motives that have been placed under the name of practical. The pointing out of motives such as these, is what we frequently mean when we talk of giving *reasons*. Your neighbour's house is on fire as before. I observe to you, that at the lower part of your neighbour's house is some wood-work, which joins on to yours; that the flames have caught this wood-work, and so forth; which I do in order to dispose you to believe as I believe, that if you stay in your house much longer you will be burnt. In doing this, then, I suggest motives to your understanding; which motives, by the tendency they have to give birth to or strengthen a pain, which operates upon you in the character of an internal motive in *esse*, join their force, and act as motives upon the will.

§ 2—*No motives either constantly good, or constantly bad*

992   IX. In all this chain of motives, the principal or original link seems to be the last internal motive in prospect; it is to this that all the other motives in prospect owe their materiality: and the immediately acting motive its existence. This motive in prospect, we see, is always some pleasure, or some pain; some pleasure, which the act in question is expected to be a means of continuing or producing: some pain, which it is expected to be a means of discontinuing or preventing. A motive is substantially nothing more than pleasure or pain, operating in a certain manner.

X. Now, pleasure is in *itself* a good: nay, even setting aside immunity from pain, the only good: pain is in itself an evil; and, indeed, without exception, the only evil; or else the words good and evil have no meaning. And this is alike true of every sort of pain, and of every sort of pleasure. It follows, therefore, immediately and incontestably, that *there is no such thing as any sort of motive that is in itself a bad one.*★

993   XI. It is common, however, to speak of actions as proceeding from *good* or *bad* motives: in which case the motives meant are such as are internal. The expression is far from being an accurate one; and

---

★ Let a man's motive be ill-will; call it even malice, envy, cruelty; it is still a kind of pleasure that is his motive: the pleasure he takes at the thought of the pain which he sees, or expects to see, his adversary undergo. Now even this wretched pleasure, taken by itself, is good: it may be faint; it may be short: it must at any rate be impure: yet while it lasts, and before any bad consequences arrive, it is as good as any other that is not more intense. See ch. iv. [Value.]

as it is apt to occur in the consideration of almost every kind of offence, it will be requisite to settle the precise meaning of it, and observe how far it quadrates with the truth of things.

XII. With respect to goodness and badness, as it is with every thing else that is not itself either pain or pleasure, so is it with motives. If they are good or bad, it is only on account of their effects: good, on account of their tendency to produce pleasure, or avert pain: bad, on account of their tendency to produce pain, or avert pleasure. Now the case is, that from one and the same motive, and from every kind of motive, may proceed actions that are good, others that are bad, and others that are indifferent. This we shall proceed to show with respect to all the different kinds of motives, as determined by the various kinds of pleasures and pains.

XIII. Such an analysis, useful as it is, will be found to be a matter of **994** no small difficulty; owing, in great measure, to a certain perversity of structure which prevails more or less throughout all languages. To speak of motives, as of any thing else, one must call them by their names. But the misfortune is, that it is rare to meet with a motive of which the name expresses that and nothing more. Commonly, along with the very name of the motive, is tacitly involved a proposition imputing to it a certain quality; a quality which, in many cases, will appear to include that very goodness or badness, concerning which we are here inquiring whether, properly speaking, it be or be not imputable to motives. To use the common phrase, in most cases, the name of the motive is a word which is employed either only in a *good sense*, or else only in a *bad sense*. Now, when a word is spoken of as being used in a good sense, all that is necessarily meant is this: that in conjunction with the idea of the object it is put to signify, it conveys an idea of *approbation*: that is, of a pleasure or satisfaction, entertained by the person who employs the term at the thoughts of such object. In like manner, when a word is spoken of as being used in a bad sense, all that is necessarily meant is this: that, in conjunction with the idea of the object it is put to signify, it conveys an idea of *disapprobation*: that is, of a displeasure entertained by the person who employs the term at the thoughts of such object. Now, the circumstance on which such approbation is grounded will, as naturally as any other, be the opinion of the *goodness* of the object in question, as above explained: such, at least, it must be, upon the principle of utility: so, on the other hand, the circumstance on which any such disapprobation is grounded, will, as naturally as any other, be the opinion of the *badness* of the object: such, at least, it must be, in as far as the principle of utility is taken for the standard.

Now there are certain motives which, unless in a few particular cases, have scarcely any other name to be expressed by but such a word as is used only in a good sense. This is the case, for example, with the motives of piety and honour. The consequence of this is, that if, in speaking of such a motive, a man should have occasion to apply the epithet bad to any actions which he mentions as apt to result from it, he must appear to be guilty of a contradiction in terms. But the names of motives which have scarcely any other name to be expressed by, but such a word as is used only in a bad sense, are many more. This is the case, for example, with the motives of lust and avarice. And accordingly, if in speaking of any such motive, a man should have occasion to apply the epithets good or indifferent to any actions which he mentions as apt to result from it, he must here also appear to be guilty of a similar contradiction.★

995 This perverse association of ideas cannot, it is evident, but throw great difficulties in the way of the inquiry now before us. Confining himself to the language most in use, a man can scarce avoid running, in appearance, into perpetual contradictions. His propositions will appear, on the one hand, repugnant to truth; and on the other hand, adverse to utility. As paradoxes, they will excite contempt: as mischievous paradoxes, indignation. For the truths he labours to convey, however important, and however salutary, his reader is never the better: and he himself is much the worse. To obviate this inconvenience, completely, he has but this one unpleasant remedy; to lay aside the old phraseology and invent a new one. Happy the man whose language is ductile enough to permit him this resource. To palliate the inconvenience, where that method of obviating it is

★ To this imperfection of language, and nothing more, are to be attributed, in great measure, the violent clamours that have from time to time been raised against those ingenious moralists, who, travelling out of the beaten tract of speculation, have found more or less difficulty in disentangling themselves from the shackles of ordinary language: such as Rochefoucauld, Mandeville, and Helvetius. To the unsoundness of their opinions, and, with still greater injustice, to the corruption of their hearts, was often imputed, what was most commonly owing either to a want of skill, in matters of language on the part of the author, or a want of discernment, possibly now and then in some instances a want of probity, on the part of the commentator.

impracticable, he has nothing left for it but to enter into a long discussion, to state the whole matter at large, to confess, that for the sake of promoting the purposes, he has violated the established laws of language, and to throw himself upon the mercy of his readers.*

§ 3—*Catalogue of motives corresponding to that of Pleasures and Pains*

★　　　★　　　★　　　★

XXV. To the pleasures of sympathy corresponds the motive which, in a neutral sense, is termed good-will. The word sympathy may also be used on this occasion: though the sense of it seems to be rather more extensive. In a good sense, it is styled benevolence: and in certain cases, philanthropy; and, in a figurative way, brotherly love; in others, humanity; in others, charity; in others, pity and compassion; in others, mercy; in others, gratitude; in others, tenderness; in others, patriotism; in others, public spirit. Love is also employed in this as in so many other senses. In a bad sense, it has no name applicable to it in all cases: in particular cases it is styled partiality. The word zeal, with certain epithets prefixed to it, might also be employed sometimes on this occasion, though the sense of it be more extensive; applying sometimes to ill as well as to good will. It is thus we speak of party zeal, national zeal, and public zeal. The word attachment is also used with the like epithets: we also say family-attachment. The French expression, *esprit de corps*, for which as yet there seems to be scarcely any name in English, might be rendered, in some cases, though rather inadequately, by the terms corporation spirit, corporation attachment, or corporation zeal.

1. A man who has set a town on fire is apprehended and committed: out of regard or compassion for him, you help him to break prison. In this case the generality of people will probably scarcely know whether to condemn your motive or to applaud it: those who

* Happily, language is not always so intractable, but that by making use of two words instead of one, a man may avoid the inconvenience of fabricating words that are absolutely new. Thus instead of the word lust, by putting together two words in common use, he may frame the neutral expression, sexual desire: instead of the word avarice, by putting together two other words also in common use, he may frame the neutral expression, pecuniary interest. This, accordingly, is the course which I have taken. In these instances, indeed, even the combination is not novel: the only novelty there is consists in the steady adherence to the one neutral expression, rejecting altogether the terms, of which the import is infected by adventitious and unsuitable ideas.

★　　　★　　　★　　　★

996

condemn your conduct, will be disposed rather to impute it to some
other motive: if they style it benevolence or compassion, they will be
for prefixing an epithet, and calling it false benevolence or false compassion.* 2. The man is taken again, and is put upon his trial: to save
him you swear falsely in his favour. People, who would not call your
motive a bad one before, will perhaps call it so now. 3. A man is at
law with you about an estate: he has no right to it: the judge knows
this, yet, having an esteem or affection for your adversary, adjudges
it to him. In this case the motive is by every body deemed abomin-
able, and is termed injustice and partiality. 4. You detect a statesman
in receiving bribes: out of regard to the public interest, you give
information of it, and prosecute him. In this case, by all who acknowledge your conduct to have originated from this motive, your
motive will be deemed a laudable one, and styled public spirit. But
his friends and adherents will not choose to account for your conduct
in any such manner: they will rather attribute it to party enmity. 5.
You find a man on the point of starving: you relieve him; and save
his life. In this case your motive will by every body be accounted
laudable, and it will be termed compassion, pity, charity, benevolence. Yet in all these cases the motive is the same: it is neither
more nor less than the motive of good-will.

997   XXVI. To the pleasures of malevolence, or antipathy, corresponds
the motive which, in a neutral sense, is termed antipathy or displeasure: and, in particular cases, dislike, aversion, abhorrence, and
indignation: in a neutral sense, or perhaps a sense leaning a little to
the bad side, ill-will: and, in particular cases, anger, wrath, and
enmity. In a bad sense it is styled, in different cases, wrath, spleen,
ill-humour, hatred, malice, rancour, rage, fury, cruelty, tyranny,
envy, jealousy, revenge, misanthropy, and by other names, which
it is hardly worth while to endeavour to collect.† Like good-will, it

---

* Among the Greeks, perhaps the motive, and the conduct it gave birth to, would,
in such a case, have been rather approved than disapproved of. It seems to have been
deemed an act of heroism on the part of Hercules, to have delivered his friend Theseus
from hell: though divine justice, which held him there, should naturally have been
regarded as being at least upon a footing with human justice. But to divine justice,
even when acknowledged under that character, the respect paid at that time of day
does not seem to have been very profound, or well-settled: at present, the respect paid
to it is profound and settled enough, though the name of it is but too often applied to
dictates which could have had no other origin than the worst sort of human caprice.

† Here, as elsewhere, it may be observed, that the same words which are mentioned
as names of motives, are also many of them names of passions, appetites, and affections:

is used with epithets expressive of the persons who are the objects of the affection. Hence we hear of party enmity, party rage, and so forth. In a good sense there seems to be no single name for it. In compound expressions it may be spoken of in such a sense, by epithets, such as *just* and *laudable*, prefixed to words that are used in a neutral or nearly neutral sense.

1. You rob a man: he prosecutes you, and gets you punished: out of resentment you set upon him, and hang him with your own hands. In this case your motive will universally be deemed detestable, and will be called malice, cruelty, revenge, and so forth. 2. A man has stolen a little money from you: out of resentment you prosecute him, and get him hanged by course of law. In this case people will probably be a little divided in their opinions about your motive: your friends will deem it a laudable one, and call it a just or laudable resentment: your enemies will perhaps be disposed to deem it blameable, and call it cruelty, malice, revenge, and so forth: to obviate which, your friends will try perhaps to change the motive, and call it public spirit. 3. A man has murdered your father: out of resentment you prosecute him, and get him put to death in course of law. In this case your motive will be universally deemed a laudable one, and styled, as before, a just or laudable resentment: and your friends, in order to bring forward the more amiable principle from which the malevolent one, which was your immediate motive, took its rise, will be for keeping the latter out of sight, speaking of the former only, under some such name as filial piety. Yet in all these cases the motive is the same: it is neither more nor less than the motive of ill-will.

*   *   *   *

XXIX. It appears then that there is no such thing as any sort of **998** motive which is a bad one in itself: nor, consequently, any such thing as a sort of motive, which in itself is exclusively a good one. And as to their effects, it appears too that these are sometimes bad, at other times either indifferent or good: and this appears to be the case with every sort of motive. *If any sort of motive then is either good*

fictitious entities, which are framed only by considering pleasures or pains in some particular point of view. Some of them are also names of moral qualities. This branch of nomenclature is remarkably entangled: to unravel it completely would take up a whole volume; not a syllable of which would belong properly to the present design.

or bad on the score of its effects, this is the case only on individual occasions, and with individual motives; and this is the case with one sort of motive as well as with another. *If any sort of motive then can, in consideration of its effects, be termed with any propriety a bad one*, it can only be with reference to the balance of all the effects it may have had of both kinds within a given period, that is, of its most usual tendency.

XXX. What then? (it will be said) are not lust, cruelty, avarice, bad motives? Is there so much as any one individual occasion, in which motives like these can be otherwise than bad? No, certainly: and yet the proposition, that there is no one *sort* of motive but what will on many occasions be a good one, is nevertheless true. The fact is, that these are names which, if properly applied, are never applied but in the cases where the motives they signify happen to be bad. The names of these motives, considered apart from their effects, are sexual desire, displeasure, and pecuniary interest. To sexual desire, when the effects of it are looked upon as bad, is given the name of lust. Now lust is always a bad motive. Why? Because if the case be such, that the effects of the motive are not bad, it does not go, or at least ought not to go, by the name of lust. The case is, then, that when I say, 'Lust is a bad motive,' it is a proposition that merely concerns the import of the word lust; and which would be false if transferred to the other word used for the same motive, sexual desire. Hence we see the emptiness of all those rhapsodies of common-place morality, which consist in the taking of such names as lust, cruelty, and avarice, and branding them with marks of reprobation: applied to the *thing*, they are false; applied to the *name*, they are true indeed, but nugatory. Would you do a real service to mankind, show them the cases in which sexual desire *merits* the name of lust; displeasure, that of cruelty; and pecuniary interest, that of avarice.

*   *   *   *

§ 4—*Order of pre-eminence among motives*

999   XXXVI. Of all these sorts of motives, good-will is that of which the dictates,* taken in a general view, are surest of coinciding with

---

* When a man is supposed to be prompted by any motive to engage, or not to engage, in such or such an action, it may be of use, for the convenience of discourse, to speak of such motive as giving birth to an imaginary kind of *law* or *dictate*, enjoining him to engage, or not to engage, in it. See ch. i.

those of the principle of utility. For the dictates of utility are neither more nor less than the dictates of the most extensive* and enlightened (that is *well-advised*†) benevolence. The dictates of the other motives may be conformable to those of utility, or repugnant, as it may happen.

XXXVII. In this, however, it is taken for granted, that in the case in question the dictates of benevolence are not contradicted by those of a more extensive, that is enlarged, benevolence. Now when the dictates of benevolence, as respecting the interests of a certain set of persons, are repugnant to the dictates of the same motive, as respecting the more important‡ interests of another set of persons, the former dictates, it is evident, are repealed, as it were, by the latter: and a man, were he to be governed by the former, could scarcely, with propriety, be said to be governed by the dictates of benevolence. On this account, were the motives on both sides sure to be alike present to a man's mind, the case of such a repugnancy would hardly be worth distinguishing, since the partial benevolence might be considered as swallowed up in the more extensive: if the former prevailed, and governed the action, it must be considered as not owing its birth to benevolence, but to some other motive: if the latter prevailed, the former might be considered as having no effect. But the case is, that a partial benevolence may govern the action, without entering into any direct competition with the more extensive benevolence, which would forbid it; because the interests of the less numerous assemblage of persons may be present to a man's mind, at a time when those of the more numerous are either not present, or, if present, make no impression. It is in this way that the dictates of this motive may be repugnant to utility, yet still be the dictates of benevolence. What makes those of private benevolence conformable upon the whole to the principle of utility, is, that in general they stand unopposed by those of public: if they are repugnant to them, it is only by accident. What makes them the more conformable, is, that in a civilized society, in most of the cases in which they would of themselves be apt to run counter to those of public benevolence, they find themselves opposed by stronger motives of the self-regarding class, which are played off against them by the laws; and that it

---

* See ch. iv. [Value.] and ch. vi. [Sensibility.] xxi.
† See ch. ix. [Consciousness.]
‡ Or valuable. See ch. iv. [Value.]

is only in cases where they stand unopposed by the other more salutary dictates, that they are left free. An act of injustice or cruelty, committed by a man for the sake of his father or his son, is punished, and with reason, as much as if it were committed for his own.

★   ★   ★   ★

BIBLIOGRAPHICAL NOTE
OF SOME BRITISH WRITERS

ADAMS, William, 1706–89, Master of Pembroke College, Oxford, and Archdeacon of Llandaff.

The Nature and Obligation of Virtue. A sermon. London, 1754.

ARBUCKLE, James, see HUTCHESON, Francis.

BALFOUR, James, of Pilrig, 1705–95, Professor of Moral Philosophy, then of the Law of Nature and Nations, at Edinburgh.

(1) *A Delineation of the Nature and Obligation of Morality* (in criticism of Hume). Edinburgh, 1753; ed. 2, 1763.

(2) *Philosophical Essays* (in criticism of Hume and Kames). London, 1768.

(3) *Philosophical Dissertations.* Edinburgh, 1782.

BALGUY, John, 1686–1748, Vicar of Northallerton.

(1) *A Letter to a Deist, concerning the beauty and excellence of moral virtue, etc.* (in criticism of Shaftesbury). London, 1726; ed. 2, 1730; ed. 3, 1732.

(2) *The Foundation of Moral Goodness.* London, 1728; ed. 2, 1731; ed. 3, 1733.

(3) *The Second Part of the Foundation of Moral Goodness.* London, 1729.
   (1), (2), and (3) included in *A Collection of Tracts Moral and Theological.* London, 1734.

(See Silvester.)

BEATTIE, James, 1735–1803, Professor of Moral Philosophy and Logic at Marischal College, Aberdeen.

Elements of Moral Science. Edinburgh, vol. i, 1790; vol. ii, 1793.

BENTHAM, Jeremy, 1748–1832.

(1) *An Introduction to the Principles of Morals and Legislation.* First printed, London, 1780, but published 1789; ed. 2, 1823.

(2) *A Table of the Springs of Action.* London, 1815.

(3) *Deontology; or the Science of Morality*, ed. J. Bowring. 2 vols. London and Edinburgh, 1834.

BERKELEY, George, 1685–1753, Bishop of Cloyne.

(1) *A Treatise concerning the Principles of Human Knowledge*. Dublin, 1710; ed. 2, London, 1734.

(2) *Passive Obedience*. London, 1712; ed. 2, 1712; ed. 3, 1713.

(3) *Alciphron: or the Minute Philosopher*. 2 vols. London and Dublin, 1732; ed. 2, 1732; ed. 3, 1752. (See Mandeville.)

BLUETT, Thomas.

An Enquiry whether a General Practice of Virtue tends to the Wealth or Poverty, Benefit or Disadvantage of a People? (in criticism of Mandeville). London, 1725.
    This is answered by [Anon.] *The True Meaning of the Fable of the Bees*. London, 1726. (Brit. Mus. 1028. c. 6 (2).)

BOTT, Thomas, 1688–1754, Rector of Spixworth and Edgefield.

(1) *The Principal and Peculiar Notion advanced in a late book, intitled 'The Religion of Nature delineated', considered and refuted*. London, 1724.
    This is answered by [Anon.] *A Defence of Mr. Wollaston's Notion of Moral Good and Evil*. London, 1725. (Brit. Mus. 480. c. 21 (2).)

(2) *Morality, founded in the Reason of Things, and the Ground of Revelation*. A sermon. London, 1730.

(3) *Remarks upon Dr. Butler's Sixth Chapter of the Analogy of Religion, . . . and also upon the dissertation of the nature of virtue*. London, 1737.

BRAMHALL, John, 1594–1663, Bishop of Derry, then Archbishop of Armagh.

(1) *A Defence of True Liberty* (in answer to Hobbes). London, 1655.

(2) *Castigations of Mr. Hobbes his last animadversions . . . concerning liberty and universal necessity. With an appendix concerning the catching of Leviathan*. London, 1658.

(See Hobbes.)

BROWN, John, 1715–66, Vicar of St. Nicholas, Newcastle.

Essays on the Characteristics (of Shaftesbury). London, 1751; ed. 3, 1752; ed. 5, 1764.

BRYANT, Jacob, 1715–1804, Fellow of King's College, Cambridge.

An Address to Dr. Priestley, upon his Doctrine of philosophical necessity illustrated. London, 1780. (See Priestley.)

Burnet, Gilbert, the younger, see Hutcheson, Francis.

Butler, Joseph, 1692–1752, Bishop of Bristol, then of Durham.

(1) *Fifteen Sermons preached at the Rolls Chapel*. London, 1726; ed. 2, 1729; ed. 3, 1736; ed. 4, 1749.

(2) *The Analogy of Religion* (including *Dissertation of the Nature of Virtue*). London, 1736; Dublin, 1736; ed. 2, London, 1736; ed. 3, 1740. (See Bott, S. Clarke.)

Campbell, Archibald, 1691–1756, Professor of Ecclesiastical History at St. Andrews.

An Enquiry into the Original of Moral Virtue (in criticism of Mandeville and Hutcheson). First published as Ἀρετη-λογία, or an Enquiry etc., and falsely claimed to be by Alexander Innes, Westminster, 1728. Republished by Campbell as *An Enquiry etc.*, Edinburgh, 1733.

Chubb, Thomas, 1679–1747.

The Ground and Foundation of Morality considered (in criticism of Rutherforth). London, 1745. (See Johnson.)

Clarke, John, 1687–1734, schoolmaster at Hull, then at Gloucester.

(1) *An Examination of the Notion of Moral Good and Evil* (in criticism of Wollaston). London, 1725.

(2) *The Foundation of Morality in Theory and Practice* (in criticism of Samuel Clarke and of Hutcheson). York, [1726].

The criticism of S. Clarke in (2) is answered by [Anon.] *A Letter to Mr. John Clarke, etc.* London, 1727. (Brit. Mus. 698. e. 8 (5).)

Clarke, Samuel, 1675–1729, Rector of St. James's, Westminster.

(1) *A Demonstration of the Being and Attributes of God* (the Boyle Lectures, 1704). London, 1705; ed. 2, 1706.

(2) *A Discourse concerning the Unchangeable Obligations of Natural Religion* (the Boyle Lectures, 1705). London, 1706.

(1) and (2) subsequently published together as *A Discourse concerning the Being and Attributes of God, the Obligations of Natural Religion, etc.* Ed. 4, 1716, contains also correspondence between Butler and Clarke about some of Clarke's arguments in the first set of lectures. Ed. 5, 1719; ed. 6, 1725.

(3) *A Collection of Papers, which passed between Mr. Leibniz, and Dr. Clarke, etc.* (together with correspondence between John Bulkeley and Clarke about liberty and necessity, and with criticism by Clarke of Anthony Collins). London, 1717.

(See J. Clarke, Cockburn.)

COCKBURN, Mrs. Catharine (*née* Trotter), 1679–1749.

Remarks upon . . . Dr. Rutherforth's Essay on the Nature and Obligations of Virtue: in vindication of the contrary principles and reasonings . . . of . . . Dr. Samuel Clarke (with preface by Warburton). London, 1747.

COKE, Roger.

Justice vindicated (in criticism of Hobbes and others). London, 1660; ed. 2, 1662.

COLLINS, Anthony, 1676–1729.

(1) *A Philosophical Inquiry concerning Human Liberty.* London, 1717; ed. 2, 1717.

(2) *A Dissertation on Liberty and Necessity.* London, 1729.

(See S. Clarke, Jackson.)

COOPER, Anthony Ashley, see SHAFTESBURY, Third Earl of.

CROFT, George, 1747–1809, Fellow of University College, Oxford, then Vicar of Arncliffe.

A Short Commentary, with Strictures, on . . . the Moral Writings of Dr. Paley and Mr. Gisborne. London and Oxford, 1797.

CUDWORTH, Ralph, 1617–88, Professor of Hebrew at Cambridge, and Master of Clare Hall, then of Christ's College.

(1) *The True Intellectual System of the Universe.* London, 1678.

(2) *A Treatise concerning Eternal and Immutable Morality.* London, 1731.

(3) *A Treatise of Freewill,* ed. J. Allen. London, 1838.

CULVERWEL, Nathanael, d. 1651(?), Fellow of Emmanuel College, Cambridge.

The Light of Nature. London, 1652; further eds., 1654, 1661.

CUMBERLAND, Richard, 1631–1718, Bishop of Peterborough.

De Legibus Naturae disquisitio philosophica. London, 1672; ed. 2, Lubeck, 1683; ed. 3, Lubeck, 1694. English translations by J. Maxwell, London, 1727; and by J. Towers, Dublin, 1750. (See Tyrrell.)

DAWES, Manasseh, d. 1829.

Philosophical Considerations (on the controversy between Priestley and Price about liberty and necessity). London, 1780.

DENNIS, John, 1657–1734.

Vice and Luxury Public Mischiefs (in criticism of Mandeville). London, 1724.

EACHARD, John, 1636(?)–97, Master of Catharine Hall, Cambridge.

(1) *Mr. Hobbes's State of Nature considered.* London, 1672; ed. 2, 1672; ed. 3, 1685; ed. 4, 1696.

(2) *Some Opinions of Mr. Hobbes considered.* London, 1673.

FERGUSON, Adam, 1723–1816, Professor of Moral Philosophy at Edinburgh.

(1) *Institutes of Moral Philosophy.* Edinburgh, 1769; ed. 2, 1773; ed. 3, 1785; new ed., Basel, 1800.

(2) *Principles of Moral and Political Science.* 2 vols. Edinburgh, 1792.

FIDDES, Richard, 1671–1725, Rector of Halsham.

A General Treatise of Morality, formed upon the principles of Natural Reason only (in criticism of Mandeville and Shaftesbury). London, 1724.

FORDYCE, David, 1711–51, Professor of Moral Philosophy at Marischal College, Aberdeen.

The Elements of Moral Philosophy. London, 1754.

GAY, John, 1699–1745, Fellow of Sidney Sussex College, Cambridge, then Vicar of Wilshampstead.

A Dissertation concerning the Fundamental Principle of Virtue or Morality (prefixed to Edmund Law's translation of William King's *Essay on the Origin of Evil*). London, 1731; ed. 2, 1732; ed. 3, 1739.

GISBORNE, Thomas, 1758–1846, Curate of Barton-under-Needwood, then Prebendary of Durham.

The Principles of Moral Philosophy (in criticism of Paley). London, 1789; ed. 2, 1790; ed. 5, 1798. (See Croft.)

GLOVER, Phillips, High Sheriff of Lincolnshire.

(1) *A Discourse concerning Virtue and Religion.* London, 1732.

(2) *An Inquiry concerning Virtue and Happiness.* London, 1751.

GODWIN, William, 1756–1836.

(1) *An Enquiry concerning Political Justice and its influence on general virtue and happiness.* 2 vols. London, 1793; ed. 2, 1796; ed. 3, 1798.

(2) *Thoughts occasioned by ... Dr. Parr's Spital Sermon* (in reply to criticism by Parr, Mackintosh, and others). London, 1801.

(See Mackintosh, Parr.)

GREGORY, James, 1753–1821, Professor of Medicine at Edinburgh.

Philosophical and Literary Essays. 2 vols. Edinburgh, 1792. Includes criticism of Hume on liberty and necessity, which is answered by 'A Necessitarian', *Illustrations of Mr. Hume's Essay concerning Liberty and Necessity*, London, 1795.

GROVE, Henry, 1684–1738, tutor at the Taunton Academy.

(1) *Wisdom the first Spring of Action in the Deity.* London, 1734.

(2) *A System of Moral Philosophy.* 2 vols. London, 1749.

HARRIS, James, 1709–80 (author of *Hermes*).

Three Treatises . . . the third concerning Happiness. London, 1744; ed. 2, 1765; ed. 3, 1772.

HARTLEY, David, 1705–57, Fellow of Jesus College, Cambridge.

Observations on Man. London, 1749; ed. 2, 1791. (See Priestley.)

HIBERNICUS, see HUTCHESON, Francis.

HOBBES, Thomas, 1588–1679.

(1) *Elementa Philosophica de Cive.* Privately printed, as *Elementorum philosophiae sectio tertia: de Cive*, Paris, 1642. Published, Amsterdam, 1647. English translation, *Philosophical Rudiments concerning Government and Society*, London, 1651.

(2) *Human Nature.* London, 1650; ed. 2, 1651.

(3) *De Corpore Politico: or the Elements of Law, moral and politic.* London, 1650; ed. 2, 1652.

(4) *Leviathan: or the Matter, Form, and Power of a Commonwealth, ecclesiastical and civil.* London, 1651. Latin version in *Opera . . . Latine . . . omnia*, Amsterdam, 1668.

(5) *A Treatise of Liberty and Necessity.* London, 1654; corrected reprint, 1654.

(6) *The Questions concerning Liberty, Necessity, and Chance . . . debated between Dr. Bramhall . . . and Thomas Hobbes*: includes Hobbes's 'animadversions' on Bramhall's reply to (5). London, 1656.

(7) *Elementorum philosophiae sectio secunda: de Homine.* London, 1658.

(8) *Tracts . . . containing . . . II. An Answer to Archbishop Bramhall's book, called the catching of the Leviathan.* London, 1682.

(See Bramhall, Coke, Eachard, Laney, Lowde, Lucy, Ross, Shafto, Sharrock, Tenison.)

HOME, Henry, see KAMES, Lord.

HUME, David, 1711-76.

(1) *A Treatise of Human Nature.* 3 vols. London, 1739-40.

(2) *Essays, Moral and Political.* Edinburgh, 1741; ed. 2, 1742; ed. 3, 1748.

(3) *An Enquiry concerning Human Understanding.* First published as *Philosophical Essays concerning Human Understanding,* London, 1748; ed. 2, 1751.

(4) *An Enquiry concerning the Principles of Morals.* London, 1751.

(3) and (4) subsequently included in *Essays and Treatises on Several Subjects,* 4 vols., London and Edinburgh, 1753-4; further eds., 1758, 1760, 1764, 1768, 1770, 1777.

(5) *Dialogues concerning Natural Religion.* [London,] 1779; ed. 2, London, 1779; ed. 3, 1804.

(See Balfour, Gregory.)

HUTCHESON, Francis, 1694-1746, Professor of Moral Philosophy at Glasgow.

(1) *An Inquiry into the original of our Ideas of Beauty and Virtue.* London, 1725; ed. 2, 1726; ed. 3, 1729; ed. 4, 1738.

(2) *Reflections upon Laughter, and Remarks upon the Fable of the Bees.* Originally published in the *Dublin Journal,* 1725-6, among 'Letters to "Hibernicus" ' [James Arbuckle]; reprinted in Arbuckle's *Hibernicus's Letters,* 2 vols., London, 1729; published separately, Glasgow, 1750.

(3) *An Essay on the Nature and Conduct of the Passions and Affections. With Illustrations on the Moral Sense.* London, 1728; ed. 2, 1730; ed. 3, 1742.

(4) *Letters between . . . Gilbert Burnet and . . . Hutcheson, concerning . . . virtue or moral goodness.* Originally published in the *London Journal,* 1728; published separately, with preface by Burnet, London, 1735.

(5) *Philosophiae Moralis Institutio Compendiaria.* Glasgow, 1742; ed. 2, 1745. English translation, *A Short Introduction to Moral Philosophy,* Glasgow, 1747.

(6) *A System of Moral Philosophy.* 2 vols. Glasgow and London, 1755.

(7) *De Naturali Hominum Socialitate.* Glasgow, 1756.

(See Campbell, J. Clarke, Reid, John Taylor.)

INNES, Alexander, see CAMPBELL, Archibald.

JACKSON, John, 1686-1763, Rector of Rossington, then Prebendary of Wherwell and Master of Wigston's Hospital, Leicester.

A Defence of Human Liberty. London, 1725. Ed. 2, London, 1730, includes also *A Vindication of Human Liberty* (in criticism of Anthony Collins).

JAMESON, William, Minister of Rerick.

An Essay on Virtue and Harmony. Edinburgh, 1749.

JOHNSON, Thomas, d. 1737, Fellow of Magdalene College, Cambridge (editor of Pufendorf's *De Officio Hominis et Civis*, 1735).

An Essay on Moral Obligation (in criticism of Chubb). Cambridge, 1731.

KAMES, Henry Home, Lord, 1696–1782, Judge of the Scottish Court of Session.

(1) *Essays on the Principles of Morality and Natural Religion*. Edinburgh, 1751; ed. 2, 1758.

(2) *Objections against the Essays on Morality and Natural Religion Examined*. Edinburgh, 1756.

(See Balfour.)

KING, William, 1650–1729, Archbishop of Dublin.
De Origine Mali. Dublin and London, 1702. English translation by Edmund Law, *An Essay on the Origin of Evil*, with preliminary *Dissertation concerning . . . Virtue* by John Gay, London, 1731. (See Gay, E. Law.)

LANEY, Benjamin, 1591–1675, Bishop of Peterborough, then of Lincoln, then of Ely.

A Letter about Liberty and Necessity . . . by Thomas Hobbes of Malmesbury: With Observations upon it. London, 1676.

LAW, Edmund, 1703–87, Bishop of Carlisle.

Notes to his *Essay on the Origin of Evil* (English translation of William King's *De Origine Mali*). London, 1731; ed. 2, 1732; ed. 3, 1739; ed. 4, 1758; ed. 5, 1781.

LAW, William, 1686–1761, Fellow of Emmanuel College, Cambridge.

Remarks upon . . . the Fable of the Bees. London, 1724; ed. 2, 1725; ed. 3, 1726.

LOCKE, John, 1632–1704.

(1) *An Essay concerning Human Understanding*. London, 1690; ed. 2, 1694; ed. 3, 1695; ed. 4, 1700; ed. 5, 1706. (See Lowde.)

(2) *Essays on the Law of Nature*, ed. and trans. W. von Leyden. Oxford, 1954; corrected reprint, 1958.

LOWDE, James.

(1) *A Discourse concerning the Nature of Man* (in criticism of Hobbes). London, 1694.

(2) *Moral Essays* (in criticism of Locke and Malebranche). London, 1699.

LUCY, William, 1591–1677, Bishop of St. David's.

Observations, Censures and Confutations of divers Errors in the 12, 13, and 14 chap. of Mr. Hobbes his Leviathan. First published under the name of William Pike, London, 1657; ed. 2, under Lucy's real name, London, 1663.

MACKINTOSH, Sir James, 1765–1832.

(1) *A Discourse on the Study of the Law of Nature and Nations* (in criticism of Godwin). London, 1799; ed. 2, 1828. (See Godwin.)

(2) *Dissertation on the Progress of Ethical Philosophy.* Edinburgh, 1830.

MANDEVILLE, Bernard, 1670–1733.

(1) *The Grumbling Hive; or, Knaves turned Honest.* [London,] 1705. Afterwards included in (2).

(2) *The Fable of the Bees; or, Private Vices Public Benefits.* (Includes *An Inquiry into the Origin of Moral Virtue.*) London, 1714; ed. 2, 1723; ed. 3, 1724; ed. 4, 1725; ed. 5 (includes a second part), 1728; ed. 6, 1729.

(3) *A Letter to Dion* (i.e. Berkeley, in answer to criticism of Mandeville in *Alciphron*). London, 1732.

(4) *An Enquiry into the Origin of Honour.* London, 1732.

(See Bluett, Campbell, Dennis, Fiddes, Hutcheson, W. Law, Thorold.)

MORE, Henry, 1614–87, Fellow of Christ's College, Cambridge.

Enchiridion Ethicum. London, 1667, 1668; ed. 2, 1669; further eds., 1679, 1695. English translation by Edward Southwell, *An Account of Virtue*, London, 1690.

PALEY, William, 1743–1805, Archdeacon of Carlisle.

The Principles of Moral and Political Philosophy. London, 1785; ed. 2, 1786; ed. 5, 1788; ed. 6, 1788; ed. 7, 1790; ed. 12, 1799. (See Croft, Gisborne, Pearson.)

PALMER, John, 1729(?)–90, Dissenting Minister at New Broad Street, London.

(1) *Observations in Defence of the Liberty of Man, as a Moral Agent* (in criticism of Priestley). London, 1779.

(2) *An Appendix to the Observations etc.* (in reply to Priestley's *Letter*). London,
1780.

(See Priestley.)

PARR, Samuel, 1747–1825, schoolmaster, then Rector of Asterby and Vicar
of Hatton.

A Spital Sermon (in criticism of Godwin). London, 1801. (See Godwin.)

PEARSON, Edward, 1756–1811, Master of Sidney Sussex College, Cambridge.

(1) *Remarks on the Theory of Morals, . . . an examination of the theoretical part
of Dr. Paley's 'Principles of Moral and Political Philosophy'*. Ipswich, 1800.

(2) *Annotations on the practical part of Dr. Paley's 'Principles of Moral and
Political Philosophy'*. Ipswich, 1801.

PIKE, William, see LUCY, William.

PRICE, Richard, 1723–91, Dissenting Minister at Stoke Newington and at
Hackney.

(1) *A Review of the Principal Questions and Difficulties in Morals*. London,
1758; ed. 2, 1769; ed. 3, 1787.

(2) *A Free Discussion of the Doctrines of Materialism and Philosophical Necessity*
(correspondence between Price and Priestley). London, 1778. (See Dawes,
Priestley.)

PRIESTLEY, Joseph, 1733–1804, Dissenting Minister at Leeds, then at
Birmingham.

(1) *Hartley's Theory of the Human Mind, on the principle of Association of Ideas*.
London, 1775; ed. 2, 1790.

(2) *The Doctrine of Philosophical Necessity illustrated*. London, 1777; ed. 2,
Birmingham, 1782.

(3) *A Free Discussion of the Doctrines of Materialism and Philosophical Necessity*
(correspondence between Price and Priestley). London, 1778.

(4) *A Letter to the Rev. Mr. J. Palmer in defence of . . . Philosophical Necessity*.
Bath and London, 1779.

(5) *A Letter to Jacob Bryant, Esq., in defence of Philosophical Necessity*. London
and Birmingham, 1780.

(See Bryant, Dawes, Palmer.)

REID, Thomas, 1710–96, Professor of Philosophy at King's College, Aberdeen, then Professor of Moral Philosophy at Glasgow.

(1) *An Essay on Quantity, etc.* (in criticism of Hutcheson's application of mathematical formulae to ethics). First published in *Philosophical Transactions*, 1748.

(2) *An Inquiry into the Human Mind, on the Principles of Common Sense.* Edinburgh, 1764; ed. 2, 1765; ed. 3, London, 1769; ed. 4, 1785.

(3) *Essays on the Intellectual Powers of Man.* Edinburgh, 1785.

(4) *Essays on the Active Powers of Man.* Edinburgh, 1788.

ROSS, Alexander, 1590–1654, schoolmaster at Southampton.

Leviathan drawn out with a Hook. London, 1653.

RUTHERFORTH, Thomas, 1712–71, Professor of Divinity at Cambridge, and Archdeacon of Essex.

An Essay on the Nature and Obligations of Virtue. Cambridge, 1744. (See Chubb, Cockburn.)

SANDERSON, Robert, 1587–1663, Bishop of Lincoln.

(1) *De Juramenti promissorii obligatione.* London, 1647. English translation (said to be by Charles I), *De Juramento: Seven lectures concerning the obligation of promissory Oaths*, London, 1655. Abridged English version, *A Discourse concerning the Nature and Obligation of Oaths*, London, 1716.

(2) *De Obligatione Conscientiae.* London, 1660; another ed., 1661. English translation by R. Codrington, *Several Cases of Conscience discussed*, London, 1660.

SHAFTESBURY, Anthony Ashley Cooper, Third Earl of, 1671–1713.

(1) *An Inquiry concerning Virtue.* London, 1699.

(2) *The Moralists, a philosophical rhapsody.* London, 1709.

(1) and (2) reprinted in *Characteristics of Men, Manners, Opinions, and Times*, vol. ii, London, 1711; ed. 2, 1714.

(See Balguy, Brown, Fiddes, Whichcote.)

SHAFTO, John.

The great Law of Nature, etc. (in criticism of Hobbes). London, 1673.

SHARROCK, Robert, 1630–84, Archdeacon of Winchester.

(1) Ὑπόθεσις ἠθική, *De Officiis secundum Naturae Jus* (in criticism of Hobbes). Oxford, 1660; further eds., 1667, 1682.

(2) *De Finibus Virtutis Christianae*. Oxford, 1673.

(3) *The Royal Table of the Laws of Human Nature*. London, 1682.

SILVESTER, Tipping, 1700–68, Vicar of Shabbington.
Moral and Christian Benevolence. A sermon (containing reflections on Balguy).
London, 1734.

SMITH, Adam, 1723–90, Professor of Moral Philosophy at Glasgow.
The Theory of Moral Sentiments. London and Edinburgh, 1759; ed. 2, 1761;
ed. 3, 1767; ed. 4, 1774; ed. 5, 1781; ed. 6, 1790.

SMITH, John, 1618–52, Fellow of Queens' College, Cambridge.
Select Discourses. London, 1660; ed. 2, Cambridge, 1673.

STEWART, Dugald, 1753–1828, Professor of Moral Philosophy at Edinburgh.

(1) *Outlines of Moral Philosophy*. Edinburgh and London, 1793; ed. 2, 1801;
ed. 3, 1808; ed. 4, 1818; ed. 5, 1829.

(2) *The Philosophy of the Active and Moral Powers of Man*. 2 vols. Edinburgh
and London, 1828.

TAYLOR, Jeremy, 1613–67, Bishop of Down and Connor.
Ductor Dubitantium or the Rule of Conscience. London, 1660.

TAYLOR, John, 1694–1761, Dissenting Minister at Norwich, then tutor at
the Warrington Academy.

(1) *An Examination of the Scheme of Morality advanced by Dr. Hutcheson*.
London, 1759.

(2) *A Sketch of Moral Philosophy*. London, 1760.

TENISON, Thomas, 1636–1715, Archbishop of Canterbury.
The Creed of Mr. Hobbes examined. London, 1670; ed. 2, 1671.

THOROLD, Sir John, Bart.
A short examination of . . . The Fable of the Bees. London, 1726.

TUCKER, Abraham, 1705–74.

(1) *Freewill, Foreknowledge, and Fate*. London, 1763.

(2) *The Light of Nature pursued*. 2 vols. London, 1768.

TUCKNEY, Anthony, see WHICHCOTE, Benjamin.

TURNBULL, George.
The Principles of Moral Philosophy. 2 vols. London, 1740.

TYRRELL, James, 1642–1718.
A Brief Disquisition of the Law of Nature (abridgement of Cumberland). London, 1692; ed. 2, 1701.

WARBURTON, William, 1698–1779, Bishop of Gloucester.
The Divine Legation of Moses demonstrated. London, vol. i, 1738; ed. 2, 1738; ed. 3, 1742; ed. 4, 1755; ed. 5, 1766: vol. ii, 1741; ed. 2, 1742; ed. 3, 1758; ed. 4, 1765. (See Cockburn.)

WHICHCOTE, Benjamin, 1609–83, Provost of King's College, Cambridge.
(1) *Select Sermons,* with a preface by Shaftesbury. London, 1698.
(2) *Moral and Religious Aphorisms.* London, 1703; ed. 2, including correspondence between Whichcote and Anthony Tuckney, London, 1753.

WILKINS, John, 1614–72, Warden of Wadham College, Oxford, then Bishop of Chester.
(1) *An Essay towards a real Character and a Philosophical Language.* London, 1668.
(2) *Of the Principles and Duties of Natural Religion.* London, 1675.

WOLLASTON, William, 1660–1724.
The Religion of Nature delineated. Privately printed, 1722. Published, London, 1724; ed. 2, 1725. (See Bott, J. Clarke.)

INDEX

The references are to the marginal sections of the text. Figures enclosed in parentheses (unless preceded by 'cf.') refer to passages opposed in sense to the preceding entry, often indicating direct criticism. References comparing an entry with passages in other authors are confined to works written earlier than the entry compared.

abilities

[*Hutcheson*]—and benevolence jointly determine the moral importance of an agent or the quantity of public good he produces, 335. perfection of virtue when the amount of good produced equals the ability, 337. the taking account of abilities in approbation demonstrates that benevolence is amiable, 340.

[*Hume*] whether natural abilities be virtues is a dispute of words, 632; cf. 608–12.

absolute,—goodness, no such thing as, 4 (227).—obligation, dist. accidental, 123–4.—fitness of beneficence and justice, 226.—necessity, dist. moral, 232. not in a man's power to promise absolutely, 288.—goodness of benevolence, 351. beauty a species of absolute truth, 443*n*. —goodness of virtue, 454.—or abstract virtue, dist. relative or practical, 719*n*., 750–1; cf. 724.

abstract,—relations of things, 374.—inquiries do not go well with moralizing, 630.—and universal ideas, perceived by the intellect, 663, 669.—ideas have a universality which is not merely nominal, 669.—or absolute virtue, dist. practical or relative, 750–1; cf. 719*n*., 724. actions in the abstract are right or wrong according to their tendency, 854*n*. actions considered abstractly are morally good in a different sense from that in which agents are, 897–900.

absurdity

[*Hobbes*] injustice or injury resembles absurdity or self-contradiction, 59, 102.

[*Clarke*]—or iniquity in practice, resembles self-contradiction, 232, 242, 257.

[*Wollaston*]—of treating things as being what they are not, 283.

[*Hutcheson*]—produced by substitut-ing definition of obligation for the term defined, 350; cf. 351.

accidental,—obligation, dist. absolute, 123–4.—consequences, dist. tendencies, 579*n*.; cf. 555, 633.

acts

[*Locke*] actions of men the best interpreters of their thoughts, 156.

[*Shaftesbury*]—depend on motive of affection or passion, being determined by the balance of stronger and weaker affections, 209.

[*Wollaston*]—moral, imply intelligence and free choice, 273.—may deny or contradict truth, 275–9.—have meaning or signification, 275–6, 279.—interfering with truth, must be wrong or unnatural, 280 (368, 494–6, 959).

[*Hutcheson*] three elements in our ideas of actions, 371.

[*Butler*] actions, including intentions but not necessarily actual consequences, are the object of the moral faculty, 430. will and design constitute the very nature of actions as such, 430.

[*Balguy*] moral actions concern behaviour toward intelligent or sensible, not toward insensible, objects, 448. actions must spring from free choice, 448.

[*Hume*] action cannot be produced by reason alone, 479–82. action and passion are influenced by morality, which therefore cannot be derived from reason, 489. an active principle can never be founded on an inactive, 489.—cannot be reasonable or unreasonable, 490 (857). —are praised only as signs of motive or inward principle, 512, 633.—of men, generally uniform, 615.—irregular or extraordinary, due to opposition of contrary causes, 617.—and motives, are regularly conjoined, 619–20; but are

acts (*cont.*):

not felt to have a necessary connection, 621.—performance of, dist. reflecting on, 623.

[*Price*] the ideas of action and of right would be incompatible if moral ideas were the effect of sensation, 681. all actions must have a nature or character, right, wrong, or indifferent, 683. actions may be described as right and wrong, agents as of good and ill desert, 695. virtue of the action, dist. virtue of the agent, 724, 755; cf. 719*n.*, 750–1.—two senses of, (1) volitions, including intentions, (2) external effect produced, 756.

[*Paley*] actions in the abstract are right or wrong according to their tendency, dist. virtue or vice of the agent, which depends on his design, 854*n.*

[*Reid*] every deliberate human action must be done either as a means or as an end, 859. actions considered abstractly are morally good in a different sense from that in which agents are, 897–900; cf. Price, 719*n.*, 750.—solitary, dist. social, 902.

[*Bentham*] act dist. consequences, both together making the action, 979.—intentionality of, in relation to that of the consequences, 980–1.

Addison,—cited by Hutcheson, 356.

admiration,—dist. approbation, 783.

advantage, see *interest, utility.*

affection, see *benevolence, desire, passion, virtue.*

[*Shaftesbury*] good or ill of a sensible creature depends on motive of passion or affection, 199.—natural and unnatural, 199, 210.—towards affections themselves, arises from reflection or reflected sense, 200.—aesthetic, compared with moral, 201. sense of right or wrong, a sentiment or judgement of what is done through good or bad affection, 202.—social, necessary to a sensible creature, 203. good affections to society as well as self, necessary for virtue, 205.—natural, directed to the good of the species or common nature, 205–6.—public, appears, but mistakenly, to conflict with private, 206–7.—necessary for action, which depends on the balance of stronger and weaker affections, 209. natural affections lead to public good, self-affections to private good, unnatural affections to neither, 210.—natural, may be too strong, 211.—private, may be too weak, and is necessary

for goodness, 212. too great weakness of public affection, or too great strength of private affection, or unnatural affection in any degree, is vice, and therefore contrary to private interest, 213–14, 221.—natural, the chief means to happiness, 215–19. natural affections, or their effects, are the mental pleasures, 216. charm of kind affection superior to all other pleasure, 217.—kind, shown in sexual love to be superior to sensual, 218.—natural or kind, pleases even in adversity, as tragedy shows, 218.—kind, effects of, are enjoyment of good by communication, and consciousness of approbation of others, 219.—connection and balance of, necessary for happiness, 222.

[*Clarke*]—natural, for kin and friends, 244.

[*Hutcheson*]—approved by the moral sense, is entirely different from self-love, 306. every action judged morally good or evil flows from some affection toward sensitive creatures, 315. all passions and affections justify themselves, 322.—disinterested, the spring of virtuous action, 327.—calm, dist. particular passions, 331, 357, 369; cf. Butler, 382–3, 414–16.—benevolent, a motive to election, 359.—instincts and, presupposed by exciting reasons for action, 361–2. all affections included under self-love, self-hatred, benevolence, and malice, 362.—instinct and, said to be necessary, not voluntary, 373.

[*Butler*]—particular, dist. self-love, 382–3, 414–16.—particular, dist. both benevolence (cf. Hutcheson, 331) and self-love, 389.—particular, has as object a particular external thing, not the pleasure arising from its gratification, 414–15.—particular, subservient to self-love, 422.

[*Balguy*]—benevolent, an aid or incentive to virtue, but not the true ground of it, 437 (336).—absence of, would not prevent us from discovering obligations, 439.—cannot be the ground of virtue, since any degree of virtue varies inversely with strength of affection, 441.

[*Gay*]— = desire of future pleasure, consequent upon the present pleasure of imagining it, 467. the passions and affections are mistakenly thought to be innate, 467.—and approbation are acquired, not innate or instinctive, 473.—public, 474, 478.

[*Hume*]—natural, the duty of a parent, 513.—excited by utility of virtue, not by that of inanimate objects, 574n.; cf. Hutcheson, 307.

[*Hartley*]—four classes of sympathetic, 642.

[*Price*]—dist. will, 661n.— = rational desire, dist. passion, 694.

[*Smith*]—or sentiment from which action proceeds, may be considered under two aspects, that of propriety, depending on cause or motive, and that of merit, depending on end or tendency, 773.—of another, is approved as proper if it corresponds with our own, 775.

agent, see *acts.*—dist. instrument, 273.—moral, dist. sensible, 460–1.—rational, has the power of governing or directing good and evil, and of acting for an end, 468.—alone, not action, may be described as of good or ill desert, 695. virtue of the action, dist. virtue of the agent, 724, 755; cf. 719n., 750–1, 897–900. agency or self-determination as free choice, 752–3. in judging my own conduct, I divide myself into two persons, the spectator and the agent, 804.—is virtuous or vicious according to his design, while actions are right or wrong according to their tendency, 854n.

agreement, see *fitness, reason.*

[*Clarke*]—or disagreement of some things with others, 226.

[*Wollaston*] some acts, like most words, have significancy by custom and agreement, 279.

[*Balguy*] moral relations of agreement and disagreement, like mathematical, perceived by the understanding, 451, 459.—or disagreement, as constituting truth, whether of ideas or of things, 452.—between bounty and gratitude, 456–8.

[*Hume*]—or convention, to ensure stability of possessions, 528.

[*Smith*] to approve of opinions, as of sentiments or passions, is to observe their agreement with our own, 771; cf. 775.

Alcibiades, 578.

Alexander (*Exegetes*),—cited by Cudworth, 144.

Allestree(?), presumed author of *Whole Duty of Man*,—referred to by Hume, 632.

amiable,—virtues, dist. respectable, 781–2; cf. 612.

animal,—motion, 2, 4.—principles of action, dist. mechanical and rational, 856, 858.—principles, commonly called passions, 863.—motives, dist. rational, 885–8.

animals,—may be considered susceptive and desirous of happiness, 300.—capable of a lower kind of virtue, 349 (440).—differ from men in lacking certain principles of action, particularly reflection or conscience, 378; cf. 430.—follow nature in gratifying appetite, 400.—may be objects but not subjects of virtue, 440 (349).—would be subject to the same morality as men if morality consisted in relations, 502. men have duties of humanity, but not of justice, towards animals, 572. the idea of having obligations as a sensible agent implies that the term 'obligation' could be applied to brutes, 717 (455, 460).—have no conception of good upon the whole, 862.

appetite, see *desire.*

[*Hobbes*]—and aversion, forms of endeavour, 3, 24.—the beginning of animal motion, 4.

[*Mandeville*]—conquest of, urged by lawgivers, 263–4.

[*Hutcheson*]—rational (dist. sensitive), often called the will, 357.

[*Butler*] appetites, passions, and particular affections, dist. self-love and benevolence, 389.—or passion, implies a direct simple tendency towards a particular object, 401, 414.—does not have as object the pleasure arising from its gratification, 415.

[*Price*]—or passion (instinctive desire), dist. affection (rational desire), 694.

approbation, see *conscience, moral sense, sentiment, sympathy, virtue.*

[*Locke*]—and disapprobation, the common measure of virtue and vice, or right and wrong, 187.

[*Shaftesbury*]—of moral qualities, produced by reflection, 204.—consciousness of, an effect of kind affection, 219.

[*Hutcheson*]—a simple idea, procured by a quality called moral goodness, 303, 358.—of affection, desire, or intention by the moral sense, 306.—excited by benevolence, not by prospect of advantage, 307, 359 (468–73).—dist. election, 358; cf. 361.—reasons for, presuppose a moral sense, 363–7.—by the moral sense, not an image of anything external, 371.

[*Butler*]—reflex, of conscience, 380. we approve or disapprove certain dispositions and actions abstracted from

approbation (*cont.*):

consideration of their tendency to the happiness or misery of the world, 427*n.*; cf. 434 (963).—faculty of, attested by common language and common behaviour, whether considered a sentiment of the understanding or a perception of the heart or both, 429.—is of action, including intention but not necessarily actual consequences, 430.—of prudence, 433.

[*Balguy*]—does not constitute merit but is produced by it, 442 (373). grounding of approbation on a moral sense is subject to the same objections as grounding virtue on affection, 444–5.—from the reasons of things, compared to assent from evidence, 450, 453.—is itself an exciting reason for choice of virtue, and is justified by its necessity, 453 (361).

[*Gay*]—and obligation, implied by virtue, 462.—is directed towards means to pleasure, 467.—of my promoting the happiness of others, is necessary as a means to exciting them to promote mine, 468.—implies desire, 468.—and affection are acquired, not innate or instinctive, 473.

[*Hume*] a sentiment of disapprobation is all that one can find in seeking a matter of fact called vice, 503; cf. 634.—of virtue, as of beauty, is implied in an immediate feeling of pleasure of a particular kind, 506.—has as its object the motive of action, 512; cf. 633.—of justice, arises from sympathy with public interest, 534, 548.—of artificial virtues, due solely to their utility, 549; cf. 566–71, 582.—of many of the natural virtues, likewise due to utility and sympathy, 549–50; cf. 564–5.—natural sentiment of, necessary before it could be excited by politicians, 550; cf. Hutcheson, 311 (263–9).—of natural virtues, more likely than that of the artificial to be the effect of sympathy with benefit produced, 552.—may be caused by reflection on utility, or by immediate taste or sentiment, 558; cf. 584–5.—of the immediately agreeable, as of the useful, depends on sympathy, 559, 585.—excited by utility of virtue, not by utility of inanimate objects, 574*n.*; cf. Hutcheson, 307.—of utility, extends beyond our own interest to the interest of those affected by the character or action approved, 575–6.—general standard of, a regard to the general interests of the community, 580.—must be founded on the sentiment of humanity, which concerns public good and is therefore shared by all and liable to be directed upon all, 589–91.—is therefore expressed by the peculiar language of morals, 592. virtue defined as whatever mental action or quality gives to a spectator the pleasing sentiment of approbation, 600.—different kinds of, produced by different virtues and different talents, 612.

[*Price*] what is the power that determines us to approve and disapprove? 656.—faculty of immediate, 657; cf. 672, 696. there are some actions that are ultimately approved, and for justifying which no reason can be assigned, 672; cf. Hutcheson, 362–3. every being must desire happiness for himself, and a rational nature must therefore approve of actions procuring it, 679.—of making the virtuous happy and discouraging the vicious, is immediate and not wholly founded on utility, 696.—of an action, is the same as discerning it to be right, as assenting to a proposition is the same as discerning it to be true, 707.—dist. obligation, 719 (346).—of gratitude, justice, and veracity is not grounded on utility, 730.—is not limited to one sort of actions, 732.

[*Smith*] to approve of the passions of another, as suitable to their objects, is the same thing as to observe that we sympathize with them, 770, 775.—of opinions, as of sentiments or passions, is to observe their agreement with our own, 771.—may depend on hypothetical, not actual, sympathy, 772; cf. 799.—of propriety, dist. admiration of virtue, 783. an action deserves reward or punishment if it is the proper and approved object of gratitude or resentment, 786–8.—and propriety of passions, depend on the sympathy of the impartial spectator, 789.—of merit, unlike that of propriety, may arise from illusive sympathy without actual correspondence of sentiments, 799. self-approbation depends on sympathy with the imagined approbation of the impartial spectator, 800.—and disapprobation of society, is the mirror in which a man can view the beauty or deformity of his mind, 801–3; cf. Hume, 593.—of virtue, is enhanced by, but is not primarily or principally due to, the beauty of utility, 832 (560, 586).—of virtue, differs from that of convenient material things (cf. Hume, 574*n*.), and includes a sense of propriety distinct from the perception of utility, 833, 844. —has been ascribed to three different sources, self-love, reason, and sentiment, 834. the dispute about the principle of approbation is of importance only for speculation, not for practice, 835; cf. Hume, 503, 634.—as sentiment, two theories of, (1) moral sense, (2) sympathy, 836. if the principle of approbation were a moral sense, it could not be itself the object of moral judgement, 838. if it were a peculiar sentiment, it would be the same in all instances, whereas in fact there are different types of approbation for different types of virtue, 840; cf. 781–2; and cf. Hume, 612.—of approbation itself, can only be explained by sympathy, 841.—is not limited in meaning to morals, but covers whatever is entirely to our satisfaction, 842.—is derived from four sources, (1) sympathy with the motives of the agent, (2) sympathy with the gratitude of the beneficiary, (3) observation that the action conforms to the general rules of sympathy, (4) thought of utility, 843.

[*Reid*] the rational principle of regard to our good upon the whole produces a kind of self-approbation, 866; cf. Butler, 433. actions deserve moral approbation only if done from a belief that they are right, 894; cf. Price, 755, 758. does approbation include judgement or is it feeling alone? 907. if moral approbation includes judgement, a statement expressing it can have, as it does have, a different meaning from that of a statement expressing feeling, 922. but if moral approbation were feeling alone, the first statement would either have the same meaning as the second, which is not the case, or would be meaningless, 923.

[*Bentham*] the principle of utility is a sentiment approving utility as the quality by which approbation ought to be governed, 947*n*.—without regard to consequences, if taken to be a standard of right and wrong, is either despotical or anarchial, 954.—reason or ground of, dist. motive or cause of action, 966; cf. 963.

Aristotle,—cited by Hobbes, 80; by Cudworth, 125, 133, 146, 153; by Hutcheson, 362–3. — criticized by Hobbes, 73.

art,—and nature, 21; cf. 510.
artificial
[*Hobbes*]—the state as, 21.—person represents another, 78.—covenant as, 80. civil laws, artificial chains, 84.

[*Hume*] sense of some virtues is artificial, of others natural, 510, 512, 546. both virtue and vice equally may be called artificial, 511. justice an artificial virtue, 512, 519, 631; but not arbitrary, 521. artifice of convention is required to bestow stability on possession of external goods, 527.—character of promises, shown by invalidity of contracts entered through force, 545.— virtues, esteemed through sympathy with the good of society, 548.
asceticism
[*Bentham*]—principle of, dist. principle of utility and principle of sympathy and antipathy, 955.—principle of, is at bottom the principle of utility misapplied, and cannot be consistently pursued, 956.
association
[*Butler*] natural association of the two ideas, moral and natural evil, wickedness and punishment, 431.

[*Gay*]—of ideas with pleasure, causes means to be mistaken for ends, 477.—of ideas is often learned from others by imitation, 478.

[*Hume*] through sympathy the mind passes immediately from effects of passion to causes, or vice versa, 546. imagination passes easily from cause to likely effect, 556. the mind is carried by a customary transition from one of two constantly conjoined objects to the other, 621.

[*Hartley*]—of sensations and ideas, as the possible source of all intellectual pleasures and pains, 635; cf. Gay, 475–8. —a more accurate and precise description than the power of habit and custom, 638–9.—as the effect of vibrations, 638–40.—of sensations, causes all the corresponding ideas to be excited by any one of the sensations, 639.—synchronous, dist. successive, 639.—causes simple ideas to run into complex ones, 640.—helps to produce intellectual pleasures and pains from sensible ones, 641.—proved by the existence of pure disinterested benevolence, which arises from associated advantages though not attended by direct explicit advantage, 644.—as the source of compassion,

association (*cont.*):
especially evident in children, 645.—can provide analysis and explanation of the pleasures and pains of the moral sense, 646–54.—the cause of all reasoning as well as affection, 654.

[*Bentham*] perverse association of ideas of good and bad with the names of motives, 995.

atheists, 146.

authority, see *conscience, law, obligation.* — = the right of doing an action, 78.— of a commonwealth, 81.—of natural law, comes from God, 106, 111.—of commanding, depends on natural justice, 122–4.—of conscience, 379–81, 399–402, 406.—dist. strength or power, 379, 402–4.—obligations arising from, a compound of moral and natural, 461.— of the moral sense, 653.—implied by the direction of rectitude, 713. reason a natural and authoritative guide, 713.— evident badges of, carried by our moral faculties, 822.

Bacon,—cited by Hume, 576.

Balguy, 436–61. see especially *obligation, reason, virtue.*—cites Clarke, 447.—cited by Price, 761*n.*—criticizes Hutcheson, 436–47, 451, 453–5; Wollaston, 452.— criticized by Price, 690, 717.—refers to Shaftesbury, 447.

beauty
[*Hobbes*]— = what promises good, 25.—or perfection of the universe, consistent with necessity, 95.

[*Shaftesbury*]—sense of, compared with moral approval, 201.—of moral acts, 203. the charm of kind affection, 217.—of virtue in adversity, shown in tragedy, 218.

[*Hutcheson*]—of actions, 305, 340.—or excellence of kind affections, 307. moral sense makes benevolent actions appear beautiful, 309 (443).—moral, 328, 331, 340.

[*Balguy*] *pulchrum*, dist. *honestum*, 443. —moral or natural, a species of absolute truth, perceived by the understanding alone, 443*n.* (309, 690).

[*Hume*]—judgement of, compared with judgement of virtue, 506–7, 554, 556–8, 561, 574, 603.—of useful objects, due to sympathy with pleasure produced for the possessor, 547.—sentiments of, depend much on the imagination, 556–7.—utility of, 574.—moral and natural, compared, 603.—does not con-

sist in relations or qualities, but is their effect on the sentiments of a spectator, 603 (937).

[*Hartley*]—natural or artificial, gives rise to pleasures of imagination; moral, gives rise to pleasures of the moral sense, 637.

[*Price*]—and deformity denote feelings of pleasure and pain, not real qualities, 685, 690 (443*n.*); but these feelings are the result of a natural aptitude of real natures to please or offend, 686–7. virtue is naturally adapted to please every observing mind, 687, 689. *pulchrum*, dist. *honestum*, 689; cf. Balguy, 443.—is the effect of, not identical with, order and regularity, 690 (443*n.*).

[*Smith*]—judgements of, do not depend on any peculiar relation to the persons judging or judged of, and so do not require sympathy based on imaginary change of situation, 776. differences in aesthetic judgement do not affect us as does lack of harmony in moral feelings, 777. our ideas of beauty and deformity, whether aesthetic or moral, depend on society, 801–2.—utility is a principal source of, 824.—afforded by utility enhances, but is not the first or principal source of, approbation of virtue, 832–3, 843 (560, 586).

[*Reid*]—and deformity are mistakenly supposed by modern philosophy to be subjective, 908, 925. the view that beauty is a feeling of the spectator, not a quality of the object, is a paradox contrary to common language and common sense, 937 (603).

benevolence, see *humanity, love, self-love, virtue.*

[*Hobbes*] good will or charity, assisting other men in their desires, evidence of power, 13 (388*n.*).— = desire of good to another, 29.

[*Cumberland*]—of each towards all, forms the happiest state of each and all, 107; cf. 118. the term is here used for effective, not ineffective, volition, 107.—a more suitable word than 'love', 107.

[*Shaftesbury*] see *affection.*

[*Clarke*]—or love, endeavouring to promote the happiness of all men, one of the two branches of duty to fellow creatures, 241, 243–4.—duty of, may be deduced from greatest fitness of greatest good, 243; and from men's natural need of friendship and society, 244.—duty of, presupposed by Hobbes's laws of nature, 254-5.

[*Hutcheson*]—approved by the moral sense, 307, 309, 328, 359.—desire of the happiness of another, a species of love, 316.—necessarily disinterested, 318.—and self-love, may be joint motives to the same action, 319. suggestions that benevolence depends on self-love, either by the voluntary or by the necessary occasioning of benevolence as a means to private happiness, 320; but neither benevolence nor any other affection or desire can be directly raised by volition, 321; and benevolence may be attended with pain, 322; further, desire of the happiness of others as a means to our own is not approved, as benevolence is, 323; and benevolence does not include an intention to obtain private pleasure, 324.—essential for moral goodness, 328.—may be overcome by mistaken self-love or other motives, which then are the ordinary spring of vice, 329.—the internal spring of virtue, 331.—three different senses of, 331-2; cf. 357, 369. a moral agent may be, in part, an object of his own universal benevolence, 332.—and ability, jointly determine the moral importance of an agent or the quantity of public good he produces, 335.—alone, not always the entire spring of good actions, but still the criterion of virtue, 336 (437).—want of, shown in crimes of ignorance owing to prior neglect, 339.—shown to be necessarily amiable by the taking account of abilities in approbation, 340.—universal, compared to gravitation, 343.—natural obligation to, 346.—the most probable means of promoting natural good, 347.—absolutely good, 351.—or desire of the public natural happiness of rational agents, 351.—of God, may be inferred from his boundless wisdom and power, 354.—universal, could exist in a nature superior to human, 357.—as well as self-love, can be a motive to election, 359.—of God, may be inferred from our approval of kind affections, which tend to the happiness of his creatures, 366.

[*Butler*]—no more opposed to self-love than is any other particular affection, 382, 384.—no more disinterested than particular passions, 384, 419.—may be blameable, 384.—natural principle of, shown in affections such as compassion,

388.—differs from, but coincides with, self-love, 388.—identified by Hobbes with love of power through confusing benevolence with ambition, 388*n.* (13).—and self-love, both dist. particular passions and affections, 389.—a natural principle of attraction in man towards man, 391; cf. Hutcheson, 343.—mistakenly alleged to be in competition with self-love, 418-23.—is in a degree its own reward, 420.—as a particular affection, is subservient to self-love, 422.—strongest obligation to, arises from religion, 423.—as the sum of virtue, is not a blind propension but a rational principle, 425.—comprises the common virtues, but with qualifications in regard to our approval of some, 427. the moral attributes of God may all be resolved into goodness, i.e. benevolence, 428.—implies piety or the love of God, 428.—is not the whole of virtue, 434-5.

[*Balguy*]—an aid or incentive to virtue, but not the true ground of it, 437 (336).—of God, cannot be an ungrounded disposition, 438 (366).

[*Hume*]—an originally implanted instinct, 485.—as the principle of humanity, 513.—public or private, cannot be the original motive to justice, 518. selfishness and limited generosity, combined with instability and scarcity of external possessions, make justice necessary, 525-6, 532, 540. an increase of benevolence, or of the bounty of nature, would render justice useless, 532, 567-8.—is esteemed even when ineffectual, owing to the working of the imagination, 555-6. no contradiction between limited generosity and extensive sympathy, 557. nothing can bestow more merit than the sentiment of benevolence, and at least a part of this merit is due to utility, 565.—natural sentiment of, causes us to approve social virtues for their utility, 581.—approved both because useful and because immediately agreeable by sympathy, 584; cf. 558.—may be excessive and so blamed (cf. Butler, 384), but is still loved, 584. relative degrees of benevolence and self-love not worth disputing, 588. were benevolence the only virtue, no characters could be mixed, 632.

[*Hartley*]—two senses of, 644.—disinterested, arises from associated advantages without there being direct explicit advantage, 644.

benevolence (*cont.*):

[*Price*]—is essential to intelligent beings, as well as self-love to sensible beings, 693.—rational and dispassionate, would be too weak a principle in man if unaided by instinct, 694; cf. 688.—is not the whole of virtue, 730–2; cf. Butler, 434–5. beneficence as one of the main branches of virtue, and as the most general and leading consideration in our inquiries concerning right, 736–7.—rational or universal, which is a principle of virtue, dist. instinctive, which is not, 760; cf. Balguy, 441–2.

[*Smith*] to restrain selfish and indulge benevolent affections constitutes the perfection of human nature, 782.

[*Bentham*] the motive of good will or benevolence may be regarded as good or bad according to circumstances, 996. the dictates of good will or benevolence are most likely to coincide with those of the principle of utility, for the dictates of utility are simply those of the most extensive and enlightened benevolence, 999. partial benevolence may be opposed to utility, i.e. to a more extensive benevolence, 999.

Bentham, 946–99. see especially *intention, motive, pleasure, utility*.—criticizes Hutcheson, 959; Wollaston, 959.—refers to Rochefoucauld, Mandeville, and Helvetius, 994n.

Berkeley,—criticized by Reid, 908.

blame, see *praise*.—implies judgement as well as feeling, 934 (597).

body,—and mind, faculties or powers of, 1.—and mind, pleasures of, 215.

Boethius,—cited by Cudworth, 132.

Bramhall,—criticized by Hobbes, 90–9.

brutes, see *animals*.

Butler, 374–435. see especially *benevolence, conscience, happiness, interest, nature, self-love, virtue*.—cites Wollaston, 375; Cicero, 382n., 430n.; Epicureans, 383, 385–6; St. Paul, 387, 395, 397–9, 410, 413, 424, 427; Hobbes, 429; Epictetus, 429n.; Marcus Aurelius, 430n.—cited by Price, 730, 737.—criticizes Shaftesbury, 380–1; Hobbes, 382, 388n., 411; Epicureans, 382; Rochefoucauld, 382; Mandeville, 391; Hutcheson, 435.—criticized by Gay, 470.

Cabalists, 129.

Caesar, 612.

calm

[*Hutcheson*]—affections, dist. particular passions, 331, 357, 369. general calm desires require reflection, 357.

[*Butler*] cool or settled selfishness, dist. passionate or sensual selfishness, 382. cool self-love, 393, 400. when we sit down in a cool hour, 423.

[*Hume*]—passion or desire, dist. violent emotions or passions, 485 (864). —and indolent judgements of the understanding, 489; cf. 607.

[*Price*] universal, calm benevolence and reasonable, calm self-love, both virtuous principles, 761.

[*Smith*] violent emotion or passion, dist. entering coolly into the sentiments of the indifferent spectator, 813–14.

[*Reid*] regard to our good upon the whole is a rational principle which operates in a calm and cool manner, 863.

Cato, 94, 311, 612.

cause

[*Hobbes*] sufficient cause also a necessary cause, 97, 99 (139–40, 152). all events have necessary causes, 99; cf. 97 (152).

[*Cumberland*] actions which have free causes are themselves necessary causes, 110, 114.—and 'effect', clearer terms, and more suitable for demonstration, than 'means' and 'end', 113.

[*Cudworth*]—efficient, dist. formal, 120. choice is a sufficient cause which is not necessary, 140. desire or love of good and happiness is the first mover of action, 147. man is not always determined by necessary causes, 150. a sufficient cause need not be a necessary cause, 152 (97, 99).

[*Hume*] causes or effects of action may be alleged to make it contradictory to reason or truth, 491–6.—and effect, discoverable only by experience, 500. will or choice can be a cause of action but not a cause of different relations from those of a similar action done without choice, 501. causes ought not to be multiplied without necessity, 549. we must stop somewhere in our examination of causes, 576n. idea of cause and necessity arises from the constant conjunction of similar objects and the consequent inference from one to the other, 614, 621–2 (667). contrariety of causes accounts for apparently irregular effects, 617. maxim of philosophers that the connection between all causes and effects is equally necessary, 617. in a chain of natural causes and voluntary actions, the mind feels no difference in passing from one link to another, 620. men mistakenly suppose that they perceive a necessary connection between cause and effect, 621. nothing exists without a cause of its existence, 625.— must be defined as including necessary connection, unless the definition is to be unintelligible or a mere synonym, 625.—and so necessity in actions, is presupposed by rewards and punishments, 628 (891).

[*Price*]—idea of, dist. occasion, perceived by the understanding, 667-8 (614, 621-2).—of (free) actions is the agent himself, 752.—dist. occasion, 753*n*.

[*Smith*]—or motive of affection, determines its propriety, while end or tendency determines its merit, 773, 785. —of affection, has been unduly neglected by philosophers in concentrating on effects, 774.

[*Reid*]—influence of, differs from that of motives, 881; cf. Price, 753*n*.—presupposed by motives, 881.

[*Bentham*] pleasure and pain supply both the causes of action and the standard of right and wrong, 946. the question whether moral sentiment always arises from thought of utility is irrelevant to the question whether it is justified thereby, 963 (427*n*., 434).—or motive of action, dist. ground or reason for approbation, 966. pleasure and pain are efficient as well as final causes, 967.

chance

[*Hume*]—a mere negative word, 625. liberty when opposed to necessity is the same as chance, which does not exist, 625.

character,— = fixed and habitual principles of action, 430. it is the constant character of human nature that the characters of men are to a certain degree inconstant, 618.

charity, see *benevolence, love.*—duty of, 286.—right of poor to, as example of imperfect rights, 353.

choice, see *freedom, will.*

[*Cudworth*]—between equal things, an argument against determinism, 140.— between better and worse, necessary for blame, 150.

[*Wollaston*]—intelligence and, implied by acts denominated morally good or evil, 273.

[*Hutcheson*] election dist. approbation,

358; cf. 361. election falsely alleged to depend always on self-love, 359.

[*Balguy*] actions must spring from free choice, 448. approbation is itself a sufficient reason for choice of a virtuous action, 453 (361).

[*Hume*] liberty and choice would not be essential to morality if immorality consisted simply in the production of false opinions, 495. will or choice as cause of an action does not produce any different relations from those of a similar action with a different cause, 501.

Cicero,—cited by Cumberland, 107; by Cudworth, 153; by Clarke, 244, 246; by Hutcheson, 359; by Butler, 382*n*., 430*n*.; by Hume, 632-3; by Smith, 809; by Reid, 900.—referred to by Wollaston, 275; by Hume, 604.

civil, see *law.*—law, dist. divine law and law of opinion or reputation, 184-8.— obligation, dist. natural, virtuous, and religious, 464.

Clarke, 224-61. see especially *fitness, nature, obligation.*—cites St. Paul, 234; Plato, 235; Cicero, 244, 246; Cumberland, 247.—cited by Balguy, 447.— criticizes Hobbes, 227, 229, 236, 244, 247, 252-60; Stoics, 250.—criticized by Hutcheson, 367.

Collier, Arthur,—criticized by Reid, 908.

command

[*Hobbes*]—and law, 20, 100, 103.— dist. counsel, 85, 100.—dist. covenant, 100, 103.

[*Cudworth*]—obligation of, depends on natural justice, 122-6.

[*Clarke*] positive will or command of God not the foundation of duty, 225, 247.

[*Paley*] obligation means being urged by a violent motive resulting from the command of another, 848.

common,—good, the end of natural law, 105, 107, 118.—good = common happiness, 108.—good, the end prescribed by reason, 115.—nature, or system of the kind, 206.—interest, not inconsistent with private, 207.—sense of mankind on the signification of acts, 276.—sense and innate principles, an infirm basis for distinction between moral good and evil, 292.—or public sense, a determination to be pleased with the happiness of others, and to be uneasy at their misery, 356.—language and behaviour, attest a moral faculty, 429.—sense tells us that right and wrong

common (*cont.*):
are perceived by the understanding, 676–80. the view that beauty is a feeling of the spectator, not a quality of the object, is a paradox contrary to common language and common sense, 937 (603). —sense, as standard of moral judgement, is simply a name for individual sentiment, 959.

commonwealth
[*Hobbes*]—an artificial man, 21.— makes covenants valid, 67.—generation and authority of, 81.

community,—of all mankind, 244.—is a fictitious body composed of the individual persons who are considered its members, 949.

compact, see *contract*, *promise*.

compassion, see *pity*.

conscience, see *moral sense*, *reflection*.
[*Cudworth*]—remorse of, an inward sense of guilt, 137.—sense of, in all men, accusing or excusing, 141.—dictate of, majestically controls other powers of the soul, 148.

[*Shaftesbury*]— = reflection of unjust action, dist. reflection of foolish action, 220.—moral or natural, presupposed by religious, 220.

[*Clarke*] judgement and conscience of a man's own mind is the truest obligation, 233.—necessarily assents to the rule of right, 234.—judgement of, concerning one's own actions, may be concealed from the world and from oneself, unlike judgements on the actions of others, 237. reason and consciences of men, 237.

[*Hutcheson*] see *moral sense*.

[*Butler*]—or reflection, 376, 378–9, 390, 399, 401, 404; cf. Shaftesbury, 200, 204, 220; Hutcheson, 314.—supremacy of, essential to idea of system of human nature, 376.—lacking in brutes, 378.— bears marks of authority, 379–81, 399–402, 406. reflex approbation or disapprobation, 380.—evidence of divine intention for human nature, 395.— cannot be wholly mistaken, but more liable to error than the external senses, 395.—a superior, indeed the supreme, principle in human nature, 399–404.— dist. cool self-love, another superior principle, 400. had it strength as it has right, it would govern the world, 402. —without supremacy of, impiety or parricide would be natural, 403.—is itself alone an obligation and carries its

own authority, 406.—is our natural guide, 406; cf. 427*n*., 429*n*.—and reasonable self-love, are the chief or superior principles in man, both leading us the same way, 409.—approves or disapproves of certain dispositions and actions abstracted from consideration of their tendency to the happiness or misery of the world, 427*n*.; cf. 434. common language and common behaviour attest a moral faculty, whether called conscience, etc., whether considered a sentiment of the understanding or a perception of the heart or both, 429. what it approves and disapproves is not in general doubtful, 429; cf. 395.

[*Balguy*] the still voice of conscience amid the bustle and tumult of appetites and passions, 455.

[*Hume*]—or a sense of morals, 490. constant habit of surveying ourselves in reflection, by considering how others regard us, keeps alive the sentiments of right and wrong, 593.

[*Hartley*] see *moral sense*.

[*Price*] in contemplating the actions of moral agents, we have both a perception of the understanding and a feeling of the heart, 688; cf. Butler, 429.

[*Smith*] imagination of the approval or disapproval of spectators is the only looking-glass by which we can scrutinize the propriety of our own conduct, 803. when I judge my own conduct, I divide myself into two persons, the spectator and the agent, 804. to feel ourselves praiseworthy, we must become the impartial spectators of our own character and conduct, 806. the judgement of mankind, the man without, is subject to appeal to the higher tribunal of conscience, the supposed impartial and well-informed spectator, the man within the breast, 811. when conscience is shaken by the different judgement of real spectators, the demi-god within the breast appears partly of immortal and partly of mortal extraction, 811. judgements of the man within the breast (dist. the real and impartial spectator) may be perverted by selfish passions, 812. this is particularly so when we are about to act, 813. when the action is over, we can enter more coolly into the sentiments of the indifferent spectator and identify ourselves with the ideal man within the breast, 814. our moral faculties carry badges of authority, 822;

cf. Butler, 379–81, 399–402, 406; Hartley, 653; Price, 713. they are therefore plainly intended to govern human nature, 823; cf. Butler, 395.—does not immediately denote, though it presupposes the existence of, a moral faculty, 842.

[*Reid*]—or sense of duty, is a distinct principle from a rational regard to our good upon the whole, though both lead to the same conduct, 866; cf. 860; and cf. Butler, 408–9.

consequences, see *end, intention.*

[*Hutcheson*]—affecting morality of actions, not limited to direct and natural effects, 334.

[*Butler*]—intention of, is a part of the action, but not necessarily the actual consequences, 430.—consideration of, does not affect our moral judgement of justice and veracity, 434–5.

[*Hume*] tendencies rather than accidental consequences are regarded in our moral judgements, 579*n.*; cf. 555, 633.

[*Price*] distant consequences are little attended to by mankind in general when making moral judgements, 731.

[*Paley*]—general, dist. particular, 855.

[*Bentham*] the general tendency of an act is to be judged by its material (or important) consequences, 978.—dist. act, both together making up the action, 979.—intentionality of, in relation to that of the act, 980–1.—are the effects of intention, 982. actual consequences need not affect the goodness or badness of intention, which depends on intended consequences, 983.

constitution, see *nature.*—of the mind, 222.—of human nature, 376–9, 404.

constitutive,—dist. intelligible essences, 133.

constraint, compulsion or restraint as a form of necessity, 166.—dist. obligation, 352.—dist. necessity, 625.

contract, see *promise.*

[*Hobbes*]— = the mutual transfer of right, 61.—in relation to covenant, 61.—dist. law, 100. contracts oblige us, laws tie us fast, being obliged, 100.

[*Clarke*]—obligatory through eternal fitness, 227–8. Hobbes's obligation to perform compacts implies antecedent obligations of justice, 254, 257.

[*Hume*] invalidity of contracts entered through force shows that promises are an artificial invention for the advantage of society, 545.

[*Reid*] contracts and promises belong to the class of social operations of the mind, 902. there can be no compact without signs, natural or invented, 904.—must be voluntary, but the will which is essential to a contract is a will to engage, not a will to perform, 905; cf. Hume, 536.—obligation of, is unaffected by the agent's purpose or intention, 906; cf. Hume, 543.

contradiction, injustice or injury resembles absurdity or self-contradiction, 59, 102, 257.—in the precept that private good be the ultimate end, 115. refusal to act equitably, or to take the necessary means to an acknowledged moral end, is equivalent to self-contradiction, 232, 242. deeds may contradict truth or true propositions, 275–7, 279 (452, 727).—of a true proposition, dist. counter-action to the truth of things, 452. a statement expressing a moral judgement, unlike one expressing a feeling, can be contradicted without offence, 921. to say that it is dangerous to consult the principle of utility is self-contradictory, 953*n.*

convention

[*Hume*]—and education, must be the source of the sense of justice, 519.—required to bestow stability on the possession of external goods, 527. this convention is not a promise but only a general sense of common interest, 528; and gives rise to ideas of justice and injustice, 529.—necessary for intelligibility of promises, 535–7; and for their obligation, 538.

cool, see *calm.*

counsel

[*Hobbes*]—in relation to deliberation, 20.—dist. command, law, and covenant, 85, 100, 103.

covenant, see *contract, promise.*

crime,—dist. sin and vice, 184–7.—of ignorance, dist. of malice, 339.—not attributable to mistakes of fact, as being involuntary, 491.

criterion, see *rules.*

[*Locke*] divine law the touchstone of moral rectitude, 185 (675).

[*Wollaston*]—for distinguishing moral good and evil, 291–3; unsatisfactory suggestions of *honestum*, following nature, 291; right reason, common sense and innate principles, 292; pleasure, 293; correct view is conformity to truth, 293 (727–8, 959).

criterion (*cont.*):

[*Hutcheson*] conformity between true proposition and its object cannot be the criterion for election or approbation, 360. reason is said to be a standard antecedent to sense and affection, 361.

[*Butler*] inquiries after some general rule of morals are useful but not necessary for practice, 405. universally acknowledged standard of virtue, 429.

[*Gay*]—of virtue, as a rule of life to which we are obliged to conform, 462. immediate rule or criterion of virtue is the will of God, 464; cf. Locke, 185.—once-removed, of virtue, is the happiness of mankind, 465.

[*Hume*] standard of reason is eternal and inflexible, that of taste is ultimately due to divine will, 607.

[*Price*]—of virtue, not afforded by such expressions as acting suitably to the natures of things or to truth, 728.

[*Smith*] rule or canon for judging propriety of affections is the correspondent affection in ourselves, 775. two standards of moral judgement, (1) complete propriety and perfection, (2) the degree of proximity to perfection which is commonly reached, 784. general rules based on experience are used as standards of judgement in dubious cases, 818.

[*Paley*]—of right is utility, 854.

[*Bentham*] pleasure and pain supply both the standard of right and wrong and the cause of actions, 946. if approbation without regard to consequences is taken to be a standard of right and wrong, it is either despotical or anarchial, 954.

Cudworth, 119–53. see especially *freedom, God, will*.—cites Plato, 119, 130, 134; Aristotle, 125, 133, 146, 153; Boethius, 132; Hobbes, 135, 139; Alexander (*Exegetes*), 144; Descartes, 147; Cicero, 153.—cited by Price, 663*n*., 664*n*.—criticizes Descartes, 127–8; Protagoras, 130–3; Hobbes, 138(?), 146, 152–3.

Cumberland, 104–18. see especially *nature*.—cites Cicero, 107.—cited by Clarke, 247; by Hutcheson, 331, 347.—criticized by Price, 718.

custom, some acts, like most words, have significancy by custom and agreement, 279.—gives us no new ideas, 312. power of habit and custom, a general and indeterminate description of the influence of association, 638–9. utility established by custom or habit is not the ground of all approbation, 730.

dead,—imaginative sympathy with, 769, 791.

decency, see *dignity*.—perceptions of, 356.

deduction, see *demonstration*.

[*Clarke*] particular duties may be deduced from general obligation to conform to the rule of right, 239, 245.

[*Balguy*]—of obligation, from relation of agreement or moral fitness, 456–60.

[*Hume*] 'ought' cannot be deduced from 'is', 504.—from abstract principle, one scientifical method, dist. the experimental method, 563.

[*Price*]—dist. intuition, as two acts of the understanding, 661*n*.; cf. 671, 704.—as one of three grounds of belief, 705.—may supply different degrees of evidence, from full certainty to lowest probability, 706.

[*Smith*] particular moral judgements are not deduced from antecedent general rules but are the ground of those rules, 817.

[*Reid*] all our knowledge of the material world is deduced from the truths immediately testified by the external senses, and all our knowledge of duty is deduced from the truths immediately testified by our moral faculty, 879. the first principles of morals are self-evident, and other moral truths are deduced from them, not from any different relations as Hume's criticism supposes, 930 (504).

definition, see *tautology*.

[*Cudworth*] moral good and evil, unless they be mere names without signification or names for willed and commanded, cannot be arbitrary things, made by will, 120.

[*Hutcheson*]—of obligation in terms of advantage, may be refuted by substituting the definition for the term defined, 350; cf. 351. election and approbation are simple ideas, which can only be explained by synonymous words or by concomitant circumstances, 358. to say that 'merit' means 'deserving approbation' is to define merely by a synonymous term, 373.

[*Butler*] best way to expose paradoxical accounts of social affections is to substitute the definitions given for the words commonly used, 411; cf. Hutcheson, 350.

[*Hume*]—of key terms can end controversy about liberty and necessity, 613.—of cause in terms of production, etc., is merely giving a synonym, 625*n.*; cf. Hutcheson, 373.

[*Price*] schemes which found morality on self-love, positive law, or divine will, may mean that 'moral good' and 'evil' are only other words for 'advantageous' and 'disadvantageous', 'willed' and 'forbidden', 658, 709; cf. Cudworth, 120. but if 'right' simply meant 'commanded' or 'useful', it would be absurd to ask whether it is right to obey a command, and the propositions 'obeying a command is right' or 'producing happiness is right' would be trifling, expressing no more than that obeying a command is obeying a command, or producing happiness is producing happiness, 658; cf. Hutcheson, 351; Butler, 411. right and wrong are simple ideas, as is shown by the impossibility of giving definitions of them that are more than synonymous expressions, 672; cf. Hutcheson, 358. 'right' and 'wrong' express simple and undefinable ideas, but that does not prove that they are perceived by sense and not reason, 674. Locke's view that rectitude signifies the conformity of actions to rules or laws makes it absurd to apply rectitude to rules and laws themselves, 675 (183–8). 'fitness', in either of its two senses, is undefinable except by synonymous words, 707; cf. Hutcheson, 358, 373; Hume, 625*n.* if virtue signified the relation of actions to private interest, it would make no sense to say that virtue tends to our happiness, since this implies that it need not necessarily do so, 710. Balguy's definition of obligation can be seen to be defective if it be substituted whenever the words 'duty', 'should', 'obliged', occur, 717; cf. Hutcheson, 350; Butler, 411. to define obligation as the necessity of doing a thing in order to be happy, would make ridiculous the statement that a man is obliged to study his own happiness, 718 (463).

[*Paley*] we need to distinguish meaning of obligation from reasons why we are obliged, 847.

[*Reid*] the notion of duty is too simple to admit of a logical definition, 869; cf. Price, 672. we can define it only by synonymous words or phrases, or by its properties and necessary concomitants, 869; cf. Hutcheson, 358; Price, 672.

[*Bentham*] interest cannot in the ordinary way be defined, since it does not have any superior genus, 949*n.*

deliberation

[*Hobbes*]— = an alternate succession of appetite and fear (or aversion), 17, 33; i.e. an alternate imagination of the good and evil sequels of an action, 96, 98.— = ending of liberty, 17, 33; cf. 96.

[*Cumberland*] while we deliberate we may be called free, 114; cf. Hobbes, 17, 33.

demonstration, see *deduction.*

[*Cumberland*] effects of action can be demonstrated, 114.

[*Cudworth*]—presupposes immutable natures and essences, 127.

[*Locke*]—moral rules capable of, 154, 189 (497–8).

[*Clarke*]—compared both with moral understanding and with moral action, 232–3.

[*Hume*]—and probability, two ways of employing the understanding, 480.— dist. will, as concerned respectively with ideas and realities, 480.—influences action only in directing judgement about causes and effects, 480–1; cf. 595. if morality is susceptible of demonstration, it must consist in some relations, 497, 498*n.*; but the only relations relevant to demonstration apply to irrational inanimate objects as well as to rational beings, and therefore cannot constitute morality, 498.

[*Price*] moral principles may be treated as axioms, but to demonstrate morality in individual instances would require universal and unerring knowledge, 747–8.

[*Bentham*] the principle of utility neither can nor needs to be directly proved, 952.

Descartes,—cited by Cudworth, 147.— criticized by Cudworth, 127–8; by Reid, 908, 915.

desert, see *merit.*

design, see *intention.*

desire, see *affection, appetite, passion, uneasiness.*

[*Hobbes*]—and aversion, forms of endeavour, 3, 24.—same as love, 24.— object of, = good, 25.

[*Cudworth*]—or love of good and happiness, the first mover of action, not

desire (*cont.*):

a mere passion but a settled principle, 147.

[*Locke*]—of happiness and aversion to misery are innate practical principles, constantly influencing all our actions, 156.—is uneasiness in the absence of pleasure or good, 161, 174 (325).—dist. bare velleity, by uneasiness, 161.—dist. will, 173.—or uneasiness, not thought of the greater good, determines the will, 174–5 (486).—moved by happiness alone, 176. the mind has a power to suspend the satisfaction of desires, and this is what is improperly called free will, 179.

[*Hutcheson*]—is uneasy rather than pleasant, 322; but is not the same as uneasiness, 325 (161, 174).—general calm, requires reflection, 357, 369.

[*Butler*]—of esteem, a public affection distinct from benevolence, 389.

[*Gay*]—of pleasure and of good, and aversion from pain and from evil, arise from reflecting upon them, 467.—of the happiness of others, implied by approbation thereof, 468.

[*Hume*] aversion or propensity arises from prospect of pain or pleasure, 481. —calm, or calm passion, dist. violent emotion or passion, 485; cf. Hutcheson, 331, 357, 369; Butler, 382.—to perform an action, dist. promising, 536.

[*Price*] every being must desire happiness for himself, 679. is all desire wholly instinctive? 691.—of private happiness, does not arise from instinct but from the nature of happiness, 692.—pain is not a possible object of, 692. a purely reasonable being would see that happiness is in itself valuable and desirable, 693.—rational (affection), dist. instinctive (passion), 694.

[*Reid*] animal principles or blind desires, 856, 863.

difference, see *agreement, relation, fitness.* —of things, the foundation of moral fitness, 225–6 (367).—natural, between good and evil, 227.

dignity

[*Hobbes*]— = public worth, 40.

[*Hutcheson*] approved actions, or the quality approved, regarded as perfection and dignity, 306, 314.—moral, of benevolence, 331.—or moral importance of persons, may compensate numbers, 333; cf. 335. perceptions of decency or dignity, 356.

disposition, benevolence of God cannot be an ungrounded disposition, 438 (366). cause of moral dispositions is irrelevant to their justification, 963.

duty, see *obligation.*

[*Locke*]—and sin, related to divine law, dist. crime and innocence, virtue and vice, 184–7.—to God, society, and self, 194.

[*Clarke*]—or obligation, arises from eternal and necessary differences of things, 225.—and necessity, compared and contrasted, 232.—three principal branches of, to God, our fellow men, and ourselves, 239–45.

[*Wollaston*] there cannot be two incompatible duties, but there can be a mixed obligation, 288.—to make oneself happy, 299.

[*Butler*]—to follow conscience, 406.— and interest, seldom inconsistent, 408.— and interest are perfectly coincident, if we take in the future world, 409.

[*Balguy*]—of gratitude and of relieving distress, can be discovered by reason without affection, 439.

[*Hume*] if duties are discovered by reason, they must exist antecedent to that discovery, 502.—sense of, cannot be the first motive of virtuous action, 513; cf. 633.—sense of, can be a motive to action, but presupposes some other virtuous motive as common in human nature, 514.—common measures of, determined by the natural and usual force of the passions, 520.—sense of, the sole motive for performance of promises, 538.—all the great lines of, determined by utility, 558.

[*Price*]—or moral obligation, necessarily connected with moral right and wrong, 683*n.*, 708.—may be said to be narrower than right, though not than wrong, 720.—general, which is coincident with right, dist. particular, which is left to our discretion, 721–3.—six main branches of, 733–45.—to God and other superiors, 733.—to self, 734–5.— of beneficence, 736.—of gratitude, 737. —of veracity, including fidelity to promises, 738–40.—of justice, 741–4.

[*Smith*]—sense of, is a regard to general rules of conduct, 820.

[*Paley*]—differs from prudence only in taking account of gain or loss in the world to come as well as in the present world, 852.

[*Reid*]—as an end of action, co-operates with interest and leads to the same course of conduct, 860, 866; cf. Butler, 408–9. sense of interest and sense of duty are the only rational inducements to obey a general rule of conduct, 867.—notion of, too simple to admit of a logical definition, 869; cf. Price, 672. we can define it only by synonymous words or phrases, or by its properties and necessary concomitants, 869; cf. Hutcheson, 358; Price, 672.—cannot be resolved into interest, 870; cf. Price, 710.—regard to, is called honour by men of rank, 871. the principle of duty is universal, being found in every language, 872; cf. Butler, 429.—is not a quality of action or agent, but a relation between the two, 873.—implies that the action is voluntary, 874; and that the agent believes it to be good, 875; cf. 894; and cf. Price,ʳ750–1, 755, 758.

education,—impressions of, mistaken for innate maxims, 292; cf. 478.—gives us no new ideas, 312.—prejudice of, a method of association and acquiring principles, 478.—and convention, must be the source of the sense of justice, 519. —a source of associations giving rise to the moral sense, 647.

election, see *choice*.

emotion, see *affection, passion*.

[*Hume*]—of aversion or propensity, arises from prospect of pain or pleasure, and sets us upon reasoning about causes and effects of their objects, 481.— violent, dist. calm passion or desire, 485; cf. Hutcheson, 331, 357, 369; Butler, 382.

[*Smith*]—sympathetic, may be roused by any passion, 765.—violent, can distort the judgements of conscience, 812–14.

end, see *desire, happiness, pleasure, reason, virtue*.

[*Hobbes*]— = good, 4.—no utmost, 4, 44 (362).

[*Cumberland*]—and 'means', ambiguous terms, may be replaced by 'effect' and 'cause', 113.

[*Cudworth*]—and good, the principle of all actions, 146.

[*Shaftesbury*] natural end for every creature, 195.

[*Hutcheson*] no end can be previous to self-love, self-hatred, benevolence, or malice, 362 (454).—ultimate, dist. subordinate, 362 (4, 44).—ultimate, no ex-

citing reasons for, 362. question whether one ultimate end can be more reasonable than another, 362.—ultimate, no justifying reasons for, 363.—fitness of, 367.

[*Butler*]—virtue to be pursued as, 386. —of particular affections, is having particular external things, 416.

[*Balguy*] moral good is one kind of ultimate end, natural good another, 455. —of a moral agent, is virtue alone, abstracted from the pleasure that accompanies and follows, 455.—of sensible agents, is interest or pleasure, of moral agents, moral rectitude or virtue, 460.

[*Gay*]— = that which is pursued for its own sake, 467.—ultimate, dist. inferior, 470. each particular action may have its proper and peculiar end (cf. Butler, 414–16), but private happiness is the ultimate end of all actions, 470. to ask a reason for an ultimate end is absurd, 470; cf. Hutcheson, 362–3. known or presumed means to happiness are often treated as ends, 475–6. the cause of this is the association of pleasure with them, 477.

[*Hume*] means to an end are only valued so far as the end is valued, 561.— ultimate, no reasons can be given for, 606; cf. Hutcheson, 362–3; Gay, 470.

[*Price*] there are some ends which are ultimately desired, and for choosing which no reason can be given; otherwise there would be an infinite progression of reasons and ends, 672; cf. Hutcheson, 362–3; Gay, 470; Hume 606.

[*Smith*]—or tendency of an action, determines its merit, while motive or cause determines its propriety, 773, 785. means come to be valued more than the end for which they were intended, 825.

[*Reid*] every deliberate human action must be done either as a means or as an end, 859. some ends, viz., what is good for us upon the whole, and what appears to be our duty, cannot even be conceived without reason, 860 (480–1, 594–5, 606–7). ultimate ends = the principles of action, 939. Hume is right in saying that there are no reasons for ultimate ends, i.e. that they are not means to further ends, 940; but it does not follow from this that ultimate ends cannot depend on the intellectual faculties, 941 (606). there are ultimate ends which are rational principles of action, requiring judgement or reason, 942; cf. 856–60. virtue is an ultimate end, but

end (*cont.*):
is not thereby independent of the intellectual faculties, 943 (606).
[*Bentham*] the happiness of the members of a community is the sole end which the legislator ought to have in view, 967, 970, 977.
envy, 10, 392*n*.
Epictetus,—cited by Butler, 429*n*.
Epicureans, 104, 146, 293, 359, 382–3, 385–6, 892.
equality, natural equality of men, 47.—acknowledgement of, a law of nature, 73.—a degree of, presupposed by society, 572.—idea of, a new simple idea acquired by the understanding, 670, 678.
equity,—a law of nature, 74.—and love, the two branches of duty to fellow creatures, 241. iniquity in action is the same as falsity or contradiction in theory, 242; cf. 59, 102, 232, 257.—proportion of, between equals, and between superiors and inferiors, 242.—eternal rule of, is right reason and the law of nature, 246.
essence,—of things, dist. existence, 120–1, 684.—intelligible, dist. constitutive, 133.
esteem,—appears to be disinterested, 317.—desire of, is a public affection, 389.—presumption of, is the only motive for meritorious action, 469.—of artificial virtues, due to sympathy with the interest of society, 548.—remains steady though sympathy varies, 553.—of virtue, does not depend on actual attainment of beneficial ends, 555.—excited by utility of virtue, not by that of inanimate objects, 574*n*.—of talents, as of virtues, 610–11.
eternal,—relations or differences of things, 225, 229–30, 449 (367).—rule of equity, 246.—and inflexible standard of reason, 607. morality is eternal and immutable, 684.
Euclid,—referred to by Locke, 189; by Hume, 603; by Reid, 918, 937.
Euripides, 286.
existence, see *essence*.
[*Hume*] 'ought' cannot be deduced from 'is', 504. nothing exists without a cause of its existence, 625.
[*Price*]—our own, known by intuition, 704.
experience
[*Price*] no actual experience of impenetrability, 665.—cannot give us our certainty that every new event requires some cause, 667.

[*Smith*] as we have no immediate experience of what other men feel, we must imagine what we ourselves should feel in the like situation, 764.—the foundation of general rules of morality, 817.

faculty, faculties of body and mind, 1.—psychology, criticized, 142–5, 163, 167–8. the man or the soul, not faculties, performs acts of understanding or willing, 145.—moral, whether called conscience, moral reason, moral sense, or divine reason, 429. the question, which power or faculty of the mind is the principle of approbation, is important for speculation but not for practice, 834–5.
falsehood, see *truth*.
feeling, see *affection*, *sentiment*.
[*Hume*]—(or sentiment) of approbation or disapprobation, constitutes virtue or vice, 503; cf. 601–2, 634. morality is more properly felt than judged of, 505. to have the sense of virtue is to feel satisfaction of a particular kind from contemplation of a character, 506. immediate feeling and finer internal sense, 562.
[*Price*] in contemplating the actions of moral agents, we have both a perception of the understanding and a feeling of the heart, 688; cf. Butler, 429.—or immediate consciousness, as one of the grounds of belief, 703.
[*Smith*] as we have no immediate experience of what other men feel, we must imagine what we ourselves should feel in the like situation, 764.
[*Reid*] does approbation include judgement, or is it feeling alone? 907.—dist. judgement, 909–12.—is not expressed by a complete proposition and is neither true nor false, 910.—and judgement are often combined, and so confused, 912. when feeling and judgement are combined, the former is usually a consequence of the latter, 916. this is true of moral feeling and judgement, 917. a statement expressing a feeling differs in meaning from one expressing a moral judgement, 919; first because it is autobiographical, 920; secondly because it cannot be contradicted without offence, 921. each of the two statements can be inferred from the other, as being causally related, but not as having the same meaning, 922. if moral approbation were feeling alone, a statement

expressing a moral judgement would either mean the same as one expressing a feeling or would be meaningless, 923. the terms 'moral sense' and 'sentiment' are abused when taken to be feeling without judgement, 927. Hume's view, that reason cannot perceive the demerit of ingratitude, mistakenly assumes either that the sentiment of blame is feeling without judgement, or that only feeling can be excited by the particular structure of the mind, 933–5 (596–7). if moral judgement were feeling, a judge ought to be called a feeler, 936 (601). the view that moral judgement is feeling implies that morality is arbitrary, and therefore that God has no moral character, 944.

felicity, see *happiness*.

fidelity,—good, reasonable, and fit in its own nature, 228; cf. 257.—approved independently of considering consequences, 427n.—to promises, included in veracity, 739–40.

fitness, see *agreement, reason*.

[*Clarke*]—or unfitness of action, arises from different relations of things independent of the will of God and of any regard to private advantage, 225–6. —ought to determine the wills of men, in imitation of the will of God, 225, 231–3. fit and reasonable, 225.—of application of things or relations one to another, of circumstances to persons, and of behaviour of some persons towards others, 226.—absolute, of beneficence and justice on the part of God and man, 226.—of keeping compacts, 227–8.—of doing good, implies duty of universal benevolence, 243.

[*Hutcheson*] perceptions of decency, dignity, suitableness to human nature, without any conception of moral good, 356.—to an end, is not the idea of moral goodness, 367.—absolute, presupposes a moral sense, 367.

[*Butler*] some actions suitable to the nature of man, 409. prior suitableness between a passion and its object is necessary for the pleasure arising from gratification, 415. vicious actions properly called incongruous, unsuitable, disproportionate, unfit, 432.

[*Balguy*]—perceived by reason, 439, 451, 457–9. rectitude is agreeableness of actions to the nature and circumstances of agents and objects, 449.—is necessarily approved, as truth necessarily receives assent, 453.—between bounty and gratitude, 456–8.—a reason for action, 459, 461.—is conformity to order and truth, 459.—strictly connected with moral obligation, 461.

[*Hartley*] suitableness of all the virtues to each other and to the beauty, order, and perfection of the world, 650.

[*Price*] 'right' and 'wrong', 'fit' and 'unfit', express simple and undefinable ideas, 674.—two senses of, (1) aptitude of means to end, (2) rightness; both are undefinable, simple perceptions of the understanding, 707. 'acting suitably to the natures of things', and similar expressions used by rationalists, cannot define virtue but presuppose it, 726. nor do they afford criteria of virtue, but simply show that morality is founded in truth and reason, 728.

[*Smith*] the suitableness or proportion which a motivating affection bears to its cause or object, constitutes the propriety of the consequent action, 773. an affection is judged to be so suitable if it corresponds with our own, 775.

[*Paley*]—of things, means their fitness to produce happiness, 846.

[*Bentham*]—of things, as standard of moral judgement, is simply a name for individual sentiment, 959.

flattery

[*Mandeville*]—contrives an imaginary reward for self-denial, 263.—the most powerful argument for instilling moral notions, 264. moral virtues are the political offspring which flattery begot upon pride, 269.—general, screens personal praise, 269.

formal,—cause, dist. efficient, 120. formality of virtue, dist. materiality of actions, 125.—ratio of moral good and evil, 293, 727. formally good actions, dist. materially good, 750, 900; cf. 875.

freedom, see *necessity, will*.

[*Hobbes*]—or liberty = the absence of external impediments, 55, 82, 96, 98.—applies only to bodies, 82; to a man, not to his will, 82, 90. free will means freedom of a man to do what he will, not freedom of the will, 82. liberty consistent with fear and with necessity, 83, 90.—of will, would contradict omnipotence and liberty of God, 83. natural liberty, dist. political, 83–4. a free agent is he that can do if he will, and forbear if he will, 90, 98.—from necessity, impossible, 99.

freedom (*cont.*):

[*Cumberland*] in mathematics and morals, action is free but its effect is caused necessarily, 110; cf. 114. the terms 'means' and 'end', unlike 'cause' and 'effect', connote free intention, 113. while we deliberate we may be called free, 114; cf. Hobbes, 17, 33.

[*Cudworth*]—of will, attested by praise, blame, sense of guilt and of retributive justice, 136–8.—of will, denied by some as impossible, by others as pertaining only to God, 139.—attested by choice between equal things, 140. contingent liberty of self-determination, dist. free will, 141; cf. 150.—confused by faculty psychology, 142.—of will, allowing praise and blame, resides in power of the soul over itself, 150.—as power to produce or not to produce an effect, 152.

[*Locke*]—a power to do or forbear, according to preference, 164; cf. Hobbes, 90, 98.—implies thought and will, but is not implied by them, 164–5. the question, whether the will be free, is improper, 167–9.—belongs only to agents, not to the will, 167; cf. Hobbes, 82, 90. the will is one power or ability, freedom another, 168.—the power to do what one wills, 169. a man is not free in respect of the act of willing, 170. absurd to ask whether a man be free to will which of two alternatives he pleases, 171. what is improperly called free will is a power to suspend the prosecution of desire, 179.—not diminished but improved by the determination of the will by judgement of good and evil, 180; otherwise only madmen and fools would be free, 181. determination to pursue true happiness is the foundation of liberty in freeing us from determination by particular desires, 182.

[*Clarke*] natural liberty of will to forbear to act rightly, contrasted with necessity to assent to speculative truth, 232.

[*Wollaston*] moral acts imply an intelligent and free agent, 273.

[*Hutcheson*] merit is said to presuppose reason and free self-determination, 373.

[*Balguy*] actions must spring from free choice, 448. obligation presupposes liberty and a motive or reason for choice, 460.

[*Hume*] liberty and choice would not be essential to morality if morality consisted simply in the production of false opinions, 495. all men have always agreed in the doctrine both of necessity and of liberty, 613, 624. false sensation of liberty or indifference in performing actions, 623. question of liberty and necessity the most contentious question of metaphysics, 624. liberty can only mean a power of acting or not acting, according to the determinations of the will, 624; cf. Hobbes, 90, 98; Locke, 164, 169. liberty, when opposed to necessity instead of to constraint, is the same as chance, 625. liberty and necessity both essential to morality, 626–9.

[*Price*] liberty is presupposed by practical virtue, 752. liberty = the power of acting and determining, i.e. self-determination, 752–3. liberty does not presuppose intelligence but is presupposed by it, 754.

[*Reid*] in order to understand in what sense men have moral liberty, we must understand the influence of motives, 880. liberty in the agent is presupposed by motives, 881. liberty is compatible with the fact that we reason from motives to actions, 889 (619).—from necessary determination by motives, does not imply that all actions are capricious, 890. liberty is presupposed by reward and punishment, since the latter imply good and ill desert, 891 (628).

friendship, to have friends is power, 39. —universal, the community of all mankind, 244.

Gay, 462–78. see especially *happiness*.— cites Hutcheson, 474.—cited by Hartley, 635.—criticizes Butler, 470; Hutcheson, 473, 476, 478.—criticized by Price, 718.

generosity, see *benevolence*.

God, see *religion, will*.

[*Hobbes*]—goodness of, is his goodness to us, 4.—laws of nature may be considered as commands of, 77. commonwealth a mortal god, 81.—as first cause, implies that voluntary actions are necessary, 83.—natural right of, derived from irresistible power, 89; cf. 101 (227, 247, 259–60).

[*Cumberland*]—cause of all necessary effects, gives authority to natural laws, 106.—included in rational agents, 107. —proved to be author of natural law, 111.

[*Cudworth*]—will of, cannot change essences, 120–2.—will of, efficient cause of all things, but formal cause only of itself, 120.—will of, determines existence but not essence, 121.—will of, cannot alone oblige, 122. if essences depended on will of God, truth and science would be arbitrary, 127.—will of, determined by his wisdom, 128.—wisdom of, determined by his goodness, 129.—creates constitutive essences with existence, but not intelligible essences, 133.—not the cause of wicked actions, 136.

[*Locke*]—will and law of, the true ground of morality, 158 (675).—has joined virtue and public happiness together, 158. divine law, dist. civil law and law of opinion or reputation, 184-8. divine law the touchstone of moral rectitude, i.e. of duty and sin, 185 (675). —existence and will of, can be inferred from the evidence of sense, 192-4; cf. Cumberland, 111.—will of, that man owes duties to God, society, and self, 194.

[*Shaftesbury*]—fear of, does not of itself imply conscience, 220.

[*Clarke*]—will of, necessarily determines itself with regard to fitness, 225, 230.—positive will or command of, not the foundation of duty, 225. manifestly fitter in itself that God should promote the universal good and benefit the innocent than that he should do the contrary, 226.—duty to, one of the three principal branches of the rule of righteousness, 240.—will of, determines existence of things, but not their abstract proportions, 247; cf. Cudworth, 121.—dominion of, founded on the law of nature, not on infinite power, 247; cf. 259-60 (89).—causes truth and right to terminate in happiness, 251.

[*Wollaston*] to deny things to be what they are is opposition to the will of God, 281 (cf. Clarke, 230, 232); and to his nature, 282.

[*Hutcheson*] to make morality depend on divine law is to imply that it is a tautology to say that the laws of God are good or just, 351.—is called morally good when we see that his providence tends to universal happiness, 351.— goodness or benevolence of, may be inferred from his boundless wisdom and power, 354.—may be supposed to have attributes resembling benevolence and the moral sense, 366 (438, 634).—benevolence of, may be inferred from our being constituted to approve kind affections, which tend to the happiness of his creatures, 366.

[*Butler*] particular passions and affections are proofs of God's intention that we be instruments of good to society and to ourselves, 389. conscience is evidence of God's intention for human nature, 395, 406.—may have as his only end the good of the creation, but has laid us under distinct particular obligations, 427*n*.; cf. 434-5.—moral attributes of, may all be resolved into goodness (i.e. benevolence), 428.

[*Balguy*]—benevolence of, cannot be an ungrounded disposition, 438 (366). obligation to act conformably to reason is superior to obligation to obey the will of God, since the latter is itself subject to the former, 450.

[*Gay*]—will of, the immediate criterion of virtue, 464; cf. Locke, 185.— could have no other design in creating mankind than their happiness, which is therefore the criterion of his will, 465.— will of, necessary to make the good of mankind an obligatory pursuit, 466.

[*Hume*]—will of, cannot alter the standard of reason, but is the ultimate cause of the standard of taste, 607. we are not justified in attributing sentiments to beings superior to men, 634 (366).

[*Hartley*]—meditations upon, as a source of associations giving rise to the moral sense, 652.—love of, indicated by the moral sense as our perfection and end, 653.

[*Price*] Locke's view that rectitude is conformity to the will of God makes it absurd to suppose that the divine will is directed by it, 675 (158, 185). it is objected that a necessary and immutable morality would make it independent of God, 699; cf. Cudworth, 127. some things must be independent of the will of God, 700.—moral attributes of, imply a necessary morality, 701.—will of, depends on his understanding, 702; cf. Cudworth, 128.—will of, dist. his nature, on which all necessity depends, 702. if obligation is made to depend on the will of God backed by sanctions, vice becomes no more than imprudence, 710. the obligations ascribed to God arise from and exist in his own nature; the law by which he is directed is himself, his own infinite, eternal, perfect understanding, 715.—duty to, the first branch of virtue, 733.

God (*cont.*):

[*Smith*]—has made man the immediate judge of mankind and has thereby created him after his own image, 810. nature and reasoning tell us that the general rules of morality are the commands and laws of God, 821-3.

[*Paley*] virtue is doing good to mankind, in obedience to the will of God, and for the sake of everlasting happiness, 845.—will of, is the rule of virtue, 845, 850; cf. Gay, 464.—will of, requires promotion of general happiness, 846, 853; cf. Gay, 465. to inquire into the will of God is the whole business of morality, 853.

[*Reid*] if moral judgement were feeling, morality would be arbitrary, and so God could have no moral character, 944.—moral excellence of, is copied by human virtue, 945.

[*Bentham*]—will of, as the standard of right and wrong, must be his presumptive will, and so simply a way of expressing either the principle of utility or that of asceticism or that of sympathy and antipathy, 965.—pleasure of, cannot be known except by pronouncing our own pleasure to be his, 965*n*.

good, see *common* (good), *end, happiness, pleasure, virtue*.

[*Hobbes*]—and evil = what please and displease, 4.— = object of desire, 25. no *summum bonum*, 44; cf. 4.—to oneself, the object of every voluntary act, 60, 68. to love and to think good is all one, 98.

[*Cudworth*]—natural and immutable, 119.—and evil, not made by will but by nature, 120-9.—natural and positive, better expressed in terms of absolute and accidental or hypothetical obligation, 123-4. every thing acts for the sake of some end and good, 146.—desire and love of, the first mover of action, not a mere passion but a settled principle, 147.

[*Locke*] things are good or evil only in reference to pleasure or pain, 160, 183.—the greater, does not determine the will in the absence of uneasiness, 175, 178 (486).—and evil = what is apt to produce pleasure and pain, 177, 183; cf. 160. morally good and evil is the conformity or disagreement of voluntary actions to some law, whereby good and evil (reward and punishment) are drawn on us, 183.

[*Shaftesbury*]—or interest, 195.— relative to a system, dist. solitary perfection, 196; cf. 198.—or ill, attributed to an agent, implies design or purpose, and motive of affection, 199.—and natural, ill and unnatural, affections, 199.—public, mistakenly appears to be inconsistent with private, 206-7. natural affections tend to public good, self-affections to private, unnatural affections to neither, 210.—promotion of general, is promotion of private, 223.

[*Clarke*]—and evil in the nature of things, presupposed by obligations of compact and law, 227-8. in their own nature, some things are good, some evil, some indifferent, 228.

[*Wollaston*] foundation of religion lies in difference between good and evil, 272. acts denominated morally good or evil imply intelligence and free choice, 273. degree of good or evil in an action is determined by importance and number of truths concerned, 290. distinction between good and evil is the same as that between true and false, 291. it cannot be adequately described by talk of *honestum*, or of following nature, 291; or of right reason, or common sense and innate principles, 292; or of pleasure and pain, 293.

[*Hutcheson*]—moral (dist. natural), a quality procuring approbation, 303.—natural, or happiness, either immediate or mediate, pursued from interest or self-love, 304. desire of public good, approved by the moral sense, 309, 315. morally good actions must flow from benevolence, 328. quantity of good produced by an action is in compound proportion to motive and ability, 335. perfection of virtue when the amount of good produced equals the ability, 337. men are presumed to be naturally inclined to public good, 339.—natural, promoted by benevolence, 347.—absence of, more easily borne than presence of misery, 353.—public, as a more reasonable ultimate end than private good, 362.

[*Butler*]—public and private, though distinct, perfectly coincide, 387-8.—private, or happiness, the object of self-love, 416.—private, may be frustrated by engrossment in self-love; disengagement is necessary to enjoyment, 417.—of the creation, may be the only end of God, 427*n*.; cf. 434. our sense of actions as morally good or evil implies a sense of them as of good or ill desert, 431.

[*Balguy*] absolute goodness of virtue, 454.—moral, one kind of ultimate end, natural good another, 455, 460.—reasons for action, 457–61. to resolve all obligations into interest is to say that virtue is not good in itself but good only as it does us good, 461.

[*Gay*]—of mankind, cannot be any obligation to me if it is contrary to my happiness, 466.— = what is apt to produce pleasure, 467; cf. Locke, 160, 177, 183. reflection upon good and evil produces love (desire of good) and hatred (aversion from evil), 467.

[*Hume*] the will may be determined either by the view of the greatest possible good or by present uneasiness, 486 (174–5).—public, the ground of approbation of all the artificial virtues, and of many, though not all, of the natural virtues, 549–50. we say of one who carries benevolence to excess, that he is 'too good', 584. all virtuous qualities have a tendency to public or private good, 633.

[*Price*] desire of private good does not arise from instinct but from the nature of happiness, 692. a purely reasonable being would see that happiness is in itself valuable and desirable, 693. 'morally good' and 'evil', when applied to actions, mean the same as 'right' and 'wrong', 707.—public, is the most general and leading consideration in our inquiries concerning right, 737. materially good actions, dist. formally good, 750.

[*Paley*] virtue is the doing good to mankind, in obedience to the will of God, and for the sake of everlasting happiness, 845.—of mankind, is the subject of virtue, 845.

[*Reid*] what is good for us upon the whole is an end of which we can only form a conception by the use of reason, 860–2. it then becomes a leading or governing principle, 863 (cf. Butler, 400, 409); which operates in a calm and cool manner, 863; cf. Butler, 382, 393, 400; Hutcheson, 357; Price, 761. it gives us the conception of a right and wrong, or at least of a wise and foolish, 866; cf. Butler, 433. actions deserving moral approbation must be done with the belief of their being morally good, 894; cf. Price, 755, 758. two senses of moral goodness, one as applied to the action considered abstractly, the other as

applied to the agent, 897–8; cf. Price, 719n., 750. the former is not affected by the agent's intention and belief, the latter is, 899–900.

[*Bentham*]— = cause or instrument of pleasure, 975; cf. Locke, 160, 177, 183; Gay, 467. only pleasure and pain are good and bad in themselves; other things are good and bad as causing or preventing pleasure and pain; but in a figurative sense a thing may be called good or bad in consideration of its cause, 982; cf. 992. motives are called good or bad only on account of their effects, 993.

goodness, see *virtue*.—no absolute, 4.—of God, is his goodness to us, 4.—and justice, natural and immutable, 119.—mere, dist. virtue or merit, 200, 202.—requires private as well as public affections, 212.

good will, see *benevolence, love.*

gratitude

[*Hobbes*]—a law of nature, 68.

[*Hutcheson*]—a strong form of benevolence, 342.—right of benefactor to, as example of imperfect rights, 353.

[*Balguy*]—obligation of, could be discovered by reason even if we had no natural affection for benefactors, 439. relation of agreement between gratitude and benefaction allows inference of obligation, 456–7 (598).—obligation of, equivalent to a self-evident proposition, 458.

[*Hume*] the same relations that exist in an instance of ingratitude or parricide exist also when a sapling overtops and destroys its parent tree, 501. selfishness the true mother of ingratitude, 540. demerit of ingratitude cannot be discerned by reason alone, 596–9 (456–8, 933–5).

[*Hartley*]—in relation to association, 644.

[*Price*]—approbation of, not grounded on utility, 730.—as one of the main branches of virtue, 737.

[*Smith*] an action deserves reward or punishment if it is the proper and approved object of gratitude or resentment, 786–8; i.e. if these passions have the sympathy of the impartial spectator, 789.—sympathy with, depends on propriety of the agent's motive, 792–6.—indirect sympathy with, gives rise to sense of merit, 797.

[*Reid*] Hume's view, that reason cannot perceive the demerit of ingratitude,

gratitude *(cont.)*:

mistakenly assumes either that the sentiment of blame is feeling without judgement, or that only feeling can be excited by the particular structure of the mind, 933–5 (596–7).

grief,— = pain of the mind, 5.

Grotius,—cited by Hutcheson, 361.—referred to by Hume, 631.

guilt,—sense of, attests free will, 137.—presupposed by ill desert, 431.—consciousness of, a natural sanction of the law of nature, 450.

habit

[*Butler*] virtue, when habitual, ceases to be confinement and becomes choice and delight, 408.

[*Gay*] habitual knowledge causes us to treat known or presumed truths as axioms, 476.

[*Hartley*] power of habit and custom, a general and indeterminate description of the influence of association, 638–9.

[*Price*] utility established by custom or habit is not the ground of all approbation, 730.

happiness, see *desire, pleasure, utility.*

[*Hobbes*] felicity consists not in having prospered but in prospering, 5. felicity = continual success or prospering, 37. felicity consists not in repose of satisfaction, but is a continual progress of desire, 44.

[*Cumberland*] greatest benevolence of each towards all forms the happiest state of each and all, 107.—of each, cannot be separated from happiness of all, 108–9. adequate rewards and punishments make pursuit of public good contribute to private happiness, 112.—private, cannot be prescribed by reason as the ultimate end, 115.

[*Cudworth*] constant desire or love of good and happiness is the first mover of action, 147.

[*Locke*]—desire of, an innate practical principle, constantly influencing all our actions, 156.—public, and virtue, inseparably connected by God, 158.—alone moves desire, 176.—in its full extent, is the utmost pleasure we are capable of, 177. determination to pursue happiness in general, our greatest good, is the foundation of liberty in freeing us from determination by particular desires, 182.

[*Shaftesbury*]—generally computed from pleasures, 215.—results chiefly from natural or social affections, 215–19. —depends on promoting general good, 223.

[*Clarke*]—of all men, the object of universal love or benevolence, 243. God causes truth and right to terminate in happiness, 251.

[*Wollaston*]—allied to truth and aimed at by the practice of truth, 295.—identified with true quantity of pleasure, 298.—ultimate, a balance of true pleasure over pain, 298.—pursuit of, a duty, 299.—animals may be susceptive and desirous of, 300.—ultimate, produced by practice of truth, 301–2.

[*Hutcheson*]—or natural good, 204. that action is best which procures the greatest happiness for the greatest numbers, 333. tendency of divine providence to universal happiness is what makes us call God morally good, 351.— = pleasant sensation of any kind, or a continued state of such sensations, 358.

[*Butler*]—or interest, consists in an appetite or affection enjoying its object, 383; cf. 417.—depends on regards to others, 407.—private, or good, the object of self-love, 416.—does not consist in self-love, but in the gratification of particular passions, 417. disengagement is necessary to enjoyment, 417.—is not exclusive, like property, 422. it may be allowed that virtue or any other pursuit cannot be justified unless it is for, or at least not contrary to, our happiness, 423. —nothing but, can be of consequence to mankind or any creature, 426.—is all we can have a right to, and all that we can be obliged to promote for other men, 426. we approve or disapprove of certain dispositions and actions abstracted from consideration of their tendency to the happiness or misery of the world, 427n.; cf. 434–5.

[*Gay*] obligation is the necessity of doing or omitting any action in order to be happy, 463 (718).—of mankind, is the criterion of the will of God, and therefore the criterion, once-removed, of virtue, 465. the good of mankind cannot be any obligation to me if it is contrary to my happiness, 466.— = the sum total of pleasure, 468; cf. Shaftesbury, 215.—is dependent on others, and therefore the promotion of their happiness must be approved as a means to their promoting mine, 468.—private, as one's ultimate end, is consistent with merit, i.e. acting for the sake of another, 469–71.—private, is the proper or ultimate end of all actions, 470.—known or presumed means to, often treated as principles or ends, 475–6.

[*Price*] every being must desire happiness for himself, and a rational nature must approve of actions procuring it, 679. desire of private happiness does not arise from instinct but from the nature of happiness, 692.—is not a possible object of aversion, 692. a purely reasonable being would see that the happiness of others is as important to them as his is to him, and that happiness is in itself equally valuable and desirable, whoever possesses it, 693. to define obligation as the necessity of doing a thing in order to be happy, would make ridiculous the statement that a man is obliged to study his own happiness, 718 (463).

[*Paley*] virtue is the doing good to mankind, in obedience to the will of God, and for the sake of everlasting happiness, 845.—everlasting private, the motive of virtue, 845, 850, 852. different theories of obligation ultimately coincide in the promotion of general happiness, 846. promotion of general happiness is what is required by the will of God, 846, 853; cf. Gay, 465.

[*Bentham*] the principle of utility or the greatest happiness principle states that the greatest happiness of all those whose interest is in question is the only right and proper end of action, 946n.—of the members of a community, is the sole end which the legislator ought to have in view, 967, 977.—consists of enjoyment of pleasures and security from pains, 977.

Hartley, 635–54. see especially *association, moral sense.*—cites Gay, 635; Newton, 638; Locke, 638–9.

Helvetius,—referred to by Bentham, 994n.

Hobbes, 1–103. see especially *freedom, natural, nature, power, promise.*—cites Plato, 13; Aristotle, 80; Velleius Paterculus, 94; St. Paul, 101.—cited by Cudworth, 135, 139; by Hutcheson, 359; by Butler, 429.—criticizes Aristotle, 73; Bramhall, 90–9.—criticized by Cudworth, 138(?), 146, 152–3; by Clarke, 227, 229, 236, 244, 247, 252–60; by Hutcheson, 310; by Butler, 382,

388n., 411.—refers to Socrates, 13; to Zeno, 91.

honestum,—as supposed criterion of moral good, 291.—not constituted, but presupposed, by affections, 438.—dist. *pulchrum,* 443, 689. honesty and justice, 514–16. *sensus recti et honesti,* 877.

honour

[*Hobbes*]—manifestation of value, 40. —a sign of power, 41.—independent of justice, 42.

[*Mandeville*]—and shame, inculcated by lawgivers, 264 (311, 550).

[*Hutcheson*]—Mandeville's theory of, 311.—an immediate good, shame an immediate evil, both evidence of a moral sense, 344.—and shame, assigned to a separate sense, 356.

[*Reid*]—principle of, is only another name for regard to duty, 871.

Horace,—cited by Hume, 583, 631.

humanity, see *benevolence.*

[*Hume*]—principle of, as the motive of benevolent actions, 513, 551.—has place, where justice has not, in the duties of men towards inferior creatures, 572.— or fellow feeling, may be taken as an original principle in human nature, 576n.—has some influence on all men, 577.—sentiment of, is alone capable of expressing the universal point of view required for moral notions, 589; for since it relates to the public good, it is a feeling shared by all, 590; and comprehends all as possible objects of approval or disapproval, 591.—sentiment of, thereby gives rise to moral language, 592.—sentiment of, produces approval of utility, while reason judges what is useful, 595.

[*Smith*]—virtues of, depend on sympathy of spectator with sufferer, 781.

Hume, 479–634. see especially *approbation, benevolence, cause, justice, natural, necessity, promise, reason, sentiment, sympathy, utility, virtue, will.*—cites Quintilian, 547n.; Bacon, 576; Plutarch, 578; Horace, 583, 631; Sallust, 612; Cicero, 632–3.—cited by Price, 657n., 667n., 689n., 739; by Smith, 824; by Reid, 859, 895, 901, 907, 913, 926, 928–9, 933, 937, 940.—criticizes Locke, 486, 497; Wollaston, 494–6; Mandeville, 550; Rochefoucauld, 610n.; Hutcheson, 631–2, 634.—criticized by Price, 668, 675, 740, 759; by Smith, 832–3, 839(?), 844; by Reid, 857, 864, 880, 895–901, 906, 908, 926–30, 933–44.

Hume (*cont.*):
—refers to Euclid, 603; to Cicero, 604; to Grotius and Pufendorf, 631; to Allestree(?), 632.

Hutcheson, 303–73. see especially *benevolence, good, moral sense, reason, self-love.*—cites Shakespeare, 309; Malebranche, 322; Cumberland, 331, 347; Stoics, 337; Pufendorf, 347; Locke, 355; Addison, 356; Plato, 356–7; Epicureans, Cicero, Hobbes, and Rochefoucauld, 359; Grotius, 361; Aristotle, 362–3.—cited by Gay, 474; by Price, 657.—criticizes Hobbes, 310; Mandeville, 311; Locke, 325; Clarke, 367; Wollaston, 368.—criticized by Butler, 435; by Balguy, 436–47, 451, 453–5; by Gay, 473, 476, 478; by Hume, 631–2, 634; by Price, 674, 689, 719; by Smith, 815, 837–43; by Reid, 908; by Bentham, 959.—referred to by Reid, 877.

ideas
[*Hobbes*] idea of love in Plato, 13.

[*Clarke*]—of first truths, natural or moral, not innate, 235; cf. Locke, 154–9.

[*Hutcheson*]—innate, not implied by the moral sense, 313.—simple, can only be explained by synonymous words, 358.—relative, do not stand for real qualities in external natures, 367.—sensible, classified as purely sensible and as concomitant, 371.—of actions, distinguished into ideas of external motion and its tendency, apprehension of affections in the agent, and perception of approbation and disapprobation, 371.

[*Balguy*]—relations between, necessary and unchangeable, 449.—natural and moral, 451.—truth of, dist. truth of words and of things, 452.—antecedent to things, 452.

[*Gay*]—innate, imagined to exist because their origin is forgotten, 476.

[*Hume*]—dist. realities, as provinces of demonstration and will respectively, 480.—dist. impressions, as the two kinds of perceptions, 487, 505 (675).—are virtue and vice distinguished by means of ideas or impressions? 487. ethical rationalists hold that morality is discerned merely by ideas, 488. since morality is not discoverable by reason or the comparison of ideas, it must be by impressions, 505.

[*Hartley*]—dist. sensations, 636.—of sensation, or simple ideas, dist. intellectual or complex ideas, 636.—and sensations, in relation to pleasures and pains,

637. simple ideas of sensation are vestiges or images of repeated sensations, 639. association of sensations causes all the corresponding ideas to be excited by any one of the sensations, 639.—simple, run into complex ones by means of association, 640.

[*Price*]—simple, do not all come from sensation and reflection, 660.—new simple, may come from the understanding, i.e. intuition, 661–71.—perceived by the understanding, correspond to external realities, 668.—universal or abstract, implied in every act of judgement, are not merely nominal, 669.—of right and wrong, are simple ideas, as is shown by the impossibility of defining them except by synonymous expressions, 672; cf. Hutcheson, 358. Hume has not proved that all ideas are either impressions or copies of impressions, and begs the question in applying his principle to moral and other ideas, 675 (489, 505).

[*Reid*] sense not only gives us ideas but is also a power of judging, 878.

ignorance,—crimes of, owing to prior neglect, argue a want of benevolence, 339.

imagination, see *sympathy.*
[*Hobbes*]—of power, produces glory, 6.—of calamity, in relation to pity, 10, 32.

[*Shaftesbury*]—of moral beauty, comes from nature, 203.

[*Mandeville*] imaginary reward needed for self-denial, 263.

[*Hutcheson*]—of private advantage or disadvantage, does not explain approbation or condemnation of actions distant in time or space, 310.—pleasures of, received from an internal sense, 356.

[*Gay*]—of future pleasure or pain, produces present pleasure or pain, i.e. passion, 467.

[*Hume*]—has a set of passions upon which the sentiments of beauty depend, 556.—passes easily from cause to likely effect, 556. sentiments must touch the heart to control passion, but need not extend beyond the imagination to influence taste, 557.—adheres to the general views of things, 557.

[*Hartley*]—pleasures and pains of, arise from beauty and deformity, 637.—as a factor in producing compassion through association, 645.

[*Price*]—a faculty nearly allied to sense, 665.

[*Smith*]—of what we should feel in the situation of another, necessary for sympathy, 764, 778.—can therefore cause us to sympathize with non-existent feelings, e.g. in the insane or the dead, 768–9; cf. 772, 791, 799.—of changed situation, and consequent sympathy, are not required for harmony of sentiments in judgements of taste, 776.—of changed situation, and consequent sympathy, are exercised reciprocally by spectator and sufferer, 778–9.

immediate

[*Gay*]—criterion of virtue, dist. mediate, 465.—approval, alleged to show that approval is independent of private happiness, 474.

[*Hume*]—pleasure, a ground of esteem, but by means of sympathy, 558–9, 585. —feeling and finer internal sense, 562.

[*Price*] faculty of immediate approval and disapproval, 657. right and wrong, being simple ideas, must be ascribed to a power of immediate perception, 672. —perception is not confined to sense, 674.—approbation of making the virtuous happy and discouraging the vicious, abstracted from consequences, 696.—consciousness or feeling, as one of the grounds of belief, 703.

[*Smith*] no immediate experience of what other men feel, 764.—and instinctive approval of retaliation, 791.

immutable,—truth, natural laws are propositions of, 194. goodness and justice, natural and immutable, 119. morality is eternal and immutable, 684, 699. the principles of morals stand upon the immutable foundation of truth, 945.

impartial, see *spectator*. men's judgements concerning the actions of others are commonly impartial, 237.

impressions

[*Hume*]—dist. ideas, as the two kinds of perceptions, 487, 505 (675). are virtue and vice distinguished by means of ideas or impressions? 487. since not by ideas, it must be by means of some impression or sentiment, 505.—arising from virtue, are agreeable, from vice, uneasy, 506.

[*Price*] Hume has not proved that all ideas are either impressions or copies of impressions, and begs the question in applying his principle to moral and other ideas, 675 (487, 505).—of pleasure or pain, accompany our perceptions of virtue and vice, but should not be confounded with them, 677.

indifference,—cannot be the first mover of action, 146.—in relation to free will, 180. false sensation of liberty or indifference, 623.

indifferent,—things, may become obligatory through promise or lawful command, 123–5.—things, made obligatory by authority of law, 228.—acts, may acquire moral significancy by usage or consent, 279.—acts, those that may be either done or not done without violation of truth, 290. if no actions are in themselves right or wrong, they must all be indifferent, 683. if an action is not indifferent, it must be subject to obligation, 723. the indifferent bystander = the impartial spectator, 789.

inducement

[*Paley*]—in common parlance, is less strong than 'obligation', 848. obligation is nothing more than inducement of sufficient strength and resulting from the command of another, 851.

[*Reid*]—necessary for obedience to law, 867. the only rational inducements to follow a general rule or law are a sense of interest or a sense of duty or both together, 867.

[*Bentham*]— = motive, but more comprehensive in its signification and sometimes more apposite, 985*n*.

injury, see *justice*.

innate

[*Locke*] moral principles not innate, 154–9.—law, dist. law of nature, 159.

[*Clarke*] ideas of first truths, natural or moral, not innate, 235.

[*Wollaston*] impressions of education mistaken for innate maxims, 292.

[*Hutcheson*]—ideas, not implied by the moral sense, 313.

[*Gay*] the passions and affections are mistakenly thought to be innate, like the power of receiving pleasure and pain, 467. approbations and affections are acquired, not innate or instinctive, 473, 478.—ideas, like instincts, imagined to exist because their origin is forgotten, 476.

innocence,—punishment of, against the law of nature, 87.—dist. duty and virtue, 184–7.—and ill desert, are inconsistent ideas, 431.

instinct

[*Cudworth*]—of nature to praise and blame, attests free will, 136–7.

[*Hutcheson*]—or determination of our nature to love others, is the spring of

instinct (*cont.*):

virtuous action, 327 (442, 473).—and affection, presupposed by exciting reasons for action, 361–2.—or affection, said to be necessary, not voluntary, 373.

[*Balguy*]—or natural affection, not the true ground of virtue, 437 (336).—would make virtue arbitrary and positive, 438.—as the ground of virtue, depreciates it, 442 (327).—necessity of, incompatible with virtue, 442 (373).—or sense, cannot account for moral approbation, 444–5.

[*Gay*] approbations and affections are acquired, not innate or implanted by instinct, 473, 478 (442).—mistakenly substituted for acquired principles, 476 (356).

[*Hume*] instincts such as benevolence, resentment, love of life, kindness to children, 485.

[*Hartley*]—can be excluded as a cause of intellectual pleasures and pains if these can be shown to arise by association from sensible pleasures and pains, 641. the moral sense is not an instinct, 654.

[*Price*]—is needed to aid reason, 688; cf. 694. is all desire wholly instinctive? 691.—desire of private happiness does not arise from, 692. instinctive desire (passion), dist. rational desire (affection), 694. instinctive benevolence, dist. rational or universal, 760–1.

[*Smith*] immediate and instinctive approval of retaliation, 791.

intellect, see *reason, understanding.* intellectual nature obliges, either absolutely or hypothetically, 123. rational or intellectual nature identified with natural justice, 123–6.—superior to sense, goes beyond appearance to reality, 133. intellectual pleasures and pains, 635. intellectual ideas, dist. ideas of sensation, 636. intellectual pleasures and pains deducible from sensible ones, 641.—superior to sense in rising above individuals to universal and abstract ideas, 663.

intelligence,—and free choice, implied by acts denominated morally good or evil, 273.—presupposed by practical virtue, 754.—presupposes liberty, though not presupposed by it, 754.

intelligible,—essences, dist. constitutive, 133.—objects, dist. visible, 670.

intention, see *consequences, motive.*

[*Hobbes*]—dist. will, 19, 96.

[*Shaftesbury*] design or purpose, and motive of affection, implied in describing an agent as good or ill, 199.

[*Hutcheson*]—approved by the moral sense, is not an intention to obtain self-approbation or any other natural good, 306.—of good, necessary for approbation, 307. unintended advantage to self does not diminish the morality of an action, 336. direct intention of public evil is not necessary to make an action evil, 339. human laws cannot examine intentions, and must judge actions by their tendencies, 339. either malicious intention or neglect of public good necessary to make an action evil, 368.

[*Butler*] will and design constitute the very nature of actions as such, 430.—of consequences, is part of the action, but not necessarily the actual consequences, 430.

[*Price*]—constitutes the actual being of virtue, 755. an agent does, strictly speaking, only what he intends to do, 756.—of virtue, essential for there to be virtue in the agent, 758. Hume's view that virtue presupposes a different intention, 759 (513–14, 633).—determines vice as well as virtue, 762.

[*Paley*] an agent is virtuous or vicious according to his design, while actions are right or wrong according to their tendency, 854n.

[*Reid*] Hume's view, that the virtue of an action cannot depend on the agent's regard for its virtue, is disproved by the fact that the agent's intention is a necessary condition of such virtues and vices as benevolence, malice, revenge, gratitude, veracity, 896 (513–14).—or purpose, does not affect the obligation of contract, 906; cf. Hume, 543.

[*Bentham*]—or will, may regard (1) the act itself, or (2) its consequences, 979. 'intentional' dist. 'voluntary', 979n. an act may be intentional without the consequences being so, and the consequences may be intentional without the act's being so throughout, 980; but the consequences cannot be intentional without the act's being so at least in the first stage, 981.—is caused by motive, and has consequences as its effects, 982.—may be called good or bad with reference to consequences or to motive, 982.—can be called good or bad with reference to intended consequences and irrespective of actual consequences and of motive, 983–4.—and motive, need to be clearly distinguished, 984.

interest, see *self-love.*

[*Shaftesbury*]—or good, 195.—and virtue agree, 195.—public, notion of, required for virtue, 202.—public or common, not inconsistent with, indeed inseparable from, self-interest, 206–7, 213–14, 223.

[*Clarke*] moral fitness independent of private advantage, 225–6; cf. 248.

[*Mandeville*]—of all, to preach public-spiritedness, 267.

[*Hutcheson*]—consequent on, not antecedent to, sense of pleasure, 304.—alleged to be the motive of virtuous actions, 305.—may concur with, or oppose, benevolence, 336.—may co-operate with, or oppose, a depraved temper, 338.—gives rise to one meaning of 'obligation', 347; but cannot be the foundation of obligation as contrasted with constraint, 352.—the ground of a non-moral meaning of 'right', 370.

[*Butler*]—is a manifest obligation, 380.—idea of, applies only to self-love, 382.—or happiness, consists in an appetite or affection enjoying its object, 383.—and virtue, to be distinguished, but not opposed to each other, 384. the goodness or badness of actions does not arise from their being interested or disinterested, 384.—men have not enough regard to, 385, 393.—and duty, seldom inconsistent, 408.—and duty, are perfectly coincident, if we take in the future world, 409.—is constituted, not by self-love, but by nature, 417. disengagement is necessary to enjoyment, 417.—consideration of, may be necessary for justifying virtue, 423.—promotion of, is a virtue or at least is approved, 433.

[*Balguy*] to promote one's own welfare, in subordination to that of the public, is virtue, 448.—considerations of, may be called external reasons, dist. internal reasons of morality, 455.—or pleasure, a fit motive and an obligatory end for men as sensible agents, 460. to resolve all obligations into interest is to confound morality with sensibility and to say that virtue is good only as it does us good, 461.

[*Gay*] merit, i.e. acting for the sake of another, is consistent with acting ultimately for private happiness, 469–70.

[*Hume*]—or present uneasiness, may either of them determine the will, 486

(174–5).—sentiment of, distinct from sentiment of morality, though the two are often confounded, 507.—private or public, cannot supply the reason or motive for acts of justice or honesty, 515–18.—the natural obligation to justice, dist. moral obligation thereto, 533; cf. Balguy, 460. self-interest is the original motive to the establishment of justice, but sympathy with public interest is the source of its moral approbation, 534; cf. 548. interested commerce of mankind, distinguished from disinterested by the invention of promising, 541.—the first obligation to performance of promises, 542.—public, the ground of all the artificial virtues, and of many, though not all, of the natural virtues, 549–50.—public, is approved even when contrary to private, 576.—general, the standard of general approbation, 580.

[*Hartley*] pleasures and pains of self-interest, 637.

[*Price*]—dist. virtue, 710–11; cf. Butler, 380.—public, is the most general and leading consideration in our inquiries concerning right, 737.

[*Smith*]—of society, is advanced unawares by the rich, led by an invisible hand, 829.

[*Paley*] we can be obliged to nothing but what we ourselves are to gain or lose something by, 849. private happiness is the motive of moral obligation, 850; cf. 845. prudence concerns gain or loss in the present world, duty concerns also gain or loss in the world to come, 852.

[*Reid*] what is good for us upon the whole, co-operates with duty and leads to the same course of conduct, 860, 866; cf. Butler, 408–9. conception of our good upon the whole, can only be formed by reason, 860–2. it then becomes a leading or governing principle, 863 (cf. Butler, 400, 409); which operates in a calm and cool manner, 863; cf. Butler, 382, 393, 400; Hutcheson, 357; Price, 761. it gives us the conception of a right and wrong, or at least of a wise and foolish, 866; cf. Butler, 433. sense of interest and sense of duty are the only rational inducements to obey a general rule of conduct, 867.—duty cannot be resolved into, 870; cf. Price, 710.

[*Bentham*]—of the community, is the sum of the interests of its members, 949.

interest (*cont.*):

a thing is said to promote the interest of the individual when it tends to add to the sum total of his pleasures, 949.—cannot in the ordinary way be defined, since it does not have any superior genus, 949*n.*

intrinsic,—worth of virtue and goodness, 248–50.—goodness of moral actions, 459.

intuition

[*Butler*] full intuitive conviction that moral perception should govern man, 377.

[*Balguy*] is the obligation of gratitude seen intuitively? 458.

[*Hume*] promises would be unintelligible naturally, even if we could perceive each other's thoughts by intuition, 535.

[*Hartley*] early formed associations may appear like axioms and intuitive propositions, 654.

[*Price*]—a spring of new ideas, 661.—dist. deduction, as two acts of the understanding, 661*n.*; cf. 671, 704. we perceive intuitively the necessary existence and the infinity of space and duration, 666.—of truth, 674.—of the natures of things, dist. powers of sensation, 678.—dist. feeling and reasoning, as three grounds of belief, 704.—the foundation of the possibility of all reasoning, 704.—varies in degree, being sometimes clear and perfect, sometimes faint and obscure, 706.

Johnson, Samuel,—cited by Reid, 930.

judgement

[*Reid*]—in addition to intention and will, is required for rational principles of action but not for animal principles, 856, 858, 942. no exercise of reason without judgement, 858. sense includes judgement as well as having ideas, 878. the moral sense similarly gives us judgements as well as conceptions, 879. Hume's argument about motives implies that judgement cannot make an action good or bad, 895; but many virtues and vices necessarily depend on the agent's belief or intention, 896. does approbation include judgement, or is it feeling alone? 907.—dist. feeling, 909–12.—must be expressed by a proposition and must be either true or false, 911.—and feeling are often combined, and so confused, 912. in perception, judgement is the consequence of sensation, 915. but when judgement is combined with feeling, the feeling is usually the consequence of the judgement, 916. this is true of moral judgement and feeling, 917. a statement expressing a moral judgement differs in meaning from one expressing a feeling, 919; first because the latter statement is autobiographical, while the former is not, 920; secondly because the former statement can be contradicted without offence, while the latter cannot, 921. each of the two statements can be inferred from the other, as being causally related, but not as having the same meaning, 922. if moral approbation were feeling alone, a statement expressing a moral judgement would either mean the same as one expressing a feeling or would be meaningless, 923. Hume abuses the word 'reason' in limiting it to speculative judgement, 926; and the terms 'moral sense' and 'sentiment' in limiting them to feeling without judgement, 927. Hume even uses the word 'judgement' itself of moral perception, although he regards this as mere feeling, 928. Hume's view, that reason cannot perceive the demerit of ingratitude, mistakenly assumes either that the sentiment of blame is feeling without judgement, or that only feeling is excited by the particular structure of the mind, 933–5 (596–7). the existence, but not the truth or falsity, of a judgement, depends on the structure of the mind, 935. if moral judgement were feeling, a judge ought to be called a feeler, 936 (601). if moral judgement were feeling, morality would be arbitrary, and so God could have no moral character, 944.

justice

[*Hobbes*]—and injustice, have no place in state of nature, relate to men in society, 53, 67 (227, 255). injustice or injury resembles absurdity, i.e. self-contradiction, 59, 102.—originates in the third law of nature, and consists in keeping valid covenants, 67; cf. 102.—of criminal law, not impugned by the doctrine of necessity, 93, 96.

[*Cudworth*]—natural and immutable, 119.—natural, the foundation of positive law, 122–6.—natural, identified with the rational or intellectual nature, 123–6.—retributive, looks to past as well as future, 138 (93).

[*Locke*]—comes nearest to being a universal moral rule, 155.—necessarily linked to property, 189.

[*Clarke*]—universal, the top and perfection of all virtues, 242. Hobbes's obligation to keep compacts implies antecedent obligations of justice, 257.

[*Butler*] injustice and pain both contrary to nature but in different senses, 377, 404. men are often unjust to themselves as to others, 394. injury dist. harm, 429. our moral judgement of justice and veracity is independent of consideration of good or bad consequences, 434–5; cf. 427*n*.

[*Hume*]—an artificial virtue, 512. motive for acts of justice and honesty cannot be originally a regard for honesty itself, 514; nor a concern for private interest, 515; nor a regard for public interest, 516; nor private benevolence, i.e. a regard to the interests of the party concerned, 518. the sense of justice must therefore arise artificially, 519.—artificial but not arbitrary, and may be called natural in the sense of being a necessary invention, 521; cf. 631.—idea of, arises from convention regarding stability of possessions, and itself gives rise to ideas of property, right, and obligation, 529.—derives its origin from the selfishness and confined generosity of man, along with the scanty provision of nature for his wants, 532; cf. 567–71. interest, the natural obligation to justice, dist. moral obligation thereto, 533; cf. Balguy, 460.—is judged a virtue, and injustice a vice, because sympathy causes us to share the satisfaction or uneasiness which they produce in society, 534, 548.—is first established through self-interest, and then receives moral approbation through sympathy, 534.—an artificial invention for the purpose of serving the good of mankind, 548. a single act of justice may be contrary to public good, but the whole system of law and justice is advantageous to society, 551; cf. 594.—has utility as its sole origin and sole ground of merit, 566–73, 582.—would be rendered useless, and so inconceivable, if there were abundance of external conveniences or an extension of human benevolence, 567–8; cf. 532.—is suspended in conditions of extreme necessity or of extreme rapaciousness, 569–71.—would be useless and non-existent in the relations between men and creatures of greatly inferior strength, 572.—would not exist if each individual were self-sufficient and solitary, 573.—single instances of, may be harmful in their immediate tendency, but advantage to society results from observance of the general rule, 594.

[*Price*]—approbation of, not grounded on utility, 730; cf. 744.—as one of the main branches of virtue, 741–4.—as concerned with property, 741–3.—as equitable distribution of rewards and punishments, 744; cf. 696–8.—not grounded solely on utility, but much influenced by it, 744.

[*Bentham*]—natural, as standard of moral judgement, is simply a name for individual sentiment, 959.

Kames,—cited by Price, 720.

knowledge, see *understanding*.

[*Cudworth*]—presupposes immutable natures and essences, 127.—the comprehension of that which necessarily is, 128. —or understanding, is active comprehension by universal reasoning, 132.

[*Price*]—dist. sense, 663.—implies an active and vital energy of the mind, 663; cf. Cudworth, 132. understanding, as the source of knowledge, must be likewise the source of new ideas, 670.—of obligation, necessary for obligation in one sense but not in another, 719*n*.; cf. 750–1.

language

[*Locke*]—the means of maintaining society, 194.

[*Wollaston*] natural gestures are a sort of universal language, 275.

[*Hutcheson*] confusion of ambiguous words, 358.

[*Butler*] common language and common behaviour attest a moral faculty, 429.

[*Hume*] a promise is a certain form of words invented by men, 541. use of language would be impossible if we did not correct the momentary appearances of things, 554; cf. 580.—of self-love, dist. language of morals, 590.—of morals, a peculiar set of terms, to express universal sentiments of censure or approbation, 592. verbal disputes common in philosophy, 608. merely verbal disputes are of no importance, 609. long continued controversy is often due to ambiguity of words, 613.

language (*cont.*):

[*Reid*] Hume is guilty of abuse of words when he makes reason the servant of the passions, 864; cf. 926 (482, 485). —a necessary condition of social operations of the mind, 902, 904. social intercourse in its beginning must be carried on by natural signs, 904. a statement expressing a moral judgement differs in meaning from one expressing a feeling, though each can be inferred from the other as being causally related, 919–22. the view that moral approbation is feeling without judgement is contrary to the rules of grammar or rhetoric in all languages, 924. if language be the expression of thought, we must reject the view that secondary qualities, beauty, and virtue are subjective, 925. Hume's view about the place of reason in morals and about the moral sense rest on an abuse of words, 926–7. the meaning of a common word is to be ascertained by common usage, 926. the view that beauty is a feeling of the spectator, not a quality of the object, is a paradox contrary to common language and common sense, 937 (603).

[*Bentham*] a perversity of structure in all languages causes the names of motives to include an imputation of goodness or badness, 994. this imperfection of language explains the violent clamour raised against moralists who have tried to disentangle themselves from the shackles of ordinary language, 994n. the only remedy is to invent a new phraseology or to use neutral circumlocutions, 995.

laughter, — = sudden glory, 11, 31.

law, see *natural, nature, obligation.*

[*Hobbes*]—natural and politic, 1.—and command, 20, 100, 103.—of nature (q.v.), 54–77.—(of nature) dist. right (of nature), 56.—dist. counsel and covenant, 100, 103. contracts oblige us, laws tie us fast, being obliged, 100.

[*Cumberland*]—natural (q.v.), or of nature (q.v.), 104–18.

[*Cudworth*]—obligation of, depends not on will but on natural justice, 122.—in a secondary sense (i.e. positive law), dist. natural law or justice, 134.

[*Locke*] will and law of God the true ground of morality, 158 (675).—of nature, dist. innate law, 159.—three sorts of, divine law, civil law, and law of opinion or reputation, 184–8.—

essentially implies reward and punishment, 184.—divine, the touchstone of moral rectitude, i.e. of duty and sin, 185 (675).—civil, determines whether actions be criminal or innocent, 186.—of opinion or reputation, the common measure of virtue and vice, 187; this law of fashion is attended by censure and dislike as its sanction, 188.—of nature, known by the light of nature, i.e. reason and sense-experience, 190. all law presupposes a legislator declaring his will, 190.—of nature, decrees that men should worship God, enter and maintain society, and preserve themselves, 194.

[*Clarke*]—validity of, depends on natural good and evil, 228.—authority of, makes indifferent things obligatory, 228; cf. Cudworth, 123–5.—of nature, = right reason, 246.—of nature, the foundation of God's dominion over creatures, 247 (89).—of nature, has obligatory power antecedent to thought of reward and punishment, 248. Hobbes is inconsistent in making some moral obligations depend on positive law, others on natural law, 256–7.

[*Wollaston*]—of our nature, the law of reason, 283.—of nature, to act so as not to contradict truth, 294.

[*Hutcheson*]—of a superior, alleged to underlie all moral qualities, 305.—human, cannot examine intentions, and must judge actions by their tendencies, 339.—of a superior, does not enter into sense of disinterested obligation, but may be necessary for interested obligation, 346–7.—does not underlie moral ideas, because laws themselves are subject to moral predicates, 351. to say that morality depends on divine law implies that it is a tautology to call divine laws good or just, 351.

[*Butler*] man is by his very nature a law to himself, 381, 399–400, 405–6.

[*Balguy*] the internal reasons of things are the supreme law, 450.—of nature, has its natural sanction in remorse, 450. laws oblige us as moral agents, sanctions as sensible agents, 461.

[*Gay*] laws of nature, and natural consequences, give rise to natural obligation, 464.

[*Hume*] rules of justice may be called laws of nature, despite being artificial, 521. invention of laws of nature, 540. whole scheme of law and justice is advantageous to society, 551. laws of nature (in the scientific sense), 614, 617. all laws founded on rewards and punishments, 628.

[*Price*]—implies antecedent right, 658; cf. 709. Locke's view, that rectitude signifies conformity of actions to rules or laws, makes it absurd to apply rectitude to rules and laws themselves, 675 (183-8). rectitude is both a rule of action to direct, and a law to bind, 713. the eternal law by which God is directed is himself, 715.

[*Smith*] sacred and necessary law of retaliation, 791. all general rules are commonly called laws, e.g. the laws of motion, but the term 'law' is more properly applied to rules for the direction of conduct, 823.

[*Reid*]—implies a general rule of conduct and an inducement to obey, 867.

[*Bentham*]—of nature or of reason, as standard of moral judgement, is simply a name for individual sentiment, 959.—of nature, is used in legislative debate to save the trouble of inquiry, 962.

liberty, see *freedom, necessity, will.*

Locke, 154-94. see especially *freedom, law, will.*—cited by Hutcheson, 355; by Hartley, 638-9.—criticized by Hutcheson, 325; by Hume, 486, 497; by Price, 660, 670, 675; by Reid, 908, 915.—refers to Euclid, 189.

love, see *benevolence, self-love.*

[*Hobbes*]— = pleasure, 3.— = desire, 24.—sexual, defined as need, 12. good will or charity, assisting other men in their desires, evidence of power, 13 (388*n*.). to love and to think good is all one, 98.

[*Cumberland*]—a less suitable name than 'benevolence', 107.

[*Cudworth*]—and desire of good, the first mover of action, not a mere passion but a settled principle, 147.

[*Shaftesbury*]—sexual, as evidence for superiority of kind to sensual affection, 218.—effects of, enjoyment of good by communication, and consciousness of approbation of others, 219.

[*Clarke*]—or benevolence, endeavouring to promote the happiness of all men, one of the two branches of duty to fellow creatures, 241, 243-4.—duty of, may be deduced from greatest fitness of greatest good, 243; and from men's natural need of friendship and society, 244.

[*Hutcheson*]—in relation to virtue, is either complacence (esteem) or benevolence, 316.

[*Butler*]—of power, mistakenly identified with benevolence by Hobbes, 388*n*. (13).—of society, dist. affection to the good of society, 389.—of God, or piety, implied by benevolence, since every good affection implies the love of itself, 389.—of our neighbour, as the sum of virtue, 424-8.

[*Gay*]—is desire of good, as hatred is aversion from evil; both arise from reflection and are not innate, 467.—of a rational object, implies desire of, and pleasure in, his happiness, 468.—of voluntary beings, dist. that of involuntary, 472.

[*Hume*] no such passion as the love of mankind merely as such, 517.

[*Smith*] as to love our neighbour as we love ourselves is the great law of Christianity, so the great precept of nature is to love ourselves only as we love our neighbour or as our neighbour is capable of loving us, 782.—dist. gratitude, 787.

lust,—consists of two appetites, to please and to be pleased, 12.—is commonly used in a bad sense to impute disapprobation, and not merely to name the motive of sexual desire, 994, 998; hence to say that lust is a bad motive is true but nugatory, 998.

Malebranche,—cited by Hutcheson, 322; by Price, 667*n*.; by Smith, 813.

malice

[*Hobbes*] to take pleasure in other men's great harm, without other end of one's own, is impossible, 32.

[*Hutcheson*] human nature seems scarce capable of malicious disinterested hatred, 326, 329, 336, 338.—crimes of, dist. crimes of ignorance, 339.

[*Butler*] disinterested cruelty the utmost depravity we can imagine, 384; cf. Hutcheson, 329. no such thing as pure ill will, 392.

[*Hume*] absolute disinterested malice had never perhaps place in any human breast, 578.

[*Bentham*] the motive of ill will or malice is still a kind of pleasure, and even this wretched pleasure, taken by itself, is good, 992*n*.—is an alternative name, in a bad sense, for the motive that is called, in a neutral sense, antipathy or ill will, 997.

man,—a compound of passions, that govern him by turns, 262.—subject to a conjunction of necessity and infirmity, 522. mankind much the same in all times and places, 615. nature has placed mankind under the governance of two sovereign masters, pain and pleasure, 946.

Mandeville, 262–71. see especially *flattery.*—criticized by Hutcheson, 311; by Butler, 391; by Hume, 550; by Reid, 926.—referred to by Bentham, 994*n*.

Manicheans, 578.

Marcus Aurelius,—cited by Butler, 430*n*.

material,—dist. formal, 125, 750, 875, 900.—or important consequences, 978.

mathematical,—operations, compared with moral actions, 110 (cf. 114), 242.—reasoning, compared with moral, 189, 232–3, 235.—relations, compared with moral, 226, 235, 238, 247, 451–2 (598–9, 601).

means,—and 'end', ambiguous terms, may be replaced by 'cause' and 'effect', 113. fitness of means to ends, 367. known or presumed means to happiness are often treated as ends, 475–6; the cause of this being the association of pleasure with the means, 477.—valued only so far as end is valued, 561.—come to be valued more than the end for which they were intended, 825. every deliberate human action must be done either as a means or as an end, 859.

merit

[*Hobbes*]—dist. worthiness, presupposes a right, 43.—two sorts of, in contract and in free gift of a prize, 63.

[*Shaftesbury*]—or virtue, possible only for man, dist. mere goodness, possible for all sensible creatures, 200.

[*Mandeville*] no merit in acting from pity, 270.

[*Hutcheson*]—said to presuppose reason and free self-determination, 373.—dist. rewardable, may denote a quality which is approved by an observer, or the approbation of which is approved by all other observers, 373 (442).

[*Butler*] our sense of actions as morally good or evil implies a sense of them as of good or ill desert, 431. desert not founded on utility; ill desert presupposes guilt, 431. our perception of good desert is weak with respect to common instances of virtue; our perception of ill desert lessens in proportion to temptation, 431. perception of desert depends

on comparison of action with nature and capacity of agent, 432. imprudence is said to deserve the calamities it brings, 433.

[*Balguy*]—a quality which not only gains approbation but also deserves it, 442 (373).

[*Gay*]—and demerit, as producing esteem or the contrary, give rise to obligations of virtue, 464.—consists in the voluntary contribution of an agent to my happiness, and entitles him to my approbation and love, 469.—is consistent with acting ultimately for private happiness, since the only motive of a meritorious action is the presumption of esteem, 469.—is not acquired if an agent promotes my happiness without having that as his particular end, 471.—gives rise to all moral likings and dislikings, 472.

[*Hume*]—applies to motive, not to external action, 512–13.—regard to, presupposes an antecedent virtuous motive, 513; cf. 633.—personal, to be analysed, 563.—of the social virtues, due at least in part to utility, 564–5, 581–2; cf. 549–50. nothing can bestow more merit than the sentiment of benevolence, 565.—of justice, has utility as its sole ground, 566–71; cf. 549.—of benevolence, arises partly from utility, partly from immediate delight communicated by sympathy, 584; cf. 558.—personal, consists of qualities useful or agreeable to self or to others, 586; cf. 560 (832–3). the term 'personal merit' preferred to 'virtue', because the latter excludes approved qualities called 'talents', 608, 612.

[*Price*] ideas of good and ill desert are a species of the ideas of right and wrong, but apply to agents, while the terms 'right' and 'wrong' are properly applied only to actions, 695. good and ill desert presuppose virtue practised or neglected, and signify the propriety of making virtuous agents happy and of discountenancing the vicious, 695.—cannot be grounded wholly on utility, 696–8.—is the virtue of an agent considered as implying the fitness that good be communicated to him preferably to others, 696. desert and obligation are presupposed by reward and punishment, 712.—of actions is due to their being done from a regard to virtue, 724.—pertains to the virtue of the agent, not to the virtue of the action, 755.

[*Smith*]—(dist. propriety) consists in the beneficial or hurtful effects which an affection aims at or tends to produce, 773, 785. an action deserves reward or punishment if it is the proper and approved object of gratitude or resentment, 786-8; i.e. if these passions have the sympathy of the impartial spectator, 789. sense of merit or demerit consists of two emotions, a direct sympathy or antipathy for the sentiments of the agent, and an indirect sympathy with the sentiments of the person affected by the action, 797-8. sense of merit can be founded on illusive sympathy and does not require actual correspondence of sentiments, as the sense of propriety does, 799.

[*Reid*] punishment and reward imply good and ill desert, and therefore presuppose liberty, not necessity, 891 (628). —depends on the agent's intention, not on the moral goodness of the action considered abstractly, 899.

mind

[*Hobbes*]—body and, faculties or powers of, 1.—pleasures of, 5, 26.

[*Locke*] all pleasures and pains are, strictly speaking, mental, 160.

[*Shaftesbury*]—pleasures of, superior to those of body, 215-16.—pleasures of, are the natural affections or their effects, 216.

[*Hume*]—passes immediately, owing to force of sympathy, from effects of passion to causes, or vice versa, 546; cf. 556.—feels no difference in passing from one link to another in a connected chain of natural causes and voluntary actions, 620.—is carried by a customary transition from one of two constantly conjoined objects to the other, 621.

[*Hartley*]—is that substance, agent, or principle to which we refer sensations, ideas, and voluntary motions, 636.

[*Price*]—knowledge implies an active and vital energy of, 663; cf. Cudworth, 132.

[*Reid*]—operations of, classified as solitary and social, 902.—social operations of, cannot be resolved into any modification or composition of the solitary, 903.

mistake

[*Hume*]—of fact, being involuntary, is not criminal, 491, 602.—of right, may be immoral but cannot be the source of immorality since it presupposes an antecedent right and wrong, 493.

[*Price*] men mistake their own sensations for the properties of objects producing them, 680.—of right and wrong, would be impossible if moral ideas came from sense, 682.

moral

[*Hobbes*]—philosophy, the science of the laws of nature, 77.

[*Locke*]—rules, not innate, because not universally received and require reasoning, 154-8.—rules, capable of demonstration, 154, 189 (497-8).—rules, not even self-evident, because always susceptible to demand for a reason, 157.—relation, the conformity or disagreement of voluntary actions to a rule, 183.—rectitude, divine law the touchstone of, 185 (675).

[*Shaftesbury*]—approval, compared with sense of beauty, 201.—or natural conscience, presupposed by religious conscience, 220.

[*Clarke*]—necessity, dist. absolute, 232.—ideas, not innate, 235.—judgements upon the actions of others, the clearest evidence of natural sense of right and wrong, 237.

[*Mandeville*]—virtues, the political offspring which flattery begot upon pride, 269.

[*Wollaston*]—acts, imply intelligence and free choice, 273.

[*Hutcheson*]—good, dist. natural, 303. —ideas, most clearly observed in reflecting on actions affecting others, 309. morally good actions must flow from benevolence, 328.—beauty, 328, 331, 340.—dignity, 331; cf. 306, 314, 333.—importance of persons, 333, 335.—ideas, do not depend on law, because laws themselves are subject to moral predicates, 351.

[*Butler*] two ways of treating morals, one from abstract relations, the other from the nature of man, 374.—rectitude, or virtue, consists in pursuit of what is right and good as such, though justification of it may require consideration of interest, 423.—faculty, whether called conscience, moral reason, moral sense, or divine reason, 429.—understanding and moral sense, 434.

[*Balguy*]—goodness, or virtue, the conformity of moral actions to the reasons of things, 448.—actions, concern behaviour toward intelligent or sensible beings, 448.—and natural ideas, 451.—good is one kind of ultimate end,

moral (*cont.*):

natural good another, 455, 460.—and natural obligations, 460.—agents, dist. sensible, 460–1.—obligation, strictly connected with moral fitness, 461.

[*Gay*]—likings and dislikings, all arise from various combinations of merit, 472.

[*Hume*]—obligation, dist. natural, 533; cf. Balguy, 460.—and natural evidence, link together and are of the same nature, 620.

[*Price*]—beauty, dist. natural, 690.—goodness, arises only from a moral motive, 758.

[*Paley*]—obligation, is like all other obligations, 851. utility of a moral rule constitutes its obligation, 854.

[*Reid*]—good, two senses of, as applied to the action considered abstractly, and as applied to the agent, 897–900; cf. Price, 719*n.*, 750.—feeling is a consequence of moral judgement, 917.

[*Bentham*]—sanction, dist. physical, political, and religious, 968; cf. Locke, 184; Gay, 464.

morality, see *virtue*.

[*Cudworth*]—anticipations of, spring from an inward, vital principle, 135.—could not exist if the soul were merely passive, 135.

[*Locke*]—capable of demonstration, 154, 189 (497–8).—true ground of, the will and law of God, 158, 185 (675).

[*Clarke*]—and speculative truth, compared and contrasted, 232.—or natural religion, 239.

[*Mandeville*]—invented by politicians, 267, 269 (311, 391, 550).—utility of, 267.—not the effect of religion, 268.

[*Butler*]—and religion at last coincide, 428.

[*Balguy*] to treat or use an insensible object conformably to reason may be a right action but is indifferent in respect of morality, 448.—confounded with sensibility if all obligations are resolved into interest, 461.

[*Hume*]—influences passion and action, and cannot therefore be derived from reason, which can have no such influence, 489.—not susceptible of demonstration, since the relations relevant to demonstration apply to irrational and inanimate objects, 497–8, 501–2.—does not consist in matter of fact inferable by reason, but in a sentiment of approbation or disapprobation, 503; cf. 634.—is more properly felt than judged

of, 505.—sentiment of, distinct from that of interest, and arises only when a character is considered in general, 507. the question whether the sentiments of morality are natural depends on the meaning given to 'natural', 510.—sense of, cannot be the first motive of virtuous action, 513; cf. 633.—language of, dist. language of self-love, 590–2.—requires both liberty and necessity, 626–9.—being determined by sentiment, regards only human nature and human life, 634.

[*Price*]—is eternal and immutable, 684, 699.—is a branch of necessary truth, 699.

[*Paley*]—whole business of, is to inquire what is the will of God, 853.

[*Reid*]—practical rules of, stand upon a firmer foundation than the theory of morals, 892.—would be arbitrary if moral judgement were feeling, 944.

moral sense, see *sentiment*.

[*Shaftesbury*] sense of right or wrong, 202, 204.

[*Clarke*] sense men naturally have of difference of right and wrong, 237.

[*Hutcheson*]—a superior sense by which we approve actions as having immediate goodness, without any view of natural advantage from them, 306.—a power of receiving perceptions of moral actions, 307.—makes benevolent actions appear beautiful, 309 (443).—does not suppose innate ideas; it is a determination of our minds to receive the simple ideas of approbation or condemnation, 313. sense of goodness distinct from advantage, demonstrated by the taking account of abilities in approbation, 340.—evidenced by feelings of honour and shame, 344.—alleged to be unnecessary since reflection would recommend the same actions from self-love, 348.—an occult quality, 348.—evidence of the goodness of God, 354.—dist. public sense, by being reflective, 356.—approves kind affection and publicly useful action flowing therefrom, 359.—presupposed by rationalist theories of morals, 359, 361, 363–7.—causes every spectator to approve pursuit of public good more than private, 362.—cannot itself be judged in moral terms but only in terms of interest, 364; cf. 370.—something analogous to, may be attributed to God, 366 (438, 634).—approbation of, not an image of anything external, 371.—said not to be a rule, 372.

[*Butler*] natural sense of moral good and evil, 395, 431. moral faculty, whether called conscience, moral reason, moral sense, or divine reason, 429. moral understanding and moral sense, 434.

[*Balguy*]—object of, insufficiently specified by Hutcheson, 443.—as the ground of approbation, is subject to all the objections applying to affection as the ground of virtue, 444–5.—no more needed than an intellectual sense, 451.

[*Gay*]—and public affection, operate immediately and are therefore alleged to be independent of private happiness, 474. Hutcheson might as well have added a pecuniary sense, and a sense of power and party, to his moral sense and senses of honour, order, etc., 476 (356). —and public affection exist, but are acquired, not innate, 478.

[*Hume*] conscience or a sense of morals, 490.—moral distinctions derived from, 505–11. to have the sense of virtue is to feel satisfaction of a particular kind from contemplation of a character, 506 (839–43). immediate feeling and finer internal sense, 562.

[*Hartley*]—pleasures and pains of, arise from moral beauty and deformity, 637.—to be explained by association through education, 647; the utility of virtue, 648; the consequent love of virtue, 649; the suitableness of all the virtues to each other and to the beauty of the world, 650; the hopes and fears of a future state after death, 651; and meditation upon the perfection of God, 652.—carries its own authority with it, 653; cf. Butler, 379–81, 399–402, 406.— carries us perpetually to the pure love of God, 653.—not an instinct or a rational capacity independent of association, 654.

[*Price*]—as understood by Hutcheson, is a positive or arbitrary principle that might have been different, 657; cf. Balguy, 438, 444. Hutcheson has proved that moral ideas are simple and undefinable, not that they are perceived by a sense, 674.

[*Smith*] sense of propriety and impropriety, dist. sense of merit and demerit, 797–8. the perversion of conscience by passion shows that there is no peculiar faculty of moral sense, since such a faculty would judge our own passions more accurately than those of other men, 815. regard to general rules of conduct is what is properly called a sense of duty, 820.—as one account of sentiment as the principle of moral approbation, 836–43.—supposed to be a peculiar power of perception analogous to the external senses, 837–8.—theory of, implies that the moral faculty itself cannot be the object of moral judgements, 838, 841.—may be mistakenly supposed to be a peculiar sentiment, 839 (506–7); but this would imply that it was the same in all instances, which is false, 840; cf. 781–2; and cf. Hume, 612. —name of, is of recent formation, 842 (877).—is superfluous when the four sources of approbation are analysed, 843.

[*Reid*] sense of duty or conscience, 866. sense of duty and sense of interest are the only rational inducements to obey a general rule of conduct, 867.— is a name given by philosophers to regard for duty, 871.—name of, is not new, 877 (842).—is reasonably regarded as analogous to the external senses, 877. —like the external senses, gives us judgements as well as conceptions, 879. the truths immediately testified by our moral faculty are the first principles of all moral reasoning, 879. Hume abuses the term 'moral sense' in taking it to mean feeling without judgement, 927.

[*Bentham*]—is simply a new name for individual sentiment, 959.

motive, see *desire, end, intention, reason.*

[*Locke*]—for continuing in same state, present satisfaction; motive to change, always some uneasiness, 172; cf. 161, 174–5, 178–9.

[*Shaftesbury*]—of passion or affection, implied in describing a sensible creature as good or ill, 199.

[*Mandeville*] performance cannot be judged without knowledge of principle and motive of action, 270.

[*Hutcheson*]—of virtuous action, is disinterested affection, 315–16, 327, 331. —of election, dist. approbation, 358–9.

[*Gay*] presumption of esteem is the only motive for meritorious action, 469, 471.

[*Hume*] reason alone can never be a motive, 479–82, 607.—the object of praise or approbation, 512; cf. 633. first motive of virtuous action must be different from a regard to its virtue or sense of its morality, 513, 633 (759, 895–901).—of an action, may be the sense of duty, but this presupposes some

motive (*cont.*):

other virtuous motive as common in human nature, 514.—may be supplied by taste, 607. regular conjunction between motives and voluntary actions, 619–20.—and action are not felt to have a necessary connection, 621. virtue can never be the sole motive to any action, 633.

[*Price*]—dist. obligation, 717 (450). motives are not causes of action, but may be occasions, 753*n*.—to action, is provided by the perception of right and wrong, 757.—of a virtuous action, must be a regard to virtue, 759 (513–14, 633).

[*Smith*]—or cause of affection, determines its propriety, while end or tendency determines its merit, 773, 785. —has been unduly neglected by philosophers in concentrating on tendency, 774. propriety or impropriety of an agent's motive is a necessary condition for sympathy with the gratitude or resentment of the person affected by the action, 792–6.—direct sympathy or antipathy for, determines propriety or impropriety, 797–8.

[*Paley*]—of virtue, is everlasting private happiness, 845, 850, 852. obligation means being urged by a violent motive resulting from the command of another, 848.

[*Reid*] advocates of the doctrine of necessity stress the influence of motives, 880. we must understand the influence of motives if we are to understand the sense in which men have moral liberty, 880. the influence of motives differs from that of efficient causes, 881; cf. Price, 753*n*. motives are not causes or agents, but presuppose an efficient cause and liberty in the agent, 881. when it is said that the strongest motive always prevails, what is meant by 'the strongest motive'? 882. if strength is measured by prevalence, it will be merely a tautology to say that the strongest motive always prevails, 883. if the strength of a motive is said to be the cause of its prevalence, this begs the question in presupposing that motives are causes, and the sole causes of actions, 884.—animal, dist. rational, 885. strength of animal motives is tested by feeling, the strongest being that to which one yields easily or which it requires an effort to resist, 886. strength of rational motives is tested by

judgement of what one ought to prefer, 887. in a conflict between animal and rational motives, each is strongest by its own test, and on neither test does the strongest motive always prevail, 888. reasoning from motives to actions is compatible with liberty as well as with necessity, 889 (619). necessary determination by motives would make reward and punishment meaningless, 891 (628). Hume is mistaken in saying that a regard to virtue cannot be the sole motive of virtuous action, 901 (513).

[*Bentham*]—or cause of action, dist. ground or reason for approbation, 966; cf. 963. pleasure and pain are the only things which can operate as motives, 968*n*.—is the cause of intention, 982.— need not be relevant to the goodness or badness of intention, 983–4.—and intention, need to be clearly distinguished, 984.—may be called inducement, 985*n*.—is anything that can contribute to produce or prevent an action, 985.—speculative, influences an act of the intellectual faculty only, 985. —practical, influences the will, 986.— literal, dist. figurative, 987.—interior or internal, dist. exterior or external, 988. —in prospect, dist. in *esse*, 989. motives influencing the understanding are what we call reasons, and may affect the will indirectly by producing a belief concerning a practical motive, 991. the principal or original link in a chain of motives is the last internal motive in prospect, which is always some pleasure or pain, 992. a motive is substantially nothing more than pleasure or pain operating in a certain manner, and therefore no motive is in itself bad, 992; cf. 998. motives are called good or bad only on account of their effects, 993. the names of motives tend to carry with them the imputing of goodness or badness, 994. the motives of good will and ill will may each be regarded as either good or bad according to circumstances, 996–7. no motive is bad in itself or exclusively good, 998. of all motives, good will or benevolence is most likely to coincide with the dictates of utility, 999.

natural, see *nature*.

[*Hobbes*]—faculties and powers, 1.— and artificial man, 21.—equality of men, 47.—right, = liberty to act for self-preservation, 55.—right to all things, 57 (253).—and artificial person, 78.—right, foundation of the right to punish, 86, 93.—right of God, derived from irresistible power, 89; cf. 101 (227, 247, 259–60).—obligation, two species of, 101.

[*Cumberland*]—laws, propositions of immutable truth, known from the nature of things and of men, 104; cf. 106.—law, fulfilled if observed to the extent of ability, 107.—laws (so-called) of motion, 111.—obligation, attended with reward and punishment, does not subordinate common good to private happiness, 116–17.—law, sum of, to seek the common good, 118.

[*Cudworth*]—and immutable goodness and justice, 119.—justice, the foundation of positive law, 122–6.—justice, identical with the rational or intellectual nature, 123–6.—and positive good, better described in terms of absolute and hypothetical obligation, 123–4.

[*Shaftesbury*]—end for every creature, 195.—and unnatural affections, 199, 210, 213–14.—affections, those directed towards the good of the species or common nature, 205–6.—affections, tend to public good, self-affections to private, unnatural to neither, 210.—affections, may be too strong, 211.—affection, the chief means to happiness, 215–19.—affection, pleases even in adversity, as tragedy shows, 218.—or moral conscience, presupposed by religious conscience, 220.

[*Clarke*]—difference between right and wrong, 227.—good and evil, presupposed by obligations of compact and law, 227–8.—and (morally) necessary for the will to be determined by the reason of the thing, 232. morality or natural religion, 239.—self-love and natural affection for kin and friends, 244.

[*Wollaston*]—signification of acts, 275–6; dist. customary, 279. acts that interfere with truth are wrong or unnatural, 280.—religion, identified with moral obligation, 294.—religion may be called, upon two accounts, 302.

[*Hutcheson*]—good, dist. moral, 303. —obligation to benevolence, 346.

[*Butler*]—authority of reflection or conscience, 379.—supremacy of conscience, 400–4.—for brutes, but not for man, to follow strongest desire, 400.—superiority of self-love, 400. conscience is our natural guide, 406; cf. 427n., 429n.

[*Balguy*]—affection or instinct, not the true ground of virtue, 437 (336). absence of natural affection would not prevent us from discovering obligations, 439.—good is one kind of ultimate end, moral good another, 455, 460.—and moral obligations, 460.

[*Gay*]—obligation, dist. virtuous, civil, and religious, 464.

[*Hume*] the question whether the sentiments of morality are natural depends on whether 'natural' is taken to mean (1) not miraculous, (2) not rare, (3) not artificial, 510; but according to such meaning, both virtue and vice are equally natural or equally unnatural, 511.—affection, the duty of a parent, 513.—and usual force of the passions determines judgement of duty, 520.—obligation of interest, dist. moral, 533; cf. Balguy, 460. obligation of promises not natural, 535–9.—virtues, dist. artificial, 546.—virtues, often tend to the good of society, and are therefore approved by sympathy, 549–50; cf. 564–5.—sentiment of approbation and blame, necessary before it could be excited by politicians, 550; cf. Hutcheson, 311 (263–9).—humanity, as the motive of a beneficent action, 551. conventions of justice, once established, are naturally attended with a strong sentiment of morals, 551.—virtues, more likely than the artificial to be the effect of sympathy with benefit produced, 552.—sentiment of benevolence, causes us to approve social virtues for their utility, 581.—and moral evidence link together and are of the same nature, 620.—should not be understood in terms of final causes, 631. justice not unnatural, 631; cf. 521. whether natural abilities is virtues is a dispute of words, 632; cf. 608–12.

[*Price*]—beauty, dist. moral, 690. reason is the natural and authoritative guide of a rational being, 713; cf. Butler, 406, 427n., 429n.

[*Smith*]—object of gratitude or resentment, is that which calls forth the sympathetic gratitude or resentment of every reasonable man or the impartial spectator, 789.—sentiments of approval and disapproval in particular instances lead us to form general rules of morality, 816–17.

[*Bentham*]—justice, as standard of moral judgement, is simply a name for

natural (*cont.*):

individual sentiment, 959. 'unnatural' should mean infrequent, and when the word is used to mean repugnant to nature it is simply an expression of antipathy or dislike, 960.

nature, see *natural*.

[*Hobbes*]—human, the sum of natural faculties, 1.—and art, 21.—state of, a state of war, 50–3, 57 (254).—dissociates men, 51.—in state of, no right or wrong, justice or injustice, or property, 53.—laws of, articles of peace, 54; precepts of reason, 56, 77; oblige *in foro interno*, not always *in foro externo*, 76 (256); immutable and eternal, 77; not properly called laws unless considered as commands of God, 77.—right of, and law of, defined and distinguished, 55–6.—in state of, every man has a right to every thing, 57 (253).—1st law of, to seek peace, 57.—2nd law of, to be willing, when others are, to lay down right to all things, 58.—3rd law of, to perform covenants, 67.—4th law of, gratitude, 68.—5th law of, complaisance, 69.—6th law of, pardon, 70.—7th law of, in retribution, to look to good consequences, 71.—8th law of, to avoid contumely, 72.—9th law of, to acknowledge equality, 73.—10th law of, modesty, 73.—11th law of, equity, 74.—sum of laws of, (not) to do to others as we would (not) be done to, 75, 79; cf. 58.

[*Cumberland*]—of things and men, supplies knowledge of natural law, 104.—law of, precepts for promoting the common good, 105.—law of, consists of necessary truths, 105, 108.—supreme law of, the greatest benevolence of each towards all forms the happiest state of each and all, 107; cf. 118.—law of, comes from God, 111.—law of, defined as both precept and sanction, 112.

[*Cudworth*]—opp. will, 120–9.—not will, the cause of essences, 120–1.—intellectual, the source of obligation, identified with natural justice, 123–6.—necessary, must be the beginner of all action, 146. love and desire of good and happiness is necessary nature in us, 147.

[*Locke*]—law of, dist. innate law, 159.—law of, known by the light of nature, which is neither tradition nor any innate principle, but reason and sense-experience, 190.—law of, decrees that men should worship God, enter and maintain society, and preserve themselves, 194.

[*Shaftesbury*]—universal, a system of all things, 197. imagination of moral beauty comes from nature, 203.—common, or system of the kind, dist. private nature, or self-system, 206.

[*Clarke*]—of things and qualifications of persons, the foundation of fitness or suitableness, 226. in their own nature, some things are good, some evil, some indifferent, 228.—and reason of things, 232.—of man, implies duty of universal benevolence, 244.—law of, = right reason, 246.—obligation of law of, antecedent to its being the positive will of God, 247. Hobbes's state of nature is a state of unnatural corruption, 254, 258 (53). Hobbes's laws of nature imply an original obligation to benevolence, 254–5. reason, the proper nature of man, 258.

[*Mandeville*] mere man, in the state of nature, 262, 268. virtue contrary to impulse of nature, 267.

[*Wollaston*] following nature cannot mean only complying with bodily inclinations without regard to truth, since truth is conformity to nature, 280.—law of our, the law of reason, 283.—and truth, require us to aim at some ends, e.g. happiness, 285. loose to talk of following nature as the criterion of moral good, 291.—religion of, identified with moral obligation, 294.—law of, to act so as not to contradict truth, 294.

[*Hutcheson*] men are presumed to be inclined, from their nature, to public good, 339.—human, formed for universal love, 342.

[*Butler*]—of man, needs explanation to understand the view that virtue consists in following nature, 375. nothing is more contrary to nature than vice, 377. to act conformably to our nature is to allow conscience absolute authority, 379. man is by his very nature a law to himself, 381, 399–400, 405–6.—of man, tends both to public and to private good, 387, 394.—of man, to be judged by what commonly appears, not by exceptional instances, 393.—of man, alleged to be shown by the strength of motives, 396.—following, different senses of, 397.—may mean following (1) any motive, or (2) the strongest motive, 398; or (3) the supreme, authoritative faculty of conscience, 399.—human, compared to a civil constitution, 404.—of man, actions suitable to, 409.

[*Balguy*]—of things, the foundation of virtue, 446, 452.—law of, has its natural sanction in remorse, 450.

[*Gay*]—laws of, and natural consequences, give rise to natural obligation, 464.

[*Hume*]—ambiguity of word, which may be opposed (1) to miracles, (2) to the rare, (3) to artifice, 510. rules of justice may be called laws of nature, despite being artificial, 521.—state of, a philosophical fiction, 531.—scanty provision of, as a partial cause of the origin of justice, 532; cf. 567. invention of laws of nature, 540.—dist. accident, 579n.—laws of (in the scientific sense), 614, 617. chief use of history is to discover the constant and universal principles of human nature, 615.—does not show complete uniformity, 616.

[*Price*]—of virtue, a different question from that of its subject-matter, 658. all actions must have a nature or character, right, wrong, or indifferent, 683.—of things, depends on necessity, not on will or power, 684; cf. Cudworth, 120.—of God, dist. his will, 702.

[*Smith*]—teaches spectators and sufferers reciprocally to imagine themselves in each other's situation, in order to produce concord of sentiments, 779. perfection of human nature is to restrain selfish and indulge benevolent affections, 782. the great precept of nature is to love ourselves only as we love our neighbour or as our neighbour is capable of loving us, 782.—by means of sympathy with resentment, can cause us to approve of retaliation antecedent to reflection on the utility of punishment, 791.—counters the delusions of self-love by leading us to form general rules of morality, 816.—and reasoning, tell us that the general rules of morality are the commands and laws of God, 821–3. moral faculties were plainly intended to be the governing principles of human nature, 823; cf. Butler, 395. the deception of nature, whereby means come to be more valued than the end which they serve, causes the rich to be led by an invisible hand to advance the interest of society, 829.

[*Paley*]—light of, as a method of coming at the will of God, 853.

[*Bentham*]—has placed mankind under the governance of two sovereign masters, pain and pleasure, 946.—law of, as standard of moral judgement, is simply a name for individual sentiment, 959.—law of, is used in legislative debate to save the trouble of inquiry, 962.

necessity, see *freedom*.

[*Hobbes*]—consistent with liberty, 83, 90.—consistent with justice of criminal law, 93, 96.—consistent with efficacy of consultation, admonition, praise, dispraise, reward, and punishment, 94.—consistent with beauty and perfection of the world, 95. all events have necessary causes, 99; cf. 97 (152).—freedom from, impossible, 99.—of a disjunctive proposition, 99 (153).

[*Cumberland*] law of nature consists of necessary truth, 105, 108. in mathematics and morals, action is free but its effect is necessarily caused, 110; cf. 114.

[*Cudworth*]—does not apply to choice, 140. the soul's power over itself shows that man is not always determined by necessary causes, 150. necessary dist. contingent cause, 152 (97, 99).—of a disjunctive proposition, compatible with contingency of its members, 153 (99).

[*Locke*] necessary not opposed to voluntary, 164–6.—when contrary to volition, = compulsion or restraint, 166.

[*Clarke*]—moral, dist. absolute, 232.—and duty, compared and distinguished, 232.

[*Hutcheson*] operation of instincts or affections is said to be necessary, not voluntary, 373.

[*Balguy*]—incompatible with virtue, 442 (373).—to approve what is right, as to assent to what is true, 453.

[*Gay*] obligation is the necessity of doing or omitting any action in order to be happy, 463 (718).

[*Hume*] causes ought not to be multiplied without necessity, 549. all men have always agreed in the doctrine both of necessity and of liberty, 613, 624.—idea of, arises from the constant conjunction of similar objects and the consequent inference from one to the other, 614, 621–2 (667). voluntary actions are subject to necessity in this sense, 614. maxim of philosophers that the connection between all causes and effects is equally necessary, 617.—physical, no different from that of other causes, 620. men mistakenly suppose that they perceive a necessary connection between cause and effect in matter, but know

necessity (*cont.*):

that they feel no such connection between motive and action, 621.—of an action, is not a quality in the agent, but is a determination in a spectator to infer the action from preceding objects, 623. question of liberty and necessity the most contentious question of metaphysics, 624.—must be included in the definition of cause, 625.—dist. constraint, 625.—constancy is the essence of, 625*n*.—and liberty, both essential to morality, 626–9.—understood as constant conjunction and inference therefrom, is no danger to morality or religion, 627.—of a cause of actions, is presupposed by rewards and punishments, 628 (891).

[*Price*]—idea of, discerned by the understanding, 666. morality is a branch of necessary truth, 699.—depends on the nature, not on the will, of God, 702.

[*Reid*] advocates of the doctrine of necessity stress the influence of motives, 880.—doctrine of, assumes that an intelligent being is an inert, inactive substance which does not act but is acted upon, 881.—is not implied by the fact that we reason from motives to actions, 889 (619).—denial of, does not imply that all actions are capricious, 890. —doctrine of, is incompatible with reward and punishment, since these imply good and ill desert, 891 (628).

Nero, 578, 602, 605.

Newton,—cited by Hartley, 638.

obligation, see *duty, reason.*

[*Hobbes*]—is thraldom, 46.—incurred by laying down a right, 59.—implied by covenant, not by counsel, 85. contracts oblige us, laws tie us fast, being obliged, 100.—natural, two species of, dist. obligation of contract, 101 (227).

[*Cudworth*]—not made by will or command, but by natural justice, 122.—arises from the intellectual nature of person obliged, 123.—absolute, dist. accidental or hypothetical, 123–4.

[*Shaftesbury*]—to virtue, 205; depends on the happiness and good of virtue, 221.

[*Clarke*]—or duty, arises from the eternal and necessary differences of things, 225.—of compacts, depends on antecedent natural fitness of fidelity, 227–8; cf. 254, 257. judgement and conscience of a man's own mind is the truest

obligation; sanction of reward and punishment is a secondary obligation or enforcement of the first, 233.—ambiguity of, 233.—original, is the eternal reason of things, 233.—of law of nature, antecedent to its being the positive will of God, 247; and to consideration of reward and punishment, 248.—Hobbes's theory of, 254–7, 260.

[*Wollaston*] there cannot be two incompatible duties, but there can be a mixed obligation, 288.—identified with natural religion, 294.—to pursue happiness, 299.

[*Hutcheson*]—different senses of, 346–7, 352.—as a determination, without regard to our own interest, to approve and perform actions, 346 (719).—as a motive from self-interest, 347.—definition of, in terms of advantage, may be refuted by substituting the definition for the term defined, 350.—dist. constraint, 352. 'ought' an unlucky word in morals, 367.

[*Butler*]—of interest, dist. obligation to virtue, 380.—a constituent part of reflex approbation, implied in the very idea of virtue, 381.—may be shown by different methods, 395.—to follow the rule of right, arises from its being the law of our nature, 406.—to other men, can only be to further their happiness, 426. though the good of the creation be the only end of God, he has laid us under distinct particular obligations, 427*n*.; cf. 434.

[*Balguy*]—of gratitude and of relieving distress, can be discovered by reason and reflection, 439; cf. 456.—external, arising from just authority, dist. internal, arising from perception of the reasons of things, which is the supreme law, superior even to obligation to obey the will of God, 450 (717).—may be deduced from relations of agreement or moral fitness, 456–60.—of gratitude, equivalent to a self-evident proposition, 458.—presupposes liberty and some perception which forms a motive or reason for choice, 460.—moral, dist. natural, 460; cf. 455 (717).—arising from authority, a compound of moral and natural, 461.—moral, strictly connected with moral fitness; to resolve all obligations into interest is to confound morality with sensibility, 461.—to perform an action, means having a good reason, moral or natural, for performance, 461.

[*Gay*]—and approbation, implied by virtue, 462.— = the necessity of doing or omitting any action in order to be happy, 463 (718).—four sorts of, natural, virtuous, civil, and religious, 464; cf. Locke, 184. the last, arising from the authority of God, is the only full and complete obligation, 464.—of virtue, requires the will of God, since the good of mankind cannot be any obligation to me if it is contrary to my happiness, 466. —of merit, 469, 471.

[*Hume*] to show that right and wrong are obligatory on all rational minds, we must prove a necessary connection of cause and effect between moral relations and the will, 500. if obligations are discovered by reason, they must exist antecedent to that discovery, 502. 'ought' cannot be deduced from 'is', 504.—idea of, presupposes idea of justice, 529.—natural, dist. moral, 533; cf. Balguy, 460. a promise, if an act of mind, would have to be willing an obligation, 536.—means that non-performance displeases in a certain manner, and cannot be willed since a change of sentiment cannot, 537–8.—of promises, first one of interest, then one of morals, 542–3. willing an obligation is a feigned act of the mind, 543.

[*Price*]—or duty, necessarily connected with moral right and wrong, 683n., 708.—to action, is coincident and identical with rightness of action, 708.—is involved in the very nature of virtue, 709; cf. Butler, 381.—dist. interest, 710; cf. Butler, 380.—presupposed by reward and punishment, 712.—of rectitude, implies that it is both a rule to direct and a law to bind, 713. it is absurd to ask why we are obliged to practise virtue, since this is to ask why we are obliged to do what we are obliged to do, 714.—ascribed to God, arises from and exists in his own nature, 715.—of religion, is a branch of universal rectitude, 716.—mistakenly defined by Balguy as state of mind brought about by perceiving a reason for action, 717 (450). Balguy's distinction between external obligation, on us as sensible agents, and internal, on us as reasonable and moral agents, implies that the former could be applied to brutes, 717 (450, 455, 460). Balguy fails to distinguish obligation and motive, 717. to define obligation as the necessity of doing a thing in order to be

happy, would make ridiculous the statement that a man is obliged to study his own happiness, 718 (463).—two senses of, corresponding to absolute and relative virtue, 719n.; cf. 724, 750–1.—dist. approbation, 719 (346). it may be objected that some actions, e.g. of beneficence, are right though not obligatory; but at least all wrong actions imply obligation, 720. in fact, beneficence in general is obligatory, though we are at liberty in applying the duty to particular instances, 721. we cannot determine the precise limits of general duties, 722. if an action is not indifferent, it is subject to obligation, 723. to aim at acting beyond obligation is to aim at acting contrary to obligation, 725.—particular or peculiar, dist. general, 737.—two senses of, one independent of judgement, the other dependent; for a man to do what he thinks he ought, is nevertheless a real obligation, 750–1.—consciousness of, is a motive to action, 757.

[*Paley*]—different theories of, ultimately coincide in the promotion of general happiness, 846.—theories of, leave unanswered the question, why am I obliged to do what is right, 847. we need to ask, (1) what we mean by 'obligation', (2) why we are obliged to do anything, 847.—means being urged by a violent motive resulting from the command of another, 848.—dist. ordinary inducement, 848. we can be obliged to nothing but what we ourselves are to gain or lose something by, 849. the reason why I am morally obliged is that I am urged by the violent motive of being rewarded or punished in the after-life, resulting from the command of God; private happiness is our motive, and the will of God our rule, 850.—moral, is like all other obligations, and does not differ from inducement except in being a strong inducement and resulting from the command of another, 851; cf. 848. duty differs from prudence only in taking account of gain or loss in the world to come as well as in the present world, 852.—of a moral rule, is constituted by its utility, 854.

[*Reid*]—is not a quality of action or agent, but a relation between the two, 873. it is a condition of moral obligation that the action be voluntary, 874; and that the agent believes it to be good,

obligation (*cont.*):

875; cf. Price, 750–1, 755.—of contract, is unaffected by the agent's purpose or intention, 906; cf. Hume, 543. 'ought' expresses judgement, but cannot be applied to mere feelings, 929. Hume is unreasonable in asking that the word 'ought' be explained, and mistaken in supposing that rationalists deduce the relation of obligation from other relations, 930 (504).

[*Bentham*] an action that conforms to the principle of utility is one that ought to be done, or at least is not one that ought not to be done, 951. 'ought' has meaning only when thus interpreted, 951. a sanction is the source of obligatory powers or motives, 968*n*.

Oedipus, 602.

opinion

[*Locke*]—law of, dist. divine law and civil law, 184–7.—or reputation or fashion, the measure of virtue and vice, 187–8.

[*Smith*] to approve of opinions, as of sentiments or passions, is to observe their agreement with our own, 771.

order,—and beauty of the world, consistent with necessity, 95.—of the universe, evidence for existence and will of God, 192–3. moral fitness is conformity to order and truth, 459. suitableness of all the virtues to the beauty, order, and perfection of the world, 650.—and regularity are the causes of beauty rather than beauty itself, 690.

ought, see *obligation.*

pain, see *pleasure, uneasiness.*—or uneasiness, always moves us, prospect of good not always, 178.—and injustice, both contrary to nature but in different senses, 377, 404.—is not a possible object of desire, 692.

Paley, 845–55. see especially *obligation.*

passion, see *affection.*

[*Cudworth*] love and desire of good and happiness not a mere passion but a settled principle, 147.

[*Locke*] pleasure and pain, and the means thereto, are the hinges on which our passions turn, 160.

[*Clarke*] wilful passion, and negligent misunderstanding, may cause action contrary to reason, 231.

[*Mandeville*] man a compound of passions, that govern him by turns, 262. —the support of society, 262.—conquest of, contrary to natural impulse, called virtue, 267.

[*Hutcheson*] all the passions and affections justify themselves, 322.—particular, dist. calm affection, 331, 357, 369; cf. Butler, 382–3, 414–16.

[*Butler*]—particular, dist. self-love, 382–3, 414–16.—particular, dist. both benevolence (cf. Hutcheson, 331) and self-love, 389.—or appetite, implies a direct simple tendency towards a particular object, 401, 414.—does not have as object the pleasure arising from its gratification, 415.—gratification of, constitutes happiness, 417.

[*Gay*]— = present pleasure or pain arising from imagination of future pleasure or pain, 467. the passions and affections are mistakenly thought to be innate, 467.

[*Hume*]—and reason, fallaciously supposed to conflict, 479, 482, 484. reason is and ought only to be the slave of the passions, 482 (859, 864).—being an original existence, and not representative like an idea, cannot contradict truth and reason, though an accompanying false judgement can, 483, 490–1.—can be (though improperly) called unreasonable, either when founded on false supposition, or when choosing insufficient means for the designed end, 483–4.—yields to reason when such mistakes are discovered, 484.—calm, dist. violent, 485; cf. Hutcheson, 331, 357, 369; Butler, 382.—calm, tends to be confused with reason, 485 (864).— and action are influenced by morality, which therefore cannot be derived from reason, 489. no such passion as the love of mankind merely as such, 517. natural and usual force of the passions determines judgement of duty, 520.

[*Price*]— = instinctive desire, dist. affection, 694.

[*Smith*] any passion may rouse sympathetic emotion, 765. to approve of the passions of another, as suitable to their objects, is the same thing as to observe that we sympathize with them, 770.— violent, can distort the judgements of conscience, 812–14. the passions all justify themselves, 813; cf. Hutcheson, 322.

[*Reid*] animal principles are commonly called passions, dist. reason, 863.—is blind desire of a particular object, 863; cf. Butler, 401, 414. Hume abuses words in including under the passions what is really a rational principle, 864 (485).

[*Bentham*]—a fictitious entity, framed by considering pleasure or pain in some particular point of view, 997*n.*; cf. 987.

perception,—understanding a power of, 162. many perceptions unrelated to external sensation, 355. sentiment of the understanding or perception of the heart, 429.—of moral relations by the understanding, 459.—comprises all operations of the mind, including moral judgement, 487.—two kinds of, impressions and ideas, 487. three different perceptions concerning moral agents, 655. ideas of right and wrong, being simple, must be ascribed to a power of immediate perception, 672.—immediate, is not confined to sense, 674.—of the understanding and feeling of the heart, 688; cf. 429.—moral sense supposed to be a peculiar power of, 837-8. in perception, judgement is the consequence of sensation, 915.

perfection,—or beauty of the universe, consistent with necessity, 95.—solitary, dist. goodness, 196.—and dignity, 306, 314.—of virtue, when a being acts to the utmost of his power for the public good, 337.—of human nature, is to restrain selfish and indulge benevolent affections, 782.—in relation to virtue and propriety, 783-4.

Peripatetics, 892.

philosophy, see *science.*—moral, the science of the laws of nature, 77. philosophers dist. plain men, 327, 405, 474, 617.—moral, two methods of, (1) beginning from abstract relations, (2) beginning from the nature of man, 374. —speculative, dist. practical, 489.— moral, should follow natural in deriving arguments only from experience, 563. philosopher dist. moralist, 630. debate about the principle of approbation is important for moral philosophy but not for practice, being a mere matter of philosophical curiosity, 835; cf. 503, 634.—moral, requires analysis and dissection, and is therefore more dubious than the practical rules of morality, 892. —modern, has concentrated on sensation and feeling to the neglect of judgement, 913.—modern, paradoxical opinions of, 925; cf. 908.

piety, see *God, religion.*—dist. love, 107. —suitable to the nature of man, 403.—

or love of God, implied by benevolence, 428.—and virtue, at last coincide, 428.

pity

[*Hobbes*]— = imagination of future calamity to ourselves, proceeding from sense of another's calamity, 10 (411).— = grief for the calamity of another, and arises from imagination of like calamity for oneself, 32 (310).

[*Mandeville*]—a frailty of our nature, may produce evil as well as good, 270. to act from pity is only to oblige oneself, 270.

[*Hutcheson*]—Hobbes's account of, does not explain its variation with opinion of worth or with former affection, 310 (10, 32). compassion proves benevolence to be natural, without view of private advantage, 345. alleged pleasure of compassion, 345. pain of compassion a feeling of the public sense, 356. compassion a particular affection, dist. reflective or general calm benevolence, 357.

[*Butler*] to compassionate the distress of others is to substitute them for ourselves, 410-11.—mistakenly identified by Hobbes with fear, 411 (10).—may be accompanied by feelings concerning ourselves, but is distinct from them, 411 (645).—unlike sympathetic joy, is an original, particular affection leading us to act, 412.

[*Hartley*] compassion arises from association of the miseries of others with previous miseries of ourselves, as is especially evident in children, 645.—a coalescence of 'selfish' and other feelings, 645 (411).—most apt to arise in calamities which we have felt or think we are in danger of feeling hereafter, 645; cf. Hobbes, 10, 32.

[*Smith*]— = fellow feeling with the sorrow of others, 763-5.—arises from imagination of what we ourselves should feel in the like situation, 764.—narrower in meaning than sympathy, 765.

plain,—men, dist. philosophers, 327, 405, 474, 617.

Plato,—cited by Hobbes, 13; by Cudworth, 119, 130, 134; by Clarke, 235; by Hutcheson, 356-7; by Price, 664.

pleasure, see *desire, happiness, utility.*

[*Hobbes*]—really motion, 3.—identical with love and appetite, 3.—appearance or sense of motion, i.e. of appetite, or of good, 26.—two sorts of, sensual, and of the mind, 5, 26.

pleasure (*cont.*):

[*Locke*]—and pain, indefinable simple ideas, 160. things are good or evil only in reference to pleasure or pain, 160, 183. all pleasures and pains are, strictly speaking, mental, 160.—and pain, and the means thereto, are the hinges on which our passions turn, 160.—utmost, is happiness in its full extent, 177. good is what is apt to produce pleasure, 177, 183; cf. 160.

[*Shaftesbury*] pleasures of mind superior to those of body (or sense), 215–16. pleasures of mind are the natural affections or their effects, 216.—social, preferred to sensual by those who know both, 217. charm of kind affection the master-pleasure, 217.

[*Mandeville*] all untaught animals solicitous only of pleasing themselves, 263.

[*Wollaston*]—and pain, not a sound test of good and evil, 293. only true pleasure, not all pleasure, an ultimate good, 293.—consciousness of something agreeable, 295.—in itself a real good, pain a real evil, 295.—calculus of, 296–7. true pleasure and pain, 297.—true, = happiness, 298.

[*Hutcheson*]—gives us idea of natural good and is antecedent to advantage or interest, 304. virtuous action gives pleasure on reflection but not necessarily otherwise, 314. desire is uneasy rather than pleasant, 322. alleged pleasure of compassion, 345.

[*Butler*] the common enjoyments of life, even the pleasures of vice, depend on regards to our fellow creatures, 407.—arises from gratification of a particular affection or appetite, and is not the object of it, 415; cf. 417.—of gratifying a particular affection, is our own pleasure but is not thereby to be attributed to self-love, 415; cf. 383. disengagement is necessary to enjoyment, 417.

[*Balguy*]—of beauty, suggests that perception of beauty requires feeling as well as understanding, 443.—accompanies and follows virtue, but is not the end of a moral agent, 455.—or interest or natural good, an obligatory end for men as sensible agents, 460.

[*Gay*]—is the only thing that man pursues for its own sake, 467. what is apt to produce pleasure is called good and approved, 467; cf. Locke, 160, 177, 183. imagination of future pleasure or pain produces present pleasure or pain, i.e. passion, 467.—sum total of, constitutes happiness, 468; cf. Shaftesbury, 215. annexing pleasure to the endeavours of others to promote my happiness is the only thing in my power to this end, 468.—association with, causes means to be mistaken for ends, 477.

[*Hume*] prospect of pain or pleasure produces emotion of aversion or propensity, 481. feeling pleasure of a particular kind constitutes moral approbation, 506 (839–43).—of moral approbation, is of a peculiar kind, arising only when a character is considered in general, without reference to our particular interest, 507.—of moral approbation, from what principles derived? 509. when any action pleases us after a certain manner, we say it is virtuous, and when its non-performance displeases after a like manner, we say we are obliged to perform it, 537.—produced by useful objects, gives rise, through sympathy in the spectator, to sense of beauty, 547.—immediate, a ground of esteem, but by means of sympathy, 558–9. every quality of the mind is denominated virtuous, which gives pleasure by the mere survey, 560. this pleasure arises from four sources, being useful to others or to self, being agreeable to others or to self, 560, 586 (832–3).—immediate, as a ground of approval, like utility, arises from sympathy, 585.

[*Hartley*] possibility of deducing all intellectual pleasures and pains from association, 635; cf. Gay, 475–8.—and pain, in relation to sensations and ideas, 637.—and pain, classified as those of sensation, imagination, ambition, self-interest, sympathy, theopathy, and the moral sense, 637. intellectual pleasures and pains are deducible from sensible ones by means of association, 641. pleasures and pains of sympathy classified so as to include grief as well as joy at the happiness of others, and joy as well as grief at the misery of others, 642; cf. 644. pleasures and pains of the moral sense, how they arise by association, 646–54.

[*Price*]—and pain, accompany perceptions of virtue and vice, but should not be confounded with them, 677, 689.—of beauty, is result of a natural aptitude of certain real natures to produce this feeling, 687, 690. creatures capable of pleasure and pain must necessarily desire the one and avoid the other, 692.

[*Bentham*] nature has placed mankind under the governance of two sovereign masters, pain and pleasure, 946.—and pain, point out what we ought to do, and determine what we shall do, supplying both the standard of right and wrong and the cause of actions, 946.—sum total of, = interest, 949.—God's, only known by pronouncing our own pleasure to be his, 965*n*.—and pain, efficient as well as final causes, 967.—and pain, four sources of, or sanctions, physical, political, moral, religious, 968; cf. Locke, 184; Gay, 464.—and pain, the only things which can operate as motives, 968*n*.—and the avoidance of pain, are the ends and instruments of a legislator, 970; cf. 967, 977.—value of, to be computed from seven elements or dimensions, intensity, duration, certainty, propinquity, fecundity, purity, and extent, 971-4. good is properly the cause or instrument of pleasure, 975; cf. Locke, 160, 177, 183; Gay, 467. happiness consists of enjoyment of pleasures and security from pains, 977.—and pain, are the only things good and bad in themselves; other things are good and bad as causing or preventing pleasure and pain, 982; cf. 992. a motive is substantially nothing more than pleasure or pain operating in a certain manner, 992. the motive of ill will or malice is still a kind of pleasure, and even this wretched pleasure, taken by itself, is good, 992*n*.—of sympathy or benevolence as a motive, 996.

Plutarch,—cited by Hume, 578.

politicians,—the inventors of morality, 263-9 (311, 391, 550). moral virtues are the political offspring which flattery begot upon pride, 269.—artifice of, a part-cause of moral sentiment concerning property and promises, 543.

positive,—law, owes its authority to natural justice, 122-6.—good, better described in terms of hypothetical obligation, 123-4.—will or command of God, not the foundation of duty, 225, 247. if virtue depended on instinct, it would be arbitrary and positive, 438; cf. 657.

power

[*Hobbes*] powers of body and mind, 1.—motive, 2.—imagination of, produces glory, 6.—evidenced by good will or charity, 13 (388*n*.).— = means to obtain future good, 38.—kinds of, 38-9. perpetual and restless desire of power after power, a general inclination of mankind, 44; cf. 5 (258).—civil, necessary for the validity of covenants, 67.—sovereign, attained by force or by agreement, 81.—irresistible, implies right to rule, 89; cf. 101 (227, 247, 259-60).

[*Cudworth*]—of the soul over itself, 150.—to produce an effect, may go along with power not to produce it, 152.

[*Locke*] will a power of preferring, understanding a power of perceiving, 162-3. liberty a power, and therefore belongs only to agents, not to the will, which is also but a power, 167.—an attribute only of substances, not of powers themselves, 168.

[*Clarke*] if infinite power were the measure of right, goodness and mercy would lack signification, 247; cf. 259 (89).

[*Butler*]—or strength, dist. authority, 379, 402-3.—love of, mistakenly identified with benevolence by Hobbes, 388*n*. (13).

[*Price*]—idea of, given by inward consciousness of activity and self-determination, 667.

practical,—understanding, dist. speculative, 148; cf. 450, 455.—prejudices, dist. speculative, 476.—philosophy, dist. speculative, 489.—or relative virtue, dist. abstract or absolute, 750-1; cf. 719*n*., 724.—reason, dist. speculative, 865.—morality, dist. theory of morals, 892.—motives, dist. speculative, 985-6.

praise,—and blame, attest free will, 136-7.—and blame, only for choice between unequal objects, 141, 150. merit or praiseworthiness, 373. laudable or blameable are not the same as reasonable or unreasonable, 490.—has as its object the motive of action, 512; cf. 633.—love of, is less the cause than the effect of the love of praiseworthiness, 806. desire of praise produces the jurisdiction of the man without, desire of praiseworthiness the jurisdiction of conscience, the man within the breast, 811.

Price, 655-762. see especially *definition, duty, God, intuition, obligation, right and wrong, sense, understanding, virtue.*—cites Hutcheson, 657; Hume, 657*n*., 667*n*., 689*n*., 739; Cudworth, 663*n*., 664*n*.; Plato, 664; Malebranche, 667*n*.; Kames,

Price (*cont.*):

720; Butler, 730, 737; Priestley, 753*n*.; Balguy, 761*n*.—criticizes Locke, 660, 670, 675; Hume, 668, 675, 740, 759; Hutcheson, 674, 689, 719; Balguy, 690, 717; Cumberland, 718; Gay, 718; Wollaston, 727.

pride

[*Hobbes*]—name for passion of glory, 6. Leviathan, king of the proud, 88.

[*Mandeville*]—inseparable from man's essence, 266. moral virtues are the political offspring which flattery begot upon pride, 269.—symptoms of, even in the most virtuous and humblest of men, 271.

[*Hume*]—may be either good or bad according to circumstances, 610*n*.

Priestley,—cited by Price, 753*n*.

principle

[*Cudworth*] love and desire of good and happiness not a mere passion but a settled principle, 147.

[*Mandeville*] performance cannot be judged without knowledge of principle and motive of action, 270.

[*Gay*] in the pursuit of truth, and in conduct, we do not always go back to first principles, 475; instead we treat known truths, and means to happiness, as resting-places, imagining substitutes of principles to be principles themselves, 476; hence philosophers mistake acquired principles for instincts, 476.

[*Hume*]—active, can never be founded on inactive, 489. actions are praised only as signs of inward principles, 512, 633. there are in every science some general principles beyond which we cannot hope to find others more general, 577*n*. chief use of history is to discover the constant and universal principles of human nature, 615.

[*Price*] principles of virtue are self-evident, 747. principles of morality are universally accepted, but particular usages differ according to opinion of their relation to the principles, 749.

[*Reid*] principles of action classified as mechanical, animal, and rational, 856. rational principles of action imply judgement as well as intention and will, 856, 858, 942. two rational principles of action, a regard to our good upon the whole, and a regard to duty, 860, 867. our good upon the whole is a leading or governing principle over animal principles or passions, 863; cf. Butler, 400,

409.—of honour (dist. interest), is only another name for regard to duty, 871. all reasoning must be grounded on first principles, and there must be in morals, as in all other sciences, first or self-evident principles on which all moral reasoning is grounded, 879; cf. 930. the principles of action = ultimate ends, 939.

[*Bentham*]—of utility, or the greatest happiness principle, 946*n*.—of utility, dist. principle of asceticism and principle of sympathy and antipathy, 955. a principle of approbation should point out some external consideration to guide internal sentiment; the so-called principle of sympathy and antipathy is therefore the negation of all principle, 957.—theological, as standard of right and wrong, is not distinct from the principles of utility, asceticism, or sympathy and antipathy, 965.

probability,—and demonstration, two ways of employing the understanding, 480. deduction may supply different degrees of evidence, from full certainty to lowest probability, 706.

promise, see *contract*.

[*Hobbes*] covenant in relation to contract, 61.—expressed by words of future time, 62.—void on reasonable suspicion in a state of nature, but not in a civil state, 64.—made through fear, obligatory, 65. performance of covenants a law of nature, 67. covenants without the sword are but words, 79.—artificial, 80. —implies obligation, 85.—dist. law, 100, 103.—breach of, a self-contradiction, 102; cf. 59.

[*Cudworth*]—obligation of, depends on natural justice, 123-6. absolute obligation to keep promises makes indifferent things, when promised, obligatory by accident, 123.—formality of performing, dist. materiality of action promised, 125.

[*Wollaston*]—breach of, contradicts or denies a true proposition, 277, 285; cf. Hobbes, 102. to promise absolutely, not in a man's power, 288.

[*Hume*] convention for stability of possessions is not a promise, for promises themselves arise from conventions, 528. —not intelligible naturally, i.e. before established by human conventions, 535-7.—if an act of mind, is not resolution, desire, or willing an action, but would have to be willing an obligation,

536 (740); but this implies the changing of sentiments by an act of will, which is impossible, 537; nor could such an act of will naturally produce any obligation, 538.—a human invention, 539.—a certain form of words by which we bind ourselves to the performance of an action, 541.—interest the first obligation to performance of, 542. this is seconded by a sentiment of morals arising from public interest, education, and artifice of politicians, 543. to explain the moral obligation of promises, we feign an act of the mind, which we call willing an obligation, 543.—artificial nature of, shown by invalidity of contracts entered through force, 545.

[Price] fidelity to promises is included in veracity, 739-40.—dist. resolution or intention, 739; cf. Hume, 536.—is not thereby willing an obligation, 740 (536).

[Reid] contracts and promises belong to the class of social operations of the mind, 902.

property, see *justice.*—not in state of nature, 53, 67.—idea of, a right to any thing, 189.—idea of, unlike that of self-love, implies exclusion, 419, 422.—idea of, unintelligible without first explaining the origin of justice, 529.—transference of, 540.—does not exist in conditions of abundance or of extensive benevolence, 567-8.—as the concern of justice, 741-3.—ideas of, are relaxed in proportion to degree of intimacy or friendship, and to degree of plenty, 743; cf. 532, 567-8.

proportion, see *fitness.*—to human nature, 400, 409, 432.—or suitableness of affection to its cause or object, constitutes its propriety, 773-5, 785.

proposition, truth of propositions is conformity of words to things, 274, 360; to ideas or things or both, 452.—true, may be denied or contradicted by deeds, 275-9 (452).—may be implied by an act, 275. judgement, but not feeling, must be expressed by a proposition, 910-11.

propriety, see *fitness, sympathy.*

[Price] ideas of good and ill desert signify the propriety of making the virtuous happy and of discountenancing the vicious, 695.

[Smith] to approve of the passions of another, as proper or suitable to their objects, is the same thing as to observe that we sympathize with them, 770,

775.—(dist. merit) consists in the suitableness of affection to the cause or object which excites it, 773; cf. 785.—deserves mere approval, dist. virtue, which deserves admiration, 783.—two senses of, (1) complete propriety or perfection, (2) the degree of proximity to perfection which is commonly reached, 784.—of gratitude and resentment, constitutes merit and demerit, 786-8.—of a passion, depends on the sympathy of the impartial spectator, 789.—or impropriety of an agent's motive, is a necessary condition for sympathy with the gratitude or resentment of the person affected by the action, 792-6.—or impropriety (dist. merit or demerit), arises from direct sympathy or antipathy for the motives of the agent, 797-8. approbation of propriety requires actual correspondence of sentiments, while the sense of merit does not, 799.—of our own sentiments and conduct, can be seen only in the mirror of the imagined approbation of society, 801-3; cf. Hume, 593. approbation of virtue includes a sense of propriety distinct from the perception of utility, 833 (560, 586). approval of approbation itself as proper can only be explained by sympathy, 841.

Protagoras,—criticized by Cudworth, 130-3.

prudence, see *interest, self-love.*

[Hutcheson]—not a virtue if only employed in promoting private interest, 315.

[Butler]—is a virtue, or at least is approved, 433.

[Balguy] to promote one's own welfare, in subordination to that of the public, is in its own kind true virtue, 448.

[Gay]—dist. virtue, 462.

[Price] those who make obligation depend on divine reward and punishment identify vice with imprudence, 710.

[Paley]—differs from duty only in that duty takes account of gain or loss in the world to come as well as in the present world, 852.

[Reid] the rational principle of a regard to our good upon the whole gives us a conception of a right and wrong, or at least of a wise and foolish, producing a kind of self-approbation and a kind of remorse or compunction,

prudence (*cont.*):
866; cf. Butler, 433.—dist. virtue, 868; cf. 870.

psychology,—of faculties, criticized, 142–5, 163, 167–8.

Ptolemy, 277.

public, see *benevolence, common* (good), *utility.*

[*Cumberland*] adequate rewards and punishments make pursuit of public good contribute to private happiness, 112.

[*Locke*]—happiness, and virtue, inseparably connected by God, 158.

[*Shaftesbury*]—interest, notion of, required for virtue, 202.—good, appears, but mistakenly, to be inconsistent with private, 206–7. natural affections tend to public good, self-affections to private, unnatural affections to neither, 210.—affection, may be too strong, 211.

[*Clarke*]—benefit, means the benefit of all men, not of one nation, 228.—utility, not the foundation of morality, 251.

[*Hutcheson*] desire of public good approved by the moral sense, 309. disposition to promote public good necessary for the cardinal virtues, 315. quantity of public good produced is in compound proportion to benevolence and abilities, 335. perfection of virtue when a being acts to the utmost of his power for the public good, 337.—good, the foundation of rights, 353.—sense, a determination to be pleased with the happiness of others, and to be uneasy at their misery, 356. publicly useful actions, dist. privately useful, 358.—good, as a more reasonable ultimate end than private good, 362.

[*Butler*]—and private good, though distinct, perfectly coincide, 387–8.

[*Gay*]—affections, 474, 478.

[*Hume*]—interest, cannot be the reason or motive for acts of justice, 516. sympathy with public interest adds moral approbation to justice, once established, 534. many, but not all, of the natural virtues tend to the public good, 550.—interest, approved even when contrary to private, 576. all virtuous qualities have a tendency to public or private good, 633.

[*Price*]—good or interest, is the most general and leading consideration in our inquiries concerning right, 737.

[*Paley*] promotion of public happiness is common to all theories of obligation, 846.

Pufendorf,—cited by Hutcheson, 347.—referred to by Hume, 631.

punishment, see *merit, reward.*

[*Hobbes*]—should look to future good, 71, 87, 93–4.—defined, 86.—right of, founded on natural right, 86, 93.—of the innocent, against the law of nature, 87.—implies sin, 89.—inflicted because crime is harmful, not because it is freely chosen, 93 (138).

[*Cudworth*]—looks to past as well as future, 138 (93).

[*Butler*]—end of civil, to prevent future mischief, 381.—desert of, not grounded on utility but on guilt, 431. natural association of the ideas of wickedness and punishment, 431.

[*Hume*]—and reward, presuppose that actions are caused and so necessary, 628 (891).

[*Price*]—may sometimes depend on possibility of reformation, but even so is not justified simply in terms of balance of advantage among consequences, 698.—and reward, presuppose desert and so presuppose obligation, 712.

[*Smith*] an action deserves punishment if it is the proper and approved object of resentment, 786, 788; i.e. if the resentment has the sympathy of the impartial spectator, 789. sympathy with resentment can be independent of reflection on the utility of punishment, 791.

[*Reid*]—and reward, imply good and ill desert, and so presuppose liberty, not necessity, 891 (628).

[*Bentham*] the business of government is to promote the happiness of the society by punishing and rewarding, 977.

Pythagoras, 677.

Quintilian,—cited by Hume, 547*n*.

rational, see *reason.*

[*Cumberland*]—agents, include God and men, 107.

[*Shaftesbury*]—creature, dist. sensible, 200, 203–4.—creature, necessarily admires virtue, 203.

[*Hutcheson*]—appetite (dist. sensitive), often called the will, 357.

[*Balguy*]—beings, the only subjects, but not the only objects, of virtue, 440;

cf. 448. the end of rational actions and rational agents is reason or moral good, 455.

[*Gay*]—agents, have the power of governing or directing good and evil, and of acting for an end, 468. love of a rational object implies desire of, and pleasure in, his happiness, 468.

[*Hume*] relations relevant to demonstration apply to irrational and inanimate objects as well as to rational beings, 498. if morality were determined by reason, that is the same to all rational beings, 634.

[*Price*] a purely reasonable being would see that the happiness of others is as important to them as his is to him, and that happiness is in itself equally valuable and desirable, whoever possesses it, 693. —and dispassionate benevolence, would be too weak a principle in man, if unaided by instinct, 694; cf. 688.— desire (affection), dist. instinctive (passion), 694.—or universal benevolence, dist. instinctive, 760-1. reasonable and calm self-love is a virtuous principle, 761.

[*Smith*] reasonable man = impartial spectator, 789.

[*Reid*]—principles of action, dist. mechanical and animal, 856, 858, 939, 942. two rational principles of human action, a regard to our good upon the whole, and a regard to duty, 860, 867.— motives, dist. animal, 885-8.

reason, see *understanding*.

[*Hobbes*]—suggests articles of peace or laws of nature, 54, 56, 77.

[*Cumberland*]—prescribes the common good as the ultimate end, 115.

[*Cudworth*] rational or intellectual nature identical with natural justice, the source of obligation, 123-6.

[*Locke*]—for a moral rule, may always be demanded, 157.—and sense-experience, are the light of nature, 190.—infers from the order of the universe that it was created by a wise and powerful God, 192; and that God wills or intends what men should do, 193; namely, worship of God, maintenance of society, and self-preservation, 194.

[*Shaftesbury*] what reason is there to follow virtue? = what obligation is there to virtue? 205.

[*Clarke*]—action contrary to, may be caused by negligent misunderstanding and wilful passion, 231.—of things, the

rule of God's actions, 231.—of the thing, and right of the case, 232. ability to grasp mathematical and moral truths by reason and without teaching, proves that natural and moral relations are certain and objective, 235.—and consciences of men, 237.—right, the law of nature, 246.—the proper nature of man, leads men to universal love and benevolence, 258.

[*Wollaston*]—law of, the law of our nature, 283.—right, not explicit enough and too narrow to be the criterion of moral good, 292.

[*Hutcheson*]—too slow to take the place of the moral sense, 348. reasonableness as conformity to truth, 360.— said to judge of senses and affections, 361, 365.—exciting, dist. justifying, 361; cf. 358.—exciting, presupposes affection, 361-2 (453).—or truth, may excite to a subordinate end as conducing to an ultimate, but cannot excite to ultimate ends themselves, 362. question whether public good as an ultimate end is not more reasonable than private good, 362.—justifying, presupposes moral sense, 361, 363-7. no justifying reasons for ultimate ends, 363.—corrects sense but is not thereby the source of original ideas, 365, 371.—employed by calm desire or affection, 369.—and free self-determination, said to be presupposed by merit, 373.

[*Butler*] when reason presides, religion must address itself to self-love, 423.— must guide and direct benevolence, 425. moral faculty, whether called conscience, moral reason, moral sense, or divine reason, whether a sentiment of the understanding or a perception of the heart or both, 429.

[*Balguy*]—and reflection, even in the absence of affection, can discover fitness and obligation, 439; cf. 451, 457-61.— a nobler principle than instinct, 442. the understanding alone can perceive beauty, moral or natural, 443*n*.—or intelligence, perceives and judges of virtue, 446. virtue is the conformity of moral actions to the reasons of things, 448. to treat or use an insensible object conformably to reason may be a right action but is indifferent in respect of morality, 448. conformity of moral actions to reason is their agreeableness to the nature and circumstances of agents and objects, 449. internal reasons

reason (*cont.*):

of things are the supreme law, inducing the strongest obligation, superior even to obligation to obey the will of God, 450. reasons of things are in respect of practice what evidence is in speculation, 450.—perceives agreement or disagreement of ideas, whether natural or moral, 451, 459. approbation is itself a sufficient reason for choice of a virtuous action, 453 (361). external reasons (of interest), dist. internal reasons (of morality), 455.—or moral good, the end of rational actions and rational agents, 455. receipt of benefit is a good reason for gratitude, and therefore obliges, 457. actions for which there is a good reason are reasonable, 459. obligation to perform an action means having a good reason, moral or natural, for performance, 461.

[*Gay*]—of any action, is the end of it; to ask a reason or end for an ultimate end is absurd, 470; cf. Hutcheson, 362–3.

[*Hume*]—and passion, fallaciously supposed to conflict, 479, 482, 484.—alone, cannot be a motive to action and therefore cannot oppose passion as a motive, 479–82.—judges either from demonstration or from probability, 480.—influences action only by directing judgement about causes and effects, 480–1 (859).—is and ought only to be the slave of the passions, 482 (859, 864).—or truth, cannot be contradicted by passion but only by an accompanying false judgement, 483, 490–1. affection or passion can be (though improperly) called unreasonable, either when founded on false supposition, or when choosing insufficient means for the designed end, 483–4. it is not contrary to reason to prefer the destruction of the whole world to the scratching of my finger, or to choose my total ruin to prevent the least uneasiness of an Indian, 483.—tends to be confused with calm passion, 485 (864). is it possible by reason alone to distinguish between moral good and evil? 488.—cannot discover the rules of morality, because morality influences passion and action while reason cannot do so, 489. actions cannot be reasonable or unreasonable, 490 (857).—being inactive, cannot be the source of so active a principle as conscience or a sense of morals, 490.

two operations of the understanding, comparing of ideas, and inferring of matter of fact, 497. demonstrative reason discovers only relations, and if that reason discovers vice and virtue, they must be relations, 498*n*. if reason is said to discover the obligations of morality, they must exist antecedent to that discovery and cannot be produced by reason, 502; cf. 599. virtue and vice do not consist in matters of fact to be inferred by reason, 503, 597. 'ought' cannot be deduced from 'is', 504. morality is more properly felt than judged of, 505. controversy whether morals be derived from reason or from sentiment, 562, 594–607.—must judge the utility of actions, 594.—cannot produce approbation of utility itself, 595.—alone, cannot discern the demerit of ingratitude, which is neither a matter of fact nor a relation, 596–9 (456–7, 933–5). reasons cannot be given for ultimate ends, 606; cf. Hutcheson, 362–3; Gay, 470.—dist. taste, 607.—conveys knowledge of truth and falsehood, discovers objects as they are in nature, is no motive to action but directs impulse by showing means to happiness, 607. if morality were determined by reason, it could be ascribed to beings superior to man, but not if determined by sentiment, 634 (366).

[*Price*] see *understanding*. those who argue against referring moral ideas to reason, have generally had in view deduction and not intuition, 661*n*.; cf. 671, 704.—acquaints us with the natures of things, while sense sees only their outsides, 663. reasoning investigates relations between objects, presupposes the possession of ideas, and cannot give rise to new ideas, as intuition can, 671. there must be ultimate approval of some actions without justifying reasons, and ultimate desire of some ends without reasons for choice; otherwise there would be an infinite progression of reasons and ends, 672; cf. Hutcheson, 362–3; Gay, 470; Hume, 606.—as well as sense, can be a power of immediate perception, 674.—being slow and deliberate, needs to be aided by instinct, 688; cf. 694. reasoning, dist. intuition, as grounds of belief, 704–5.—is the natural and authoritative guide of a rational being, 713; cf. Butler, 406, 427*n*., 429*n*.

[*Smith*]—as the alleged source of approbation, 834.

[*Reid*] see *judgement*.—has two offices, to regulate belief and to regulate conduct, 857, 931. 'to act reasonably' is a phrase common in all languages and therefore has a meaning, 857 (490–1). no reason without judgement, 858.—can determine ends as well as means, 859–60 (480–2, 594–5, 606–7). some ends cannot even be conceived without reason, 860.—is required for a conception of our good upon the whole, 861–2.—dist. passion, 863. Hume calls reason the servant of the passions only because he includes under the passions what is really a principle of reason, 864; cf. 926 (482, 485).—speculative, dist. practical, 865.—comprehends both the principle of self-interest and the moral principle or conscience, 866. all reasoning must be grounded on first principles, and there must be in morals, as in all other sciences, first or self-evident principles on which all moral reasoning is grounded, 879. Hume abuses the word 'reason' in limiting it to speculative judgement, 926. all vice is contrary to reason, but vice cannot be defined as conduct contrary to reason, because this definition would apply equally to folly, 931–2. Hume's view, that reason cannot perceive the demerit of ingratitude, mistakenly assumes either that the sentiment of blame is feeling without judgement, or that only feeling can be excited by the particular structure of the mind, 933–5 (596–7). in the final act of moral judgement, there is a point to determine, and this requires reason, not feeling, 936 (601). Hume is right in saying that ultimate ends cannot be accounted for by reason, in the sense that they are not means to further ends, 940; but it does not follow from this that ultimate ends cannot depend on the intellectual faculties, 941 (606). there are ultimate ends which are rational principles of action, requiring judgement or reason, 942; cf. 856–60.

[*Bentham*]—or ground for approbation, dist. motive or cause of action, 966; cf. 963. what we call giving reasons is pointing out speculative motives which indirectly affect the will by producing a belief about a practical motive, 991.

rectitude,—moral, divine law the touchstone of, 185 (675); cf. 464. virtue or moral rectitude consists in pursuit of what is right and good as such, 423.—moral, perceived by understanding, 444.—of actions, is their agreeableness to the nature and circumstances of agents and objects, 449.—is a law as well as a rule, 713.—six main branches of, 733–45.

reflection, see *conscience*.

[*Shaftesbury*]—or reflected sense, necessary for virtue, produces affection towards affections themselves, 200.—produces approval of moral qualities, 204.—of unjust action, is conscience, 220.

[*Hutcheson*]—gives a virtuous agent pleasure, 314; cf. Shaftesbury, 200, 204.—upon principles of self-love, alleged to make a moral sense unnecessary, 348.—as a source of ideas, 355.—distinguishes the moral sense from the public sense, 356; cf. 314.—necessary for general calm desires, as contrasted with particular passions, 357.

[*Butler*]—or conscience, 376, 378–9, 390, 399, 401, 404. reflex approbation, 380; cf. Shaftesbury, 200, 204; Hutcheson, 314.—principle of, by which we approve and disapprove, 390.—approves and disapproves of certain dispositions and actions, abstracted from consideration of their tendency to the happiness or misery of the world, 327*n*.; cf. 434.—and self-love, 414; cf. 400. reflex sense of actions, 430; cf. Shaftesbury, 200.

[*Gay*]—upon pleasure and good, produces desire of them, upon pain and evil, aversion from them, 467.

[*Hume*]—on actions, dist. performance, 623.

[*Price*]—sensation and, mistakenly thought by Locke to be the sources of all our ideas, 660, 675.—necessary for virtue, 759.

[*Bentham*]—as the ground of moral sentiment, must relate to utility, 954.

Regulus, 250, 311.

Reid, 856–945. see especially *duty, feeling, judgement, language, motive, reason*.—cites St. Paul, 896; Cicero, 900; Hume, 859, 895, 901, 907, 913, 926, 928–9, 933, 937, 940; Samuel Johnson, 930.—criticizes Hume, 857, 864, 880, 895–901, 906, 908, 926–30, 933–44; Descartes and Locke, 908, 915; Arthur Collier, Berkeley, and Hutcheson, 908;

Reid (*cont.*):
Mandeville, 926; Adam Smith, 927.—
refers to Shaftesbury and Hutcheson,
877; to Euclid, 918, 937.

relation, see *agreement, fitness.*
[*Locke*]—moral, the conformity or
disagreement of voluntary actions to
a rule, 183.
[*Clarke*] necessary and eternal different relations the foundation of fitness or
unfitness, 225–6; cf. 247 (367).—eternal,
appear to the understanding as they are
in themselves, 230 (367).
[*Hutcheson*] relations are not real
qualities in external natures, but only
ideas accompanying our perception of
two objects, 367 (449).—eternal, in the
natures of things, unintelligible, 367.
[*Butler*] relations essential to the idea
of a system, 376.
[*Balguy*] relations, necessarily arising
from different natures or circumstances,
whether or not they be qualities inherent in external natures, are real,
unalterable, and eternal, 449 (367); cf.
452.—of agreement between gratitude
and benefaction, allows inference of
obligation, 456–7 (598–9).
[*Hume*] if morality is susceptible of
demonstration, it must consist in some
relations, 497, 498n. but the only
relations relevant to demonstration apply to irrational and inanimate objects
as well as to rational beings, 498. if
moral distinctions arise from relations,
the relations must lie only between
internal actions and external objects,
not within one or other of these, 499.
the relations must also have a necessary
connection with the will, as cause and
effect, if they are to be obligatory on
every rational mind, 500. the same
relations that exist in an instance of
parricide or ingratitude exist also when
a sapling overtops and destroys its parent
tree, 501; cf. 605 (938). likewise the
relations of incest are the same in animals
as in human beings, though only the
latter is immoral, 502. the absence of
reason in animals may prevent them
from discovering moral relations or
duties but cannot prevent the latter from
applying to animals, 502.—of contrariety between receipt of good offices
and return of ill offices, cannot constitute the immorality of ingratitude, 598
(456–8). comparison of mathematical
with moral relations is unintelligible,

599. relations and qualities do not constitute beauty but are the cause of it in
the mind of a spectator, 603 (937).
[*Price*] relations and circumstances of
agent and objects determine whether an
action is right, wrong, or indifferent,
726.
[*Reid*] moral obligation belongs to
the category of relation, 873. Hume is
mistaken in thinking that rationalists
deduce the relation of obligation from
other relations, 930 (504). many relations, including moral ones, can apply
only to moral agents and not to inanimate objects, 938 (605).
relative,—or practical virtue, dist.
absolute or abstract, 719n., 750–1; cf.
724.
religion, see *God.*
[*Hobbes*]— = fear of power invisible,
30.
[*Shaftesbury*] religious conscience presupposes moral or natural conscience,
220.
[*Clarke*] morality or natural religion,
239. moral virtue the foundation, sum,
essence, and life of true religion, 261.
[*Mandeville*]—not the source of moral
notions, 268.
[*Wollaston*]—foundation of, lies in
difference between good and evil, 272.
—identified with obligation, and properly called religion of nature or natural
religion, 294.—may be called natural
upon two accounts, 302.
[*Butler*]—appeals to self-love, 423.—
and morality, at last coincide, 428.
[*Gay*] religious obligation, dist.
natural, virtuous, and civil, 464; cf.
Locke, 184.
[*Hume*]—danger to, irrelevant to
philosophical dispute, 626.—not endangered by the doctrine of necessity
understood as constant conjunction and
inference therefrom, 627.
[*Hartley*] pleasures and pains of theopathy, 637, 651–3. hopes and fears of a
future state, and meditation upon the
perfection of God, as sources of associations giving rise to the moral sense,
651–2.
[*Price*]—obligation of, a branch of
universal rectitude, 716.
[*Smith*]—terrors of, enforce the
natural sense of duty, 821.
[*Bentham*] religious sanction, dist.
physical, political, and moral, 968; cf.
Locke, 184; Gay, 464.

reputation, law of opinion or reputation or fashion, dist. divine law and civil law, 184–8.—the measure of virtue and vice, or right and wrong, 187–8.—love of, adds force to moral sentiment, 593.

resentment

[*Smith*] an action deserves punishment if it is the proper and approved object of resentment, 786, 788; i.e. if the resentment has the sympathy of the impartial spectator, 789.—sympathy with, depends on impropriety of the agent's motive, 792–6.—indirect sympathy with, gives rise to sense of demerit, 798.

[*Bentham*] the motive of ill will or resentment may be regarded as good or bad according to circumstances, 997.

resolution

[*Hume*]—dist. promise, 536. a promise expresses a resolution but adds obligation by a conventional form of words, 541.

[*Price*]—or intention, dist. promise, 739.

respectable,—virtues, dist. amiable, 781–2; cf. 612.

retaliation,—sacred and necessary law of, approved through sympathy with resentment, 791.

reward, see *merit, punishment.*

[*Cumberland*] adequate rewards and punishments make pursuit of public good contribute to private happiness, 112. divine reward and punishment of virtue and vice do not subordinate common good to private happiness, 116–17.

[*Locke*]—and punishment, are pleasure and pain attending the observance or breach of a law, 183.—and punishment, essential to all law, 184.

[*Clarke*] regard to private advantage or reward not the foundation of duty, 225, 248.—and punishment, nevertheless necessary to maintain the practice of virtue, 249–50.

[*Mandeville*]—imaginary, needed for self-denial, 263. when virtue is said to be its own reward, the satisfaction that constitutes the reward is a sign of pride, 270–1.

[*Hutcheson*] 'rewardable' denotes a quality which inclines a superior nature to make an agent happy, or which makes a spectator approve such a superior nature for conferring happiness, 373.

[*Butler*] endeavouring to do good is in a degree its own reward, 420.

[*Hume*]—and punishment, presuppose that actions are caused and so necessary, 628 (891).

[*Price*]—and punishment, presuppose desert and consequently presuppose obligation, 712.

[*Smith*] an action deserves reward or punishment if it is the proper and approved object of gratitude or resentment, 786–8; i.e. if these passions have the sympathy of the impartial spectator, 789.

[*Paley*]—and punishment in the afterlife, constitute the motive of moral obligation, 850.

[*Reid*]—and punishment, imply good and ill desert, and so presuppose liberty, not necessity, 891 (628).

[*Bentham*] the business of government is to promote the happiness of the society by punishing and rewarding, 977.

right and wrong, see *duty, fitness, obligation, merit, virtue.*

[*Hobbes*]—have no place in state of nature, 53 (227).

[*Locke*]—or virtue and vice, commonly determined by the law of opinion or reputation, 187.

[*Shaftesbury*]—sense of, a sentiment or judgement of what is done through good or bad affection, 202, 204.

[*Clarke*]—natural difference between, 227.—difficulty of defining bounds of, 229. truth and right are necessarily the same to every man's understanding, 251. it cannot be right to act in breach of another man's right, 253.

[*Wollaston*] acts that interfere with truth are wrong in nature, 280.—may mean either what we approve and disapprove, or what tends to our happiness or misery, 370.

[*Balguy*] to treat or use an insensible object conformably to reason may be a right action but is indifferent in respect of morality, 448. right actions are suitable to the nature and relations of persons concerned, 449. morally good action may be called a true or a right action, 452.

[*Hume*] mistake of right, dist. mistake of fact, 493, 602.

[*Price*] are right and wrong real characters of actions, or only qualities of our minds? 657. 'right' cannot just mean 'commanded' or 'useful'. since the

right and wrong (*cont.*):
propositions 'obeying a command is right' or 'producing happiness is right' would then be trifling tautologies, 658; cf. Hutcheson, 350–1; Butler, 411.—distinctions of, perceived by the understanding, 659, 673.—can be shown to be simple ideas by the impossibility of defining them except by synonymous expressions, 672; cf. Hutcheson, 358.—may be ideas of the understanding, since others are, 674.—are simple and undefinable ideas, but that does not prove that they are perceived by sense and not reason, 674.—acknowledged by common sense to be perceptions of the understanding, 676–80.—perception of, is accompanied by impressions of pleasure or pain, but should not be confounded with them, 677. if right and wrong were the effects of sensation, they would be incompatible with the idea of action, 681; and would preclude the possibility of mistake, 682. if no actions are in themselves right or wrong, they must all be indifferent, 683.—necessarily connected with moral obligation or duty, 683*n*., 708.—denote what actions are by nature and necessity, 684.—as epithets, are properly applied only to actions, dist. good and ill desert, which apply to agents, 695. rightness of action is coincident and identical with obligation to action, 708. it may be objected that some actions, e.g. of beneficence, are right though not obligatory; but at least all wrong actions imply obligation, 720. further, beneficence in general is obligatory as well as right, 721.—two senses of, corresponding to abstract and practical virtue, 750; cf. 719*n*. both constitute real virtue, and it is absolutely right that a man should do what he thinks right, 751.—perception of, is a motive to action, 757.
[*Paley*] 'right' means conformity to the rule we go by, 846. whatever is expedient is right, 854. rightness of an action depends on its tendency, while virtue of an agent depends on his design, 854*n*.
[*Reid*] actions are virtuous only if done from a belief that they are right, 894; cf. Price, 755, 758.
[*Bentham*]—standard of, supplied by pleasure and pain, 946. an action that conforms to the principle of utility is right or at least is not wrong, 951.—have

meaning only when thus interpreted, 951, 954. if approbation without regard to consequences is taken to be a standard of right and wrong, it is either despotical or anarchial, 954.—rule of, is simply a name for individual sentiment, 959.
rights
[*Hobbes*] right of nature is liberty to act for self-preservation, 55. right distinguished from law as liberty from obligation, 56. in state of nature, every man has a right to every thing, 57 (253). to lay down a right is to incur obligation, 59.—some, cannot be laid down, 60. right of God derived from irresistible power, 89; cf. 101 (227, 247, 259–60).
[*Cudworth*] right or authority of commanding depends on natural justice, 122–4.
[*Clarke*] Hobbes's doctrine that every man has a right to every thing implies a self-contradiction, 253 (57).—are limited to an equal proportion of things necessary or useful to life, except by consent of one's fellows and for public benefit, 253.
[*Hutcheson*]—depend on tendency to the public good, 353.—perfect, necessary to prevent universal misery, dist. imperfect, which tend to promote positive good, 353.
[*Butler*] natural right of conscience to govern, 402.—can be only to happiness, 426.
[*Hume*]—idea of, presupposes idea of justice, 529.
[*Price*]—in relation to property, 741–4.
Rochefoucauld,—cited by Hutcheson, 359.—criticized by Butler, 382; by Hume, 610*n*.—referred to by Bentham, 994*n*.
rules, see *criterion.*
[*Cudworth*] wisdom has the nature of a rule and measure, 128.
[*Locke*]—moral, not innate, because not universally received and require reasoning, 154–8.—moral, capable of demonstration, 154, 189.—moral, not self-evident, always susceptible to demand for a reason, 157.—moral, often approved simply from self-interest, 158.—moral (or laws), three sorts of, divine law, civil law, and law of opinion or reputation or fashion, 184–8 (675).
[*Wollaston*] there must be a rule for distinguishing good and evil, 272.

[*Hutcheson*] universal rule to compute the morality of actions, 335. moral sense not a rule, 372.

[*Butler*] virtue and religion said to require that actions be directed by a rule other than the strength of motives, 396. man has the rule of right within, 405. inquiries after some general rule of morals are useful but not necessary for practice, 405.

[*Balguy*] the original law or rule of action, viz., to conform to reason, 450.

[*Gay*] rule of life, as the criterion of virtue, 462. immediate rule or criterion of virtue is the will of God, 464; cf. Locke, 185.

[*Hume*] general rule of justice reaches beyond the instances from which it arose by sympathy, 534. justice is advantageous to society by observance of the general rule, although single instances may be harmful in their immediate tendency, 594.

[*Price*] Locke's view, that rectitude signifies conformity of actions to rules or laws, makes it absurd to apply rectitude to rules and laws themselves, 675 (183–8). rectitude is both a rule of action to direct, and a law to bind, 713.

[*Smith*] rule or canon for judging propriety of affections is the correspondent affection in ourselves, 775. general rules of morality are formed from experience of our natural sentiments in particular instances, 816–17. these rules may then be used as standards of judgement to check the misrepresentations of self-love, 818–19. regard to general rules is what is properly called a sense of duty, 820. nature and reasoning tell us that the general rules of morality are the commands and laws of God, 821–3. all general rules are commonly called laws, whether they be the rules which bodies observe or rules laid down to direct conduct, 823.

[*Paley*] the rule of virtue is the will of God, 845, 850; cf. Gay, 464. 'right' means conformity to the rule we go by, 846. utility of a moral rule constitutes its obligation, 854. violation of a necessary or useful general rule is a general bad consequence of an apparently useful action, 855.

[*Reid*] law implies a general rule of conduct and an inducement to obey, 867.

[*Bentham*] rule of right is simply a name for individual sentiment, 959.

St. Paul,—cited by Hobbes, 101; by Clarke, 234; by Butler, 387, 395, 397–9, 410, 413, 424, 427; by Reid, 896.

Sallust,—cited by Hume, 612.

sanction, see *law, obligation, punishment, reward.*

[*Cumberland*]—and precept, both included in definition of a law of nature, 112.

[*Locke*] three different enforcements attaching to the three sorts of moral rules or laws, 184–7. commendation and disgrace the sanction of the law of opinion or fashion, 188.

[*Clarke*]—of reward and punishment, is a secondary obligation or enforcement of an original obligation depending on conscience, 233.

[*Hutcheson*] when sanctions co-operate with our moral sense, we say we are obliged; when they oppose it, we say we are constrained, 352.

[*Balguy*] remorse a natural sanction of the law of nature, 450. laws oblige us as moral agents, sanctions as sensible agents, 461.

[*Price*] reward and punishment are the sanctions of virtue, not its efficients, 712.

[*Bentham*] four sources of pleasure or sanctions, physical, political, moral, religious, 968; cf. Locke, 184; Gay, 464. —the source of obligatory powers or motives, 968n.

satisfaction,—or pleasure, 215.—or happiness, 417. approbation is not limited to morals but covers whatever is entirely to our satisfaction, 842.

Sceptics, 104, 682n.

Schoolmen, 6, 37, 67, 102, 120, 133, 144–6, 357, 881, 900.

science, see *philosophy.*—natural, includes investigation of the mind, 106.— enables us to prove existence of God and authority of natural law, 111.—can demonstrate effects of action, 114.— presupposes immutable natures and essences, 127.—the comprehension of that which necessarily is, 128.—question of abstract, dist. question of fact, 563.— experimental method of, dist. inference from abstract principle, 563. there are in every science some general principles beyond which we cannot hope to find others more general, 576n.

self

[*Locke*] natural law decrees duties to God, society, and self, 194.

self (*cont.*):

[*Gay*] where self is only concerned, a man is called prudent, not virtuous, 462.

[*Price*]—duty to, as one of the main branches of virtue, 734-5.

self-command,—virtues of, dist. those of sensibility, 781-3.

self-denial,—imaginary reward needed for, 263.—lauded both by those who practise it and by others, 266.—virtues of, depend on toning down natural feelings to those of the spectator, 781.

self-determination, see *freedom, necessity, will.*

[*Cudworth*]—contingent or fortuitous, dist. free will, 141.

[*Price*] will as the power of acting and determining, 661n.—and activity, are essential to spirit, and consciousness of them gives us the idea of power, 667. liberty = the power of acting and determining, i.e. self-determination, 752-3.

self-evident, moral rules not self-evident, because always susceptible to demand for a reason, 157. that a man ought to be grateful to benefactors is equivalent to a self-evident proposition, 458.—moral distinctions in general are, 688.—the principles of virtue are, 747. there must be first or self-evident principles in morals as in all other sciences, 879; cf. 930.

self-improvement, 286.

selfish

[*Mandeville*] man an extraordinary selfish animal, 263. supposed classes of selfish and unselfish men, 265-6.

[*Hutcheson*]—motives, denoted by the word 'interest', 336. particular selfish passions, dist. general calm desire of private good of any kind, 357.

[*Butler*] cool or settled selfishness, dist. passionate or sensual selfishness, 382. the word 'selfish', like 'property', often used to exclude regard to the good of others, 419.

[*Hume*] selfishness and limited generosity, combined with instability and scarcity of external possessions, make justice necessary, 525-6, 532, 540; cf. 567-71. selfishness the true mother of ingratitude, 540.

[*Hartley*] compassion arises from association of what may be called selfish feelings, 645.

[*Smith*] to restrain selfish and indulge benevolent affections constitutes the perfection of human nature, 782.—passions, may pervert the judgements of conscience, 812.

self-love, see *benevolence, desire, interest.*

[*Clarke*]—natural to every one, 244.

[*Hutcheson*]—or interest, the motive for pursuit of natural good, 304.—entirely different from the principle of action approved by the moral sense, 306.—not the ground of approval of characters in history, 310-11.—not the motive of virtuous action, 316.—and benevolence, may be joint motives to the same action, 319, 336.—some try to deduce benevolence from, 320. hatred is the effect of self-love, not of disinterested malice, 326.—cannot explain parental affection, 327.—mistaken, overcoming benevolence, is often the ordinary spring of vice, 329.—of itself, is morally neutral, and is within limits necessary for the good of the whole, so that a neglect of our own good may be morally evil, 330.—with neglect of the good of others, may make an action evil, 339.—and reflection, alleged to make a moral sense unnecessary, 348.—falsely supposed to be the sole source of affections, 355. general calm desire of private good, dist. particular selfish passions, 357; cf. Butler, 382-3, 414-16.—alleged to be sole motive both of election and of approbation, 359.

[*Butler*]—dist. particular passions (cf. Hutcheson, 357), which it presupposes, 382-3, 414-16.—mistakenly supposed to be the sole motive, 382-3.—can be as just and morally good as any affection, 384. no reason to wish self-love were weaker than it is, 385, 393; cf. Shaftesbury, 212.—not the moral institution of life, but a better guide than passion, 385, 400.—and benevolence, both dist. particular passions and affections, 389.—cool, a cool and reasonable concern for oneself, 393.—reasonable and cool, a superior principle to passion, 400.—in general coincides with virtue, 408.—reasonable, and conscience, are the chief or superior principles in man, both leading us the same way, 409. Hobbes's account of pity makes it no more an instance of self-love than of benevolence, 411.—engrossment in, may contradict its own end of private good, 413, 417.— = a general desire of one's own happiness, dist. particular affections towards particular external objects, 414.

—does not determine our interest or good, but only puts us upon obtaining it, 417.—mistakenly alleged to be in competition with benevolence, 418–23. —does not exclude regard to the interests of others, as the idea of property does, 419, 422.—benevolence is subservient to, 422.—often appealed to by religion; it may be allowed that virtue cannot be justified without consideration of interest, 423.

[*Hume*]—cannot be the legitimate motive for acts of justice, 515. self-interest is the original motive to the establishment of justice, but sympathy with public interest is the source of its moral approbation, 534.—cannot account for moral approbation, since we approve of tendencies to public interest even when contrary to private, 576. relative degrees of benevolence and self-love not worth disputing, 588. the passions that are commonly, though improperly, comprised under self-love cannot account for moral notions, because they do not express the universal point of view required for that purpose, 589.—language of, expresses sentiments peculiar to oneself and one's private situation, dist. language of morals, 590–2.—confused with vanity by Rochefoucauld and others, 610n.

[*Price*] desire of happiness for ourselves does not arise from instinct but from the nature of happiness, 692. benevolence is essential to intelligent beings, as well as self-love to sensible beings, 693. reasonable and calm self-love is a virtuous principle, 761.

[*Smith*] as to love our neighbour as we love ourselves is the great law of Christianity, so the great precept of nature is to love ourselves only as we love our neighbour or as our neighbour is capable of loving us, 782.—is liable to pervert the judgements of conscience when we are about to act, 813.—misrepresentations of, are corrected by general rules of morality, 816, 819.—as the alleged source of approbation, 834.

self-preservation
[*Hobbes*]—the principal end of man, 48; cf. 55.
[*Locke*]—a duty of man, willed by God, 194.
[*Shaftesbury*]—affections for, necessary for goodness or virtue, 212.
[*Clarke*]—care for, natural to every

one, 244.—one of the three principal branches of duty, 245.
sense, see *moral sense, reason, understanding*.
[*Hobbes*]—pleasures of, 5, 26.
[*Cudworth*]—cannot judge of itself or of what really exists, 131.—is passive perception of individuals, dist. active knowledge of universals, 132.
[*Locke*]—and reason, are the light of nature, 190.—shows us that the material world exists and is orderly, 191.
[*Shaftesbury*]—reflected, or reflection, necessary for virtue, produces affection towards affections themselves, 200.—of right or wrong, a sentiment or judgement of what is done through good or bad affection, 202, 204.—pleasure of = pleasure of body, 215–16.
[*Clarke*]—men naturally have of right and wrong, 237.
[*Wollaston*]—common, of mankind, on the signification of acts, 276.—common, an infirm basis for distinction between moral good and evil, 292.
[*Hutcheson*]—of pleasure, 304.— = a determination of the mind to receive ideas independent on our will, 307, 356. sensation and reflection as sources of ideas, 355.—classified into external, internal, public, moral, of honour, and of decency, 356 (476).—said to be judged of by reason, 361.—is corrected by reason but does not therefore owe its ideas to reason, 365, 371.
[*Butler*] natural sense of moral good and evil, 395.—external, compared with conscience, 395. reflex sense of actions, 430; cf. Shaftesbury, 200.—or discernment of actions as morally good or evil, and as of good or ill desert, 431.
[*Balguy*]—moral, no more needed than an intellectual sense, 451.
[*Gay*] Hutcheson might as well have added a pecuniary sense, and a sense of party and power, to his moral sense, sense of honour, order, etc., 476 (356).
[*Hume*] conscience or a sense of morals, 490.—of morality, supposed to be the discovery of some relation, 498. —of virtue, is to feel a particular kind of pleasure, 506.—of duty or morality, cannot be the original motive of virtuous action, 513; cf. 633.—of duty, may be a motive to action, but presupposes some other virtuous motive as common in human nature, 514.—of duty, always follows the common and natural course of our passions, 520.—of duty, the sole

sense (*cont.*):

motive for performance of promises, 538. immediate feeling and finer internal sense, 562.

[*Hartley*] sensations dist. ideas, 636. ideas of sensation or simple ideas, dist. intellectual or complex ideas, 636. sensation and ideas in relation to pleasures and pains, 637. repeated sensations leave vestiges or images, viz., simple ideas of sensation, 639. association of sensations causes all the corresponding ideas to be excited by any one of the sensations, 639.

[*Price*] sensation and reflection mistakenly thought by Locke to be the sources of all our ideas, 660, 675.—dist. understanding, 661-4. one sense cannot judge of the objects of another, 662; cf. Cudworth, 131.—consists in the obtruding of impressions, independently of our wills, presents particular forms to the mind, but cannot rise to general ideas, 663; cf. Cudworth, 132.—cannot give us the ideas of solidity (which includes impenetrability), inactivity, or substance, 665.—perceives the constant conjunction of events, but not the causation of one by another, 667; cf. Hume, 614, 621-2.—is not the only power of immediate perception, 674.—ideas of, are incompatible with ideas of real things such as matter and action, 681. all sensation must be true sensation, precluding the possibility of mistake, 682. does sense give us the ideas of beauty and deformity? 685.

[*Reid*]—of interest, dist. sense of duty, 867; cf. 860, 866, 870. if we have just notions of the office of the external senses, the moral sense is seen to be analogous to them, 877.—not only gives us ideas, but is also a power of judging, 878, 927. the moral sense similarly gives us judgements as well as conceptions, 879, 927. the truths immediately testified by the external senses are the first principles from which we reason with regard to the material world, 879. sensation or feeling, dist. judgement, 910. in perception, judgement is the consequence of sensation, 915.

sensible

[*Shaftesbury*]—creature, is good or ill when moved by passion or affection towards the good or ill of the system to which he has relation, 199.—creature, capable of goodness but not of virtue,

200 (349).—creature, dist. rational, 200, 203-4.—creature, necessarily has social affection, 203.

[*Balguy*] moral actions concern our behaviour to intelligent or sensible beings, 448; cf. 440; and cf. Hutcheson, 315.—agents, dist. moral, 460-1 (717).

[*Hartley*]—pleasures and pains, dist. intellectual, 641; cf. 635-7.

[*Price*]—qualities, are mistakenly supposed to be properties of objects, 680.—qualities, are incompatible with the idea of matter, 681. as merely sensible beings we are incapable of obligation, 717 (455, 460).

sentiment, see *feeling, taste*.

[*Butler*]—of the understanding, or perception of the heart, 429.

[*Hume*]—of approbation or disapprobation, constitutes the virtue or vice of an action, 503, 505, 634.—of morals, and that of interest, are distinct though often confounded, 507. the question whether the sentiments of morality are natural depends on the meaning given to 'natural', 510. all morality depends on sentiments, and since we cannot change our sentiments naturally, we cannot will an obligation, 537. natural sentiment of approbation and blame necessary before it could be excited by politicians, 550; cf. Hutcheson, 311 (263-9).—of morals, naturally attends the conventions of justice, once established, 551. sentiments vary, but are corrected for moral and aesthetic judgement by taking a general point of view, 553-4; cf. 579-80.—must touch the heart to control passion, but need not extend beyond imagination to influence taste, 557. immediate taste or sentiment is one cause of moral judgement, reflection on utility is another, 558. controversy whether morals be derived from reason or from sentiment, 562, 594-607. nothing can bestow more merit than the sentiment of benevolence, 565. different sentiments are excited by the utility of a man and by that of an inanimate object, 574*n*.; cf. Hutcheson, 307. natural sentiment of benevolence causes us to approve social virtues for their utility, 581.—of right and wrong, is kept alive by the habit of surveying ourselves in reflection, i.e. by considering how others regard us, 593.—of humanity, produces approval of utility, while reason judges what is useful, 595.

virtue defined as whatever mental action or quality gives to a spectator the pleasing sentiment of approbation, 600.—aesthetic or moral, an affair of taste, adds a new creation to objects in nature and is a motive to action, 607. we are not justified in ascribing sentiments to beings superior to man, 634 (366).

[*Smith*] approbation of the sentiments of another, as of his opinions, is to observe their agreement with our own, 771.—or affection from which action proceeds, may be considered under two different aspects, that of propriety, depending on cause or motive, and that of merit, depending on end or tendency, 773, 785. sentiments of gratitude and resentment in relation to the sense of merit and demerit, 786–98.—actual correspondence of, not necessarily required for the sense of merit, as it is for the sense of propriety, 799. our natural sentiments of approval and disapproval in particular instances lead us to form general rules of morality, 816–17.—of approbation for virtue, is enhanced by, but not primarily or principally due to, utility, 832 (560, 586).—of approbation for virtue, differs from approbation of a convenient material thing, and includes a sense of propriety distinct from the perception of utility, 833, 844.—as the source of approbation, according to one type of theory, 834.—as the principle of approbation, two theories of, (1) moral sense, (2) sympathy, 836.—supposedly peculiar, as a variation of the theory of moral sense, 839–43 (506–7). if the principle of approbation were a peculiar sentiment, it would be the same in all instances, whereas in fact approbation differs for different types of virtue, 840; cf. 781–2; and cf. Hume, 612. a peculiar sentiment of morals, if it existed, would have acquired a special name, 842. sentiments of approbation have four sources, (1) sympathy with the motives of the agent, (2) sympathy with the gratitude of the beneficiary, (3) observation that the action conforms to the general rules of sympathy, (4) thought of utility, 843.

[*Reid*] the term 'sentiment' is abused when taken to mean feeling without judgement, 927.—of blame, is mistakenly supposed by Hume to be feeling without judgement, 933–4 (597).

[*Bentham*] the principle of utility is a sentiment approving utility as the quality by which approbation ought to be governed, 947*n*. theories which say the standard of right and wrong is moral sense, common sense, understanding, rule of right, fitness, law of nature, truth, or conformity to nature, are all concealed ways of expressing individual sentiments of sympathy and antipathy, 959–60. moral sentiment may not arise from thought of utility, but that is irrelevant to its justification, 963; cf. 966 (427*n*., 434).

Shaftesbury, 195–223. see especially *affection*, *virtue*.—criticized by Butler, 380–1.—referred to by Balguy, 447; by Reid, 877.

Shakespeare,—cited by Hutcheson, 309.

shame, see *honour*.— = dejection at discovery of defect, 6.—honour and, inculcated by lawgivers, 264.—honour and, evidence of a moral sense, 344.—feeling of, given to man to prevent shameful actions, 395.

significancy,—of actions, 275, 279, 368.

sin,—dist. crime and vice, 184–7.

Smith, Adam, 763–844. see especially *approbation*, *conscience*, *moral sense*, *propriety*, *sentiment*, *spectator*, *sympathy*, *utility*, *virtue*.—cites Cicero, 809; Malebranche, 813; Hume, 824.—criticizes Hutcheson, 815, 837–43; Hume, 832–3, 839(?), 844.—criticized by Reid, 927.

social, see *affection*, *benevolence*.

[*Shaftesbury*]—affection, necessary to a sensible creature, 203.—passion, approved by any reflecting creature, 204.—pleasures, preferred to sensual, by those who know both, 217.

[*Mandeville*] man, though extraordinarily selfish, the only creature that can be made sociable, 263.

[*Butler*]—nature of man, 387–94.

[*Balguy*]—action, is right when suitable to the nature and relations of the persons concerned, 449.

[*Hume*] man's very first state and situation may justly be esteemed social, 531.—virtues, bear the greatest figure among moral qualities, 550.—virtues, approved for their utility, 574, 581–2.

[*Hartley*] sociality as a species of sympathetic affection, 643.

[*Reid*]—operations of the mind, dist. solitary, and require the use of language, 902.—operations of the mind, cannot be resolved into any modification or composition of the solitary, 903.

society

[*Locke*]—maintenance of, as much a duty as self-preservation, 194.

[*Shaftesbury*] to be well affected to society, as well as to oneself, is virtue, 205.

[*Clarke*]—need for, natural to men, 244.—universal friendship or, 244.

[*Mandeville*]—passions the support of, 262.

[*Butler*]—is not to be compared with the body alone, but with the whole nature of man, 387. we are as much made for society as for the care of ourselves, 387, 391.—love of, dist. affection to the good of, 389. men are so much one body that in a peculiar manner they feel for each other, these feelings being cements of society, 391.

[*Hume*]—supplies man with force, ability, and security, 523.—arises from sexual appetite and parental affection, 524.—endangered by the opposition between selfishness and generosity, 525; and by the instability and scarcity of possessions, 526.—is maintained by a convention bestowing stability on possessions, 527, 530.—necessities and interests of, the foundation of the invention of promises, 539-40, 545.—sympathy with the interest of, the source of esteem for all the artificial virtues, and likewise for many, but not all, of the natural virtues, 548-50.—extensive concern for, can only come from sympathy, 550-1. the whole system of law and justice is advantageous to society, though a single act of justice may not be, 551.—supposes a degree of equality, and could not exist between men and a greatly inferior species of creatures, 572.

[*Smith*]—harmony of, assisted by sympathy between spectator and sufferer, 778.—is thereby a remedy for restoring mental tranquillity, 780. approval and disapproval of society form the mirror in which a man can view the propriety or impropriety of his own sentiments and conduct, 801-3; cf. Hume, 593.—interest of, is advanced unawares by the rich, led by an invisible hand, 829.

Socrates, 13, 235, 445.

soul

[*Cudworth*]—is not a *rasa tabula*, a passive thing without activity, 135.—nature of, must be known for under- standing of morality, 135.—one and the same, understands and wills, 145.—first moving principle of, 146-7.—has power over itself, 150.

[*Price*] some divide the powers of the soul into understanding and will, 661*n*. activity and self-determination are as essential to spirit, as the contrary are to matter, 667.

spectator, see *sympathy*.

[*Shaftesbury*] the mind, spectator or auditor of other minds, 201.

[*Clarke*] men's judgements concerning the actions of others are commonly impartial, 237.

[*Hutcheson*] virtue is called amiable or lovely from its raising good will or love in spectators toward the agent, 314. every spectator approves, by the moral sense, the pursuit of public good more than private, 362, 370. 'merit' denotes a quality which is approved by an observer, or the approbation of which is approved by all other observers, 373. 'rewardable' may denote a quality which makes a spectator approve a superior nature when he has conferred happiness on the agent, 373.

[*Hume*] useful objects please the spectator by a delicate sympathy with the possessor, and give rise to sense of beauty, 547. the esteem of a judicious spectator does not vary with variation of sympathy, 553.—has a more lively sympathy with real than with imagined benefit, 556. the only interest or pleasure which appears the same to every spectator, is that of the character examined or of persons connected with him, 560. conduct hurtful to society is disapproved by every spectator, 574. we cannot remain indifferent spectators of anger, even though it be not harmful, 584. virtue defined as whatever mental action or quality gives to a spectator the pleasing sentiment of approbation, 600.—sentiments of, give rise to beauty, 603 (937). —can commonly infer actions from motives and character, though the performer feels no determination to do so, 623.

[*Smith*] any passion can give rise to fellow feeling in every attentive spectator, 765. when observed passions are in concord with the sympathetic emotions of the spectator, he approves of them as proper, 770.—can sympathize only by trying to perfect imaginary change of situation, 778. conversely the sufferer, desiring concord of sentiments, is led to imagine himself in the position of the spectator and thereby to view his situation in a candid and impartial light, 779. sympathy of spectator with sufferer produces the virtues of humanity; of sufferer with spectator those of self-control, 781. the impartial spectator can entirely enter only into moderated passions, 783. the merit or demerit of an action is determined by the sympathy of the impartial spectator with gratitude or resentment, 789. the impartial spectator = the indifferent bystander or every reasonable man, 789. self-approbation depends on sympathy with the imagined approbation of a fair and impartial spectator, this supposed equitable judge, 800. we suppose ourselves the spectators of our own behaviour and thereby judge its propriety, dividing ourselves into two persons, the spectator and the agent, 803-4. to feel ourselves praiseworthy, we must become the impartial spectators of our own character and conduct, 806. conscience is the supposed impartial and well-informed spectator, the man within the breast, whose judgement may differ from that of the real spectator, the man without, 811. the real and impartial spectator, dist. the man within the breast, whose judgements may be perverted by selfish passions, 812. when we are about to act, passion often removes the candour of an indifferent person, the complete impartiality of an equitable judge, 813. when the action is over, we can enter more coolly into the sentiments of the indifferent spectator and identify ourselves with the ideal man within the breast, viewing our conduct with the severe eyes of the most impartial spectator, 814.

[*Reid*] the view that beauty is a feeling of the spectator, not a quality of the object, is a paradox contrary to common language and common sense, 937 (603).
speculative, see *reason.*—understanding, dist. practical, 148.—truth, resembles morality, except that assent is necessary while action is voluntary, 232. speculation, dist. practice, 450, 455, 835.—prejudices, dist. practical, 476.—philosophy, dist. practical, 489.—reason, dist. practical, 865; cf. 857, 926.—motives, dist. practical, 985-6.

spirit, see *soul.*
standard, see *criterion, rule.*
Stoics, 152-3, 250, 337, 633, 892.
suitableness, see *fitness.*
sympathy
[*Shaftesbury*]—with the kind or species, a form of natural affection, 215. —the highest delight, 218.—pleasures of, essential part of almost all satisfaction, 219.
[*Hutcheson*] alleged pleasure of compassion mistakenly said to be superior to the pain of sympathy, 345. public sense, 356.
[*Butler*] correspondence between the inward sensations of men; in a peculiar manner they feel for each other, these feelings being cements of society, 391.—substituting the interest of another for our own, 410-11. Hobbes's account of pity implies sympathy in reverse, i.e. substituting ourselves for others, 411.—with distress, i.e. pity, differs from sympathetic joy in being an original, particular affection leading us to act, 412.
[*Hume*] see *humanity.*—with public interest, is the source of the moral approbation of justice, 534.—aroused by causes or effects of passion, 546.—produces sense of beauty for what is useful, 547.—the source of the esteem paid to all the artificial virtues, 548.—may be presumed to account also for approbation of many of the natural virtues, 549-50.—essential to produce an extensive concern for society, 550-1.—varies when esteem does not, 553; but we correct our sentiments, or at least our language, by taking a steady and general point of view, 554; cf. 579-80.—interests us in the good of mankind, while virtue is approved even when not actually beneficial, 555; cf. 579*n.* this is because imagination passes easily from cause to likely effect, 556.—is more lively when actual beneficial effects are produced, 556; cf. 579*n.*—extensive, not contradictory to limited generosity, 557.—necessary for approbation of the immediately agreeable, as well as for approbation of the useful, 559.—the chief source of moral distinctions, 561. natural sympathy or contagion, whereby agreeable and disagreeable qualities are shared, 583-4.—gives rise to the two kinds of approbation, of the useful and of the immediately agreeable, 585. the force of many sympathies, when **we**

sympathy (*cont.*):
consider how others regard us, adds to moral sentiment, 593. all virtuous qualities have a tendency to public or private good, and therefore their merit is derived from sympathy, 633.

[*Hartley*]—pleasures and pains of, 637. sympathetic affections classified so as to include grief as well as joy at the happiness of others, and joy as well as grief at the misery of others, 642; cf. 644. sociality, benevolence, and compassion as species of sympathetic affection, 643–5.

[*Smith*]—or fellow feeling, requires imagination of what we ourselves would feel in the situation of others, 764, 779.— = fellow feeling with any passion, not merely with sorrow, as is pity, 765.—usually requires knowledge of the cause of the emotion to be shared, 766–7.—arises therefore less from seeing a passion than from seeing the situation which excites it, 768.—can therefore be for a non-existent but imagined feeling, e.g. in the insane or the dead, 768–9; cf. 772, 791, 799. to approve of the passions of another, as suitable to their objects, is the same thing as to observe that we sympathize with them, 770.—underlying approval, may be hypothetical, not actual, 772.—based on imaginary change of situation, is not required for harmony of sentiments in judgements of taste, 776. lack of sympathy in moral sentiments affects us as difference in judgements of taste does not, 777. complete sympathy between sufferer and spectator cannot be reached, but is approached by each imagining himself in the place of the other, 778–9.—of spectator with sufferer, produces virtues of humanity; of sufferer with spectator, those of self-control, 781.—of the impartial spectator with gratitude or resentment, determines the merit or demerit of an action, 789.—with resentment, can be independent of reflection on utility of punishment, 791.—with gratitude or resentment, depends on propriety or impropriety of the agent's motive, 792–6. direct sympathy or antipathy for the motive of the agent determines propriety or impropriety of action, while indirect sympathy with gratitude or resentment of the person affected determines merit or demerit, 797–8. illusive sympathy can give rise to sense of merit, but not to sense of

propriety, 799. self-approbation depends on sympathy with the imagined approbation of the impartial spectator, 800.— as one account of sentiment as the principle of approbation, 836.—explains why approbation differs in different types of virtue, 840 (506–7).—also explains how we can approve approbation itself as proper, 841. Hume's account of approbation, in terms of utility and sympathy with the happiness of those affected by a useful action, fails to distinguish virtue from the utility of a machine, 844; cf. 833.

[*Bentham*] principle of sympathy and antipathy, dist. principle of utility and principle of asceticism, 955. principle of sympathy and antipathy approves of actions merely because of personal disposition, and so is really the negation of principle, 957–8. principle of sympathy and antipathy underlies various theories of the standard of right and wrong, such as moral sense, common sense, understanding, rule of right, fitness of things, law of nature, conformity to truth, conformity to nature, 959–60. to say that wrong acts are unnatural is simply to express antipathy, 960. these theories are all a cloak for despotism, 961; cf. 954.—dictates of, frequently coincide with those of utility, though perhaps unintentionally, 964. pleasure of sympathy or benevolence as a motive, 996.

system
[*Shaftesbury*]—goodness relative to, 196.—one, may be part of another, and of system of all things, 197. if any being be wholly and really ill, it is with respect to the universal system, 198. a sensible creature is supposed good only when moved by affection for good of the system, 199.—of the kind, or common nature, dist. self-system, or private nature, 206.

[*Hutcheson*] a determination to mutual love implies that each individual is part of a great whole or system, 327. every moral agent considers himself part of a rational system, 332.

[*Butler*] every work both of nature and of art is a system, 376.—idea of, includes relations as well as parts, and conduciveness to an end, 376.—complexity of, evidence of design, 395.—or constitution of human nature, 404*n*.

[*Hume*]—of law and justice, is advantageous to society, though a single act of justice may not be, 551. men are now cured of their passion for hypotheses and systems in natural philosophy, 563.

tabula rasa, the soul is not a *rasa tabula,* 135.

talents

[*Hume*]—held to be excluded from the virtues, 608.—cannot be clearly distinguished from virtues, 609.—like virtues, are esteemed, 610–11.—included in personal merit, 612. different talents, like different virtues, produce different kinds of approbation, 612. whether natural abilities be virtues is a dispute of words, 632; cf. 608, 612.

taste, see *feeling, sentiment.*

[*Hume*] immediate taste or sentiment a source of approbation, 558.—decisions of, or aesthetic sentiment, compared with moral, 603.—dist. reason, 607.— produces aesthetic and moral sentiment, adding a new creation to objects in nature, and is a motive to action, 607.

[*Price*] the theory of moral sense makes virtue an affair of taste, 657.

[*Smith*]—and good judgement, are ascribed where there is a correspondence of sentiments, but this does not require sympathy and imaginary change of situation, 776. disagreement in matters of taste does not affect us as does lack of harmony in moral sentiments, 777.

tautology, see *definition.*

[*Hutcheson*] to say that morality depends on divine law implies that it is an insignificant tautology to call divine laws themselves good or just, 351; cf. 350.

[*Price*] if 'right' simply meant 'commanded' or 'useful', it would be absurd to ask whether it is right to obey a command, and the propositions 'obeying a command is right' or 'producing happiness is right' would be trifling, expressing no more than that obeying a command is obeying a command, or producing happiness is producing happiness, 658.

[*Reid*] if the strength of motives is measured by prevalence, the proposition that the strongest motive always prevails will be true but identical, meaning simply that the strongest motive is the strongest motive, 883.

[*Bentham*] it is a tautology to say that the more consistently the principle of

utility is pursued, the better it must be for mankind, 956. since the word 'lust' imputes disapprobation, to say that lust is a bad motive is true but nugatory, 998.

temptation,—ill desert lessened by, 431.

tendency

[*Hutcheson*]—to public good, as the ground of rights, 353.

[*Smith*]—or end of an action, determines its merit, while cause or motive determines its propriety, 773, 785.— of affections, has unduly engaged the attention of philosophers, 774.

[*Paley*]—of actions, determines their rightness or wrongness, while design of an agent determines his virtue or vice, 854*n.*

[*Bentham*] the general tendency of an act is to be judged by its material (or important) consequences, 978.

Theocritus,—cited by Wollaston, 278.

truth, see *reason.*

[*Cudworth*]—and falsehood, independent of the will of God, 127–8.

[*Clarke*]—and right, are necessarily the same to every man's understanding, 251.—speculative, resembles morality, except that assent is necessary while action is voluntary, 232. falsity or contradiction in theory is the same as iniquity in action, 242.

[*Wollaston*]—of propositions, is conformity of words to things, 274. —may be denied or contradicted by deeds, 275–9 (452, 727); such as breach of promise, 277, 285; cf. Hobbes, 102. one who lives above his means, lives a lie, 278 (452, 494).—acts interfering with, wrong or unnatural, 280 (368, 494–6, 959).—is conformity to nature, 280.—may be denied by omissions to act, 284–6.—nature and, 285. there cannot be opposite truths or incompatible duties, but there can be truths on opposite sides, requiring their importance to be compared, 288. importance and number of truths violated determine degrees of evil or guilt, 290 (368). only true pleasure, not all pleasure, is an ultimate good, 293.— conformity to, an intelligible and practicable foundation of morality, 293 (361, 727).—not to contradict, the great law of religion or nature, 294.—practice of, aims at happiness, 295. true pleasure and pain, 296–7. true pleasure = happiness, 298.—practice of, coincides with production of ultimate happiness, 301–2.

truth *(cont.)*:

[*Hutcheson*]—as conformity between proposition and its object (cf. Wollaston, 274), cannot be the criterion of election or approbation, 360, 363.—reason or, may excite to a subordinate end, but not to an ultimate end, 362.—conformity to, cannot supply ground for approving an ultimate end, 363.—or falsehood signified by action, does not constitute virtue or vice, if abstracted from intention, 368 (280). importance of truth in action is the quantity of good or evil produced, 368 (290).

[*Butler*] our moral judgement of veracity and justice is independent of consideration of good or bad consequences, 434–5; cf. 427*n*. no designed falsehood without design to deceive, 435.

[*Balguy*]—absolute, beauty a species of, 443*n*.—either of words, ideas, or things, 452.—of words or propositions, is their conformity to ideas or things or both, 452.—of things, as of ideas, is their agreement or disagreement with one another, 452. to act contrary to the truth of things should not be called acting a lie or contradicting a true proposition, because that confuses objective and subjective truth, 452 (278–9).—of things, is the ground of moral goodness of an action, which may therefore be called a true or a right action, 452. moral fitness is conformity to order and truth, 459.

[*Gay*] in pursuit of truth, as in conduct, we do not always go back to first principles, but treat known or presumed truths as resting-places, 475–6.

[*Hume*] passion, being an original existence, and not representative like an idea, cannot contradict truth and reason, though an accompanying false judgement can, 483, 490–1.— = agreement either to real relations of ideas or to real existence and matter of fact, 490. if moral distinctions were derived from truth or falsehood of judgements, it would make no difference whether an error was avoidable or unavoidable, and since truth does not admit of degrees, all virtues and vices would be equal, 492. an action which causes a false judgement in others, differs from a lie if the effect is not part of the intention, and cannot be the source of all immorality, 494; cf. Hutcheson, 368 (278, 280). Wollaston's view implies that an error of judgement caused by the action of inanimate objects would make such action immoral, and that a person who concealed an immoral action so as to cause no false conclusions in others would thereby make his action innocent, 495. Wollaston's view is also circular, since it presupposes the morality of justice or gratitude, and especially of truthfulness itself, 496.

[*Price*] understanding defined as the power in the soul which apprehends truth (i.e. reality), 664; cf. Cudworth, 128.—intuition of, 674. all sensation must be true sensation, 682. morality is a branch of necessary truth, 699. assenting to a proposition is the same as discerning it to be true, 707. signifying truth does not constitute the whole of morality and presupposes moral ideas, 727 (280, 293).—does not afford criterion of virtue, 728. approbation of truth-telling, not grounded on utility, 730. veracity, including fidelity to promises, as one of the main branches of virtue, 738–40.

[*Bentham*]—as the standard of moral judgement, is simply a name for individual sentiment, 959 (280, 293).

understanding, see *reason.*

[*Cudworth*]—faculty of, in relation to faculty of will, 142–5.—speculative, dist. practical, 148.

[*Locke*]—a power of perception, 162.

[*Clarke*]—of natural relations and fitnesses, directs the wills of intelligent beings, 230. negligent misunderstanding and wilful passion may cause action contrary to reason, 231.

[*Hutcheson*]—mistakenly supposed to be conative as well as cognitive, 357.

[*Butler*] sentiment of the understanding or perception of the heart, 429. moral understanding and moral sense, 434.

[*Balguy*]—unlike will, has no power to rebel, 450.

[*Hume*]—judges either from demonstration or from probability, 480.—two operations of, the comparing of ideas, and the inferring of matter of fact, 497.

[*Price*]—perceives the distinctions of right and wrong, 659, 673.—a spring of new simple ideas, 661.—two acts of, intuition and deduction, 661*n*.; cf. 671.—dist. sense, 661–4.—judges the perceptions of sense, to which it must be superior, 662; cf. Cudworth, 131.—rises above individuals to universal and abstract ideas, and discovers general truths; implies an active and vital energy of the mind, 663, 669; cf. Cudworth, 132.—defined as the power in the soul which apprehends truth (i.e. reality), 664; cf. Cudworth, 128.—gives us the ideas of solidity (including impenetrability), inactivity, and substance, 665; likewise the ideas of duration (dist. succession), space, necessity, infinity, contingency, possibility, and impossibility, 666; and the idea of causation, though not that of power, which comes from inward consciousness of activity and self-determination, 667 (614, 621–2).—as the source of knowledge, must be likewise the source of new ideas, 670.—the eye of the mind, 670.—may be the source of moral ideas, since it is of other ideas, 674.—acknowledged by common sense to be the source of moral ideas, 676–80. in contemplating the actions of moral agents, we have both a perception of the understanding and a feeling of the heart, 688; cf. Butler, 429.—of God, regulates his will, 702; cf. Cudworth, 128.

[Bentham]—as standard of moral judgement, is simply a name for individual sentiment, 959.—acts of, influenced by speculative motives, 985; cf. 991.

uneasiness, see desire.

[Locke]—in the absence of pleasure or good, is desire, 161, 174 (325).—the chief if not the only spur to industry and action, 161.—the motive for change, 172.—determines the will, 174–5 (486), 178–9.

[Hutcheson]—generally attends desire, 322; but is distinct from it, 325 (161, 174).—at having acted contrary to the moral sense, 346–7.

[Hume]—not the sole determinant of the will, 486 (174–5).

universal,—notions, dist. individuals, 132. moral rules not universally received, 154–6.—system and nature, 197–8.—good, the fit end of God's action, 226; cf. 251.—justice, the top and perfection of all virtues, 242.—love or benevolence, endeavouring to promote the happiness of all men, 243.—friendship or society, 244.—benevolence, dist. limited, 331–2, 357; cf. 369.—tendencies of actions, rather than utility of particular instances, may determine rightness, 334.—rule, to compute the morality of actions, 335.—benevolence, compared to gravitation, 343.—happiness, the object of divine providence, 351.—principles of human nature, discovered by history, 615.—and abstract ideas, perceived by the intellect, 663, 669.— ideas are not merely nominal, 669.—principles of morality, dist. particular usages, 749.—or rational benevolence, 761.

utility, see consequences, good, happiness, interest, pleasure.

[Hobbes]— = good as means, 25.

[Locke] good is what is apt to produce pleasure, 177, 183; cf. 160.

[Clarke]—not the foundation of morality, though universal good coincides with the truth and reason of things, 251.

[Mandeville]—of morality, 267 (311).

[Hutcheson]—of inanimate things, or of self-interested actions, does not arouse moral approbation, 307. that action is best which procures the greatest happiness for the greatest numbers, 333. useful particular actions may be wrong because universal allowance would be harmful, 334.—of gratitude, 342.—as the ground of rights, 353.—private, dist. public, 358.—flowing from kind affection, approved by the moral sense, 359.

[Butler] though the good of the creation be the only end of God, he has laid us under particular obligations distinct from consideration of their tendency to the happiness or misery of the world, 427n.; cf. 434.—cannot account for the desert of punishment, 431. our moral judgement of justice and veracity is independent of consideration of good or bad consequences, 434–5 (963).

[Balguy] the perfections of virtue are not those of a mere cornucopia, 454.

[Gay] the happiness of mankind is the criterion of the will of God, and therefore the criterion, once-removed, of virtue, 465. what is apt to produce pleasure is called good and approved, 467; cf. Locke, 160, 177, 183. annexing pleasure to the endeavours of others to promote my happiness is the only thing in my power to this end, and therefore I must approve my promotion of their happiness, 468.

[Hume] necessities and interests of

utility (*cont.*):

society are the foundation of the invention of promises, 539–40, 545.—beauty of, due to sympathy, 547. sympathy with the interest of society is the source of the esteem paid to all the artificial virtues, 548.—the sole cause of approbation of artificial virtues, 549; cf. 566, 582.—also the ground of approbation of many, though not all, of the natural virtues, 549–50; cf. 564–5, 582.—of the whole system of law and justice, though a single act of justice may be contrary to public good, 551.—and immediate taste or sentiment, are both causes of moral judgement, the former having the greatest influence, 558; cf. 584. virtue or personal merit consists of qualities useful or agreeable to others or to oneself, 560, 586 (832–3).—as a ground of virtue, requires admission of the force of sympathy, 561.—forms at least a part of the merit of benevolence and other social virtues, 564–5, 581–2, 584.—the sole origin, and sole ground of the merit, of justice, 566–73, 582.—and existence of justice, would cease if there were abundance of external conveniences, or if human benevolence were enlarged, 567–8; cf. 532.—of justice, likewise ceases, and causes its suspension, in conditions of extreme necessity or extreme rapaciousness, 569–71.—and application of justice, would not exist in the relation between men and creatures of greatly inferior strength, 572.—of social virtues, compared with that of beauty, 574.—of virtue, does not imply that useful inanimate objects should be called virtuous, 574*n.*; cf. Hutcheson, 307.—approval of, extends beyond our own interest to the interest of those affected by the character or action approved, 575–6.—general, the standard of approval, 580.—approval of, due to the natural sentiment of benevolence, 581, 595.—is one ground of approbation, immediate pleasure is another, both being founded on sympathy, 585. the monkish virtues, being neither useful nor agreeable, are rejected by men of sense, 587.—of actions, must be judged by reason, 594.—of observance of justice as a general rule, single instances of justice being often harmful in their immediate tendency, 594.—the mother of justice, 631. all virtuous qualities have a tendency to public or private good, 633.

[*Hartley*]—of virtue, a source of associations giving rise to the moral sense, 648.

[*Price*]—not the whole foundation of merit, 696–8. even when punishment requires to be justified by reformation, this is not simply in terms of the balance of advantage among consequences, 698.—established by custom or habit, is not the ground of disapprobation of ingratitude, injustice, or violation of truth, 730.—the most general and leading consideration in inquiries concerning right, 737.—is not the sole ground of justice but is one important ground, 744.

[*Smith*] beneficial or harmful tendency of an action constitutes its merit or demerit, while cause or motive constitutes its propriety, 773, 785. philosophers have lately concentrated on tendency to the neglect of cause, 774. sympathy with resentment can be independent of reflection on utility of punishment, 791.—a principal source of beauty, 824.—is often more valued than the end for which it was intended, 825–8. this deception of nature promotes industry, and the rich are led by an invisible hand to advance the interest of society, 829.—of virtue, strikes us when we consider it in an abstract and general manner, 831. hence Hume mistakenly attributes the whole of our approbation to the useful and agreeable, 832 (560, 586).—enhances approbation, but is not the first or principal source of it, 832; cf. 843.—of a material thing, does not produce the same sentiment of approbation as does virtue, 833, 844; cf. Hume, 574*n.* approbation includes a sense of propriety distinct from the perception of utility, 833.—the last of four sources of approbation, 843.

[*Paley*] different theories of obligation ultimately coincide in the promotion of general happiness, 846. to learn the will of God concerning any action, by the light of nature, is to inquire into its tendency to promote or diminish general happiness, 853. whatever is expedient is right; the utility of a moral rule constitutes the obligation of it, 854.—the criterion of right, 854. wrong actions which are apparently useful are not really useful, 854. this can be seen by distinguishing particular and general consequences; the violation of a necessary or useful general rule is a general bad consequence, 855.

[*Bentham*]—principle of, recognizes the subjection of mankind to pleasure and pain, 946.—principle of, or the greatest happiness principle, i.e. the principle that the greatest happiness of all those whose interest is in question is the only right and proper end of action, 946*n*.; cf. 947.—is that property in any object whereby it tends to produce happiness or prevent unhappiness, 948. an action is conformable to the principle of utility when its tendency to augment happiness is greater than any tendency it has to diminish happiness, 950. an action conformable to the principle of utility is one that ought to be done or is right, or at least is not wrong, 951.— principle of, neither can nor needs to be directly proved, 952. attempts to disprove the principle of utility presuppose the principle itself, e.g. in saying that it is a dangerous principle, 953. if approbation without regard to utility is taken as a standard of right and wrong, it is either despotical or anarchial, 954.— principle of, dist. principle of asceticism and principle of sympathy and antipathy, 955.—is misapplied in reverse by the principle of asceticism, 956.—is capable, as asceticism is not, of being consistently pursued, 956.—is opposed in legislative debate by appeal to the law of nature to save the trouble of inquiry, 962.—is the only justification for moral sentiment, and it is irrelevant that the sentiment may not always arise from thought of it, 963; cf. 966 (427*n.*, 434). the happiness of the members of a community is the sole end which the legislator ought to have in view, 967, 970. the business of government is to promote the happiness of the society by punishing and rewarding, 977. the dictates of utility are simply those of the most extensive and enlightened benevolence, though they may conflict with partial benevolence, 999.

value, see *worth.*—of pleasure and pain, to be computed from seven elements or dimensions, 971–4.
vanity, or vain-glory, 6, 31, 610*n.*
Velleius Paterculus,—cited by Hobbes, 94.
vice, see *virtue.*—dist. sin and crime, 184–7.—can result either from too great

weakness of public affection, or from too great strength of private affection, or from unnatural affection; and leads to private misery, 213–14, 221. even vicious men prefer profit without crime to profit with it, 236.—is action injurious to society, 267.—ordinary spring of, is not malice but the overcoming of benevolence by mistaken self-love or other motives, 329. nothing is more contrary to nature than vice, 377.— pleasures of, depend on regards to our fellow creatures, 407.—like virtue, depends on intention, 762. all vice is contrary to reason, but vice cannot be defined as conduct contrary to reason, because this definition would apply equally to folly, 931–2.
Virgil,—cited by Wollaston, 278.
virtue, see *good, goodness, merit.*
[*Cudworth*]—formality of, dist. materiality of action, 125.
[*Locke*]—and public happiness, inseparably connected by God, 158. morally good and evil, the conformity or disagreement of voluntary actions to some law, whereby good and evil (pleasure and pain) are drawn upon us from the will and power of the lawmaker, 183.—and vice, dist. duty and sin, crime and innocence, 184-7.—and vice, coincident with divine law if referring to actions right and wrong in their own nature, but otherwise and in general determined by opinion or reputation, 187-8; cf. 184.
[*Shaftesbury*]—and interest agree, 195. —or goodness, what? 196.—or merit, possible only for man, dist. mere goodness, possible for all sensible creatures, 200.—requires reflection or reflected sense, whereby affections become themselves the object of affection, 200, 202. —or worthiness, implies notion of public interest, 202.—admiration of, necessary to a rational creature, 203. to be capable of virtue is to approve, through reflection, of social affections, 204.—what obligation to? 205.—is to be well affected to society as well as to oneself, 205.—the advantage of every creature, 207, 221-3.—requires private as well as public affections, 212.—is to one's own interest, 213-14.—beauty of, seen even in adversity, as tragedy shows, 218.—leads to happiness, and therefore obliges, 221.
[*Clarke*]—and goodness, are to be

virtue (*cont.*):

chosen for their own sakes and intrinsic worth, 248–50; yet not self-sufficient, 249.—moral, the foundation, sum, essence, and life of true religion, 261.

[*Mandeville*]—is endeavouring the benefit of others or the conquest of passion, contrary to impulse of nature, 267.—and vice, not the effect of religion, 268.—moral, the political offspring which flattery begot upon pride, 269. when virtue is said to be its own reward, the satisfaction that constitutes the reward is a sign of pride, 270–1.

[*Hutcheson*]—gives pleasure on reflection, 314.—presupposes affection and disposition to promote public good, 315.—degree of, depends on quantity of happiness expected to result, and on the number of persons affected; that action is best which procures the greatest happiness for the greatest numbers, 333.—perfection of, when a being acts to the utmost of his power for the public good, 337.—whether animals capable of, 349 (440).

[*Butler*]—consists in following nature, i.e. in conforming to conscience, 375–9. —and interest, to be distinguished, but not opposed to each other, 384, 408.— to be pursued as an end, 386.—when habitual, ceases to be confinement and becomes choice and delight, 408.— coincides in general with self-love, 408. —is in a degree its own reward, 420.— consists in pursuit of what is right and good as such, though justification of it may require consideration of interest, 423.—and piety, at last coincide, 428.— universally acknowledged standard of, 429.—common instances of, produce only weak perception of good desert, 431. prudence is virtue, or at least is approved, 433.—benevolence is not the whole of, 434–5.

[*Balguy*]—not grounded on benevolent affection, 437 (336).—would be arbitrary and positive if dependent on instinct, 438. animals may be objects but not subjects of virtue, 440 (349).— cannot be grounded on affection, since degree of virtue varies inversely with strength of affection, 441.—is depreciated if grounded on instinct, 442 (327). —cannot be reconciled with necessity, 442 (373).—rooted in the nature of things, 446, 452.—defined as conformity of moral actions to the reasons of things,

448.—to promote one's own welfare, in subordination to that of the public, 448. —absolute goodness of, 454.—has pleasure as its consequence, but they are distinct objects and distinct ends, 455. to resolve all obligations into interest is to say that virtue is good only as doing us good, 461.

[*Gay*]— = conformity to a rule directing actions of rational creatures with respect to each other's happiness, 462.—implies relation to others, obligation, and approbation, 462.—obligations of, arise from merit and demerit, as producing esteem or the contrary, 464; cf. Locke, 184.—immediate rule or criterion of, is the will of God, 464; cf. Locke, 185.—mediate criterion of, is the happiness of mankind, 465.

[*Hume*] are virtue and vice distinguished by means of ideas or impressions? 487. if morality consisted in truth or falsehood, which does not admit of degrees, all virtues and vices would be equal, 492. it is one thing to know virtue, and another to conform the will to it, 500.—and vice, are not matters of fact to be inferred by reason; to call an action vicious means that you have a feeling or sentiment of blame, 503; cf. 634. impression arising from virtue is agreeable, from vice uneasy, 506. to have the sense of virtue is to feel satisfaction of a particular kind from contemplation of a character, 506. the question whether virtue is natural depends on the meaning given to 'natural', 510; but according to such meaning, both virtue and vice are equally natural or equally unnatural, 511.—justice an artificial, 512.—depends on motive, 512–13. first motive of virtuous action must be different from a regard to its virtue, 513; cf. 633 (759, 895–901). the idea of virtue is annexed to justice, and that of vice to injustice, because we share through sympathy the satisfaction caused by justice and the uneasiness caused by injustice, 533–4. when any action pleases us after a certain manner, we say it is virtuous, 537.— natural, dist. artificial, 546.—artificial, esteemed through sympathy with the interest of society, 548.—natural, often likewise approved for utility, 549–50. social virtues bear the greatest figure among the moral qualities, 550. not all virtues and vices tend to public advantage and loss, 550.—natural, more likely than the artificial to be the effect of sympathy with benefit produced, 552.—is approved even when ineffectual, 555; cf. 579n. every quality of the mind is denominated virtuous, which gives pleasure by the mere survey, 560.—utility of social, compared with that of beauty, 574.—utility of, does not imply that the utility of inanimate objects is properly called a virtue, 574n.; cf. Hutcheson, 307. the monkish virtues, being neither useful nor agreeable, are rejected by men of sense and are accounted vices, 587.—defined as whatever action or quality gives to a spectator the pleasing sentiment of approbation, 600.—held to exclude talents, 608.—cannot be clearly distinguished from talents, 609. different virtues, like different talents, produce different kinds of approbation, 612. whether natural abilities be virtues is a dispute of words, 632; cf. 608, 612.—always has a tendency to public or private good, and therefore its merit is derived from sympathy, 633.—can never be the sole motive to any action, 633; cf. 513.

[Hartley]—love of, as a source of associations giving rise to the moral sense, 648-9. suitableness of all the virtues to each other and to the beauty of the world, 650.

[Price]—is an affair of taste, according to the theory of moral sense, 657.—nature of, dist. its subject-matter, 658. it has not been proved that virtue is factitious, to be felt, not understood, 674.—presupposed by the idea of good desert, 695.—in its very nature involves obligation, 709; cf. Butler, 381.—dist. interest, 710-11; cf. Butler, 380. it is absurd to ask why we are obliged to practise virtue, since this is to ask why we are obliged to do what we are obliged to do, 714.—absolute, dist. relative, 719n.; cf. 724, 750-1.—regard to, determines merit, 724.—of the action, dist. virtue of the agent, 724, 755.—cannot be defined by such expressions as 'acting suitably to the natures of things', 726.—cannot be identified with signifying truth, 727 (280).—criteria of, not afforded by these expressions, 728.—does not consist wholly in benevolence, 730-2; cf. Butler, 434-5.—is not limited to one sort of actions, 732.—six main branches of, 733-45; (1) duty to God,

733; (2) duty to self, 734-5; (3) beneficence, 736; (4) gratitude, 737; (5) veracity, which includes fidelity to promises, 738-40; (6) justice, 741-4.—the different branches of, all run up to one general idea, 745.—the branches of, can interfere with each other, 746.—principles of, are self-evident, 747.—abstract or absolute, dist. practical or relative, 750-1. both are real virtue, and it is absolutely right that a man should do what he thinks right, 751.—practical, presupposes liberty, 752.—practical, presupposes intelligence, 754.—practical, presupposes acting from a regard to rectitude as one's rule and end, 755.—actual being of, constituted by intention, 755.—motive to, must be a regard to virtue, 758-9 (513-14, 633).—may arise from rational or universal benevolence, but not from instinctive, 760-1; cf. Balguy, 441-2. reasonable and calm self-love is a virtuous principle, 761.

[Smith]—of an action, depends on affection, which may be considered under two aspects, one of propriety, depending on cause or motive, the other of merit, depending on end or tendency, 773, 785.—amiable, dist. respectable, 781-2; cf. Hume, 612.—consists in an uncommon, not an ordinary, degree of certain qualities, 782.—deserves admiration, dist. propriety, which deserves mere approval, 783. the two great characters of virtue are to be amiable and to be meritorious, i.e. to excite the sentiments of love and gratitude in other men, 804.—approbation of, is enhanced by, but is not primarily or principally due to, utility, 832, 843 (560, 586).—approbation of, differs from approbation of a convenient material thing (cf. Hume, 574n.), and includes a sense of propriety distinct from the perception of utility, 833, 844.—different types of, arouse different types of approbation, 840; cf. 781-2; and cf. Hume, 612.

[Paley]—is the doing good to mankind, in obedience to the will of God, and for the sake of everlasting happiness, 845.—subject of, the good of mankind, 845-6.—rule of, the will of God, 845, 850; cf. Gay, 464.—motive of, everlasting private happiness, 845, 850, 852.—of an agent, depends on his design, while rightness of an action depends on its tendency, 854n.

virtue (*cont.*):

[*Reid*]—dist. prudence, 868; cf. 870. virtuous action must be done from the belief that it is right, 894; cf. Price, 755, 758. Hume's argument to the contrary is disproved by the fact that the agent's intention is a necessary condition of such virtues and vices as benevolence, malice, revenge, gratitude, veracity, 896 (513–14). two senses of moral goodness, one as applied to the action considered abstractly, the other as applied to the agent, 897–8; cf. Price, 719*n.*, 750. the latter depends on the agent's belief, the former not, 900.—can have as its sole motive a regard to virtue, 901 (513).—is an ultimate end, but is not thereby independent of the intellectual faculties, 943 (606).—is a faint but true copy of the moral excellence of God, 945.

voluntary, see *will.* object of all voluntary acts is good to oneself, 60, 68.—not opposed to necessary, 166. operation of instincts or affections is said to be necessary, not voluntary, 373, 442.—beings, as means to our happiness, give rise to different feelings from those produced by involuntary means, 468, 472. mistake of fact, being involuntary, is not criminal, 491, 602.—actions are subject to necessity in the sense of uniformity, 614, 619. in a connected chain of natural causes and voluntary actions, the mind feels no difference in passing from one link to another, 620.—can mean intentional, or uncoerced, or spontaneous, 979*n.*

war, see *nature.*—condition of, 50–3.
whole, and part, see *system.*—of the mind, as of the body, 208, 222.
will, see *choice, freedom, voluntary.*

[*Hobbes*]— = the last appetite or fear (aversion) in deliberation, 17, 34, 96.—not voluntary, 18.—free, implies liberty of the man, not of the will, 82, 90.—the necessary and necessitated cause of voluntary actions, 97.

[*Cudworth*]—cannot be cause of essences, hence of good and evil, just and unjust, 120–9.—of God, determines existence but not essence, 121.—alone, cannot oblige, 122–6.—cannot change nature, 125–6.—of God, does not determine truth and falsehood, 127–8.—of God, determined by his wisdom, 128.—freedom of, attested by praise and blame,

sense of guilt and of retributive justice, 136–8.—free, dist. contingent liberty of self-determination, 141; cf. 150.—faculty of, in relation to faculty of understanding, according to scholastic psychology, 142–5.—the blind, falsely supposed free, 142–4.—blind, impossible, 146.

[*Locke*]—and law of God, the true ground of morality, 158 (675).—a power to act or forbear, 162.—a power of preferring, misleadingly called a faculty, 163, 168. the question, whether the will be free, is improper, 167–9.—not precisely identical with preference, 167.—is one power or ability, freedom is another, 168. no freedom to will or prefer, 170.—determined by the mind, and the mind by satisfaction or uneasiness, 172.—dist. desire, 173.—determined by uneasiness or desire, not by the greater good in view, 174–5 (486). determination of the will by judgement is not an abridgement of liberty, but the end and use of it, 180–1.—of God, may be inferred by reason from the evidence of sense, 193–4.—of God, that men owe duties to God, society, and self, 194.

[*Clarke*]—of God, necessarily determines itself with regard to fitness, 225, 230.—of men, ought to be similarly determined, 225, 231.—or command of God, not the foundation of duty, 225.—of intelligent beings, directed by their understanding of necessary relations and fitnesses, 230. those whose will is corrupted, will things to be what they are not and cannot be, 230.—natural liberty of, contrasted with necessity of assent, 232.—of God, determines existence of things, but not their abstract proportions, 247; cf. Cudworth, 121.

[*Wollaston*] agreeable to the will of God that we should own things to be as they are, 281; cf. Clarke, 230, 232.

[*Hutcheson*] neither benevolence nor any other affection or desire can be directly raised by volition, 321.—identified with rational appetite, 357.

[*Butler*]—and design, constitute the very nature of actions as such, 430.

[*Balguy*]—of God, is subject to the original law or rule of action, viz., to conform to reason, 450.—unlike understanding, has power to rebel, 450.—influenced and inclined by a motive or reason for choice, 460.

[*Gay*]—of God, is the immediate rule

or criterion of virtue, 464; cf. Locke, 185.—of God, happiness of mankind is criterion of, 465.—of God, necessary to make the good of mankind an obligatory pursuit, 466.

[*Hume*] reason alone can never be a motive to any action of the will, nor can it prevent volition, 479–82.—dist. demonstration, as concerned respectively with realities and ideas, 480.—may be determined either by the view of the greatest possible good or by present uneasiness, 486 (174–5).—cannot be true or false, conform to or contradict reason, 490. a rationalist theory of morals has the impossible task of showing a necessary connection between moral relations and the will, as cause and effect, if right and wrong are to be obligatory on every rational mind, 500.—or choice, as cause of an action, does not produce any different relations from those of a similar action with a different cause, 501. a promise, if an act of mind, could not be willing an action but would have to be willing an obligation, 536; but this implies the changing of sentiments by an act of will, which is impossible, 537; nor could such an act of will naturally produce any obligation, 538. willing an obligation is a feigned act of the mind, 543.—of God, cannot alter the standard of reason, but is the ultimate cause of the standard of taste, 607; cf. 634.—actions of, are regularly conjoined with motives, circumstances, and characters, and are therefore necessary, 622.

[*Price*]—the power of acting and determining, dist. affection, 661*n*. idea of power is given by inward consciousness of activity and self-determination, 667. Locke's view, that rectitude is con-

formity to the will of God, makes it absurd to suppose that the divine will is itself directed by it, 675 (158, 185).—of God, some things must be independent of, 700.—of God, depends on his understanding, 702; cf. Cudworth, 128.—of God, dist. his nature, 702.

[*Paley*] virtue is the doing good to mankind, in obedience to the will of God, and for the sake of everlasting happiness, 845.—of God, is the rule of virtue, 845, 850; cf. Gay, 464.—of God, requires the promotion of general happiness, 846, 853; cf. Gay, 465. to inquire into the will of God is the whole business of morality, 853.

[*Reid*]—is essential to contract, but it is the will to engage, not the will to perform, 905; cf. Hume, 536.

[*Bentham*]—of God, as standard of right and wrong, must be his presumptive will, and so is simply a way of expressing either the principle of utility or that of asceticism or that of sympathy and antipathy, 965.—or intention, 979.—is influenced by practical motives, 986.—can be indirectly influenced by speculative motives or what are called reasons, through the production of a belief about a practical motive, 991.

wisdom,—of God, 128–9.

Wollaston, 272–302. see especially *truth.*—cites Virgil and Theocritus, 278.—cited by Butler, 375.—criticizes Epicurus, 293.—criticized by Hutcheson, 368; by Balguy, 452; by Hume, 494–6; by Price, 727; by Bentham, 959.

worth,—or value of a man, is his price, 40.—public, called dignity, 40.—dist. worthiness, 43.—instrinsic, of virtue, 248–50.

Zeno, 91.